AF305381

Magritte
in 400 images

Julie Waseige

Ludion

Introduction

There is a familiar feeling of mystery, experienced with the things it is usual to call: mysterious. But the supreme feeling is the 'unfamiliar' feeling of mystery experienced with the things it is usual to 'find natural,' familiar (our own thoughts among, for example).[1]

For decades, the Belgian artist René Magritte has been the object of a constant fascination that transcends borders. His life's endeavour – to divert everyday objects and ordinary phenomena from their usual function in order to 'evoke the mystery of the world' – resulted in a body of poetic work with a universality that touches a wide audience. His decision to represent objects in accurate detail makes them easily recognisable to the viewer and his choice of pictorial repertoire is intentionally trivial: a green apple, an umbrella, a glass of water and a man wearing a suit all appear in strange compositions that lead the viewer to reconsider their subjects' utilitarian, social and moral roles. Removed from their usual contexts, the most familiar objects take on a profound sense of the unknown. Magritte's images raise new questions. They disturb our habits and unsettle our certainties. 'There is no explainable mystery in my painting,' Magritte liked to say.[2] With this in mind he chose poetic titles that were unconnected to the images represented, as a way of both shielding his works from interpretation and 'enchanting' the viewer.

Although his images cannot be explained, they bring us face to face with an ordinariness that force of habit and overuse have caused us to overlook. They open our eyes to the objects that surround us, to the conditions in which they exist and appear, and to the arbitrary nature of language. They prod us into developing a critical spirit, by freeing us from predetermined codes and instigating a thorough re-examination of the system in which we navigate as social beings.

When Magritte wrote 'This is not a pipe' under a very faithful pictorial representation of the object 'pipe', he invited us to become aware of the fundamental difference between reality and representation. 'This is not a pipe' is accurate because it refers to an image of a pipe, not the real object. At a time when human beings are confronted by an infinite mass of written and visual information every day via the media and social networks, making it difficult for us to distinguish reality from its treatment as an image or in discourse, the 'object lesson' Magritte provides us with is crucial. The relevance of Magritte's work today is that he teaches us to *see*, to analyse an image and to take distance from the fundamentally arbitrary nature of language, thus delivering a powerful message of freedom through a unique, poetic form of painting.

1   René Magritte, 'Nature et mystère', leaflet published by Maurice Rapin and
     Mirabelle Dors in *La Tendance populaire surréaliste*, 22 January 1958.
2   René Magritte, Letter to Maurice Rapin and Mirabelle Dors, 20 June 1957, in René Magritte *et al.*,
     Quatre-vingt-deux lettres de René Magritte à Mirabelle Dors et Maurice Rapin (Paris, 1976).

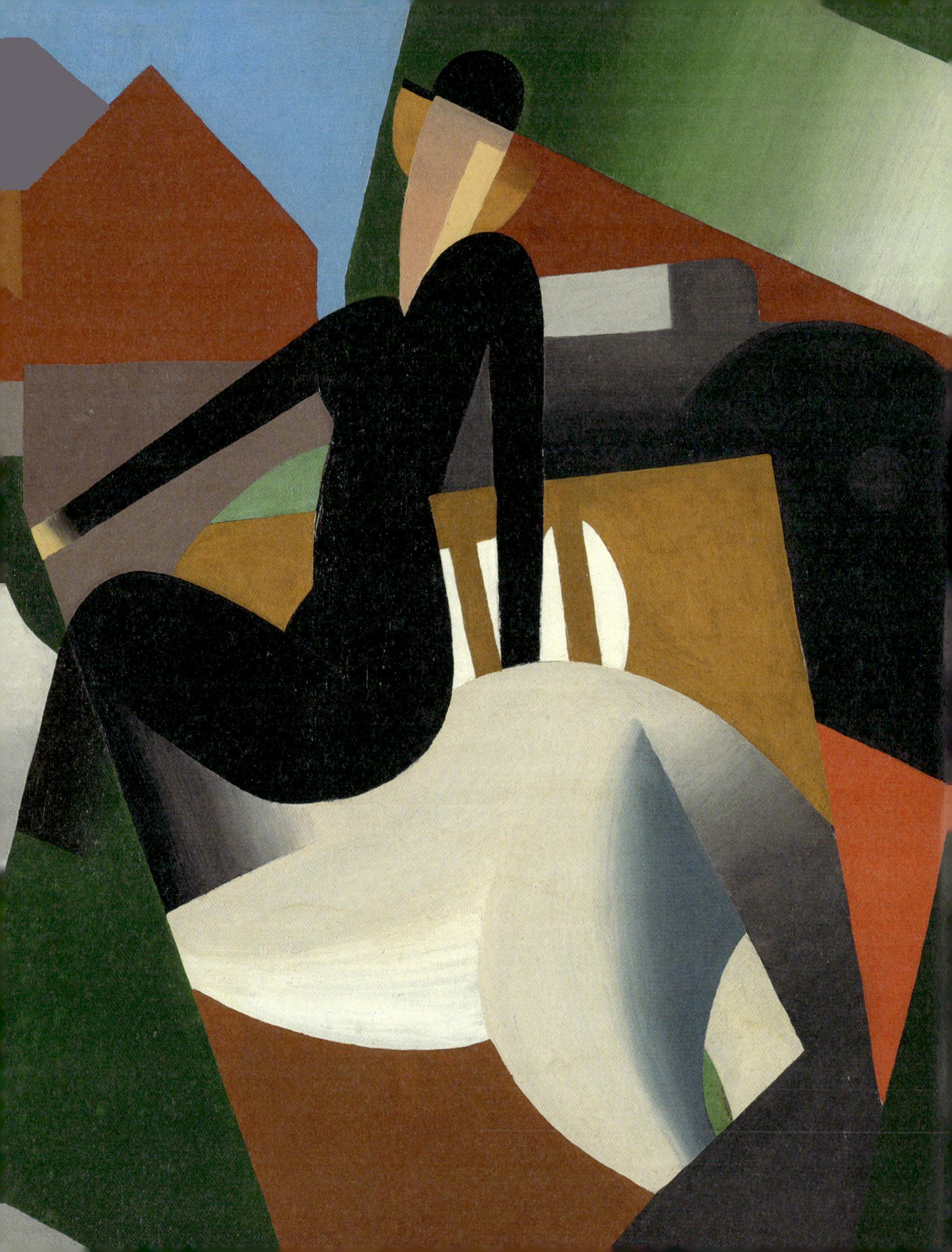

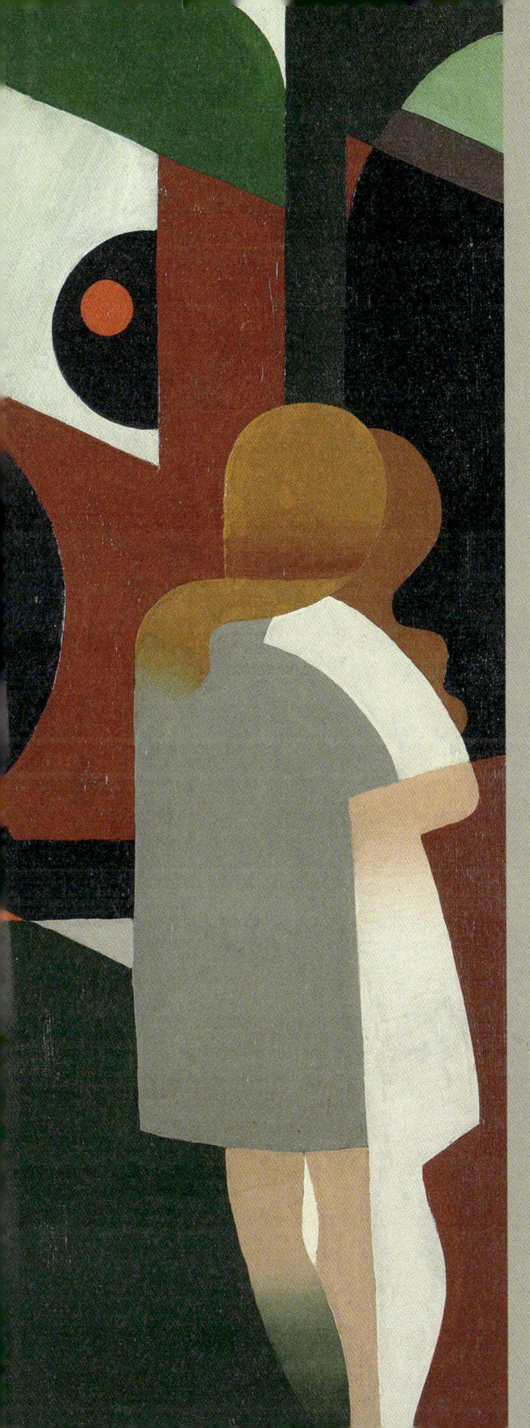

Abstract and
Pre-Surrealist
Experiments

1919–1925

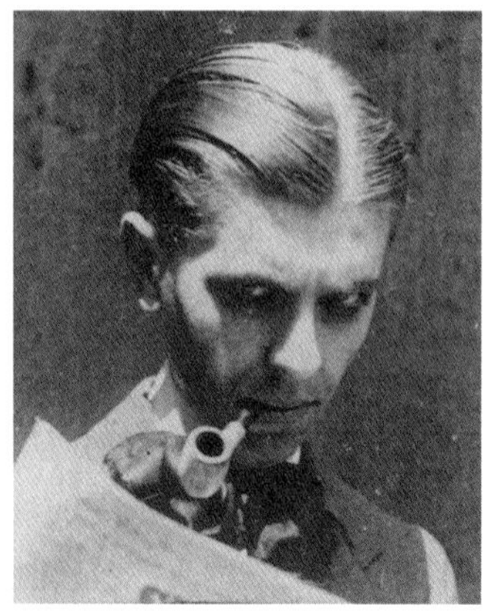

René Magritte, *c.* 1915.

Between October 1916 and 1921, Magritte attended drawing and painting classes at the Brussels Royal Academy of Fine Arts. There he met several students who gravitated towards the Brussels avant-garde and, with them, discovered contemporary modernist trends. Among his circle of friends were Pierre-Louis Flouquet (1900–67), the brothers Victor (1897–1962) and Pierre Bourgeois (1898–1976), and Victor Servranckx (1897–1965), with whom Magritte shared a distinct interest in abstract painting.

Futurism and Cubism were two major art movements that fulfilled Magritte's aspirations and greatly influenced him during these years. He first discovered Futurism in a catalogue that his friend Pierre Bourgeois showed him. Looking at these bold geometric compositions and exploded figures, and tired of the academic teaching meted out in Brussels, Magritte declared, 'I saw before my eyes a strong challenge to the common sense that bored me so,' adding, 'I painted a whole series of Futurist pictures in a state of total euphoria.'[3] Although he destroyed most of his work from this period and sometimes re-used canvases, both the form and content of a few extant paintings demonstrate this Futurist manner.

Magritte, however, was more interested in the aesthetic of Futurism, rather than in the Italian art movement's emphasis on labour, military life and modern machinery. Nonetheless, he opted for some of its characteristic subjects – train stations and steam-belching locomotives (*The Locomotive*, 1922 [6]), the automobile (*Modern*, 1923 [8]), scenes from the military sphere (*Military Tattoo*, 1920 [3]) and the working world (*The Blacksmiths*, 1920 [1]) – treating them in colourful, exploded compositions that particularly recall Futurist works.

Abstract and Pre-Surrealist Experiments

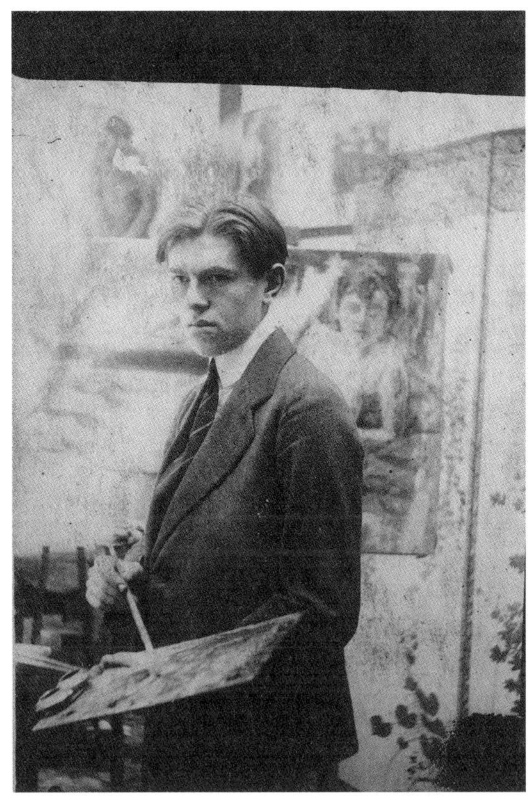

René Magritte at the Royal Academy of Fine Arts, Brussels, *c.* 1918.

Magritte pursued his interest in Futurism with the musician and composer E. L. T. Mesens (1903–71), whom he met in January 1920 at the Brussels Centre d'art, where he was exhibiting a collection of posters alongside his first abstract paintings. That year, after contacting Futurism's headquarters in Milan, Magritte and Mesens received a series of manifestos and quickly became aware that the movement's values, which were drawing nearer and nearer to Mussolini, were diametrically opposed to everything they wished to support. This realisation spelled the end of their contact with the Futurists.

Cubism, too, opened the door to Magritte's exploration of the possibilities of abstract painting. He became better acquainted with it by reading Albert Gleizes's book *Du cubisme et des moyens de le comprendre* (1920) and paying regular visits to Sélection, a new gallery in Brussels. *The Man at the Window* (1920) [2] and *Woman on Horseback* (1922) [5] tend more towards this Cubist vein, as does *Bathers* (1921) [4], in which the treatment of the female body recalls, to a degree, the work of Fernand Léger (1881–1955).

Although contact with new trends allowed Magritte to detach himself from his academic training, it did not fully satisfy him. He turned to Dadaism through Mesens, with whom he published a series of essays and reviews attesting to this influence. But the discovery of a painting by Giorgio de Chirico (1888–1978) completely reoriented his career as a painter.

In 1923 or 1924, his friend Marcel Lecomte showed him a reproduction of a painting by de Chirico entitled *The Song of Love* (1914). Magritte stated that, on seeing it, he could not restrain his tears.[4] In 'La Ligne de vie', a lecture he gave at the Museum of Fine Arts in Antwerp in 1938, he recalled the shock of encountering this image: 'It is a complete break with the mental habits of artists imprisoned by talent, virtuosity and all the little aesthetic specialities. It is a new vision, where viewers find their isolation and hear the silence of the world.'[5] Magritte realised that the attention that was currently being paid to the geometric deconstruction of a subject and the choice of colours was insignificant in the face of the deep mystery inspired by the metaphysical painting of de Chirico.

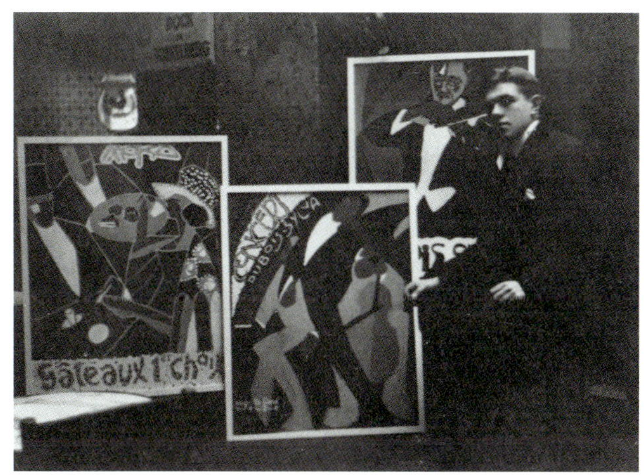

René Magritte in front of three poster designs for the Antwerp violinist Dubois-Sylva, *c*. 1920.

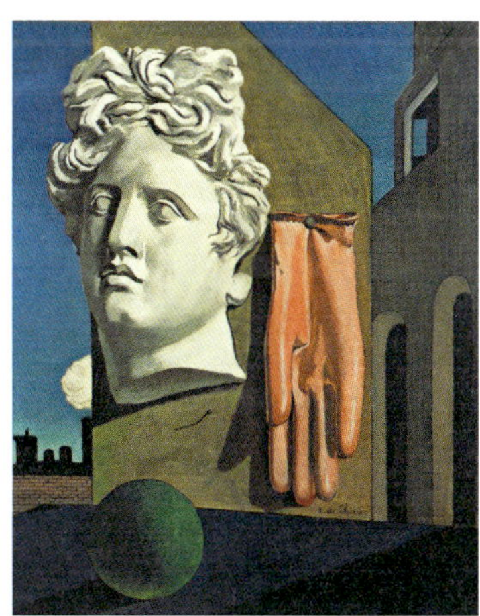

Giorgio de Chirico, *The Song of Love*, 1914.

1919–1925

Magritte felt the need to return to a focus on the subject matter of an artwork, and to the importance of representing objects 'with their visible details'.[6] *Woman with a Rose instead of a Heart* [10], painted in 1924, attests to this period of transition: for the first time, Magritte used an object out of context. Isolating an object by removing it from its usual setting was a means Magritte then began employing to redirect the viewer's perception of everyday objects. He said he was not satisfied with this painting, which he felt was still under the influence of his previous experiments with abstraction, and within a short time he painted several works that declared his intention to return to figuration. Though *The Window* [12], painted in 1925, still demonstrates a certain schematisation of forms, it is a work in which Magritte introduces the first elements of a new visual vocabulary, soon to be designated 'Surrealist', that would occupy his works: a curtain painted at the left or right of the composition to give a scene a theatrical feel; a window that opens onto a landscape recalling the slag heaps of Charleroi, the region of Belgium where Magritte grew up; a hand dissociated from the body; a bird in flight. When, in 1925, Magritte set out on this path once and for all, the question was no longer *how* to paint, but *what* to paint.

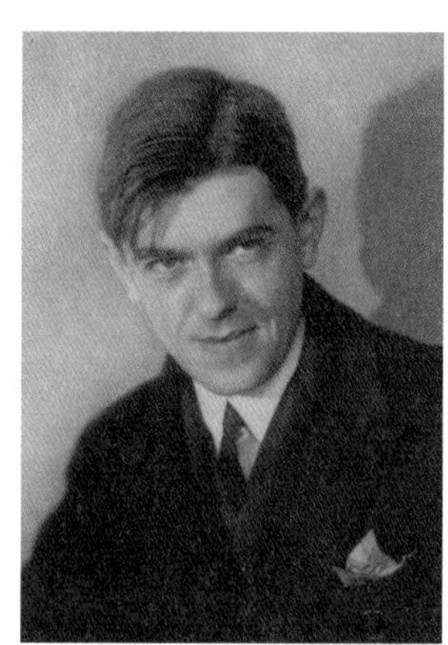

René Magritte, 1925.

3   René Magritte, 'La Ligne de vie', lecture given at the Musée royal des Beaux-Arts, Antwerp, 20 November 1938, quoted in René Magritte, *Écrits complets*, annotated by André Blavier (Paris: Flammarion, 1979), p. 105.

4   René Magritte, 'Esquisse autobiographique', in *Magritte*, exh. cat. (Brussels, Palais des Beaux-Arts, 7 May – 1 June 1954), p. 10.

5   Magritte, 'La Ligne de vie', op. cit., p. 104.

6   Ibid., p. 107.

   Abstract and Pre-Surrealist Experiments

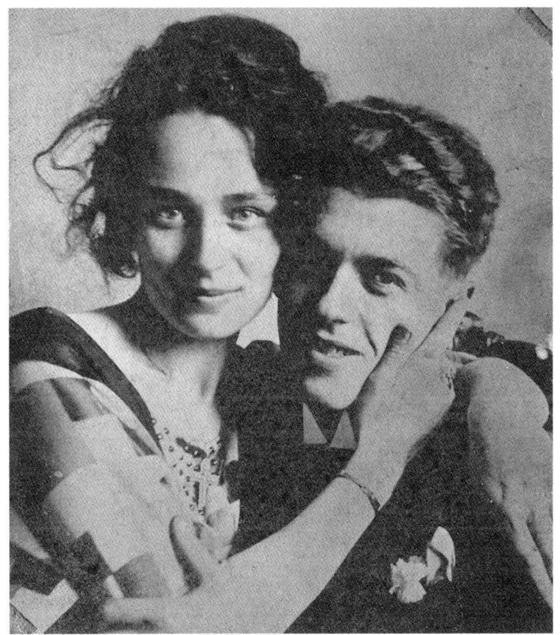

Georgette and René Magritte in June 1922.

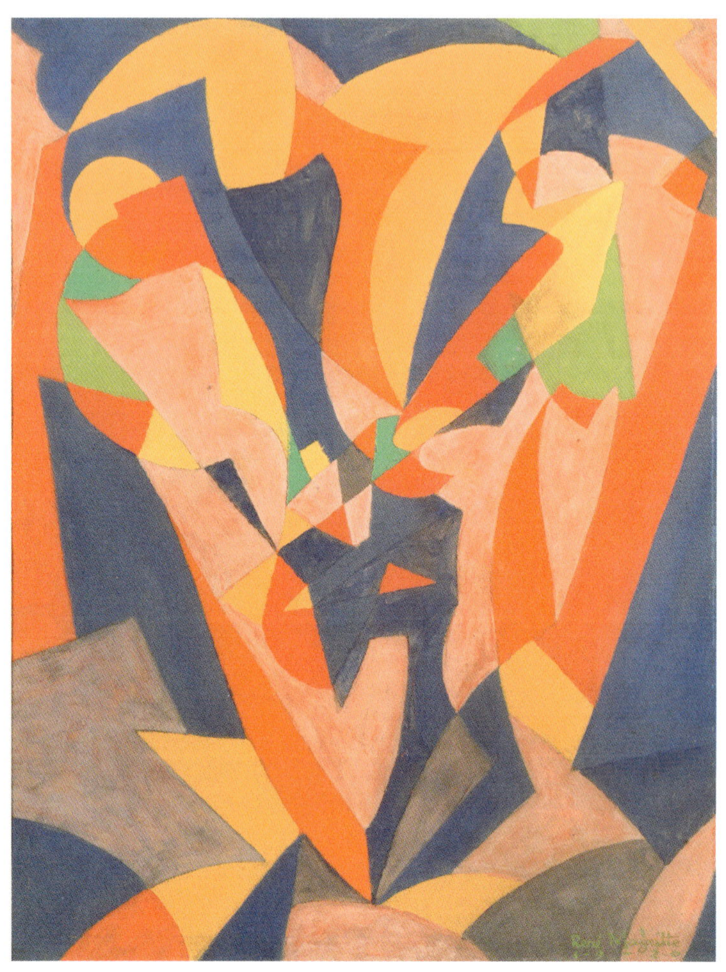

1
The Blacksmiths
1920
tempera on board, 89.5 × 70.5 cm

   Abstract and Pre-Surrealist Experiments

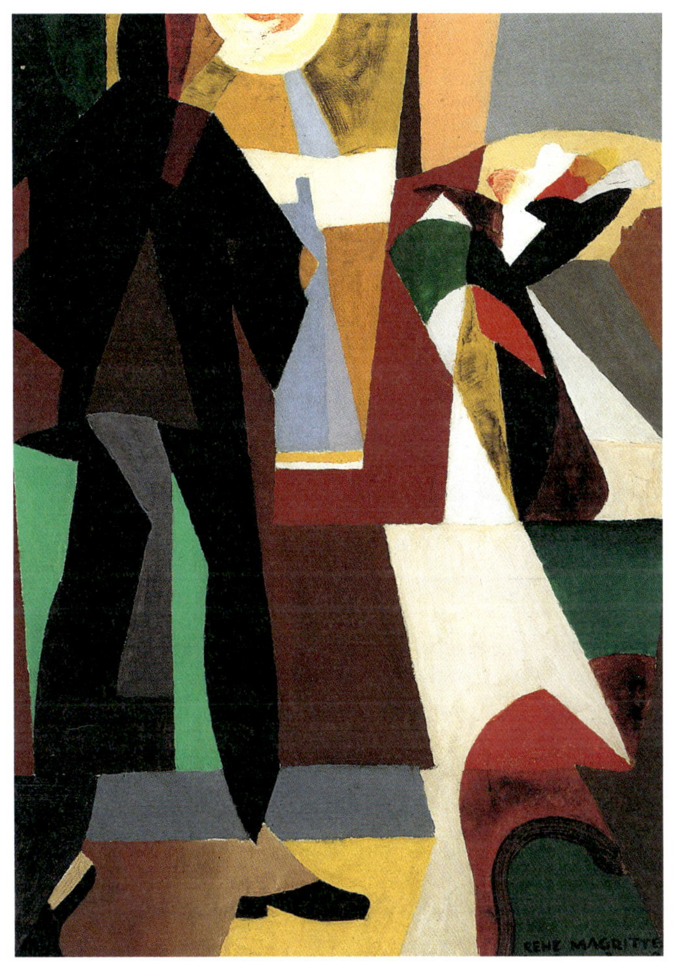

2
The Man at the Window
1920
oil on canvas, 92 × 65 cm

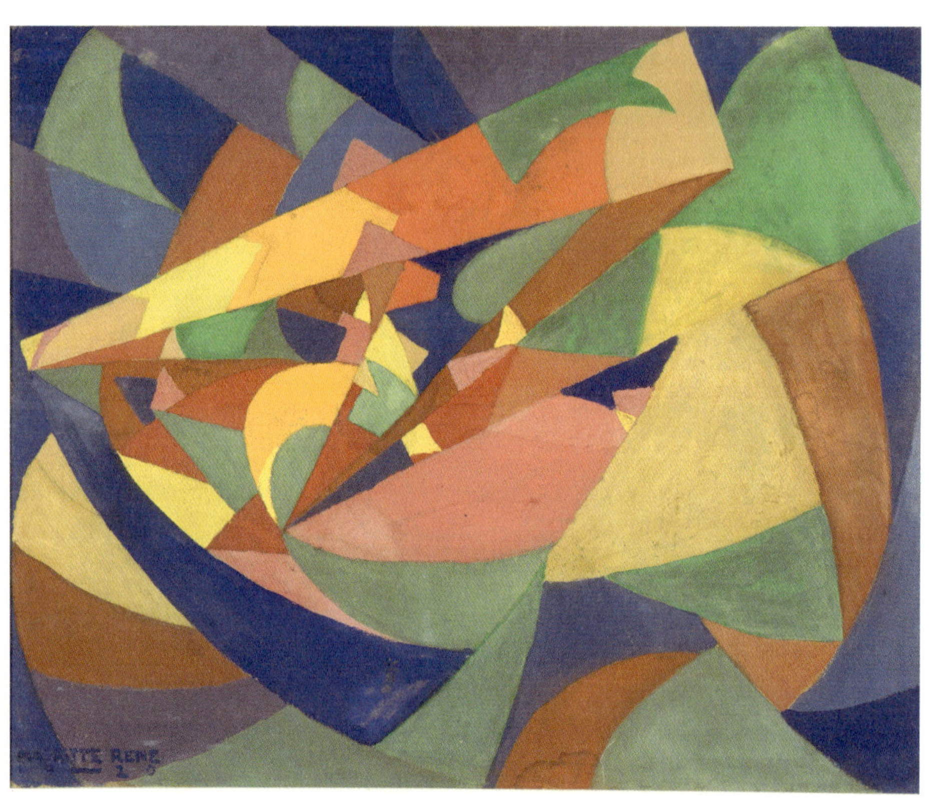

3
Military Tattoo
1920
tempera on paper mounted on board, 72 × 89.3 cm

 Abstract and Pre-Surrealist Experiments

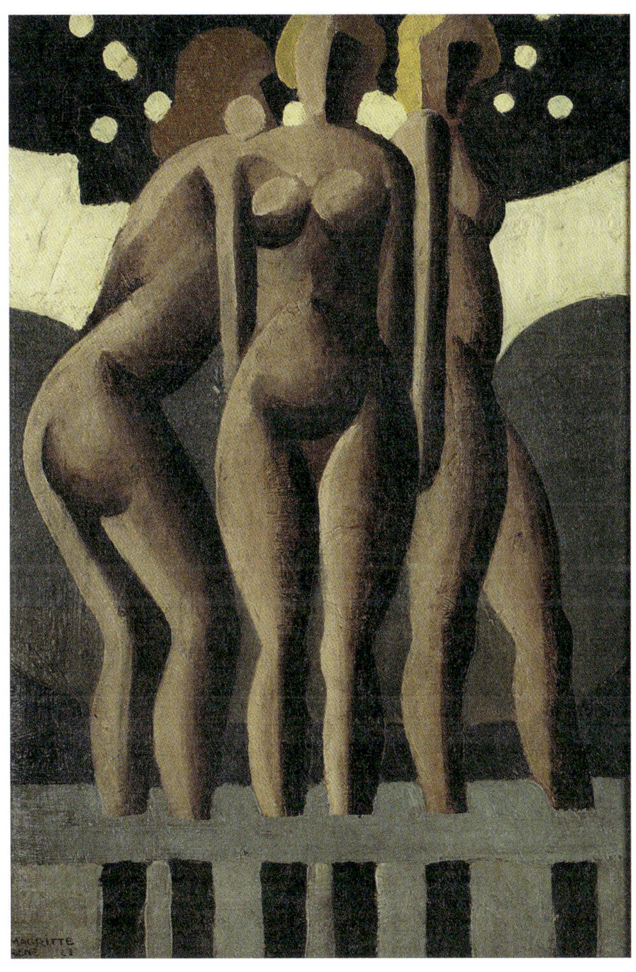

4
Bathers
1921
oil on canvas, 55 × 38 cm

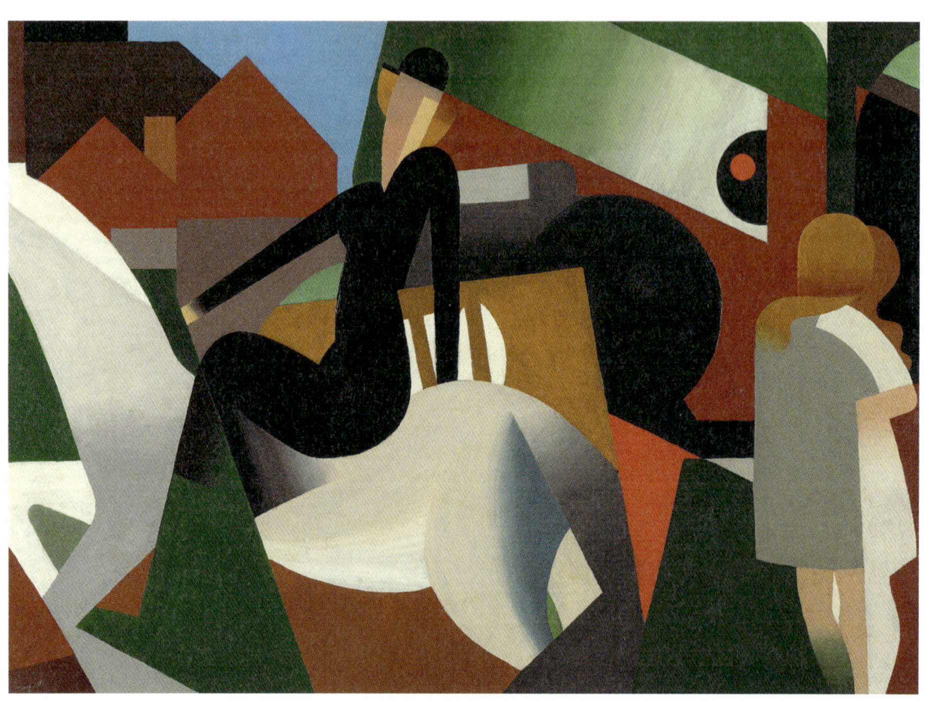

5
Woman on Horseback
1922
oil on board mounted on panel, 63 × 90 cm

  Abstract and Pre-Surrealist Experiments

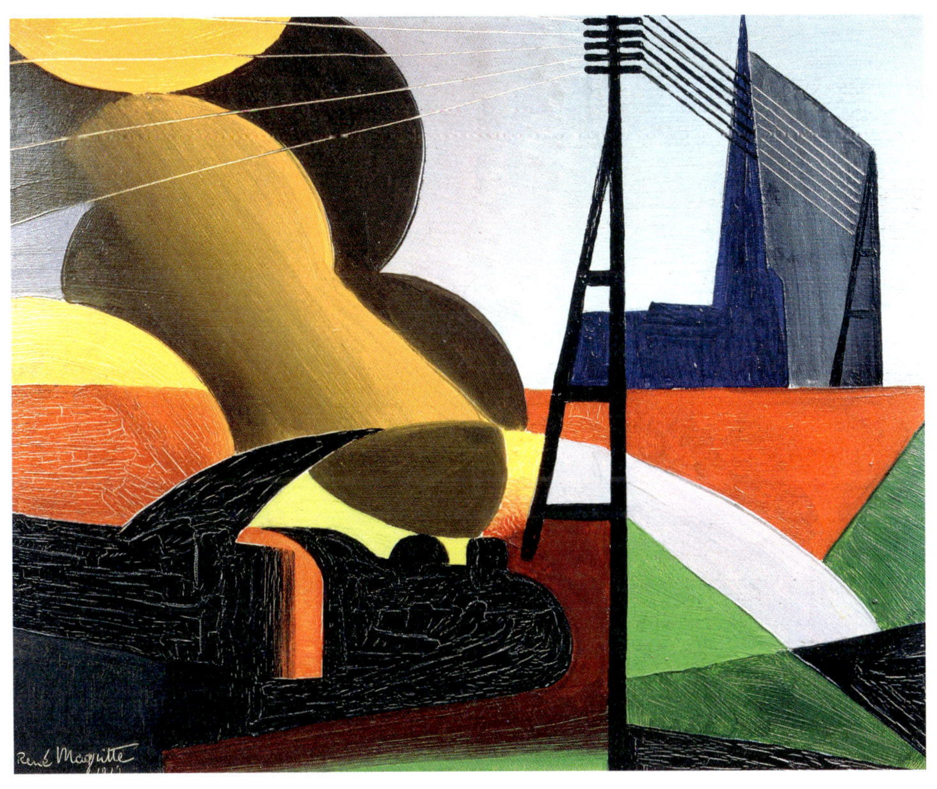

6
The Locomotive
1922
oil on cardboard, 36 × 44 cm

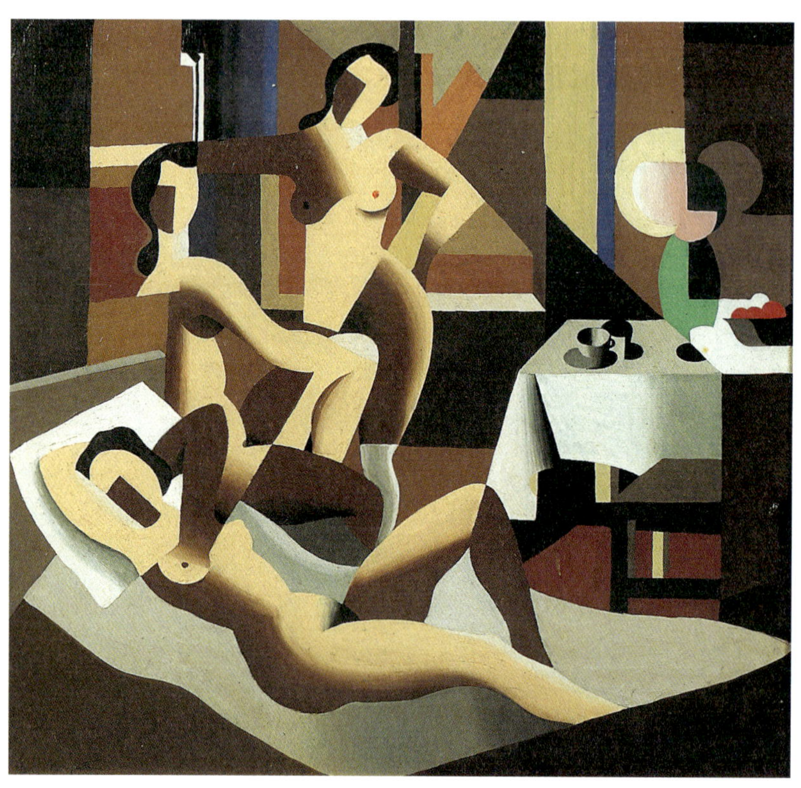

7

(Three Nudes in an Interior)

1923
oil on board, 55.5 × 59.5 cm

 Abstract and Pre-Surrealist Experiments

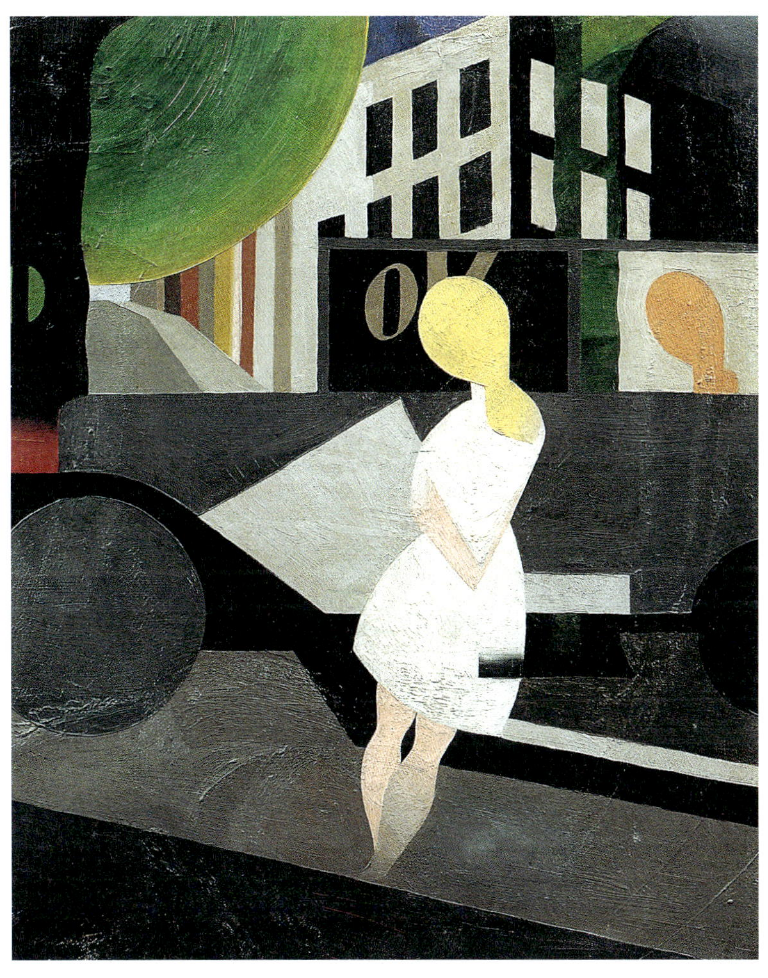

8
Modern
1923
oil on canvas, 55 × 45 cm

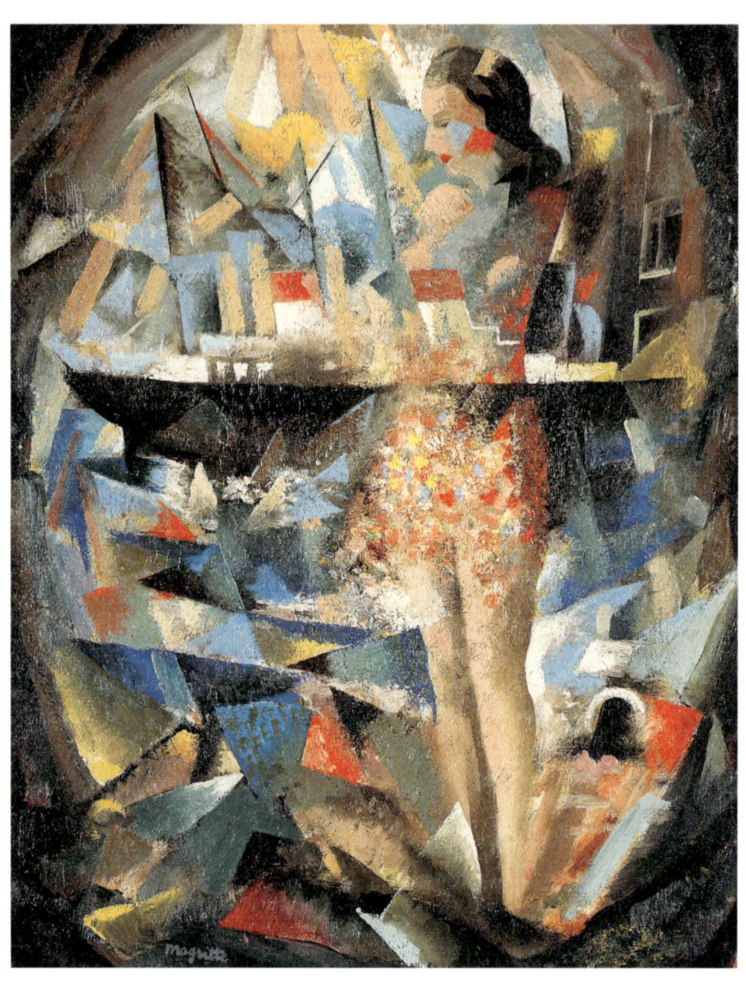

9

Youth

1924?
oil on canvas, 50 × 40 cm

  Abstract and Pre-Surrealist Experiments

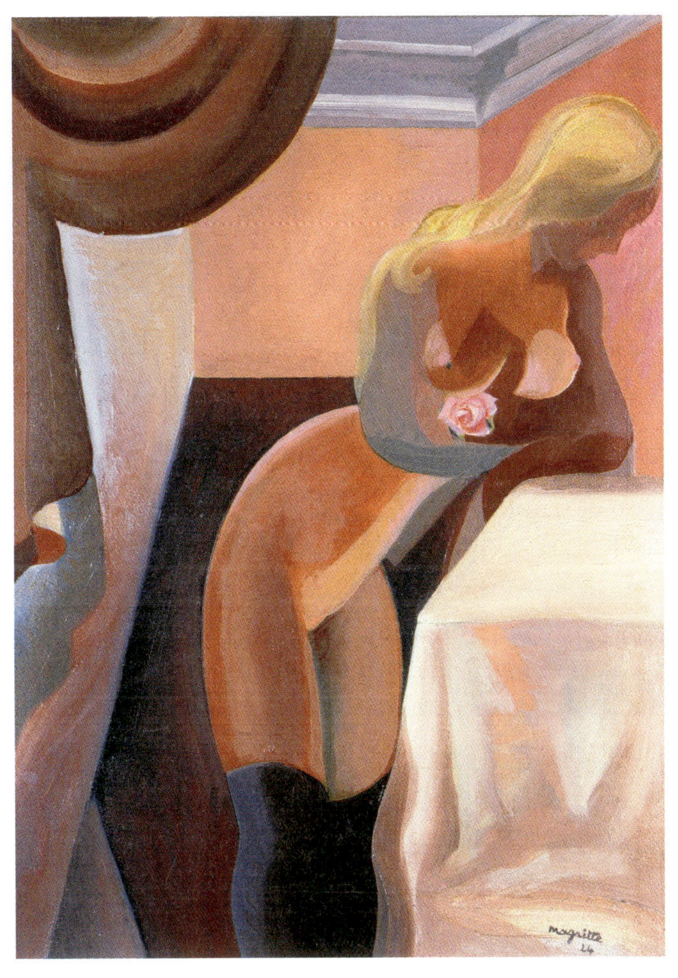

10
Woman with a Rose instead of a Heart
1924
oil on canvas, 55 × 40 cm

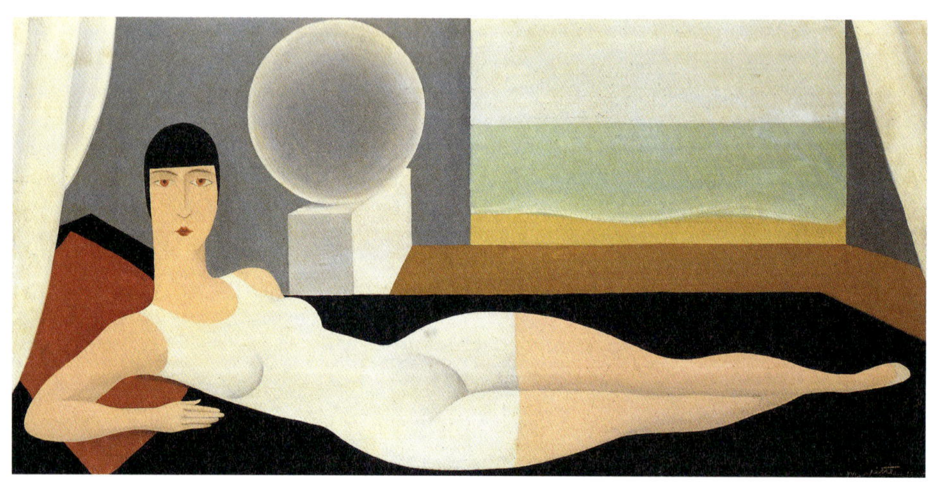

11
Bather
1925
oil on canvas, 50 × 100 cm

     Abstract and Pre-Surrealist Experiments

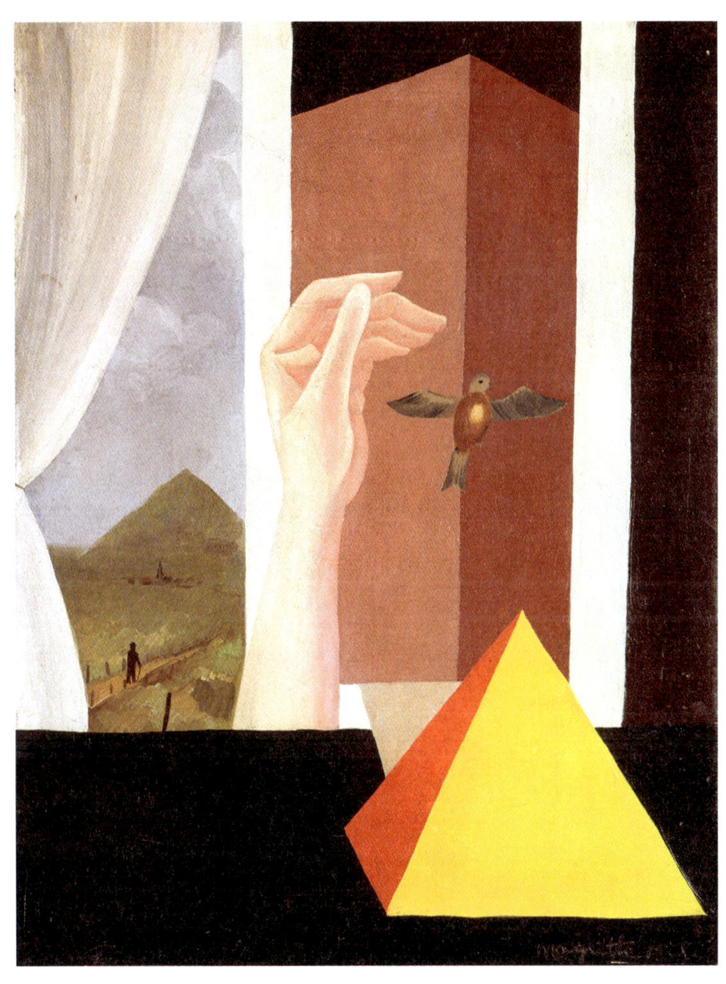

12
The Window
1925
oil on canvas, 65 × 50 cm

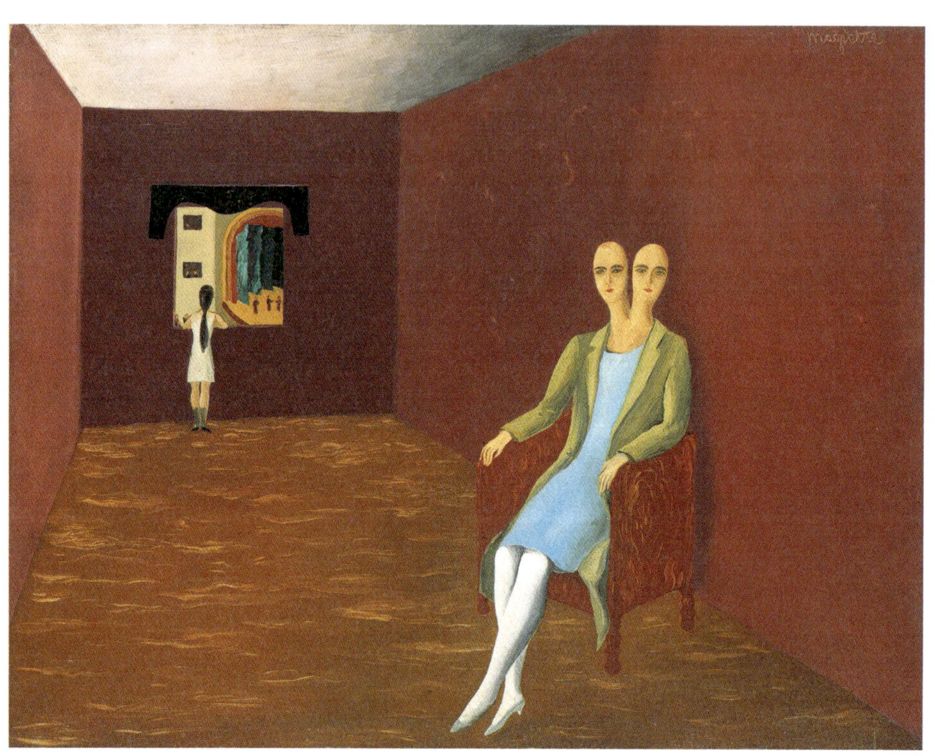

13
(A Box at the Theatre)
1925
oil on canvas, 63 × 82 cm

     Abstract and Pre-Surrealist Experiments

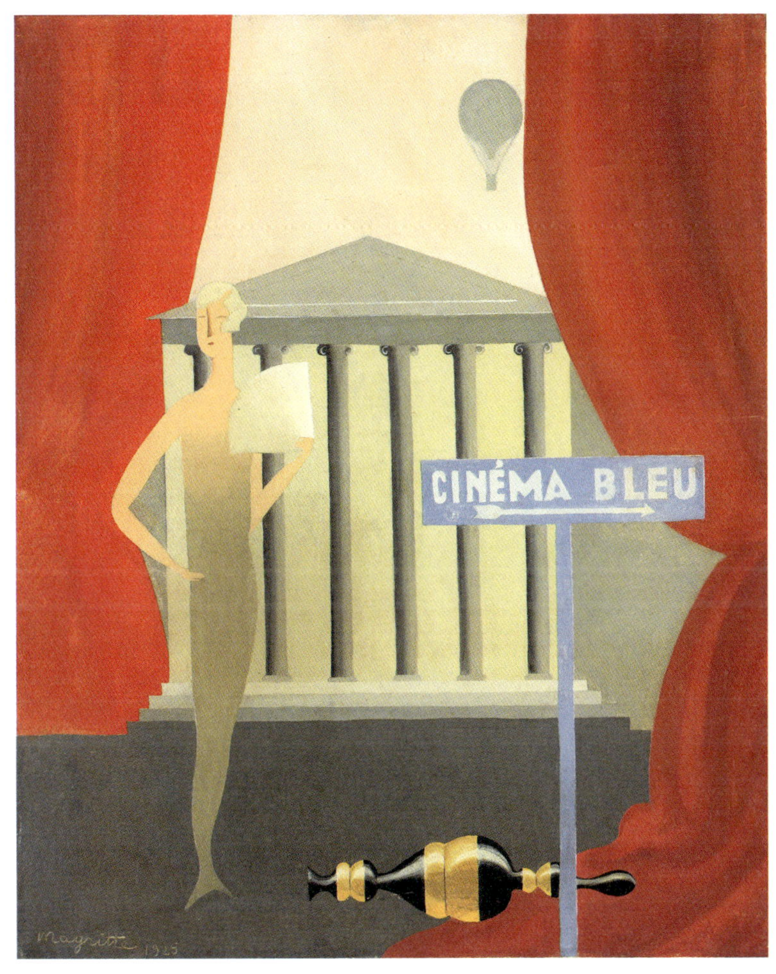

14
Cinéma bleu
1925
oil on canvas, 65 × 54 cm

 1919–1925

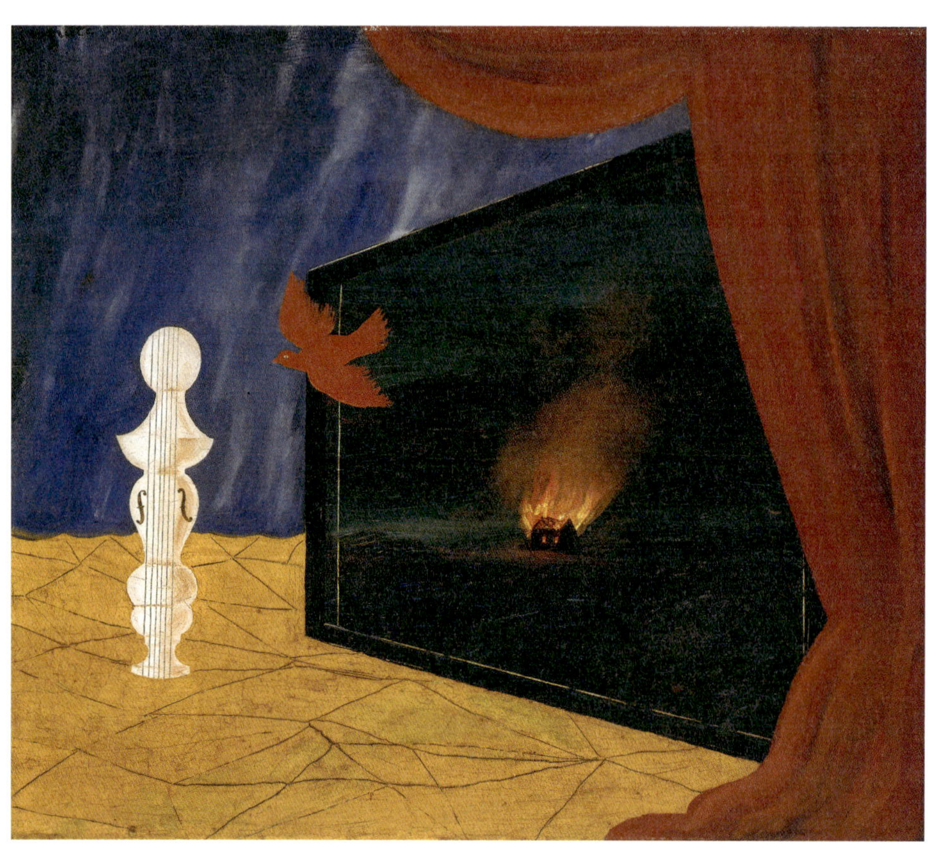

15
Nocturne
1925
oil on canvas, 65 × 75 cm

 Abstract and Pre-Surrealist Experiments

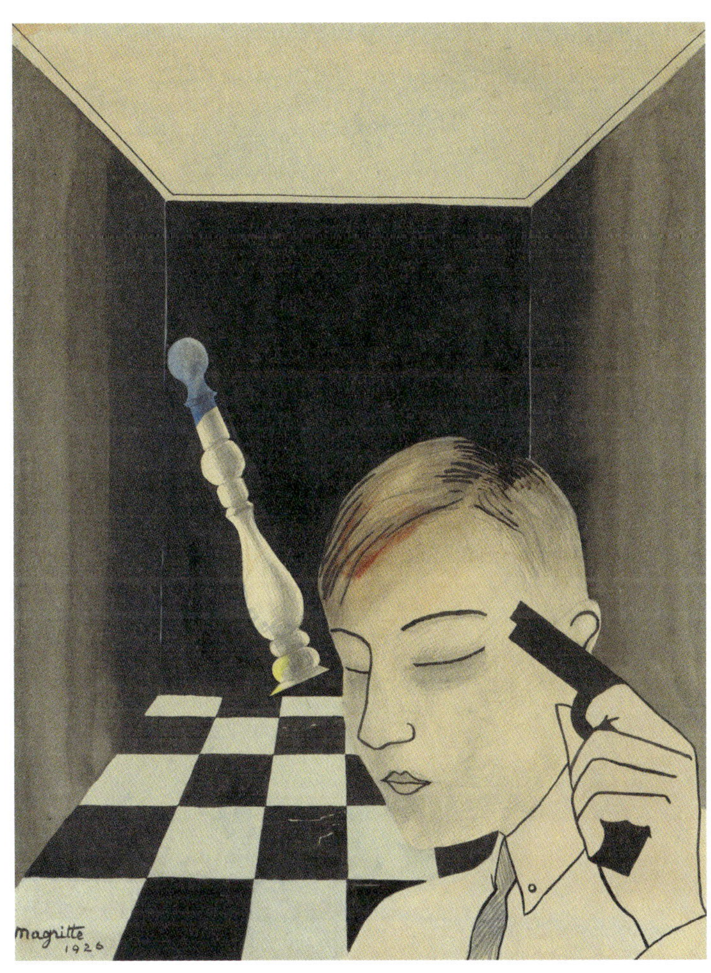

16
(Checkmate)
1926
watercolour, ink and pencil on paper, 39.2 × 29.4 cm

                              1919–1925

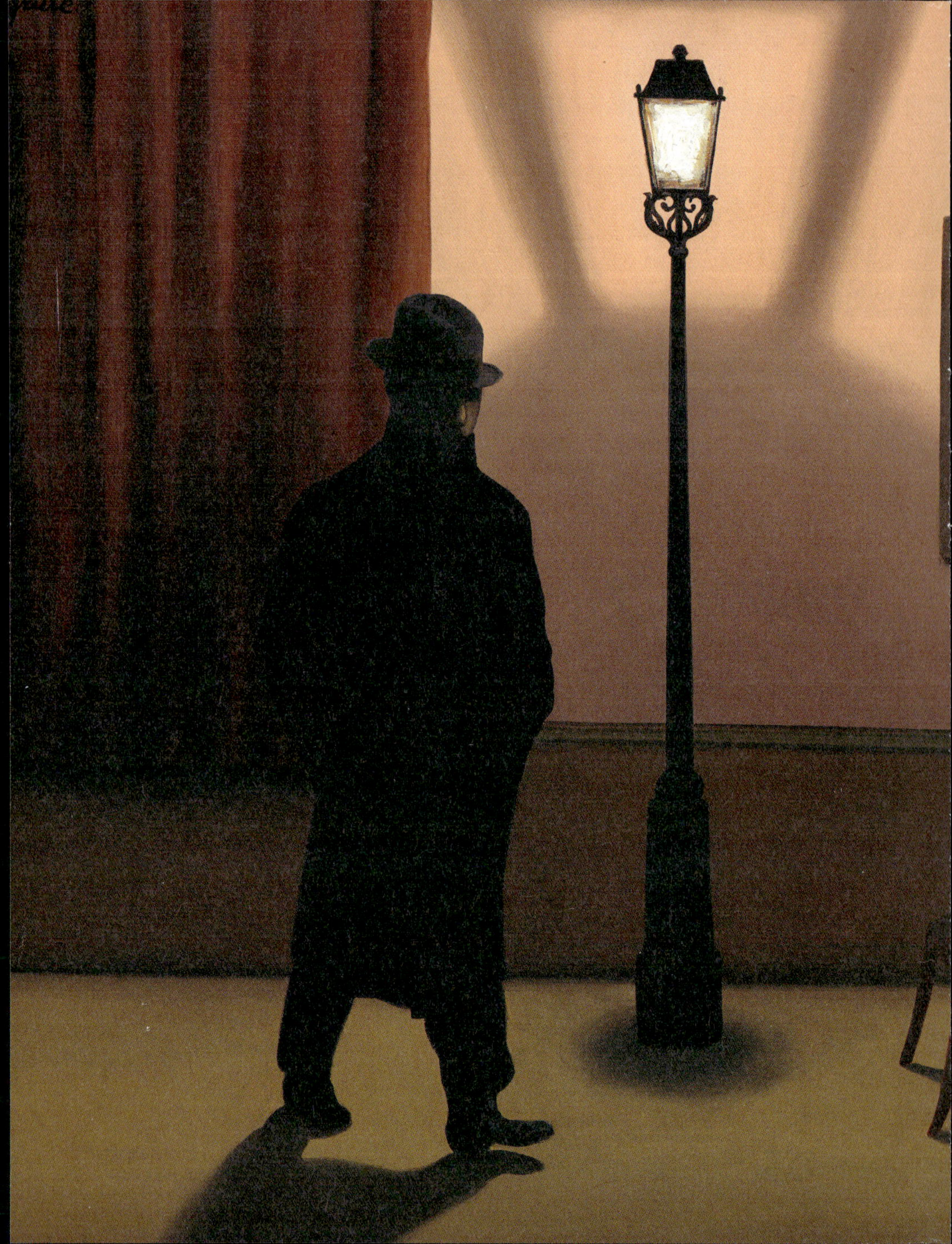

The Dark Period

1926–1930

In the interviews Magritte gave throughout his career, he referred on several occasions to one painting in particular, *The Lost Jockey* (1926) [20], which he considered to be his first Surrealist picture. His *Esquisse autobiographique*, written in the third person in 1954, states, 'He painted the picture "The Lost Jockey", conceived without aesthetic concerns, for the sole purpose of RESPONDING to a mysterious feeling, an anxiety "for no reason".'[7] This image was executed first as a collage, then in oils in 1926. Again, there is a curtain at the edge of the composition, and Magritte has depicted a forest of giant bilboquet-trees with a jockey galloping through it. The change of scale and the fusion of an inanimate element (the bilboquet) with a living element (the tree) are two further means Magritte employed to transform a familiar object into an out-of-the-ordinary *something else*.

Magritte's first Surrealist canvases still show the influence of de Chirico, through the representation of interiors with vanishing-point perspective and the presence of wooden mannequins, wigs, plaster faces (*The Face of Genius*, 1926 [33]) and empty frames that resemble flats from a stage set placed here and there (*The Silent Group*, 1926 [21]).

The atmosphere is heavy, the skies are leaden, the seas turbulent. The palette favours blacks, greys, browns, blues and dark greens. Sometimes called the 'Dark Period', this period covering the second half of the 1920s is characterised by a unique and mysterious kind of painting in which Magritte tries to confer upon the objects a 'disturbing poetic effect', a concept theorised by his like-minded friend Paul Nougé (1895–1967), who was an influential figure in the Surrealist group in Brussels.

This new direction that Magritte intended to take his painting in received a boost from two events in 1926: first, the signing

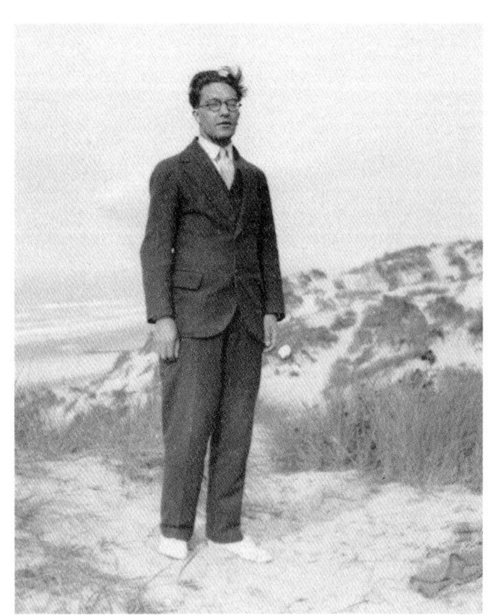

Paul Nougé, c. 1925.

The Dark Period

of a contract with the dealer Paul-Gustave van Hecke (1887–1967), which allowed the painter to devote himself entirely to his art, and secondly, by the formation of the Brussels Surrealist group, whose founding members, including E. L. T. Mesens, André Souris (1899–1970), Camille Goemans (1900–60) and Paul Nougé, assembled around Magritte. Nougé became the group's leader and theoretician. From prefaces to the catalogues of Magritte's exhibitions, to the book *René Magritte ou Les images défendues* (1943), Nougé succeeded better than anyone else at putting into words what had been at play in Magritte's works since the mid-1920s.

While under contract, Magritte entered the most prolific phase of his career, executing no less than one-quarter of his entire production of oil paintings in a mere four years. During this period, he added a number of objects central to his pictorial repertoire, defining them more clearly from one work to the next.

The sleigh bell, which appears for the first time in *The Silvered Chasm* (1926) [24], was one of his favourite objects. These small metal bells, designed to be attached to a workhorse's collar, fitted perfectly into the painter's compositions, sometimes as flowers growing from nowhere (*The Flowers of the Abyss*, 1928 [84]), sometimes outsized and floating in the sky (*The Voice of the Air*, 1931 [131]).

At the same time, Magritte introduced an object variously identified as a bilboquet, a bowling pin or a baluster. In various sizes, it abundantly populates his first Surrealist images – decked out with branches in a forest (*The Secret Player*, 1927 [50]) or with human features animated by a gaze (*The Difficult Crossing*, 1926 [22]; *The Encounter*, 1926 [29]).

It was also during this period that the man wearing a bowler hat entered Magritte's pictorial vocabulary. The man's appearance from the back and the artist's refusal to reveal his subject's face make him impenetrable in *The Musings of a Solitary Walker* (1926) [39], a strange work in which an emaciated white nude body floats, as if by magic, in the foreground of a typical landscape of the Châtelet area of Belgium, where Magritte was born. This withholding of the face is recurrent in Magritte's iconography at that time. It is not rare for a figure to be represented from the back (*The Ordeal of Sleep*, 1926 or 1927 [43]), for a face to be replaced by something else (*The Conqueror*, 1926 [34]) or for a wig to suggest the outline of a missing face (*The Midnight Marriage*, 1926 [36]). In 1928, Magritte introduced a white veil as a way of masking the face (*The Central Story*, 1928 [86]; *The Lovers*, 1928 [87]). Although some people relate this to the suicide of his mother, found dead with her face hidden by her nightgown, Magritte never spoke of this tragic episode from his youth, and no one can state with certainty that the veil is a reference to this event, rather than a new means of investing the image with a profound sense of mystery.

The face is revealed in *The Meaning of Night* (1927) [48], where the man in the bowler hat turns around, his eyes closed. He appears impassive, his features impersonal, scarcely human. He is accompanied by another man, standing on a beach strewn with clouds, while an indefinite furry silhouette floats in the air.

The atmosphere of the paintings from this period is heavy, sometimes even violent. *Girl Eating a Bird* (1927) [53], also cruelly entitled *Pleasure*, is a striking example of the almost criminal ambiance that then reigned in his images. In fact, Magritte derived several iconographic elements from his reading of crime stories. As a teenager, he had discovered the adventures of Fantômas, the elusive criminal character whose escapades were first dreamed up by French writers Pierre Souvestre and Marcel Allain in 1911, before they were adapted for the cinema by Louis Feuillade in 1913. The iconography of *The Man from the Sea* (1927) [47] was directly inspired by the closing scene of *Juve contre Fantômas*, in which the famous criminal pulls a lever that sets off an explosion. *The Murderer Threatened* (1927) [49], also a direct quotation from one of Feuillade's films, alludes as well to a scenario written by Paul Nougé in the series 'Images peintes'.[8]

Magritte regularly called up references to film and literature through his images and choice of titles. He rejected explanatory titles and instead considered them a poetic feature that protected the work from being interpreted. 'A poetic title has nothing to teach us, but must surprise and enchant us.'[9] Paul Nougé even said that the titles, which

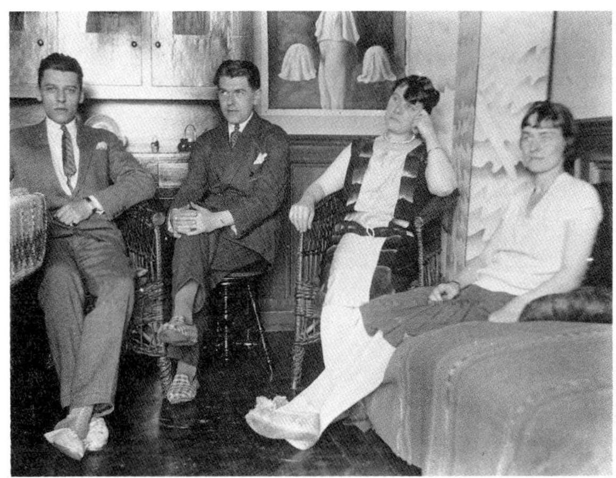

Paul, René and Georgette Magritte and an unidentified woman, Le Perreux-sur-Marne, 1928.

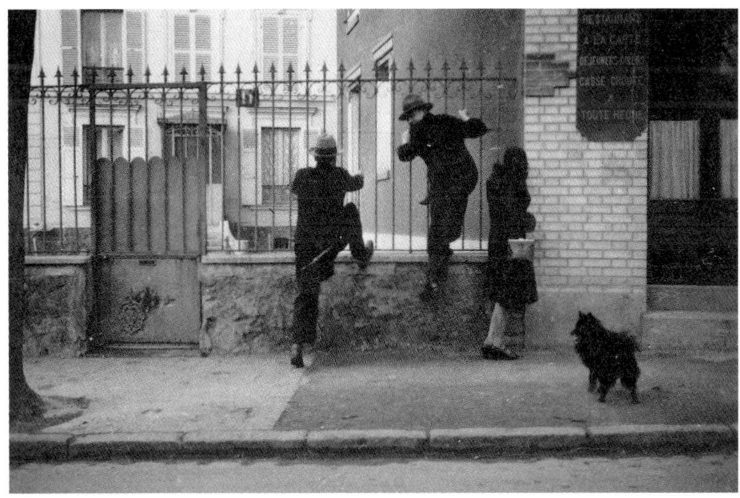

The Descent from La Courtille, Le Perreux-sur-Marne, 1928. Camille Goemans and René and Georgette Magritte.

were completely unrelated to the images, were intended only as a means to facilitate a conversation about a painting.[10]

Beyond the development of his pictorial vocabulary, Magritte also introduced new ways of making objects disturbing. With *Great Journeys* (1926) [31], objects are no longer juxtaposed in a collage-like effect but actually merged. A woman's legs are transformed into a cityscape, while her face is replaced by a strange and disturbing mollusc-like form. In a letter of November 1927 to Paul Nougé, Magritte described the concept of the metamorphosis in *Discovery* (1927) [72]: 'I think I have made a really striking discovery in painting. Up to now, I have used composite objects, or else the place of an object was sometimes enough to make it mysterious. But as a result of the experiments I've made here, I have found a new potential in things – their ability to become *gradually* something else, an object *merging into* an object other than itself. For instance, the sky in certain places allows wood to show through. This seems to me to be something quite different from a composite object, since there is no break between the two substances, and no limit. By this means I produce pictures in which the eye must "think" in a completely different way from the usual one: things are tangible and yet a few planks of solid wood become imperceptibly transparent in certain places, or else a naked woman has parts which also change into a different substance.'[11]

Besides oil paintings and gouaches, Magritte also made collages, cutting out shapes from sheet music with a pair of scissors. This practice, inherited from Max Ernst (1891–1976), whom he admired as much as de Chirico, is recalled in some paintings that look like hand-painted collages. Using isolation as a favourite means of overwhelming the object, Magritte employed the collage principle to form strange compositions through juxtaposition. *Dawn at Cayenne* (1926) [37], for example, brings together a pair of hands, a piece of cloth, a tube, a lit candle, a spider, two wooden boards and tree branches, all arranged in a peculiar order. The objects are combined freely in a way that is meant to astonish. In some cases, the object itself disappears, to be replaced by cut-out forms that resemble paper (*The Finery of the Storm*, 1927) [68] or shapeless metallic drippings (*Let Out of School*, 1927 [61]; *The Light-Breaker*, 1927 [70]) that recall works by Jean Arp (1886–1966).

   The Dark Period

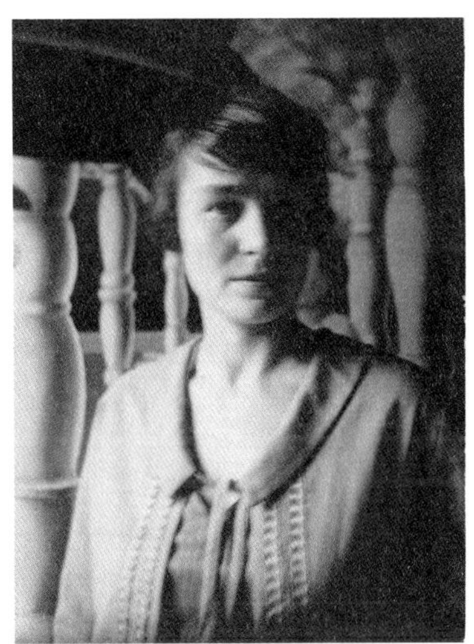

Georgette Magritte in front of *The Secret Player*,
Le Perreux-sur-Marne, *c.* 1927.

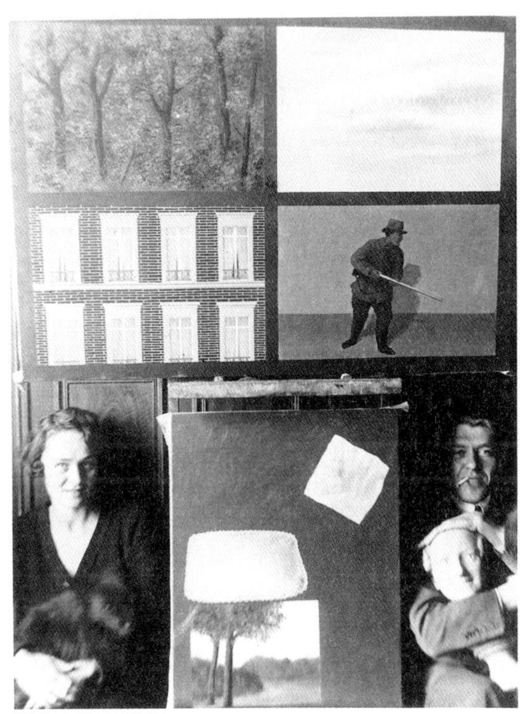

The Holy Family, Le Perreux-sur-Marne, 1928.

Magritte made the majority of these paintings at his new residence in Le Perreux-sur-Marne, on the outskirts of Paris, where he moved with his wife, Georgette, in September 1927. This move was not without an effect on the iconography of his works. The artist, whose everyday surroundings were a main source of inspiration, began to place his objects and figures in rooms similar to those of this new dwelling. Photographs from that period show the kind of wainscotting that is seen in *The Night Owl* [98], *The Voice of Silence* [99] and *Attempting the Impossible* [100], all from 1928.

Rootedness in a poetical form of the everyday became more and more marked. Magritte abandoned abstraction, turning first to a strange and disquieting form of figuration before taking up an iconography of ordinary realism. This new orientation was accompanied by an increasing desire to represent objects in thorough detail: a chair with carefully painted caning (*The Automaton*, 1928 [102]) or a cannon painted so precisely that its make can be identified (*On the Threshold of Freedom*, 1930 [108]).

Magritte was not content to represent objects with almost photographic fidelity – a necessary condition for the success of his work. He wanted to make them 'shout'.[12] Capitalising on the viewer's inability to notice the objects around them because of their ordinariness, Magritte used various means to 'disorient' these objects and give them, one after another, a new existence. In 'La Ligne de vie', Magritte listed the ways he 'forced objects to become sensational', namely 'the creation of new objects; the transformation of known objects, the change of material for some objects: a sky of wood, for example; the combination of words with images; the false identification of an image; the implementation of ideas suggested by friends; the representation of visions from a half-waking state'.[13]

7   Magritte, 'Esquisse', op. cit., p. 10.
8   Paul Nougé, 'Images peintes' (1927), in Paul Nougé, *Histoire de ne pas rire* (Brussels: Les Lèvres nues, 1956), pp. 289–90.
9   René Magritte, 'Question du titre', copy of an unpublished manuscript, Archives de l'Art contemporain en Belgique (AACB), inv. 342.
10 Paul Nougé, 'Avertissement', in *René Magritte* (Brussels: Salle Giso, February 1931), p. 12.
11 René Magritte, Letter to Paul Nougé, November 1927, quoted in David Sylvester and Sarah Whitfield, *René Magritte. Catalogue raisonné*, vol. 1 (Antwerp: Fonds Mercator, 1992), p. 245.
12   Magritte, 'La Ligne de vie', op. cit., p. 109.
13   Ibid., p. 110.

   The Dark Period

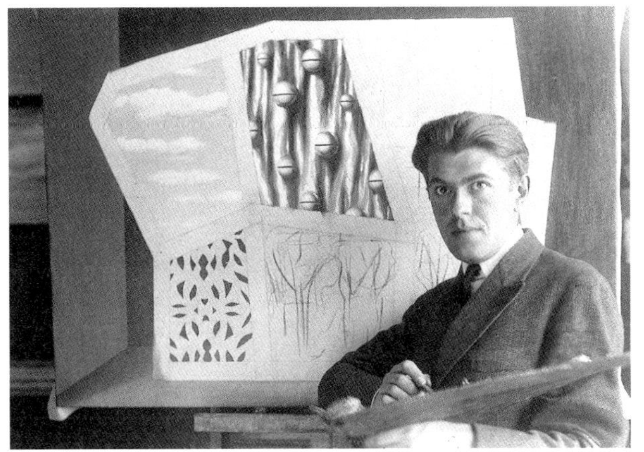

René Magritte painting *The Empty Mask*,
Le Perreux-sur-Marne, 1928.

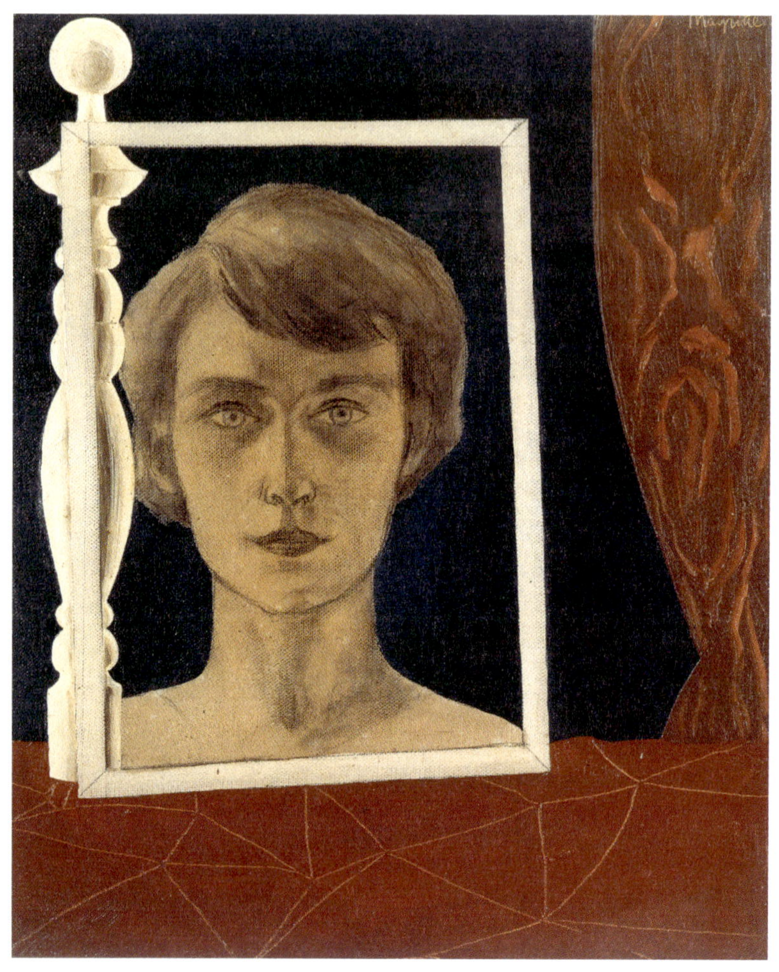

17
(Portrait of Georgette Magritte)
1926
oil and pencil on canvas, 55 × 45 cm

        The Dark Period

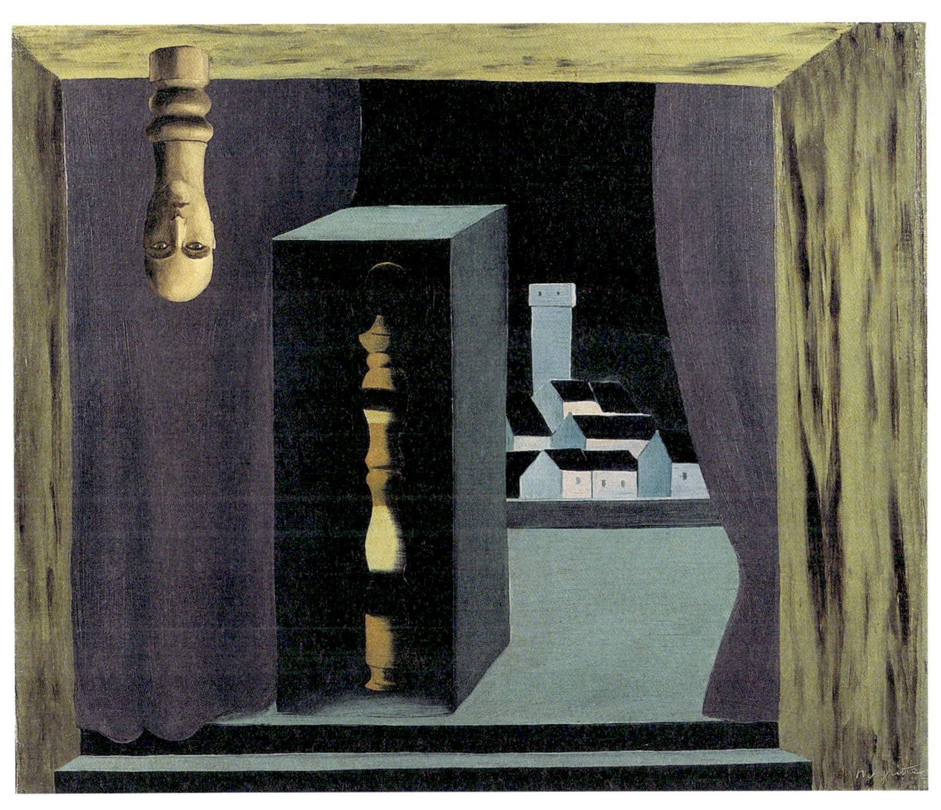

18
The Famous Man
1926
oil on canvas, 65 × 81 cm

1926–1930

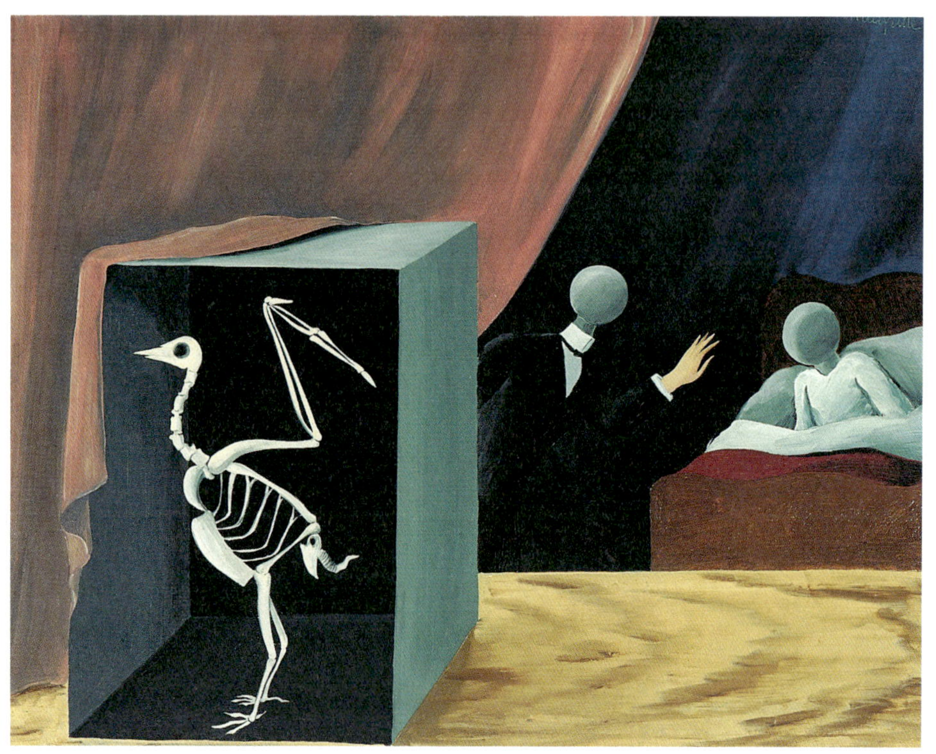

19
Sensational News
1926
oil on canvas, 62 × 81 cm

     The Dark Period

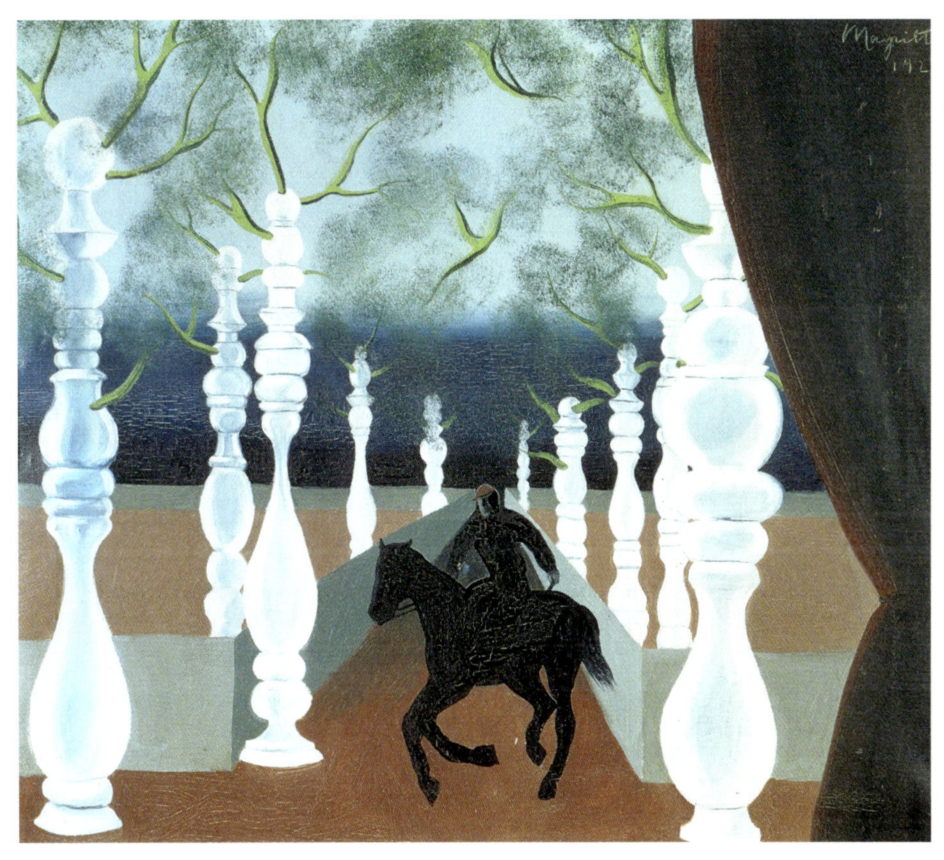

20
The Lost Jockey
1926
oil on canvas, 65 × 75 cm

                    1926–1930

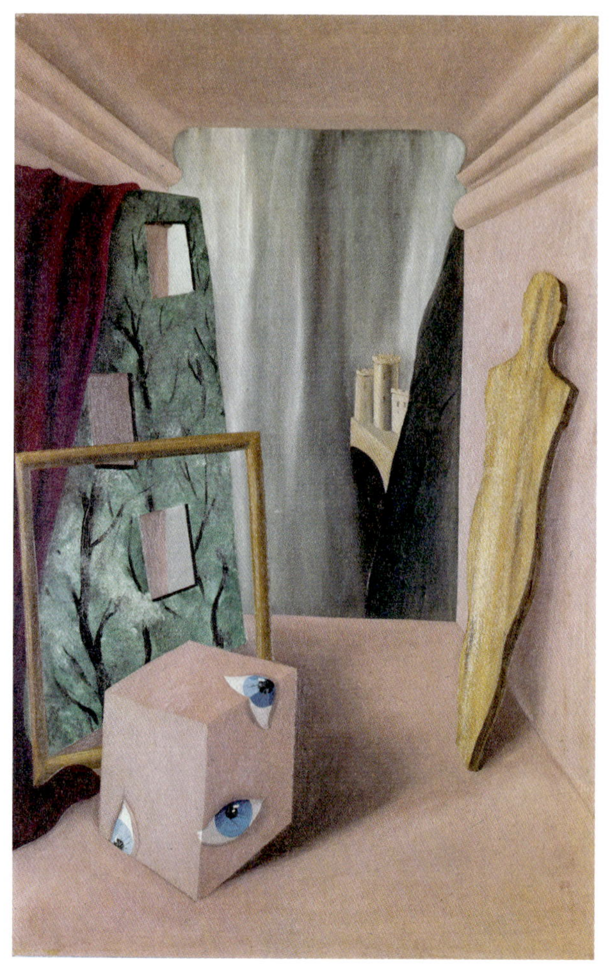

21
The Silent Group
1926
oil on canvas, 120 × 80 cm

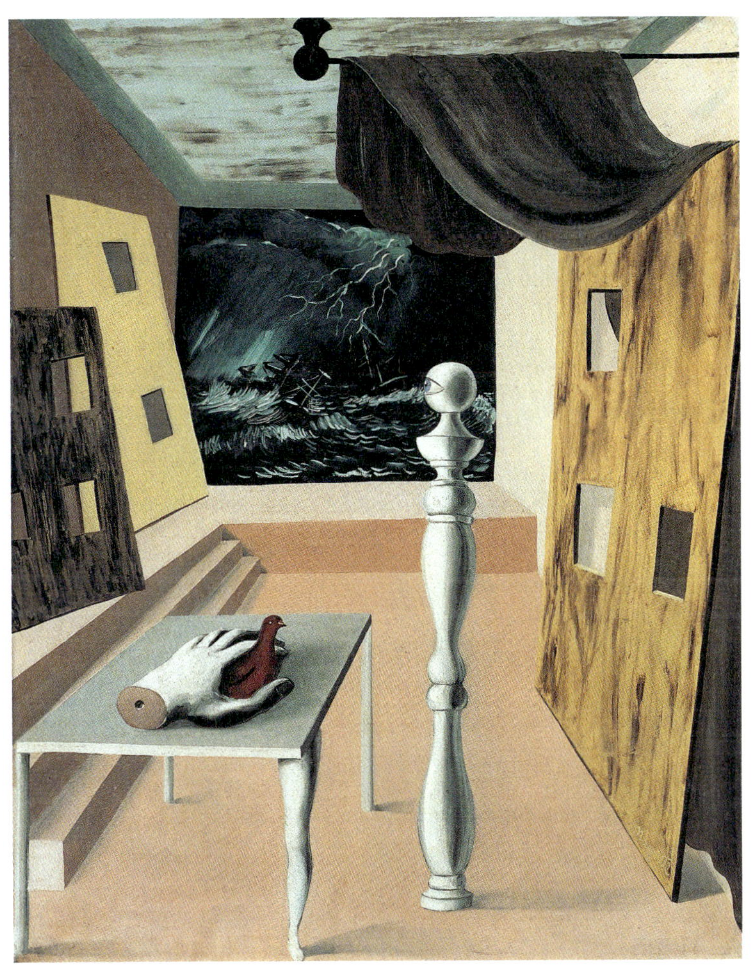

22
The Difficult Crossing
1926
oil on canvas, 80 × 65 cm

1926–1930

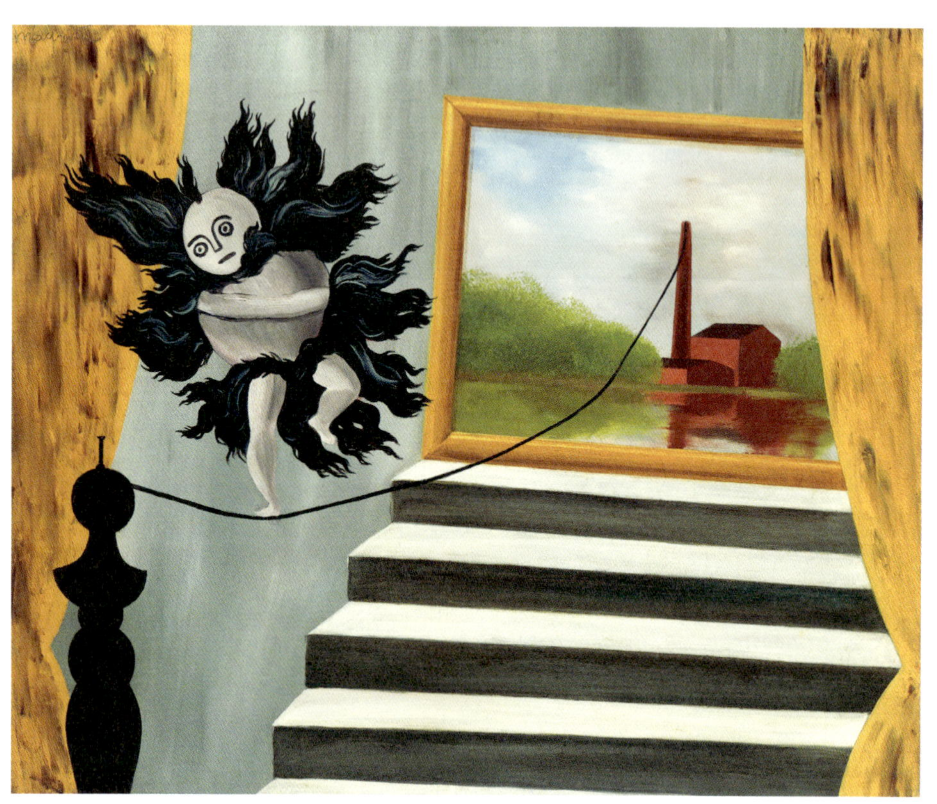

23
The Master of the Revels
1926
oil on canvas, 65 × 80 cm

The Dark Period

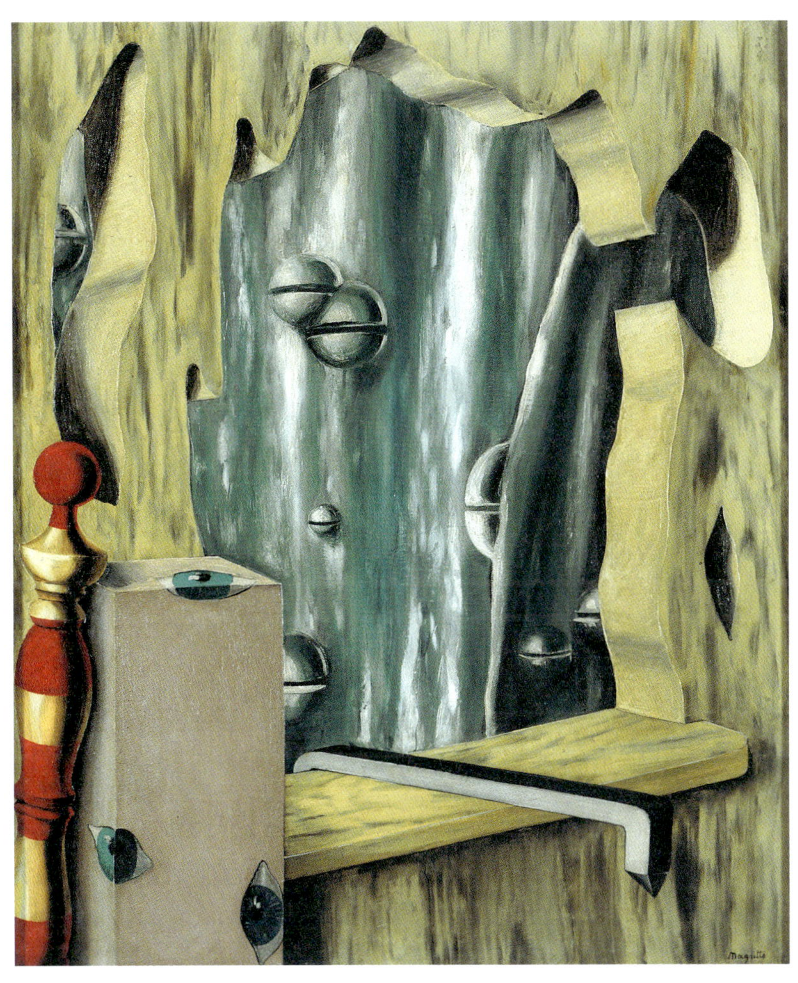

24
The Silvered Chasm
1926
oil on canvas, 75 × 65 cm

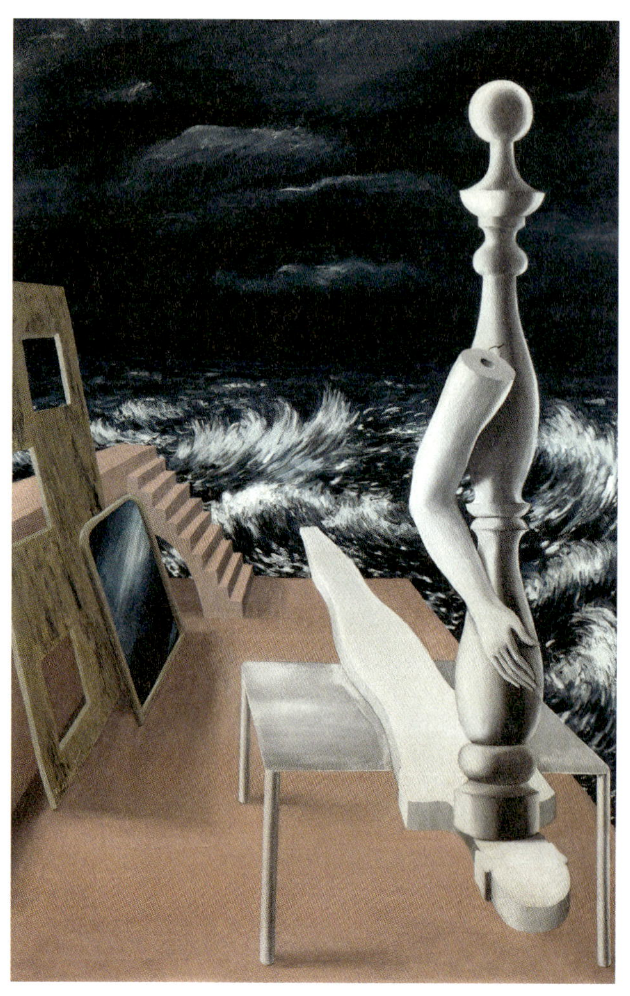

25
The Birth of the Idol
1926
oil on canvas, 120 × 80 cm

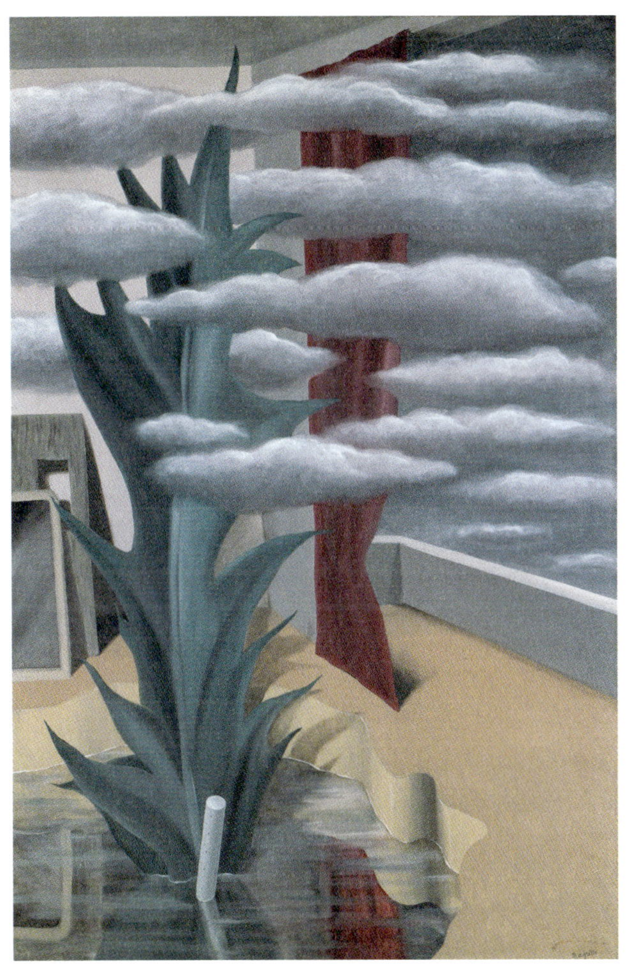

26
After the Water, the Clouds
1926
oil on canvas, 120 × 80 cm

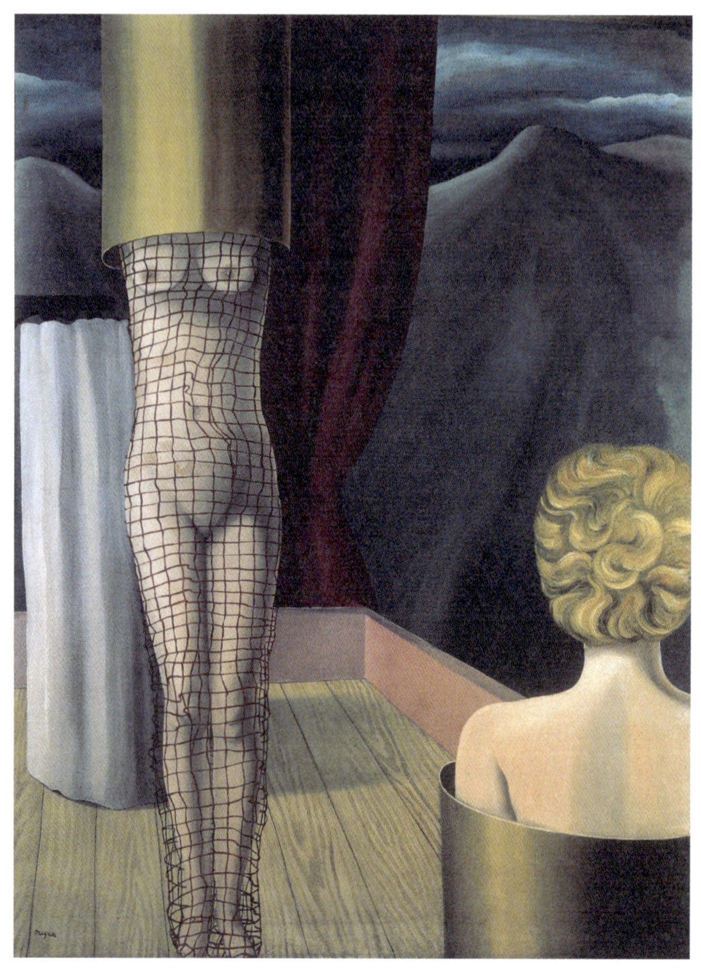

27
The Magician's Accomplices
1926
oil on canvas, 139 × 105 cm

       The Dark Period

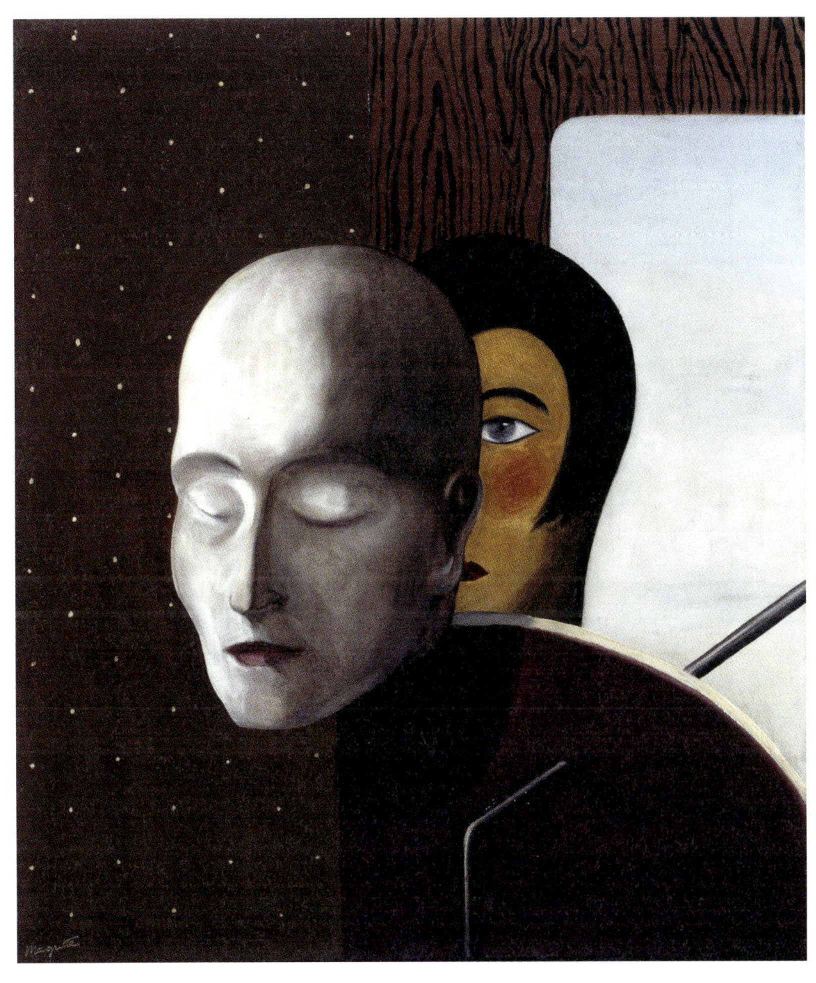

28
He is Not Speaking
1926
oil on canvas, 75 × 65 cm

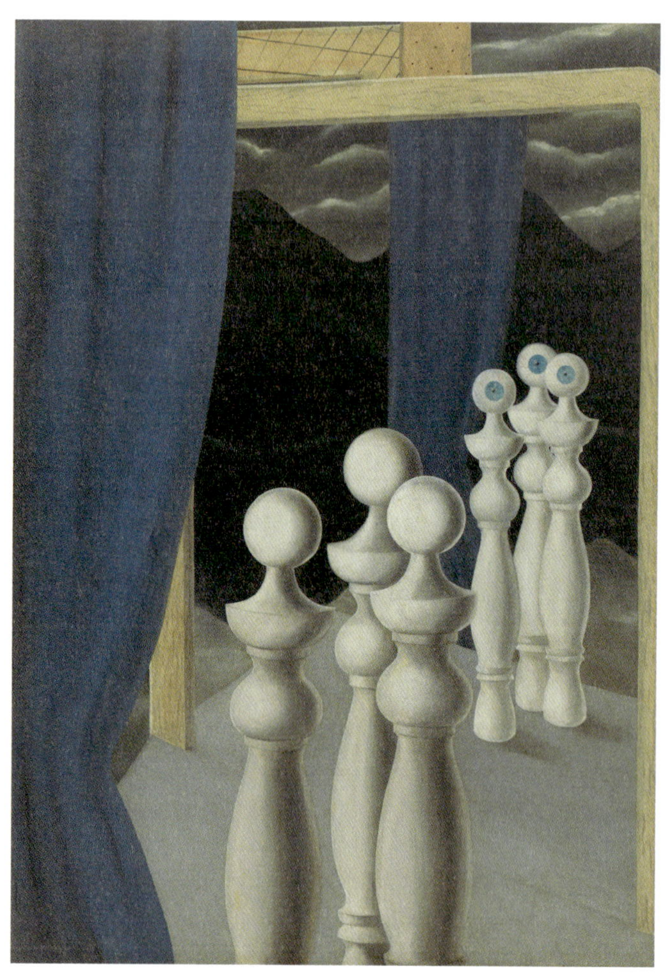

29
The Encounter
1926
oil on canvas, 139.5 × 99 cm

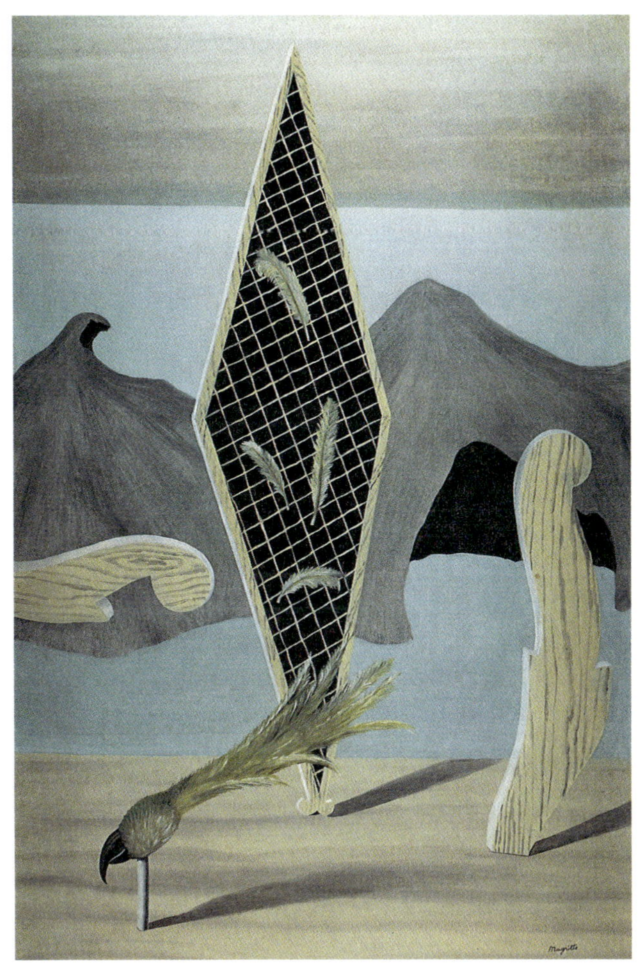

30
The Wreckage of the Dark
1926
oil on canvas, 120 × 80 cm

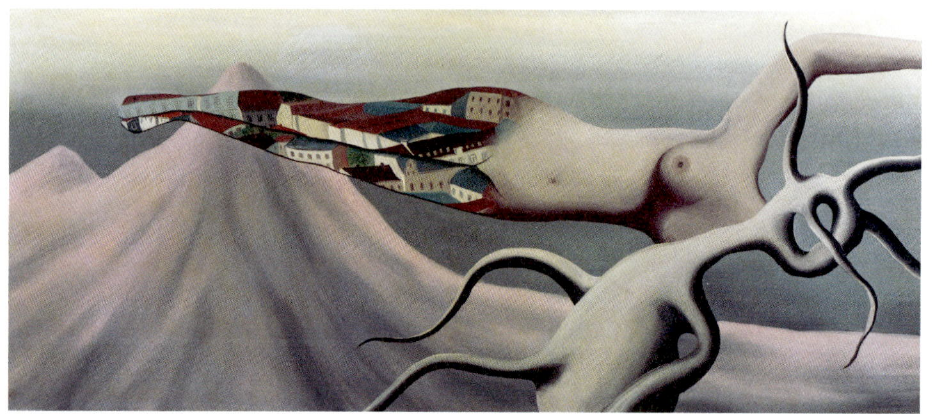

31
Great Journeys
1926
oil on canvas, 65 × 150 cm

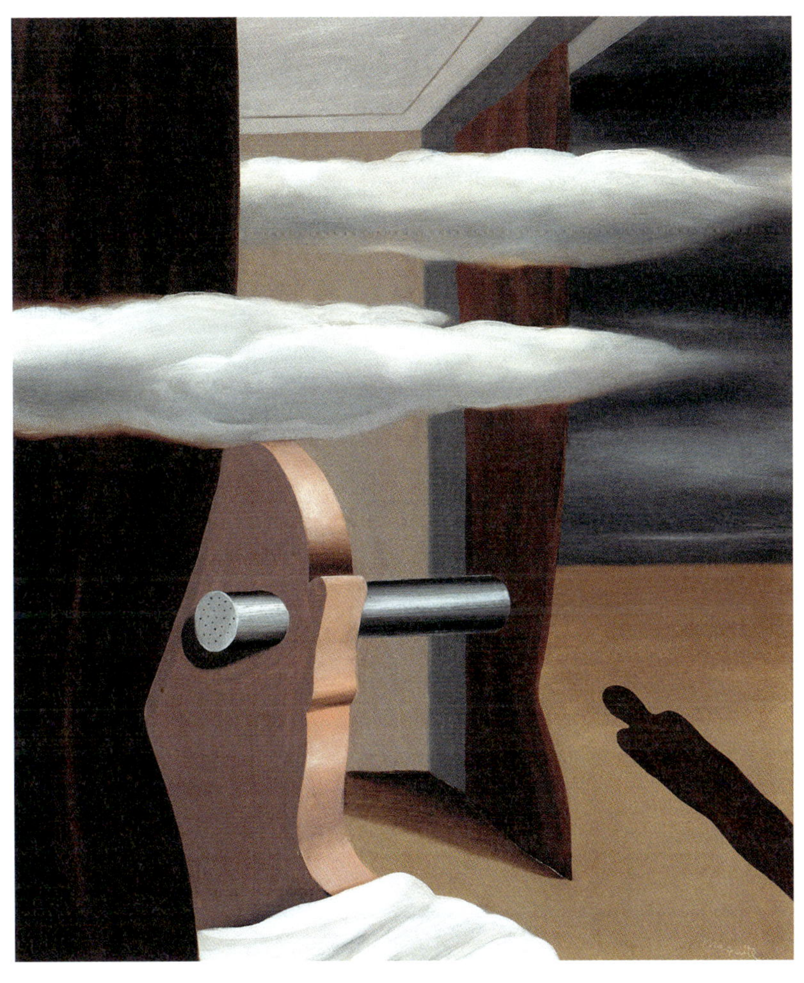

32
The Desert Catapult
1926
oil on canvas, 75 × 65 cm

 1926–1930

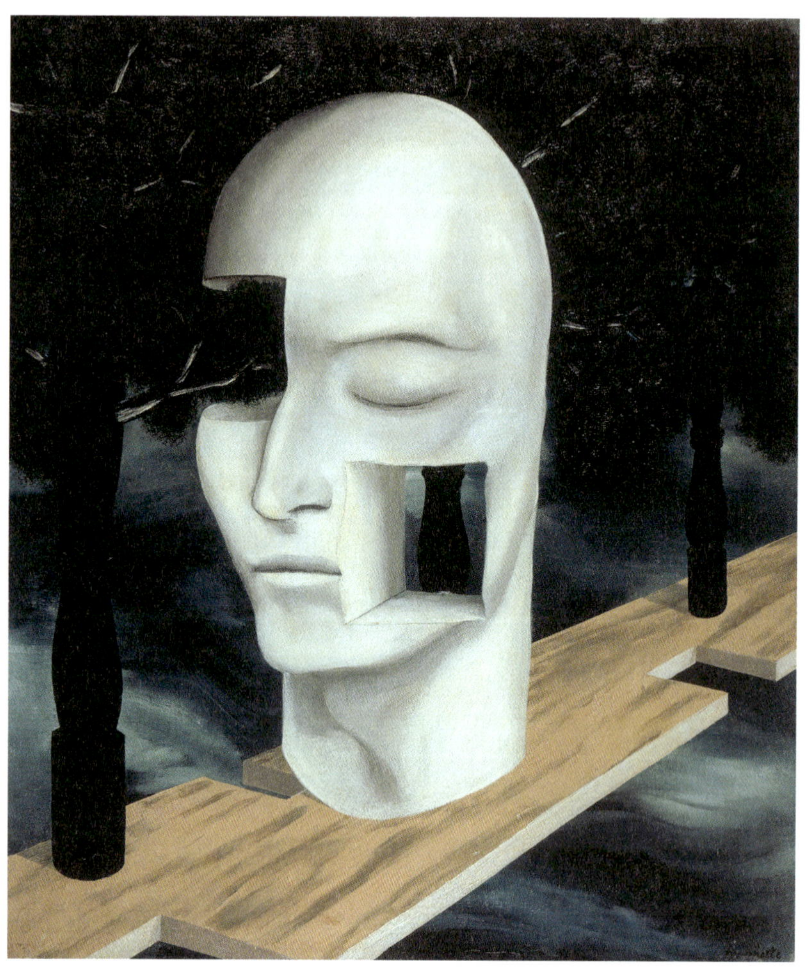

33
The Face of Genius
1926
oil on canvas, 75 × 65 cm

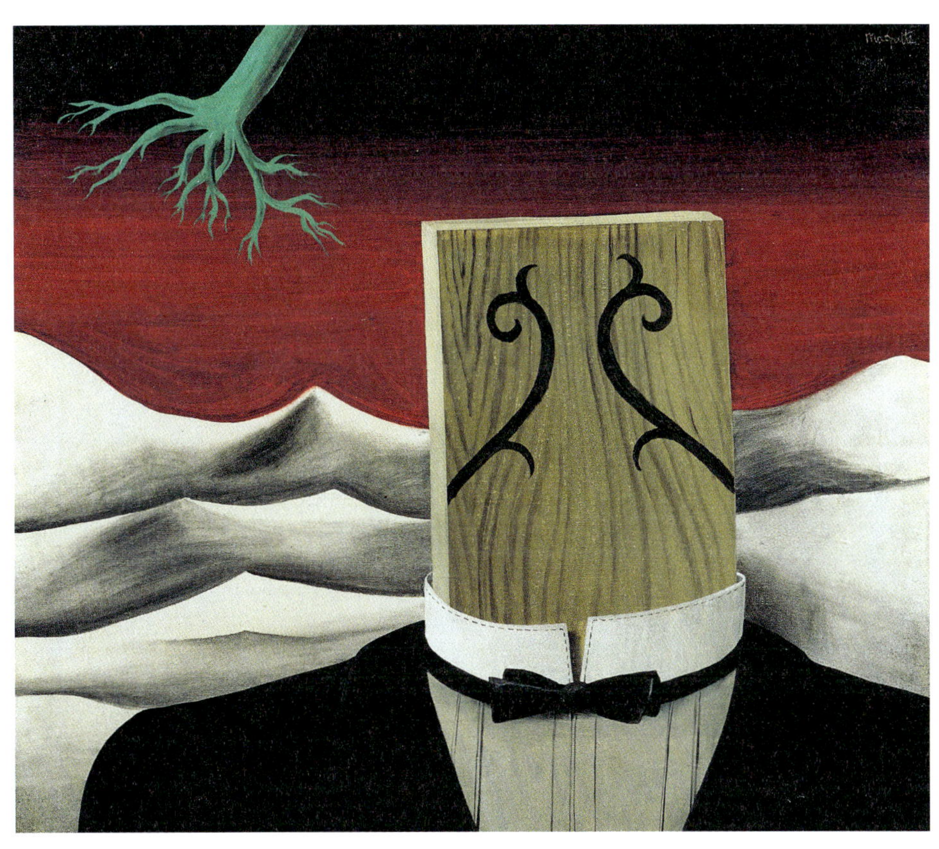

34
The Conqueror
1926
oil and Ripolin on canvas, 65 × 75 cm

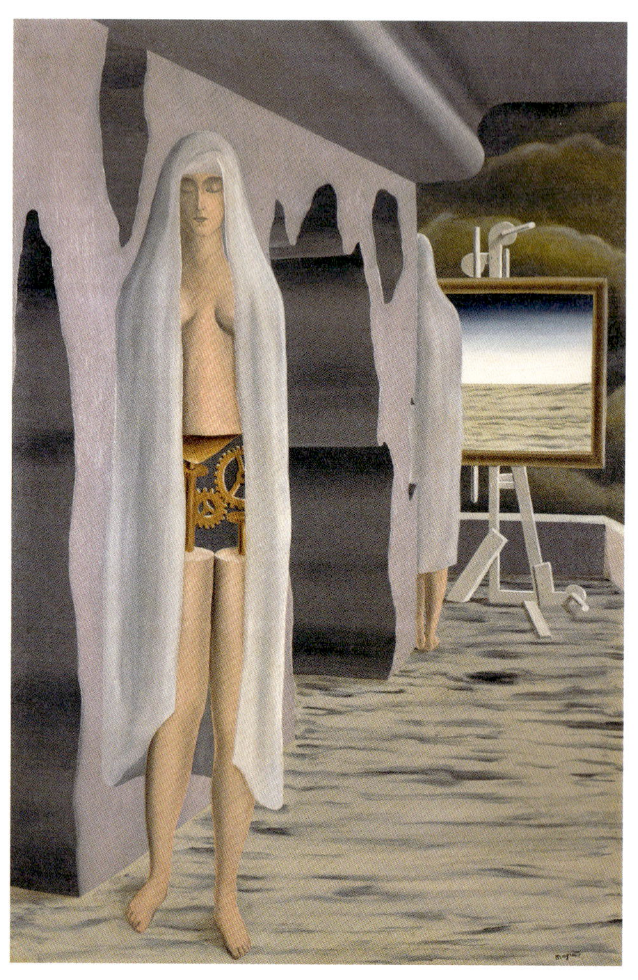

35
The Age of Marvels
1926
oil on canvas, 120 × 80 cm

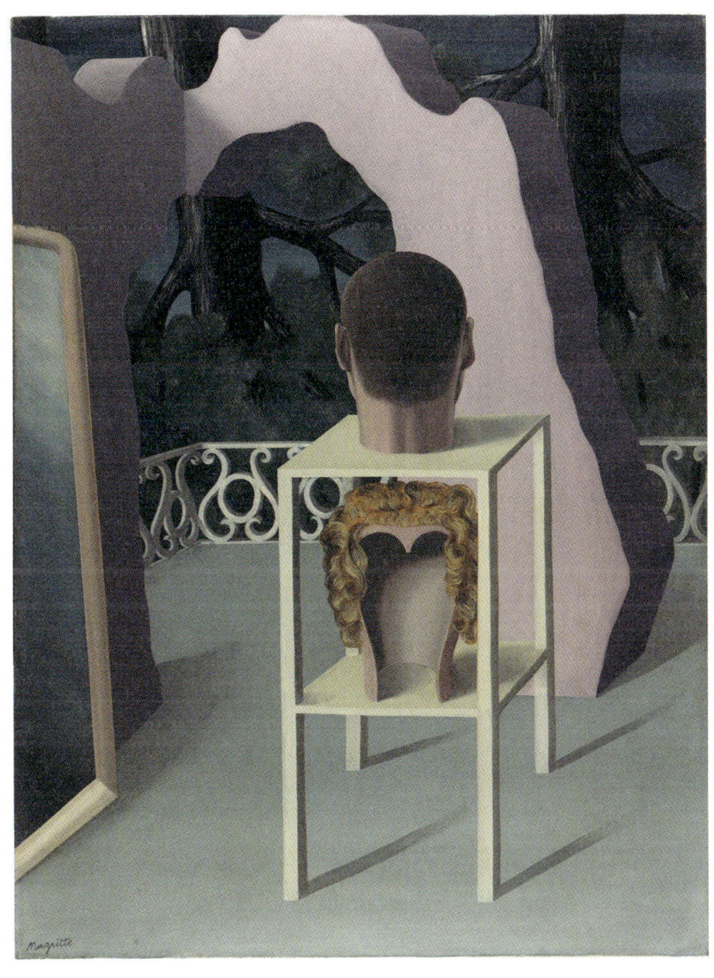

36
The Midnight Marriage
1926
oil on canvas, 139 × 105 cm

          1926–1930

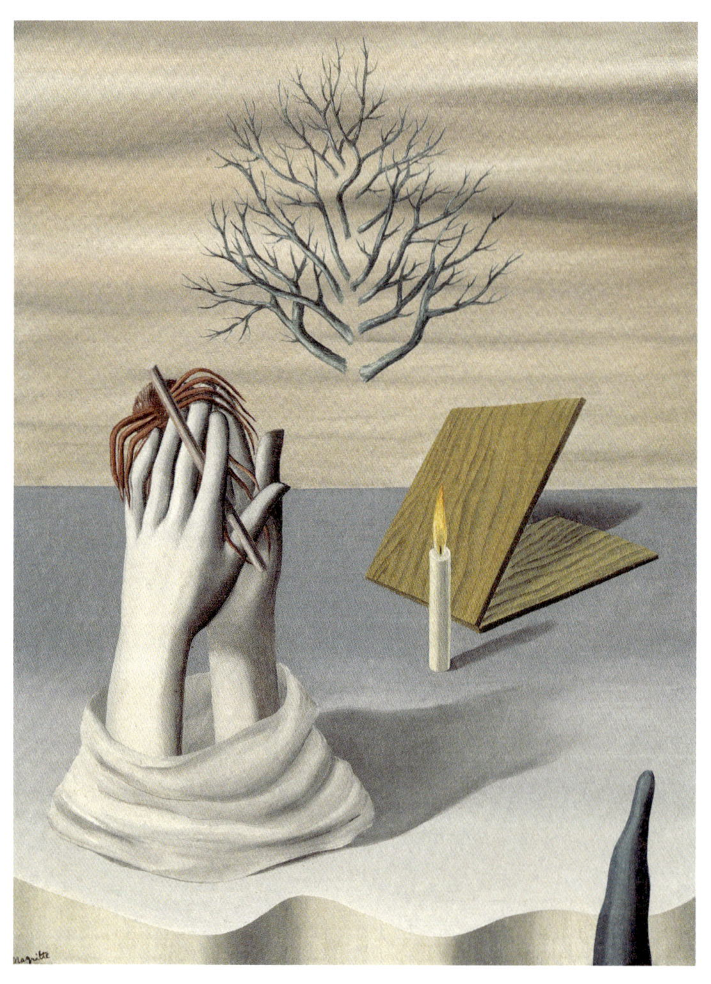

37
Dawn at Cayenne
1926
oil on canvas, 97 × 74 cm

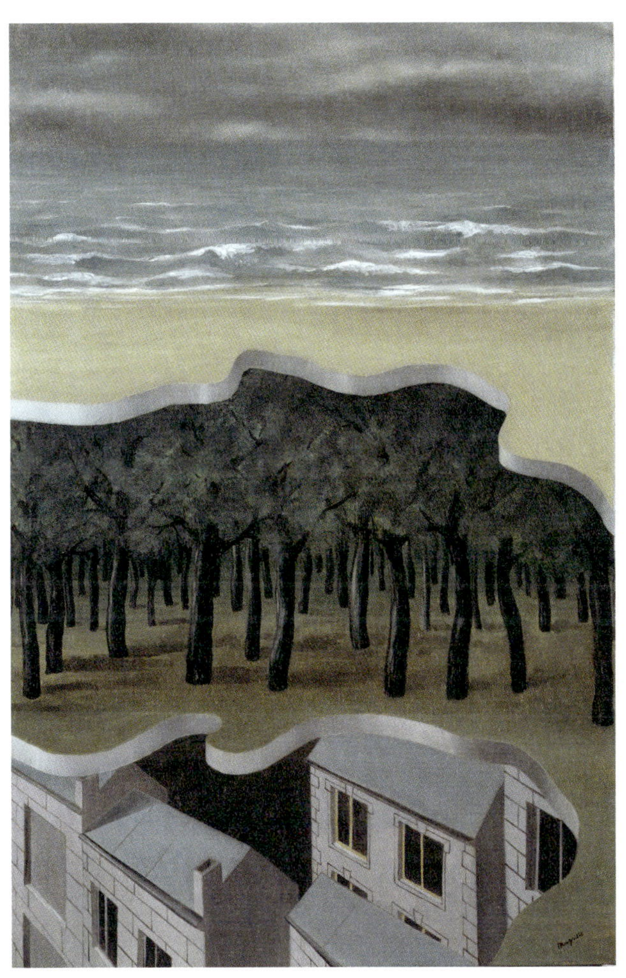

38
Panorama for the Populace
1926
oil on canvas, 120 × 80 cm

　　　1926–1930

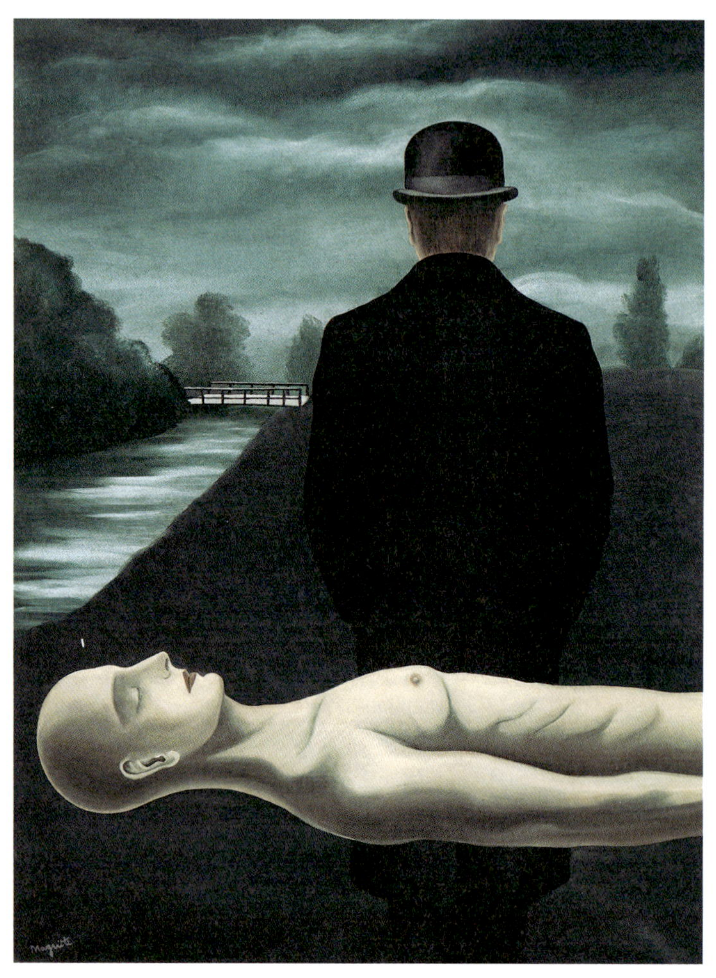

39
The Musings of a Solitary Walker
1926
oil on canvas, 139 × 105 cm

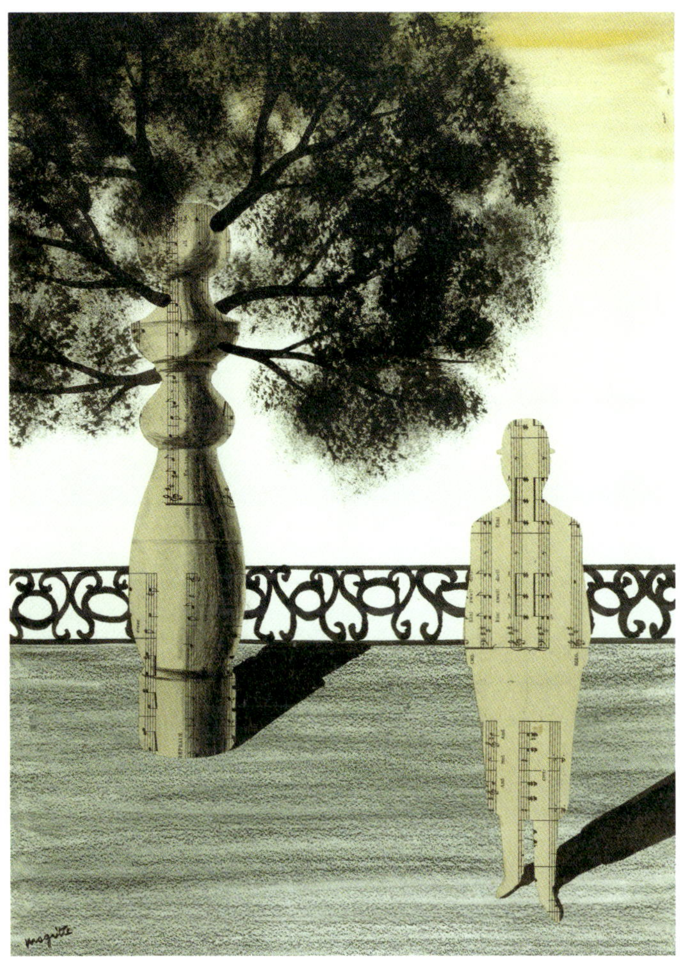

40
Untitled
1926
pasted paper, gouache, watercolour on paper, 55 × 40 cm

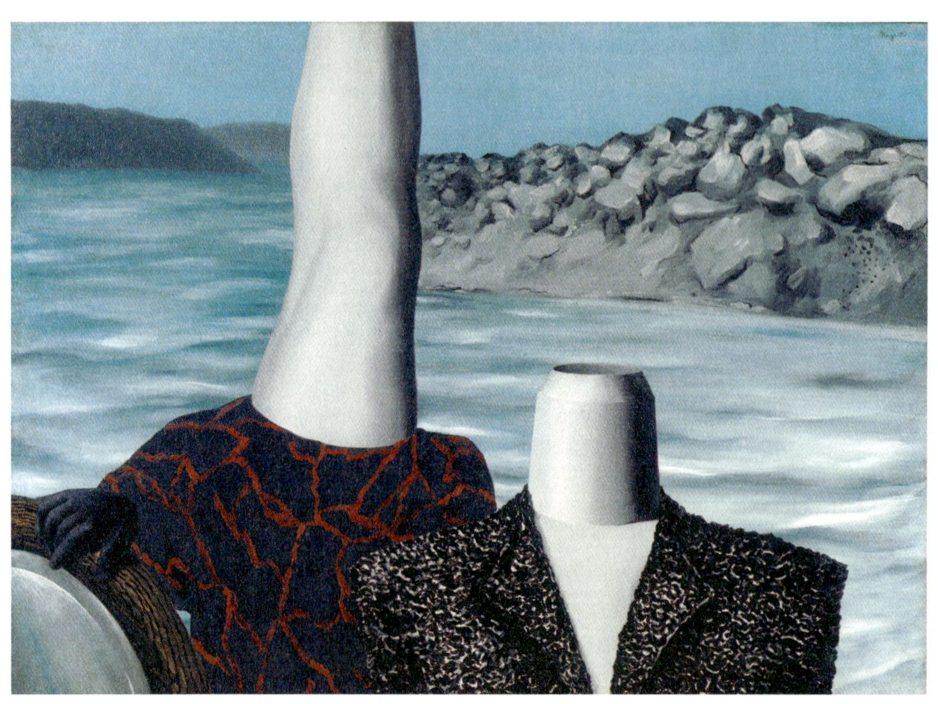

41
The Denizens of the River
1926
oil on canvas, 73 × 100 cm

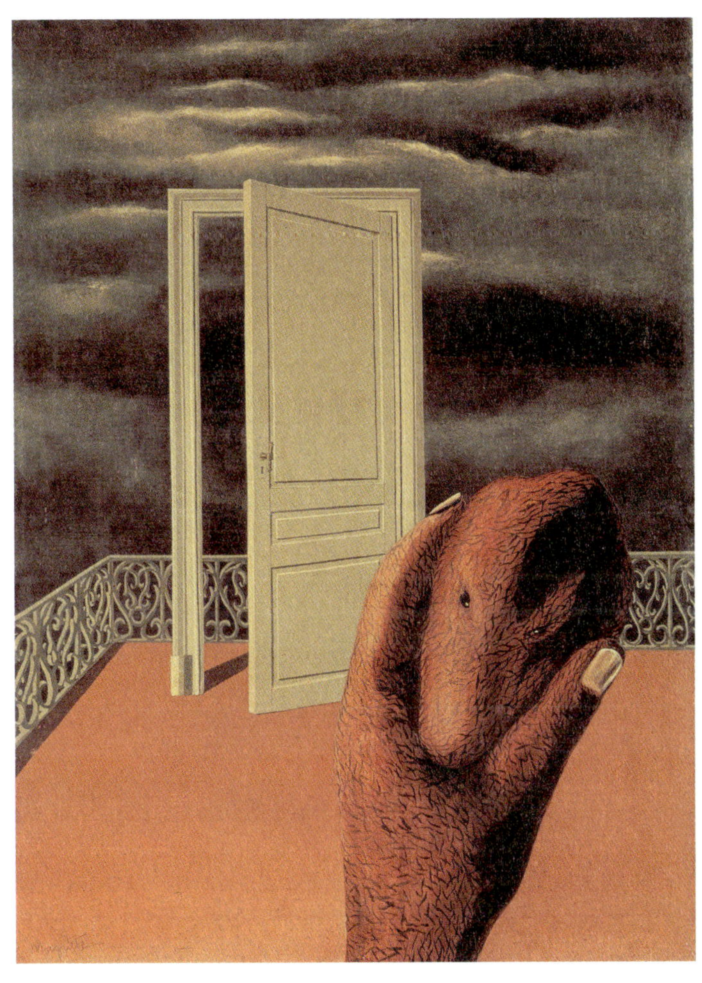

42
(The Scars of the Memory)
1926 or 1927
oil and pencil on canvas, 73 × 54 cm

                    1926–1930

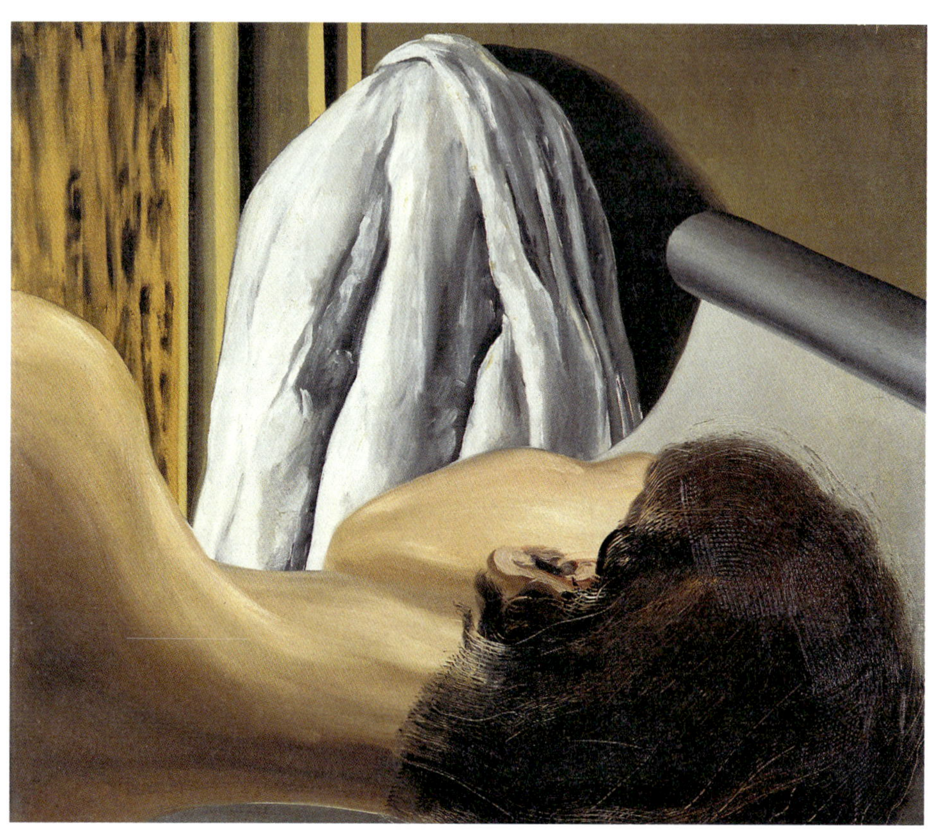

43
The Ordeal of Sleep
1926 or 1927
oil on canvas, 64 × 75 cm

The Dark Period

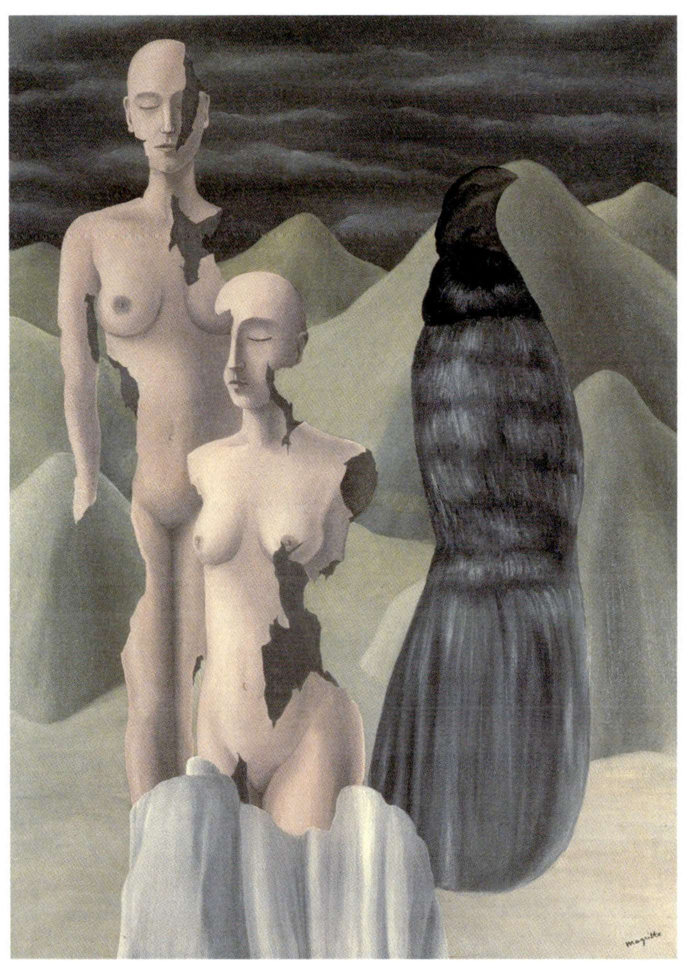

44
Polar Light
1926 or 1927
oil on canvas, 139 × 105 cm

 1926–1930

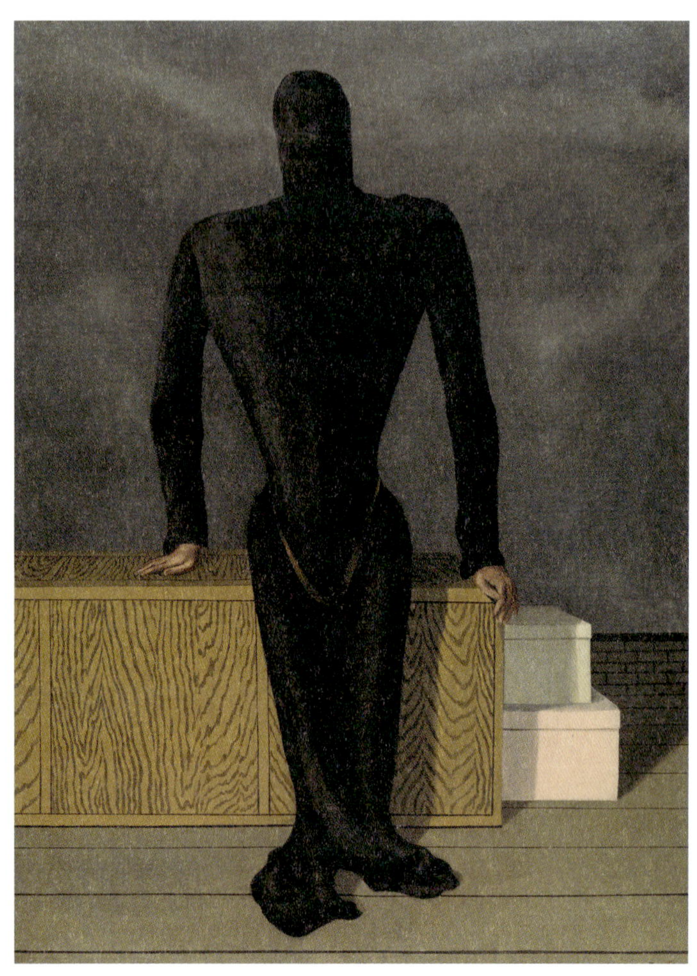

45
The Female Thief
1927
oil on canvas, 100 × 73 cm

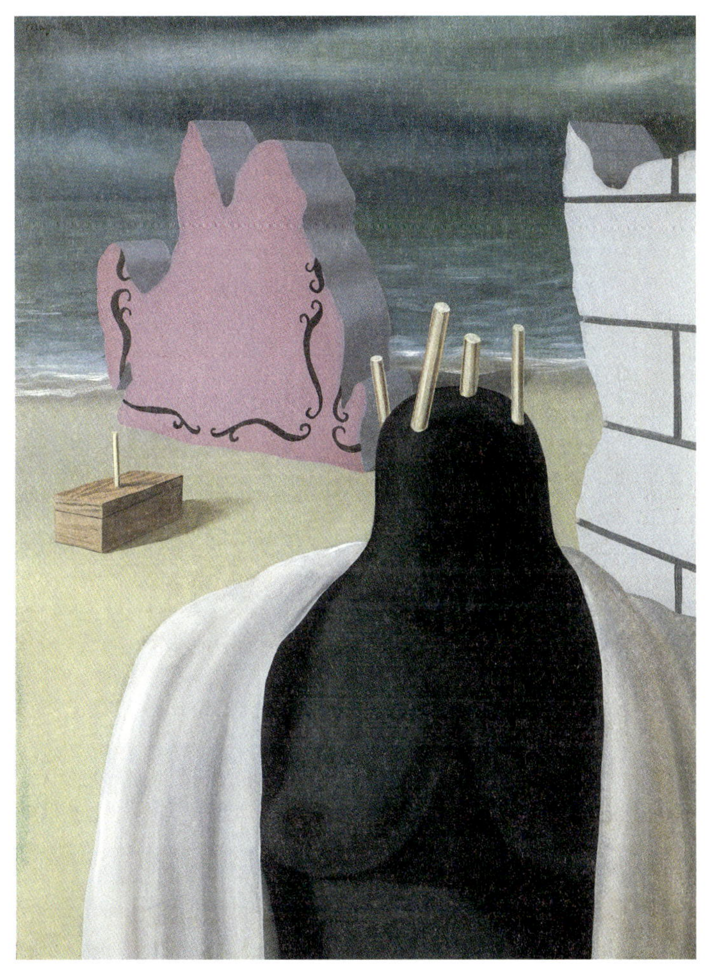

46
The Torturing of the Vestal Virgin
1927
oil on canvas, 97.5 × 74.5 cm

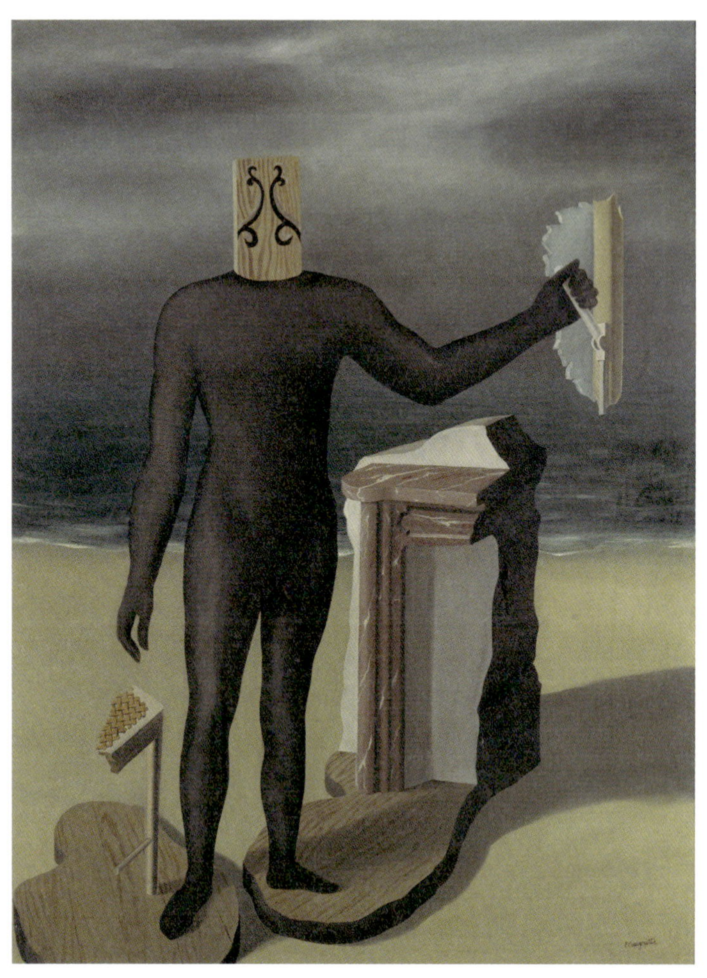

47
The Man from the Sea
1927
oil on canvas, 139 × 105 cm

    The Dark Period

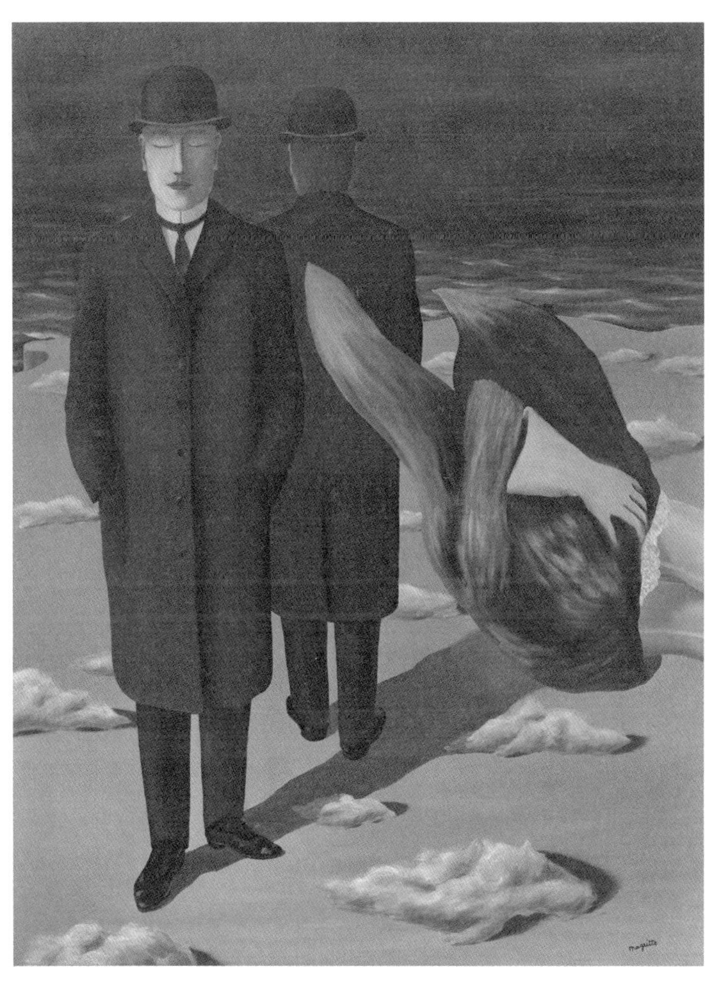

48
The Meaning of Night
1927
oil on canvas, 139 × 105 cm

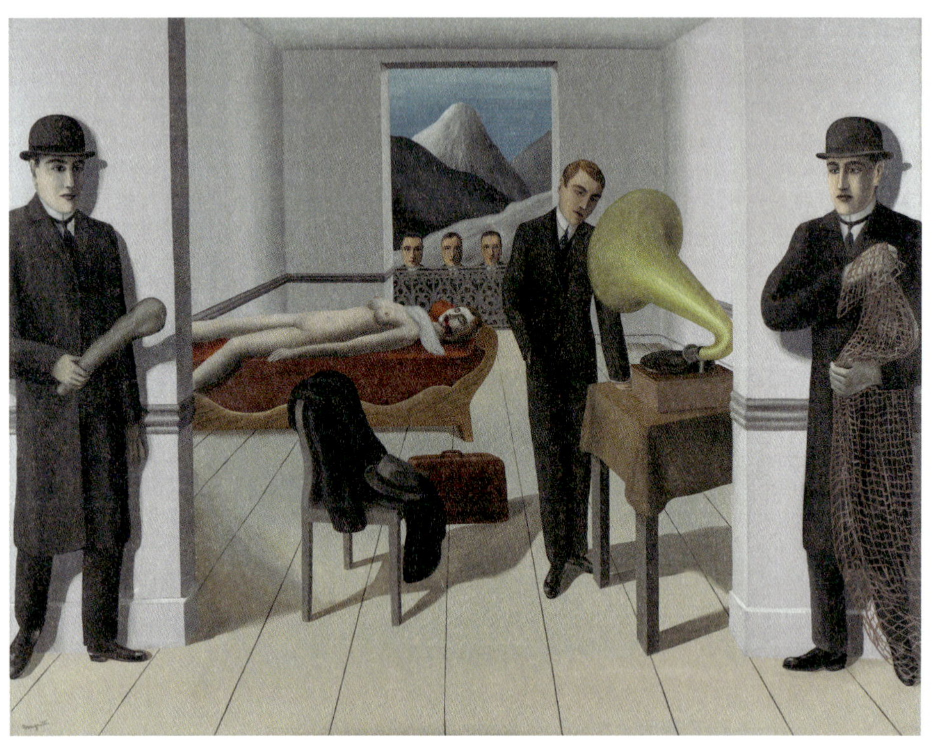

49
The Murderer Threatened
1927
oil on canvas, 152 × 195 cm

  The Dark Period

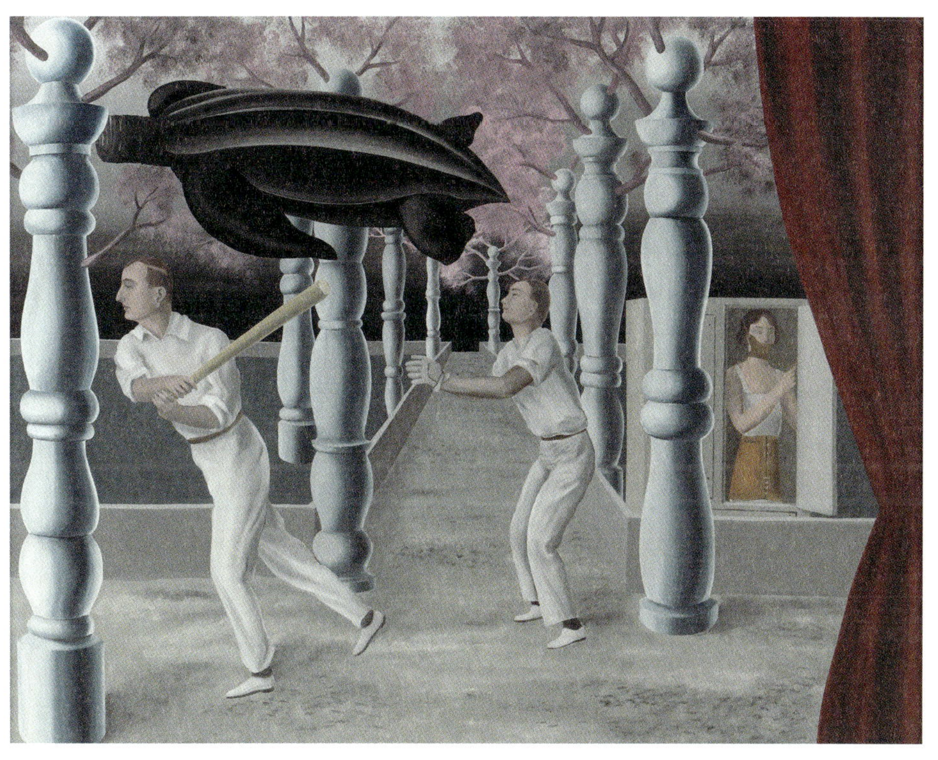

50
The Secret Player
1927
oil on canvas, 152 × 195 cm

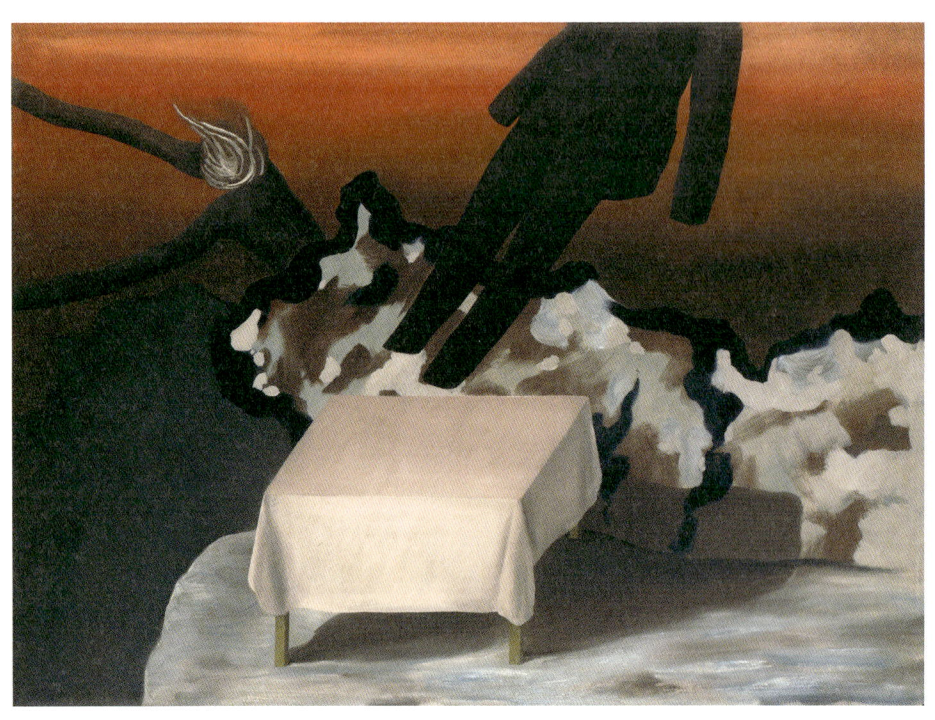

51
The Weariness of Life
1927
oil on canvas, 73 × 100 cm

 The Dark Period

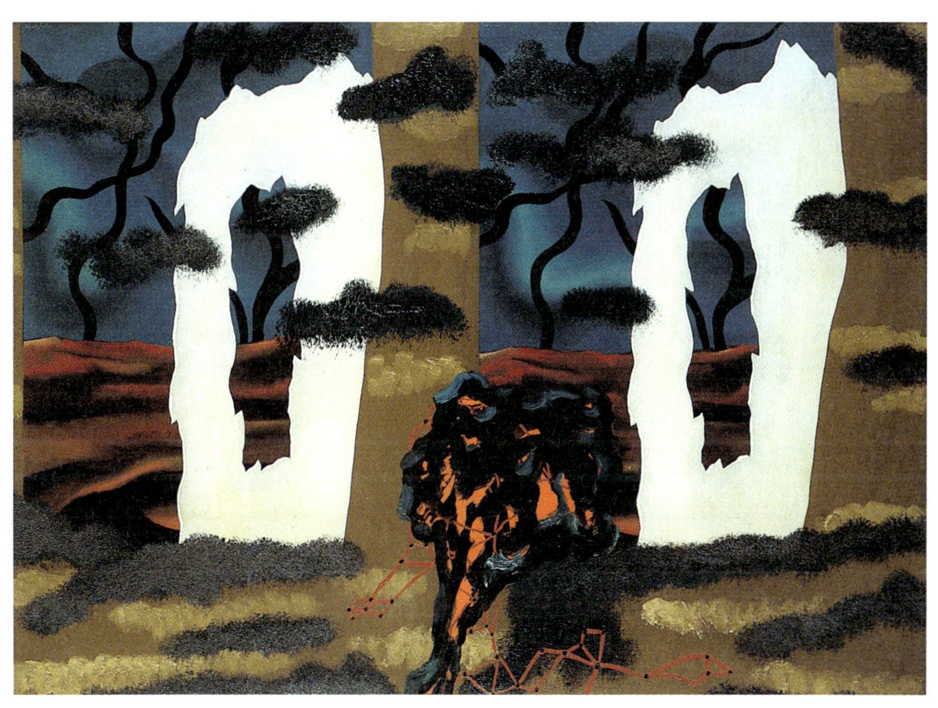

52
A Taste for the Invisible
1927
oil on canvas, 73 × 100 cm

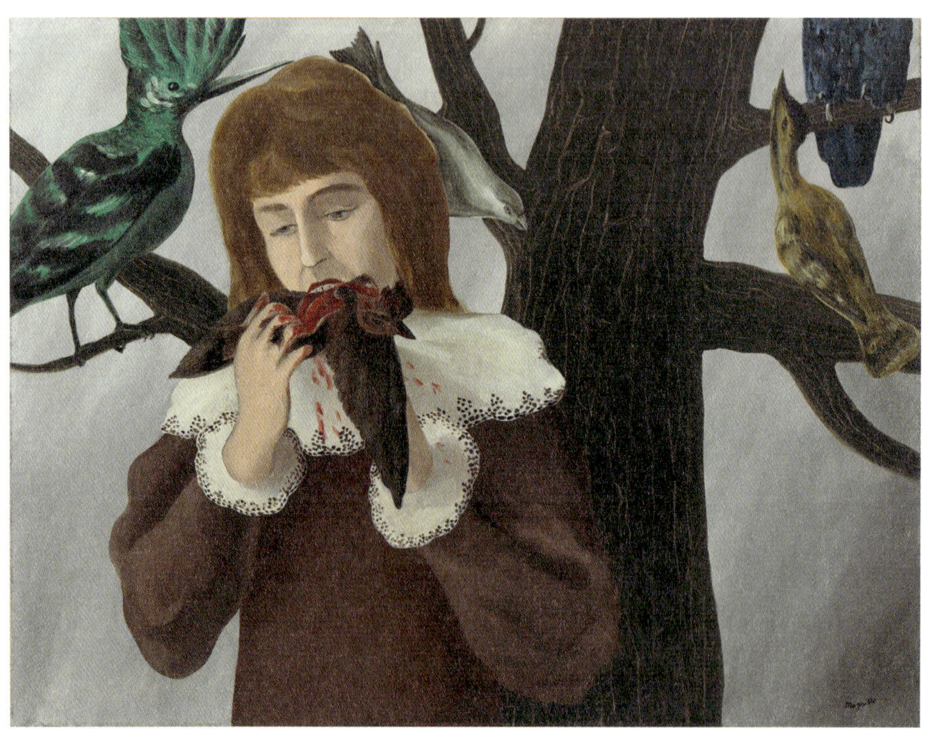

53
Girl Eating a Bird (Pleasure)
1927
oil on canvas, 74 × 97 cm

The Dark Period

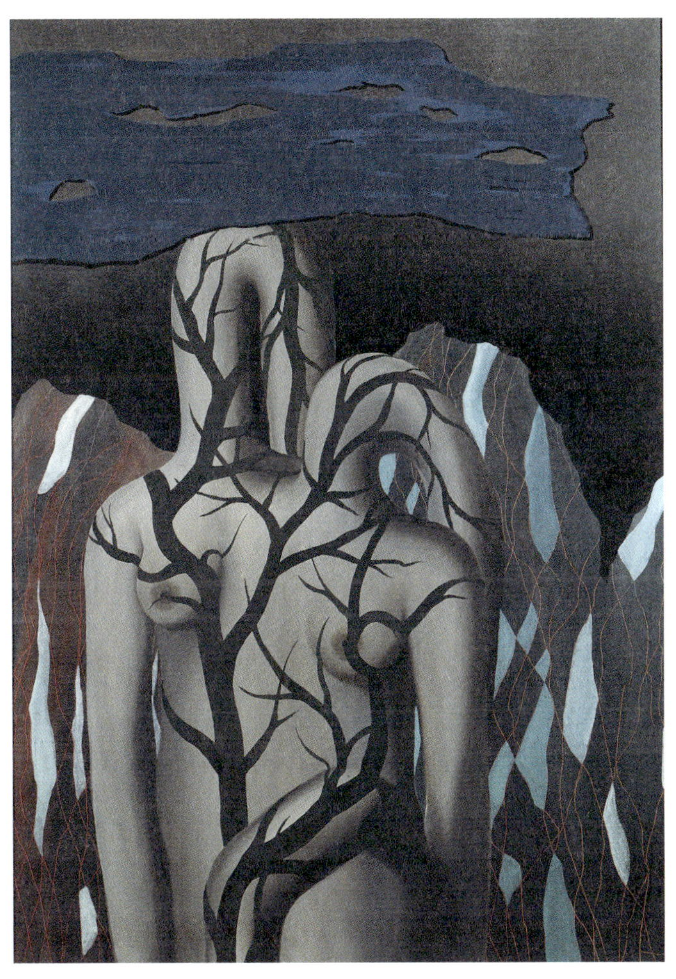

54
Landscape
1927
oil on canvas, 100 × 73 cm

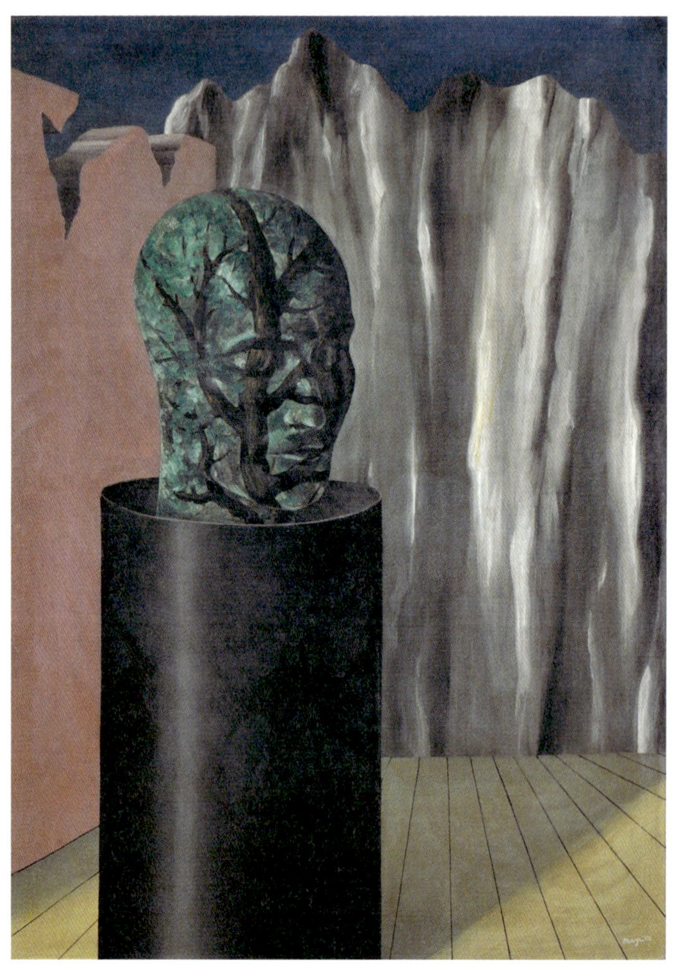

55
The Forest
1927
oil on canvas, 100 × 73 cm

The Dark Period

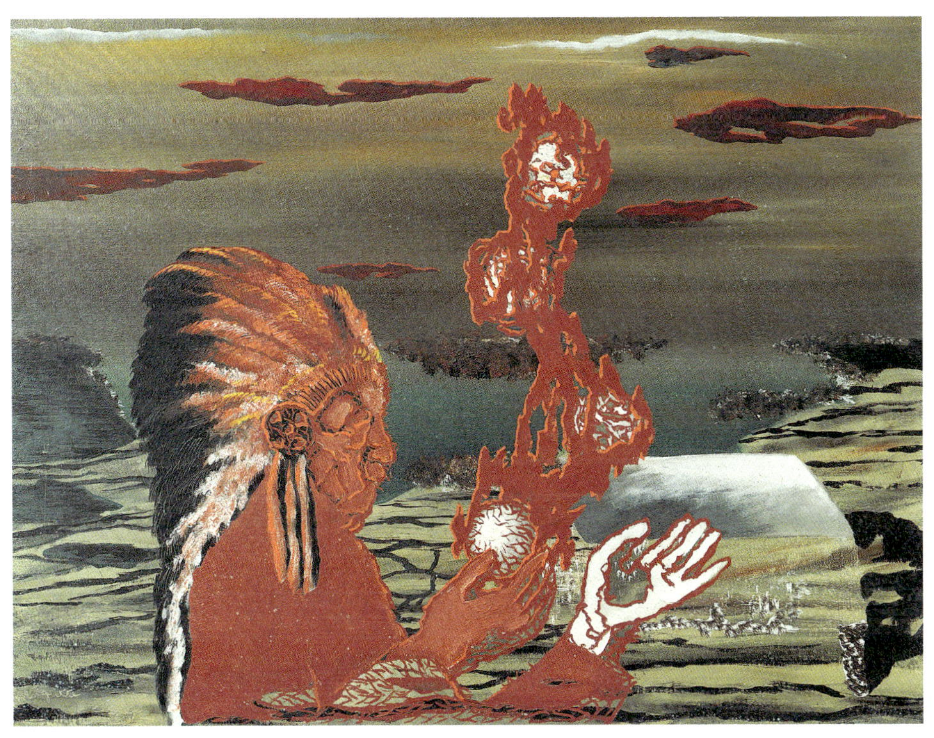

56
The Age of Fire
1927
oil on canvas, 73 × 100 cm

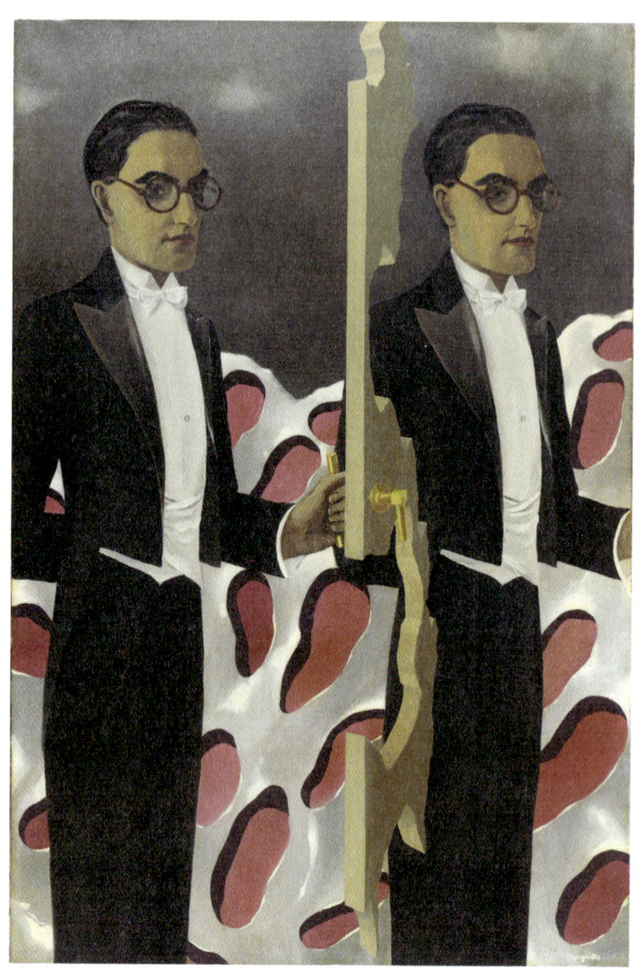

57
(Portrait of Paul Nougé)
1927
oil on canvas, 95 × 65 cm

The Dark Period

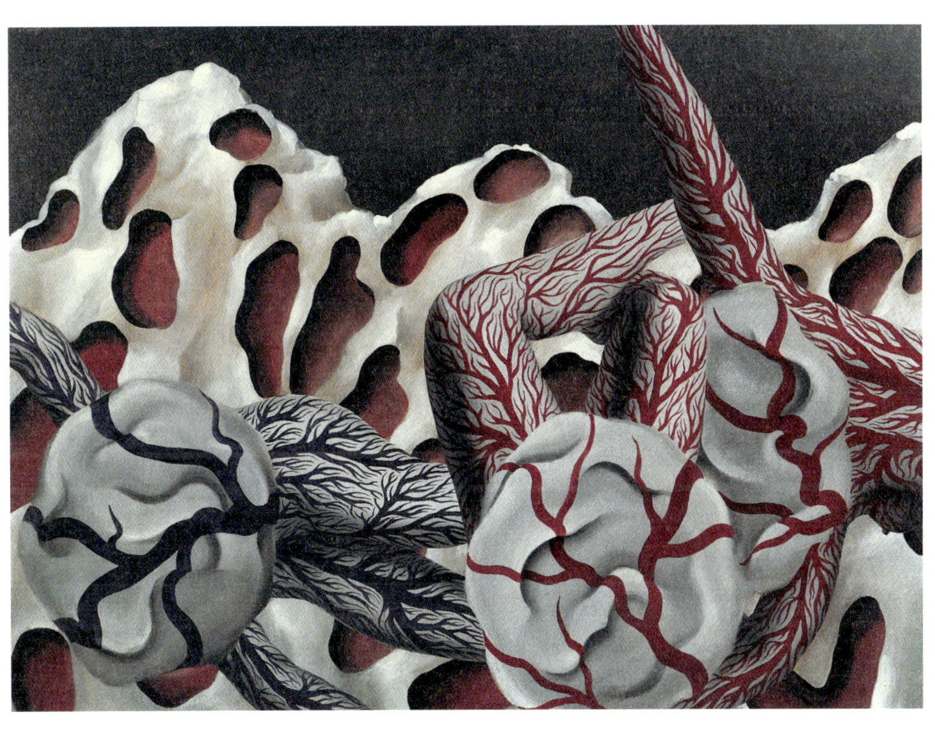

58
The Blood of the World
1927
oil on canvas, 73 × 100 cm

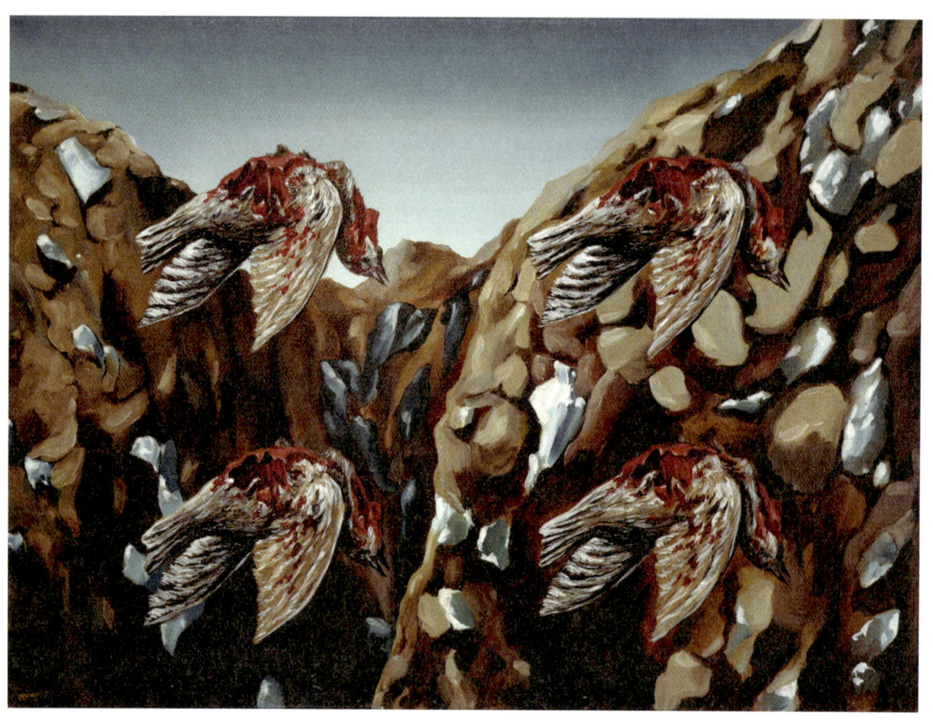

59
The Murderous Sky
1927
oil on canvas, 73 × 100 cm

The Dark Period

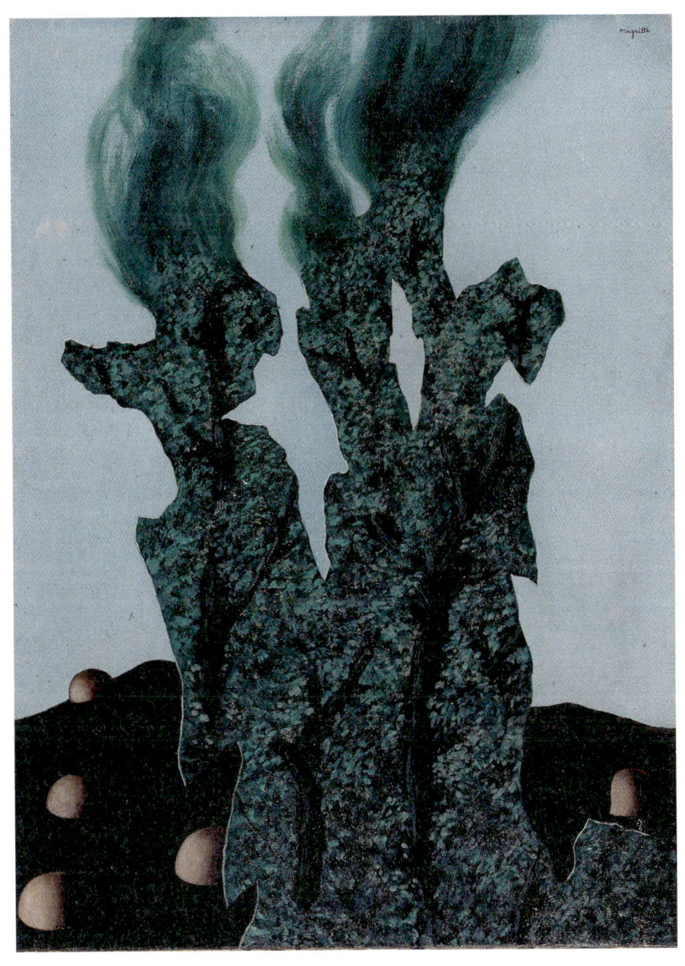

60
Countryside
1927
oil on canvas, 73 × 54 cm

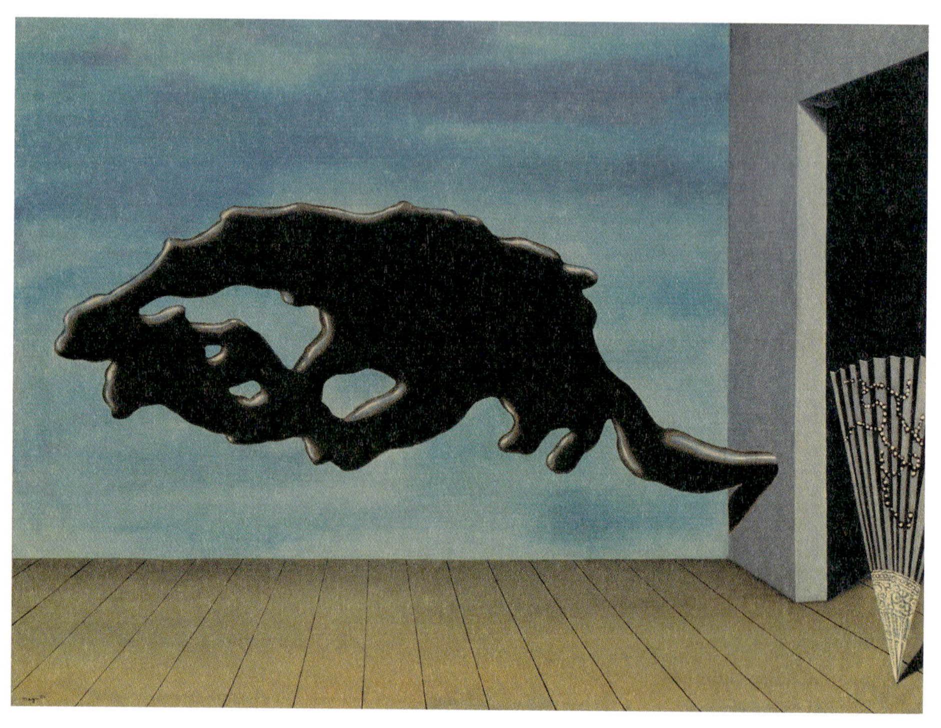

61
Let Out of School
1927
oil on canvas, 73 × 100 cm

The Dark Period

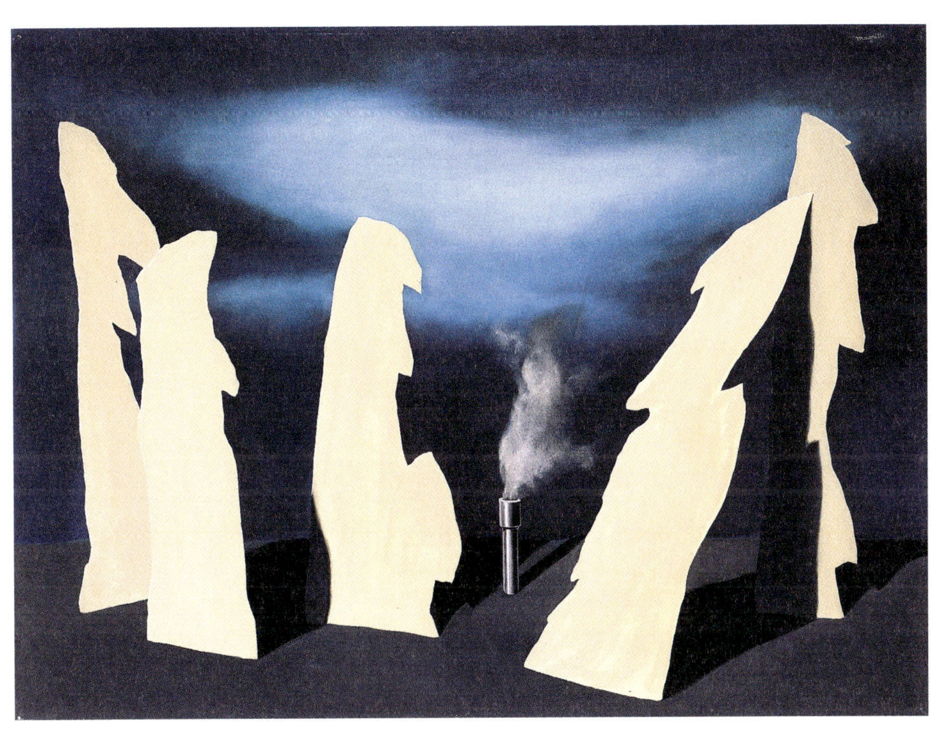

62
The Secret of the Procession
1927
oil on canvas, 73 × 100 cm

                              1926–1930

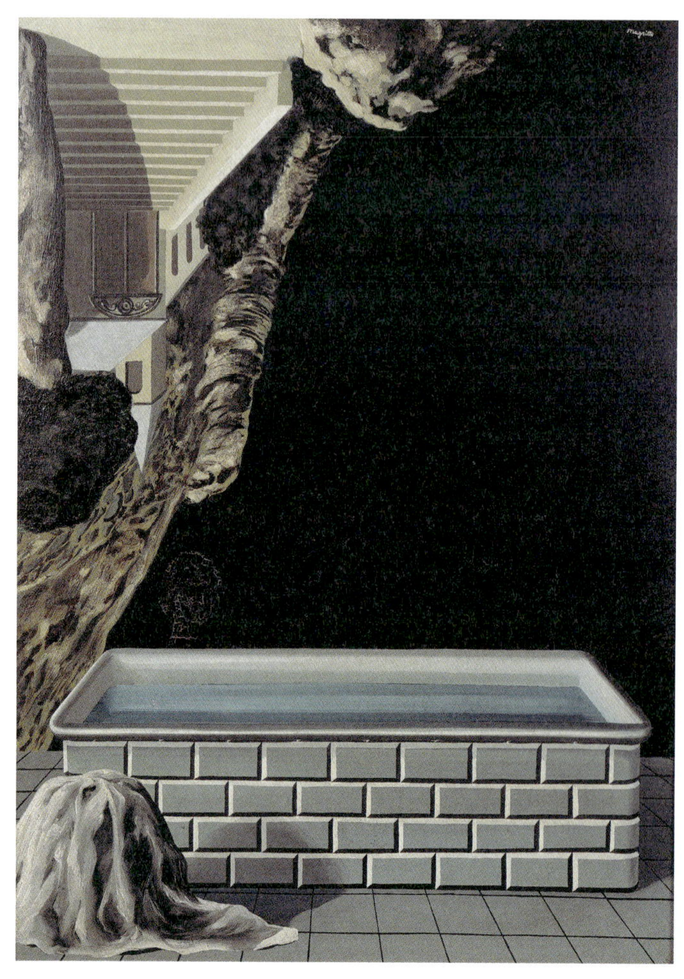

63
Atlantis
1927
oil on canvas, 100 × 73 cm

The Dark Period

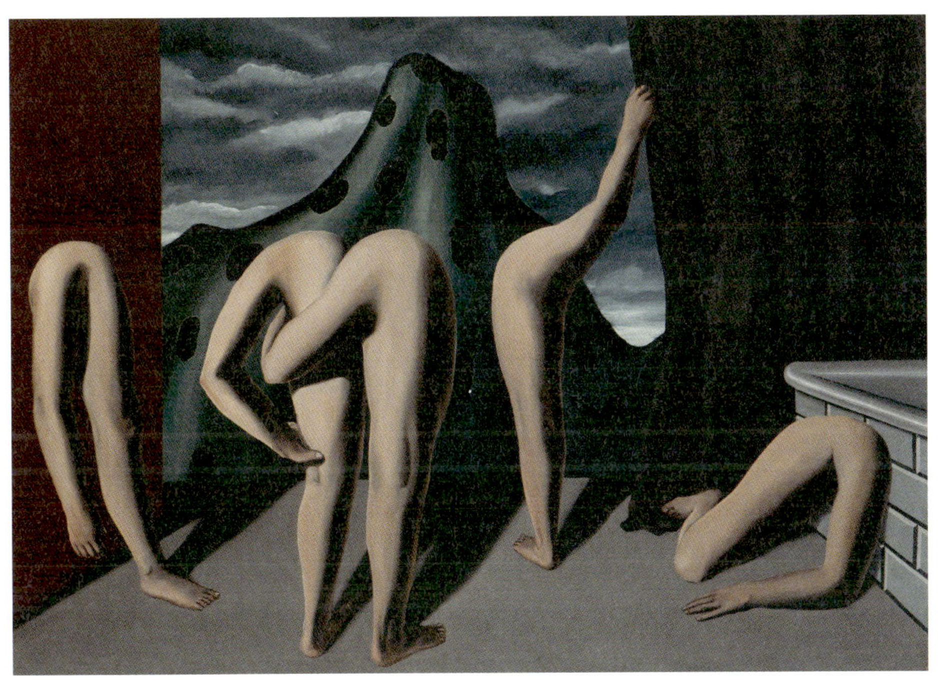

64
Entracte
1927
oil on canvas, 114 × 162 cm

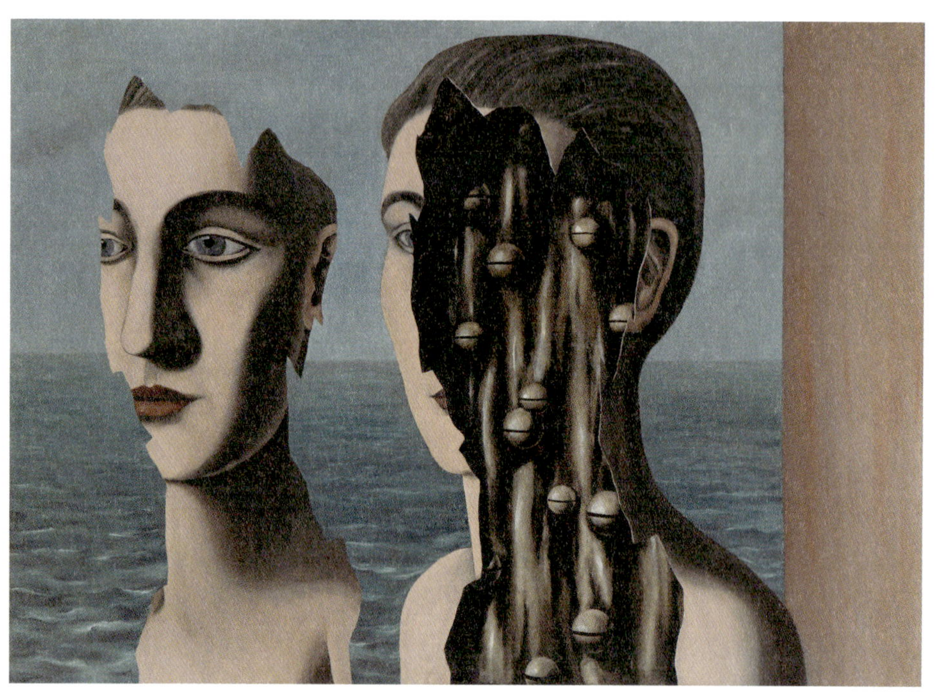

65
The Secret Double
1927
oil on canvas, 114 × 162 cm

The Dark Period

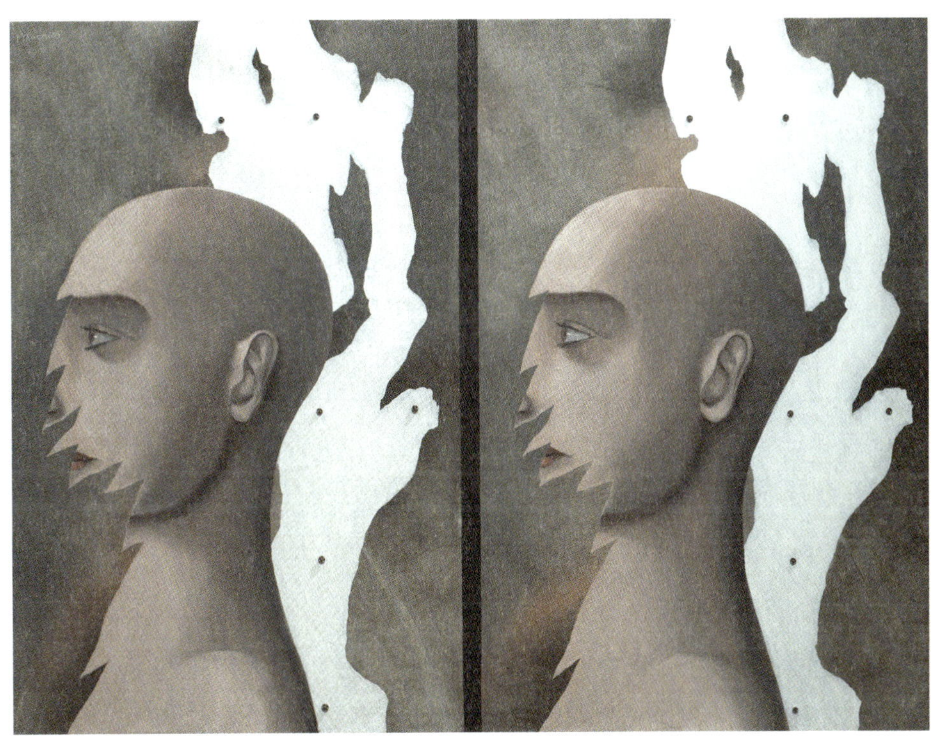

66
An End to Contemplation
1927
oil on canvas with metal snap fasteners, 73 × 100 cm

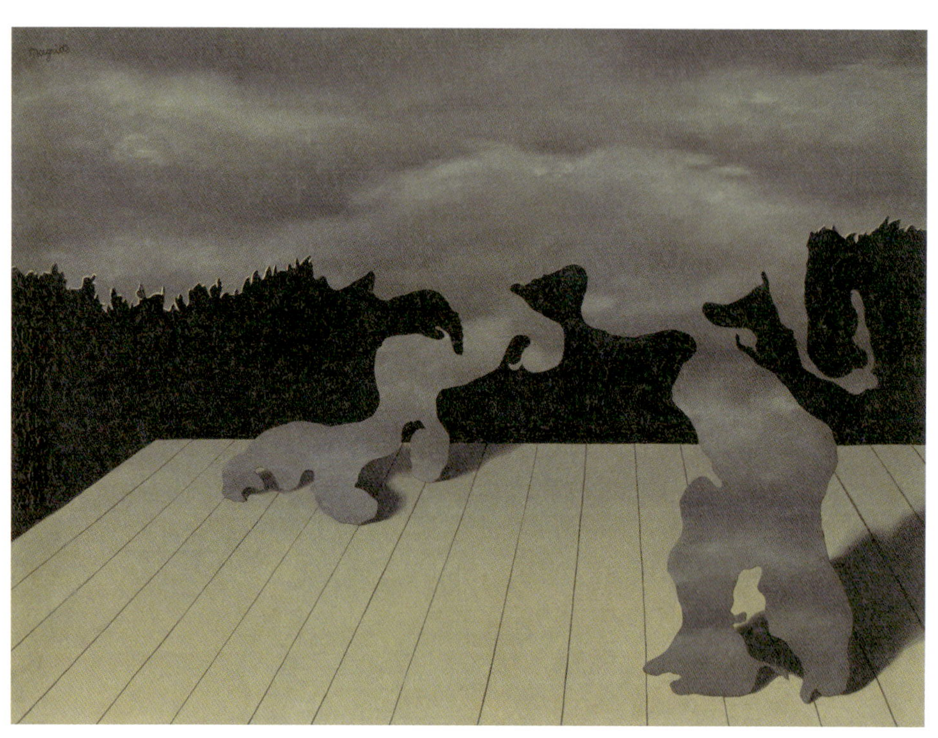

67
The Muscles of the Sky
1927
oil on canvas, 54 × 73 cm

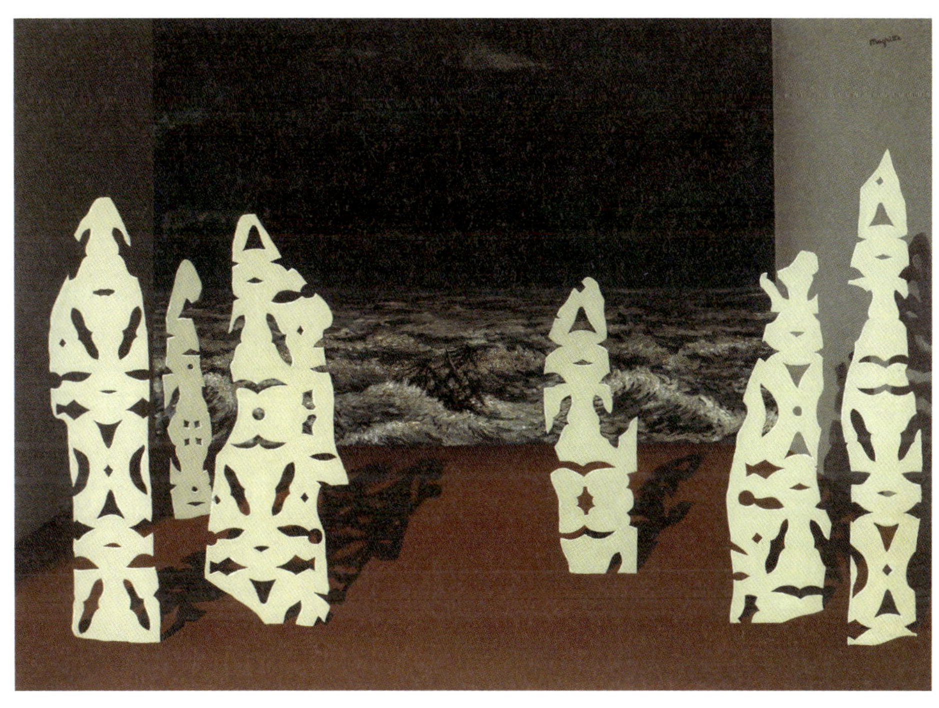

68
The Finery of the Storm
1927
oil on canvas, 81 × 116 cm

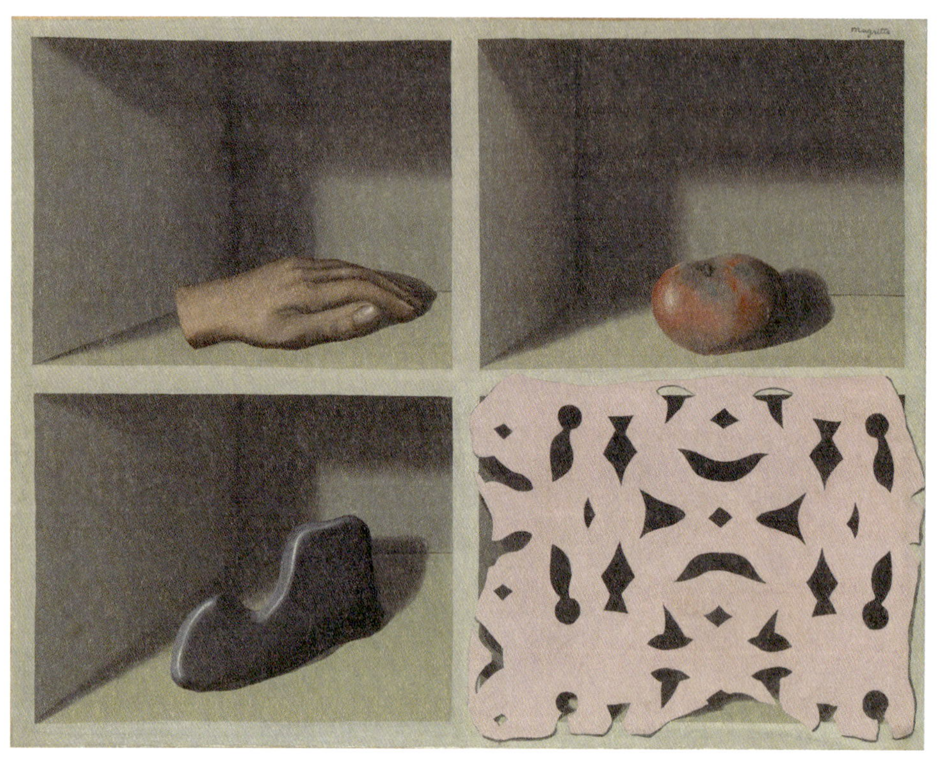

69
One-Night Museum
1927
oil on canvas, 50 × 65 cm

The Dark Period

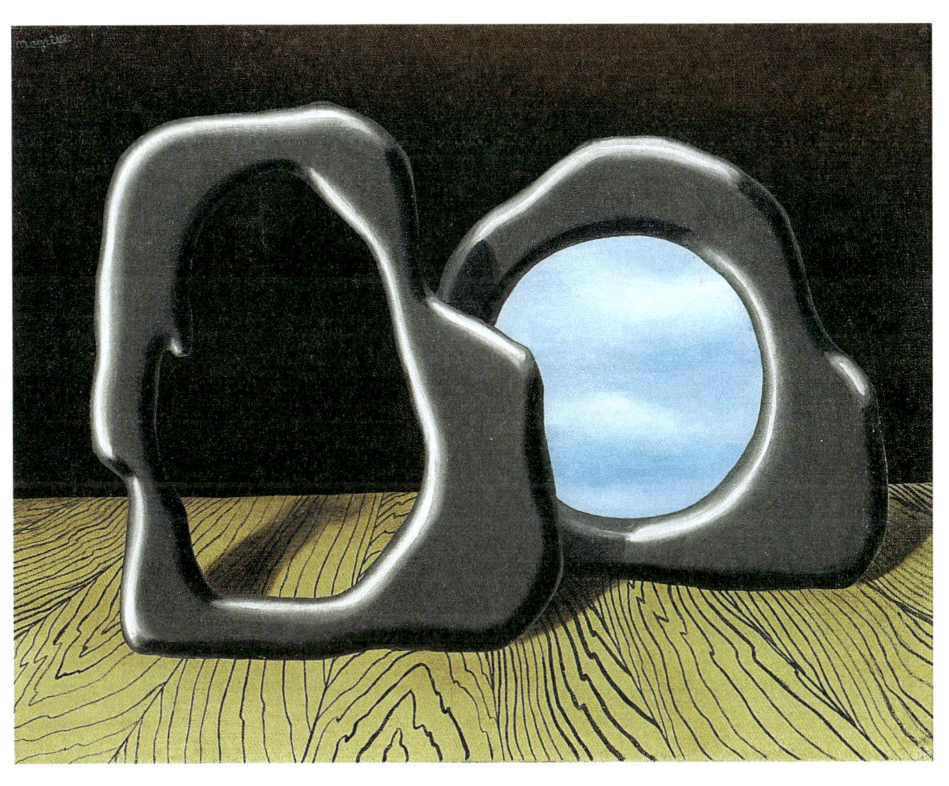

70
The Light-Breaker
1927
oil on canvas, 50 × 65 cm

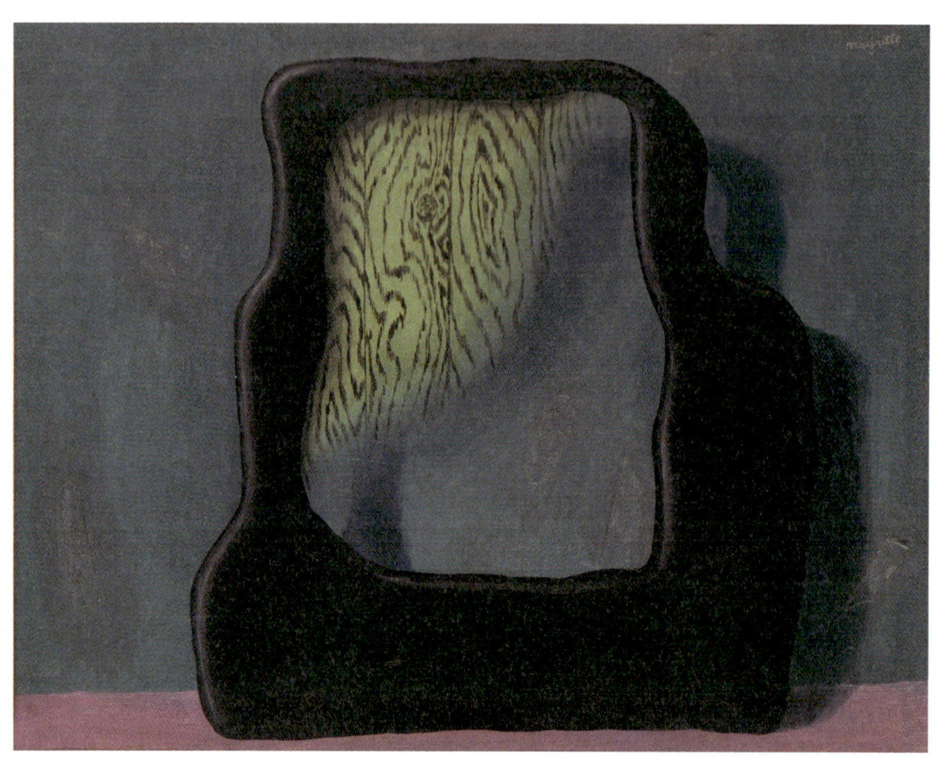

71
The Prince of Objects
1927
oil on canvas with collaged canvas, 50 × 65 cm

    The Dark Period

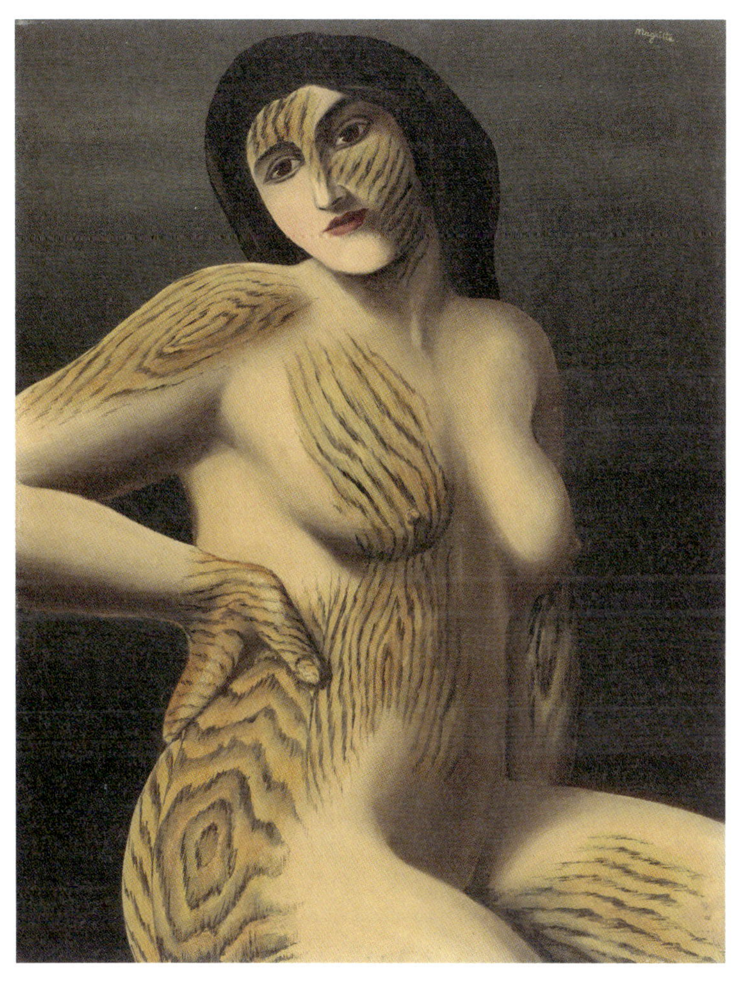

72
Discovery
1927
oil on canvas, 65 × 50 cm

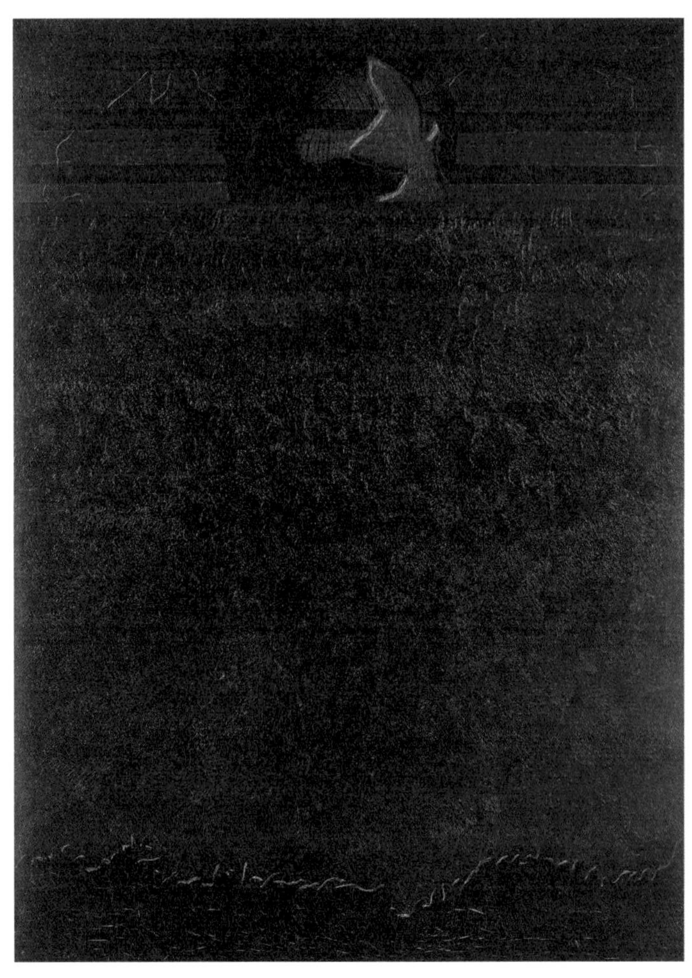

73
The Fruit of Dreams
1927
oil on canvas, 73 × 54 cm

The Dark Period

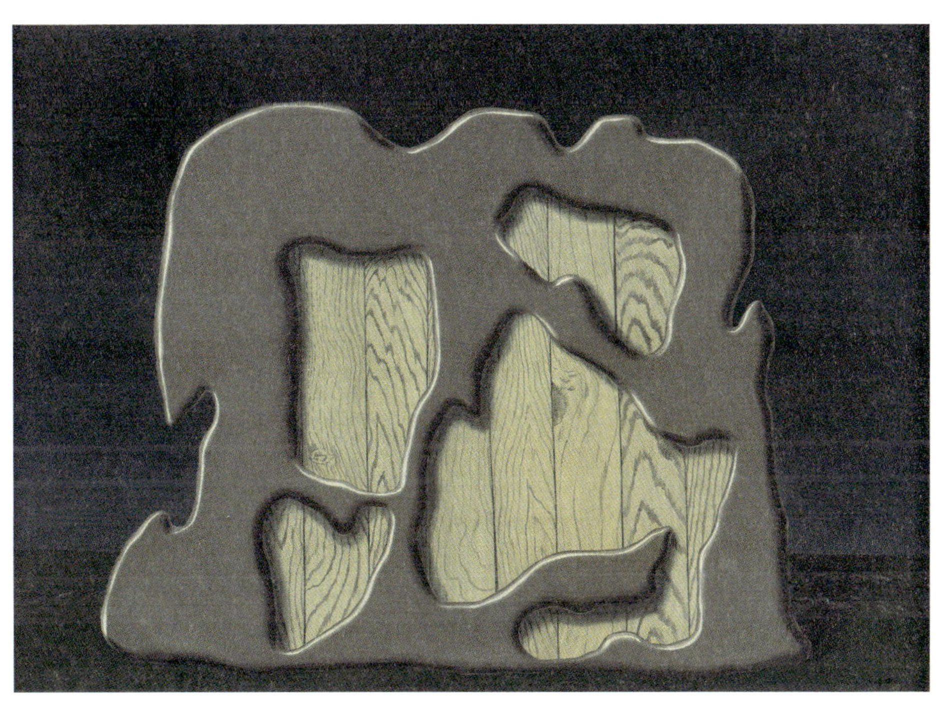

74
The Imp of the Perverse
1927
oil on canvas, 81 × 116 cm

1926–1930

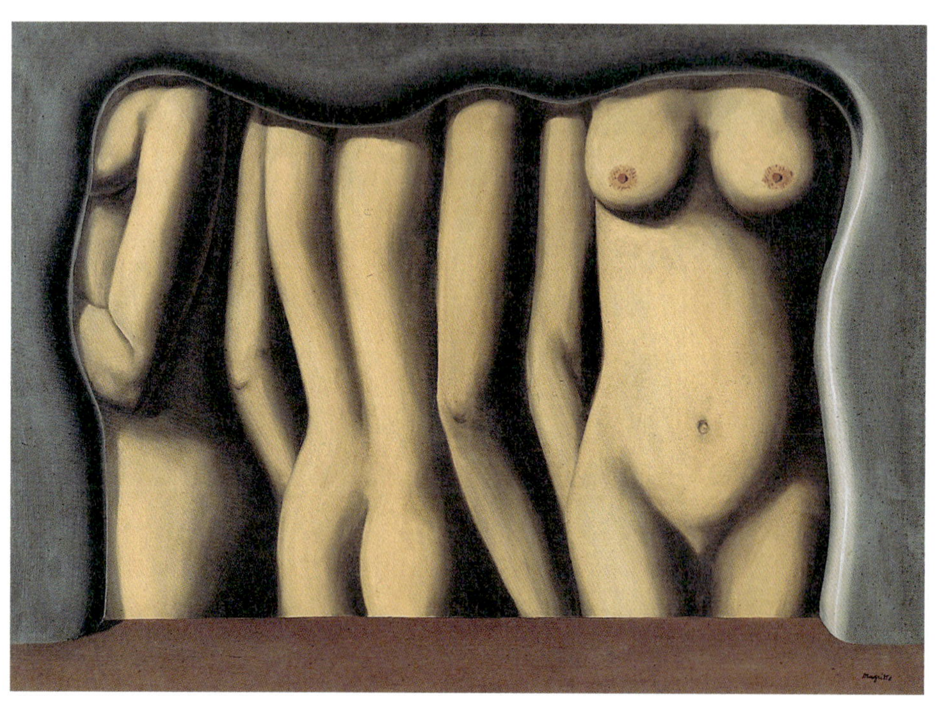

75
The Adulation of Space
1927 or 1928
oil on canvas, 81 × 116 cm

 The Dark Period

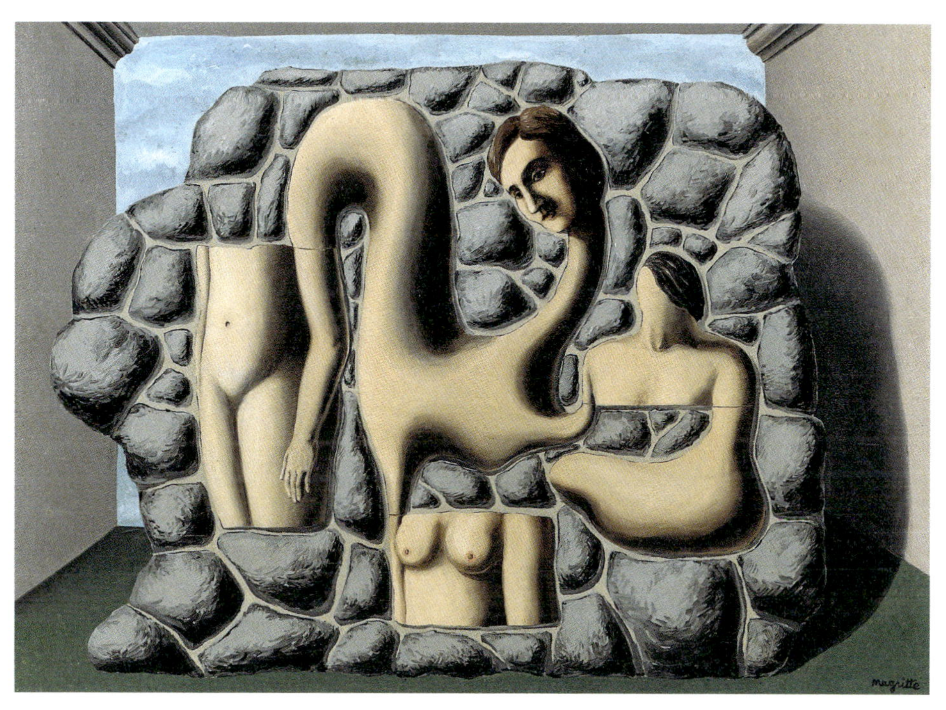

76
The Acrobat's Rest
1928
oil on canvas, 54 × 73 cm

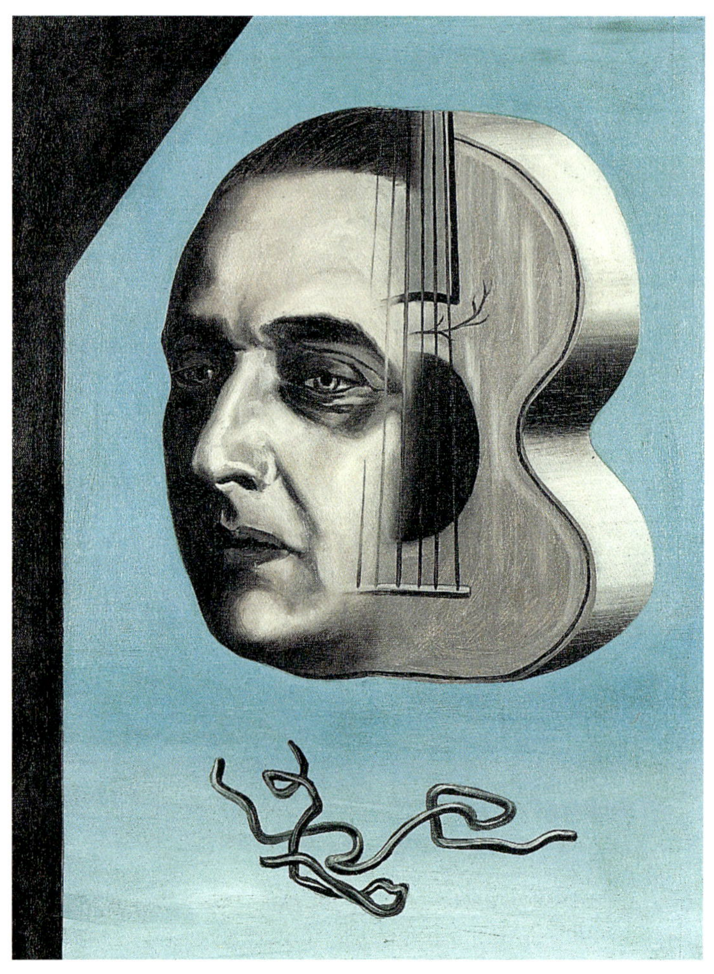

77

(Portrait of Paul-Gustave Van Hecke)

1928
oil on canvas, 65 × 50 cm

The Dark Period

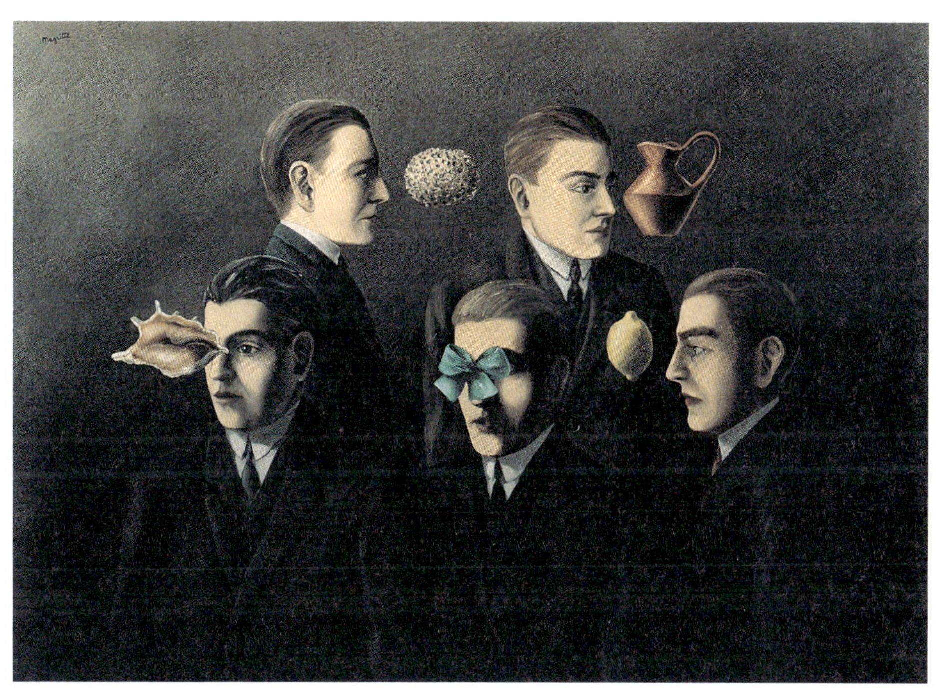

78
Familiar Objects
1928
oil on canvas, 81 × 116 cm

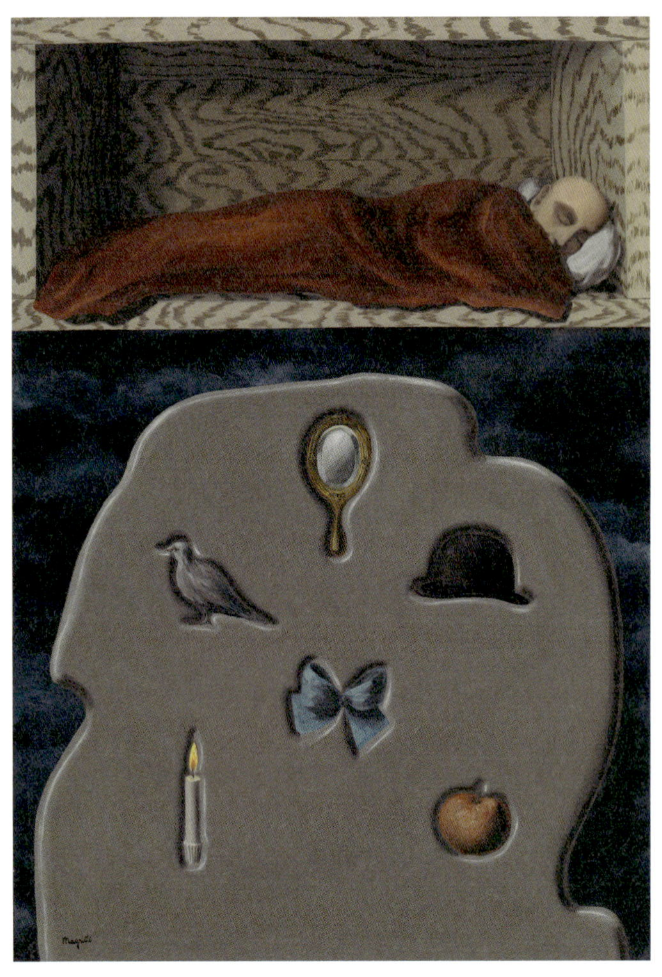

79
The Daring Sleeper
1928
oil on canvas, 116 × 81 cm

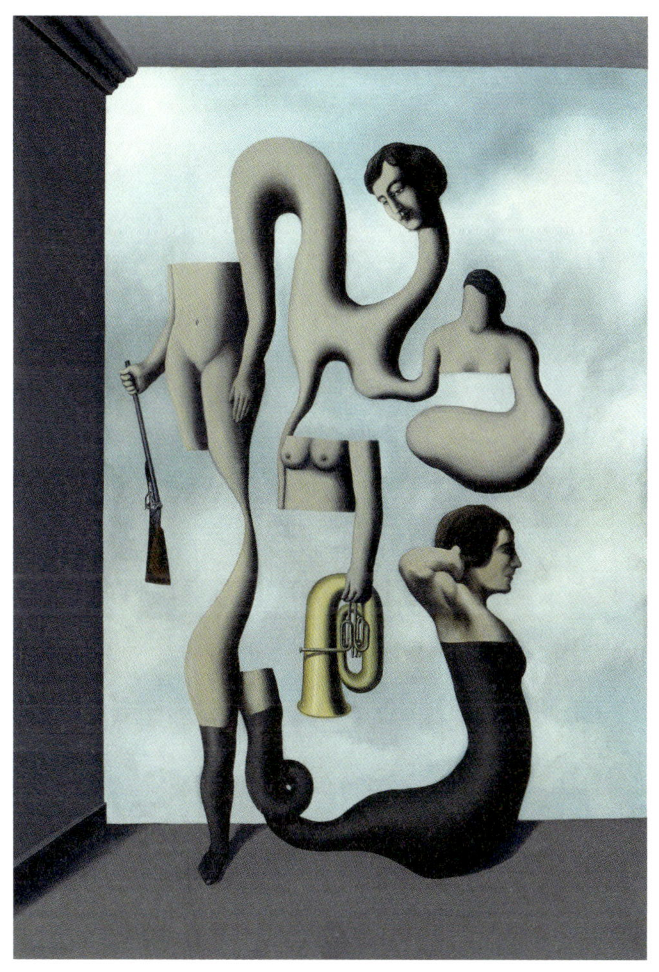

The Acrobat's Ideas

1928
oil on canvas, 116 × 81 cm

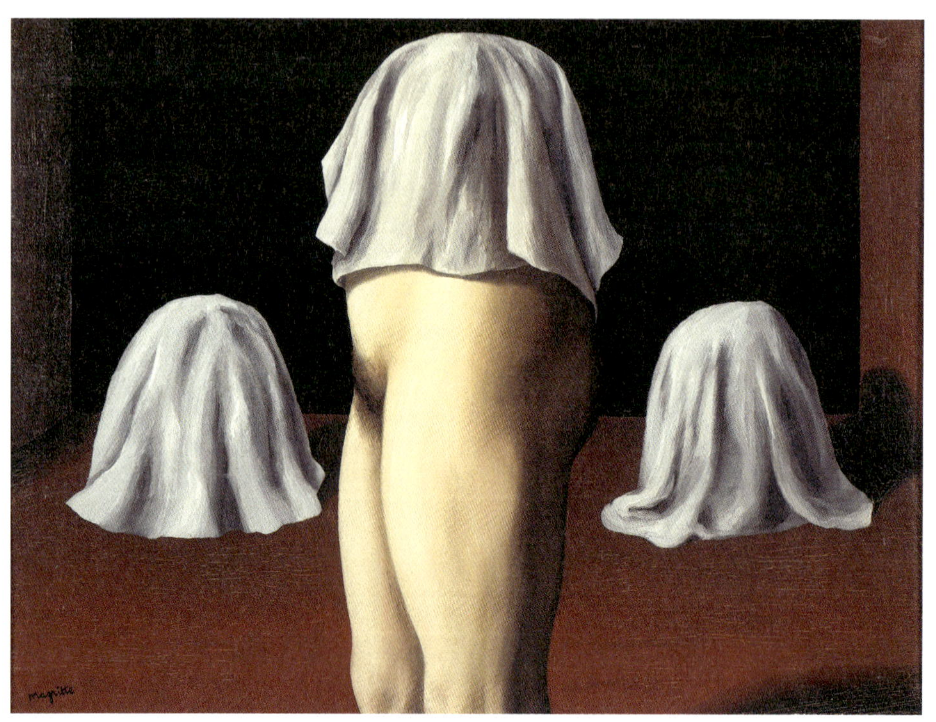

81
The Symmetrical Trick
1928
oil on canvas, 54 × 73 cm

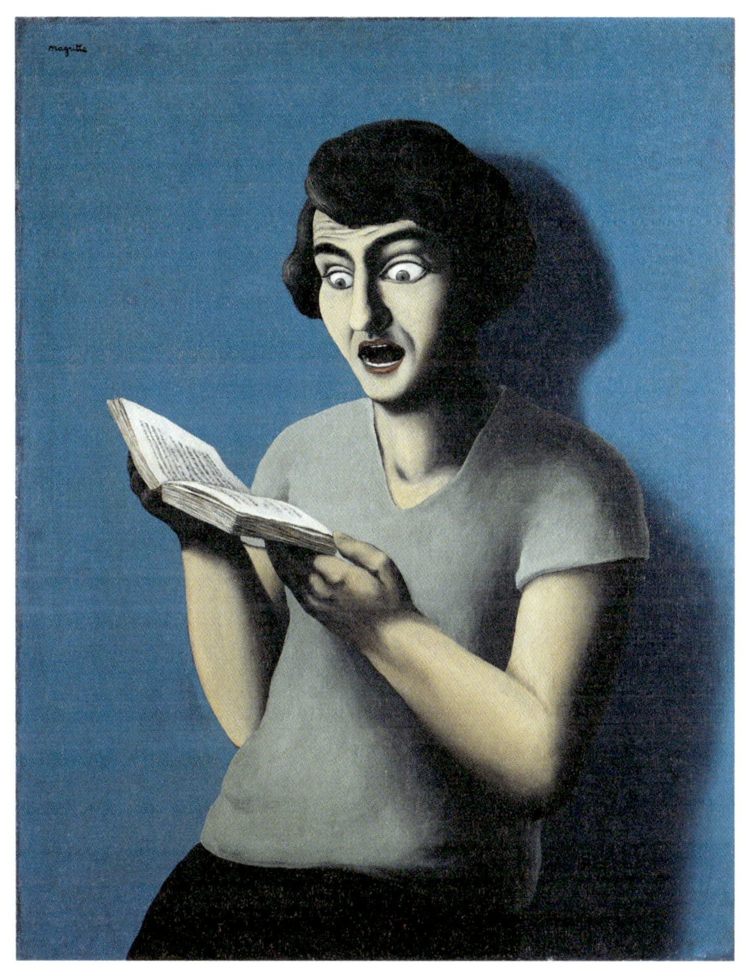

82
The Subjugated Reader
1928
oil on canvas, 92 × 73 cm

1926–1930

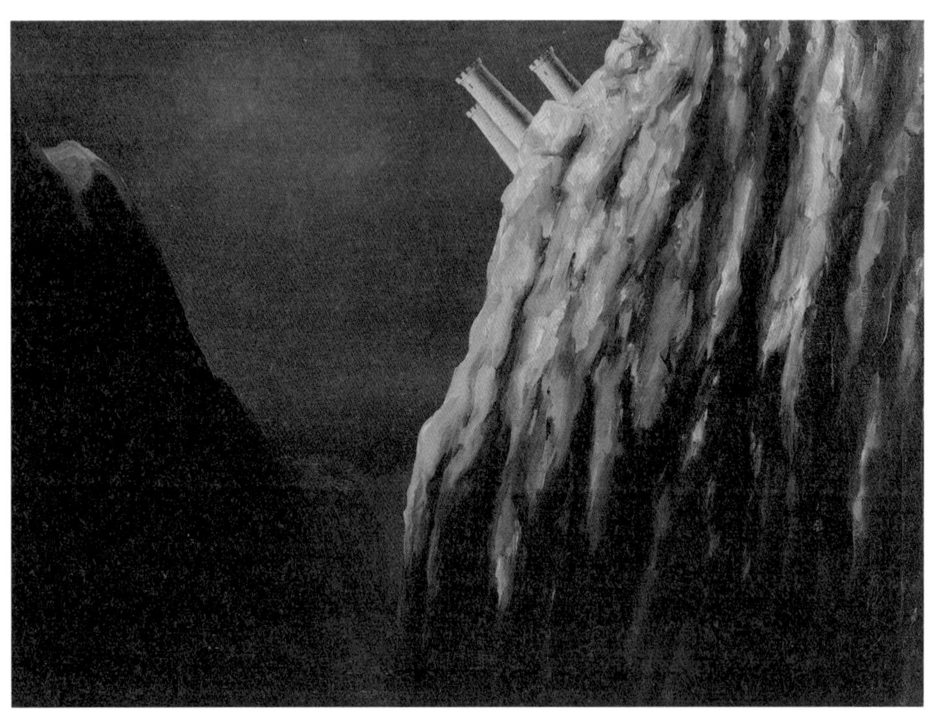

The Scent of the Abyss
1928
oil on canvas, 54 × 73 cm

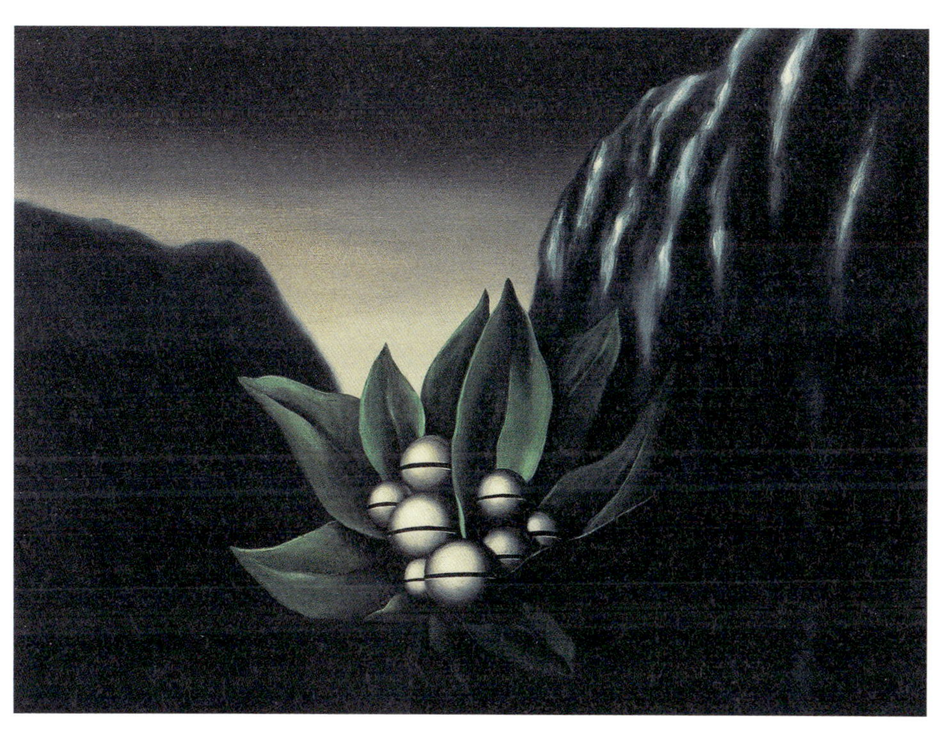

84
The Flowers of the Abyss (I)
1928
oil on canvas, 54 × 73 cm

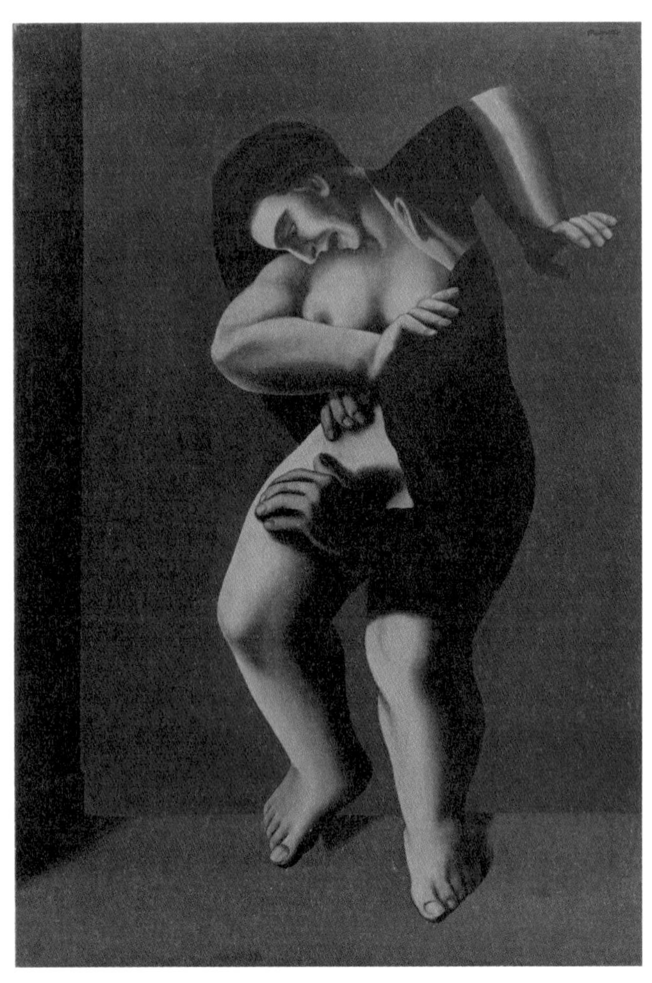

85
The Titanic Days
1928
oil on canvas, 116 × 81 cm

     The Dark Period

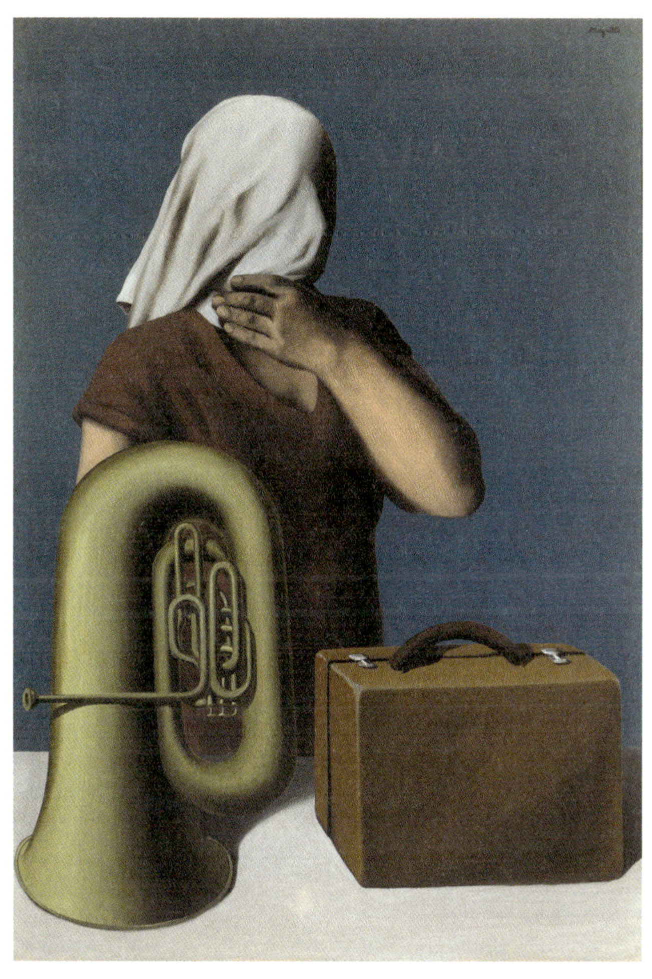

86
The Central Story
1928
oil on canvas, 116 × 81 cm

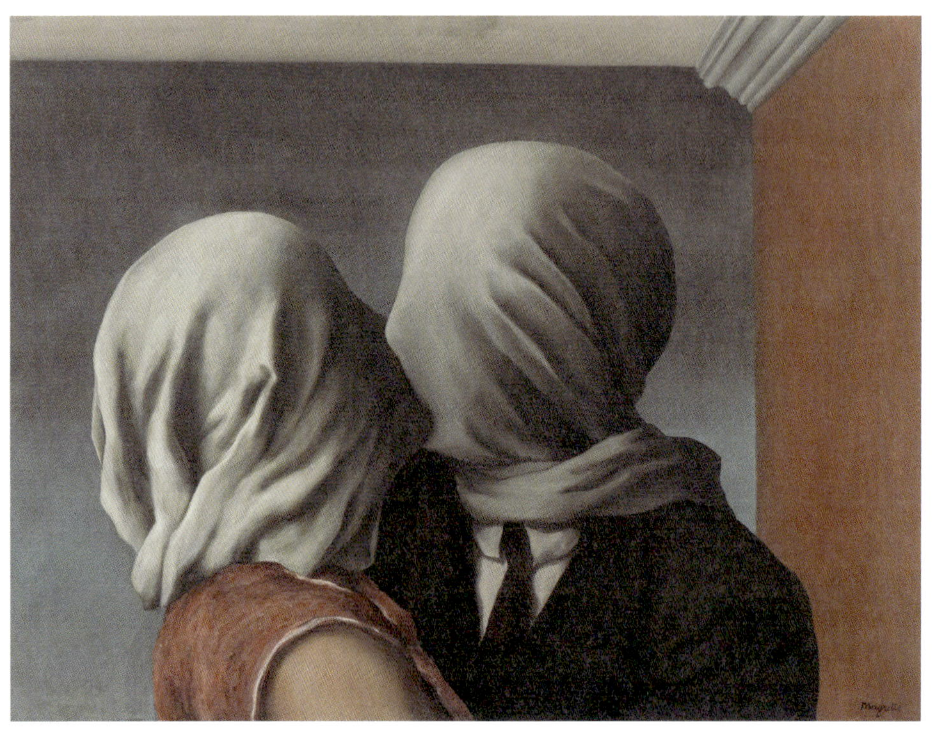

87
The Lovers
1928
oil on canvas, 54 × 73 cm

The Dark Period

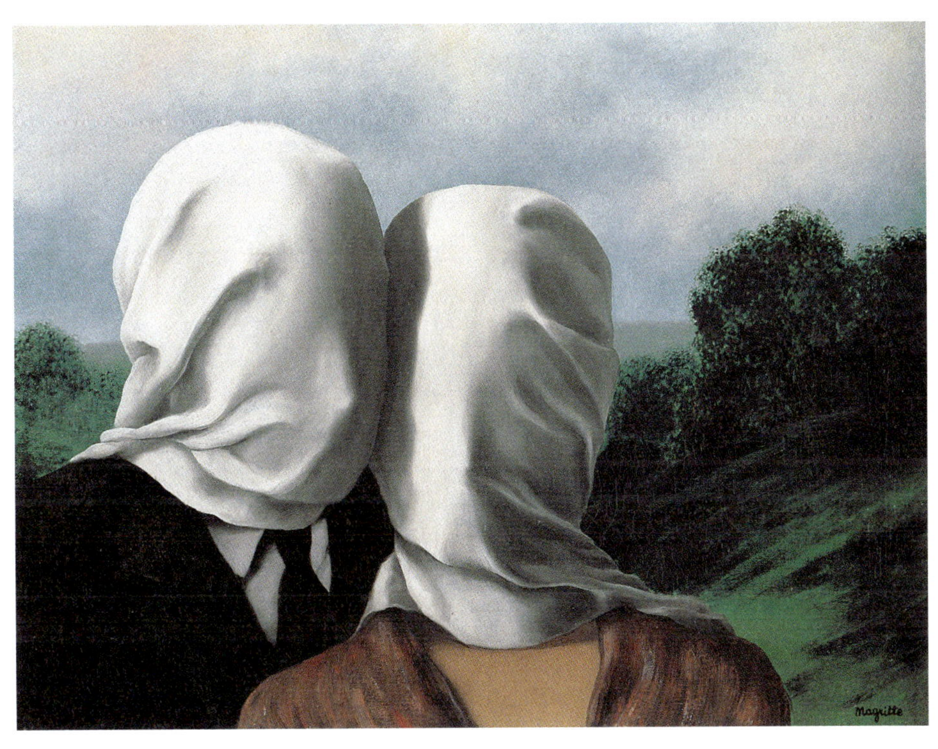

88
The Lovers (II)
1928
oil on canvas, 54 × 73 cm

1926–1930

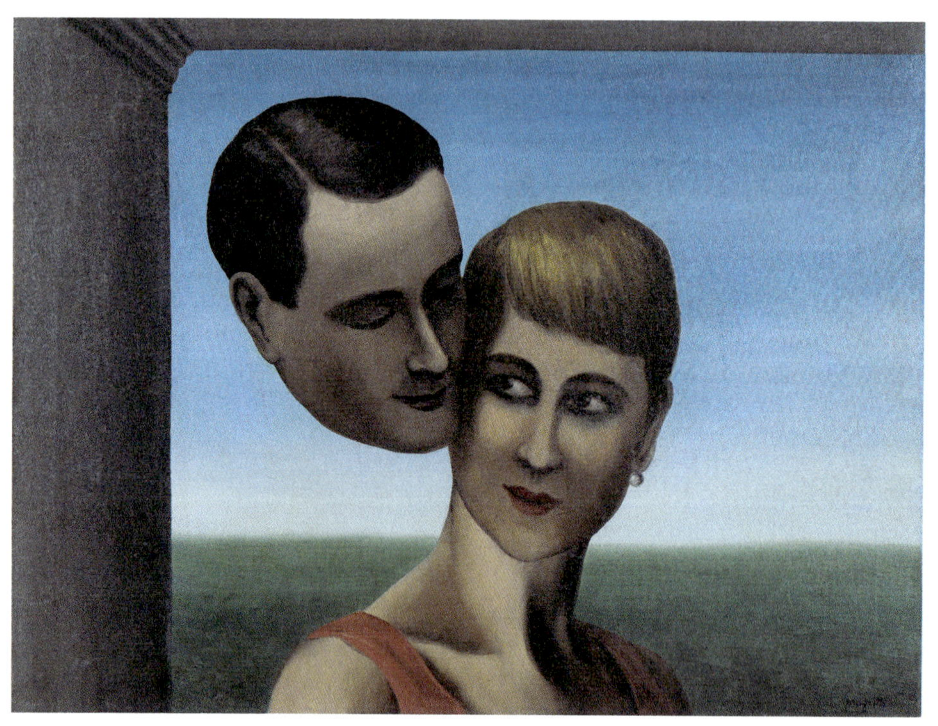

89
The Lovers (III)
1928
oil on canvas, 54 × 73 cm

The Dark Period

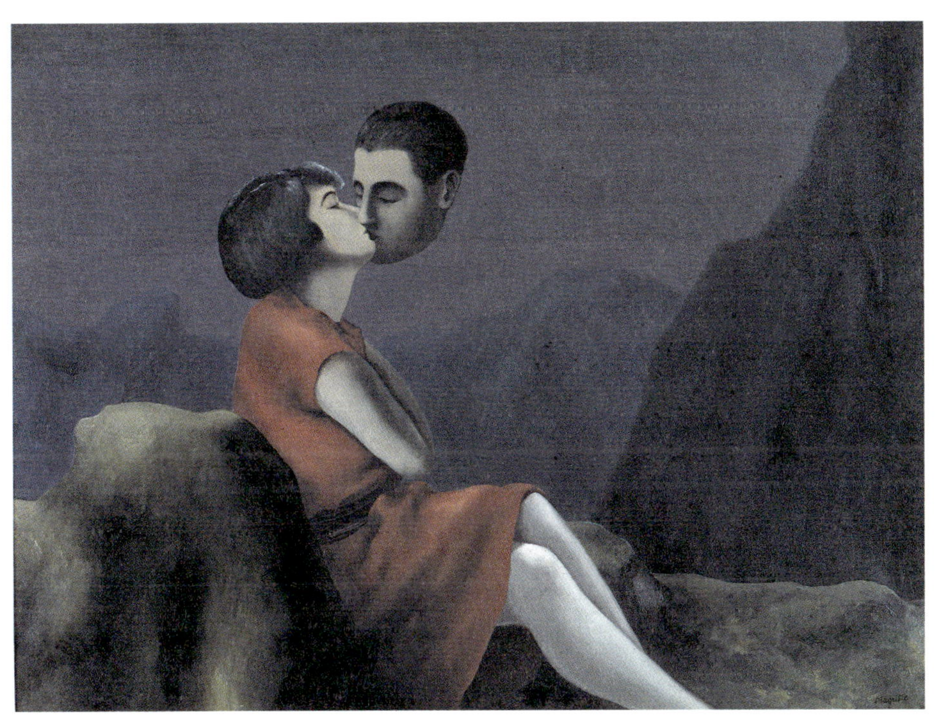

90
The Lovers (IV)
1928
oil on canvas, 54 × 73 cm

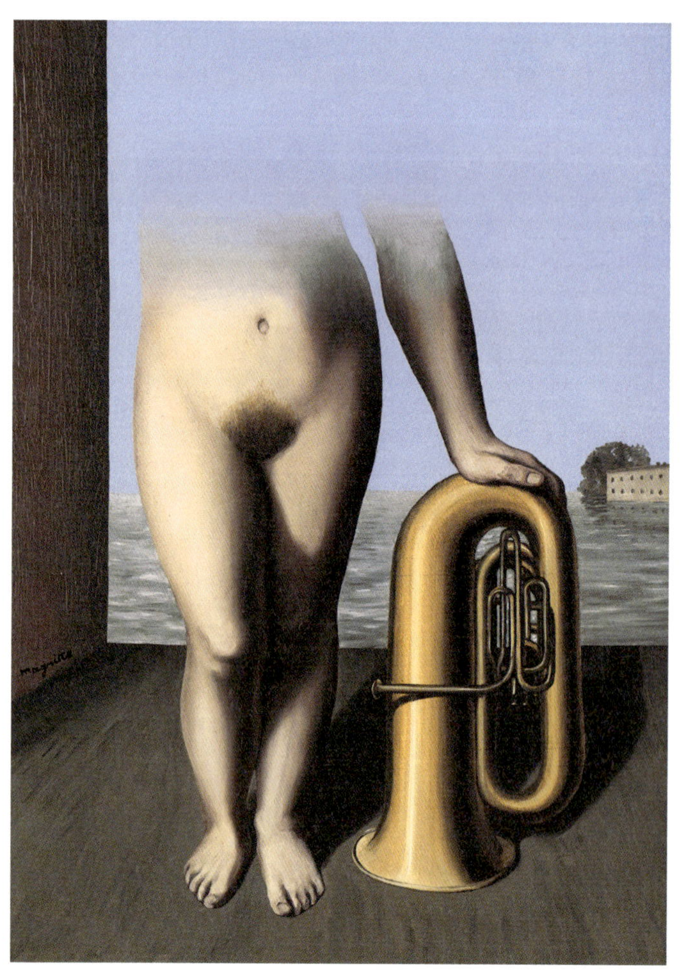

91
The Flood
1928
oil on canvas, 73 × 54 cm

The Dark Period

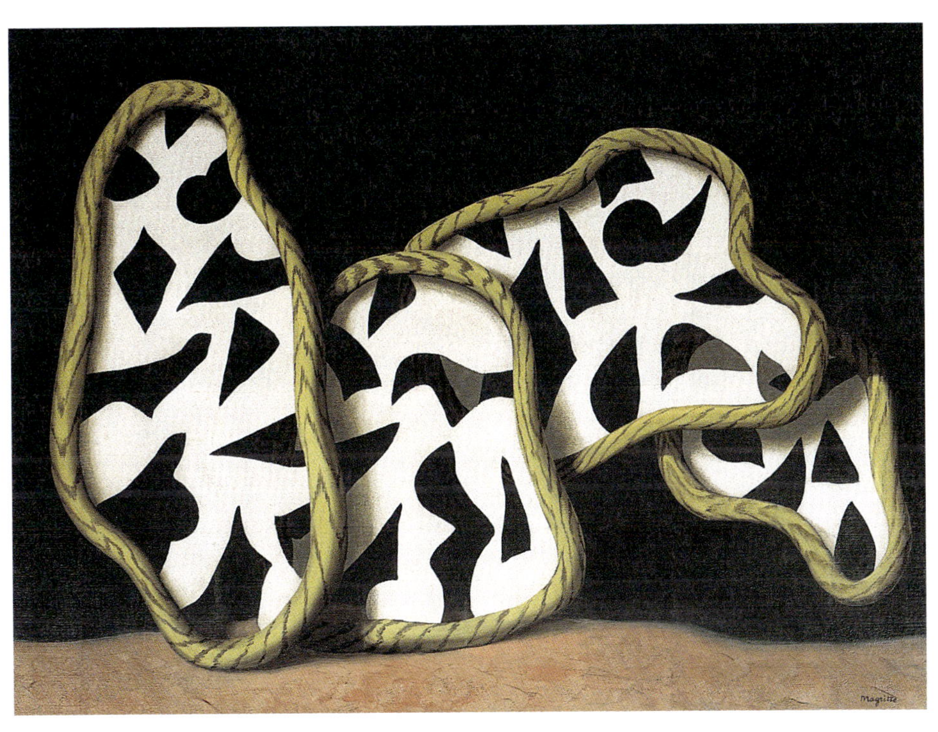

92
Magic Light
1928
oil on canvas, 54 × 73 cm

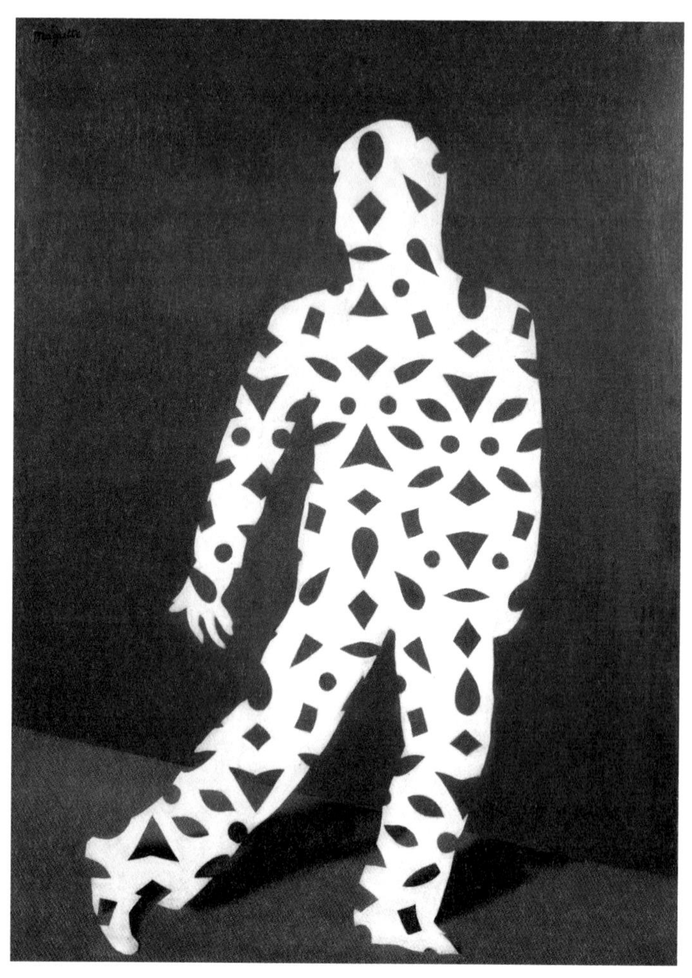

93
The Spirit of Comedy
1928
oil on canvas, 73 × 54 cm

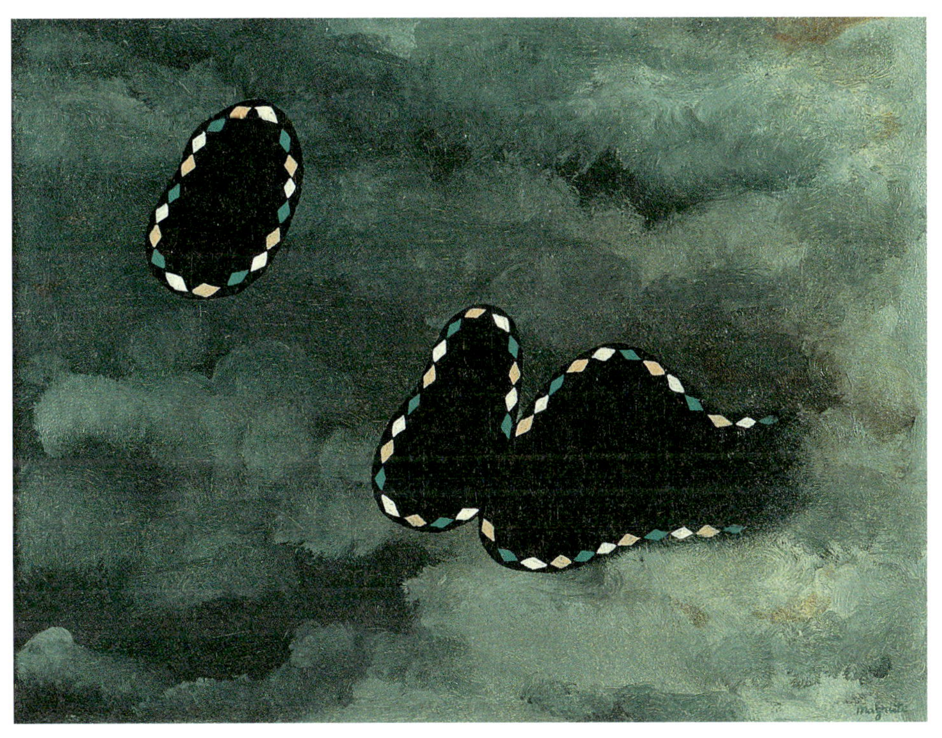

94
The Apparition
1928
oil on canvas, 54 × 73 cm

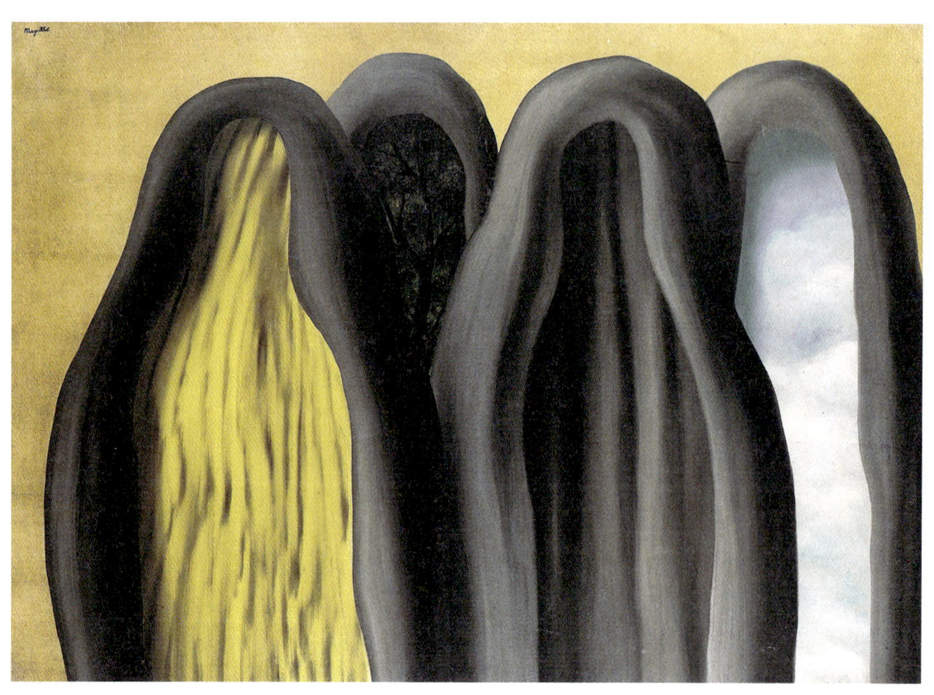

95
The Palace of Curtains
1928
oil on canvas, 81 × 116 cm

 The Dark Period

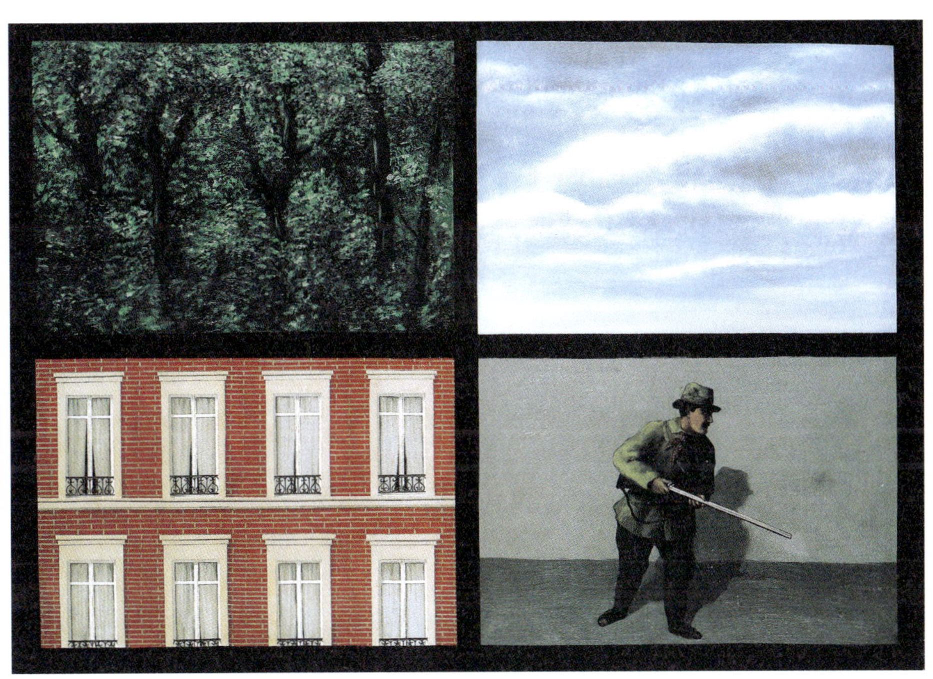

96
The Obsession
1928
oil on canvas, 81 × 116 cm

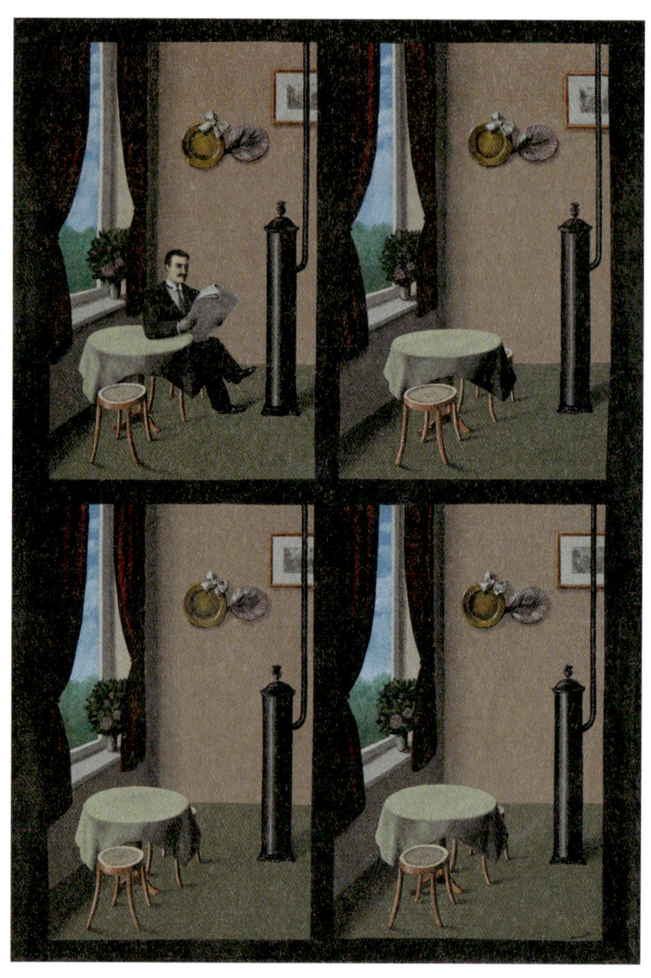

97
The Man with the Newspaper
1928
oil on canvas, 116 × 81 cm

 The Dark Period

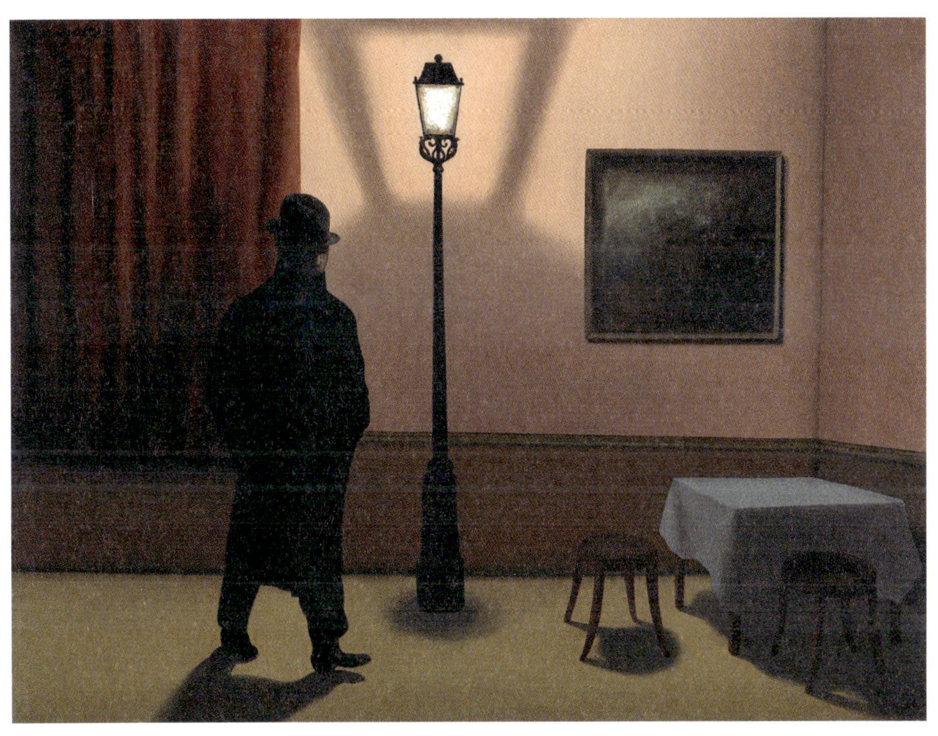

98
The Night Owl
1928
oil on canvas, 54 × 73 cm

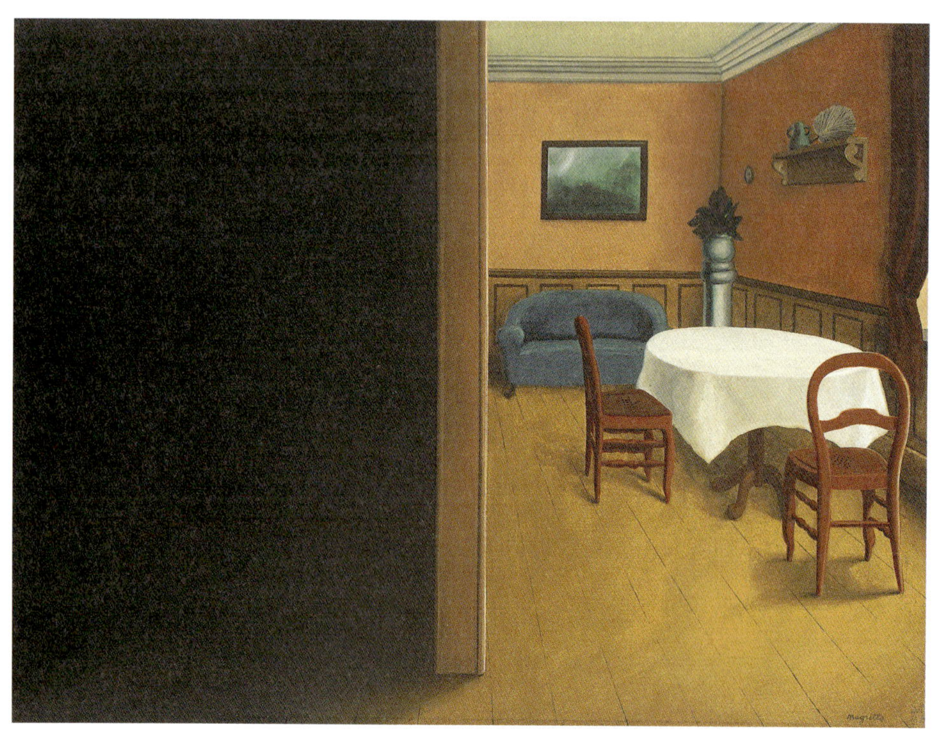

99
The Voice of Silence
1928
oil on canvas, 54 × 73 cm

     The Dark Period

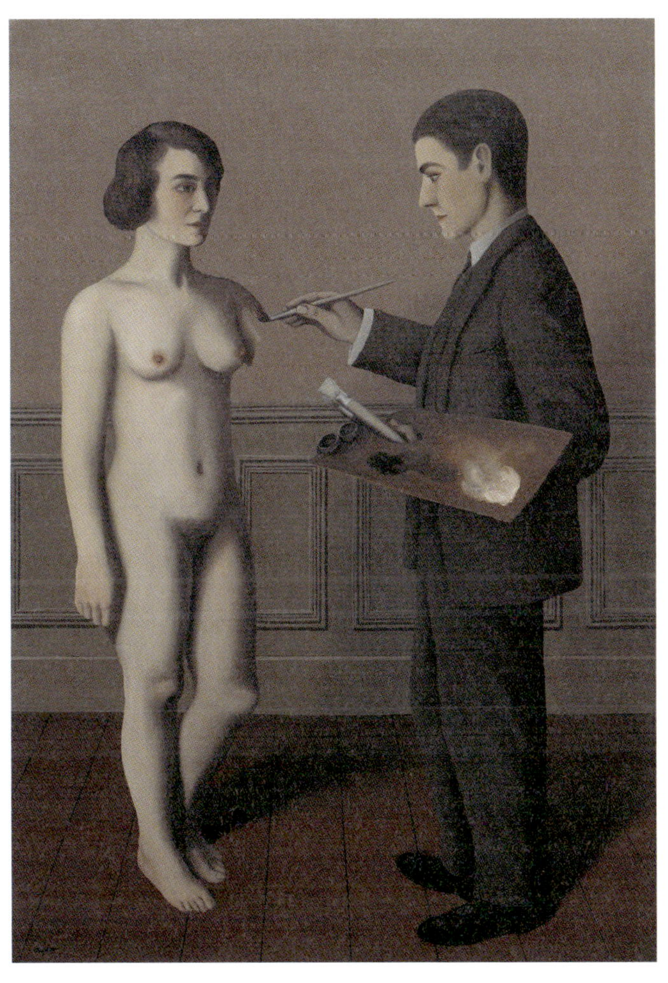

100
Attempting the Impossible
1928
oil on canvas, 116 × 81 cm

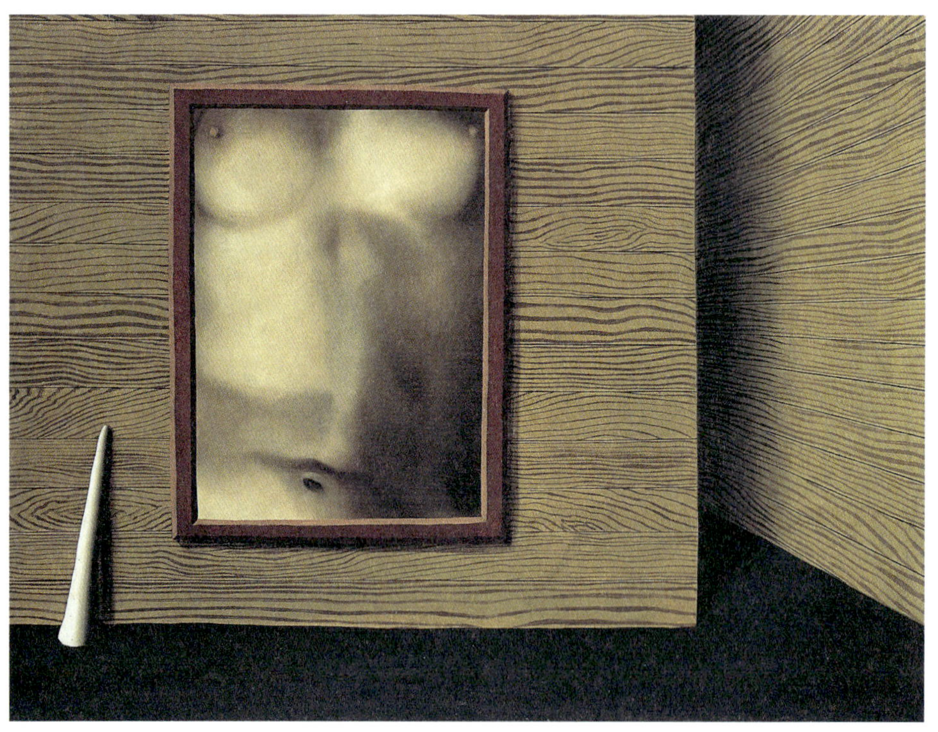

A Courtesan's Palace
1928
oil on canvas, 54 × 73 cm

 The Dark Period

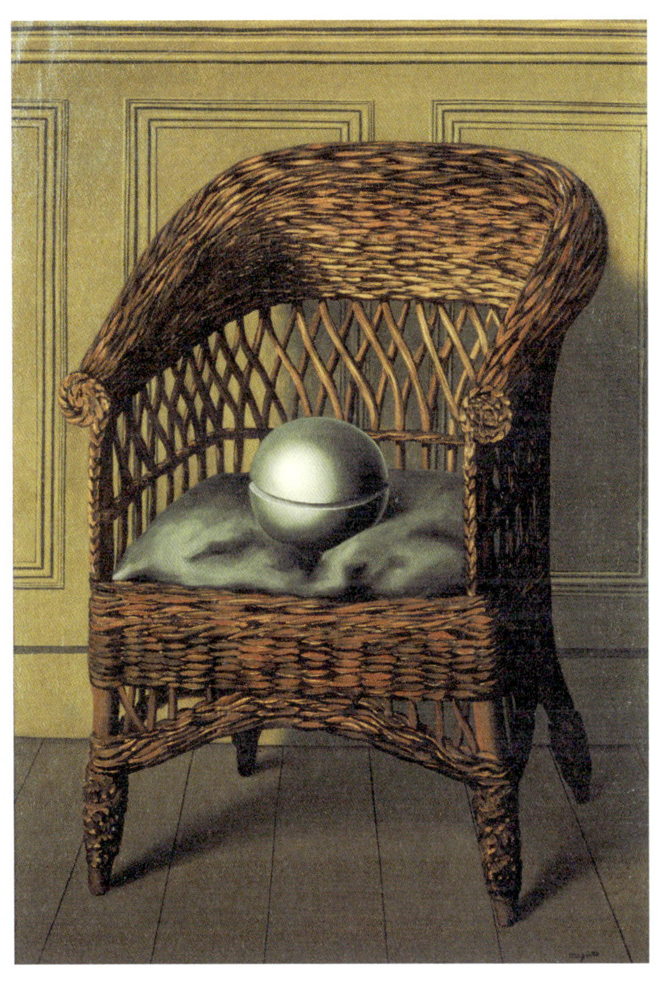

102
The Automaton
1928
oil on canvas, 116 × 81 cm

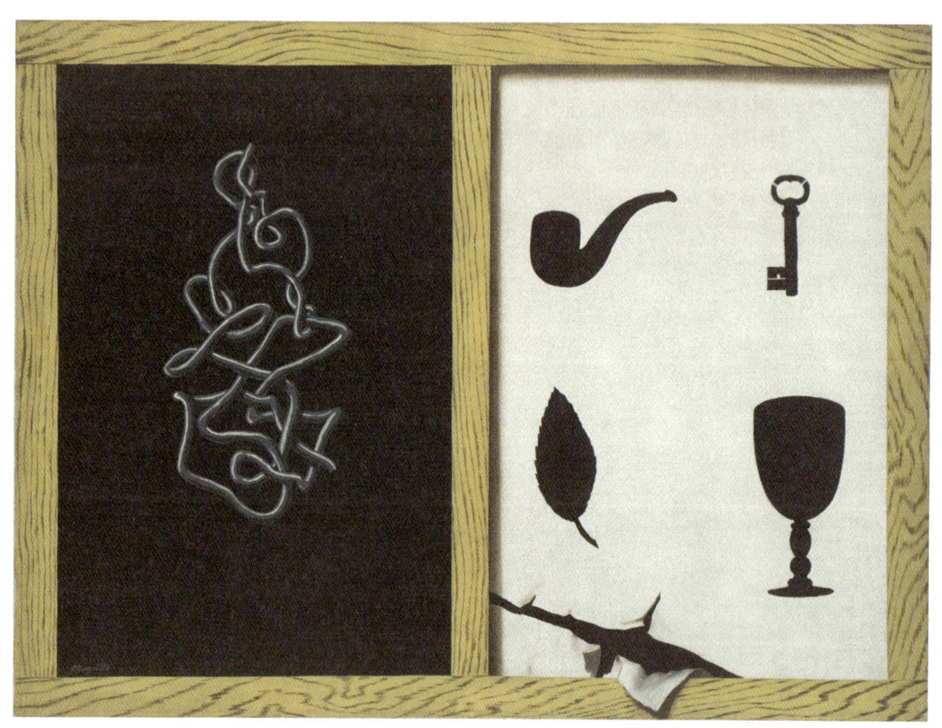

103
The Alphabet of Revelations
1929
oil on canvas, 54 × 73 cm

          The Dark Period

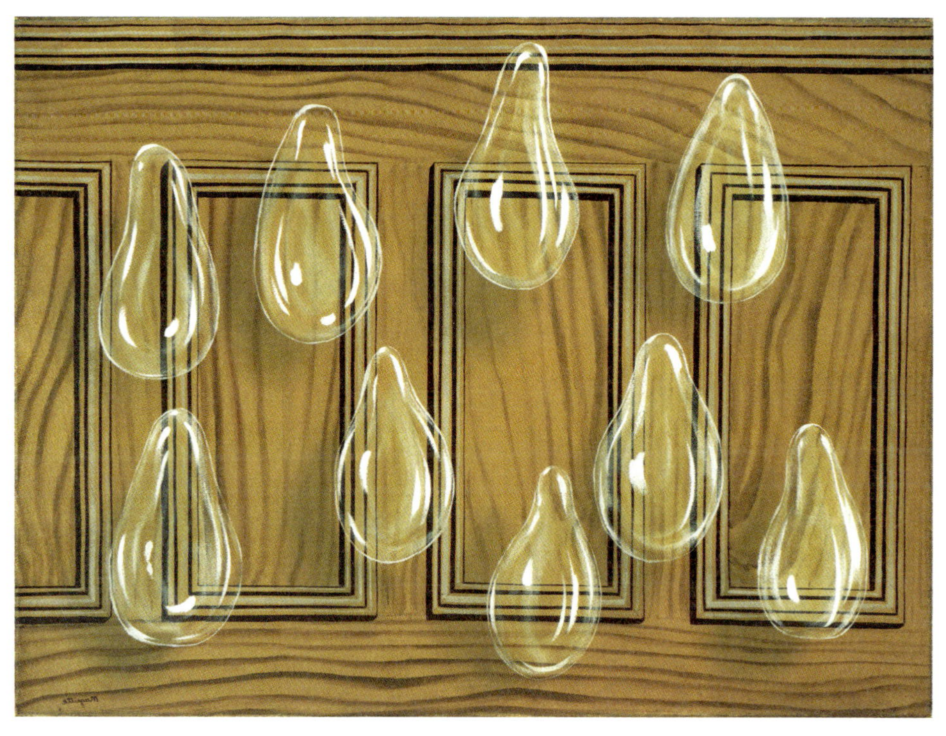

104
Surrender
1929
oil on canvas, 54 × 73 cm

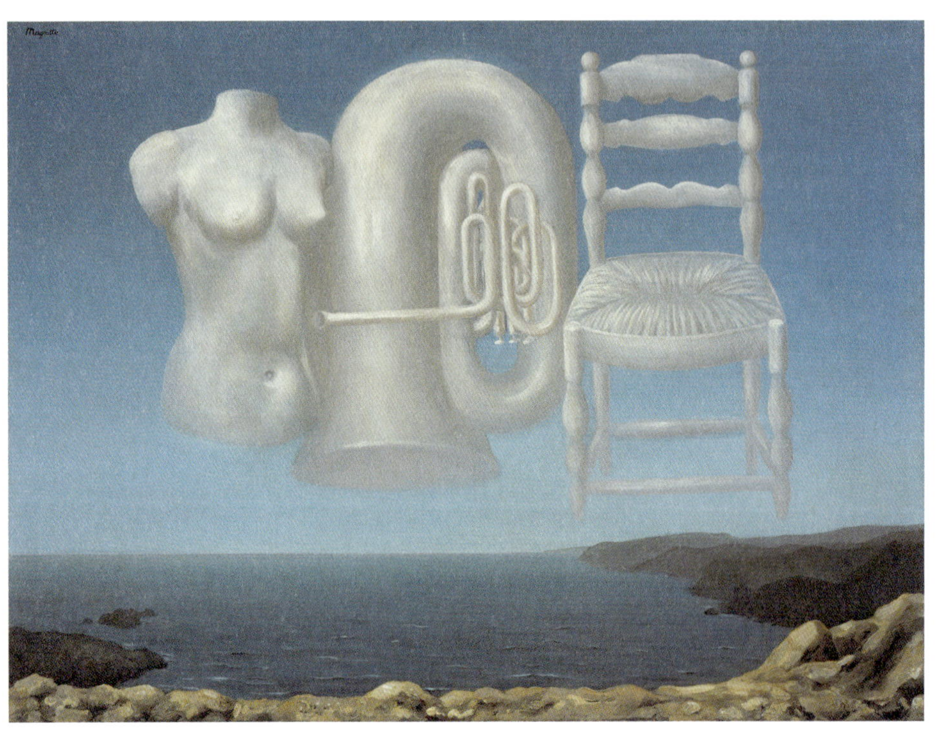

105
Threatening Weather
1929
oil on canvas, 54 × 73 cm

 The Dark Period

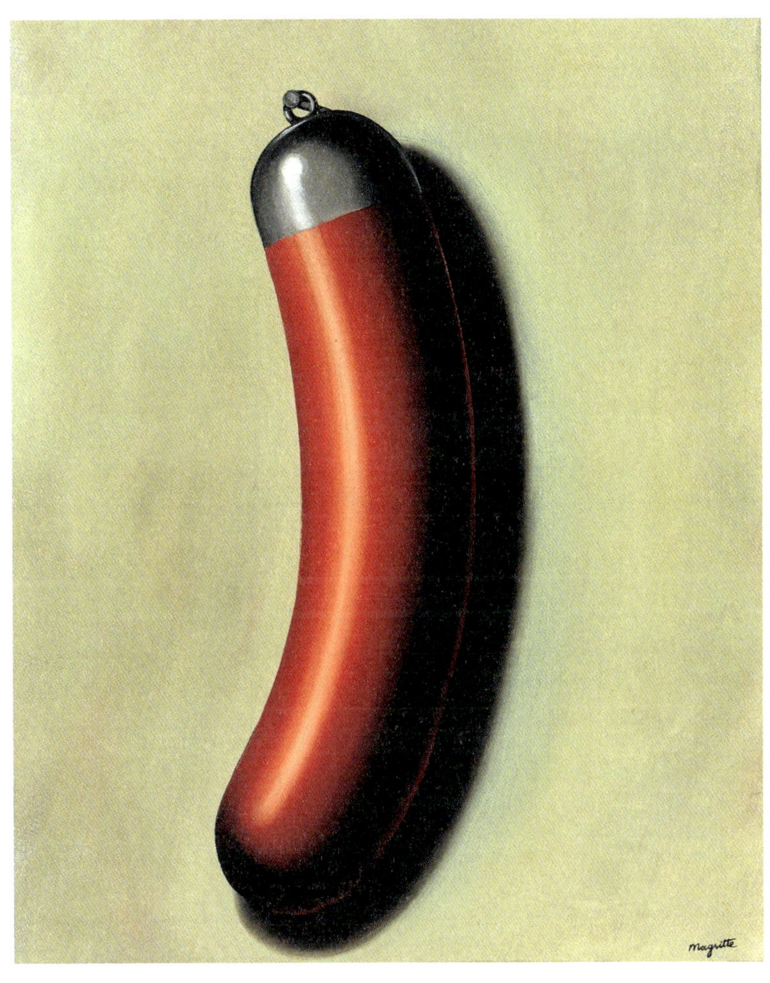

106
Helmeted Sausage
1929
oil on canvas, 55 × 46 cm

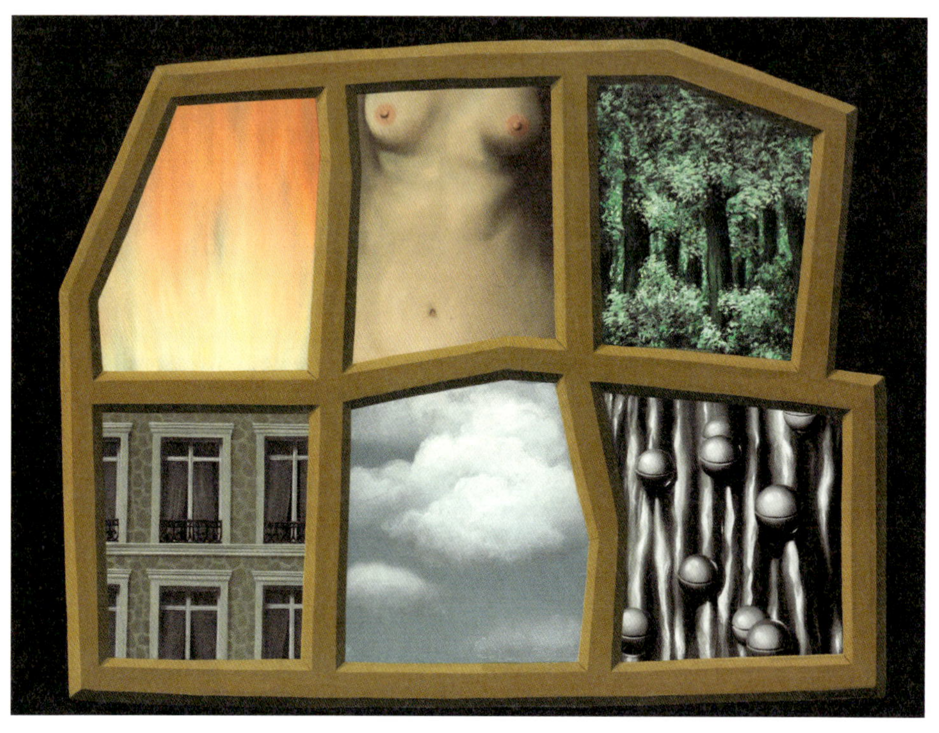

107
The Six Elements
1929
oil on canvas, 73 × 100 cm

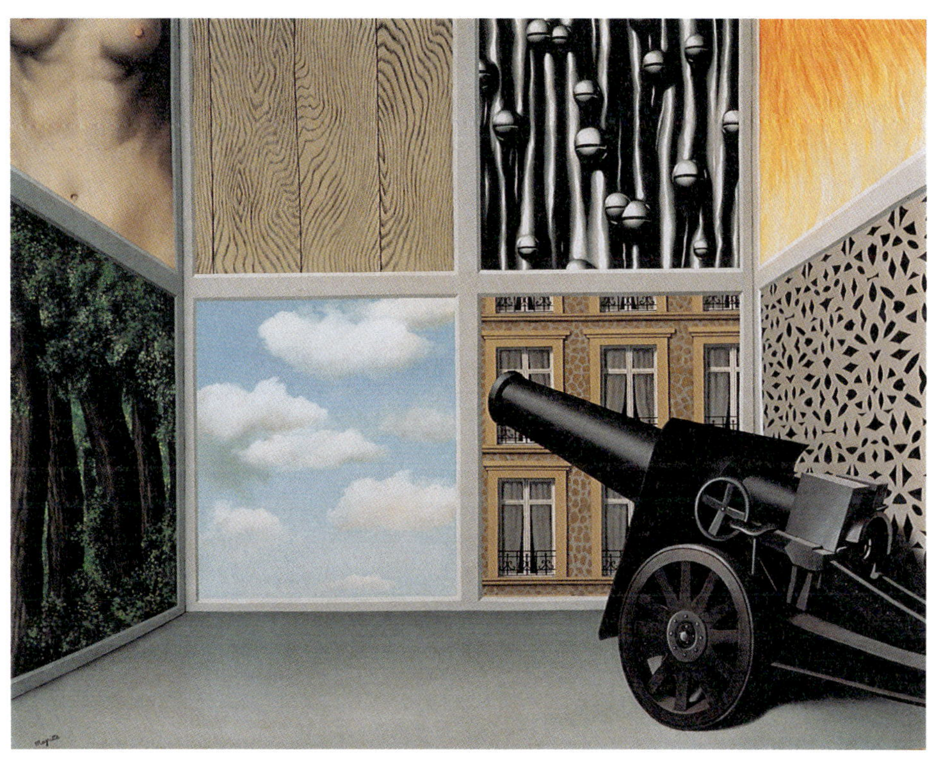

108
On the Threshold of Freedom
1930
oil on canvas, 114 × 146 cm

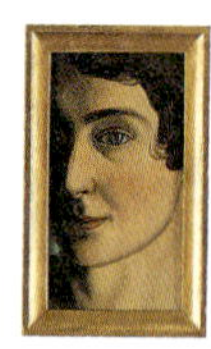

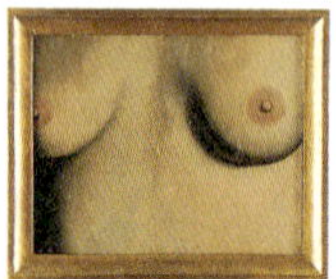

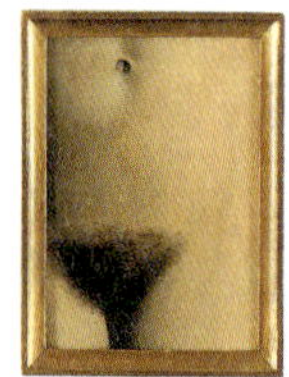

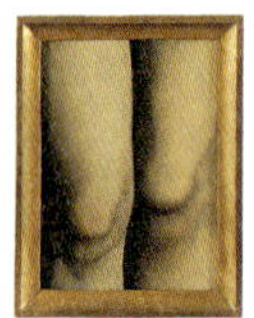

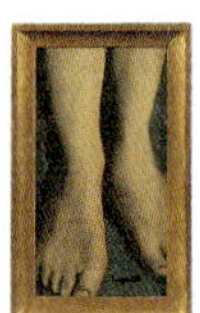

109
The Eternally Obvious
1930
oil on five canvases, 22 × 12 cm; 19 × 24 cm; 27 × 19 cm; 22 × 16 cm; 22 × 12 cm

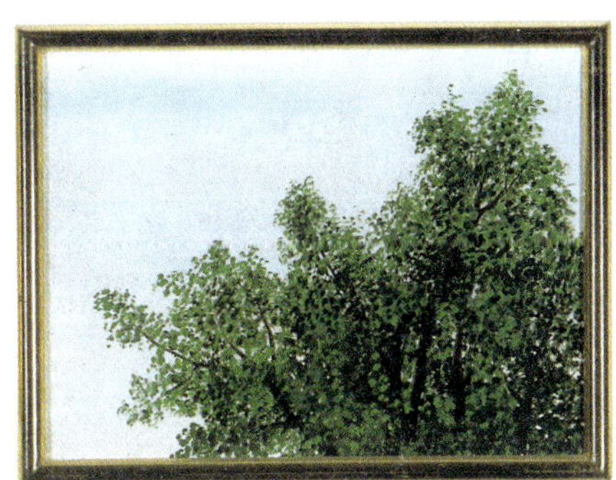

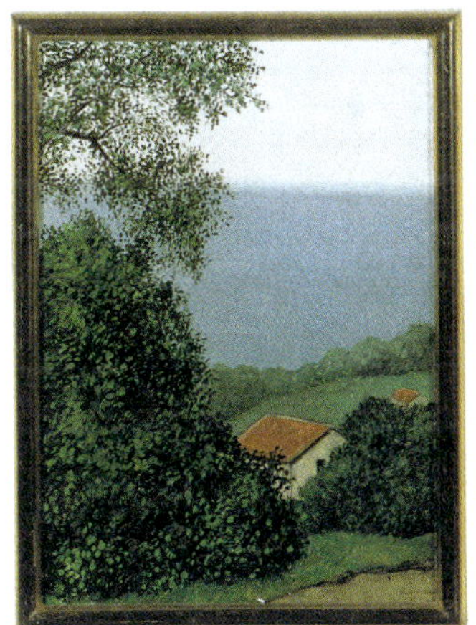

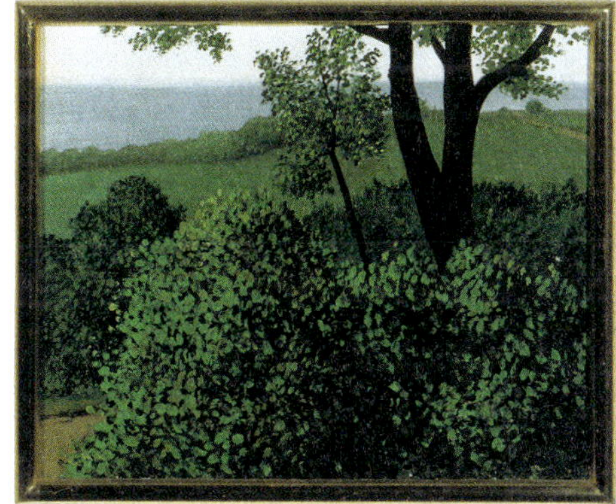

110
The Depths of the Earth
1930
oil on four canvases, 12 × 22 cm; 16 × 22 cm; 22 × 16 cm; 19 × 24 cm

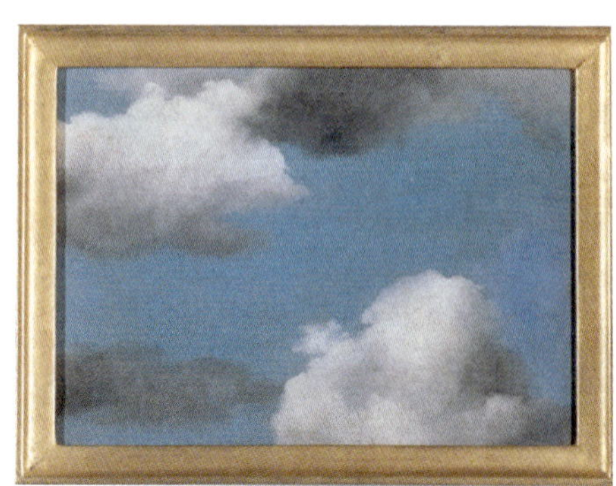
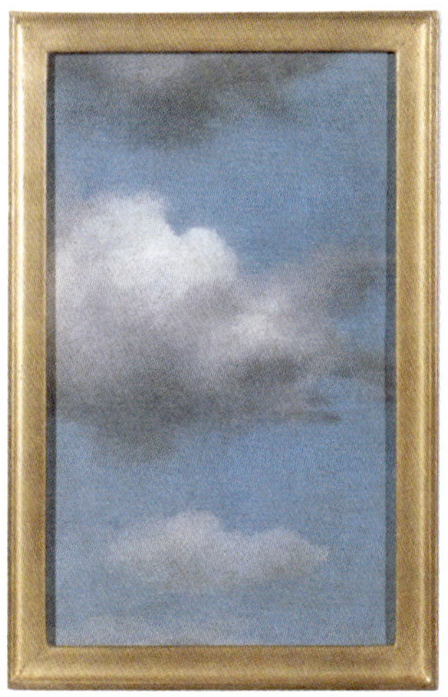
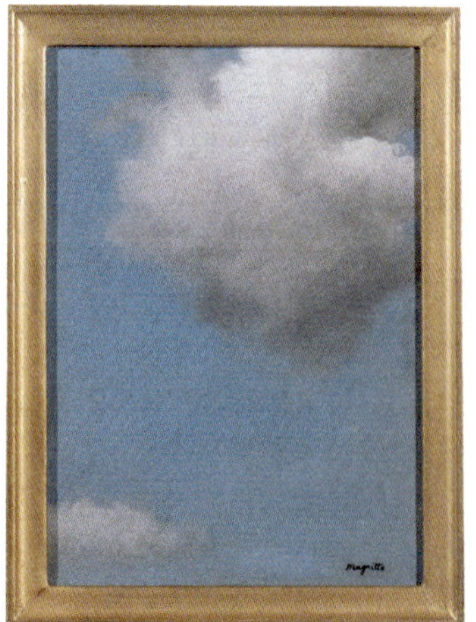

111
Celestial Perfections
1930
oil on four canvases, 27 × 22 cm; 24 × 33 cm; 35 × 22 cm; 33 × 24 cm

The Dark Period

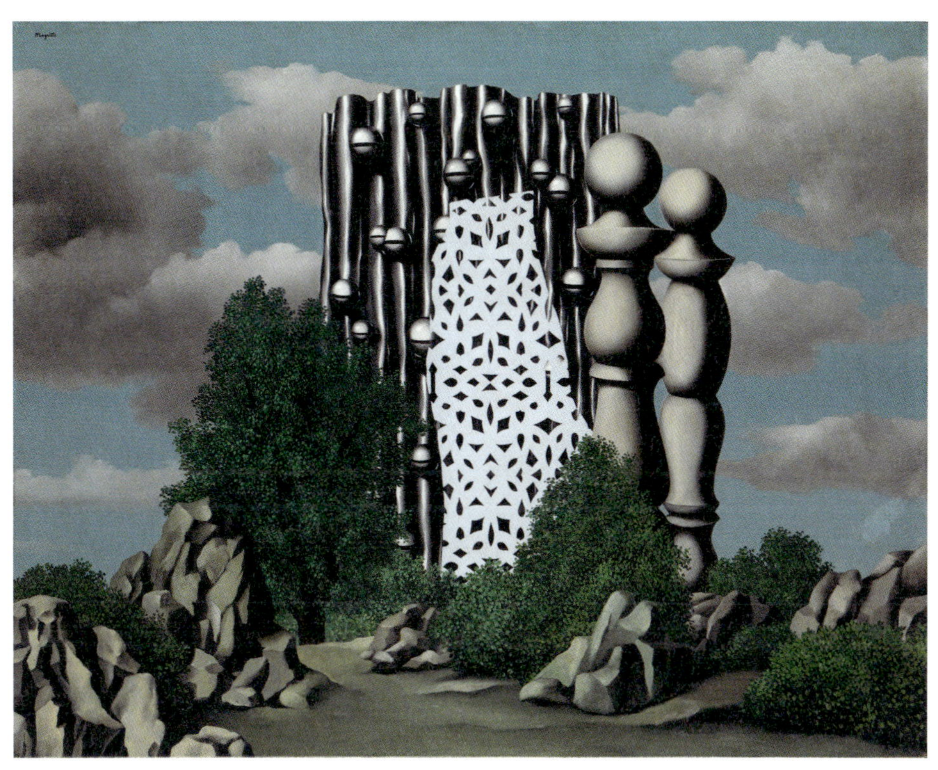

112
The Annunciation
1930
oil on canvas, 114 × 146 cm

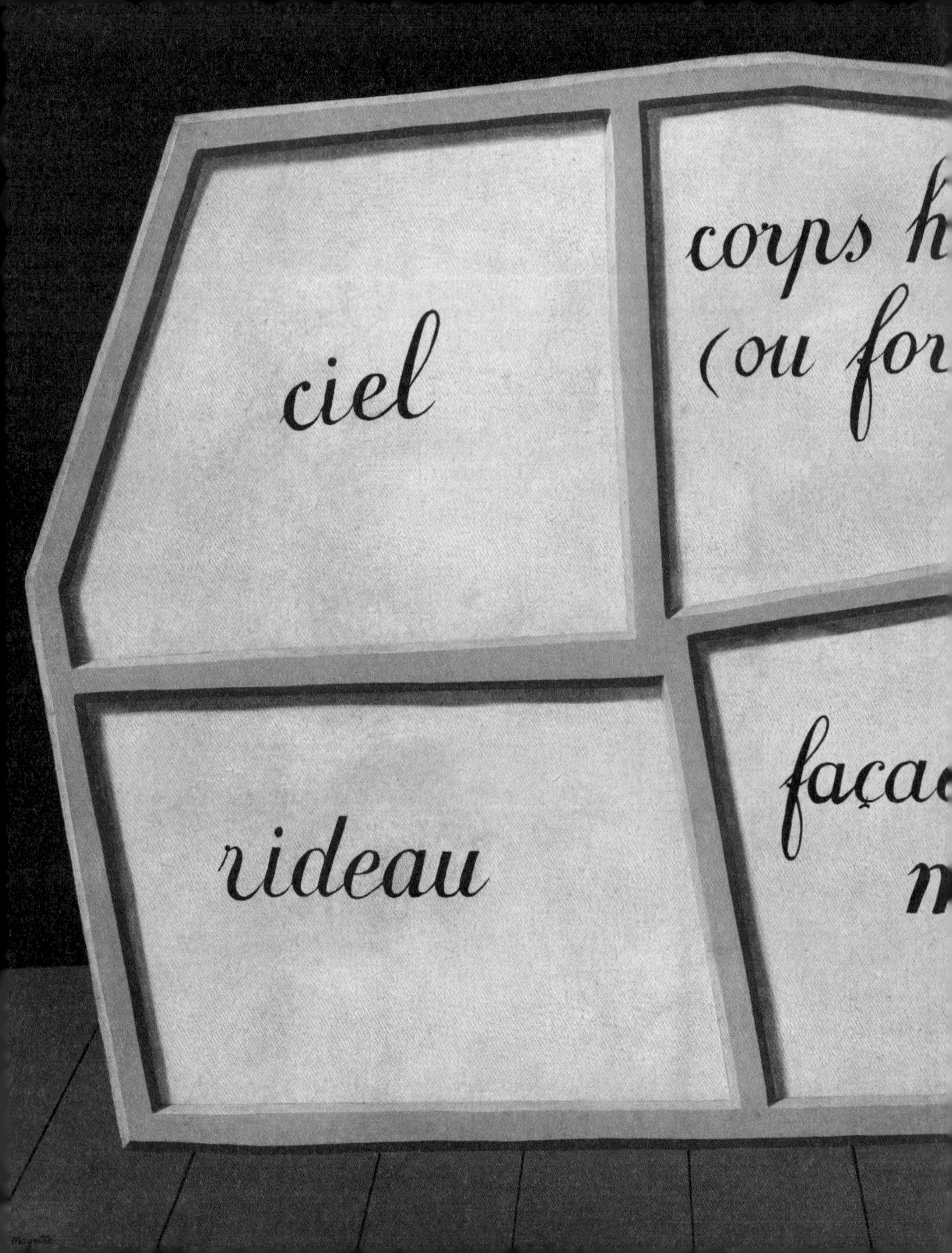

ciel

corps h

(ou for

rideau

faça

m

Magritte

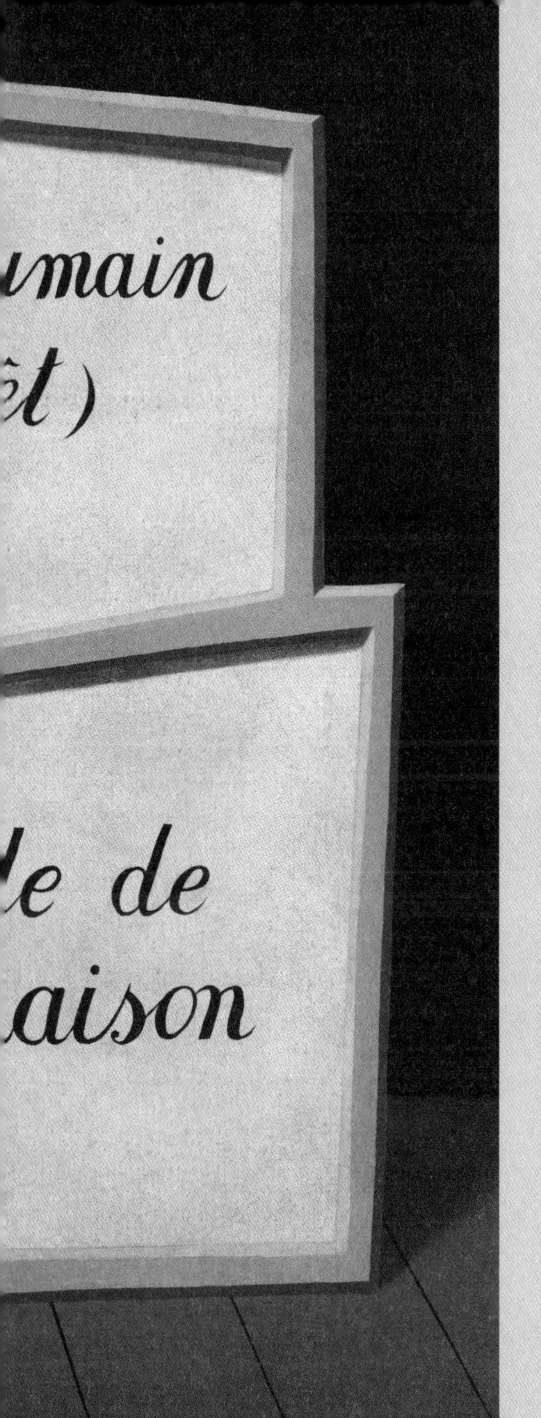

Words and Images

1927–1930

Magritte did not actually join the Paris Surrealist group led by André Breton (1896–1966) during the three years that he lived in Paris. He was not invited to take part in the big exhibitions that introduced Surrealism to Paris, and nor does Breton refer to him in his book *Surrealism and Painting*, published in 1928. That year, however, Breton purchased four of Magritte's paintings, evidence of an interest in his work.

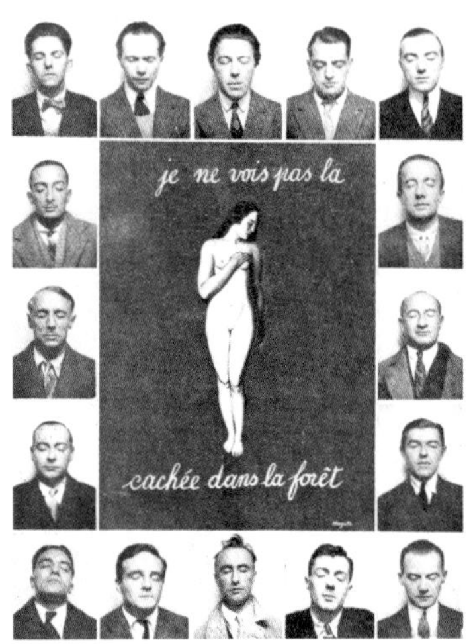

La Révolution surréaliste, no. 12, 15 December 1929.

Magritte was invited to take part in the twelfth and last issue of the Paris review *La Révolution surréaliste*, in December 1929. Of greatest note among his submissions is a text of major importance entitled 'Les Mots et les images' (Words and Images), which would become one of Magritte's most influential contributions to art in the twentieth century.

When Magritte gave his lecture 'La Ligne de vie' in Antwerp, ten years later, among the ways he named of making objects sensational were 'the combination of words with images' and 'the false identification of an image'.[14] He was referring to the results of research he had been carrying out since 1927 into the possible relationships between a real object, a represented object and the words used to name it. While the linguist Ferdinand de Saussure (1857–1913) and the philosopher Ludwig Wittgenstein (1889–1951) were also interested in this question, Magritte was the first to apply these concepts to painting.

In 'Les Mots et les images', Magritte listed eighteen possible relationships between an object, its representation and its name:

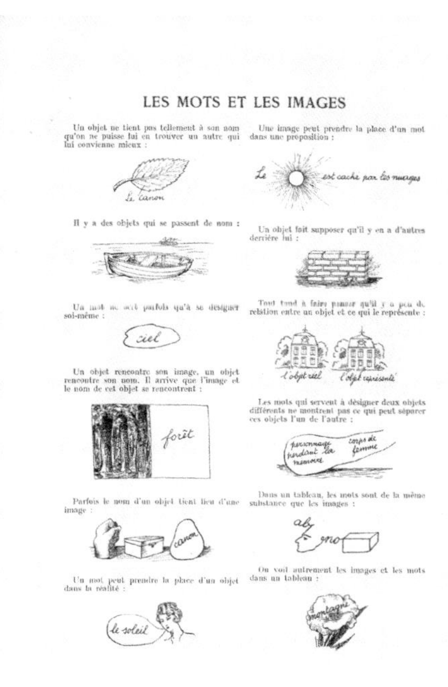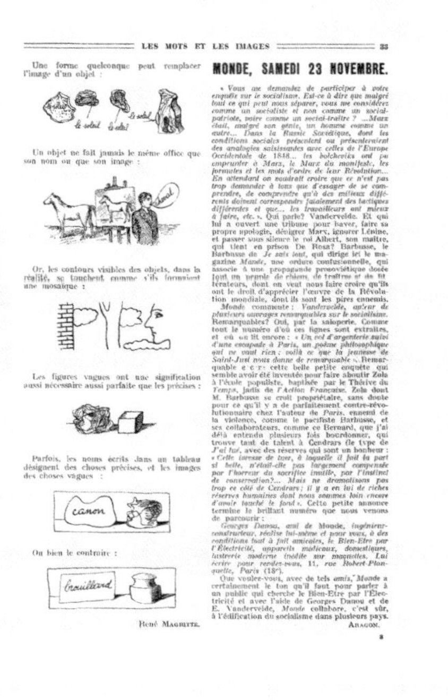

René Magritte, 'Les Mots et les images' from *La Révolution surréaliste*, no. 12, December 1929.

No object is so tied to its name that we cannot find another one that suits it better.

Some objects do without a name.

Sometimes a word merely serves to designate itself.

An object encounters its image, an object encounters its name.

The object's image and name happen to meet.

At times the name of an object stands in for an image.

A word can take the place of an object in reality.

An image can take the place of a word in a statement.

An object hints at other objects behind it.

Everything tends to suggest that there is little connection
  between an object and what represents it.

The words referring to two different objects do not show what

can separate these objects from each other.
In a picture words have the same substance as images.
Images and words are seen differently in a picture.
Any old shape can replace the image of an object.
An object never does the same job as its name or image.
Now, the visible outlines of objects touch in reality as if they make up a mosaic.
Indefinite shapes have a significance that is as
   necessary, as perfect as precise ones.
Sometimes written words in a picture refer to precise
   things, and images refer to indefinite things.
Or else, the opposite.[15]

These statements provide a user's guide to a better understanding of some of the essential issues at stake in Magritte's work. From his first paintings, he had sought to emphasise, via the canvas, the fundamental difference between reality and representation. *Nocturne* [15], from 1925, introduces the motif of the painting within a painting. For this reason, Marcel Mariën (1920–93) considers it Magritte's first Surrealist picture.[16] The image shows a bird in flight, which appears to be fleeing a house on fire in another space – that of a framed painting behind a curtain. As the bird leaves the painted space of the picture, it seems to penetrate the real space of a room, thereby becoming real itself, while at the same time remaining an image.

With *Attempting the Impossible* (1928) [100], Magritte repeated the exercise, by representing a painter at work, apparently the artist himself, as his paintbrush gives life to a naked woman who clearly resembles his own wife, Georgette. Still unfinished, the woman's body is nonetheless located in the same 'real space' as the painter.

The introduction of language into painted images allowed Magritte to take this thought process even further, as seen in the series of 'word-paintings' created in Paris between 1927 and 1930. The most influential of these, *The Treachery of Images* (1929) [124], illustrates the aphorism 'Everything tends to suggest that there is little connection between an object and what represents it.' Magritte writes explicitly, 'This is not a

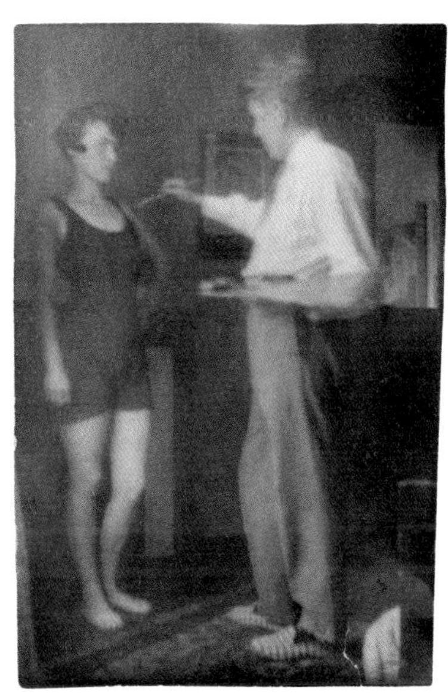

Love, Le Perreux-sur-Marne, 1928.
Study for *Attempting the Impossible*.

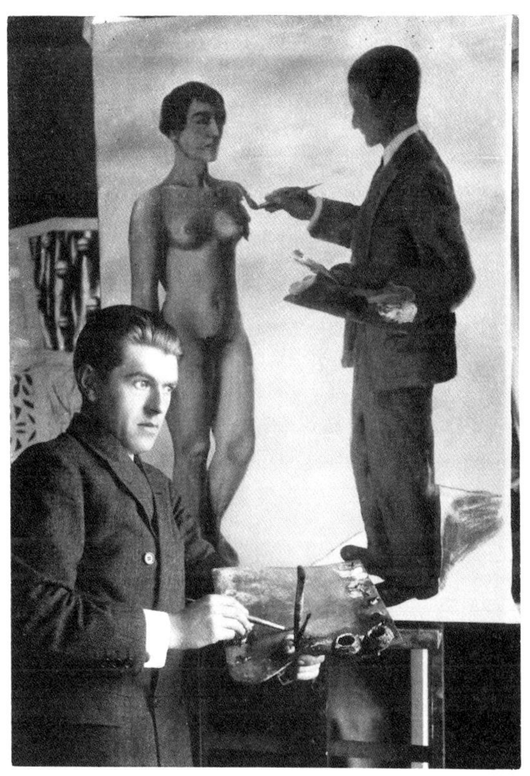

René Magritte painting *Attempting the Impossible*,
Le Perreux-sur-Marne, 1928.

pipe': it is the *image* of a pipe, not the real object. While pursuing his wish to distinguish reality from representation, Magritte demonstrates his rejection of language as a tool of knowledge and communication. Here, couched in the negative, language provides no information and raises other questions: If it isn't a pipe, then what is it? An image, yes. But why isn't it an apple? Or a tree? Who decided that this object should be called 'pipe'? And in fact, Magritte asserts in his text that, 'no object is so attached to its name that we cannot find another one that suits it better'. This question recurs in the multiple paintings entitled *The Interpretation of Dreams* [113, 129], in which Magritte paints the image of various objects and labels them with words that are incorrect according to the system of communication in effect: the word 'moon' identifies the image of a shoe, while the word 'ceiling' identifies a lit candle (*The Interpretation of Dreams*, 1930 [129]). In this simple but effective way, Magritte demonstrates the profoundly arbitrary nature of language.

In other works, Magritte empties language of its meaning and keeps only the shell. In *The Phantom Landscape* (1928) [115], for example, the word 'mountain' is inscribed across the face of a woman. True to his aphorisms, Magritte means to show not only that 'in a picture words have the same substance as images' but also that 'images and words are seen differently in a picture'. Though the word is expressed in the same pictorial matter from the same brush as the woman's portrait, we cannot help separating the word from the image. Nor can we help imagining a mountain, or trying to understand why Magritte chose this particular word, or else trying to find some connection with the face or the angle at which the word is written. Magritte's intention is to draw attention to our dependence on an established system of communication. He plays on the word's power of suggestion by emptying out its image as well. In *Swift Hope* (1927) [114], the viewer mentally completes the composition, imagining the 'tree' at the left and the 'village on the horizon' at the right, responding to the statement that 'any old shape can replace the image of an object'.

Magritte made about forty word-paintings, each illustrating one of the aphorisms in his famous text.

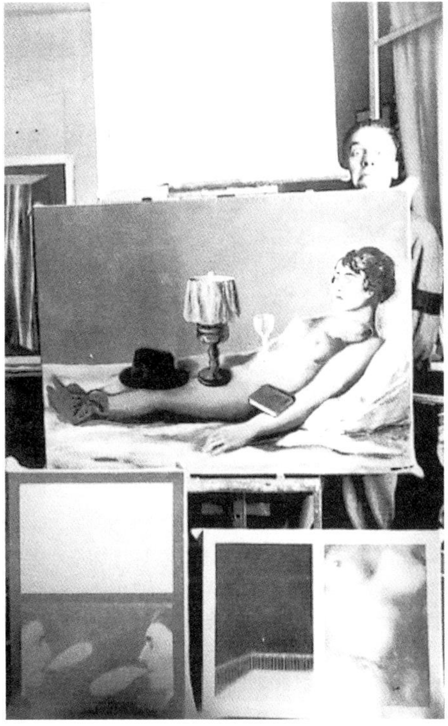

Paul Magritte, Le Perreux-sur-Marne, 1928.

14   Ibid.
15   René Magritte, 'Les Mots et les images', *La Révolution surréaliste*, no. 12 (15 December 1929).
      Quoted in English from Kathleen Mooney and Eric Plattner, eds, *René Magritte: Selected Writings*,
      trans. Jo Levy and Adam Elgar (Minneapolis: University of Minnesota Press, 2016).
16   Interview with Marcel Mariën, 9 March 1981, Brussels, in Silvano Levy, *Decoding Magritte*
      (Bristol: Sansom & Company, 2015), p. 215.

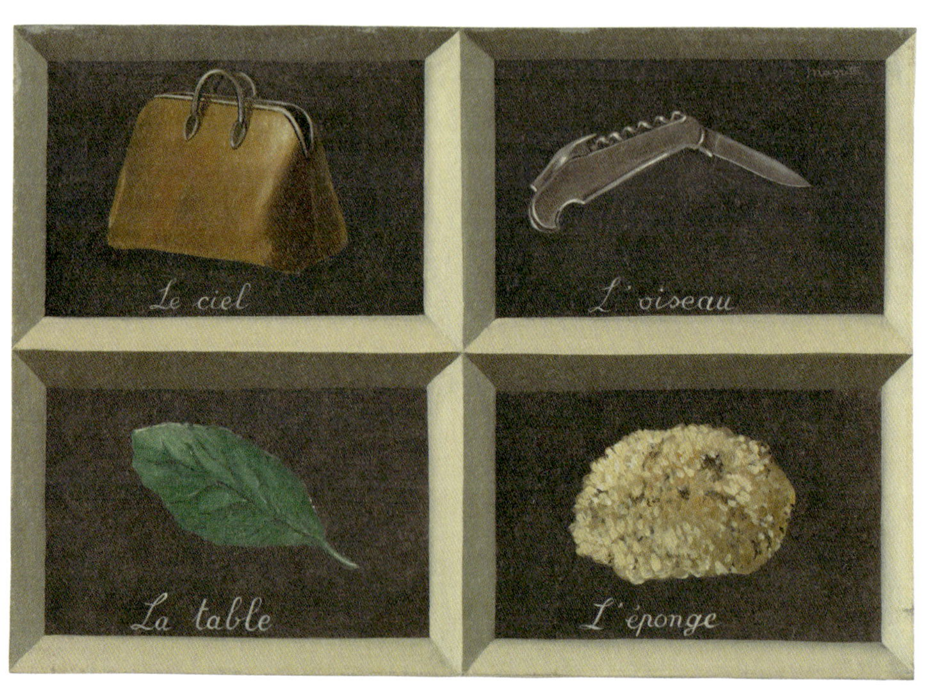

113
The Interpretation of Dreams
1927
oil on canvas, 38 × 55 cm

Words and Images

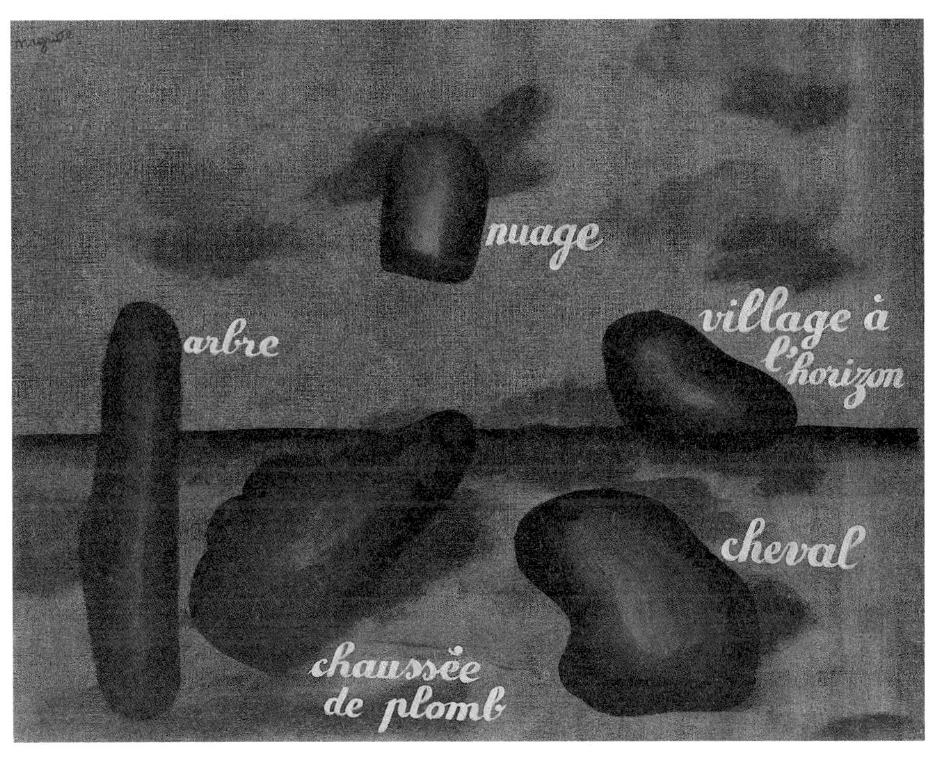

114
Swift Hope
1927
oil on canvas, 50 × 65 cm

1927–1930

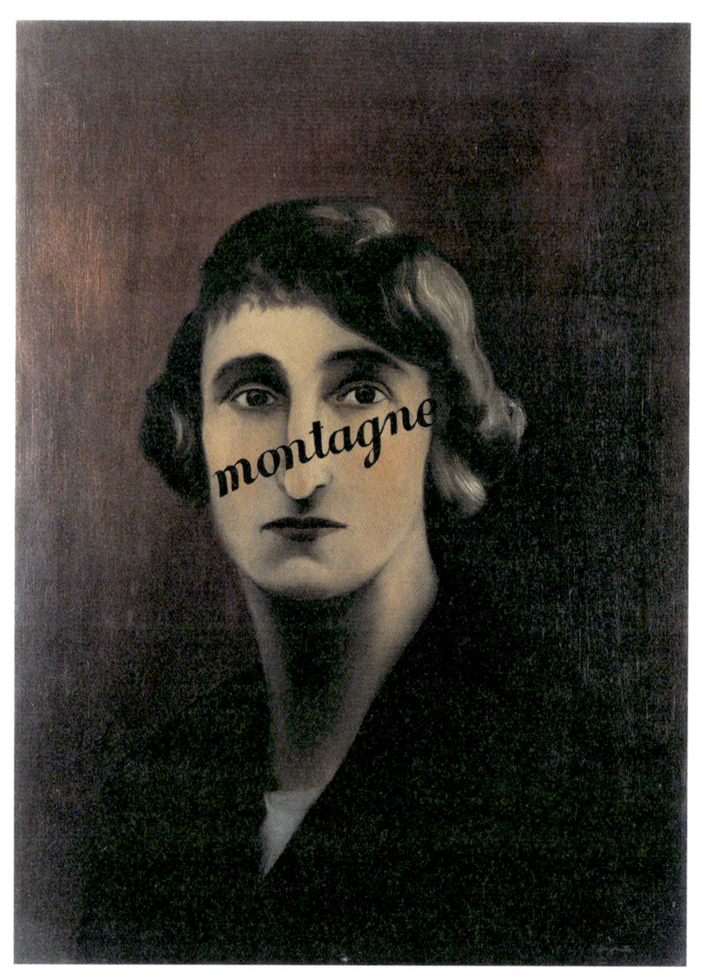

115
The Phantom Landscape
1928
oil on canvas, 73 × 54 cm

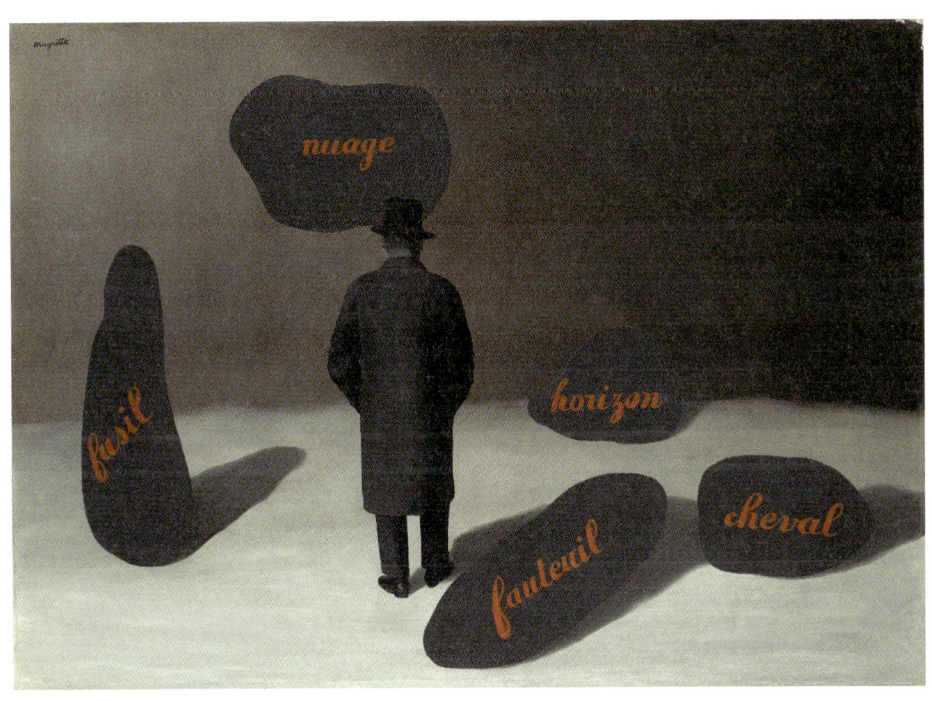

116
The Apparition
1928
oil on canvas, 81 × 116 cm

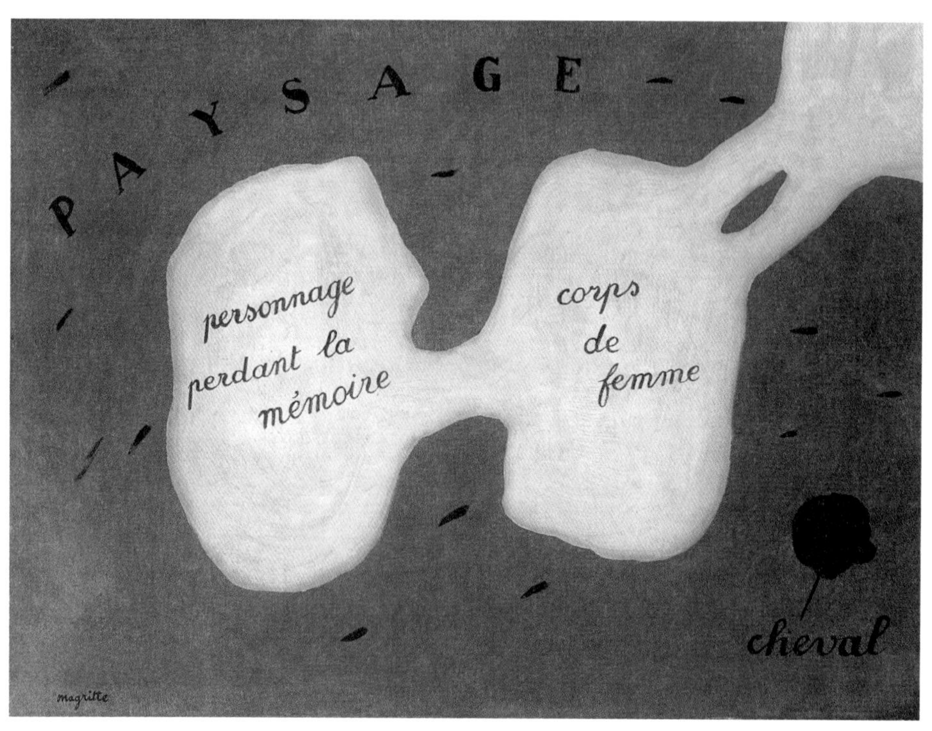

117
The Lost World
1928
oil on canvas, 54 × 73 cm

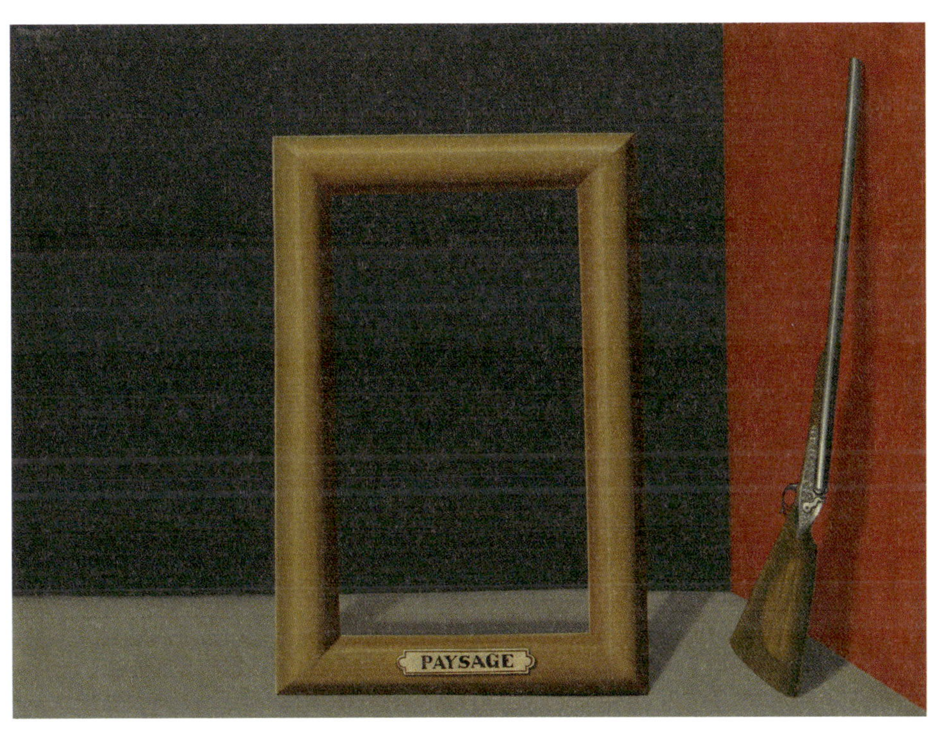

118
The Delights of Landscape
1928
oil on canvas, 54 × 73 cm

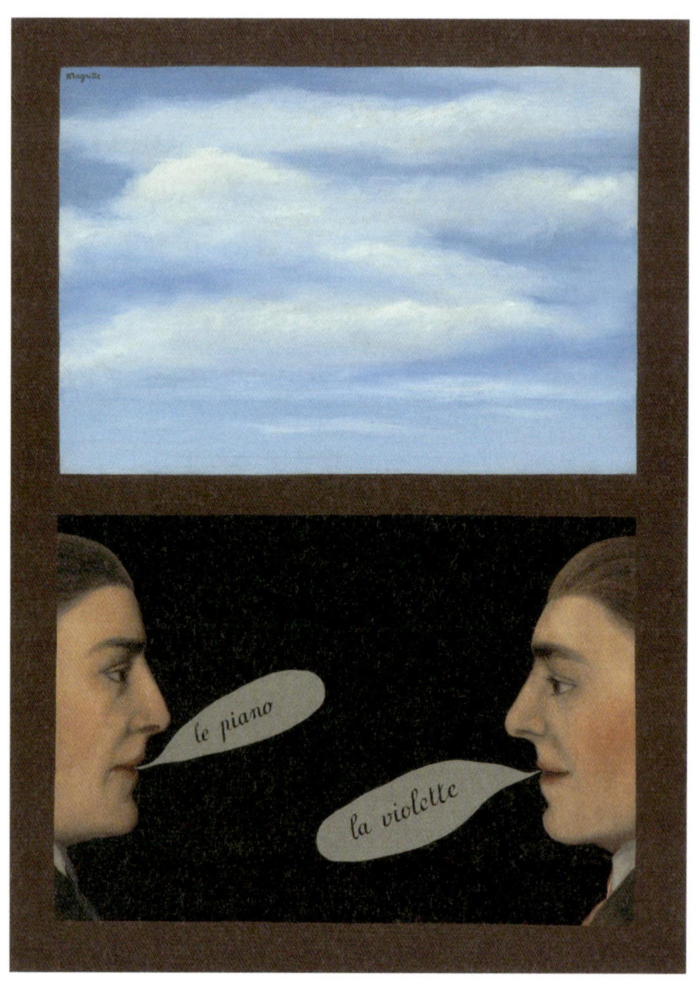

119
The Use of Speech (I)
1928
oil on canvas, 73 × 54 cm

 Words and Images

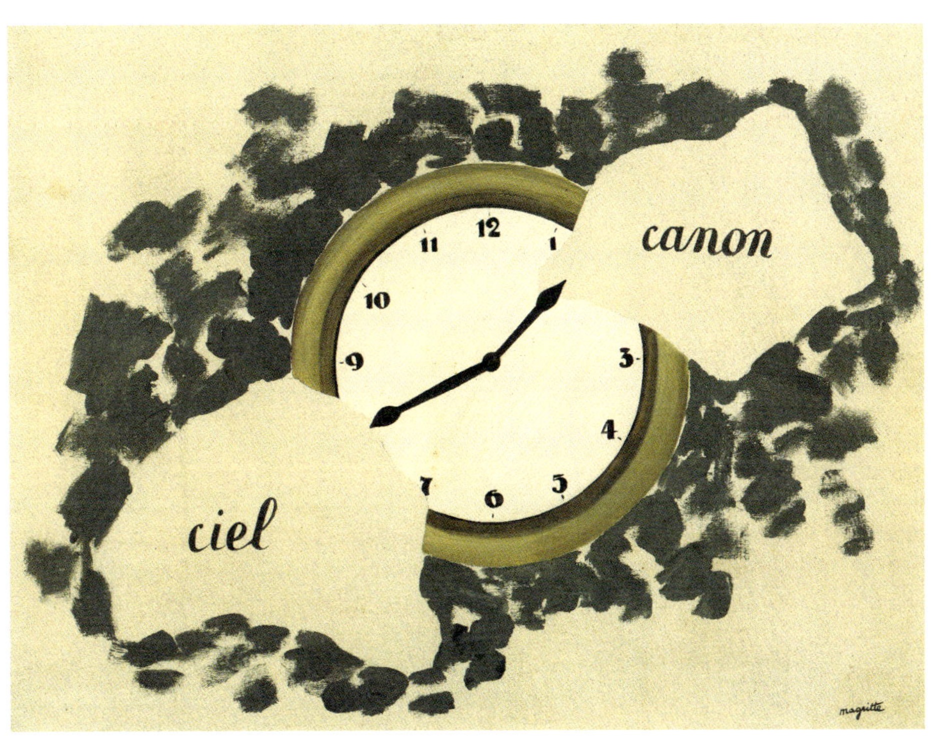

120
Reflections of Time
1928
oil on canvas, 54 × 73 cm

1927–1930

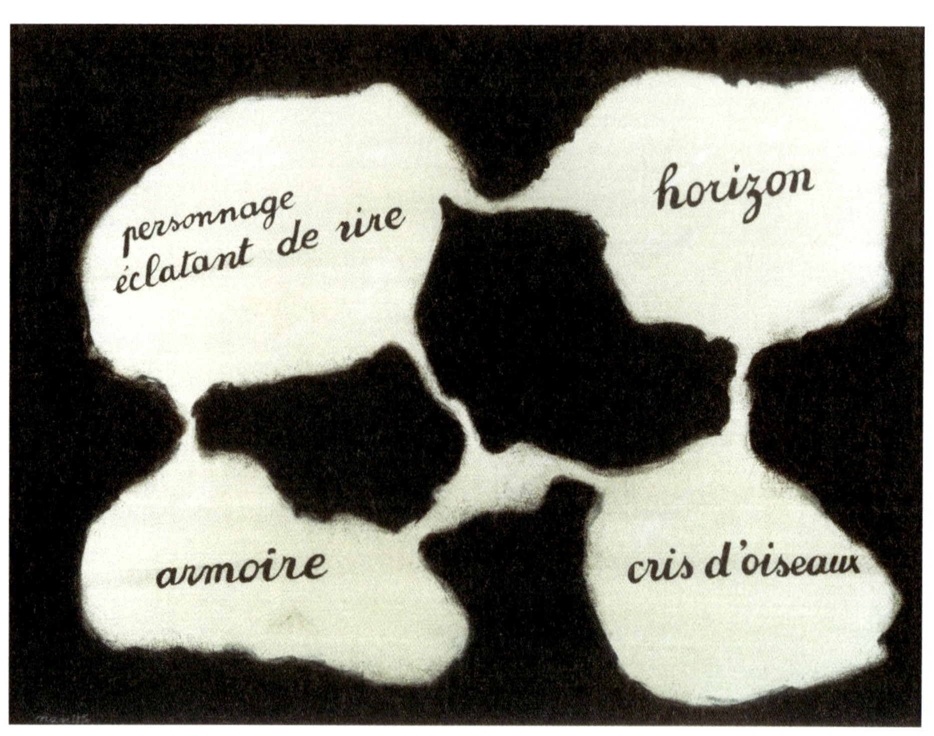

121
The Living Mirror
1928
oil on canvas, 54 × 73 cm

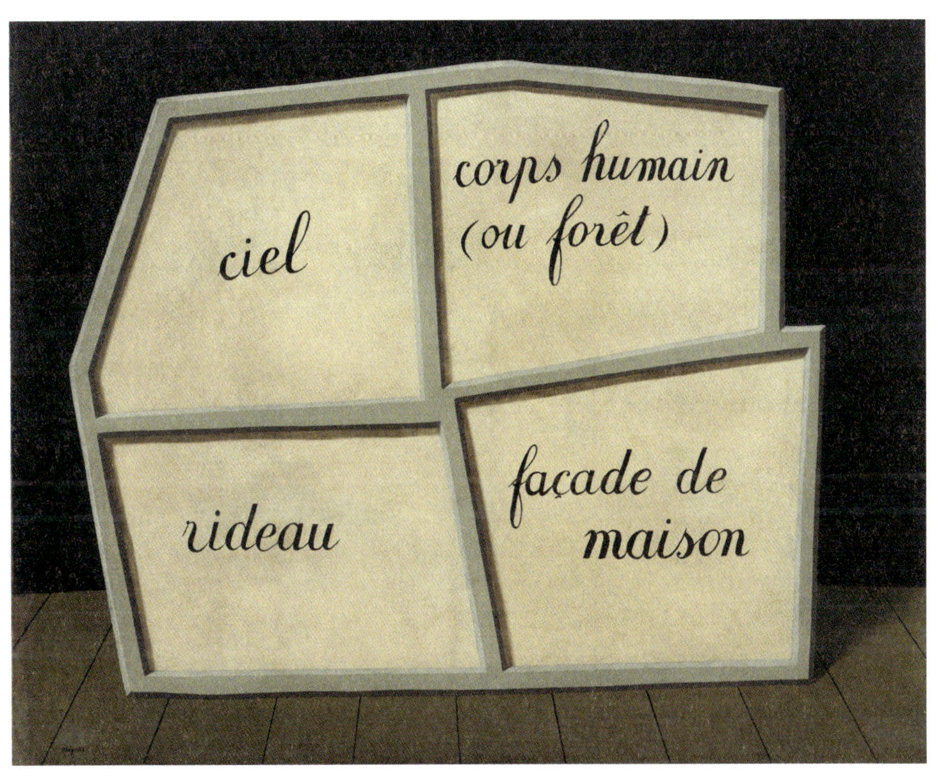

122
The Empty Mask (II)
1928
oil on canvas, 73 × 92 cm

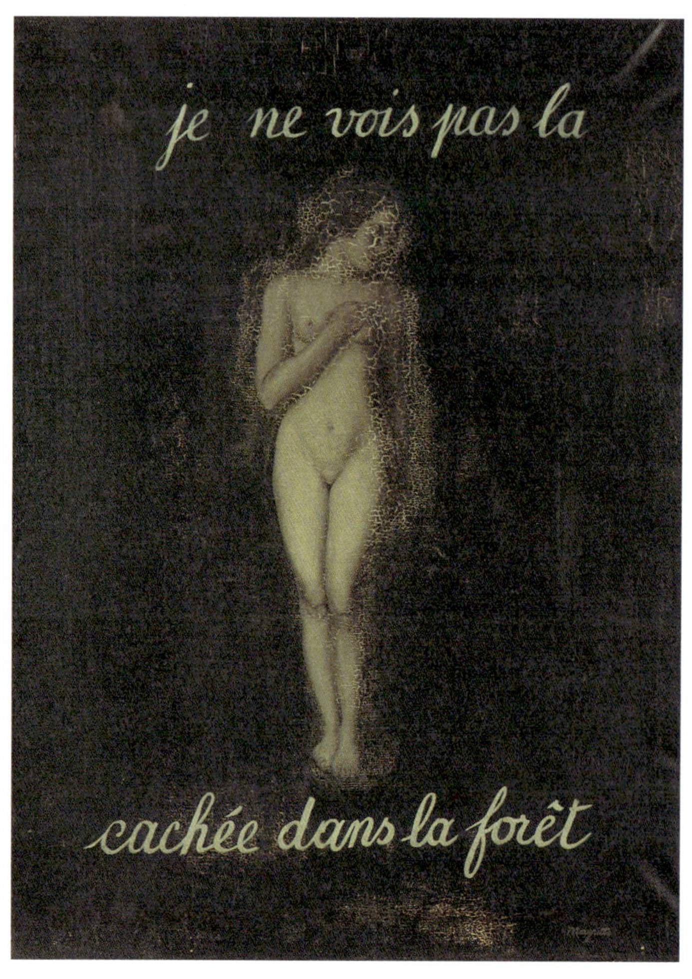

123
The Hidden Woman
1929
oil on canvas, 73 × 54 cm

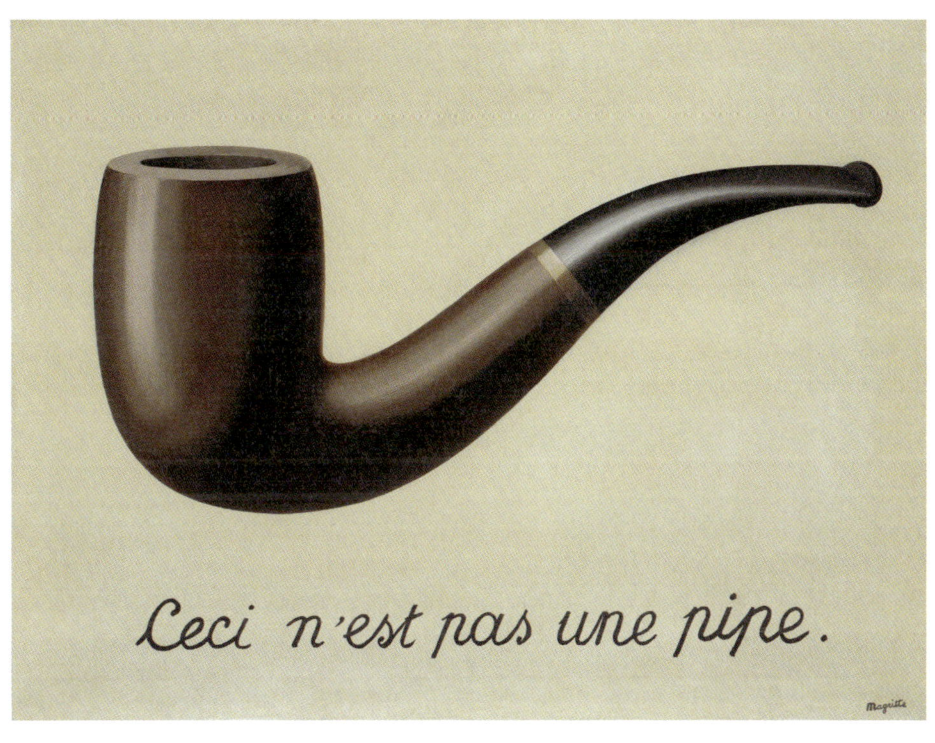

124
The Treachery of Images
1929
oil on canvas, 60 × 81 cm

 1927–1930

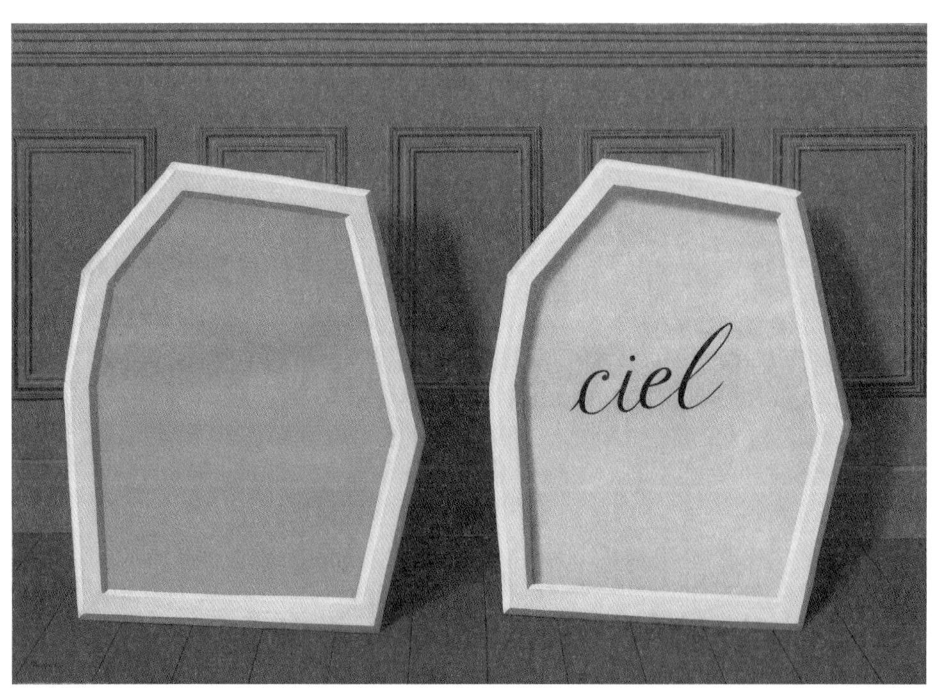

125
The Palace of Curtains
1929
oil on canvas, 81 × 116 cm

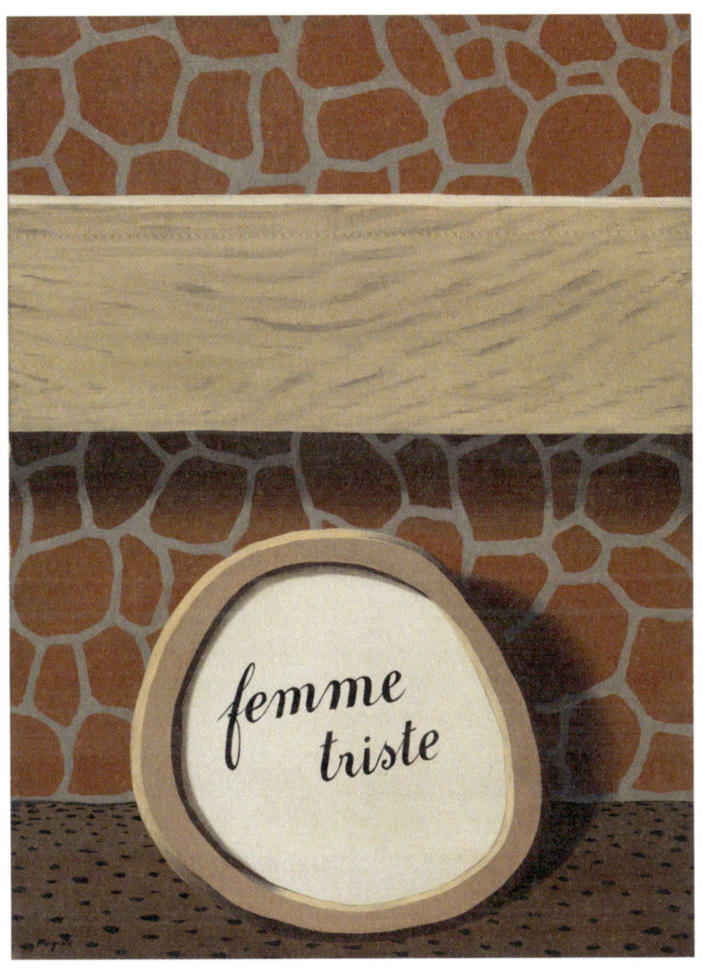

126
The Literal Meaning (IV)
1929
oil on canvas, 73 × 54 cm

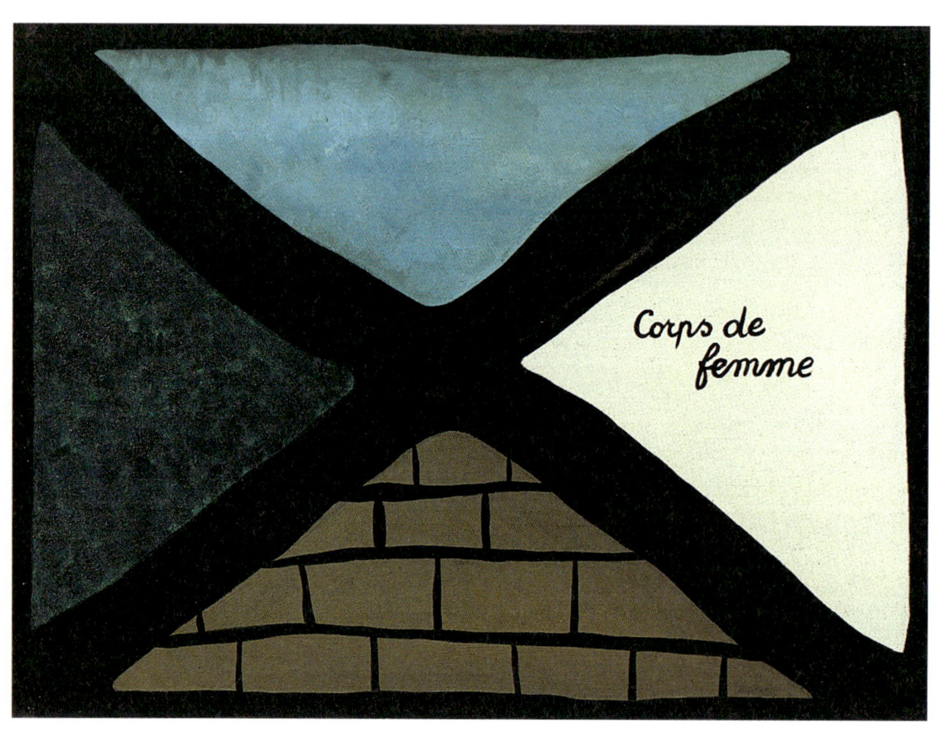

127
The Literal Meaning (VI)
1929
oil on canvas, 54 × 73 cm

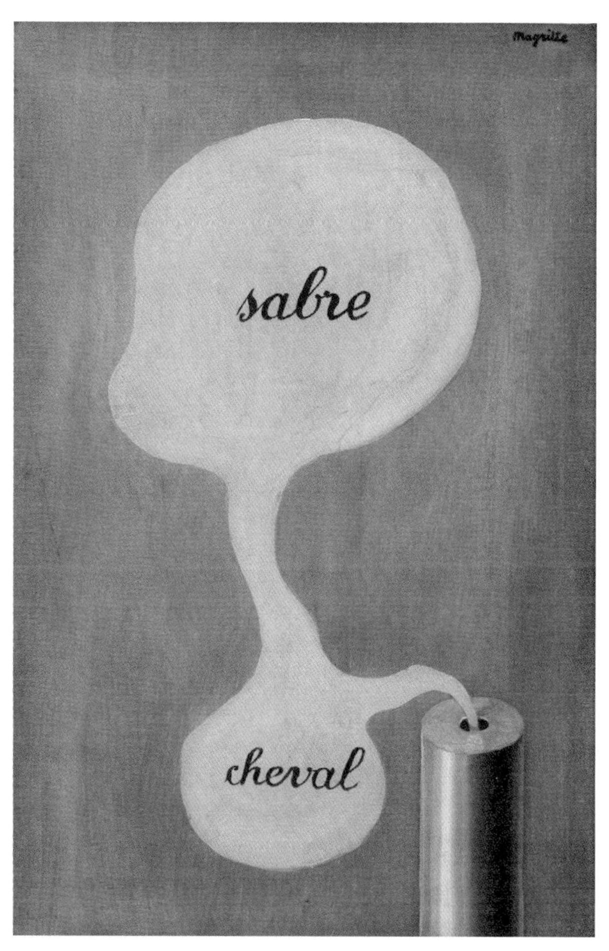

128
The Tree of Knowledge
1929
oil on canvas, 41 × 27 cm

1927–1930

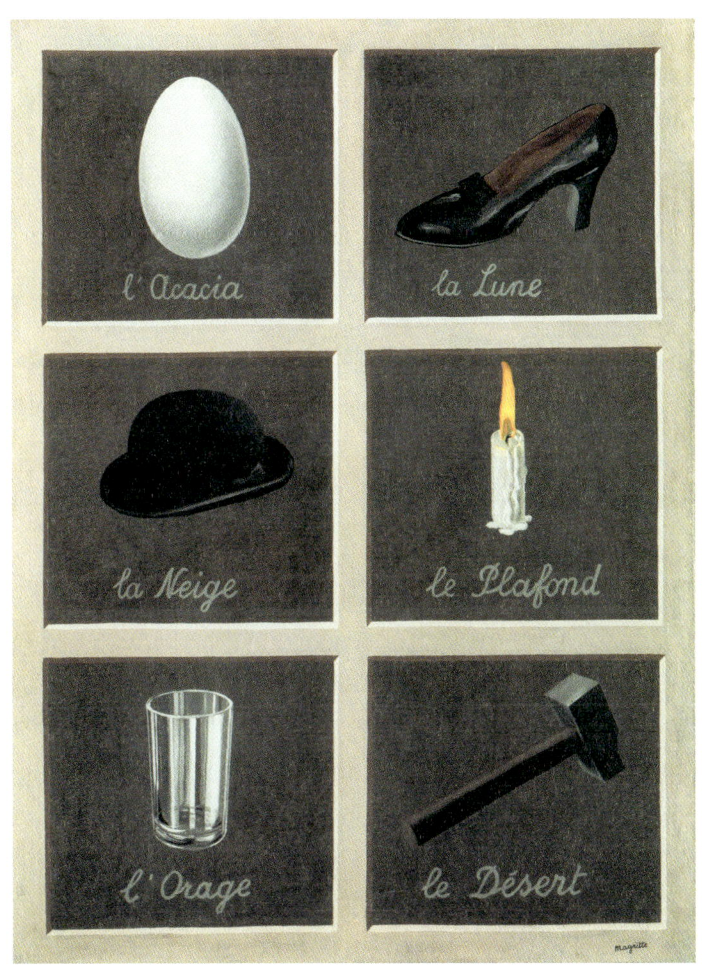

129
The Interpretation of Dreams
1930
oil on canvas, 81 × 60 cm

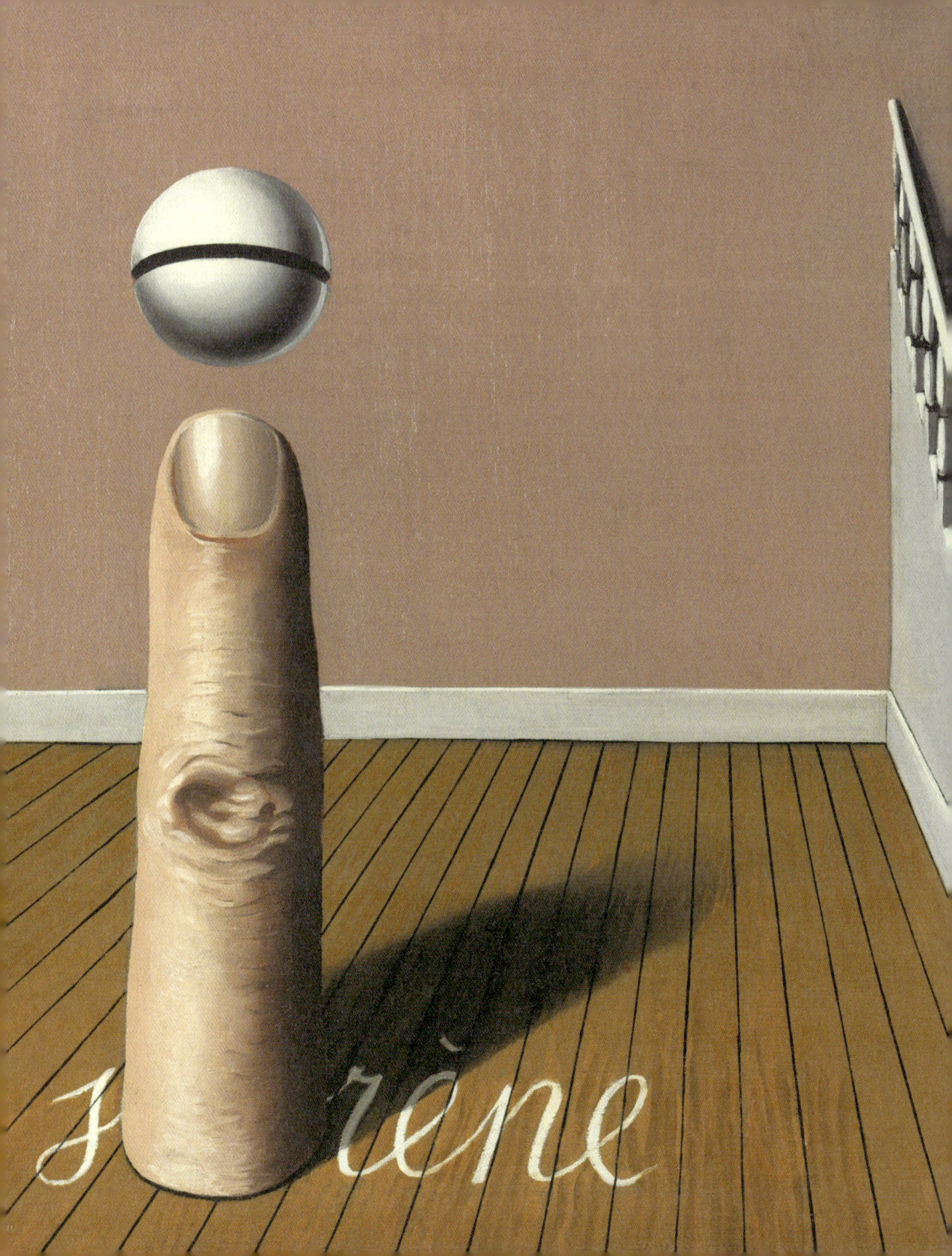
rêne

Elective Affinities

1931–1942

In July 1930, after the closing of the Galerie Goemans in Paris, with which Magritte held a contract, he and his wife, Georgette, were forced to return to Brussels. Without an income, he again took up his 'idiot work', as he called the commercial art activity he pursued in times of financial need. With his brother Paul, he founded Studio Dongo, an advertising agency installed at the end of the garden of the house in Jette, where the Magrittes had recently moved. In the context of this new enterprise, Magritte made drawings and designed advertising posters and sheet music covers.

Although the work necessitated by his straitened circumstances led to a considerable reduction in his output of paintings between 1931 and 1934, he nonetheless carried on with his investigations, inaugurating a new method of exploring the everyday world. This method, named after the title of a picture painted in 1933 – *Elective Affinities* [139] – consisted of a systematic search for 'affinities' between objects. In his 1938 lecture in Antwerp, Magritte described the vision that prompted this new orientation: 'One night in 1936,[17] I woke up in a room that contained a cage with a sleeping bird. A splendid error made me see the bird gone from the cage and replaced by an egg. I held an astonishing new poetic secret, for the shock I felt was caused precisely by the affinity of the two objects, the cage and the egg, whereas previously the shock was caused by the encounter of objects alien to each other. Based on this revelation, I wanted to discover whether, by shedding light on an element proper to them and strictly preordained for them, objects other than the cage could manifest the same obvious poetry as the egg and cage had produced by their encounter. In the course of my research, I acquired the certainty that this element to be discovered – this one thing among all others, obscurely attached to every object – I always knew in advance, but that this knowledge was buried in the back of my mind. As these investigations could lead to only one exact answer for each object, they resembled the pursuit of the solution to problems, for which I had three givens: the object, the thing attached to it in the shadows of my consciousness, and the light in which this thing was to emerge.'[18]

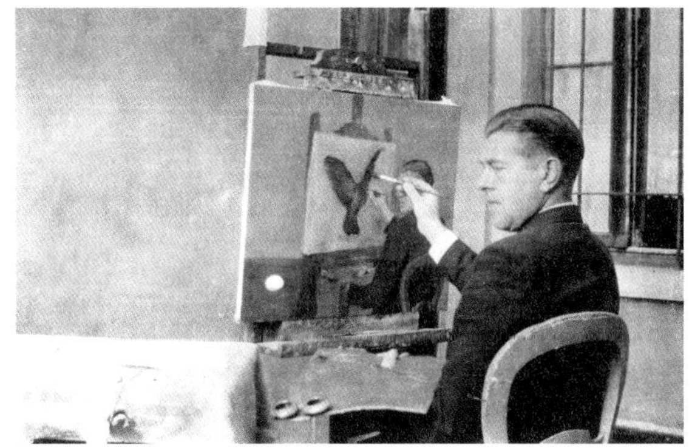

René Magritte painting *Clairvoyance*, Brussels, 4 October 1936.

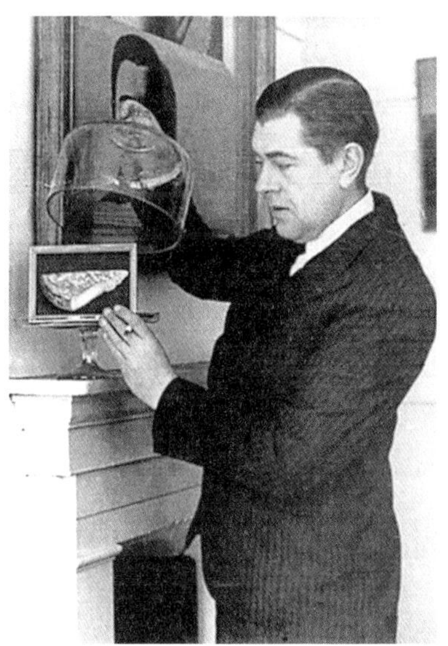

René Magritte, London Gallery, London, 1938.

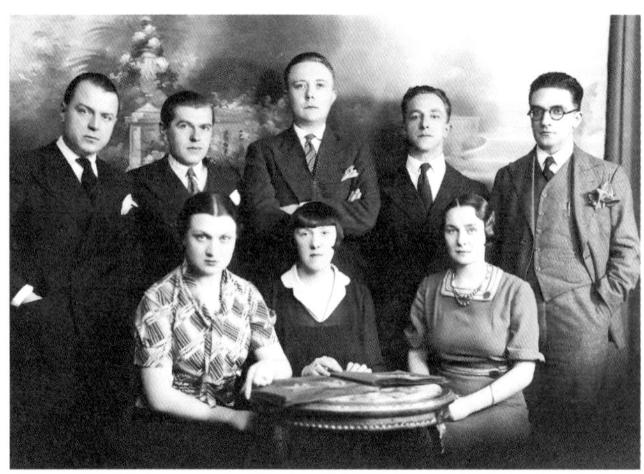

The Hunters' Gathering, 1934. Left to right: E. L. T. Mesens, René Magritte, Louis Scutenaire, André Souris and Paul Nougé. Seated: Irène Hamoir, Marthe Beauvoisin and Georgette Magritte. Studio Jos Rentmeesters.

Unlike the other paintings he had done before, in these new works, Magritte did not intentionally combine unrelated objects in order to disorient and create strange compositions. Instead, he sought to make obvious what binds objects inextricably together. Magritte claims he received the image for *Elective Affinities* (1933) [139] in a vision while half asleep, which makes it a rare example of a work by the artist inspired by a dream. To the French Surrealists, the notions of the dream and the unconscious were key concerns. Through their use of automatic writing, among other methods, these concerns were placed at the core of the emergence of images and texts. The dream for Magritte, however, has no role in the appearance of his images. For him, it was more a matter of 'presence of mind' or 'inspired thought', concepts he likened to inspiration and developed broadly in his later texts. In exceptional cases, a 'Eureka!' moment offered him an image. Most times, however, the image took form on the canvas or paper and was the result of long research developed in many drawings. This period of reflection was necessary for Magritte to obtain the image that would provide the most accurate solution to the problem raised by an object.

Elective Affinities

Through his new way of approaching the everyday and representing familiar objects, Magritte was questioning the roles assigned to them by society. He examined how they appeared in their surroundings, as well as how they were perceived. He forced viewers to reflect, opening their eyes to the existence of these objects that go entirely unnoticed, so deeply rooted are they in daily life.

The Unexpected Answer [140], painted shortly after *Elective Affinities* in 1933, solves the problem of the door. It depicts a closed door with an opening through which an indeterminate dark space is visible. This opening in the panel of a closed door is the work's key, the discovery that reveals the intrinsic role of the object 'door' – that of opening the way.

With *The Red Model* [154, 173], the first version of which dates to 1935, Magritte emphasises our dependence on objects. By metamorphosing a pair of shoes into feet – or vice versa – he invites viewers to question their habits. He even goes so far as to question the sense of propriety that requires us to wear shoes: 'The problem of shoes shows how, under the effect of inattentiveness, the most frightful things can pass as completely inoffensive. Thanks to *The Red Model*, we feel that the combination of a human foot and a shoe is in reality a hideous custom.'[19]

Other cases deal with the specific properties of an object. In *The Ladder of Fire* (1934) [145], a crumpled sheet of paper, a wooden chair and a tuba are in flames. The viewer realises that paper and wood are combustible, but senses the strangeness of the sight of a metal tuba catching alight. Magritte has turned the logic of things inside out.

In the 1930s, he analysed the 'problems' of light (*The Light of Coincidence*, 1933 [142]), the woman (*The Rape*, 1934 [144]), the tree (*The Giantess*, 1935 [149]), the sea (*Collective Invention*, 1935 [147]), the house (*In Praise of the Dialectic*, 1937 [168]) and rain (*The Song of the Storm*, 1937 [180]). It was not unusual for him to reconsider older problems, reworking images and adjusting compositions. He sometimes added new elements, at times combining several object-solutions in a single painting. *The Amorous Vista* (1935) [156], in which a hole through a doorway exposes a view of a landscape dominated by a hybrid leaf-tree – a form comprised of a single leaf in the shape of a tree that Magritte used as a solution for the problem of the tree – is a variant of the painting *The Unexpected Answer* [140].

By systematically choosing objects and phenomena from daily life, but representing them in an unexpected way, Magritte overturned the viewer's mental habits, thus bringing these objects back to life. The viewer can finally see the objects that are surrounding him. The objects exist. 'And now, for the world to be repopulated,' as his steadfast friend Louis Scutenaire (1905–87) wrote.[20]

Using the same problematological approach, Magritte also focused on the way we perceive our environment. He explained how he solved the problem of the window and what he wished to demonstrate in the painting *The Human Condition* (1933) [141]: 'In front of a window seen inside a bedroom, I placed a painting representing the exact part of the landscape that the painting masks. Thus, the tree represented in this painting hides the tree behind it, outside the room. For the viewer, it is at once inside the room and outside in the real landscape. This is how we see the world. We see it outside ourselves, and yet all we have of it is a representation inside us. In the same way, we sometimes locate in the past something that is occurring in the present. Then time and space lose the crude meaning that is all everyday experience takes into account.'[21]

Magritte reused the idea of the painted canvas revealing the landscape hidden behind it in variants of *The Human Condition* [157, 159] and *The Fair Captive* [132, 270]. A canvas presented in this way also underscores one of the principles Magritte expressed in his text 'Les Mots et les images': 'An object hints at other objects behind it.' The painted canvas corresponds to the limits of human vision by revealing what it is supposed to hide and by recalling to the viewer that the apparent invisibility of things is not the same as nonexistence.

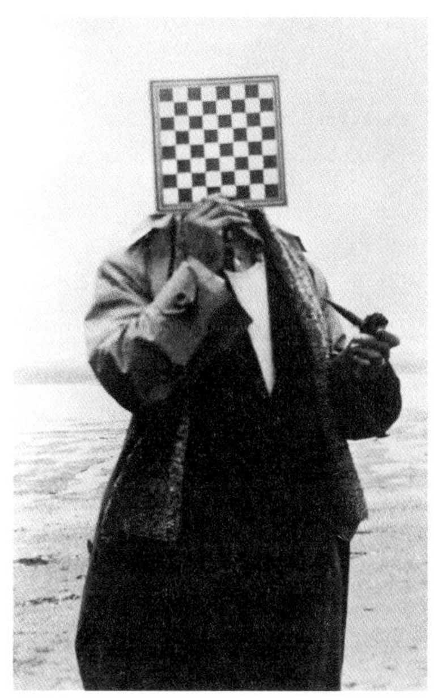

The Giant, 1937. Paul Nougé on the Belgian coast.

During the 1930s Magritte also executed some of his most interesting portraits, whereas later, in the 1950s and 1960s, when, owing to his growing success, his portrait commissions became more frequent, he fulfilled them not without a certain tedium and systematisation, placing his sitters in Surreal landscapes typical of his world. In 1937, however, he conceived a number of particularly intriguing portraits. The first two were commissioned by Edward James (1907–84), an English art collector. Both are 'failed' portraits, in that neither shows the sitter's face, as if Magritte was insisting yet again on the illusory character of the portrait as only the image of a person and not their reality. In *The Pleasure Principle* (1937) [179], Magritte replaced James's face with a dazzling light. In *Not to be Reproduced* (1937) [177], he reversed the logic of the mirror, duplicating the back of James's silhouette in the reflection instead of showing his face. Magritte introduced the object-mirror again that year, in the portrait he painted of his wife, Georgette, her face surrounded by assorted objects. Based on this work, entitled *Georgette* [178], Magritte delivered an enlightening commentary on the overall concept of his art: 'There is no explainable mystery in my painting. The word "Wave" written in the portrait manifests the inexplicable mystery. The objects that accompany my wife's face are no more symbols than the face is. "Why?" is not a "serious" question. It is too easy to reply, for example, that familiar objects have been brought together in the portrait to produce a sensational result.' [22]

Magritte always refused to explain his works. He rejected out of hand all symbolic and psychological interpretations of his images. In this regard, he later stated that his art resisted psychoanalysis, which he believed had nothing to say about works that evoke the mystery of the world.[22]

171

At the same time, Magritte began recycling objects (for example painted bottles) and fashioning objects (plaster sculptures). *The Future of Statues* (c. 1932) [137] depicts Napoleon's death mask, covering it with a cloudy blue sky. With *This is a Piece of Cheese* (1936 or 1937) [171], Magritte tips his hat to his famous statement 'This is not a pipe' (*The Treachery of Images*, 1929 [124]). Once again, he plays on the difference between reality and representation, mixing the reality of the glass dome with the representation of a piece of cheese, and deliberately confusing the viewer with the title, which states 'This is a piece of cheese.'

Marked by the change of context, Magritte's painting altered during World War II. Pervaded with a gravity (*The Plain of the Air*, 1940 [200]), melancholy (*Homesickness*, 1941 [205]) and threatening atmospheres (*The Misanthropes*, 1942 [215]), vacillating between *The Last Fine Days* (1940) [201] and *Great Expectations* (1940) [202], his paintings, and most of their titles, evoke a gloomy, anxiety-inducing everyday. Magritte was on the eve of a radical stylistic reversal that he called 'Sunlit Surrealism'.

17   This date is erroneous, as the painting *Elective Affinities*, which resulted from this vision, is in fact from 1933.
18   Magritte, 'La Ligne de vie', op. cit., pp. 110–11.
19   Ibid., p. 112.
20   Louis Scutenaire, *Avec Magritte* (Brussels: Éditions Lebeer-Hossmann, 1977), p. 10.
21   Magritte, 'La Ligne de vie', op. cit., p. 144.
22   Magritte, Letter to Maurice Rapin and Mirabelle Dors, 20 June 1957, op. cit.
23   René Magritte, preface to the exhibition catalogue *The Vision of René Magritte* held at the Walker Art Center, Minneapolis, from 16 September to 14 October 1962.

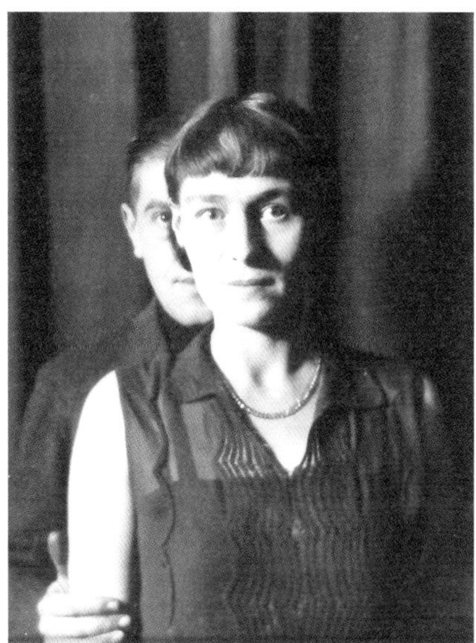

The Shadow and Its Shadow, Brussels, 1932.
Georgette and René Magritte.

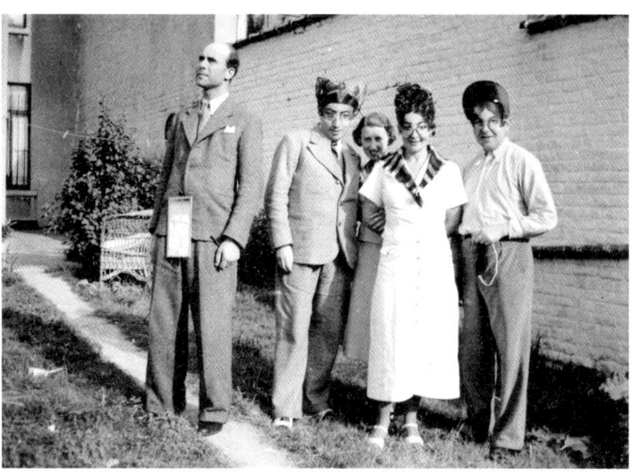

The Extraterrestrials IV, Rue Esseghem, Brussels, 1935. Left to right: Paul Colinet,
Marcel Lecomte, Jacqueline Nonkels, and Georgette and René Magritte.

1931–1942

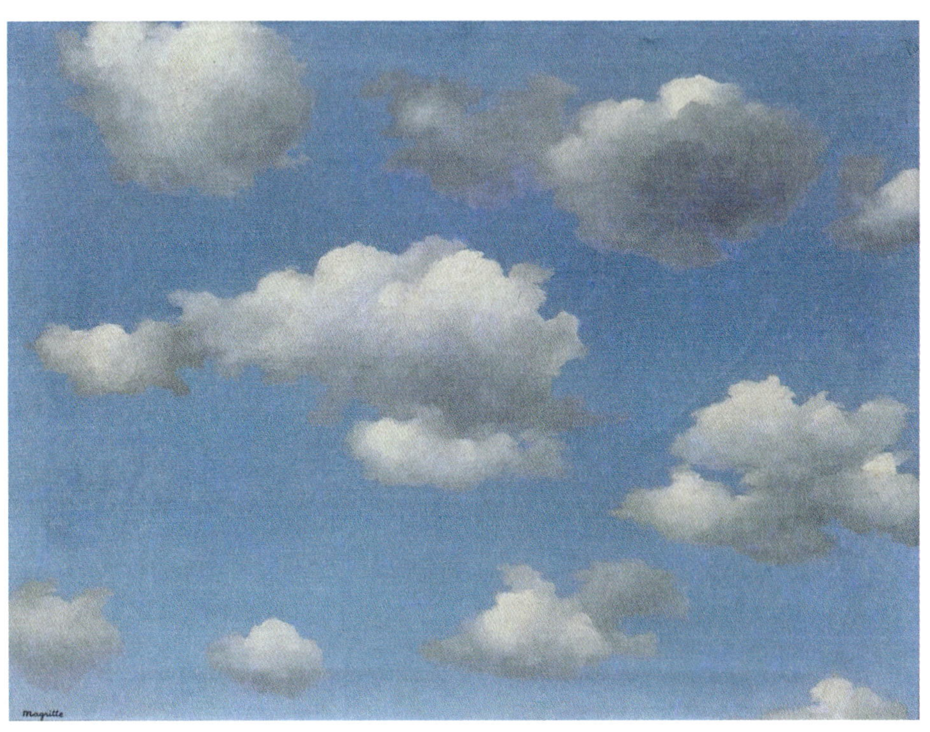

130
The Curse
1931
oil on canvas, 54 × 73 cm

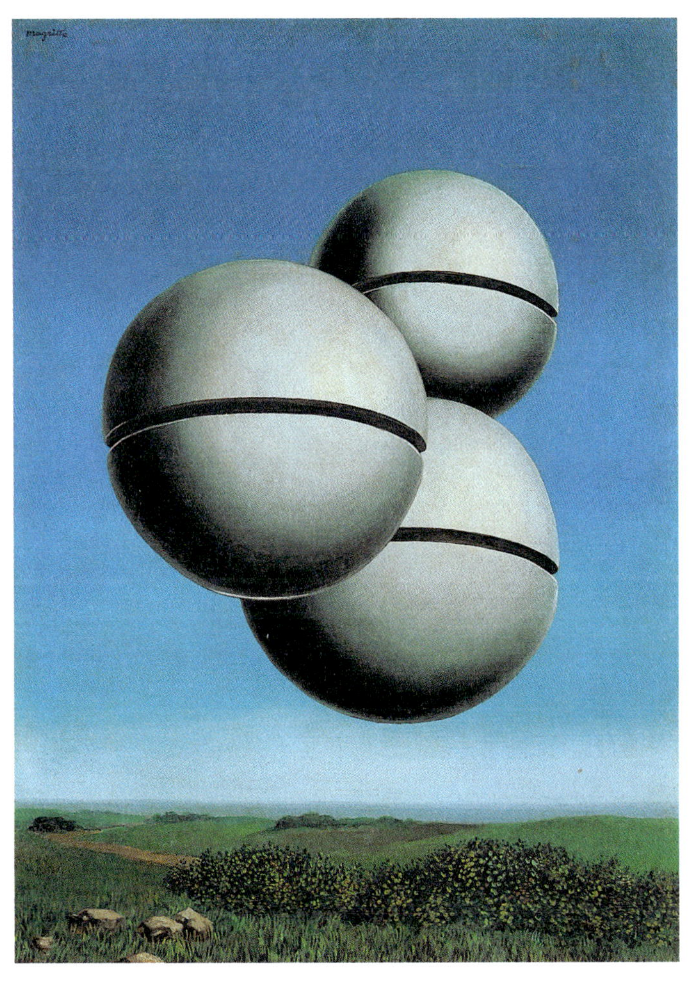

131
The Voice of the Air
1931
oil on canvas, 73 × 54 cm

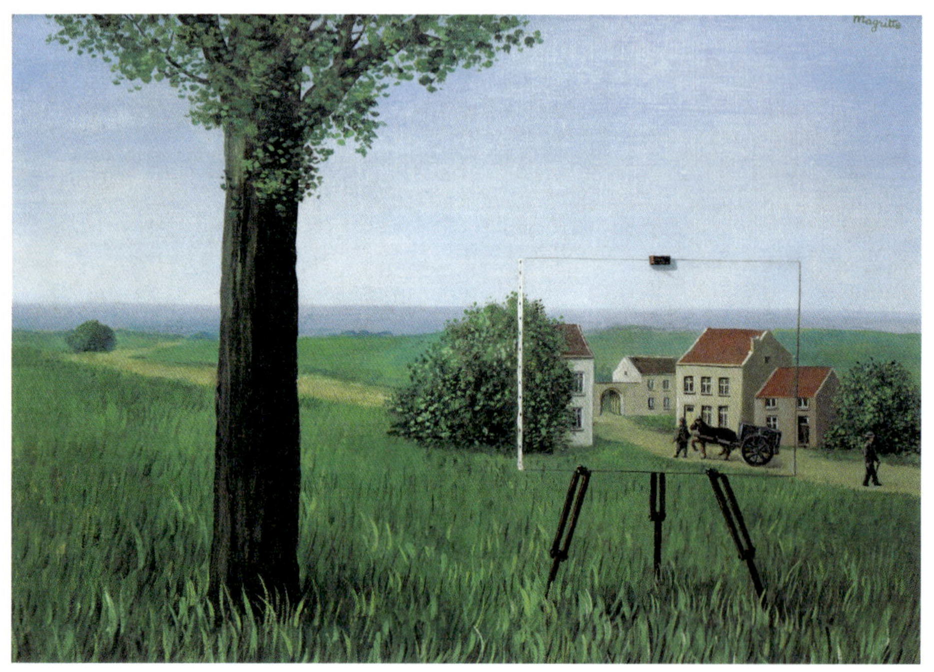

132
The Fair Captive
1931
oil on canvas, 38 × 55 cm

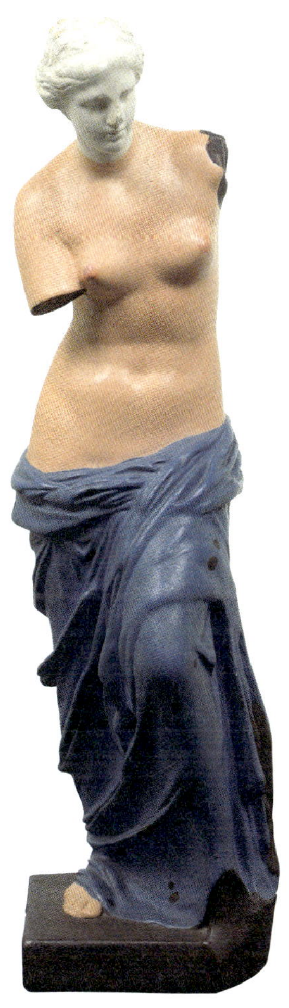

133
The Copper Handcuffs
1931
oil on plaster reproduction of the Venus de Milo, ht. 37 cm

1931–1942

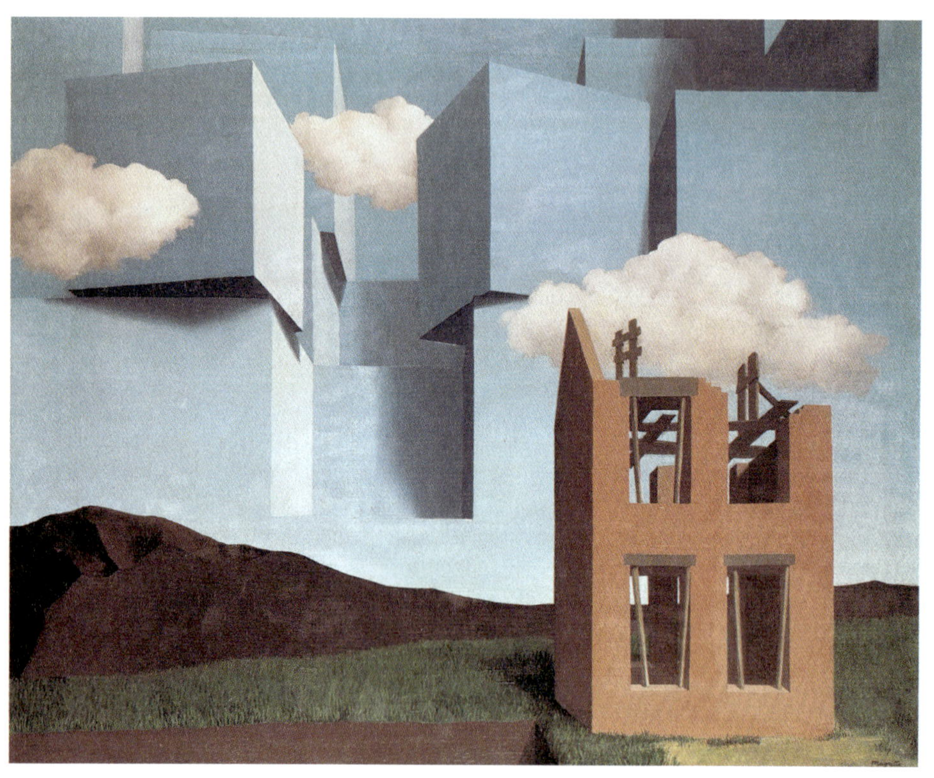

134
The Universe Unmasked
1932
oil on canvas, 73 × 92 cm

     Elective Affinities

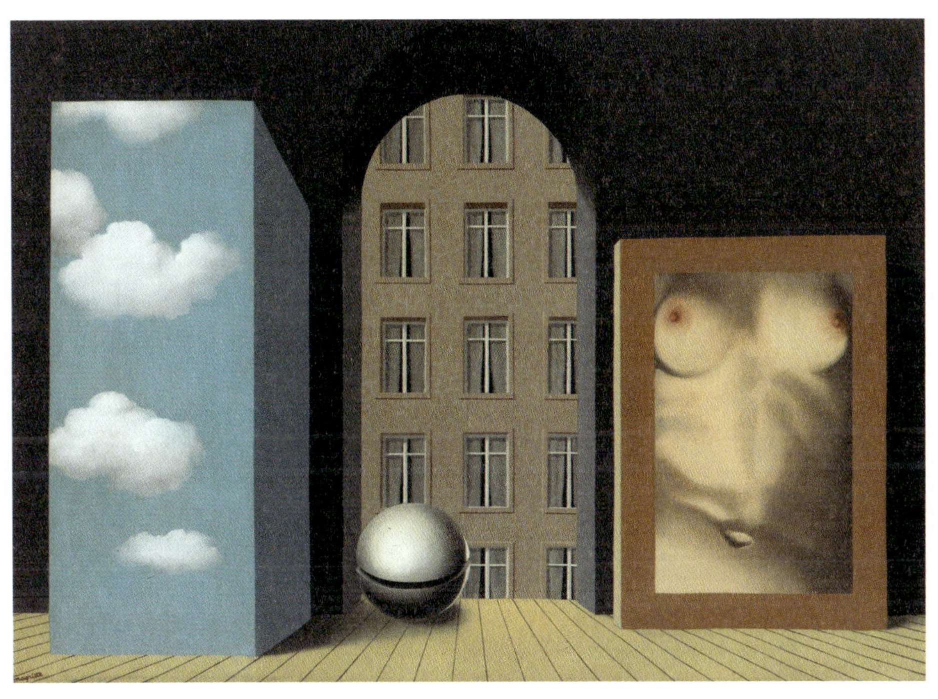

135
Act of Violence

1932
oil on canvas, 70 × 100 cm

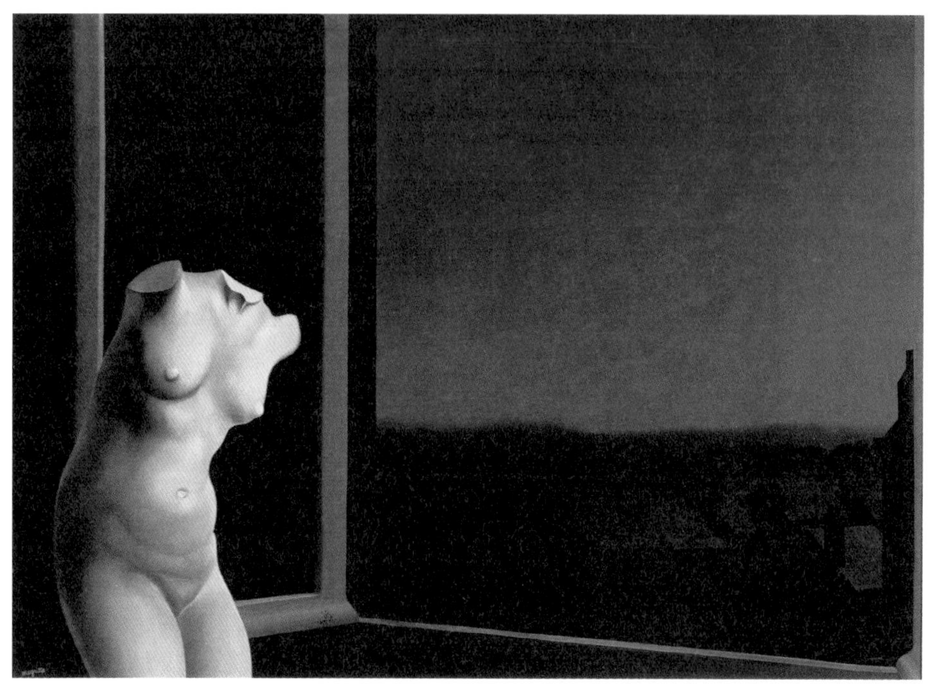

136
Lady of the Night
1932
oil on canvas, 81 × 116 cm

 Elective Affinities

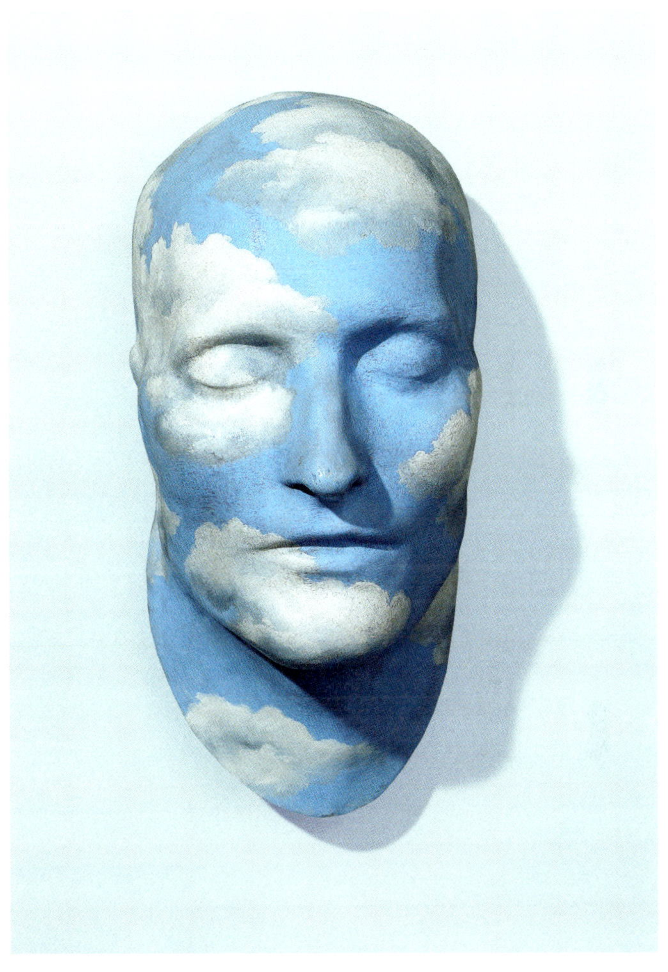

137
The Future of Statues
c. 1932
oil on plaster cast of Napoleon's death mask, ht. 32 cm

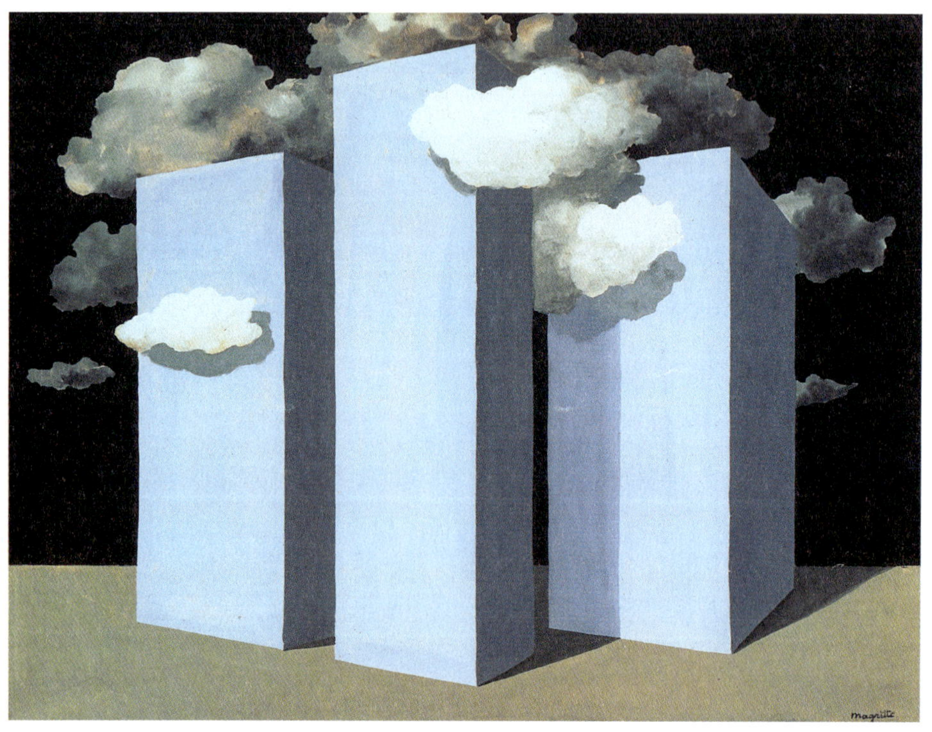

138
The Tempest
1932
gouache on paper, 40.8 × 56 cm

Elective Affinities

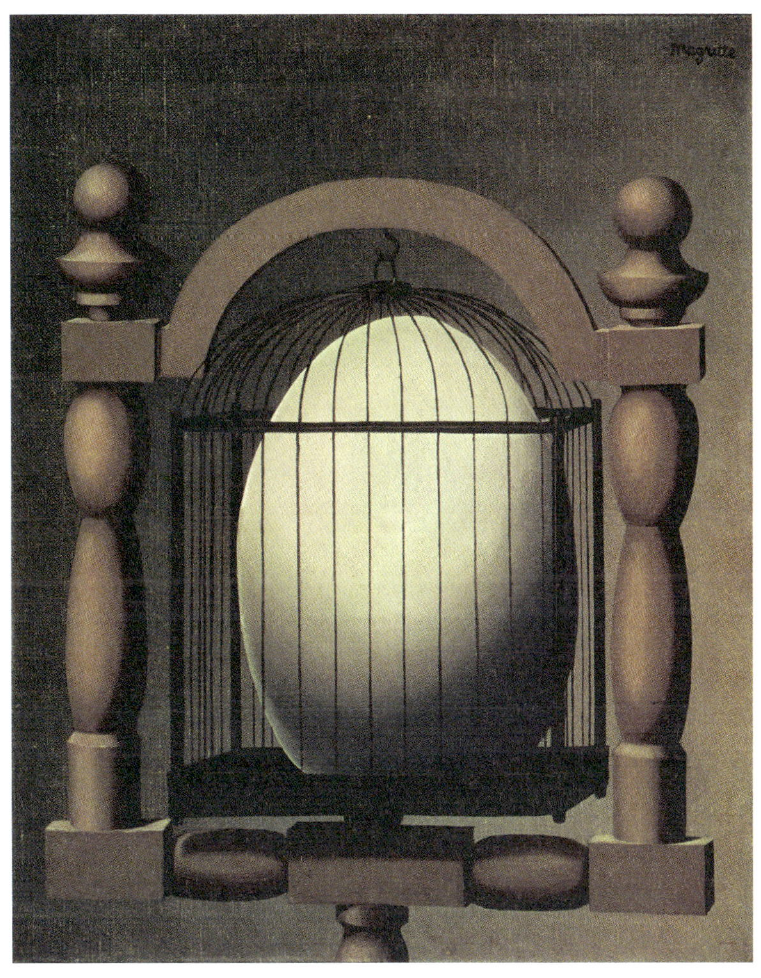

139
Elective Affinities
1933
oil on canvas, 41 × 33 cm

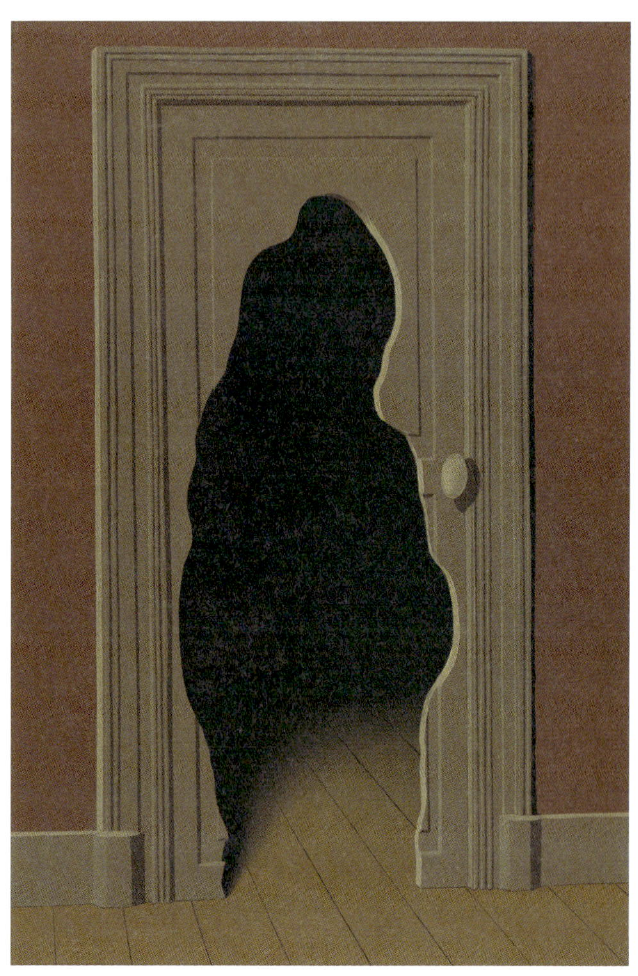

140
The Unexpected Answer
1933
oil on canvas, 81 × 54 cm

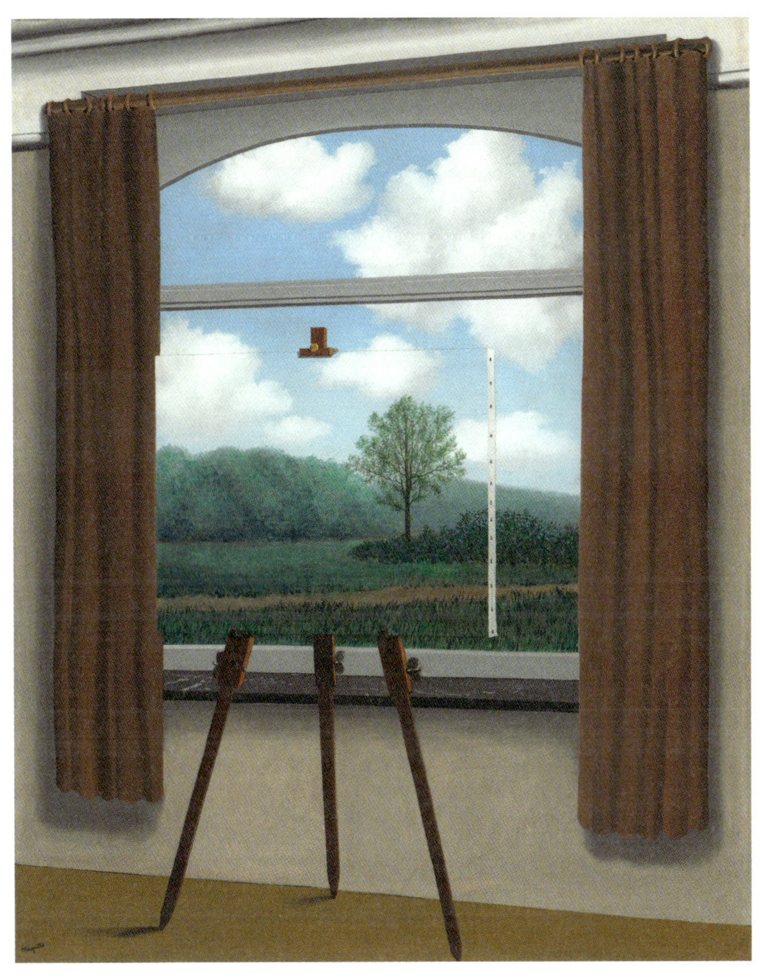

141
The Human Condition
1933
oil on canvas, 100 × 81 cm

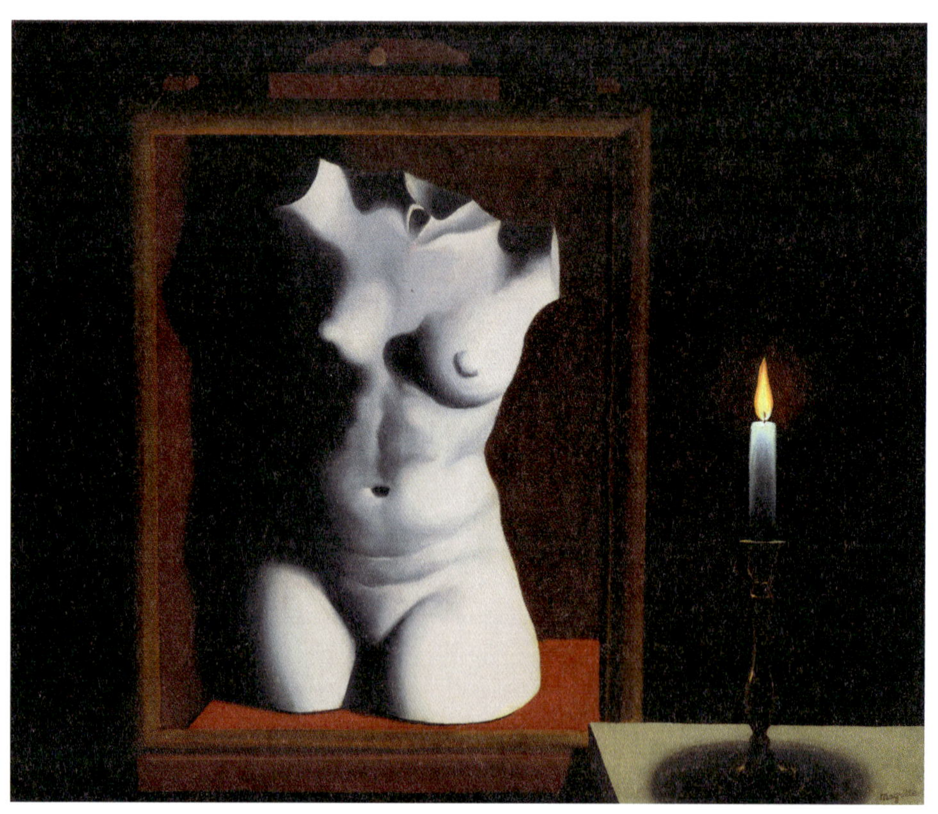

142
The Light of Coincidence
1933
oil on canvas, 60 × 73 cm

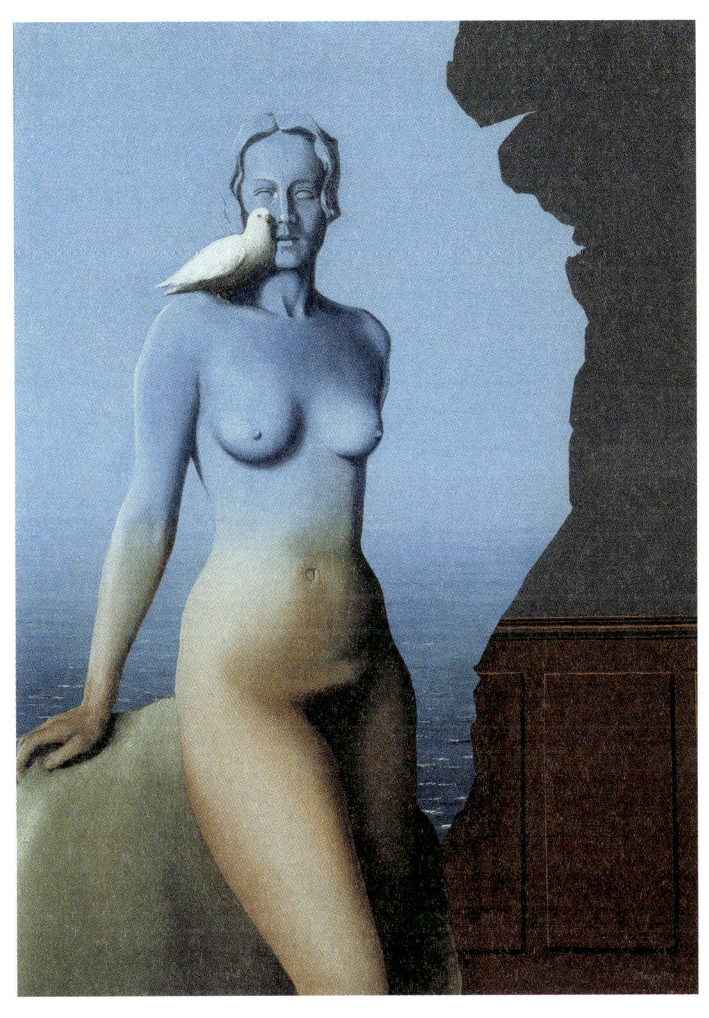

143
Black Magic
1934
oil on canvas, 73 × 54 cm

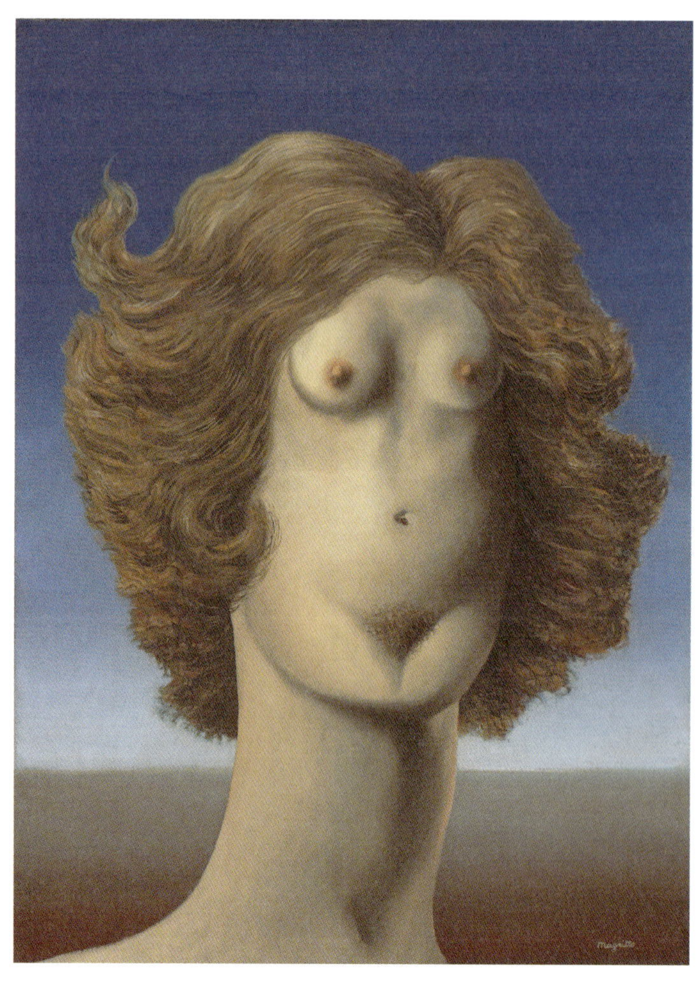

144
The Rape
1934
oil on canvas, 73 × 54 cm

 Elective Affinities

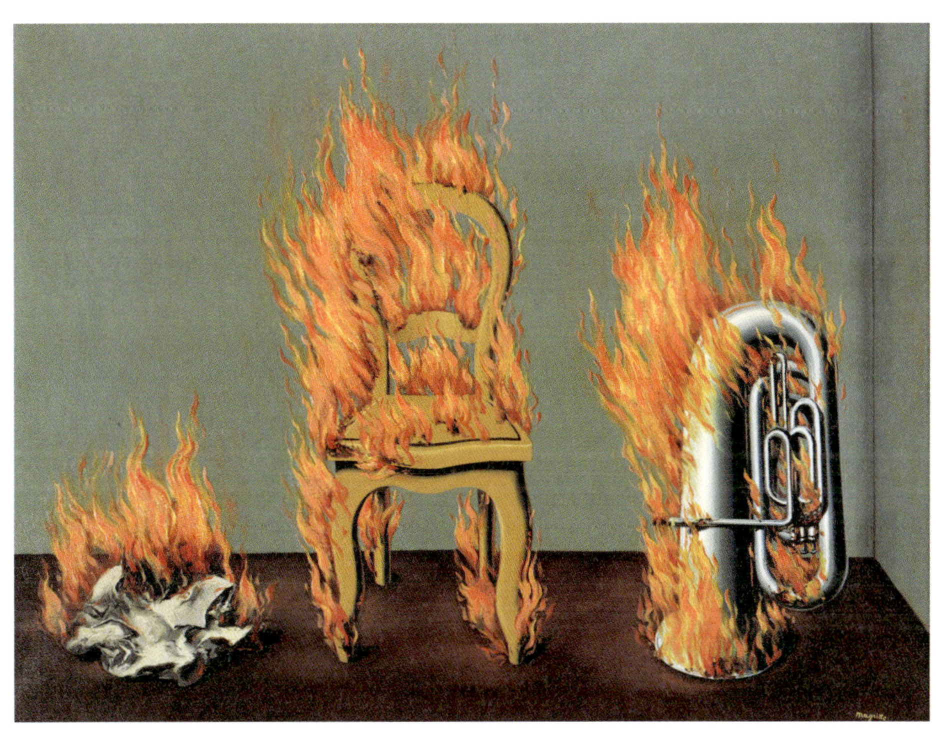

145
The Ladder of Fire
1934
oil on canvas, 54 × 73 cm

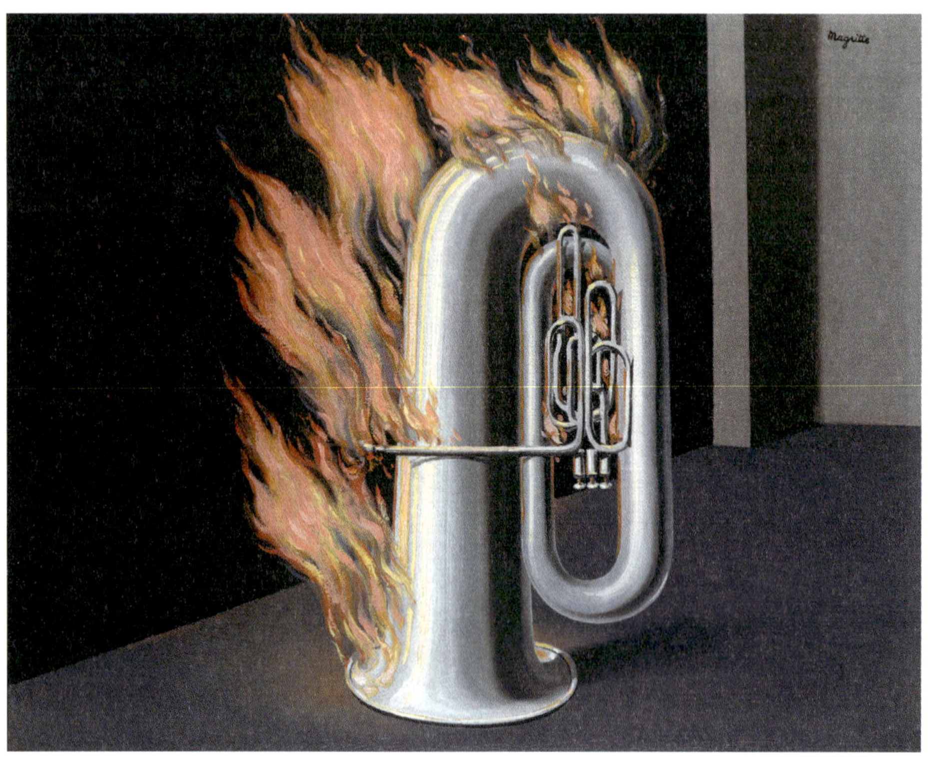

146
The Discovery of Fire
1934 or 1935
oil on canvas, 33 × 41 cm

Elective Affinities

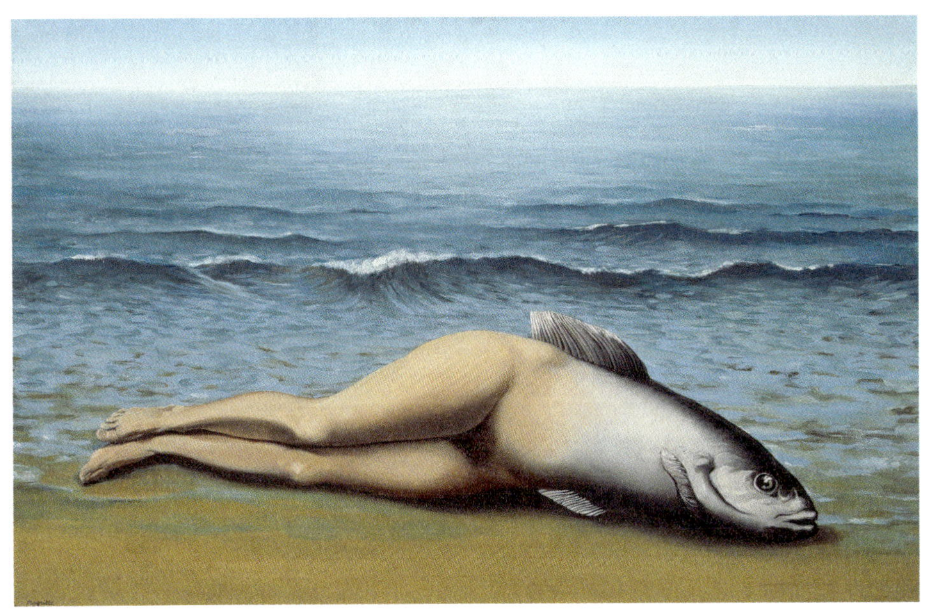

147
Collective Invention
1935
oil on canvas, 73 × 116 cm

1931–1942

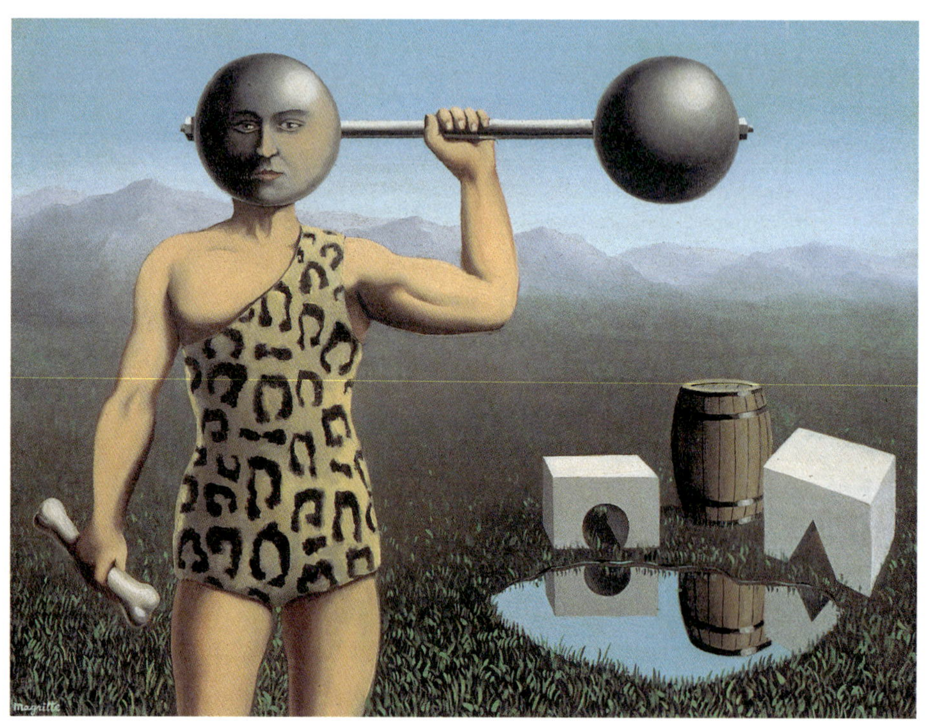

148
Perpetual Motion
1935
oil on canvas, 54 × 73 cm

     Elective Affinities

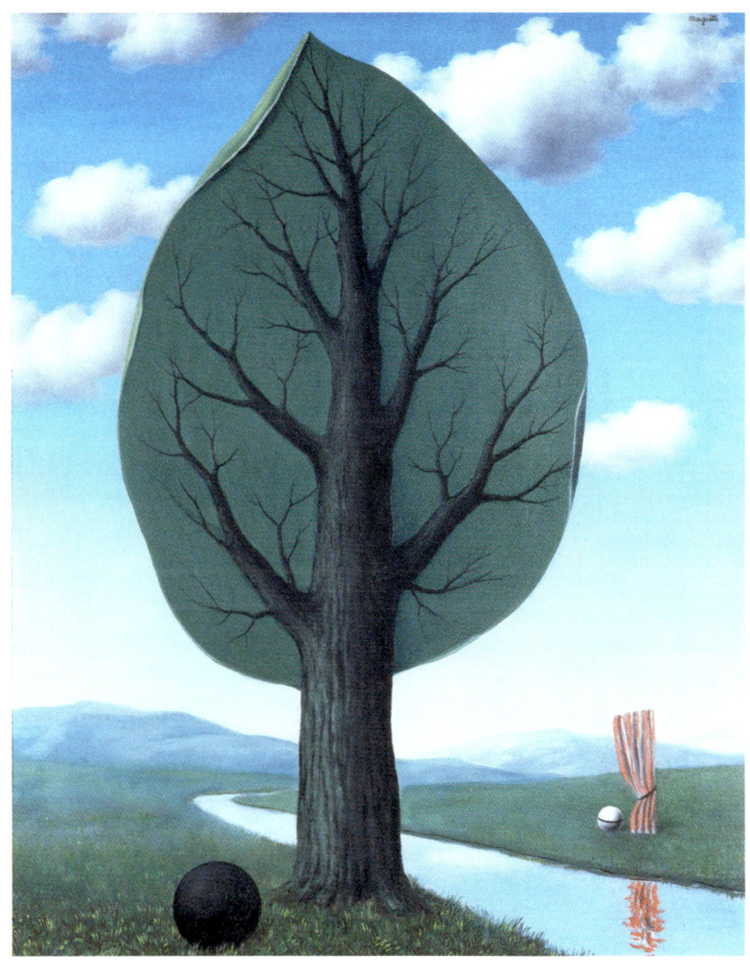

149
The Giantess
1935
oil on canvas, 73 × 60 cm

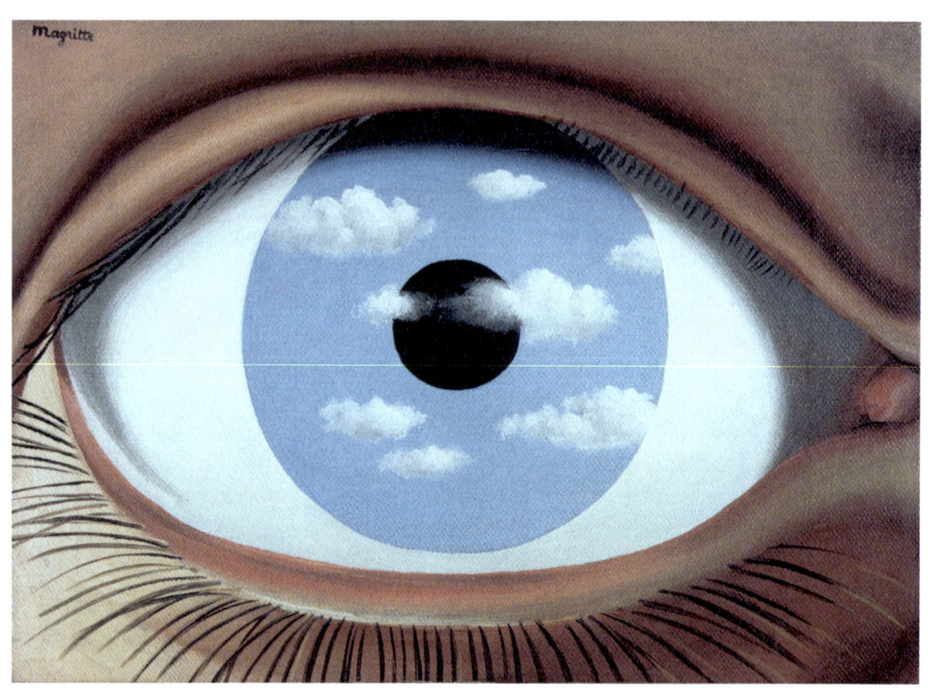

150
The False Mirror
1935
oil on canvas, 19 × 27 cm

 Elective Affinities

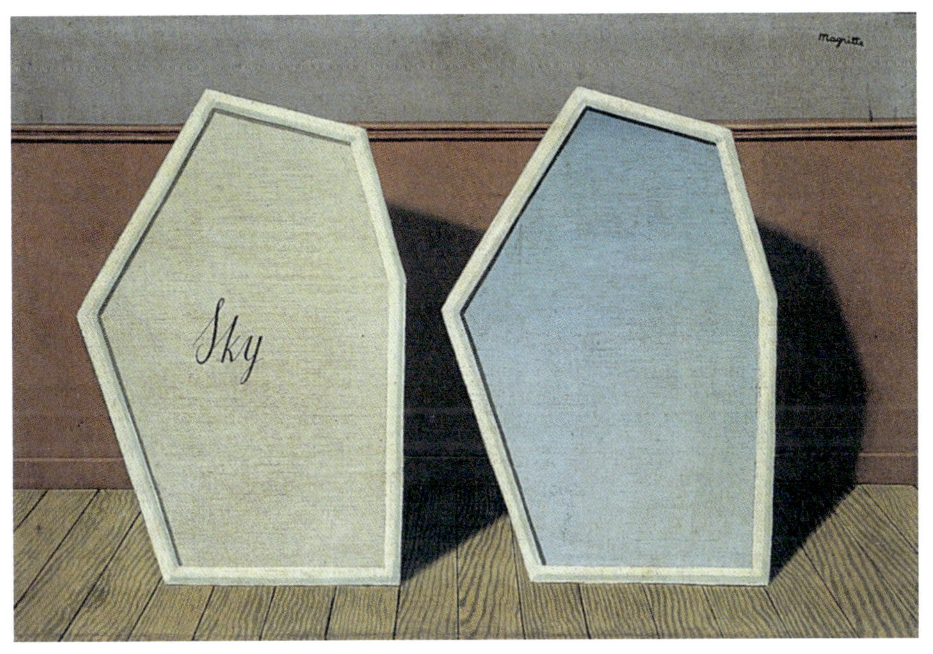

151
The Palace of Curtains
1935
oil on canvas mounted on board, 27 × 41 cm

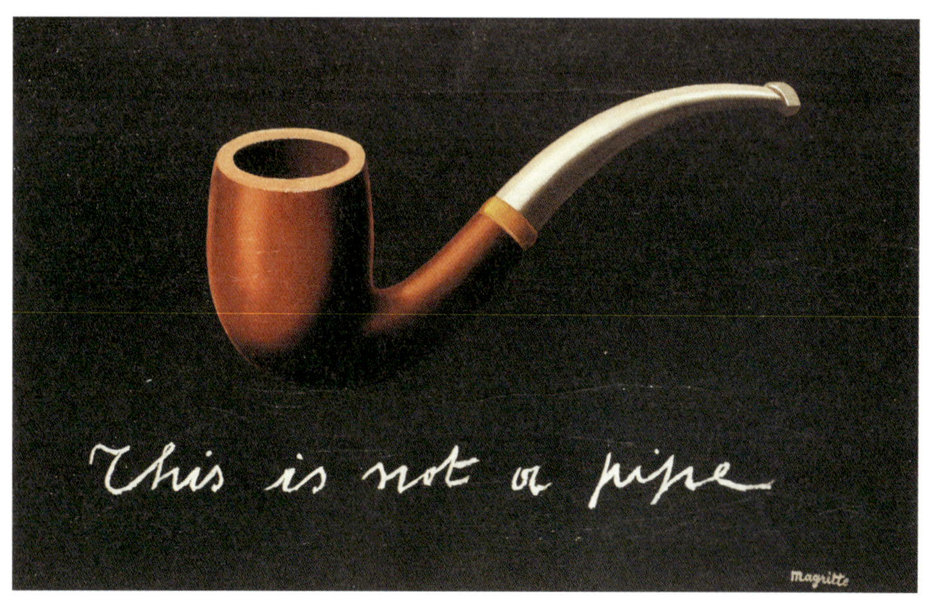

152
The Treachery of Images
1935
oil on canvas, 27 × 41 cm

Elective Affinities

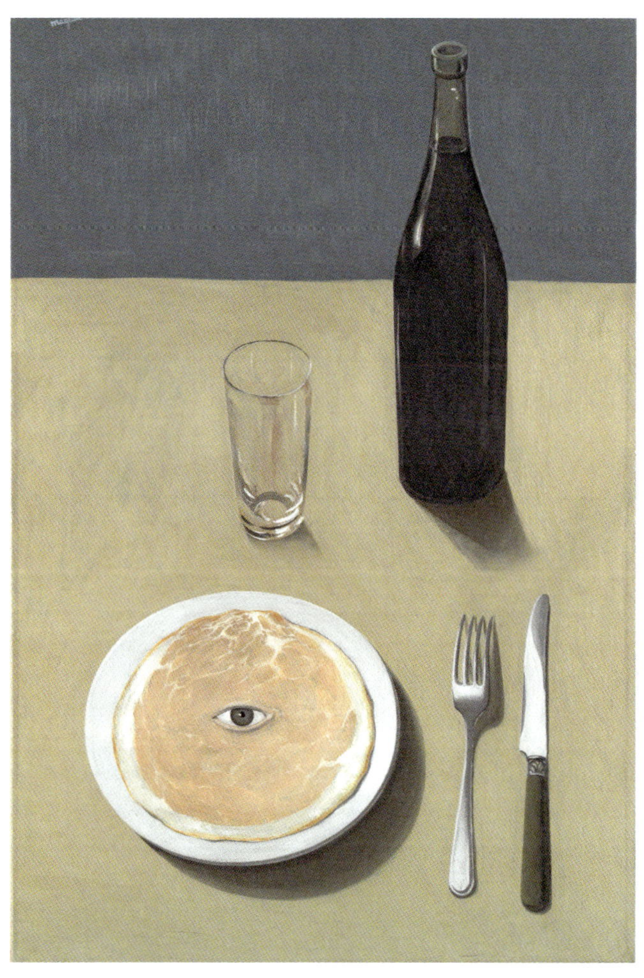

153
The Portrait
1935
oil on canvas, 73 × 50 cm

1931–1942

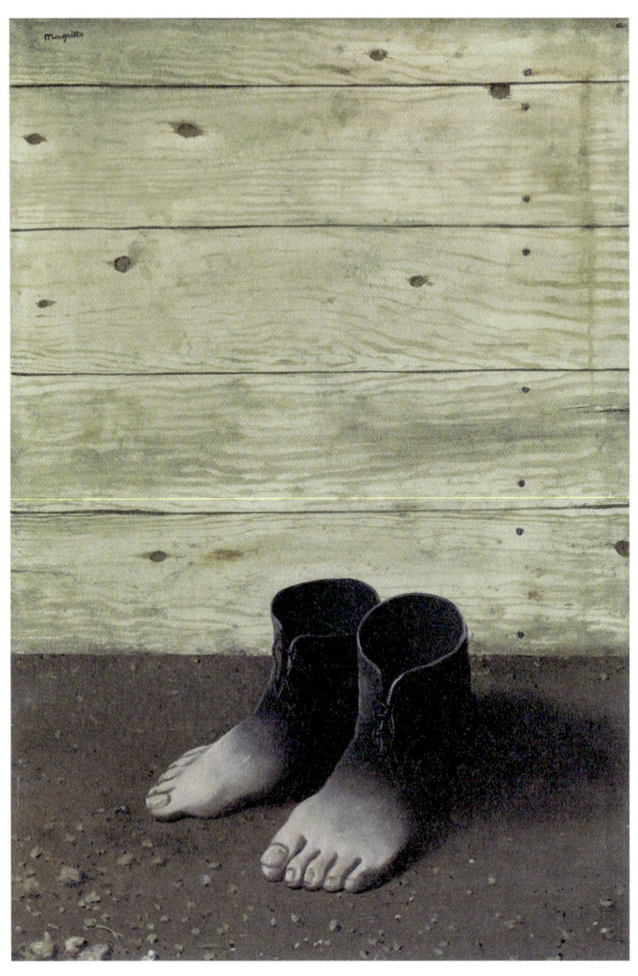

154
The Red Model
1935
oil on canvas, 74 × 50 cm

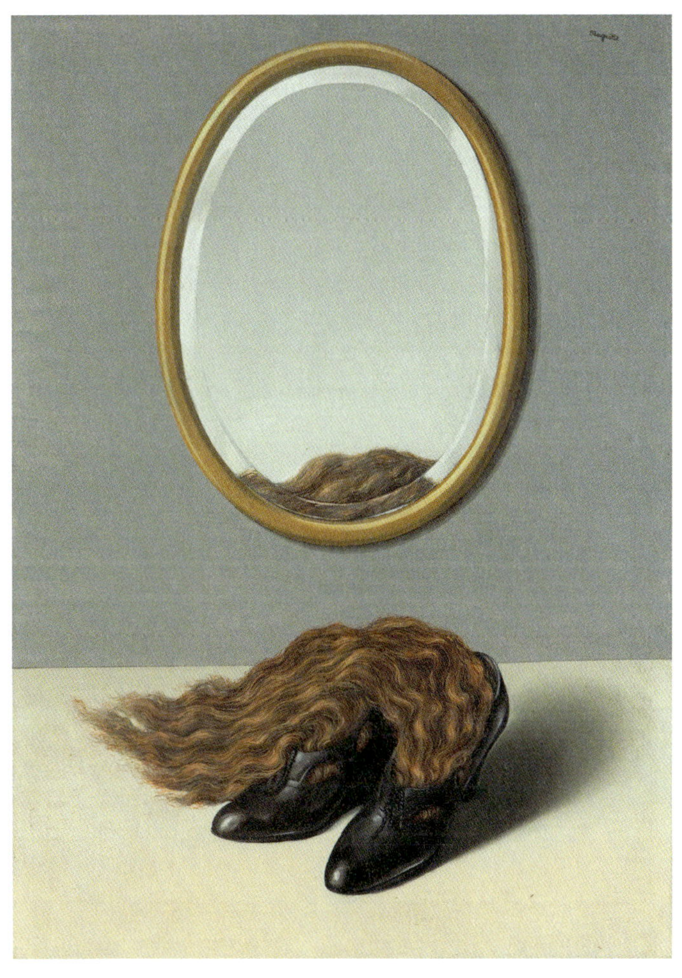

155
Love Disarmed
1935
oil on canvas, 72 × 54 cm

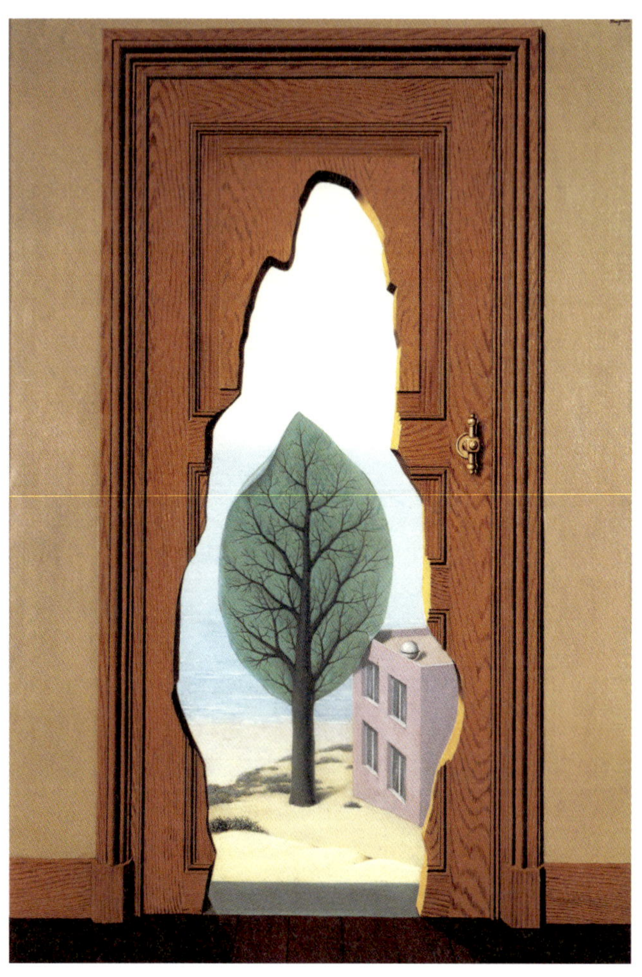

156
The Amorous Vista
1935
oil on canvas, 116 × 81 cm

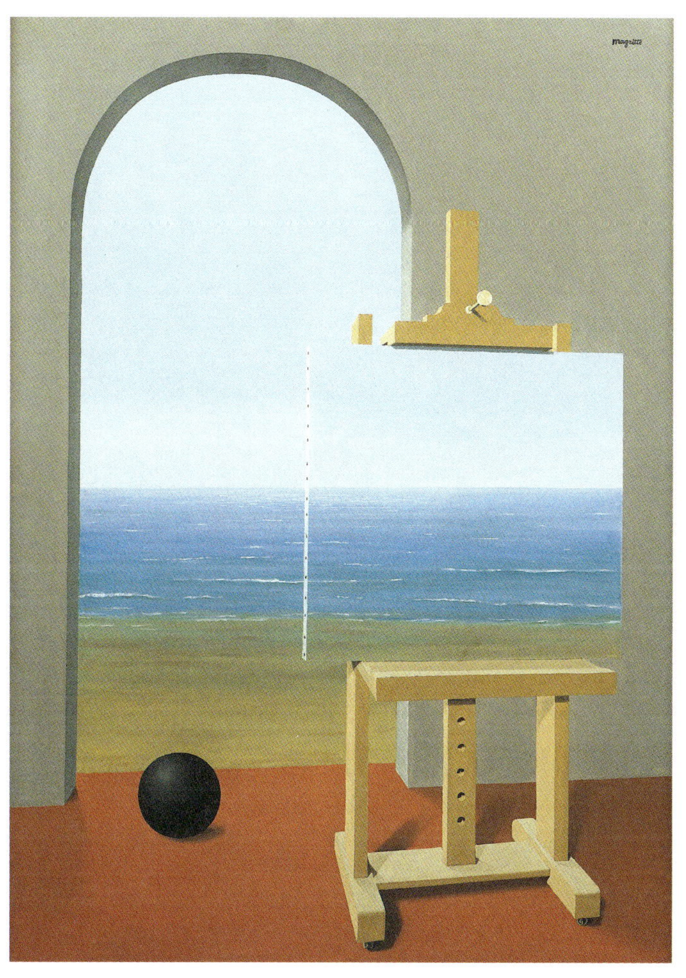

157
The Human Condition
1935
oil on canvas, 100 × 73 cm

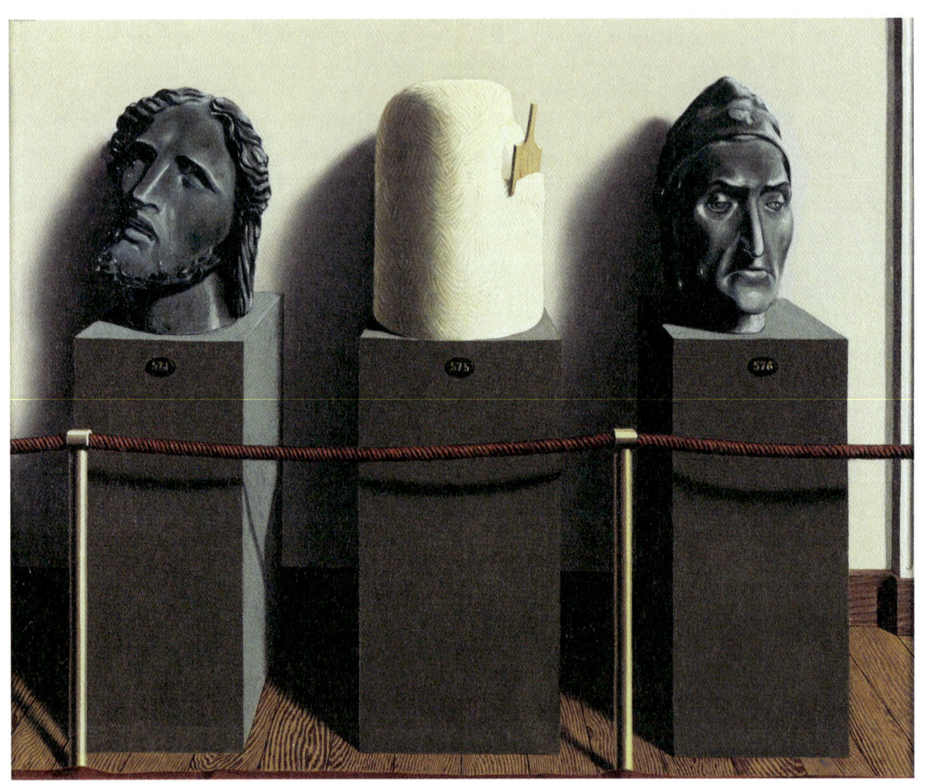

158
Eternity
1935
oil on canvas, 65 × 81 cm

    Elective Affinities

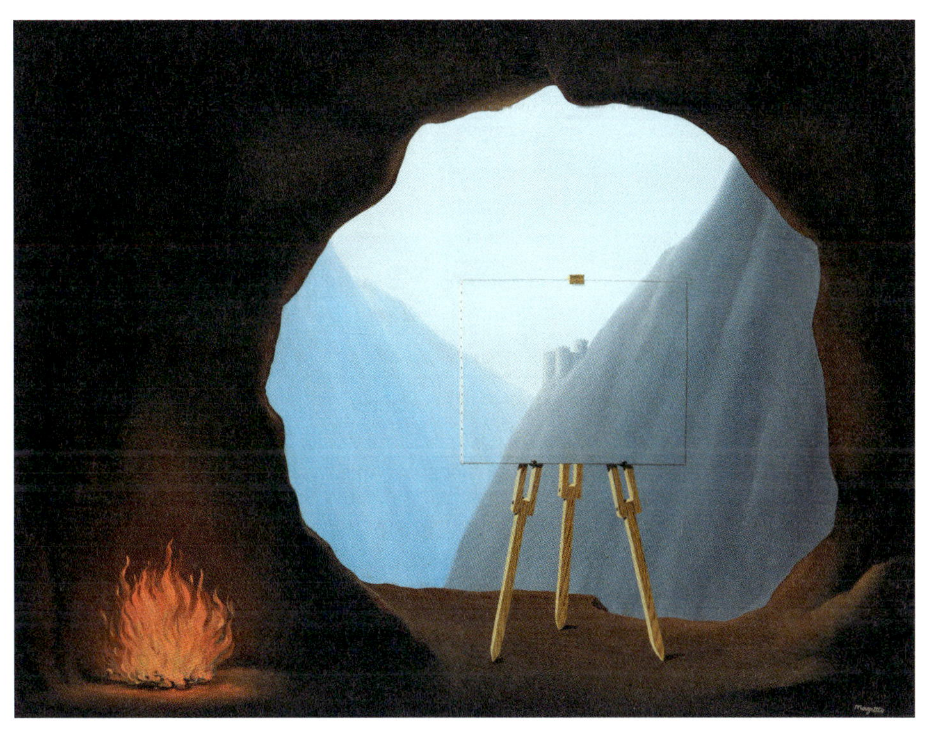

159
The Human Condition
1935
oil on canvas, 54 × 73 cm

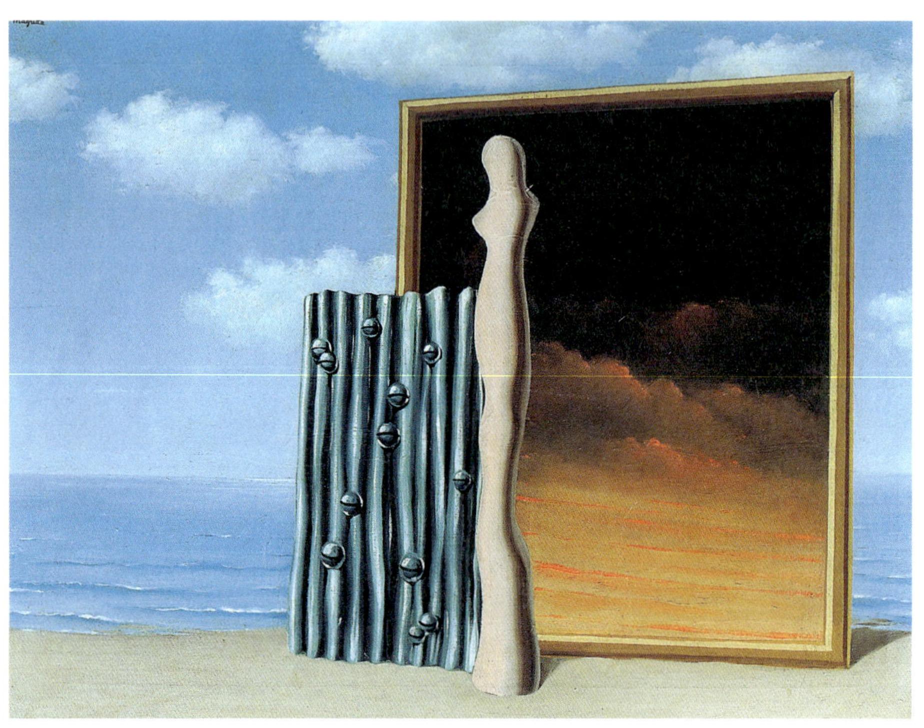

160
(Composition on a Seashore)
1935 or 1936
oil on canvas, 54 × 73 cm

Elective Affinities

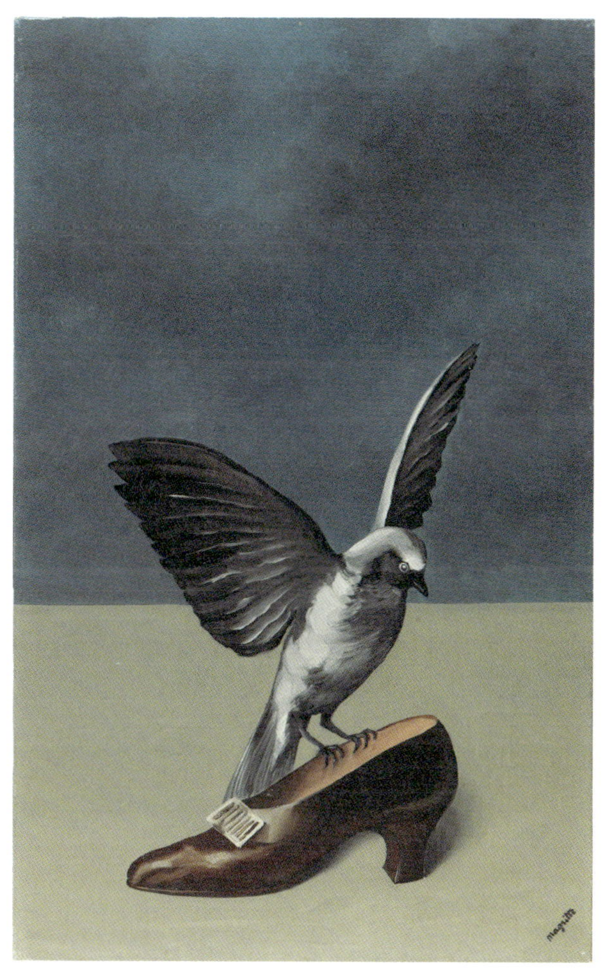

161
God is No Saint
1935 or 1936
oil on canvas, 67 × 43 cm

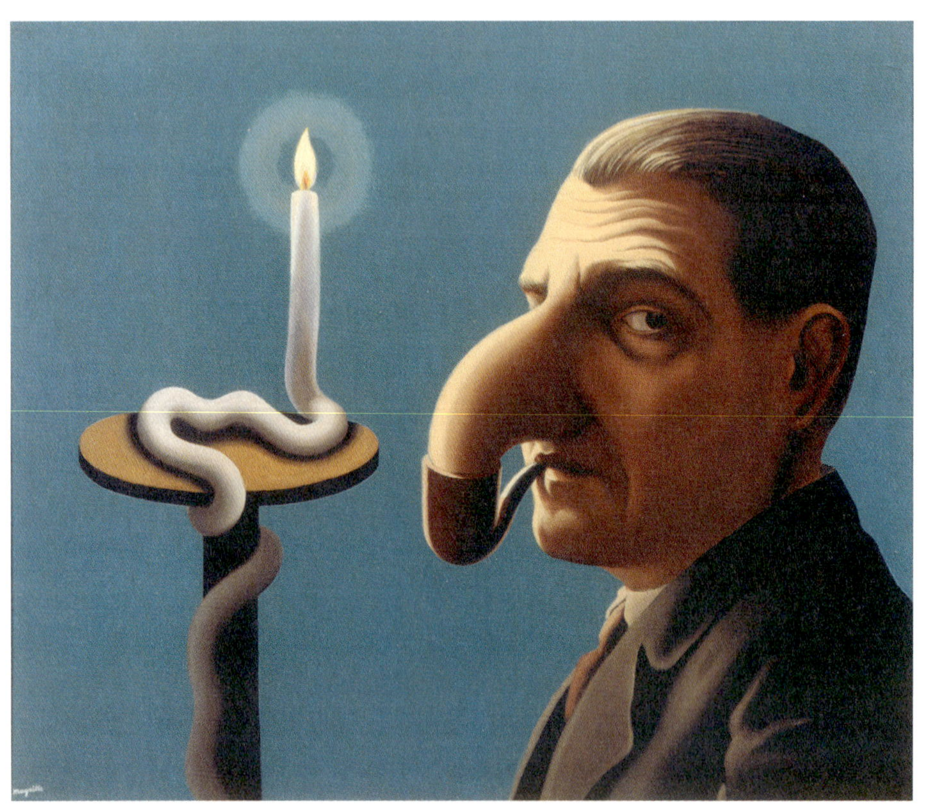

162
The Philosopher's Lamp
1936
oil on canvas, 46 × 55 cm

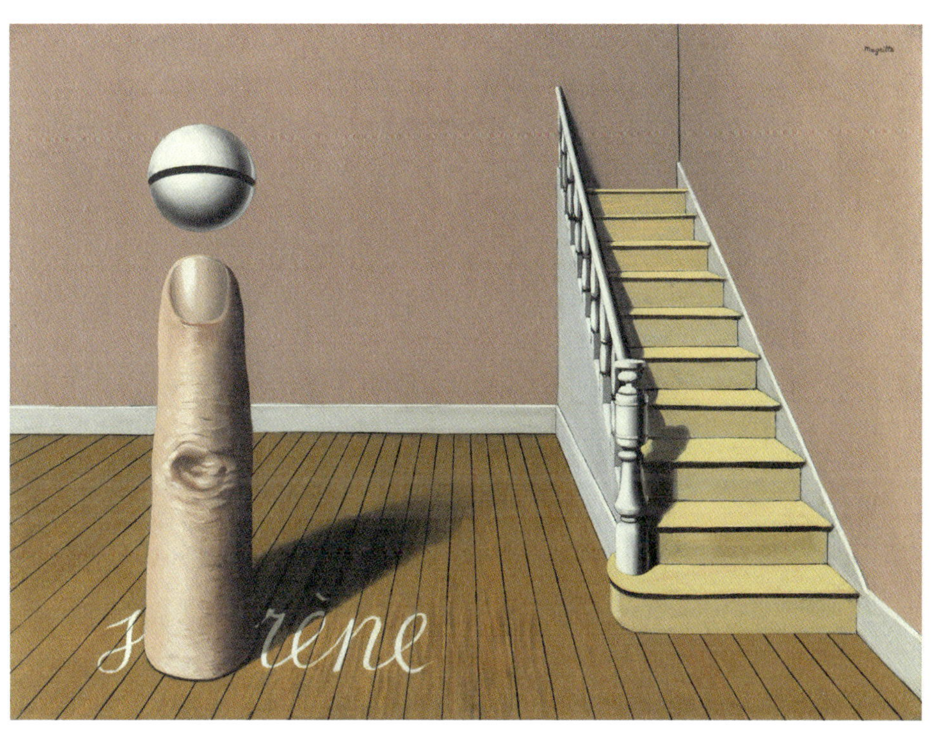

163
(Forbidden Literature)
1936
oil on canvas, 54 × 73 cm

1931–1942

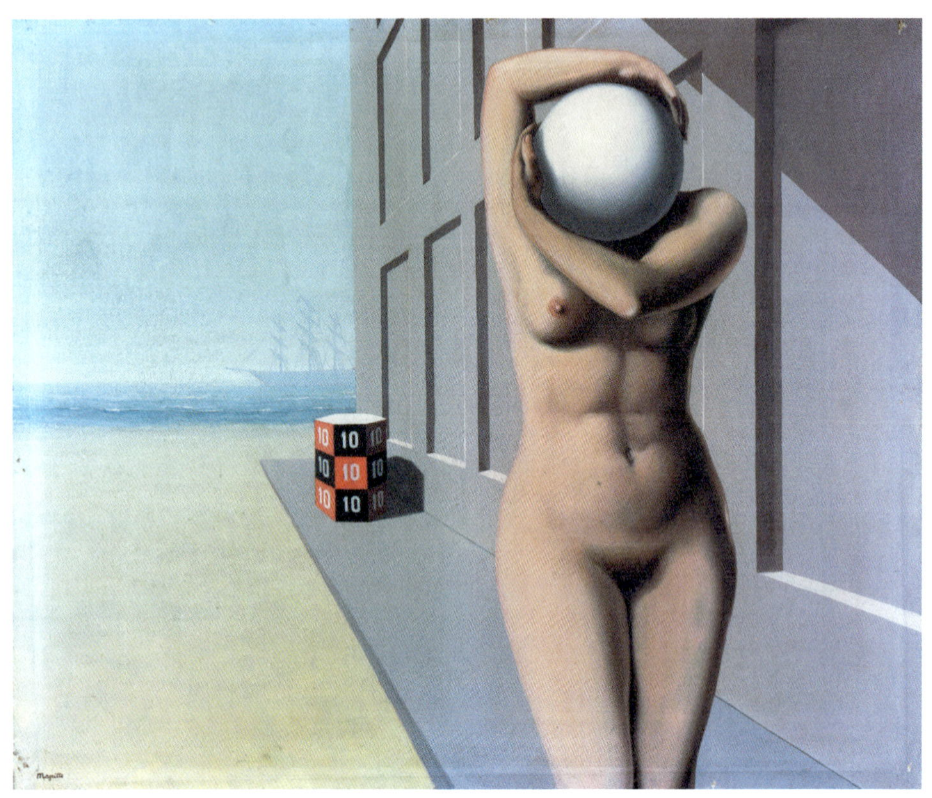

164
Spiritual Exercises
1936
oil on canvas, 60 × 73 cm

    Elective Affinities

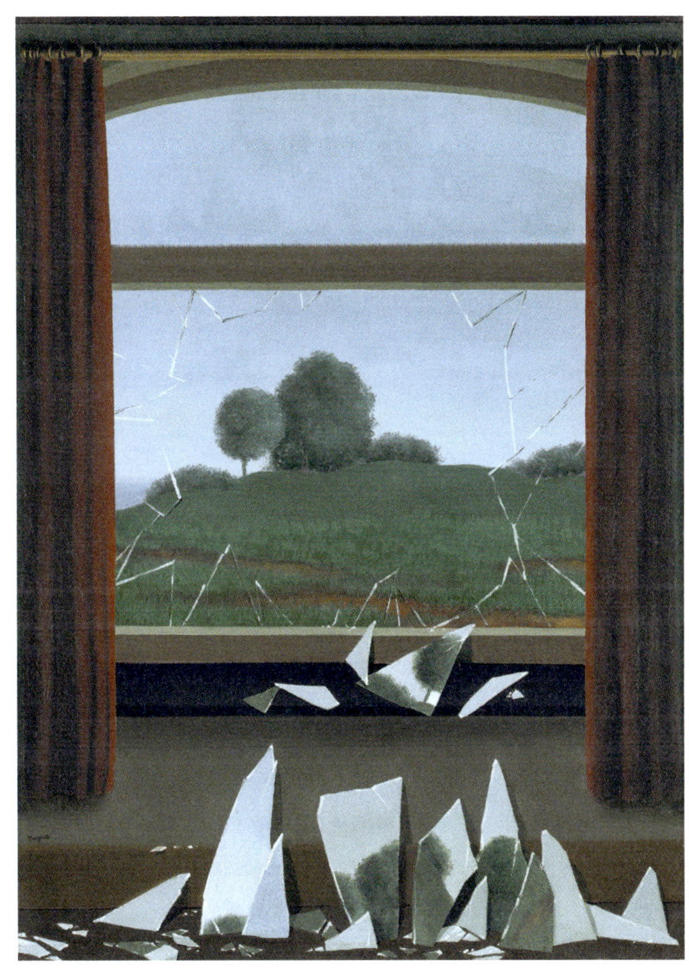

165
The Key to the Fields
1936
oil on canvas, 81 × 60 cm

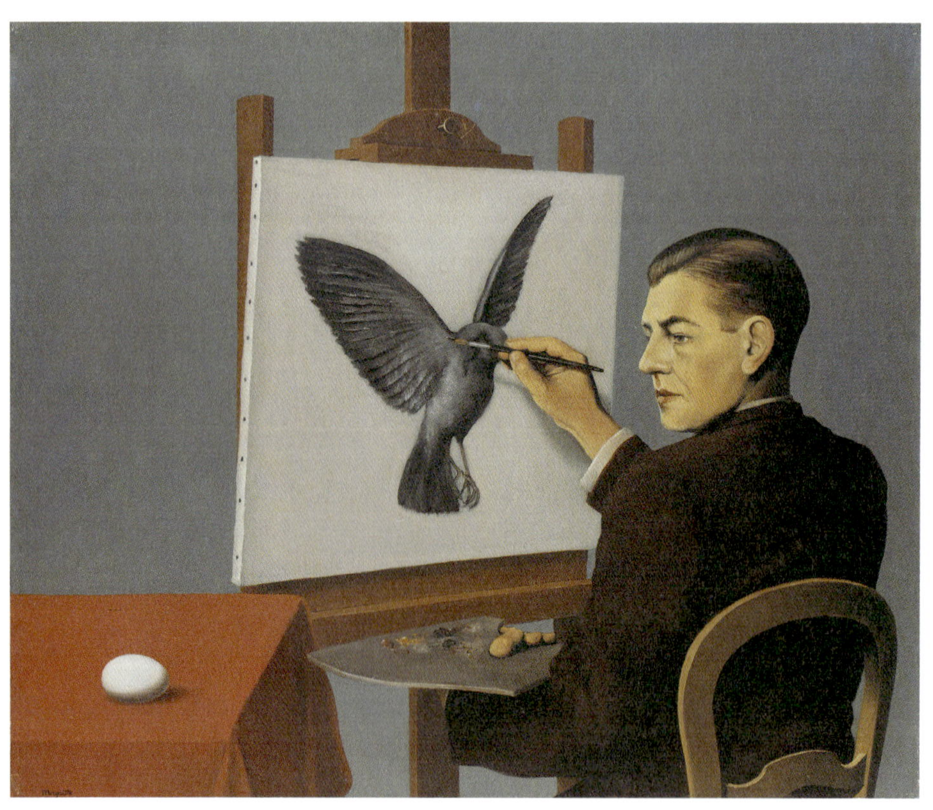

166
Clairvoyance
1936
oil on canvas, 54 × 65 cm

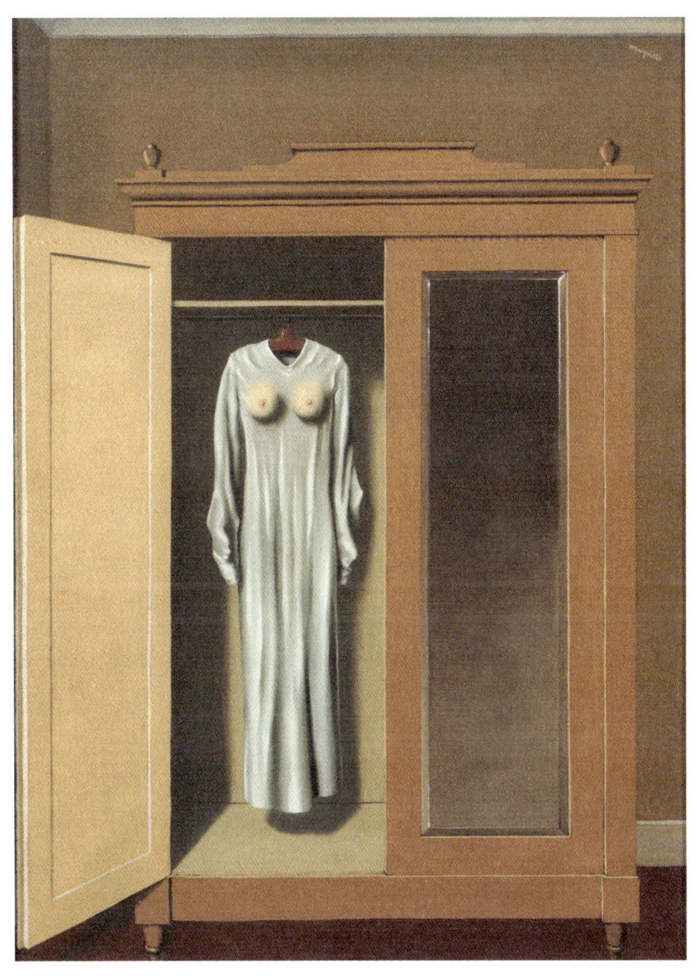

167
In Memory of Mack Sennett
1936
oil on canvas, 73 × 54 cm

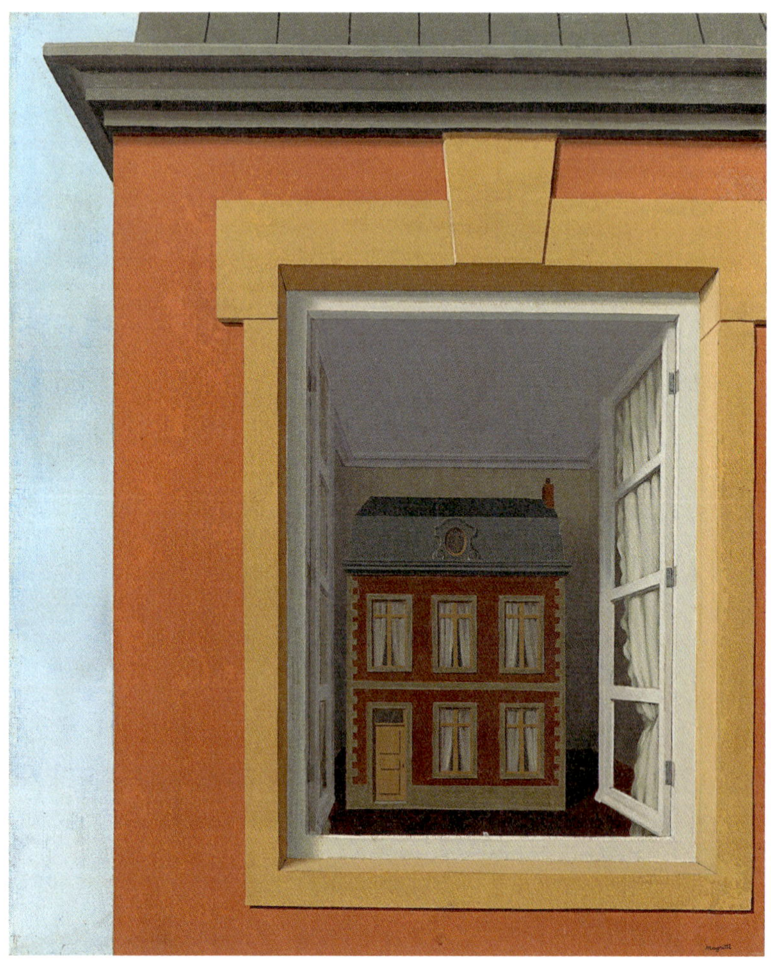

168
In Praise of the Dialectic
1937
oil on canvas, 65 × 54 cm

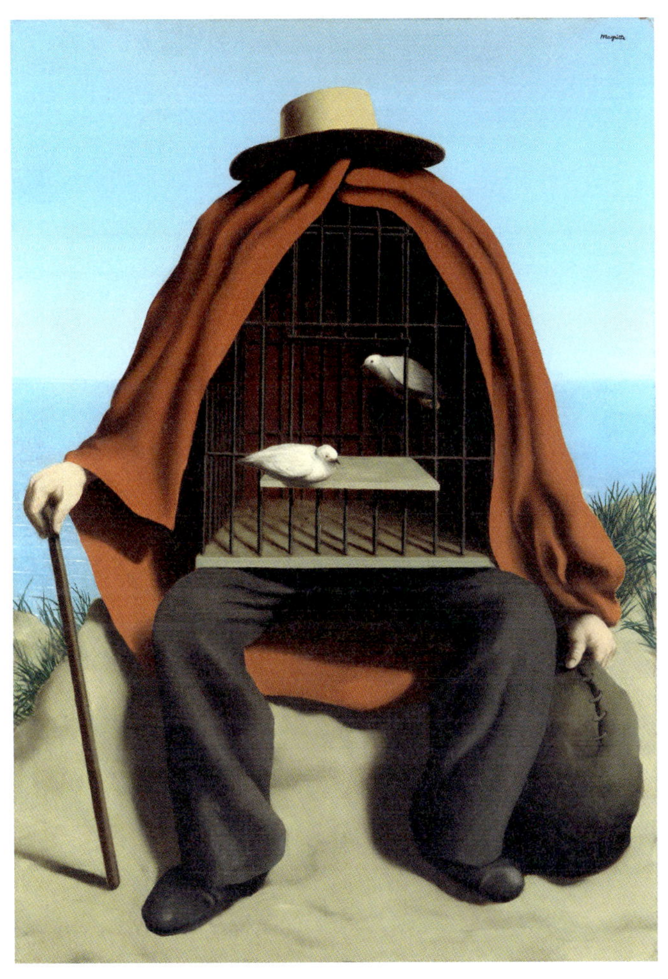

169
The Healer
1937
oil on canvas, 92 × 65 cm

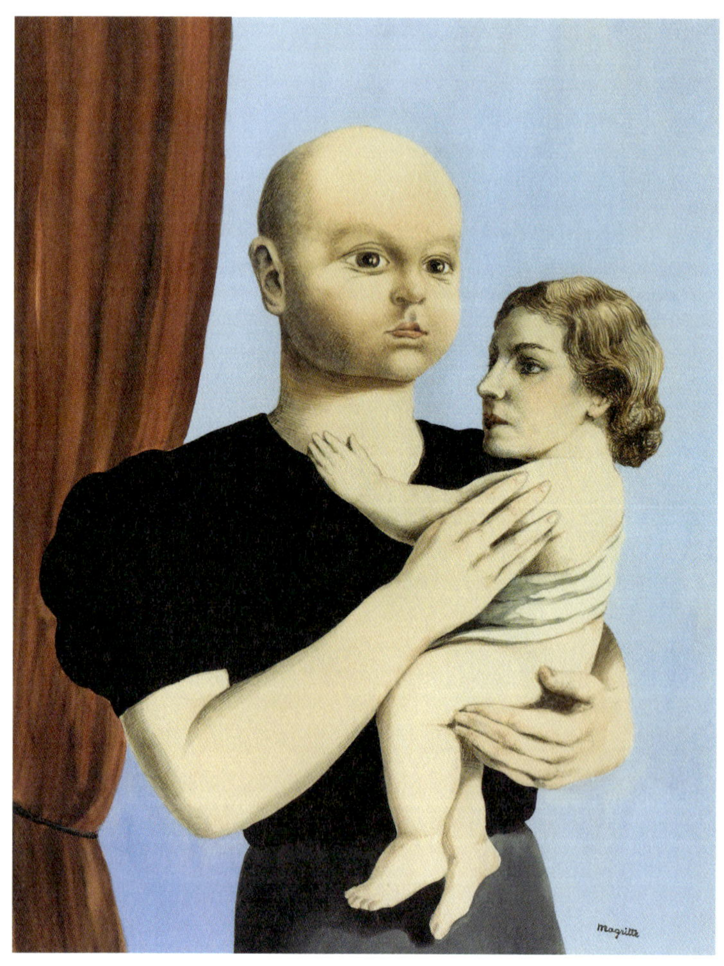

170
The Mathematical Mind
1936 or 1937
gouache on paper, 37.5 × 29.4 cm

Elective Affinities

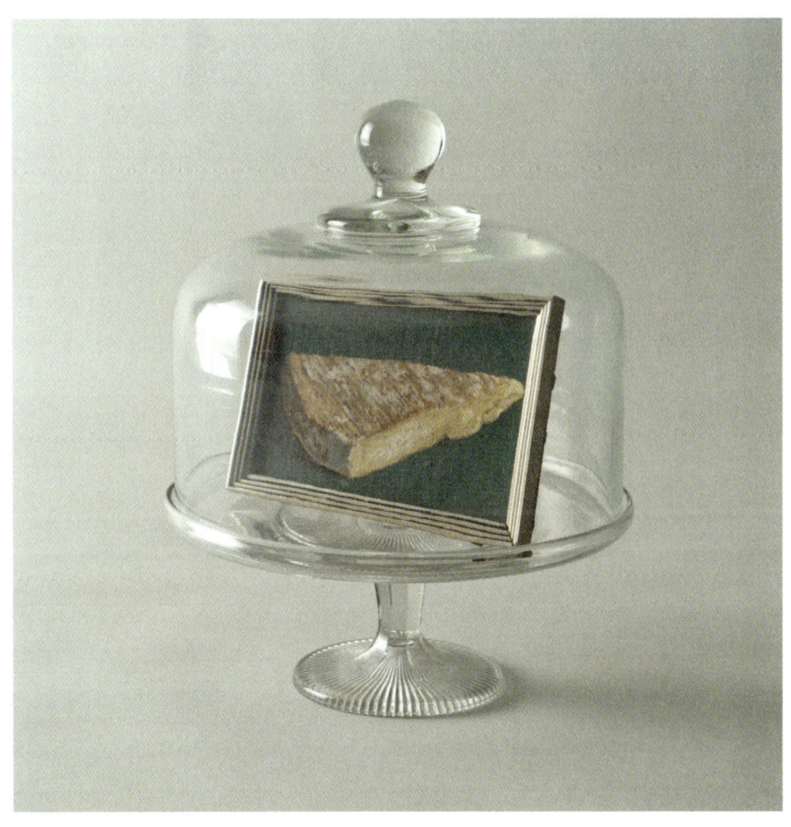

171
This is a Piece of Cheese
1936 or 1937
oil on canvas board, 12.5 × 18.4 cm, in gilded wooden frame;
glass dome and pedestal, ht. 30.5 cm, diam. 25.4 cm

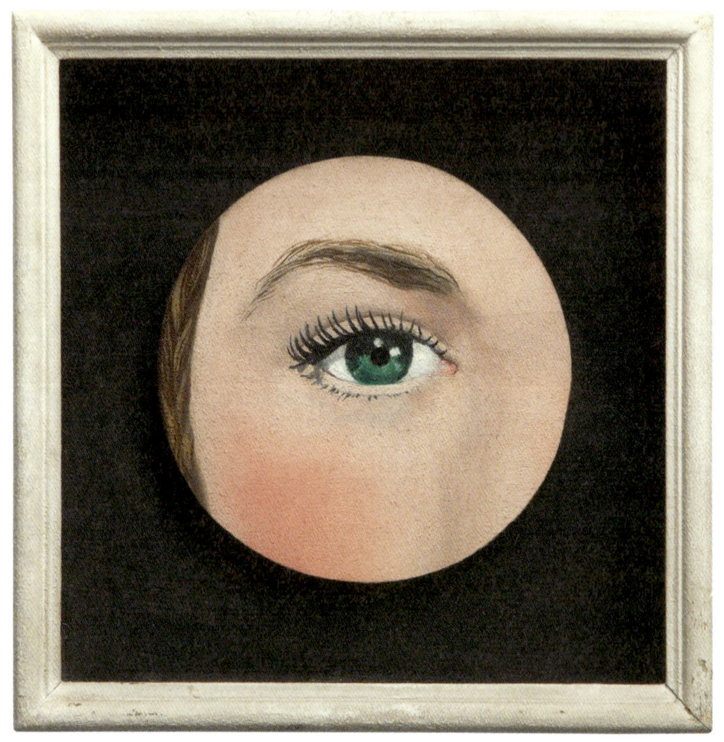

172
Painted Object: Eye
1936 or 1937
oil on panel glued to wooden base,
diam. 15.3 cm; base: 25.4 × 25.4 × 5.1 cm

Elective Affinities

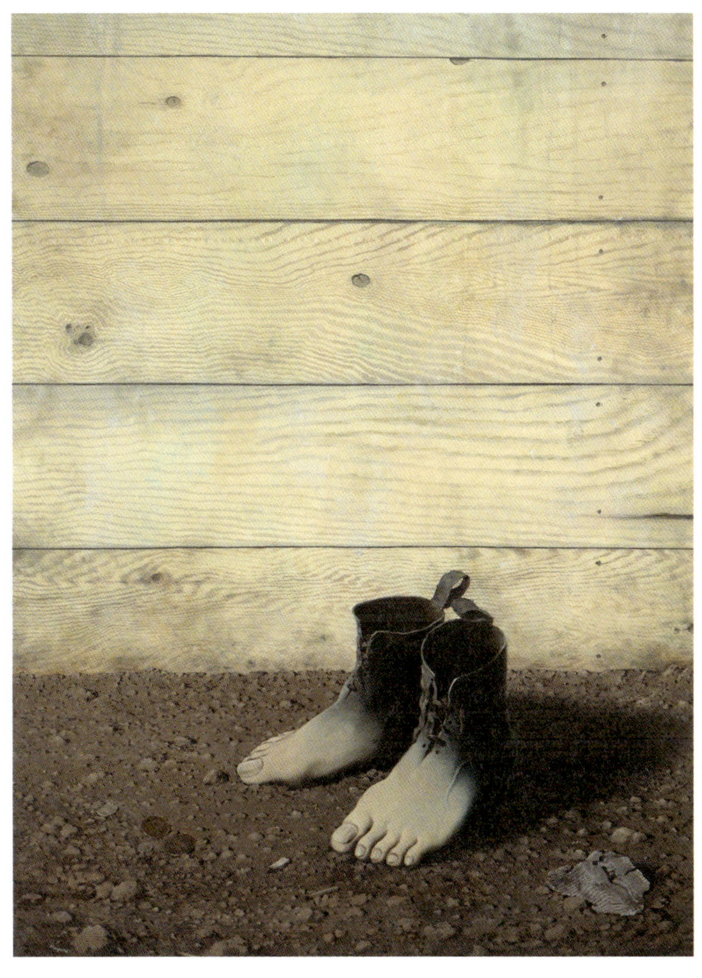

173
The Red Model
1937
oil on canvas, 183 × 136 cm

    1931–1942

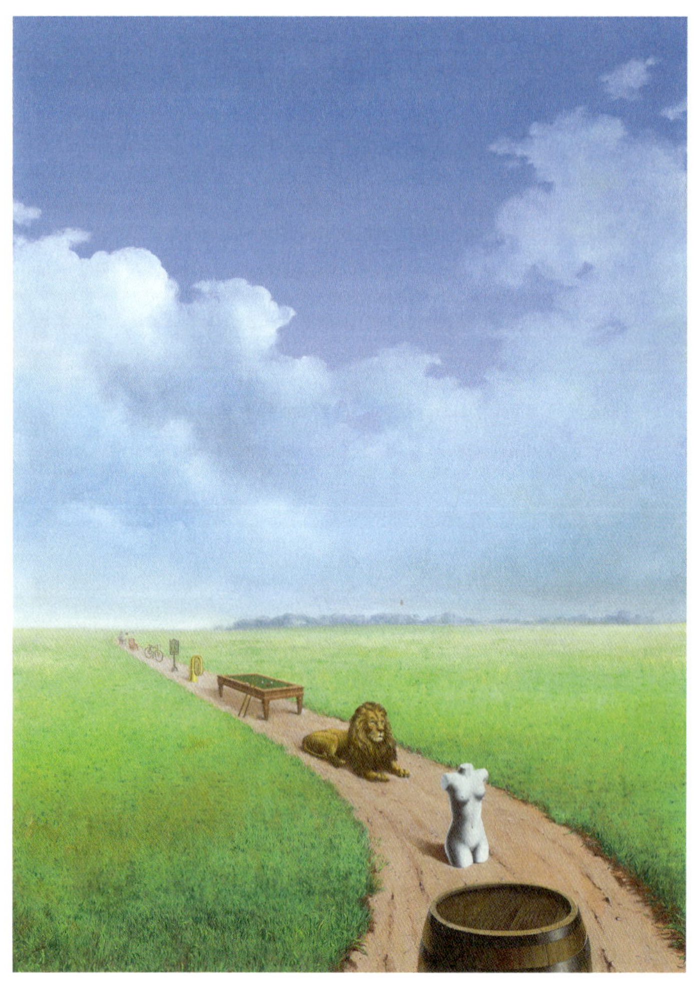

174
Youth Illustrated
1937
oil on canvas, 183 × 136 cm

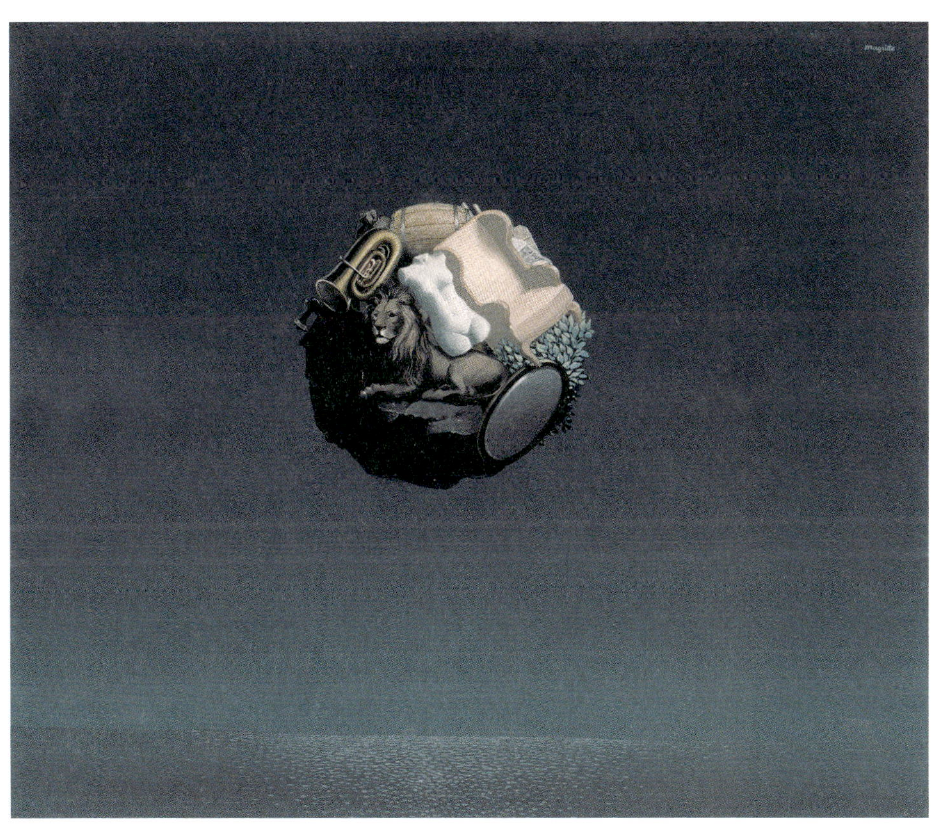

175
The Traveller
1937
oil on canvas, 54 × 65 cm

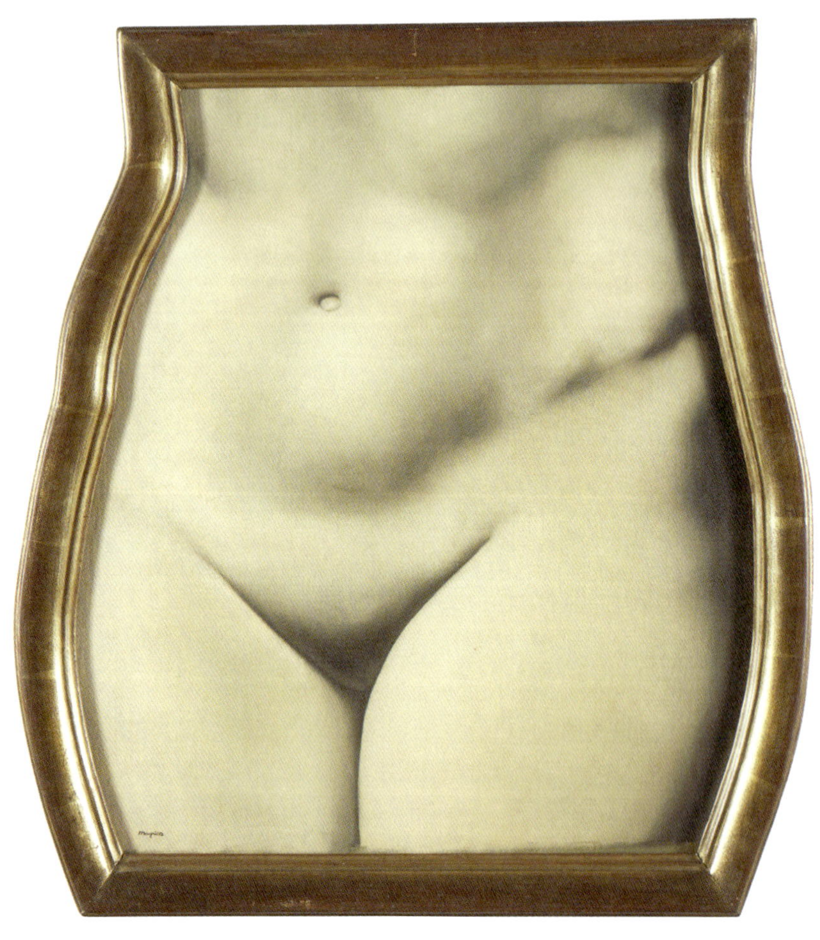

176
Representation
1937
oil on canvas mounted on panel, 48.5 × 44 cm

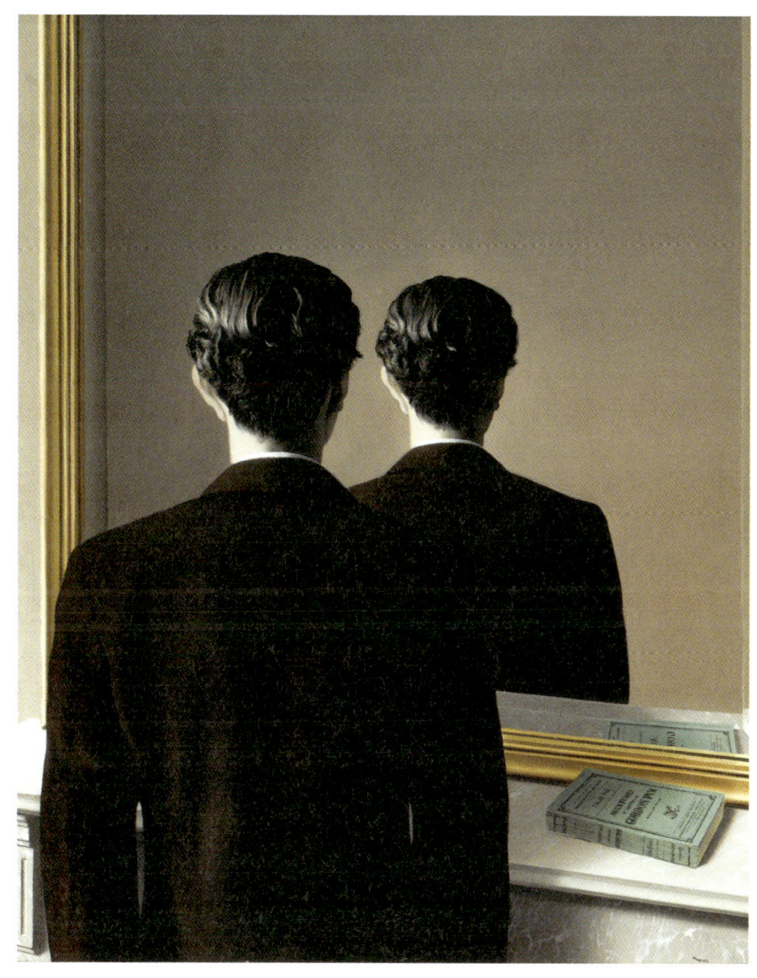

177
Not to be Reproduced
1937
oil on canvas, 81 × 65 cm

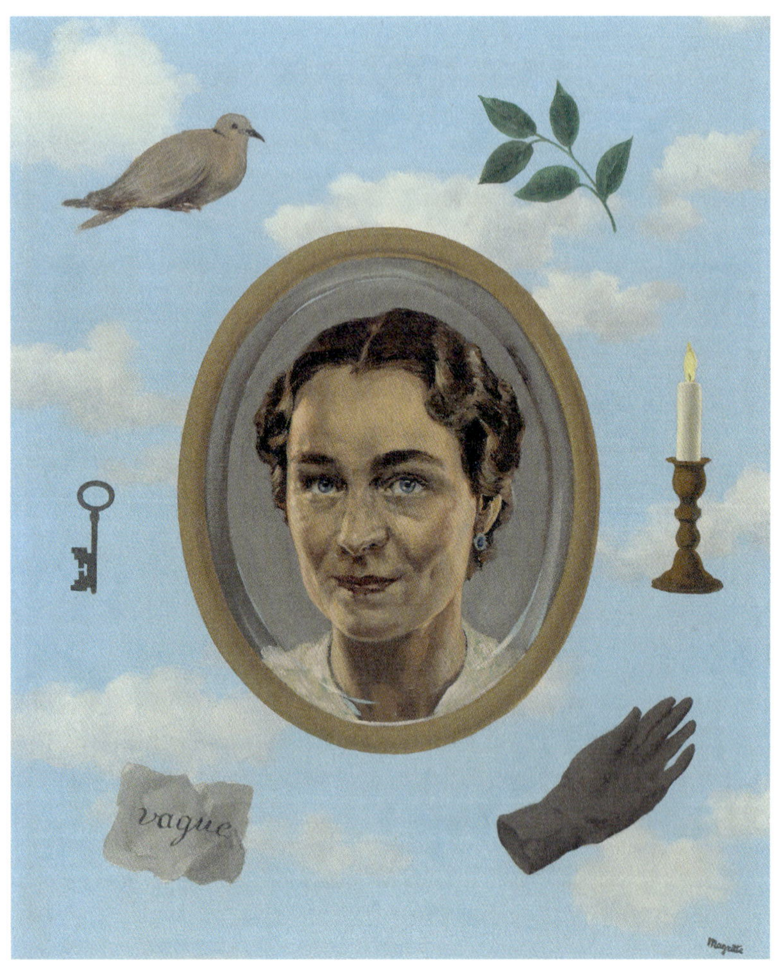

178
Georgette
1937
oil on canvas, 65 × 54 cm

 Elective Affinities

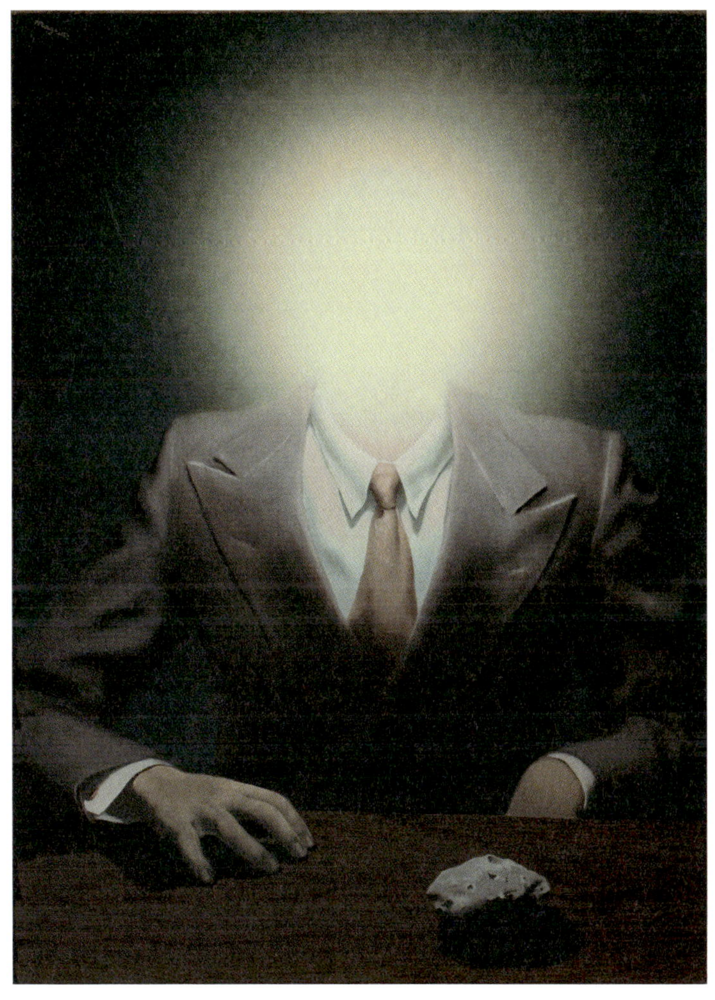

179
The Pleasure Principle
1937
oil on canvas, 73 × 54 cm

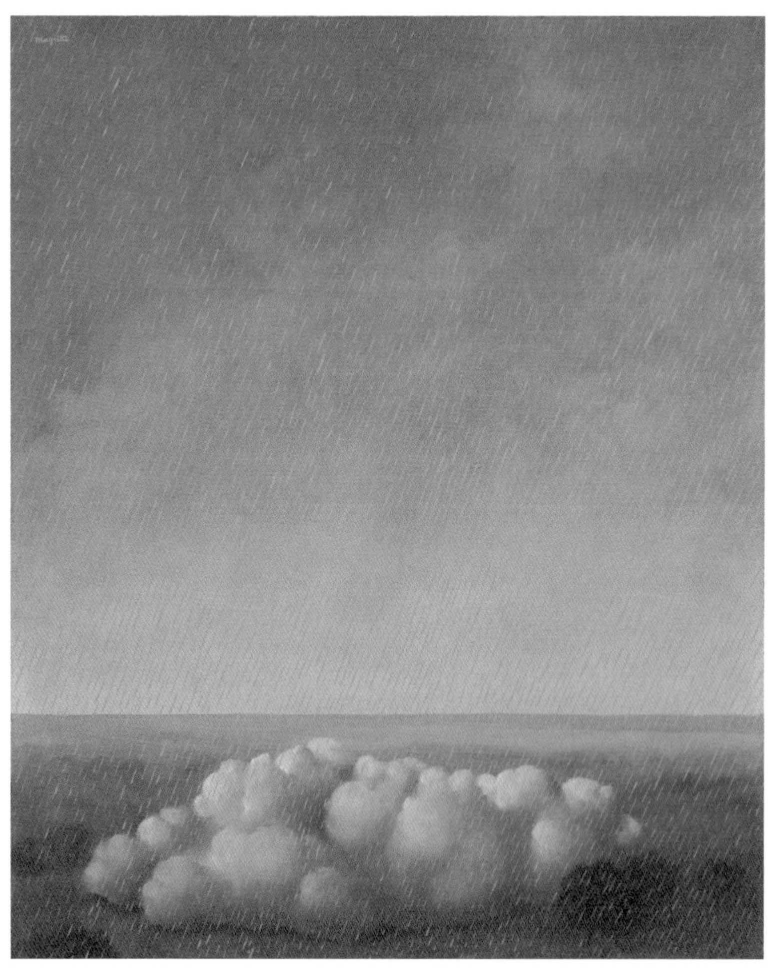

180
The Song of the Storm
1937
oil on canvas, 65 × 54 cm

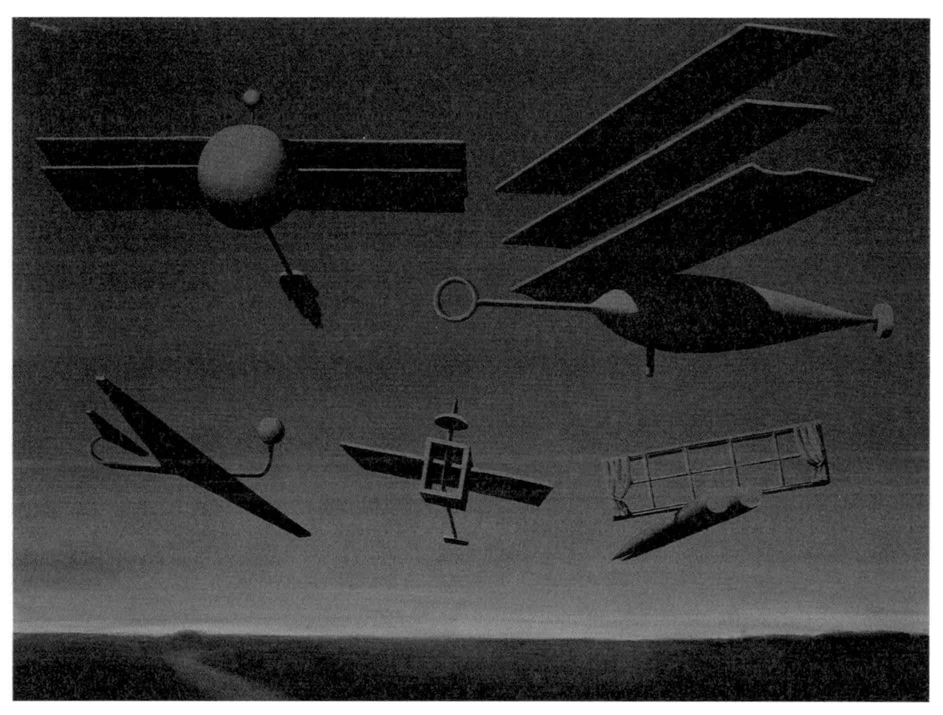

The Black Flag

1937
oil on canvas, 54 × 73 cm

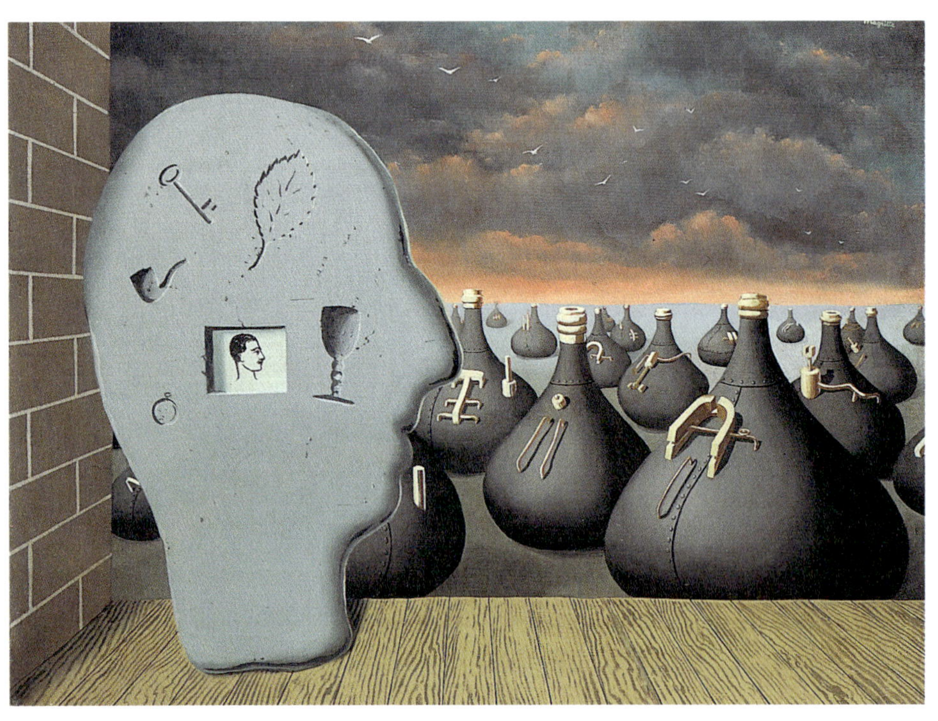

182
Spontaneous Generation
1937
oil on canvas, 54 × 73 cm

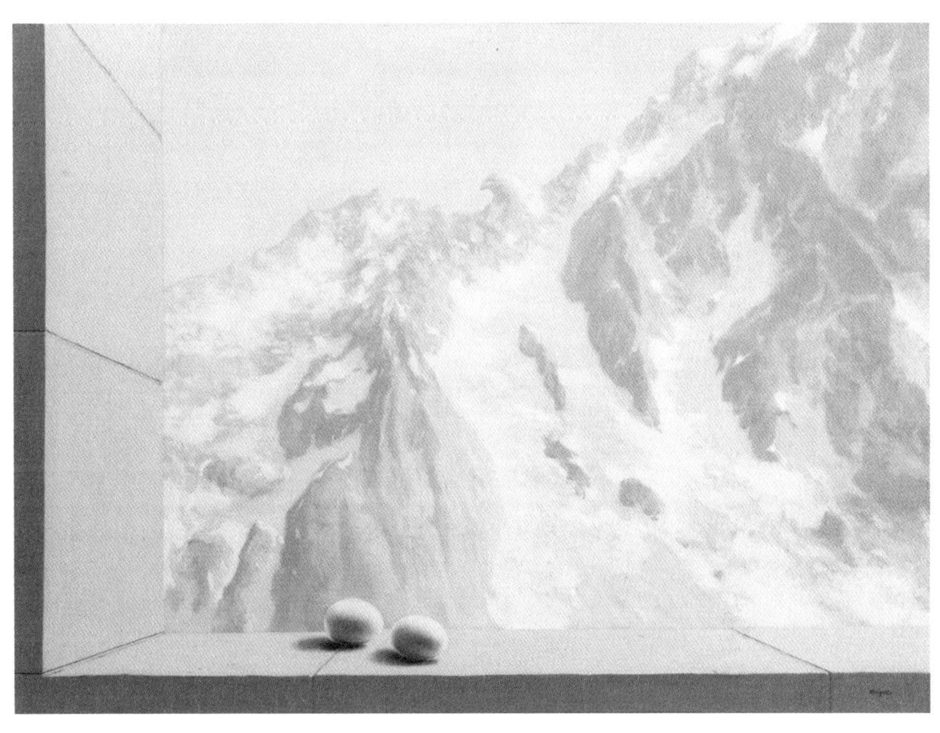

183
The Domain of Arnheim
1938
oil on canvas, 73 × 100 cm

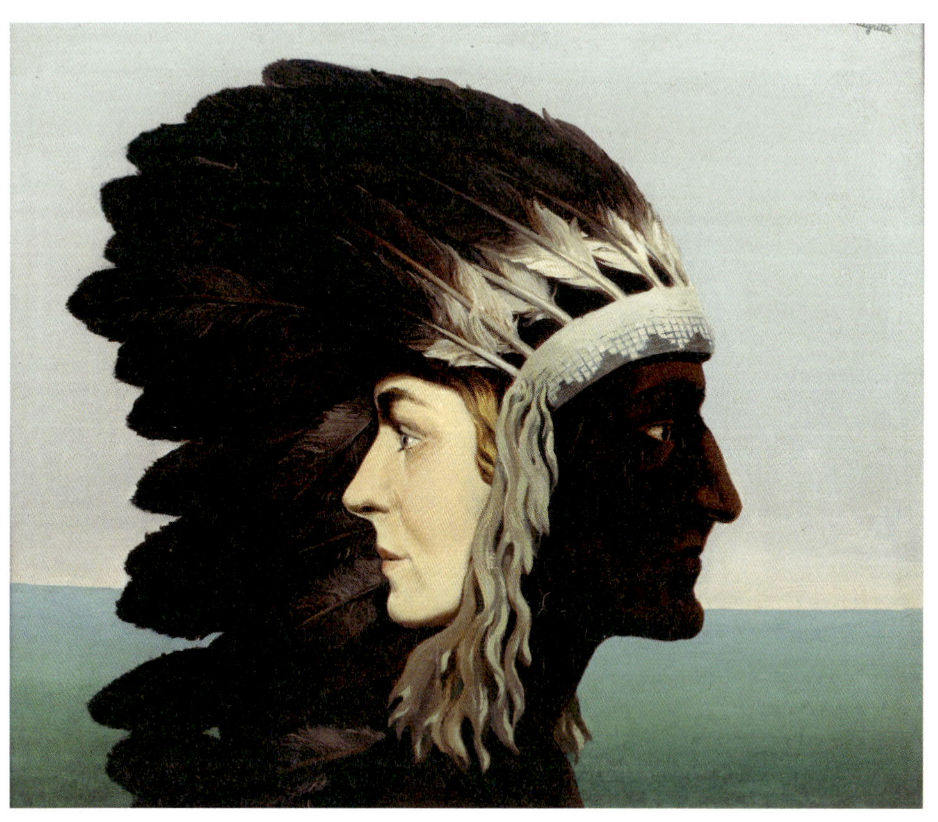

184
The Morning Star
1938
oil on canvas, 50 × 61 cm

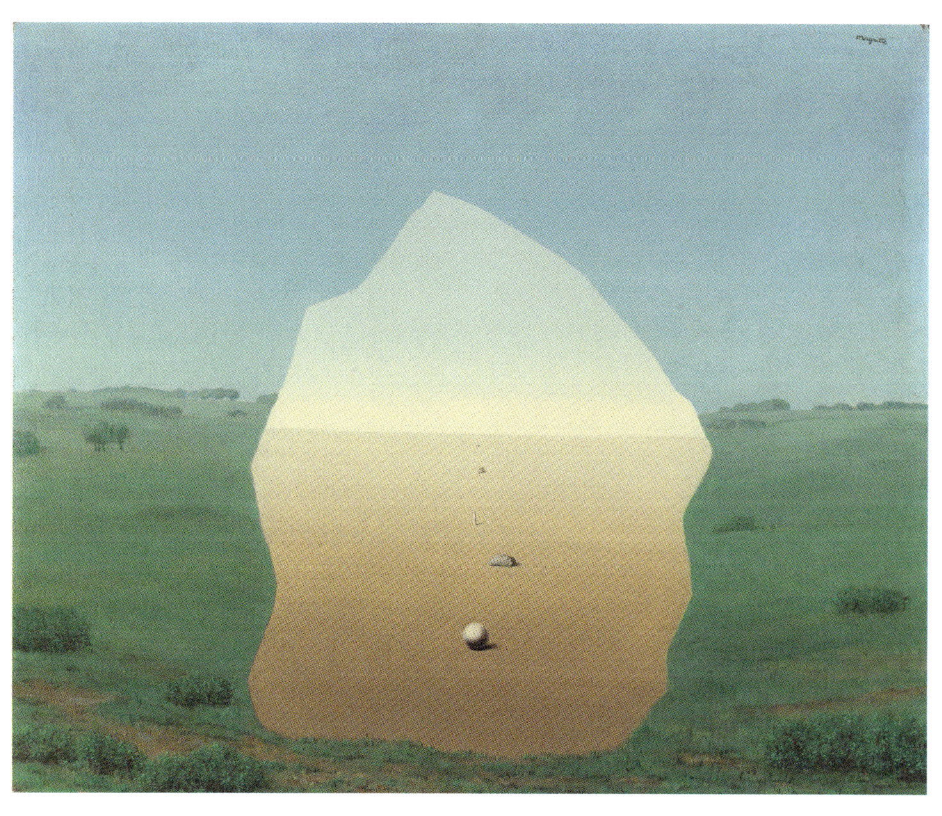

185
The Kiss
1938
oil on canvas, 60 × 73 cm

186
The Beyond
1938
oil on canvas, 73 × 50 cm

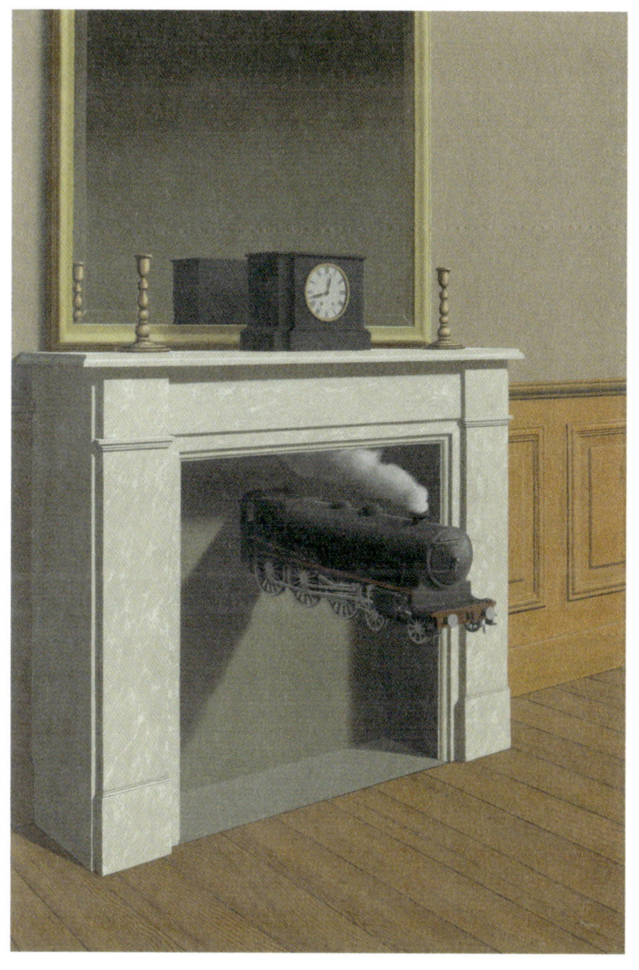

187
Time Transfixed
1938
oil on canvas, 147 × 99 cm

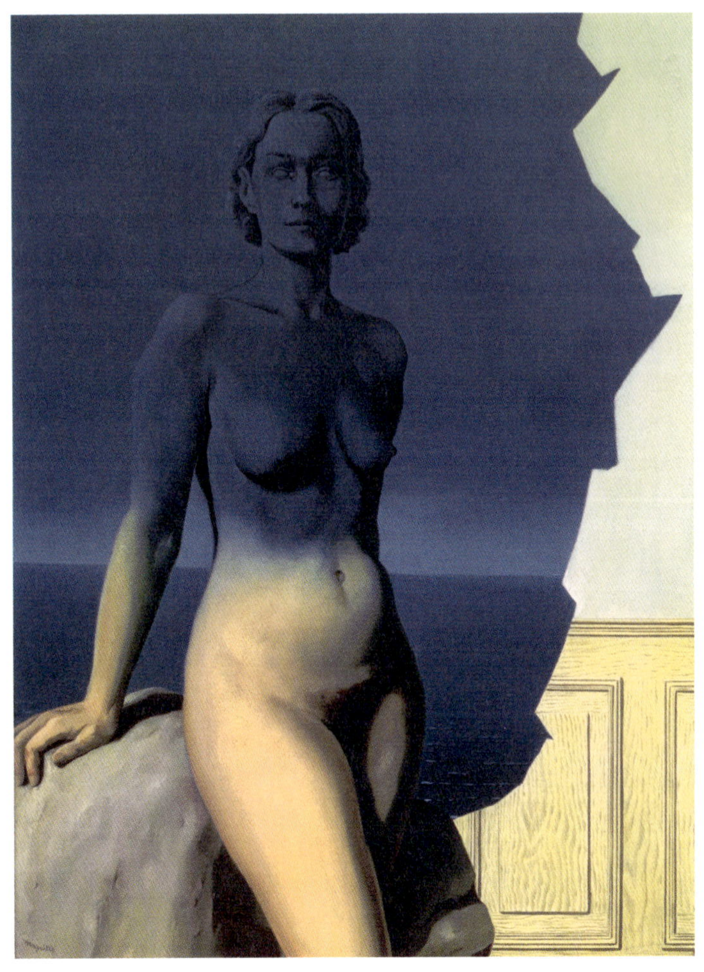

188
The Invasion
1938
oil on canvas, 73 × 54 cm

Elective Affinities

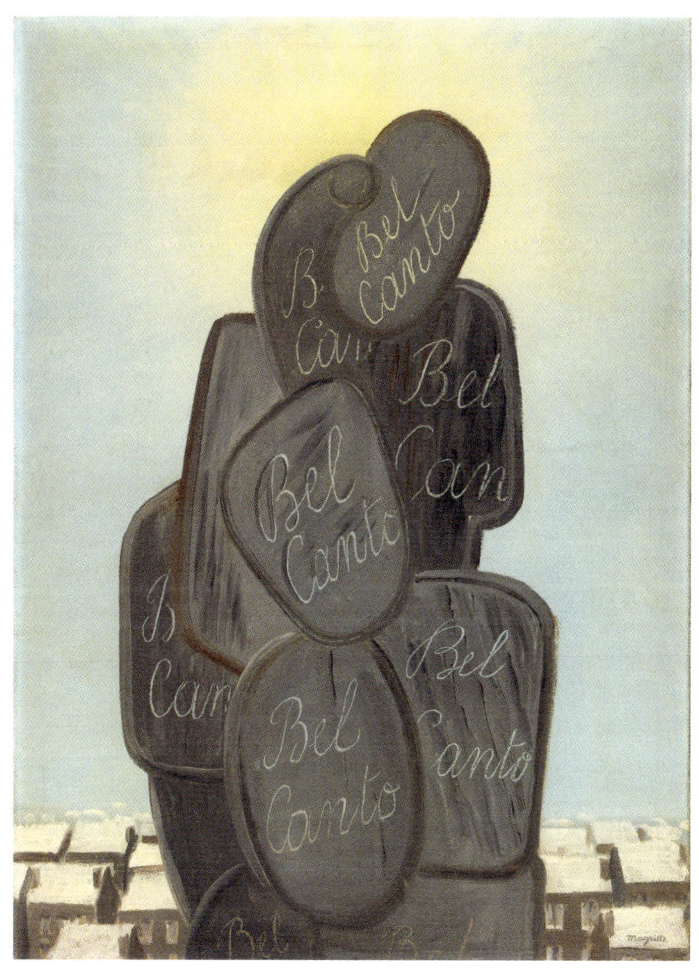

189
Bel Canto
1938
oil on canvas, 73 × 54 cm

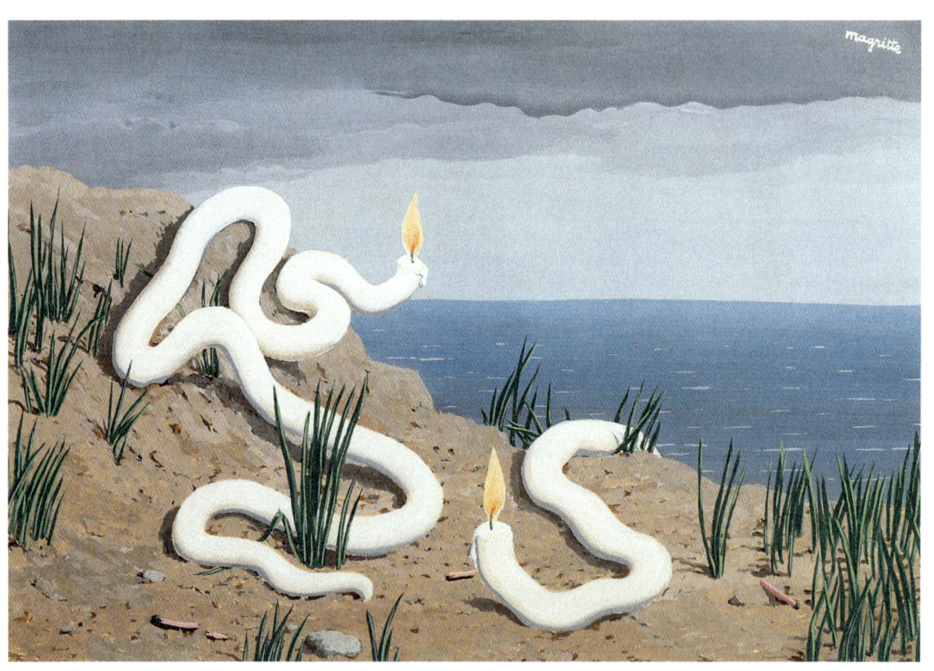

190
The Return to Nature
1938 or 1939
gouache on paper, 27.4 × 39.5 cm

     Elective Affinities

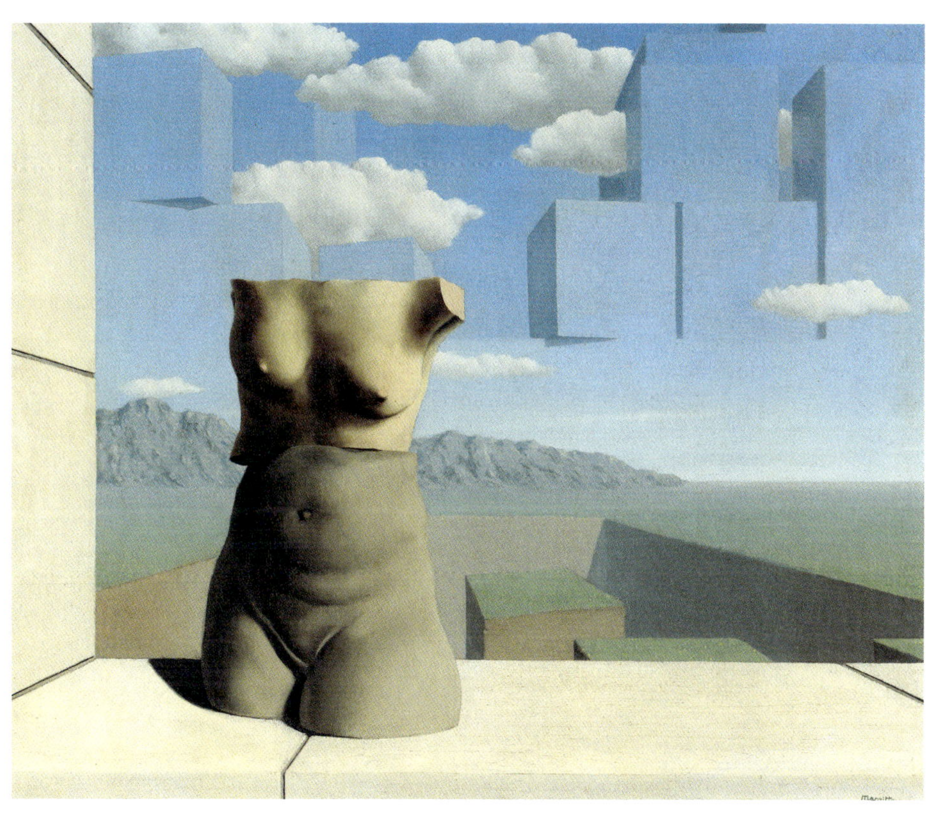

191
The Marches of Summer
1938
oil on canvas, 60 × 73 cm

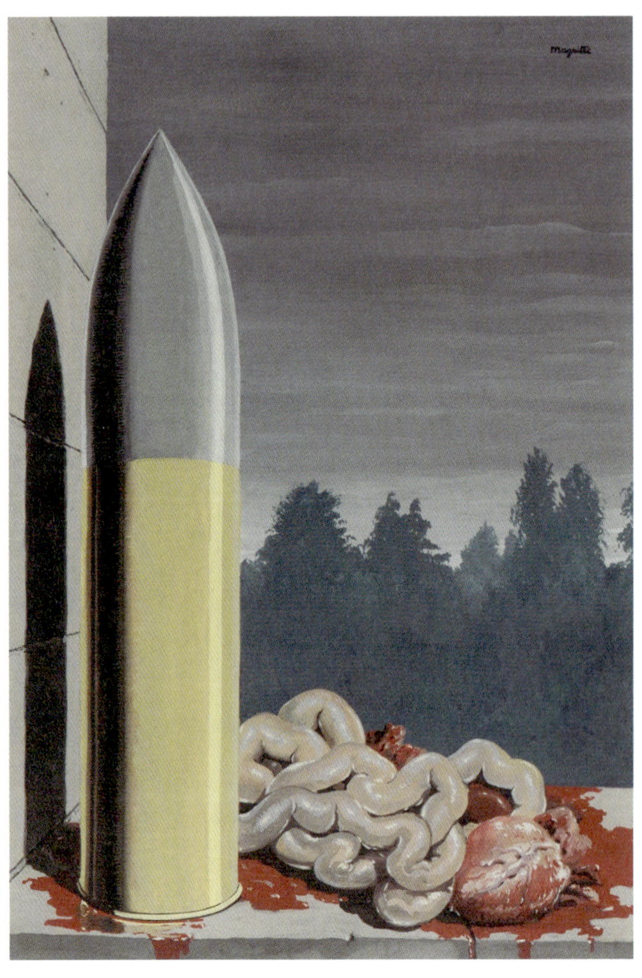

192
The Witness
1938 or 1939
gouache on paper, 42 × 29 cm

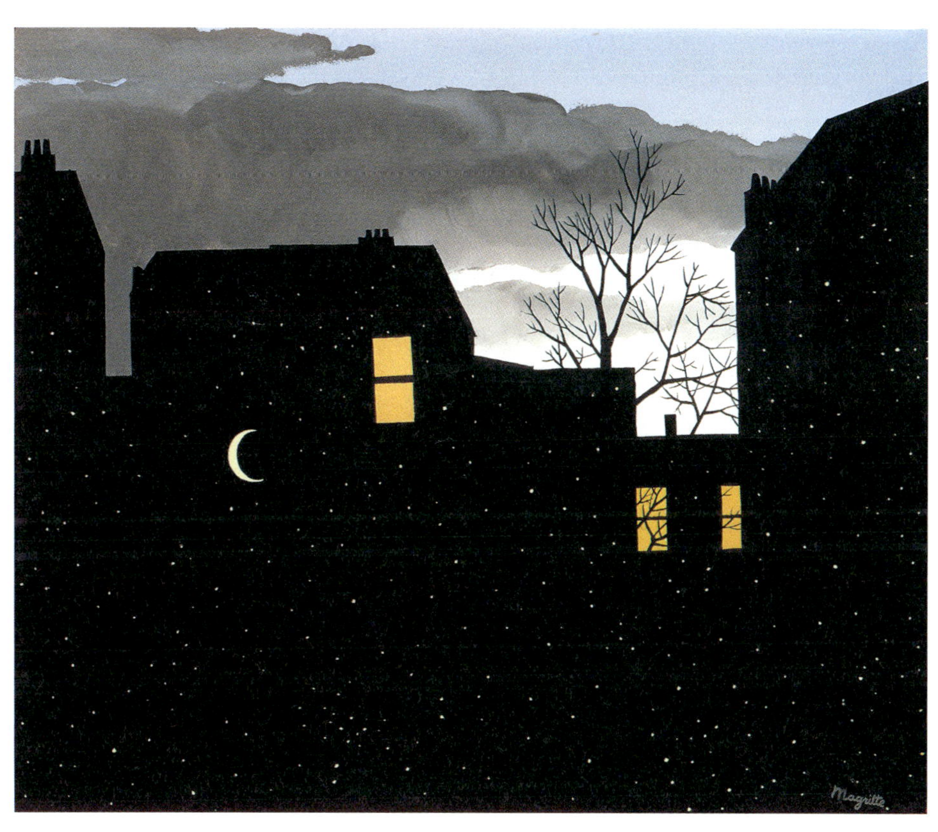

193
Poison
1938 or 1939
gouache on paper, 33.5 × 40.7 cm

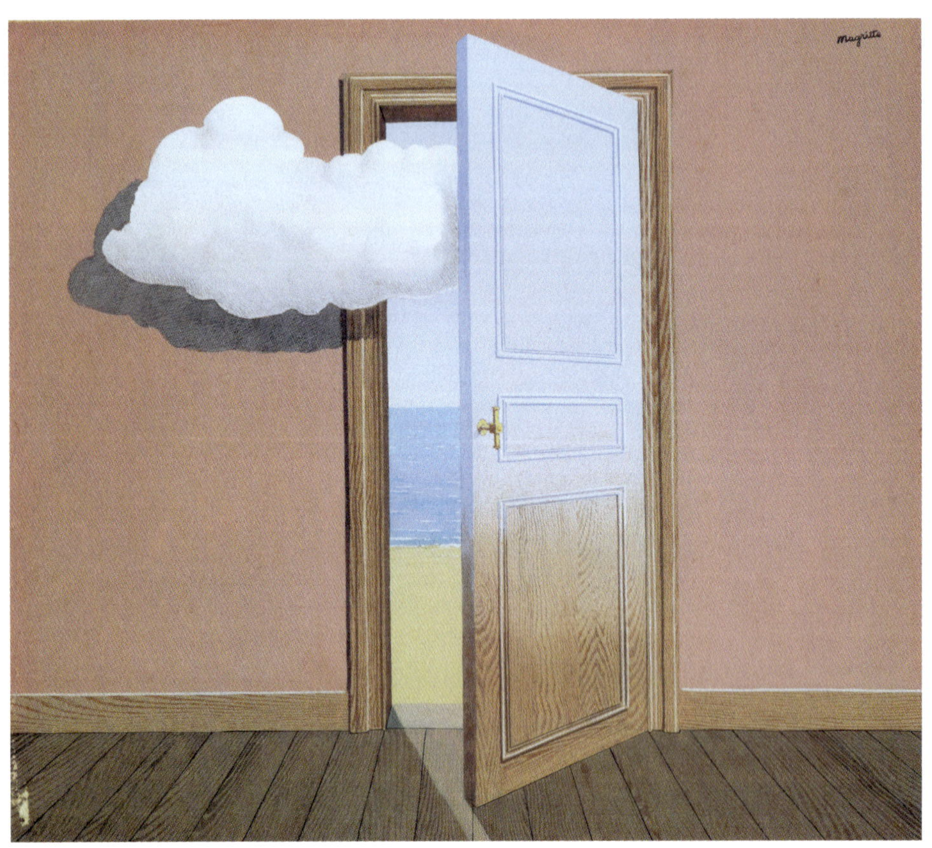

194
Fortune Telling
1938 or 1939
gouache on paper, 36 × 41.5 cm

 Elective Affinities

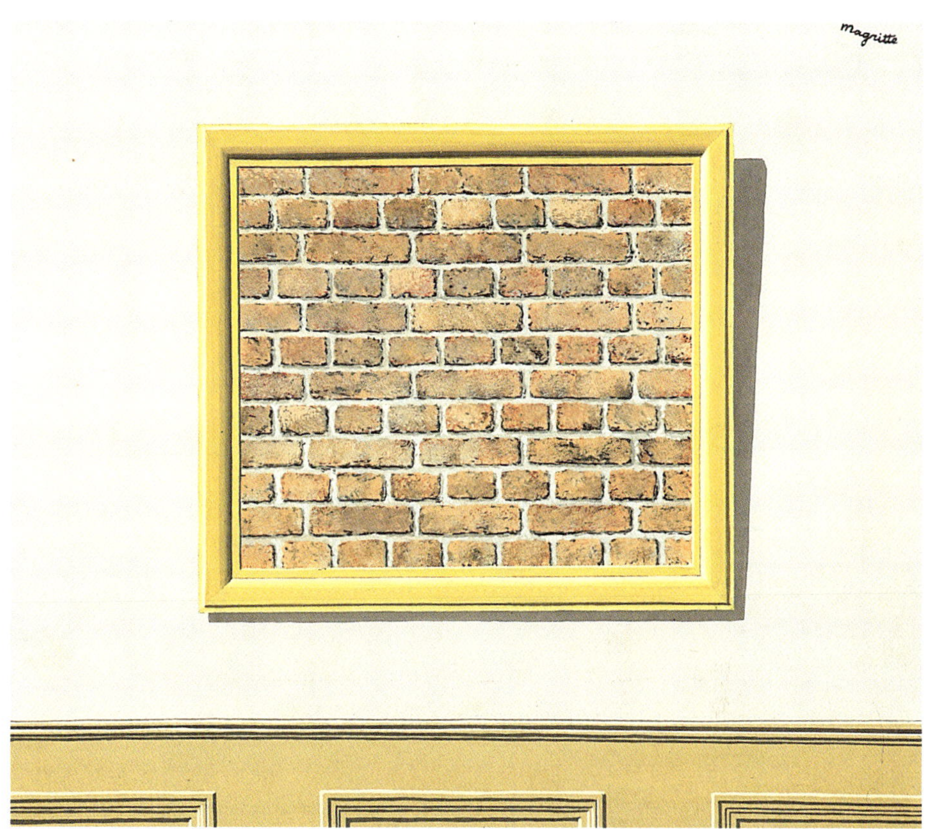

195
Bloodletting
1938 or 1939
gouache on paper, 37 × 43 cm

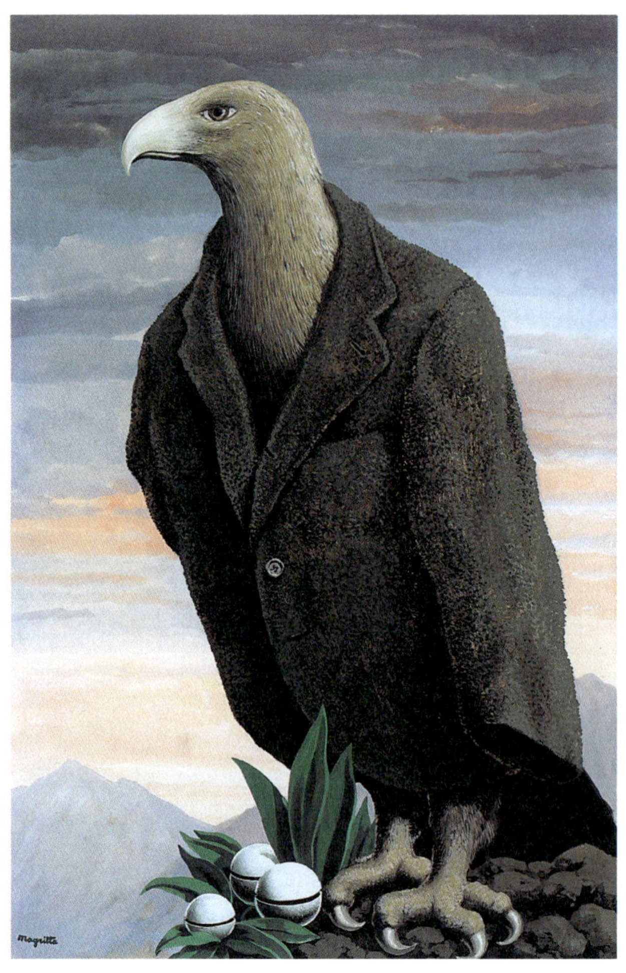

196
The Present
1938 or 1939
gouache on paper, 48.3 × 32.4 cm

 Elective Affinities

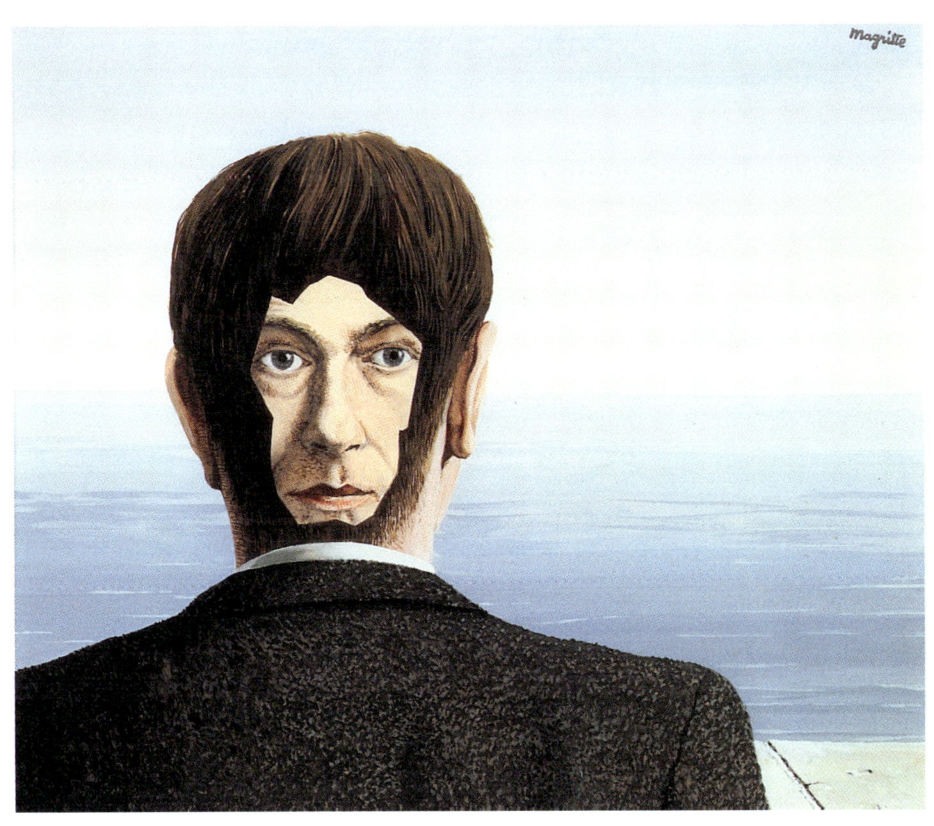

197
The Glass House
1939
gouache on paper, 33.6 × 40.2 cm

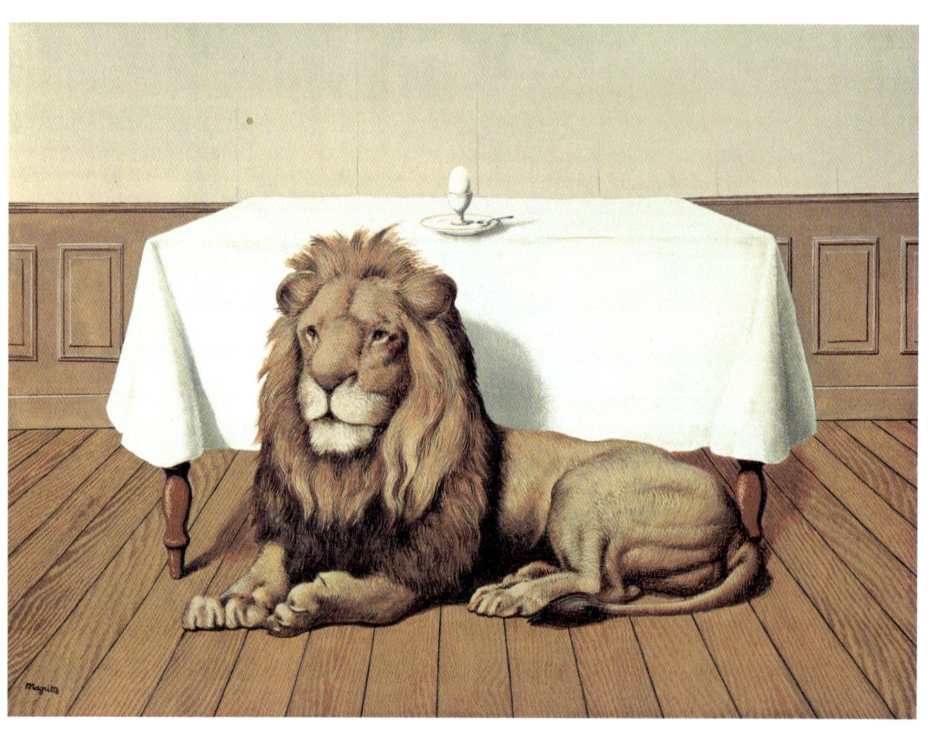

198
(The Wedding Breakfast)
1939 or 1940
gouache on paper, 31 × 41.5 cm

 Elective Affinities

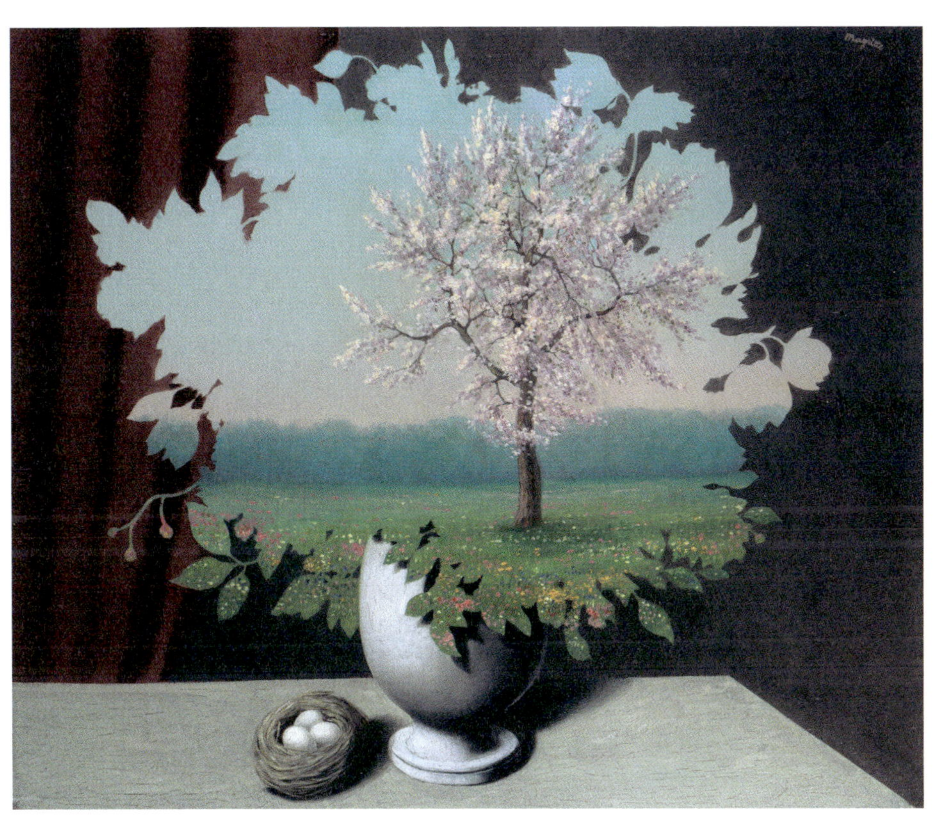

199
Plagiary
1940
oil on canvas, 54 × 65 cm

     1931–1942

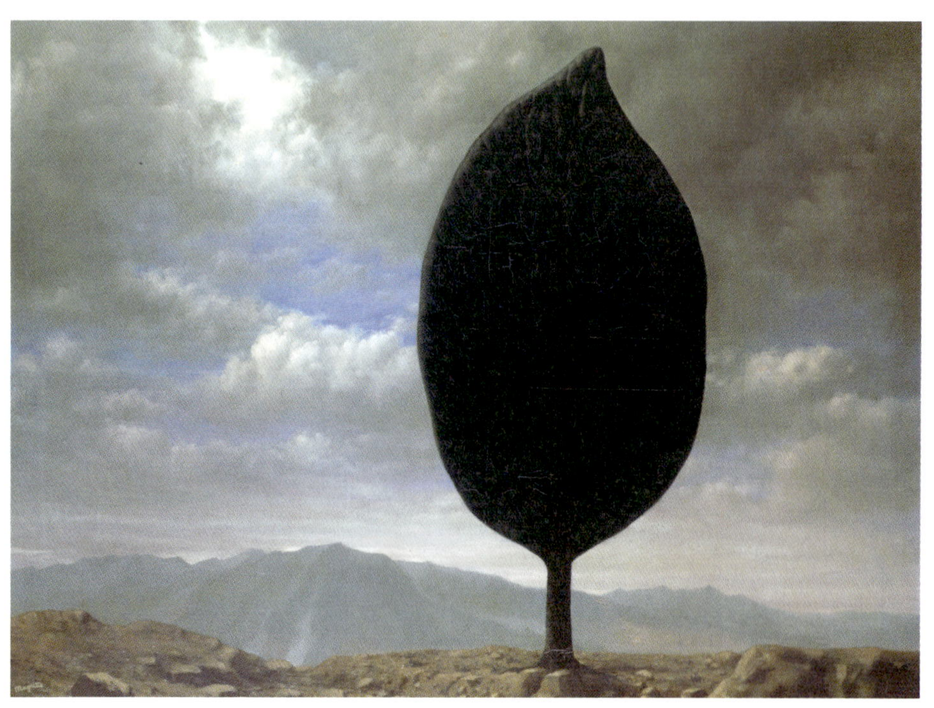

200
The Plain of the Air
1940
oil on canvas, 73 × 100 cm

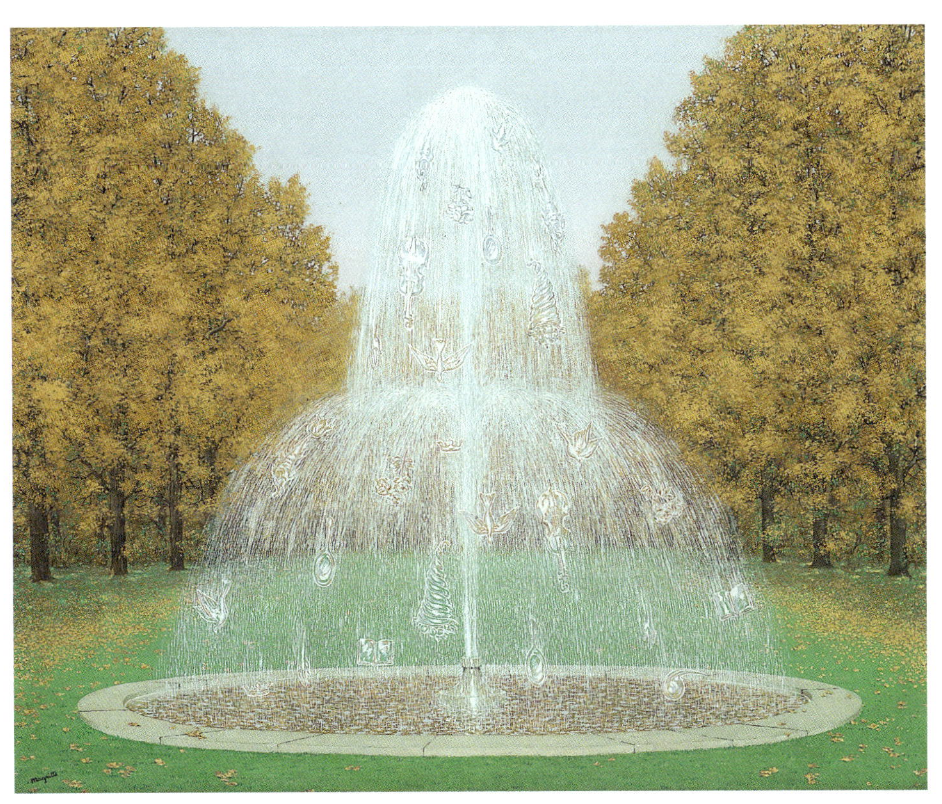

201
The Last Fine Days
1940
oil on canvas, 81 × 100 cm

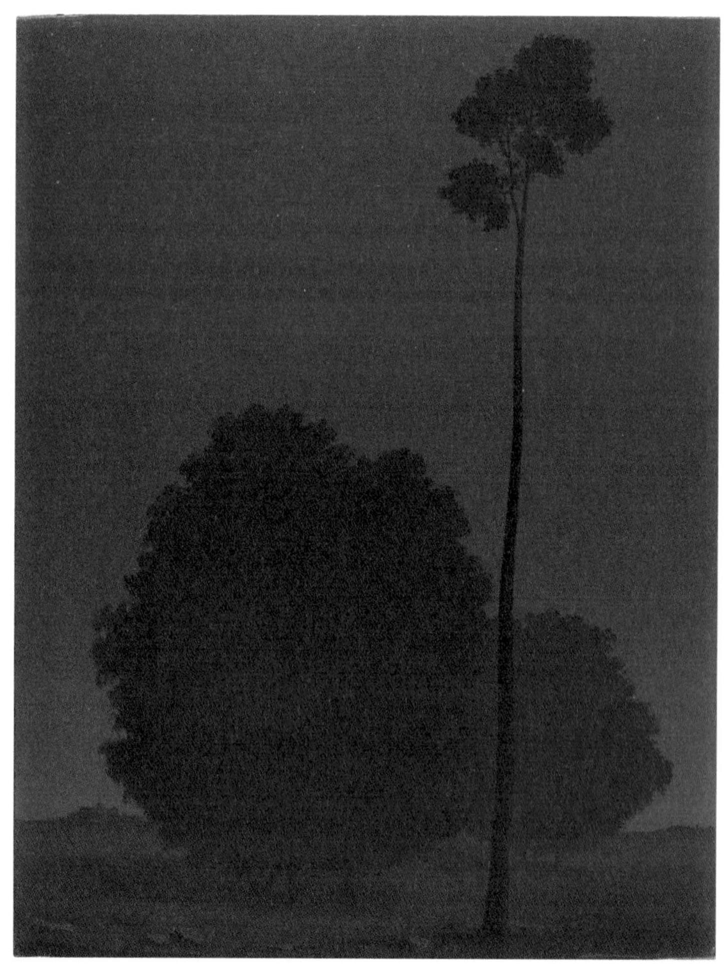

202
Great Expectations
1940
oil on canvas, 65 × 50 cm

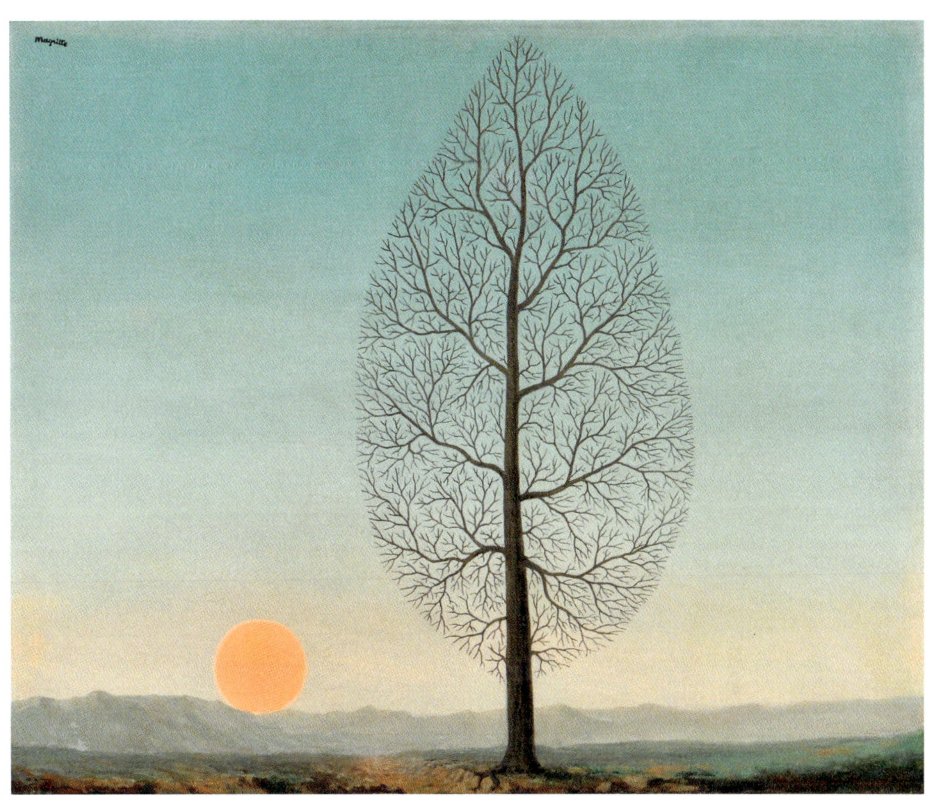

203
The Search for the Absolute
1940
oil on canvas, 60 × 73 cm

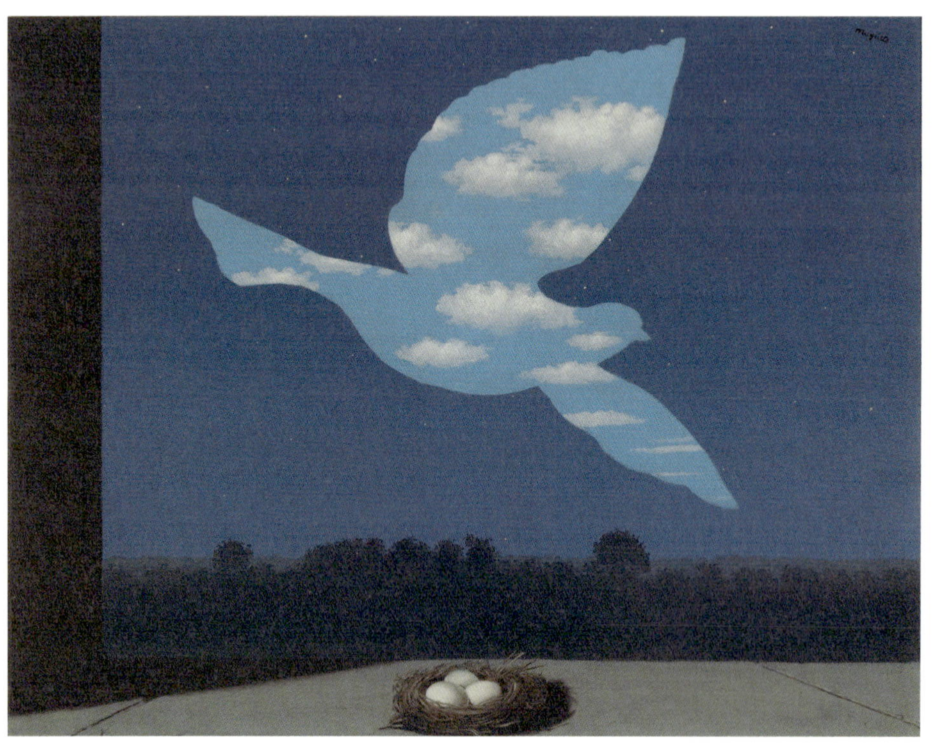

204
The Return
1940
oil on canvas, 50 × 65 cm

 Elective Affinities

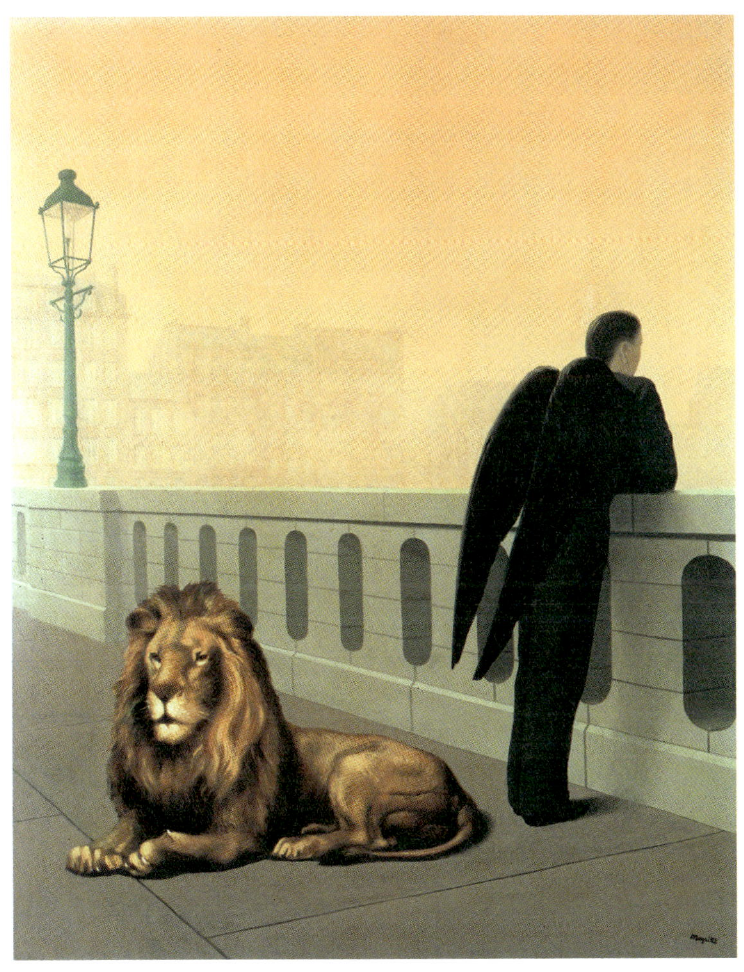

205
Homesickness
1941
oil on canvas, 100 × 81 cm

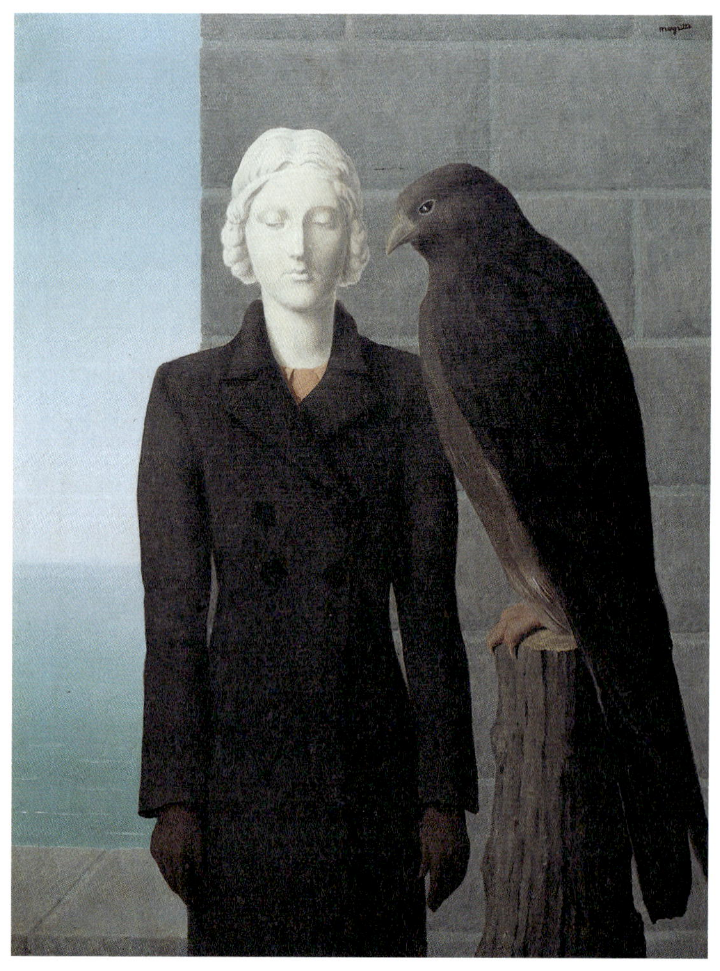

206
Deep Waters
1941
oil on canvas, 65 × 50 cm

Elective Affinities

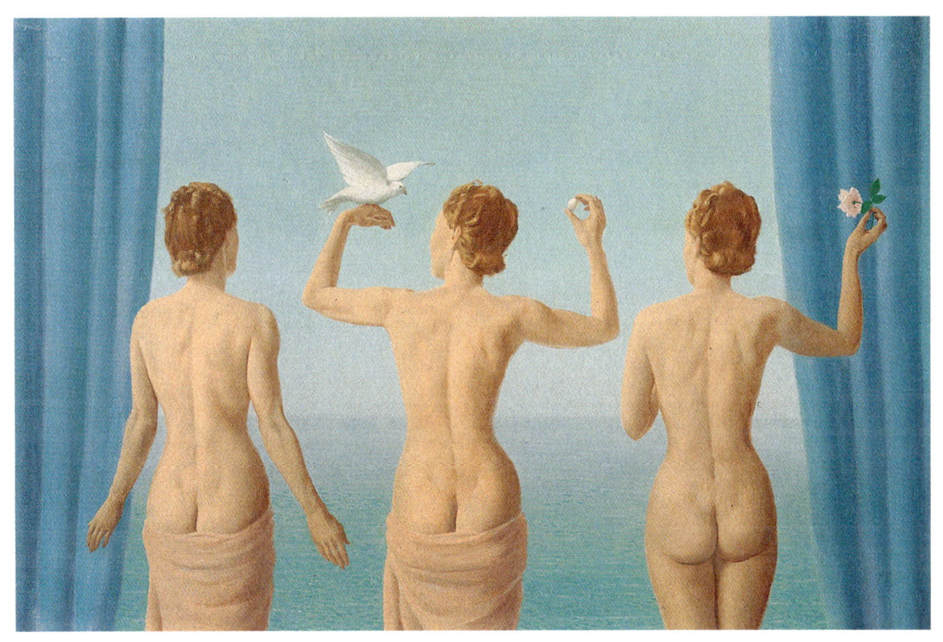

207
The Break in the Clouds
1941
oil on canvas, 65 × 100 cm

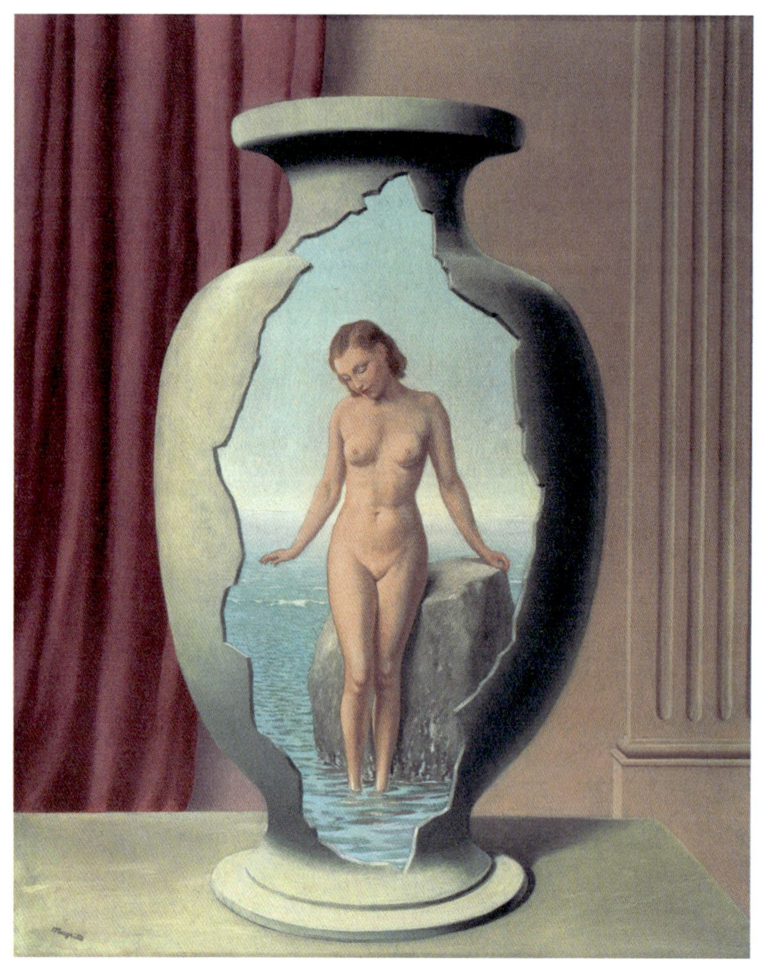

208
The Orient
1941
oil on canvas, 81 × 65 cm

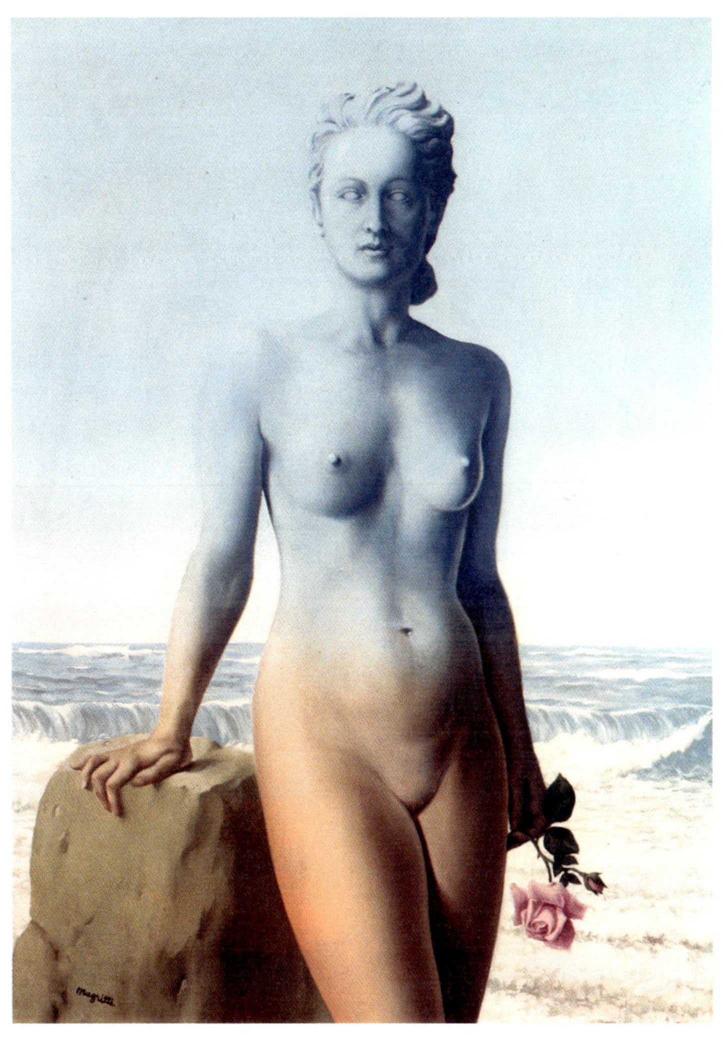

209
The Proud Ship
1942
oil on canvas, 92 × 70 cm

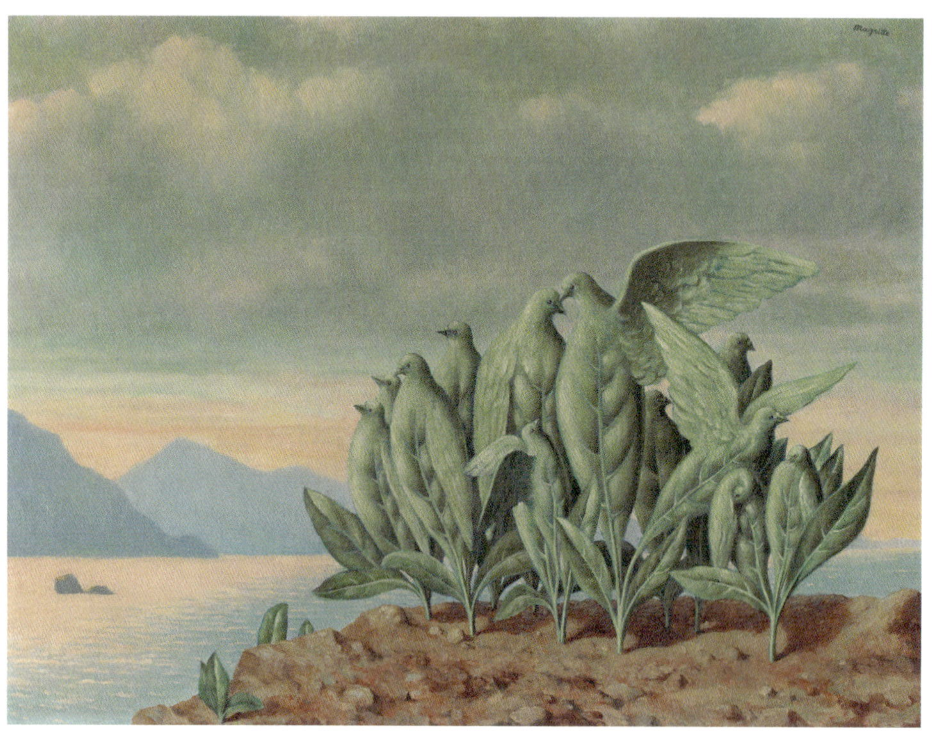

210
Treasure Island
1942
oil on canvas, 60 × 81 cm

     Elective Affinities

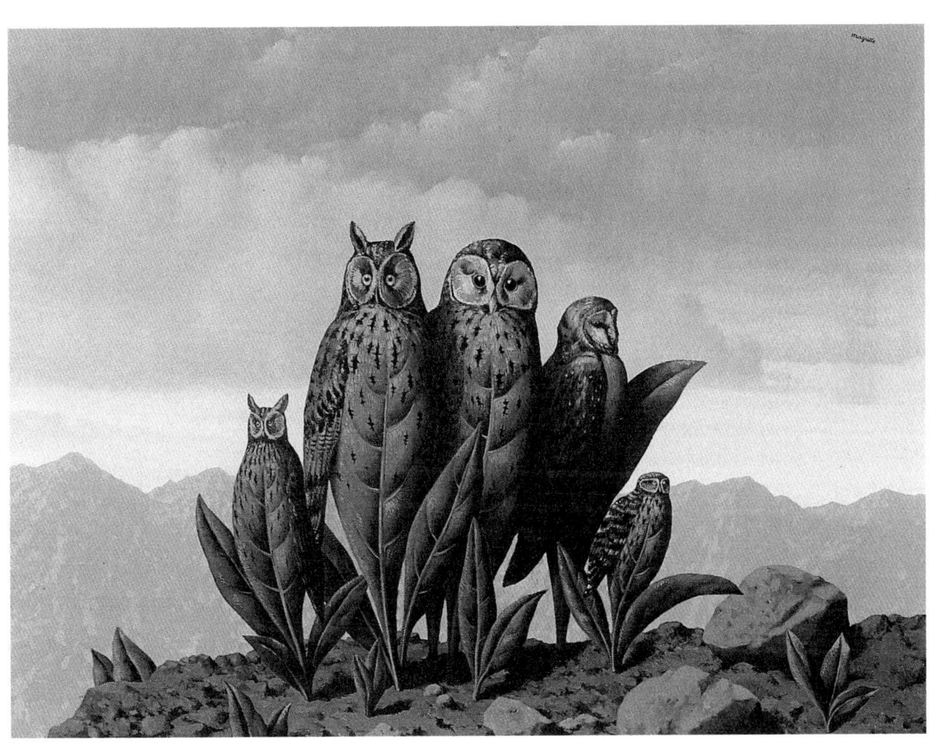

211
The Companions of Fear
1942
oil on canvas, 70.5 × 92 cm

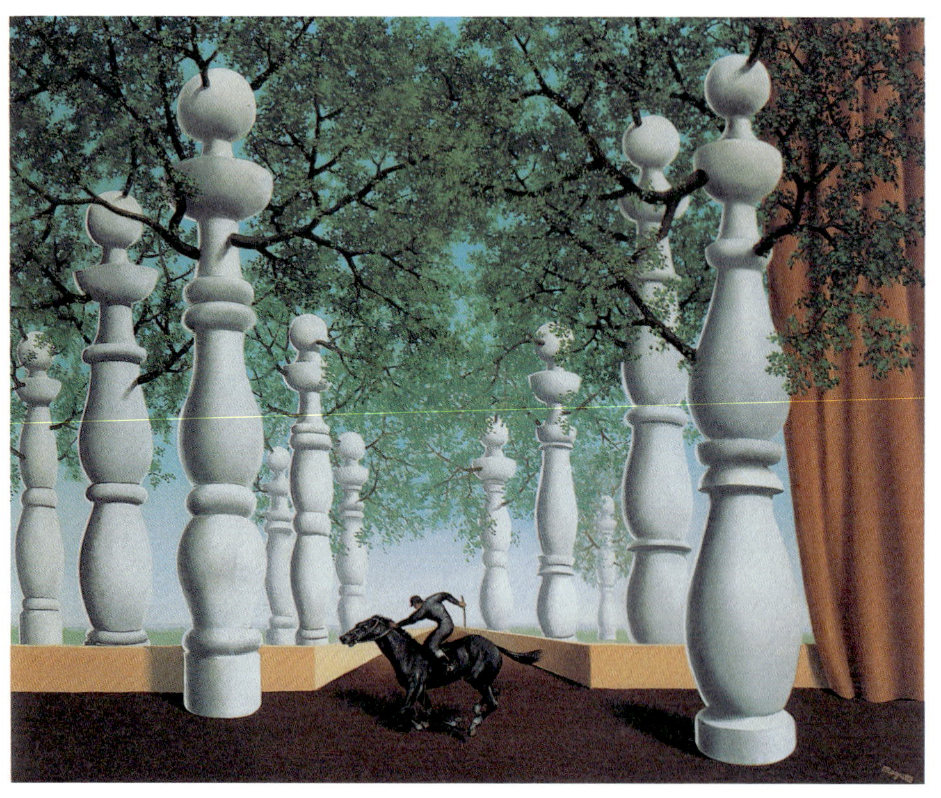

212
The Lost Jockey
1942
oil on canvas, 60 × 73 cm

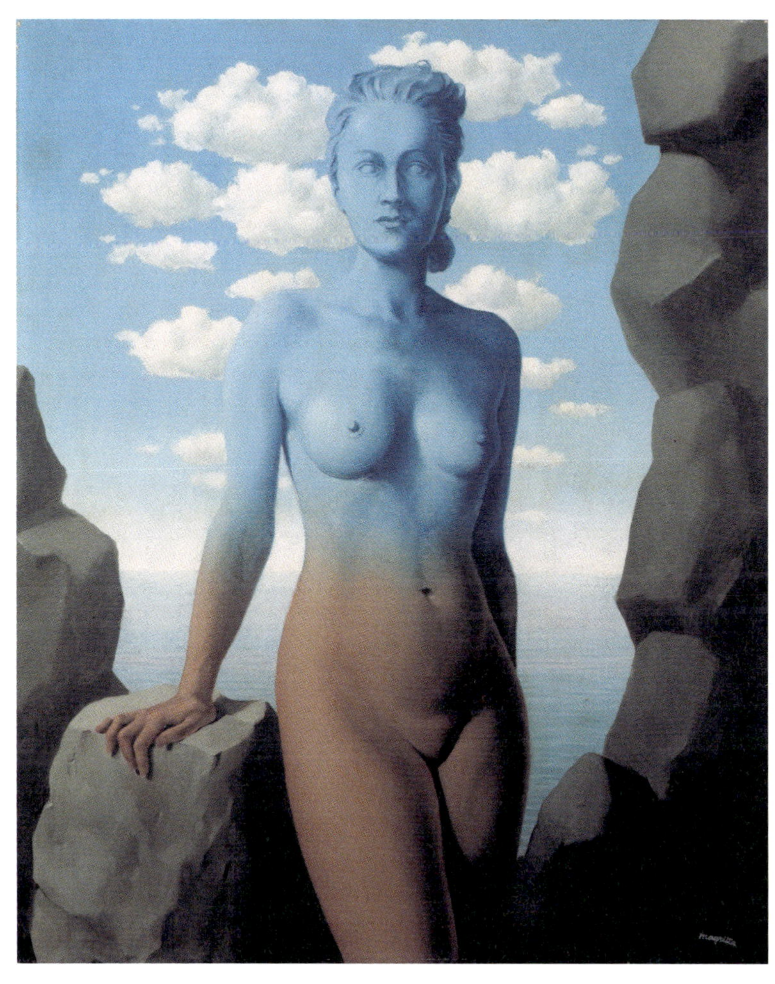

213
(Black Magic)
1942
oil on canvas, 65 × 54 cm

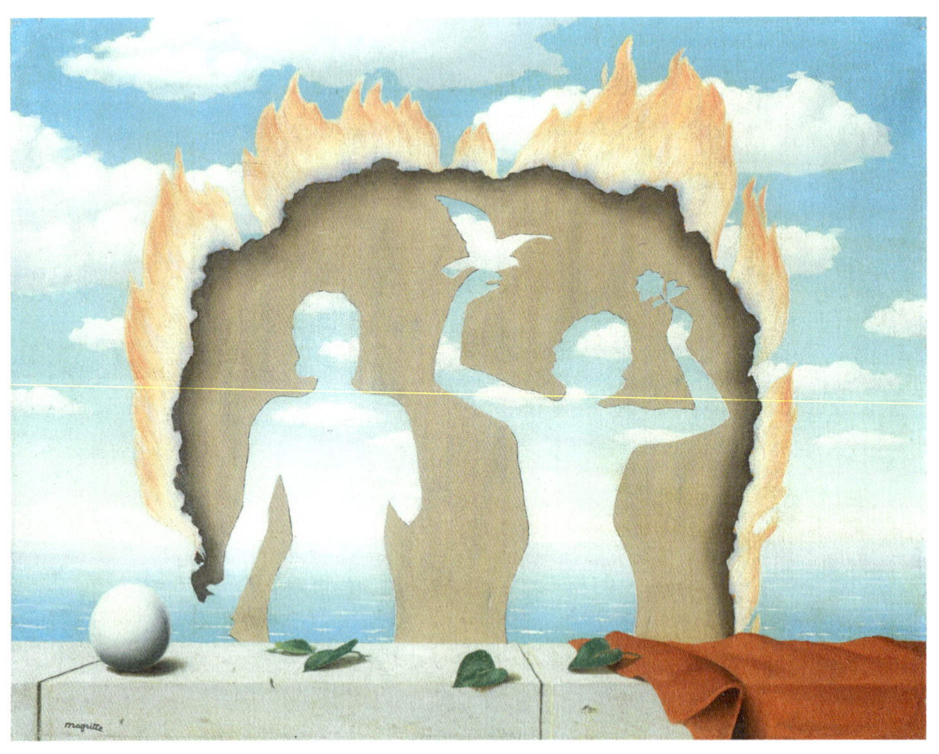

214
Misses de L'Isle Adam
1942
oil on canvas, 50 × 65 cm

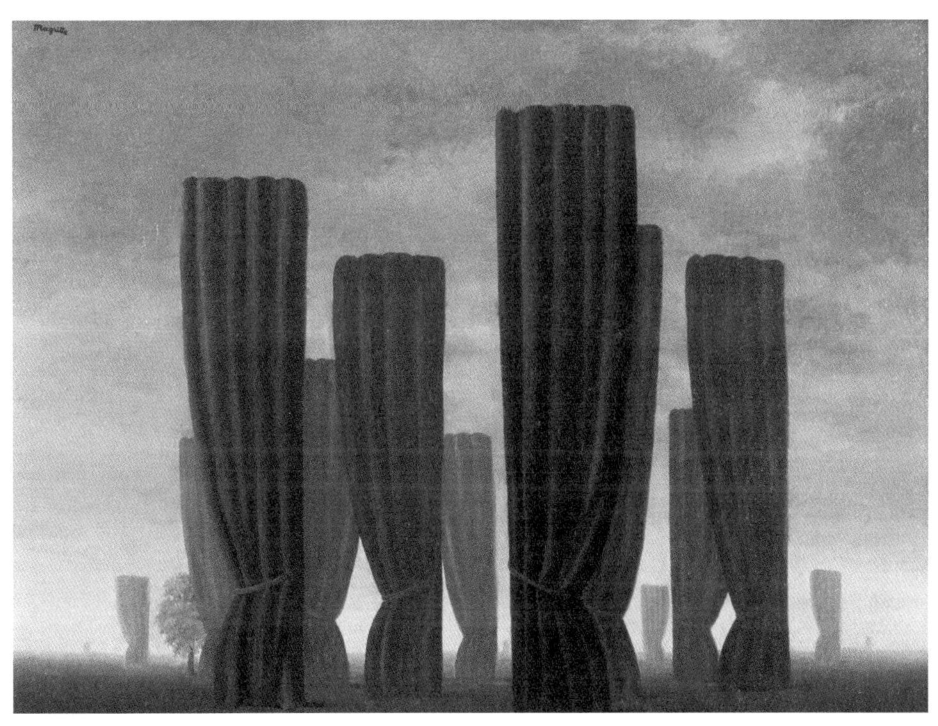

215
The Misanthropes
1942
oil on canvas, 54 × 73 cm

1931–1942

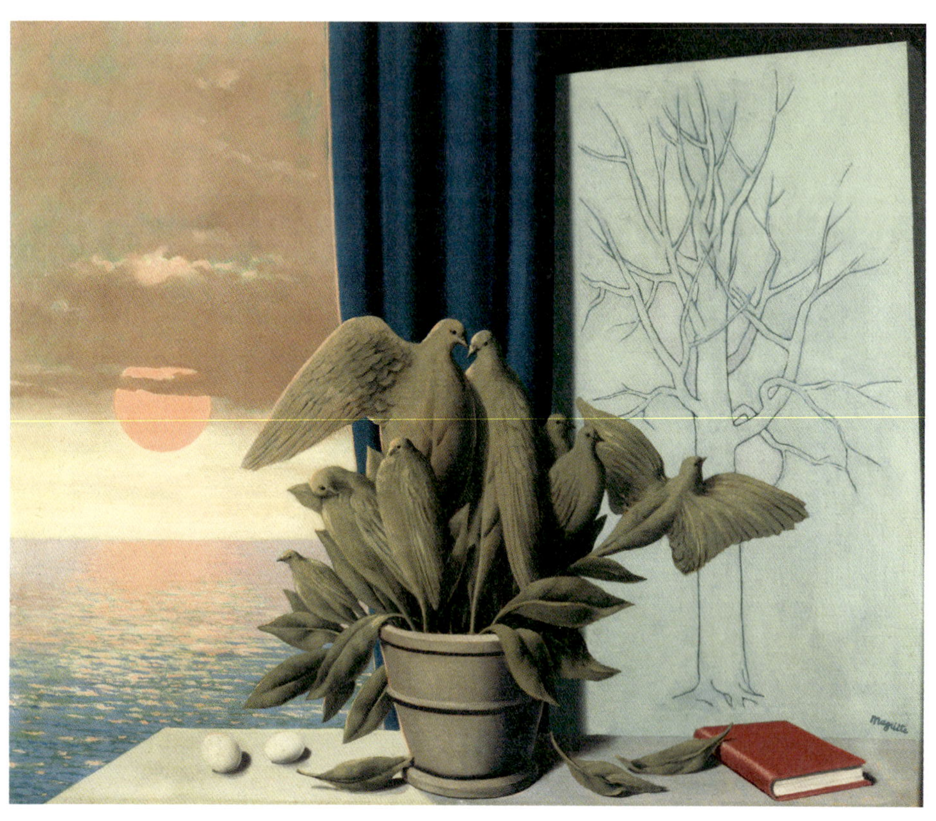

216
The Hyphen
1942
oil on canvas, 60 × 73 cm

Elective Affinities

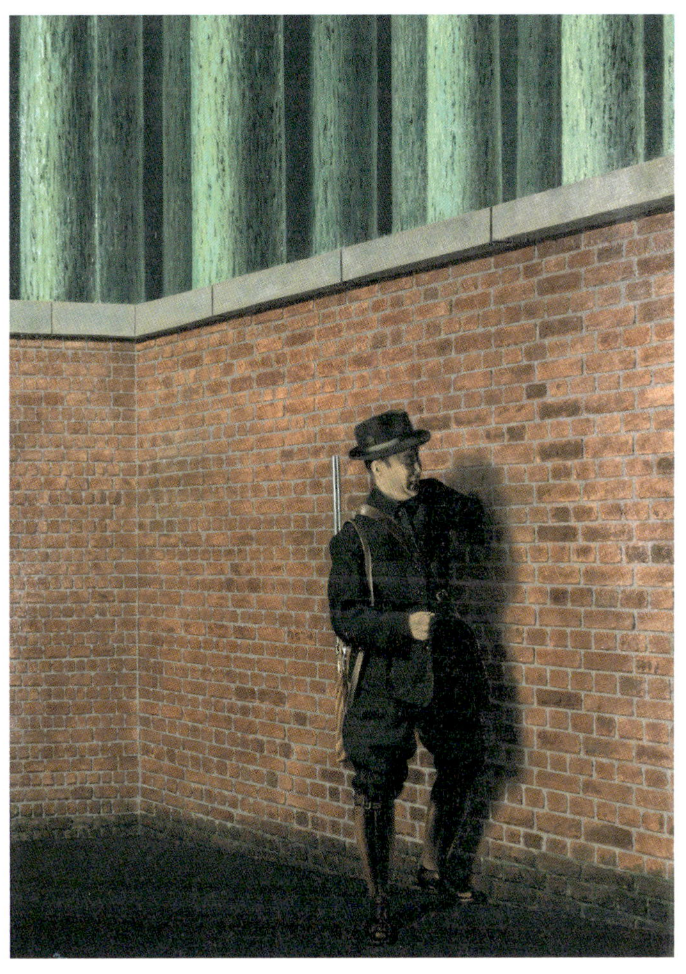

217
Universal Gravitation
1943
oil on canvas, 100 × 73 cm

         1931–1942

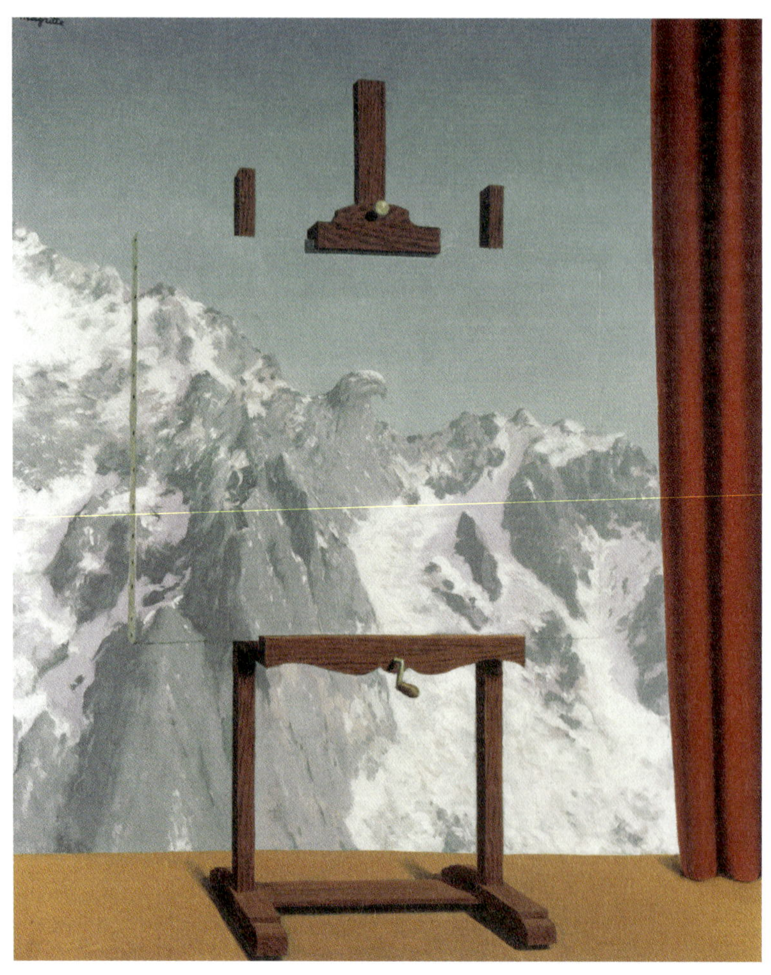

218
The Call of the Peaks
1943
oil on canvas, 65 × 54 cm

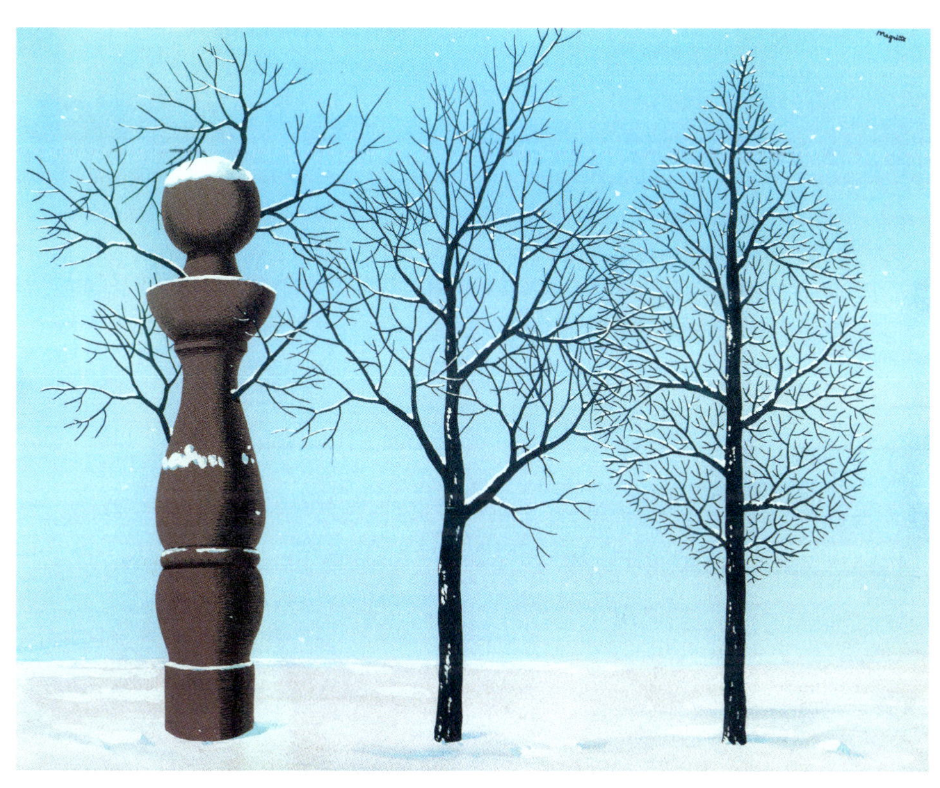

219
The New Years
1942
gouache on paper, 50 × 62 cm

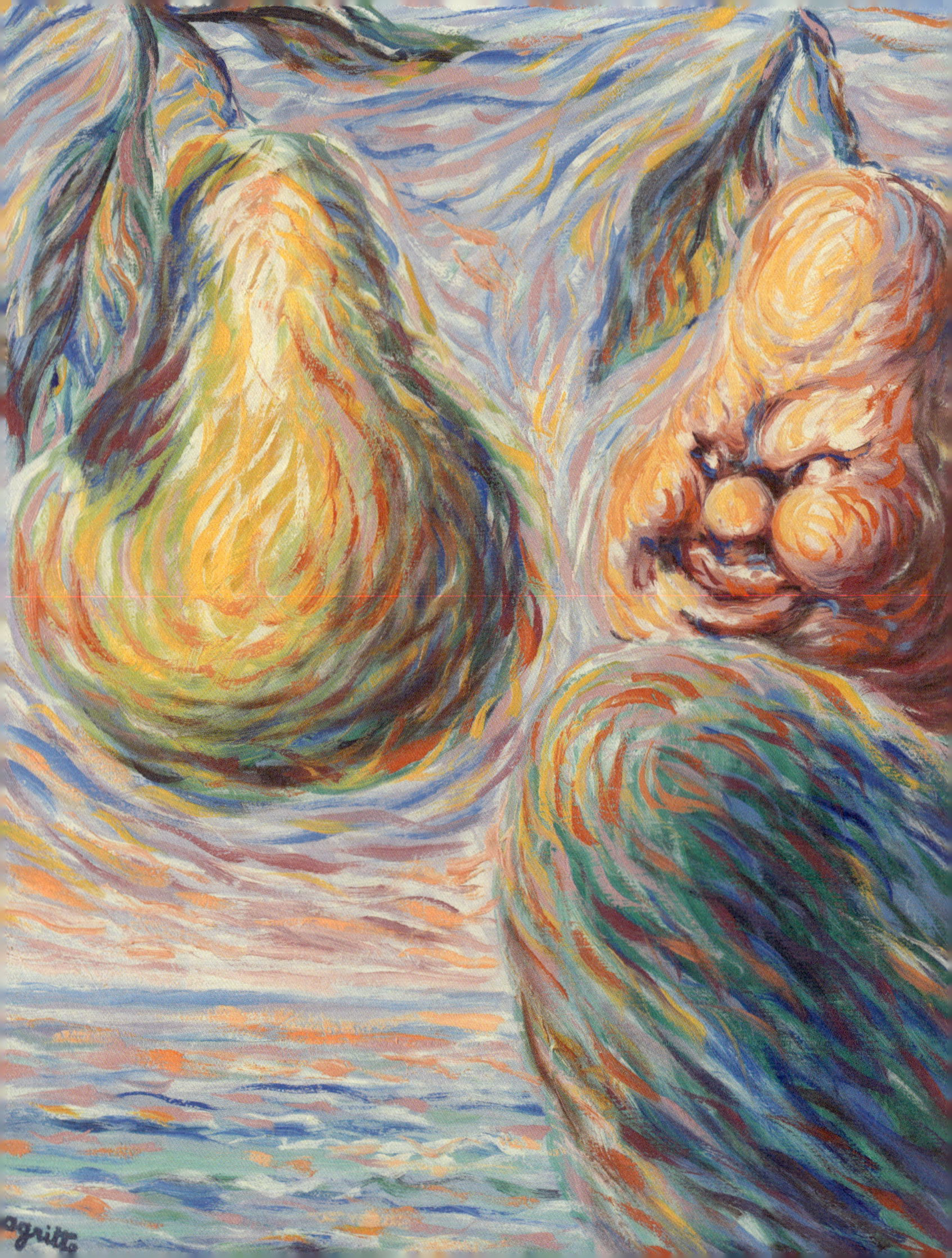
agritte

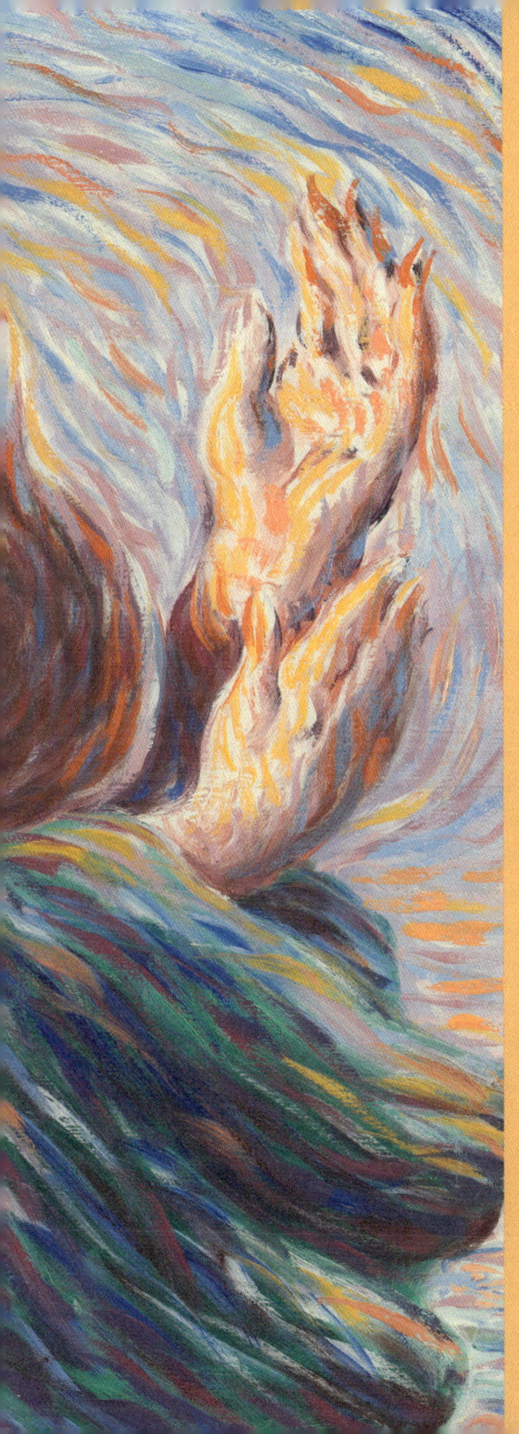

Sunlit Surrealism

1943–1947

In 1937, Magritte painted *The Black Flag* [181], eerily foreshadowing the bombardments to come. He referred to the painting in a letter to André Breton in June 1946: 'I painted a picture, "The Black Flag", which gave a foretaste of the terror that would result from flying machines and I am not proud of it. That and the need for change that is not necessarily to be considered as "progress" seemed to warrant this "sudden outburst" of a new mood in my pictures and my desire to experience it in real life. To the general mood of pessimism, I opposed the quest for joy, for pleasure.'[24]

In this letter, Magritte justifies the new direction he has taken. From the start of the war, he intended to align himself with '"the bright side" of life'.[25] In reaction to the German offensive, he armed himself with his paintbrush. Rather than being active politically, beginning in 1943, his engagement was reflected in his paintings. That year, Magritte broadened his repertoire of pleasing and enchanting subjects. At the centre of warm, colourful compositions, often featuring flowers, are pearl-women, whose facial contours are composed of pearls (the 'Sheherazade' series [255, 272]), musicians and dancers (*The First Day*, 1943 [223]), animals with human features (*The Meteor*, 1944 [233]; *The Civilizer*, 1944 [237]), fortress-forests (*A Previous Life*, 1944 [234]), curious trees and laughing fruit (*Alice in Wonderland*, 1946 [248]), sleeping mermaids (*The Forbidden Universe*, 1943 [231]), and so on.

The feeling of optimism that emanates from these new images is sustained by a radical change in style. Magritte put aside the meticulously smooth brushwork that had enabled him to depict objects with almost photographic realism and turned to an Impressionist technique. For the first time, the gesture of his brush is visible in the myriad comma-shaped strokes that energise the composition. The range of colours also changed, with luminous warm tones replacing the cold and sometimes drab palette of previous works.

Treatise on Light (1943) [220] is the first painting in this new 'Impressionist' style. It is a direct reference to *The Bathers* (1918–19) by Auguste Renoir (1841–1919), which accounts for the name 'Renoir Period' that was used to designate this new style, but

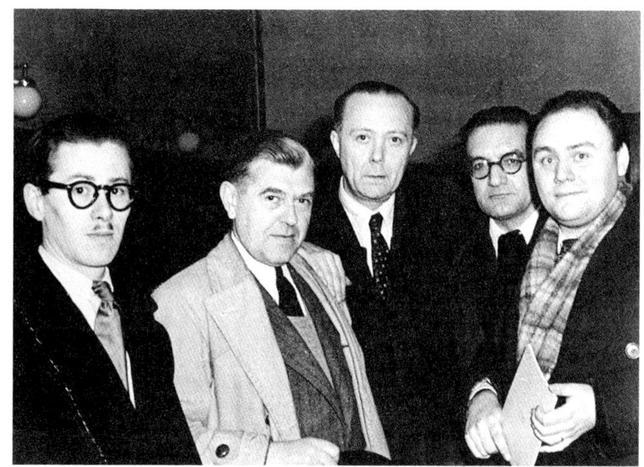

Left to right: Marcel Mariën, René Magritte, Louis Scutenaire, Paul Nougé and Noël Arnaud. Congrès des écrivains et artistes communistes, Antwerp, November 1947.

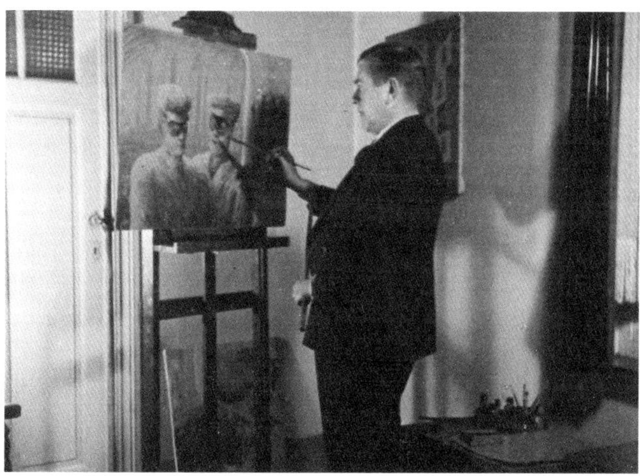

René Magritte painting *Intelligence*, Brussels, 1946.

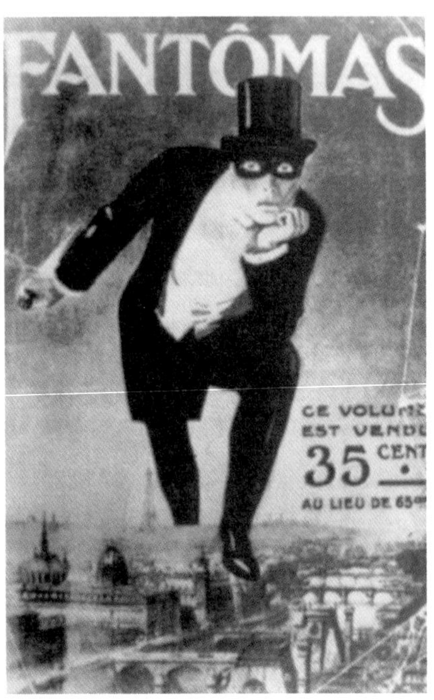

Cover of Pierre Souvestre and Marcel Allain's *Fantômas*, 1911.

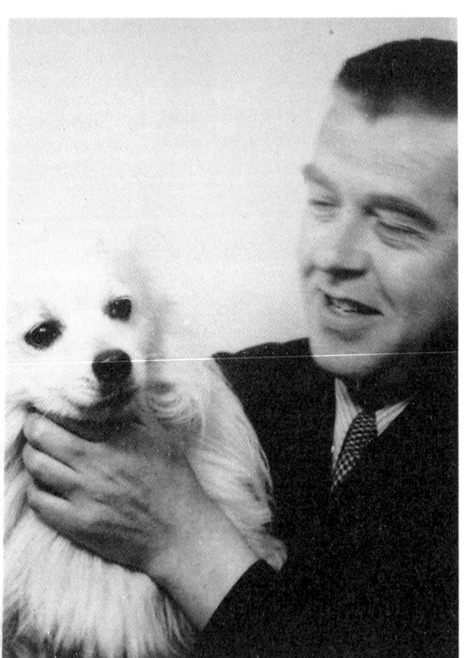

René Magritte and his dog, 1946.

    Sunlit Surrealism

which Magritte himself preferred to refer to as 'Sunlit Surrealism'. Renoir is not the only painter to whom Magritte referred in those years. He also executed *Monsieur Ingres's Good Days* (1943) [230], an Impressionist variant of *The Spring* (1820–56) by Jean-Auguste-Dominique Ingres (1780–1867). Magritte's references also came from popular culture. *The Flame Rekindled* (1943) [226] reuses the cover of the first novel in the 'Fantômas' series (1911). One detail is different, however: the dagger in Fantômas's hand is replaced by a rose, rendering that most formidable of criminals harmless.

In the works of this period, Magritte was implementing more than a simple transposition into Impressionist language; he was pursuing his investigation of language and the problem of objects. There are many examples. *The Blaze* (1943) [222] depicts a forest of leaf-trees in bright shimmering colours, the solution he had found to the problem of the tree and developed eight years earlier in *The Giantess* (1935) [149]. *A Previous Life* (1944) [234] again responds to the problem of the forest by showing a group of trees sculpted into the shape of a castle. *Vertigo* (1943) [225] returns to the series of word-pictures and echoes the principle developed in *The Phantom Landscape* (1928) [115], again superimposing a word on a figure.

Although Magritte himself was convinced of the importance of this new orientation, as the excerpt from his letter to Breton shows, it did not receive general approval. Except from Paul Nougé and Marcel Mariën, both of whom defended Sunlit Surrealism in several important texts,[26] Magritte received only tepid support. The few semi-clandestine exhibitions organised during the war had little success. However, Magritte saw it as a means of relaunching Surrealism after the war, and he was counting on Breton to back him up. In his letter of June 1946, he explains why he felt it was so important to pursue this path: 'The painting of my "solar period" is obviously in contradiction to many things we were convinced of before 1940. This, I think, is the main explanation of the resistance it has met with. I believe however that we no longer exist to prophesy (our prophecies were always unpleasant, it must be admitted); at the International Surrealist Exhibition in Paris visitors had to find their way around with electric torches. We had this experience during the occupation and it wasn't funny. The confusion and panic that Surrealism wanted to create in order to bring everything into question were achieved much better by the Nazi idiots than by us, and there was no question of avoiding the consequences.'[27]

In order to consolidate this new optimistic impulse that he intended to promote, in October 1946, Magritte wrote a manifesto entitled 'Le Surréalisme en plein soleil', in which he set out his purpose. Among the signatories were his like-minded friends Paul Nougé, Marcel Mariën and Louis Scutenaire. Although the manifesto was ultimately not distributed, its conclusion is enlightening: 'We must not fear the sun's light on the pretext that it has almost always shone only on a world of misery. Mermaids, doors, phantoms, gods, trees – all these objects of the spirit will be restored, with new and attractive traits, to the intense life of bright lights in the isolation of the world of the mind.'[28]

Magritte's attempts to convince Breton were to no avail. Breton expressed virulent disapproval at the *Exposition internationale du surréalisme* held at the Galerie Maeght in Paris in 1947. Nor did the public take to it. Alexander Iolas, Magritte's new dealer in the United States, made it clear that it would be pointless to send him works from this period because they would not sell in America. Compelled to accept the obvious, in 1947 Magritte returned to his earlier smooth, classical style for good. But he kept a memory of his sunny adventure in the lightening of his palette.

24   René Magritte, Letter to André Breton, 24 June 1946, quoted in Magritte, *Écrits complets*, op. cit., p. 200.
25   René Magritte, Letter to Paul Éluard, 4 December 1941, quoted in Sylvester and Whitfield, *René Magritte. Catalogue raisonné*, op. cit., vol. 2, p. 290.
26   See Marcel Mariën, *Magritte* (Brussels: Les Auteurs associés, 1943) and Paul Nougé, *René Magritte ou Les images défendues* (Brussels: Les Auteurs Associés, 1943).
27   René Magritte, Letter to André Breton, 24 June 1946, quoted in Sylvester and Whitfield, *René Magritte. Catalogue raisonné*, op. cit., vol. 2, p. 132.
28   René Magritte, *Le Surréalisme en plein soleil. Manifeste n° 1*. L'expérience continue (Brussels: Le Miroir infidèle, October 1946).

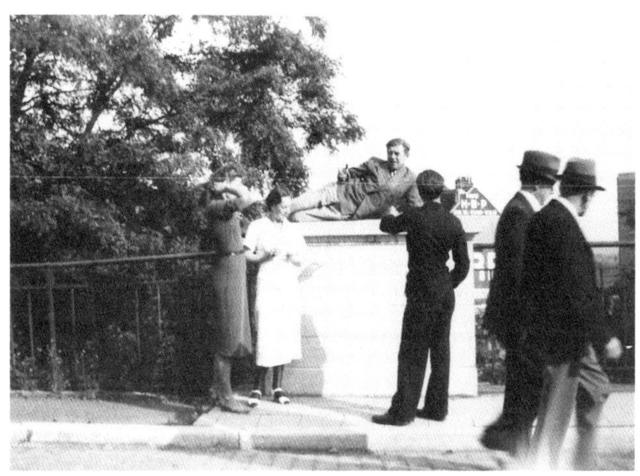

The Soothsayer, Brussels, 1942. Left to right: Betty Magritte, Georgette Magritte, René Magritte and Marcel Mariën.

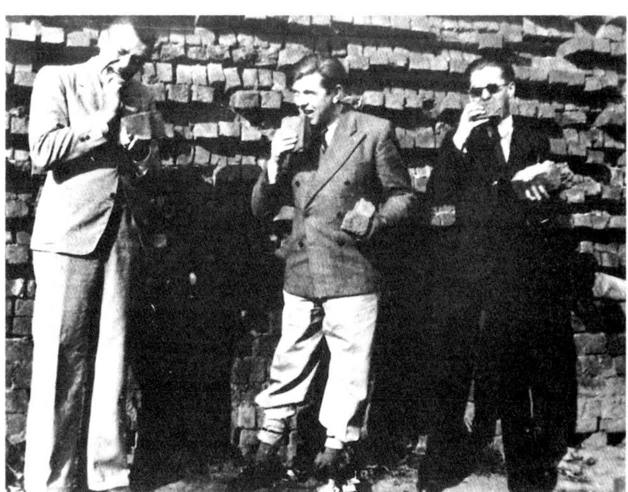

The Feast of Stones, Brussels, 1942. Left to right: Paul Magritte, René Magritte and Marcel Mariën.

1943–1947

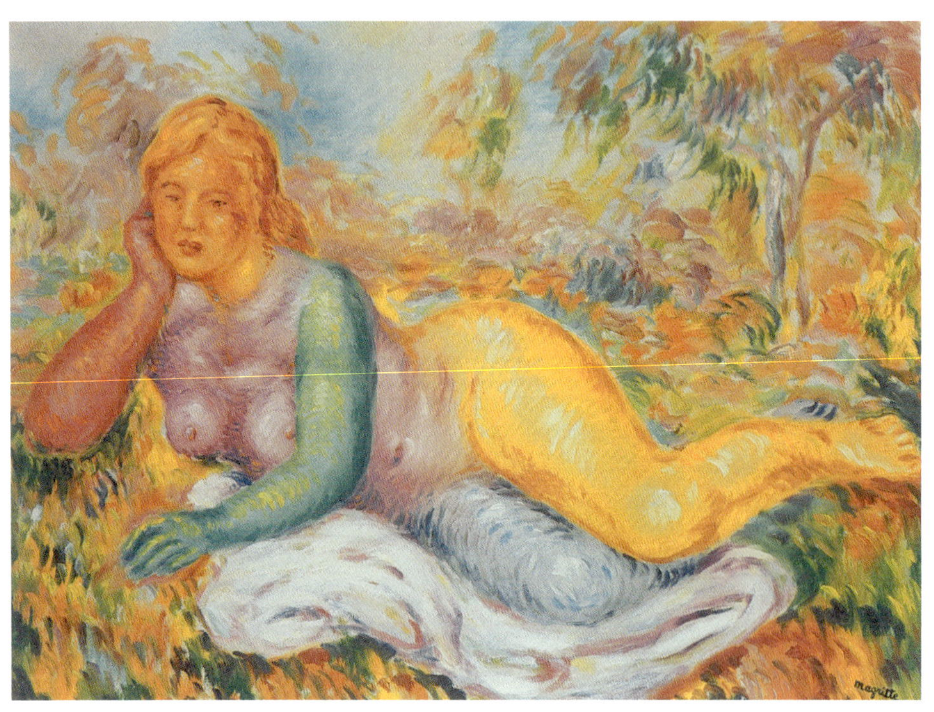

220
Treatise on Light
1943
oil on canvas, 55 × 75.5 cm

Sunlit Surrealism

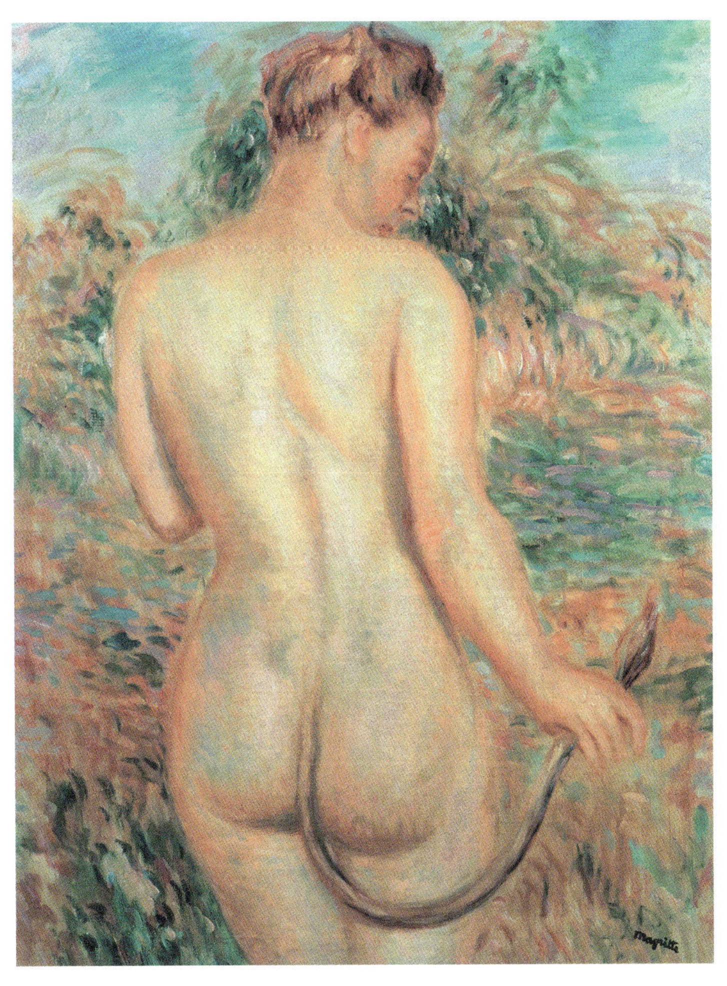

221
The Goad
1943
oil on canvas, 65 × 50 cm

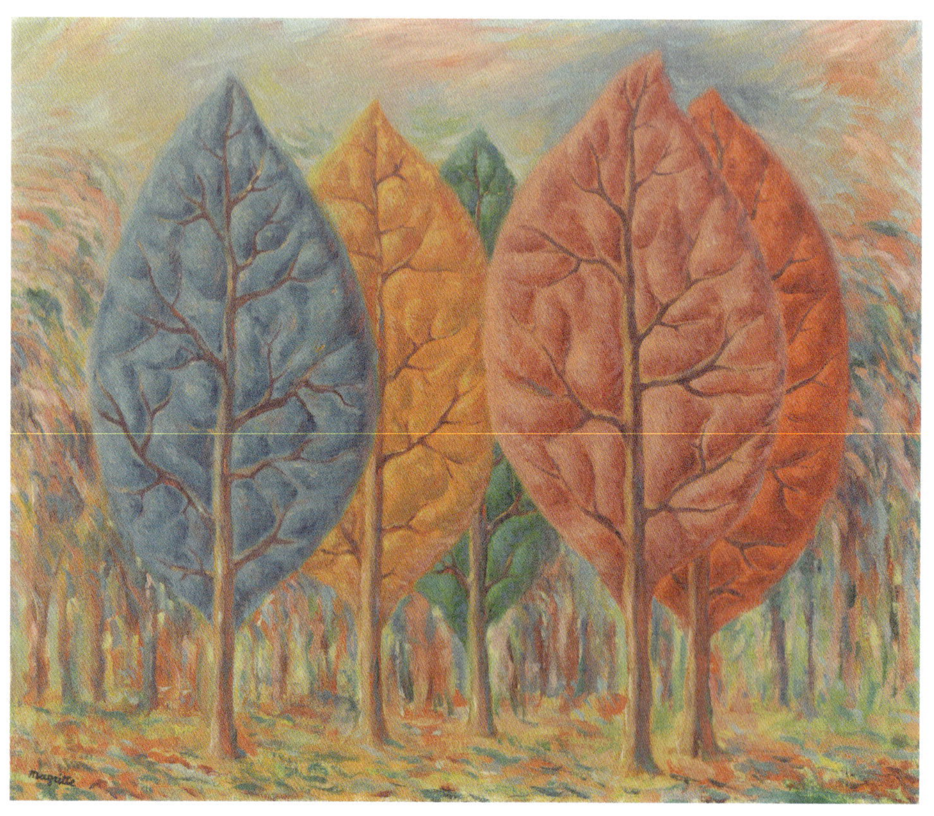

222
The Blaze
1943
oil on canvas, 54 × 65 cm

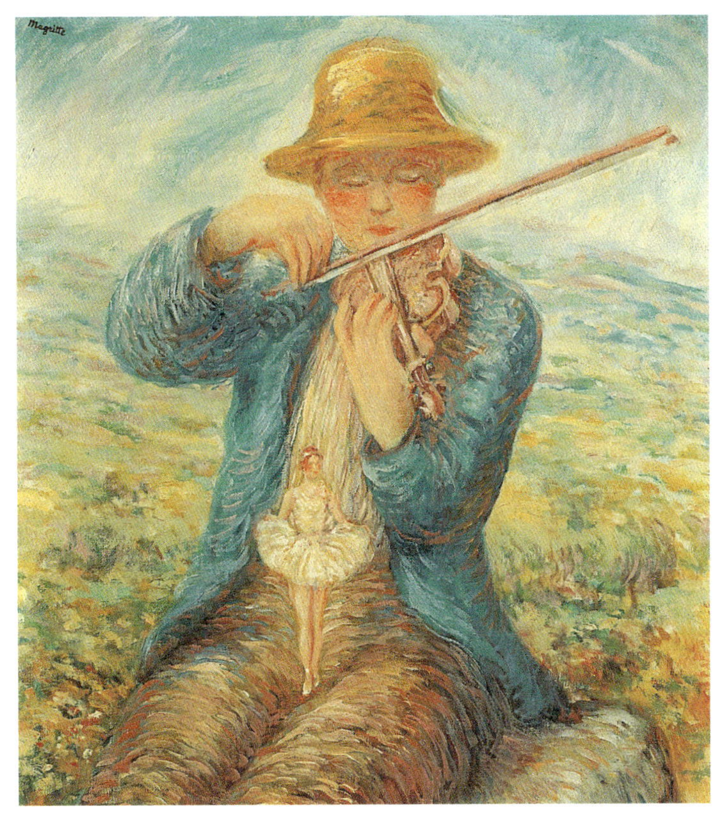

223
The First Day
1943
oil on canvas, 60.5 × 55.5 cm

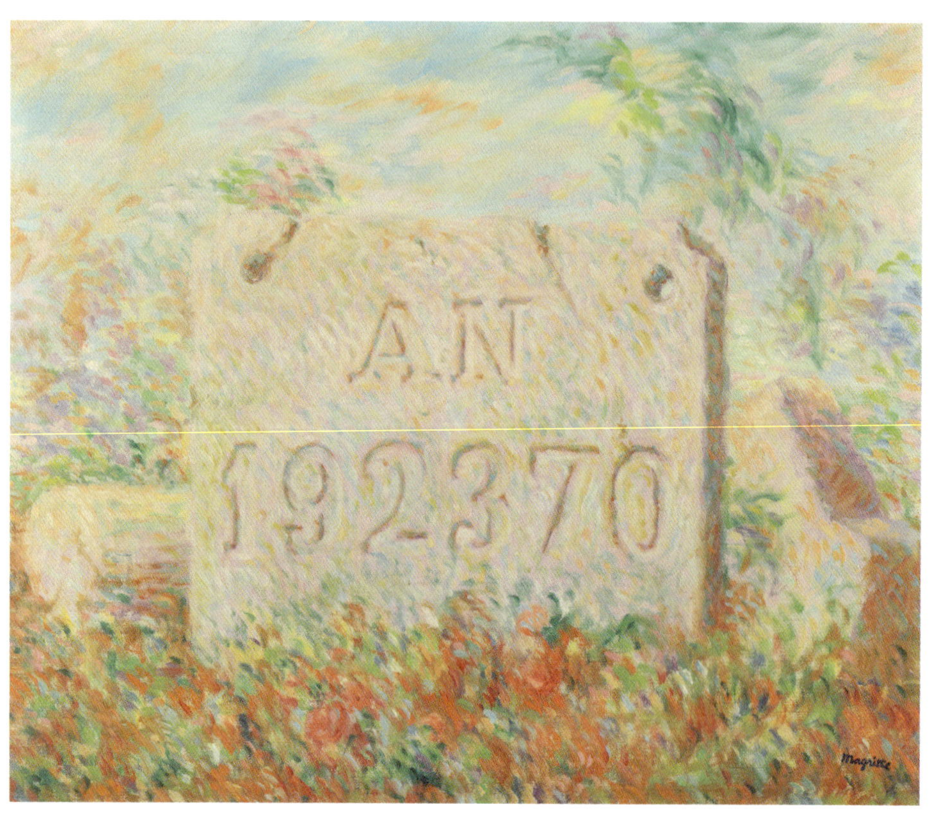

224
The Smile
1943
oil on canvas, 54 × 65 cm

 Sunlit Surrealism

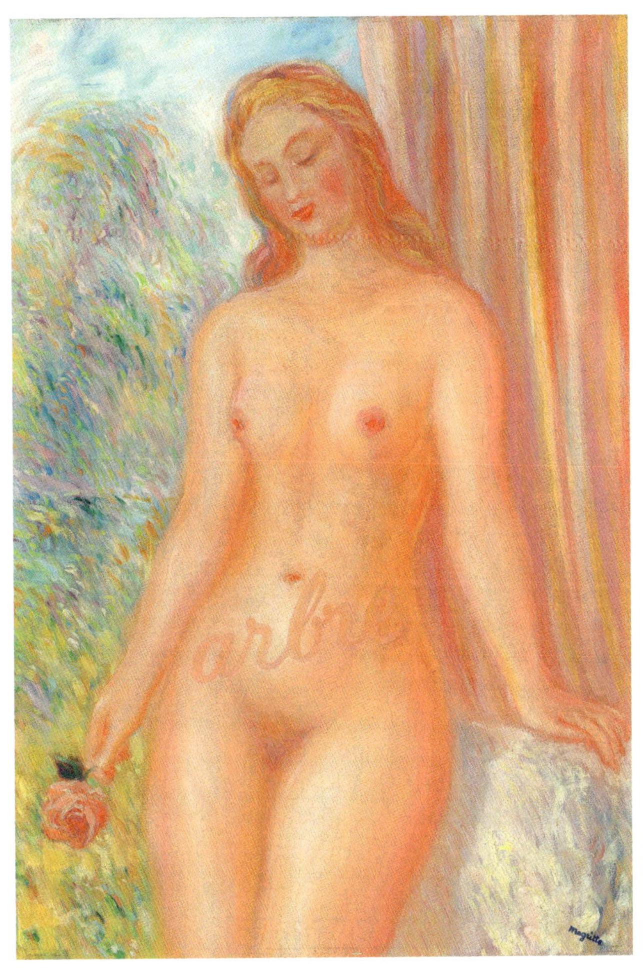

225
Vertigo
1943
oil on canvas, 73 × 50 cm

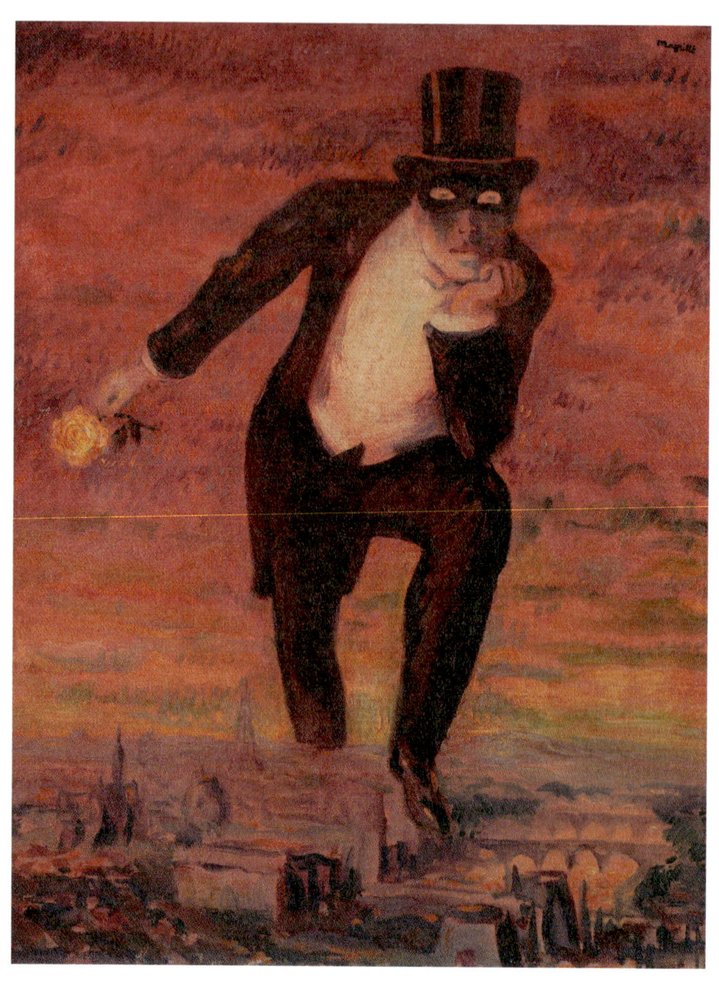

226
The Flame Rekindled
1943
oil on canvas, 65 × 50 cm

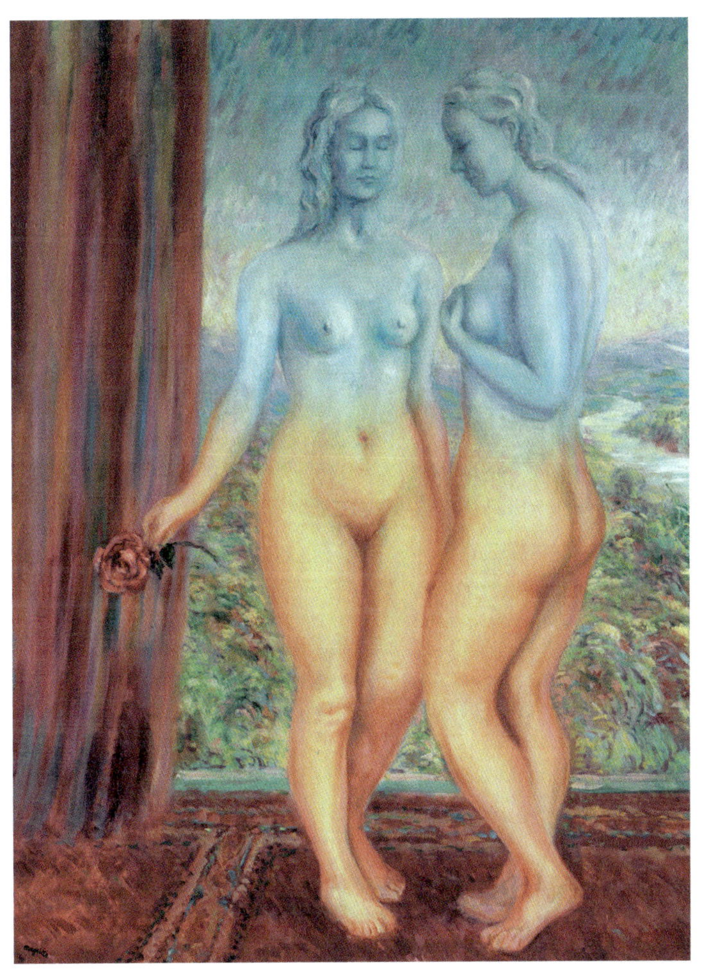

227
The Felicity of Images
1943
oil on canvas, 130 × 97 cm

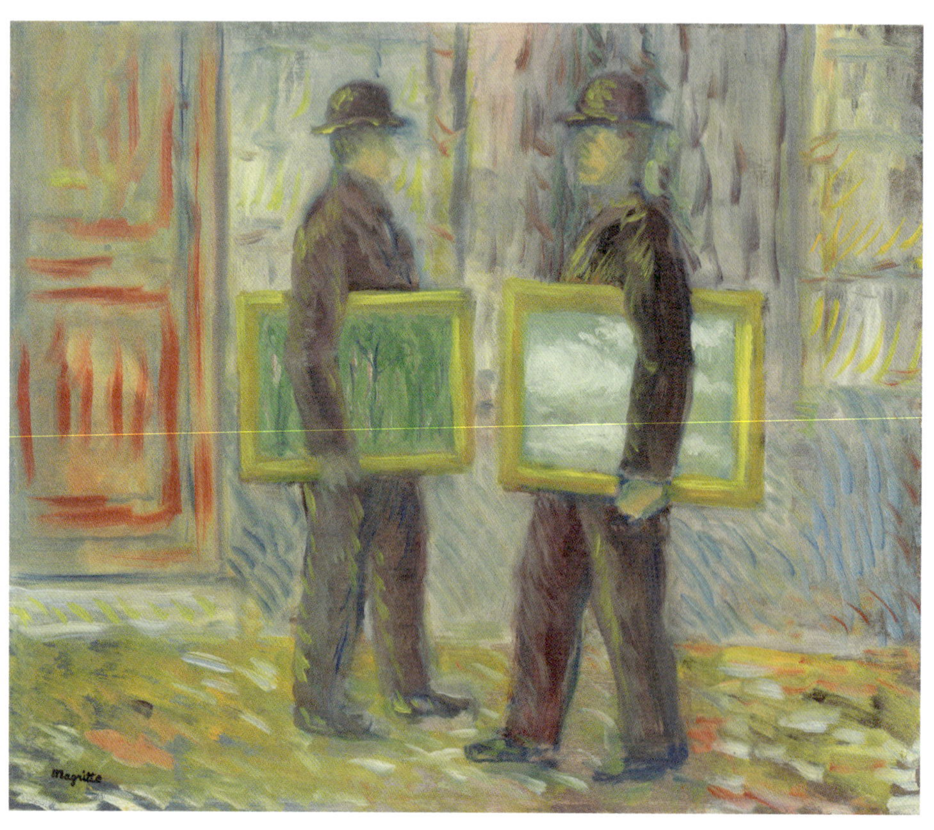

228
The Fifth Season
1943
oil on canvas, 50 × 60 cm

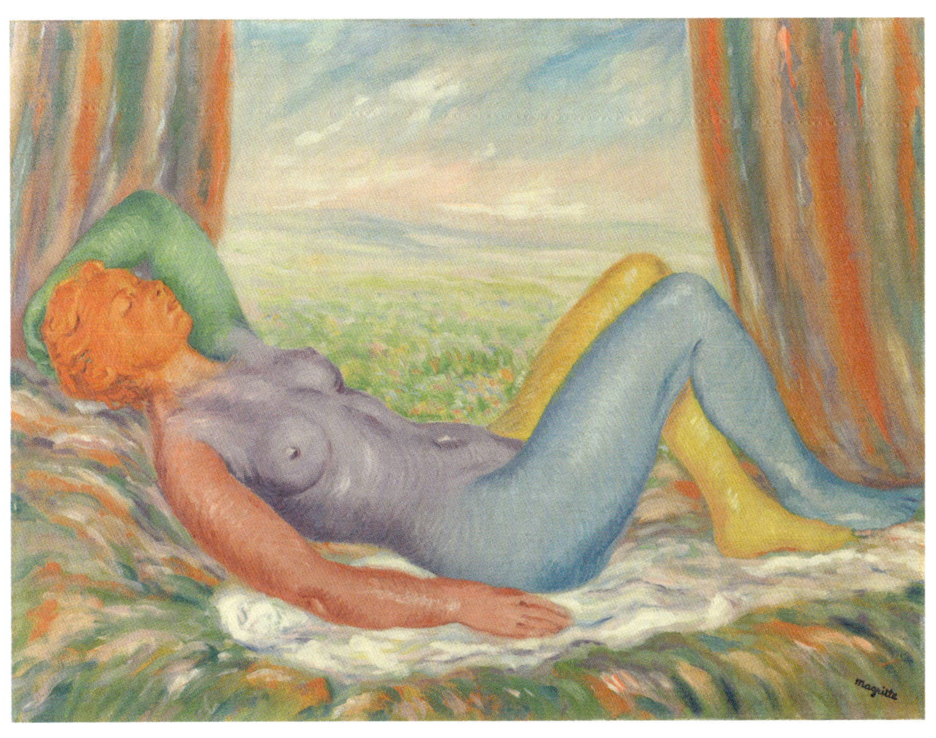

229
The Harvest
1943
oil on canvas, 60 × 80 cm

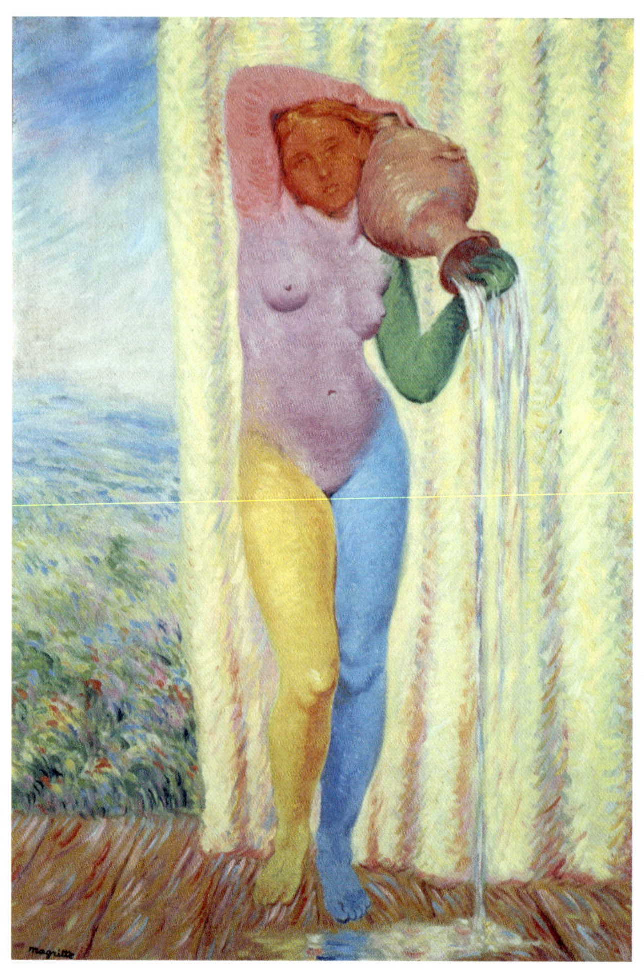

230
Monsieur Ingres's Good Days
1943
oil on canvas, 73 × 50 cm

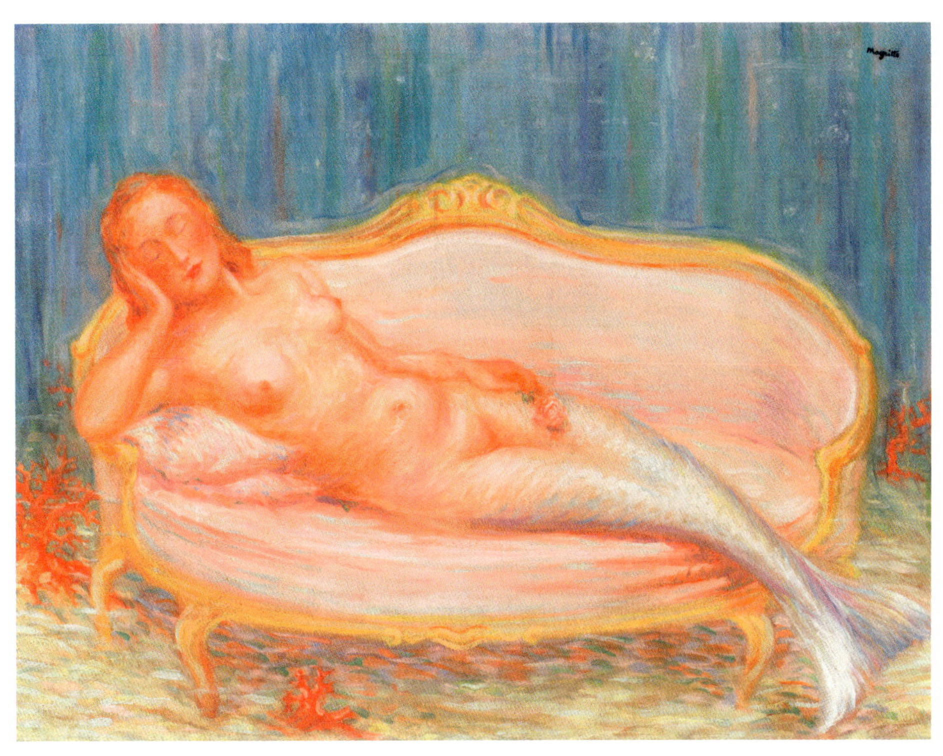

231
The Forbidden Universe
1943
oil on canvas, 60 × 81 cm

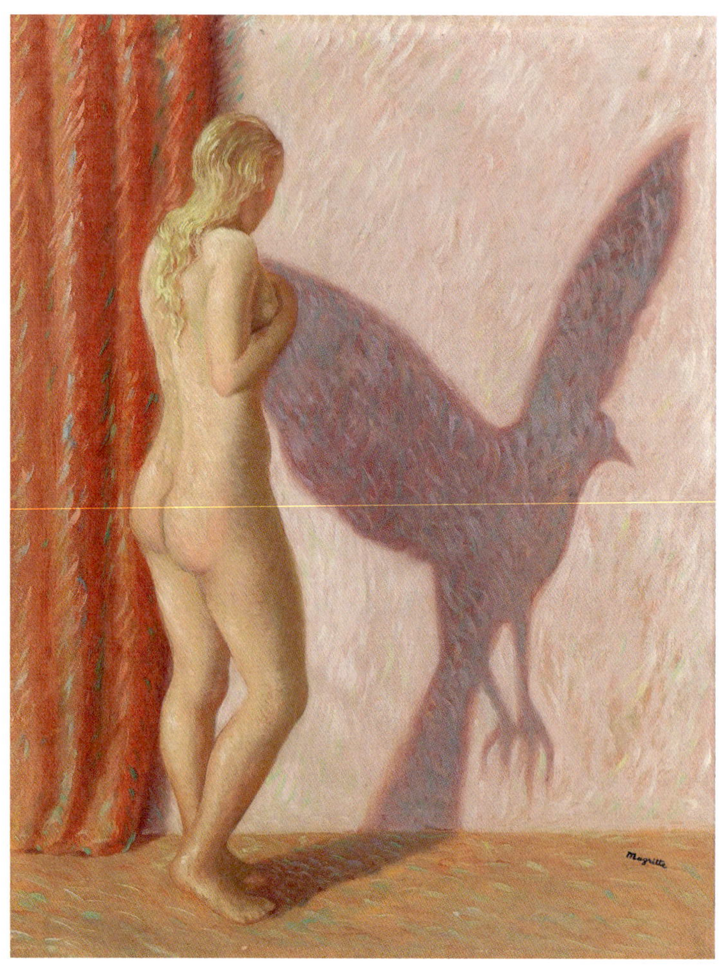

232
The Uncertainty Principle
1944
oil on canvas, 65 × 50 cm

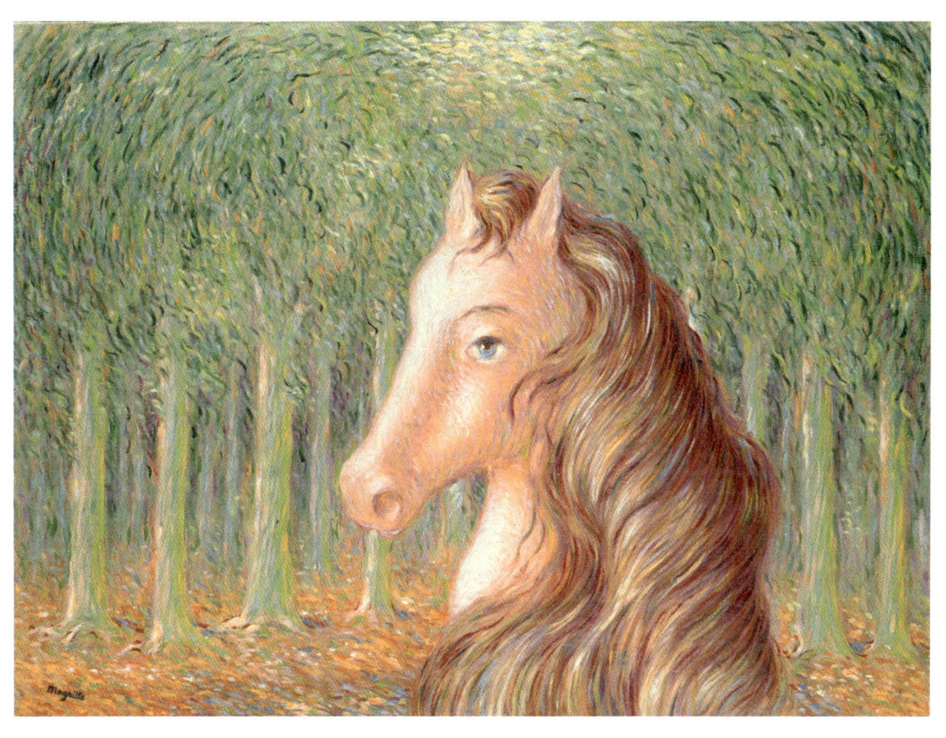

233
The Meteor
1944
oil on canvas, 54 × 73 cm

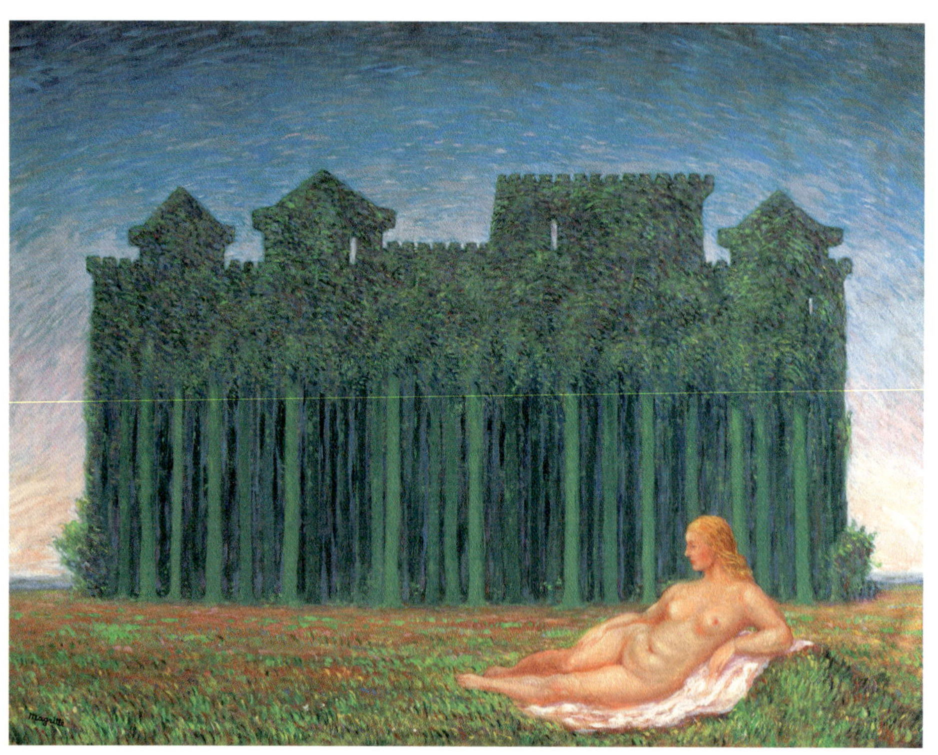

234
A Previous Life
1944
oil on canvas, 60 × 81 cm

Sunlit Surrealism

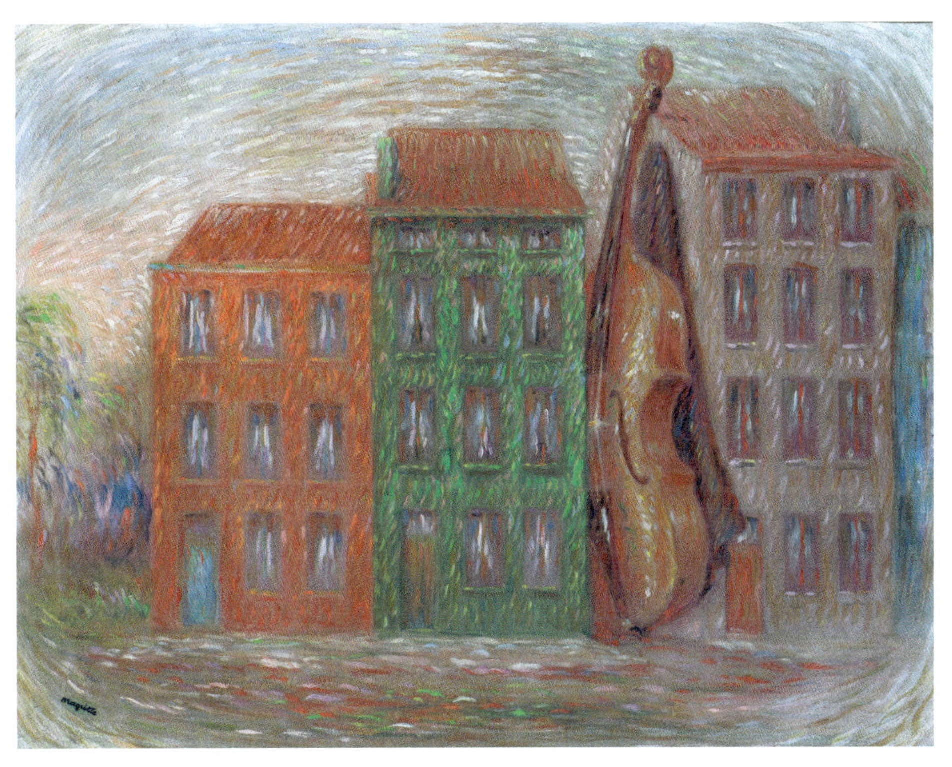

235
Image with a Green House
1944
oil on canvas, 60 × 81 cm

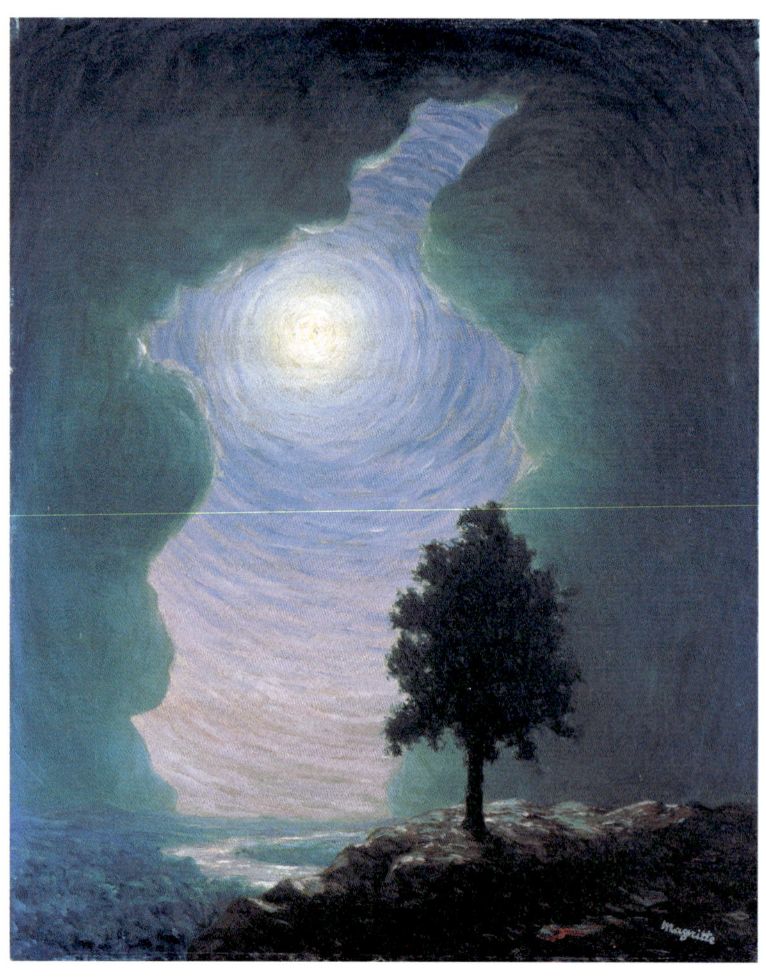

236
The Echo
1944
oil on canvas, 55 × 46 cm

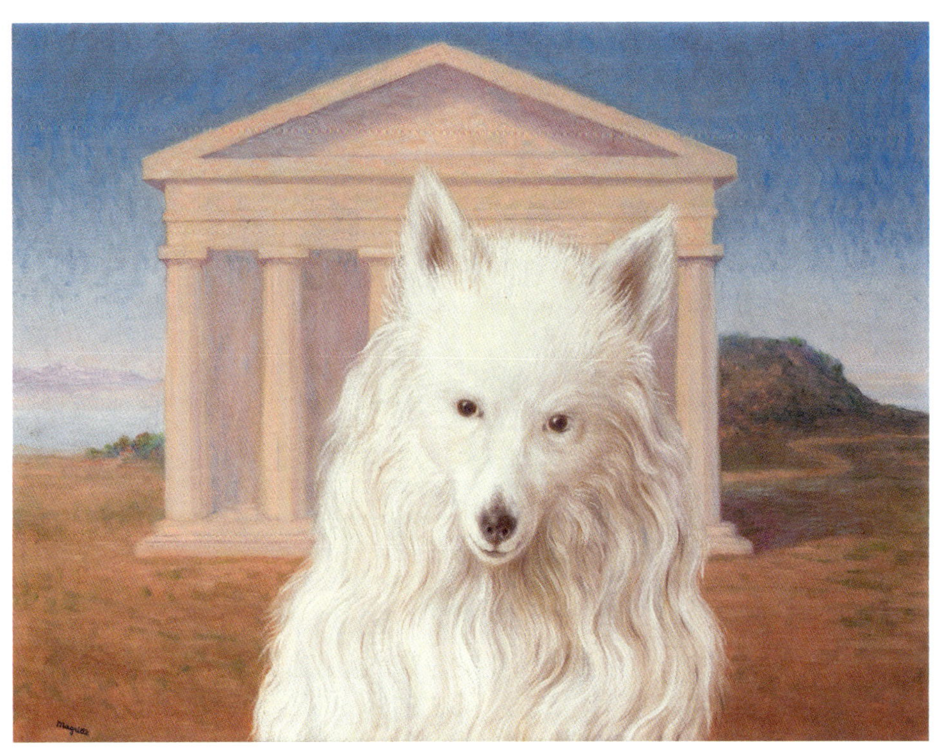

237
The Civiliser
1944
oil on canvas, 60 × 80 cm

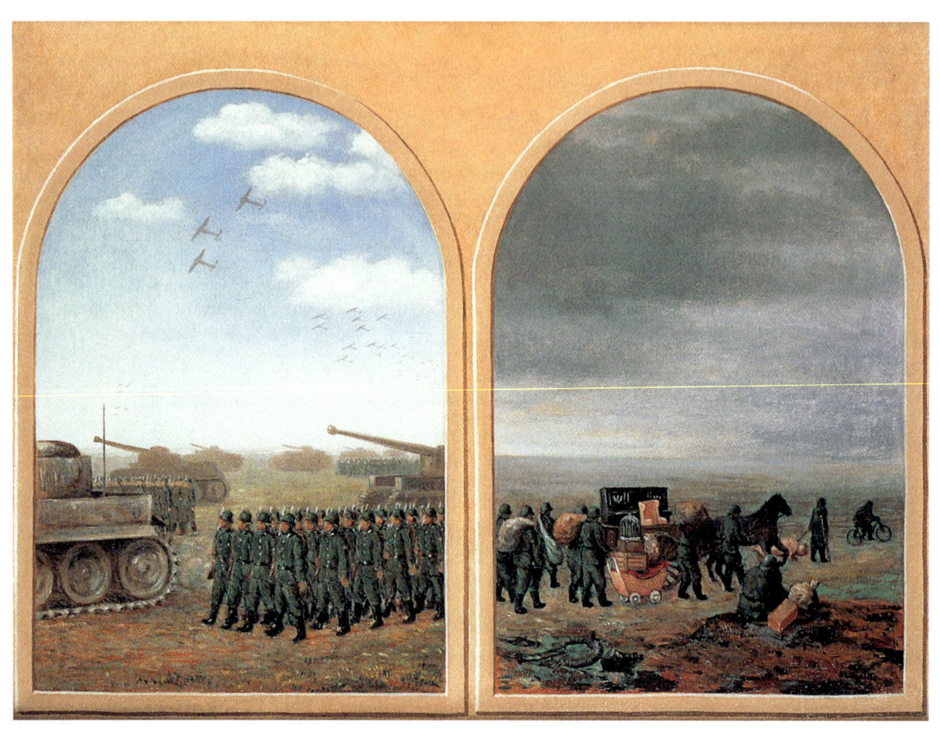

238
Applied Dialectics
1944 or 1945
oil on canvas, 60 × 80 cm

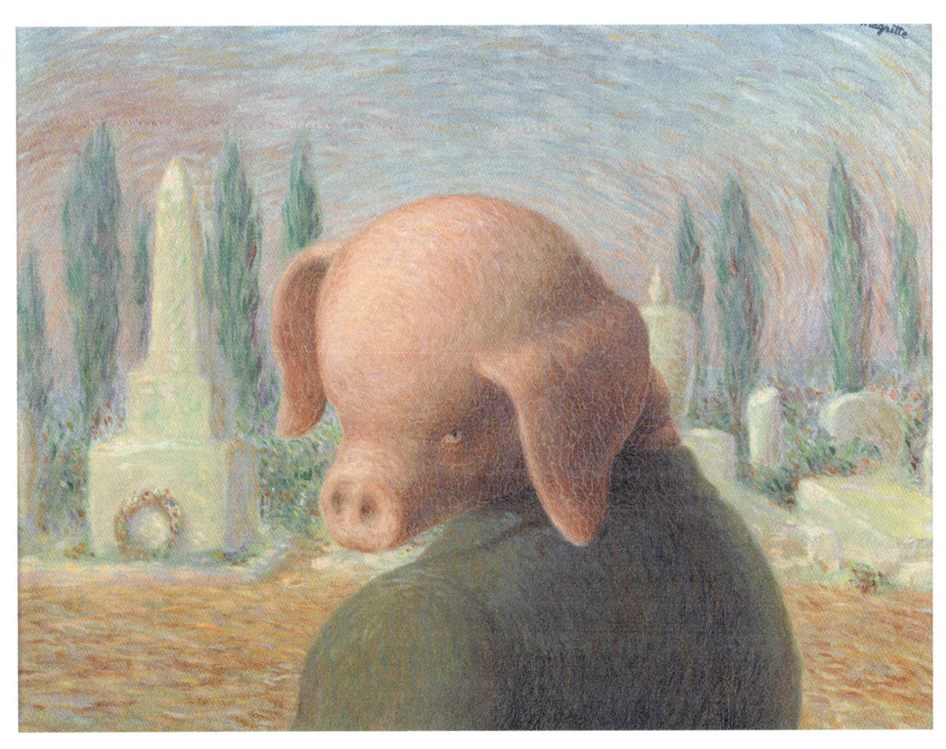

239
A Stroke of Luck
1945
oil on canvas, 60 × 80 cm

1943–1947

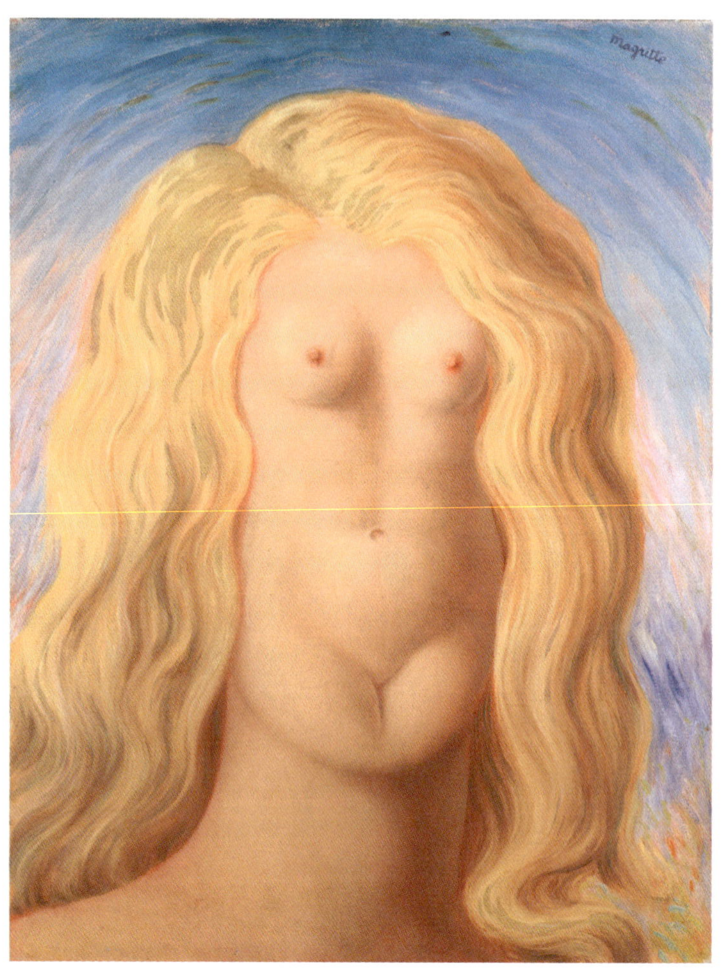

240
The Rape
1945
oil on canvas, 65 × 50 cm

    Sunlit Surrealism

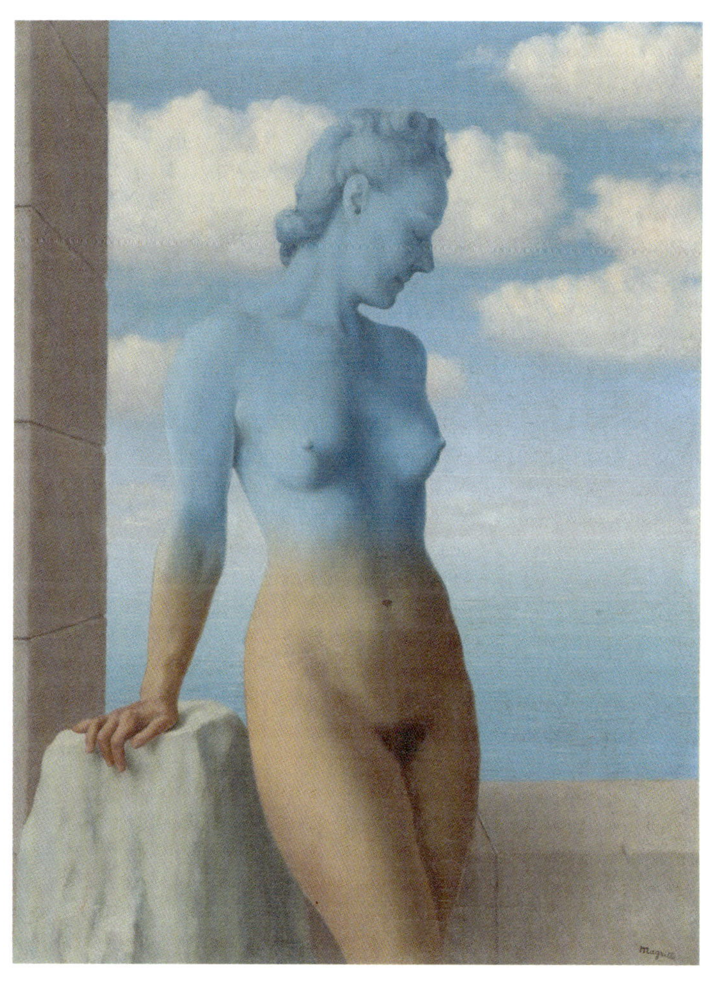

241
Black Magic
1945
oil on canvas, 80 × 60 cm

1943–1947

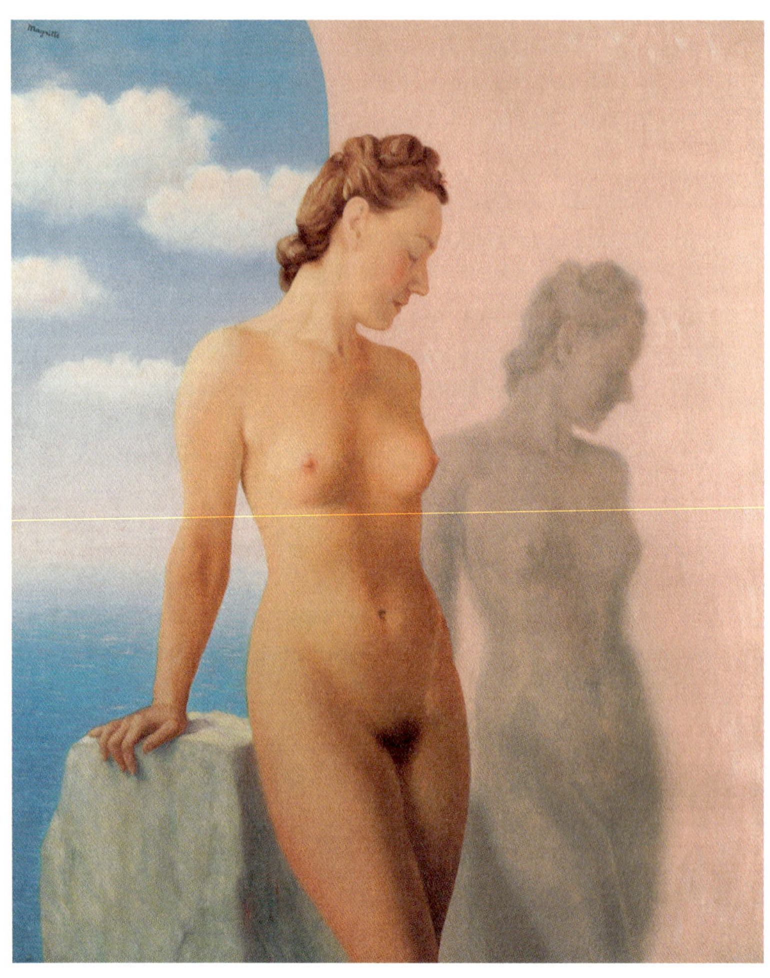

242
The Dream
1945
oil on canvas, 83 × 69 cm

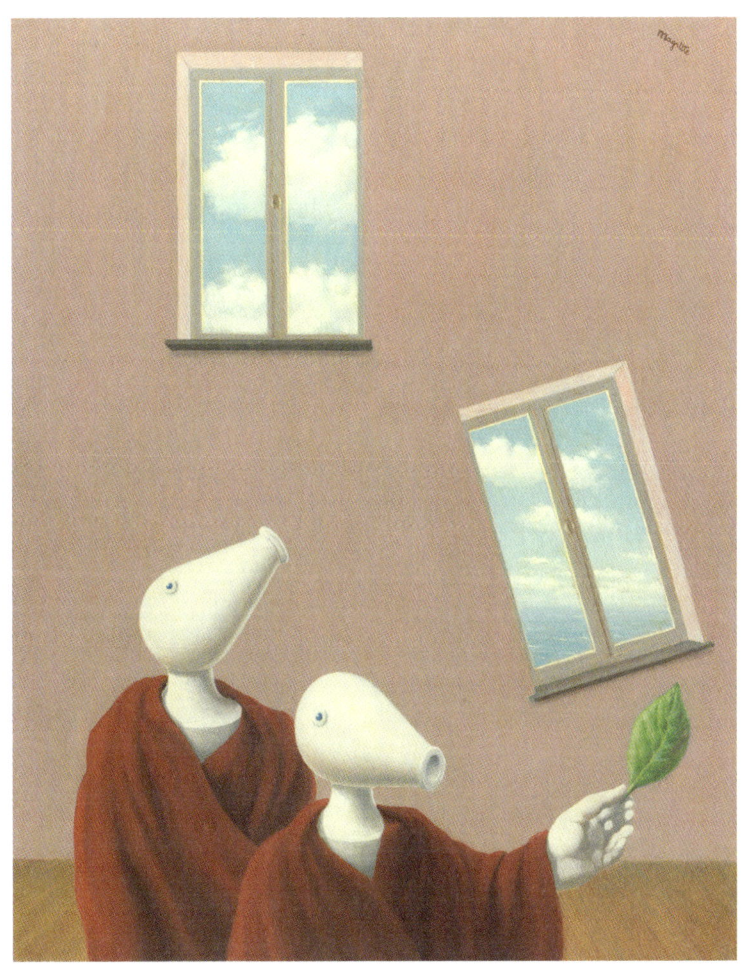

243
Natural Encounters
1945
oil on canvas, 81 × 65 cm

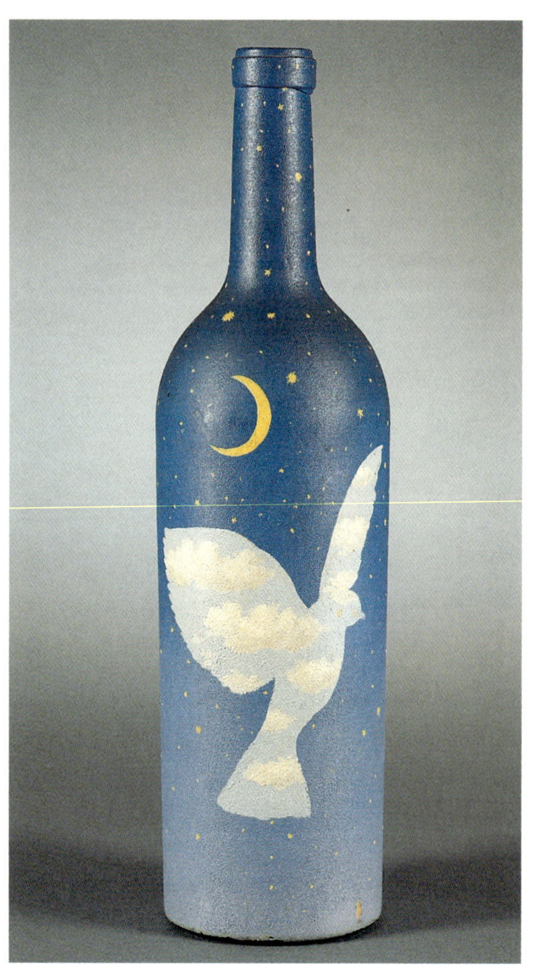

244
Night Sky with Bird
1945
oil on glass bottle, ht. 30.7 cm

 Sunlit Surrealism

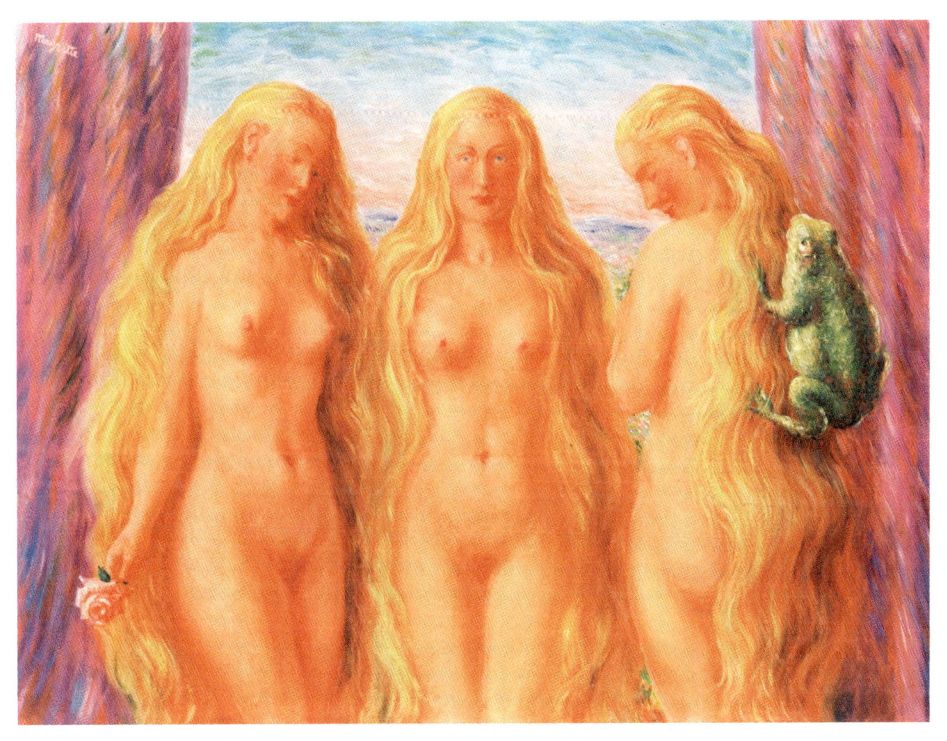

245
The Fire
1945 or 1946
oil on canvas, 60 × 80 cm

1943–1947

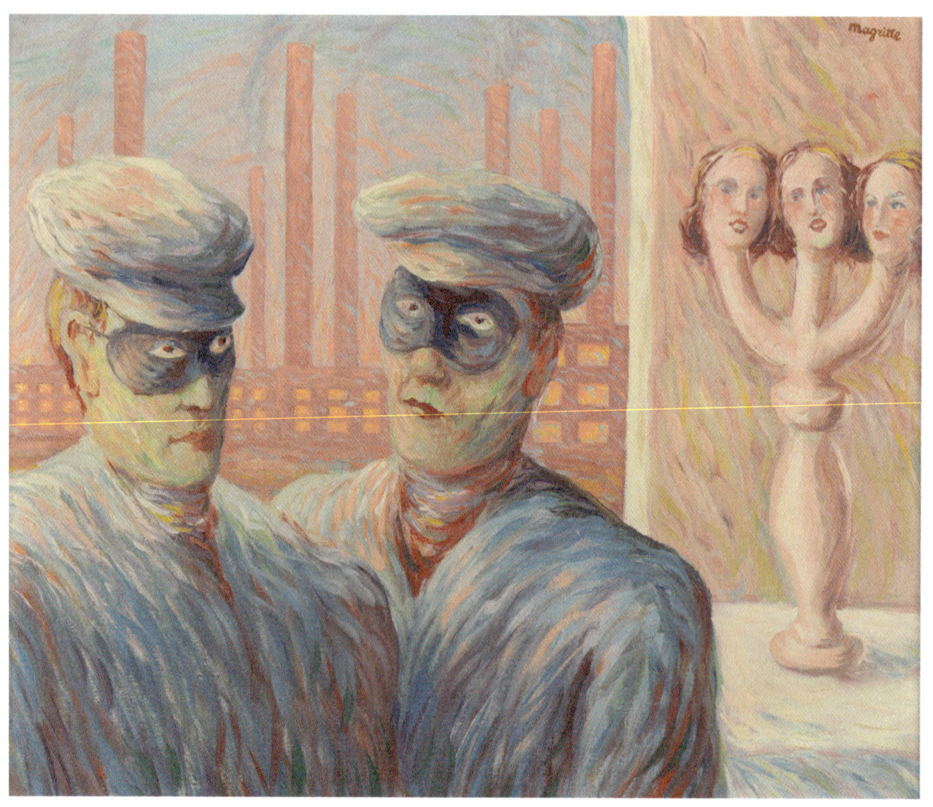

246
Intelligence
1946
oil on canvas, 54 × 65 cm

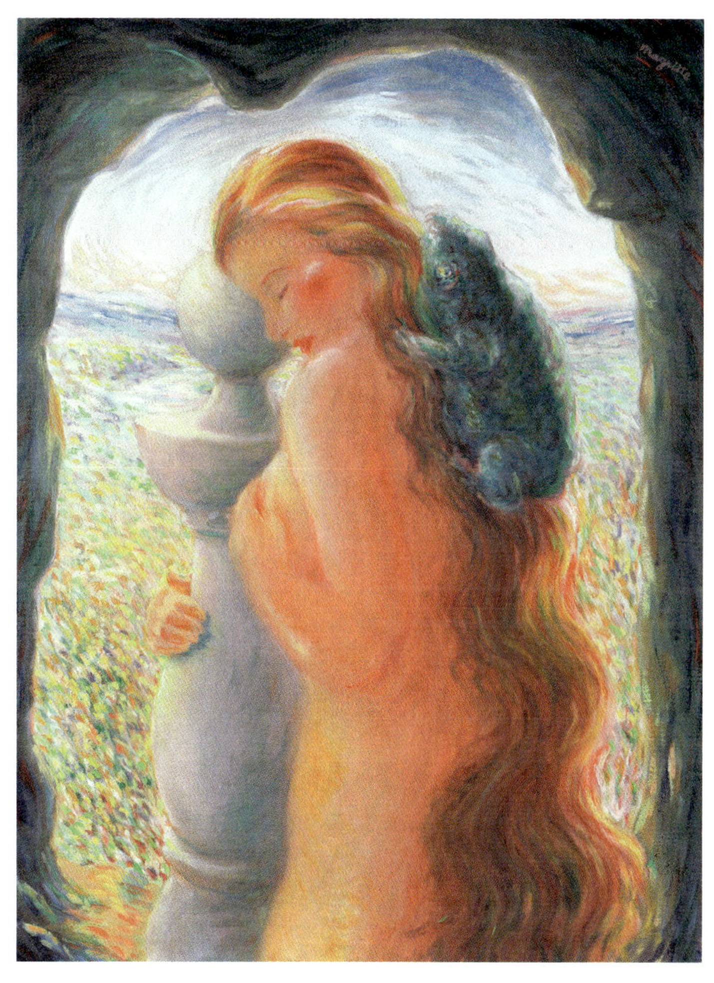

247
The Age of Pleasure
1946
oil on canvas, 80 × 60 cm

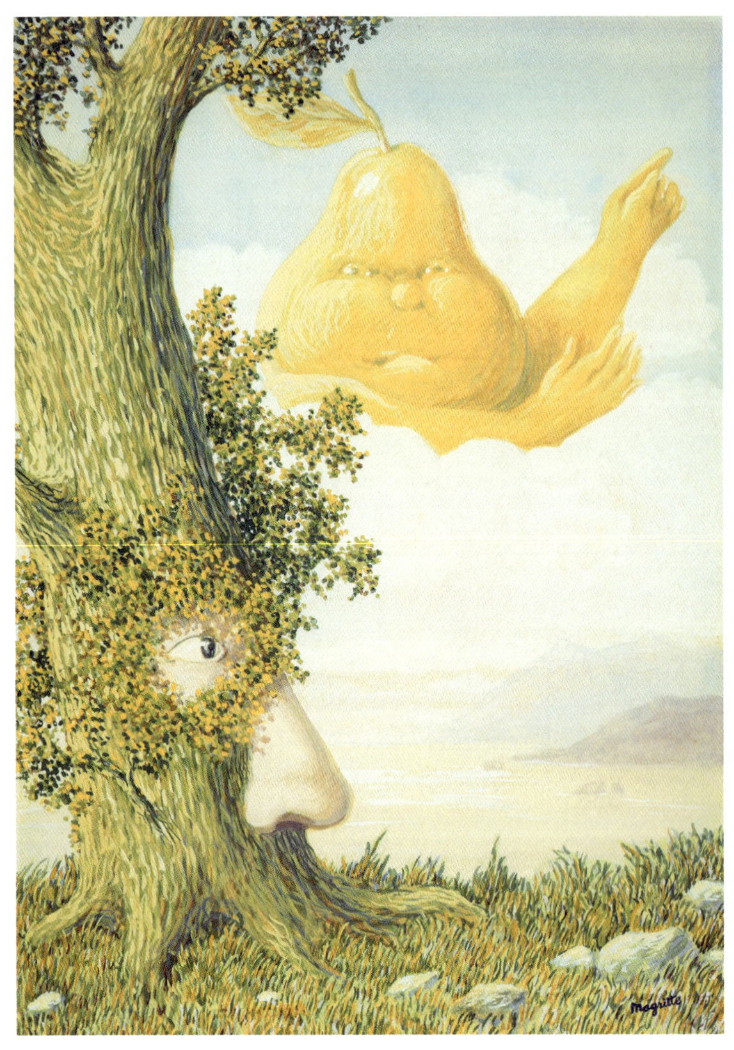

248
Alice in Wonderland
1946
gouache on paper, 48 × 34.7 cm

     Sunlit Surrealism

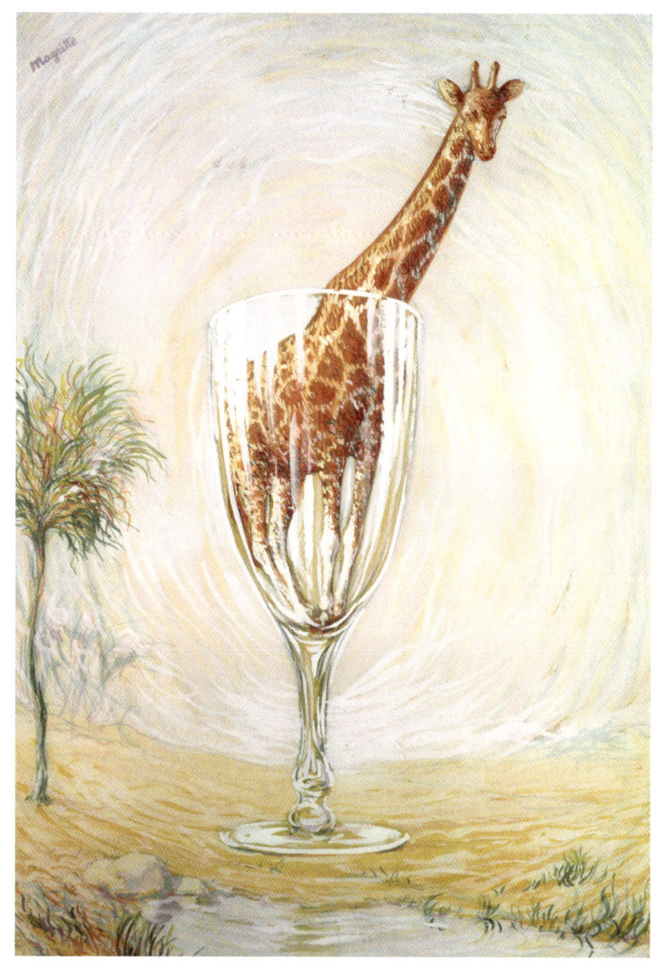

249
The Cut-Glass Bath
1946
gouache on paper, 48.5 × 34 cm

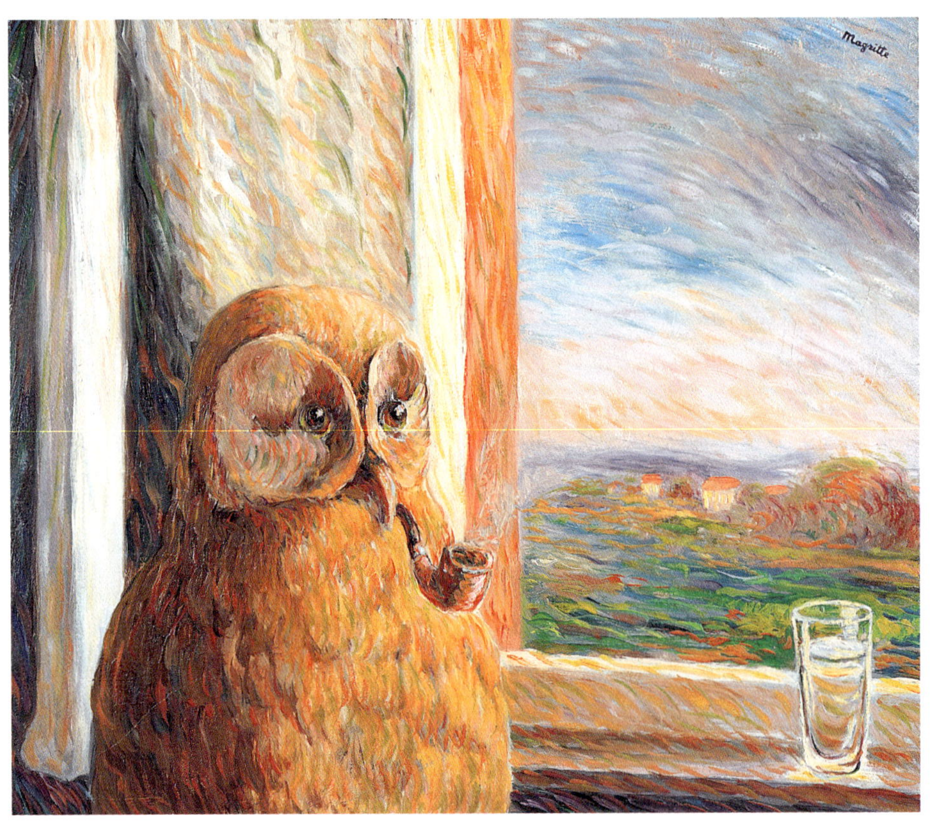

250
The Sleepwalker
1946
oil on canvas, 54 × 65 cm

Sunlit Surrealism

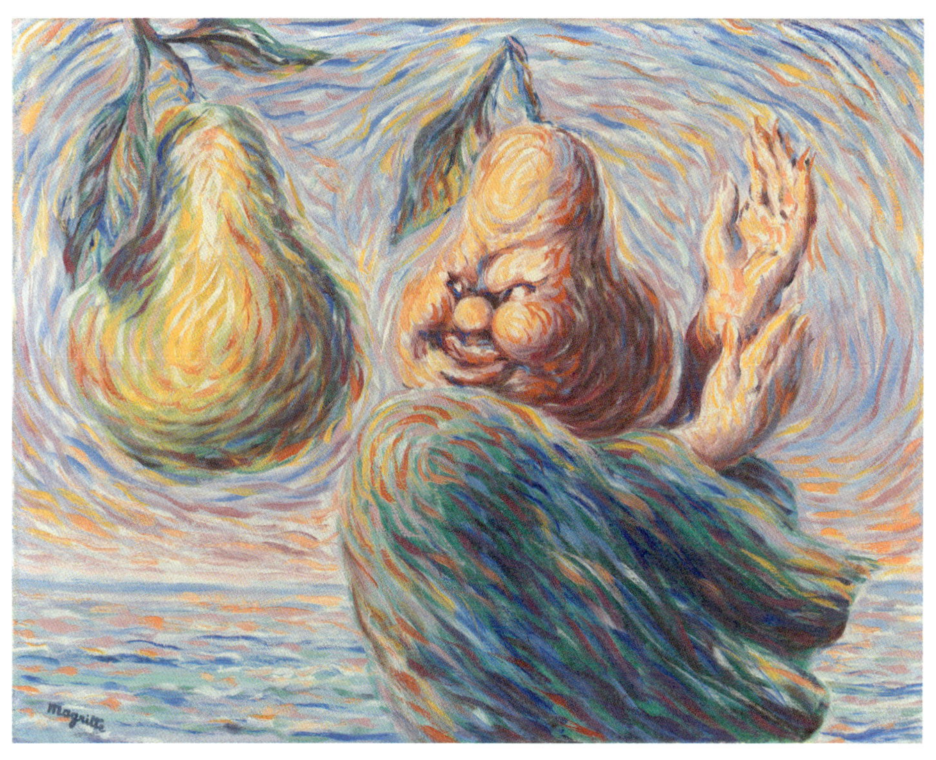

251
Lyricism
1947
oil on canvas, 50 × 65 cm

1943–1947

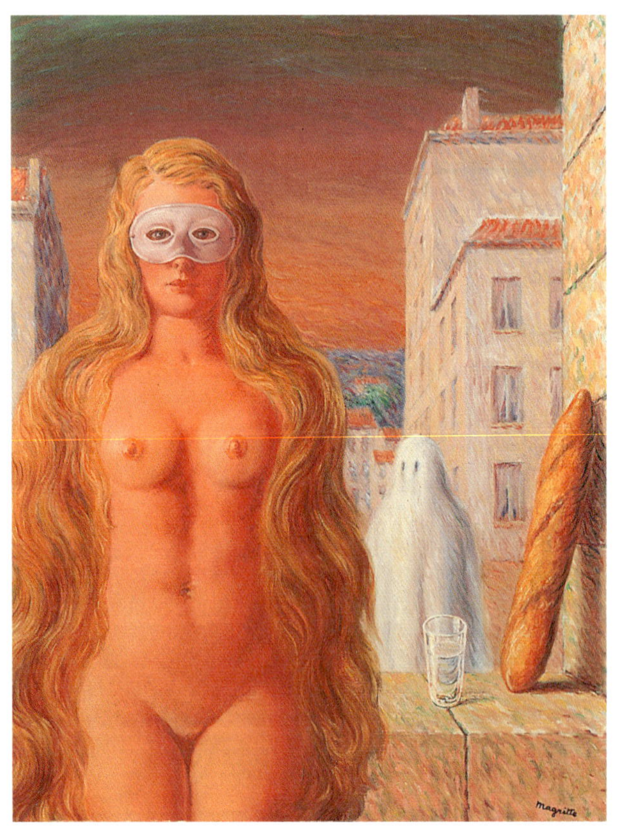

252
The Sage's Carnival
1947
oil on canvas, 65 × 50 cm

     Sunlit Surrealism

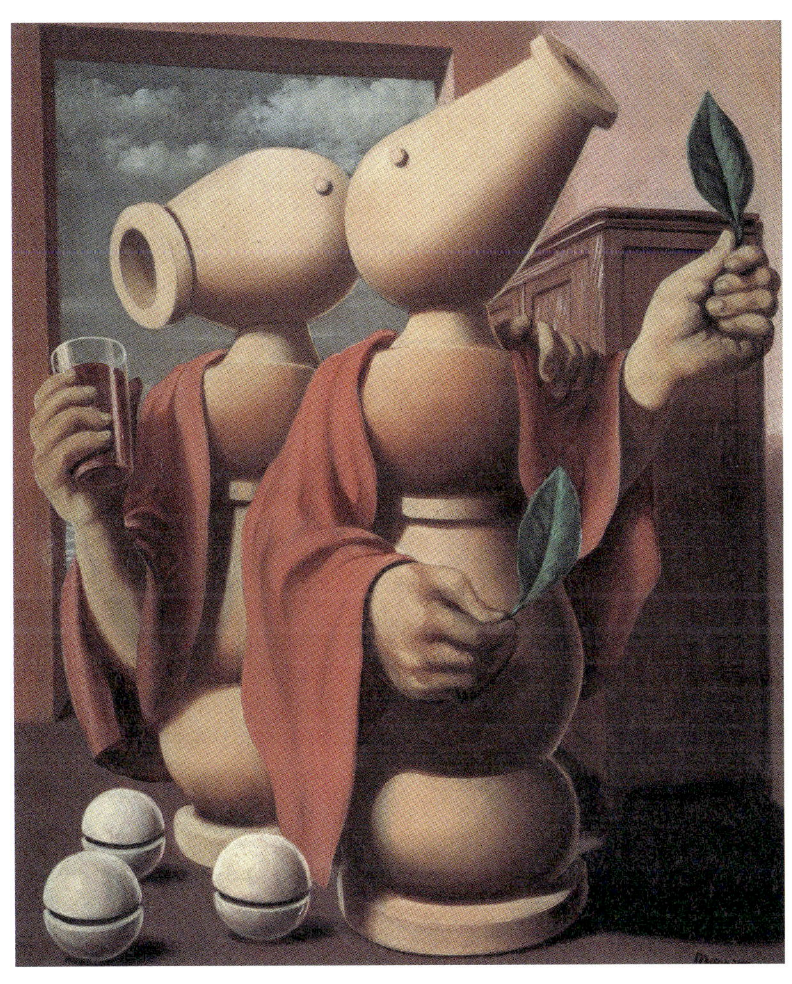

253
The Promised Land
1947
oil on canvas, 60 × 50 cm

     1943–1947

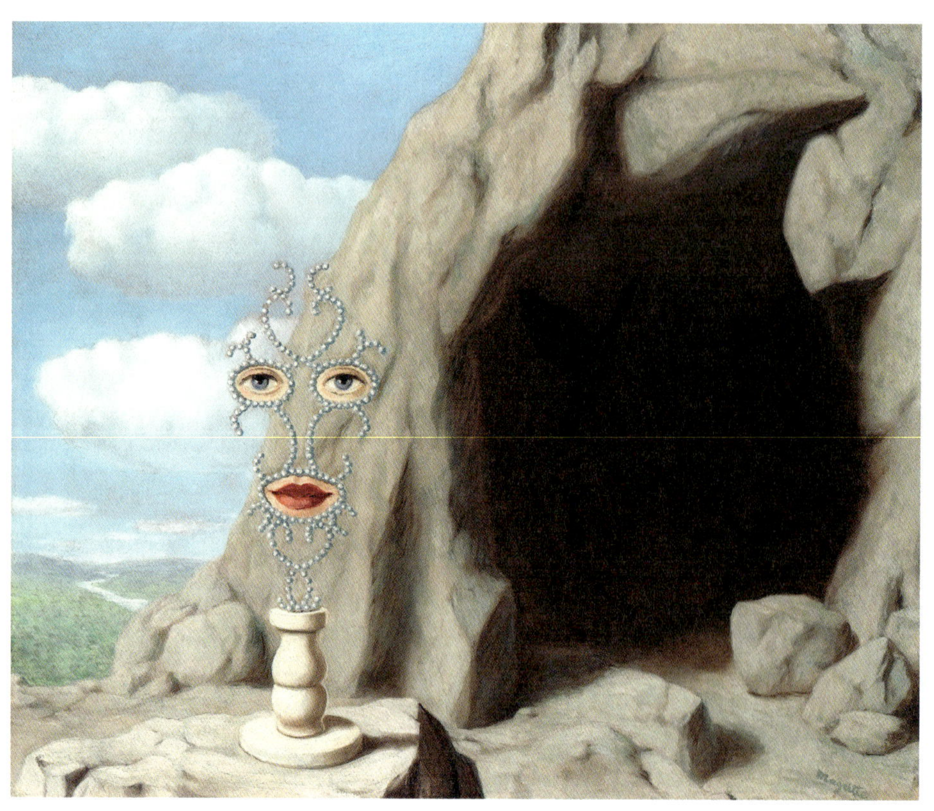

254
High-Level Meetings
1947
oil on canvas, 54 × 65 cm

     Sunlit Surrealism

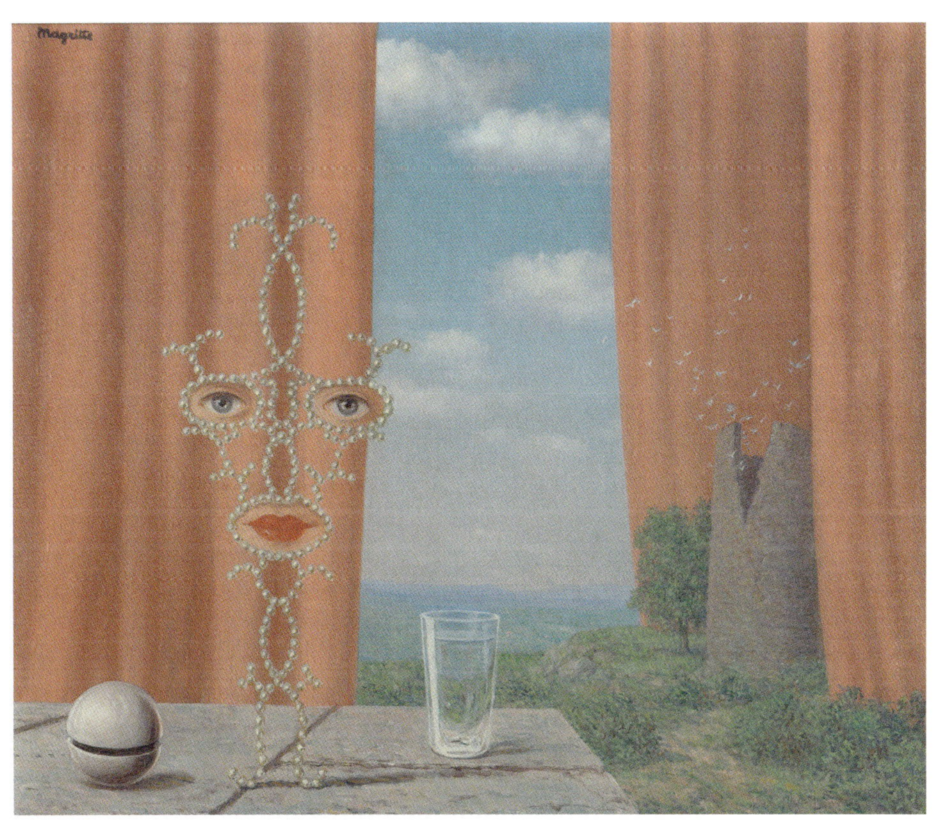

255
Sheherazade
1948
oil on canvas, 50 × 60 cm

                    1943–1947

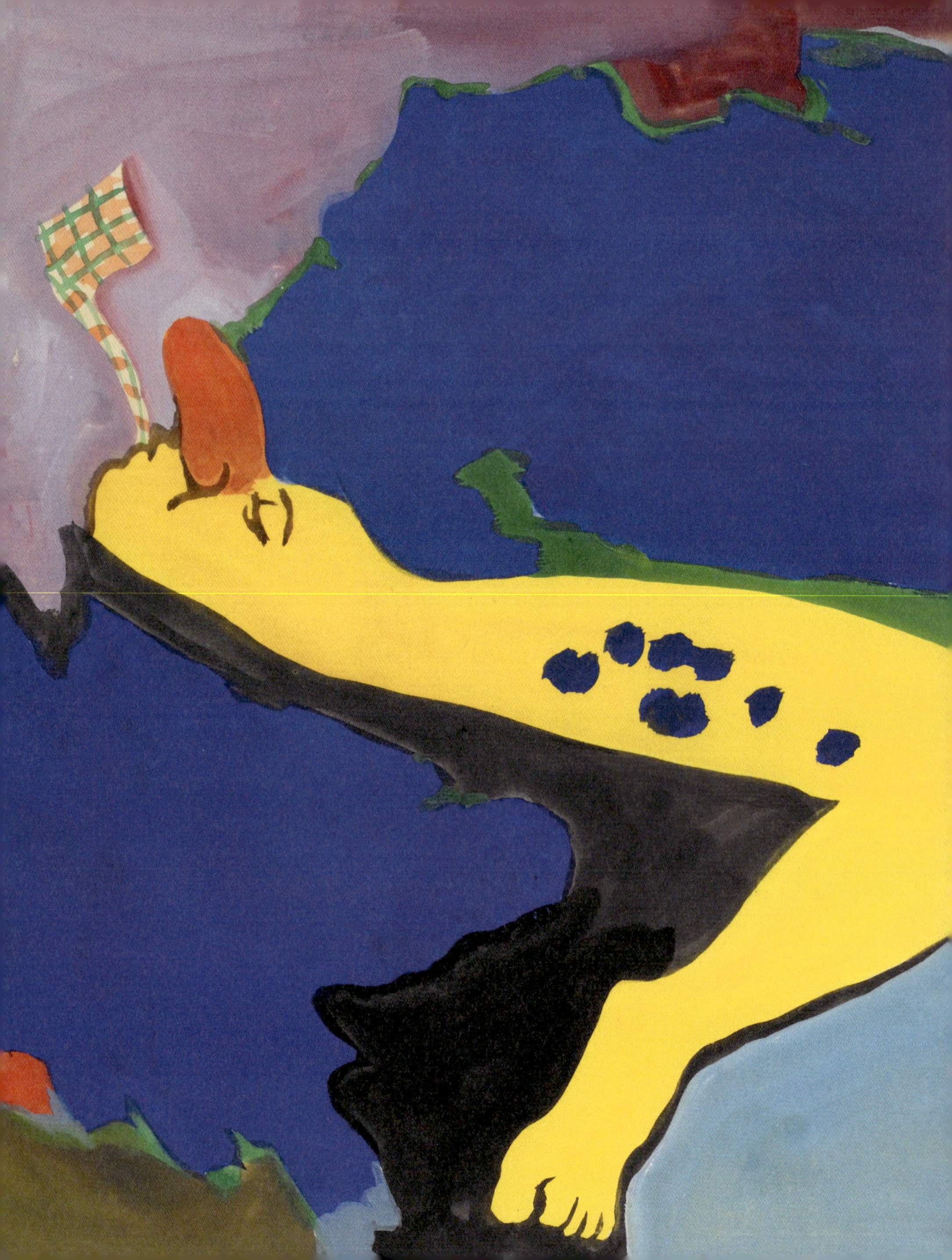

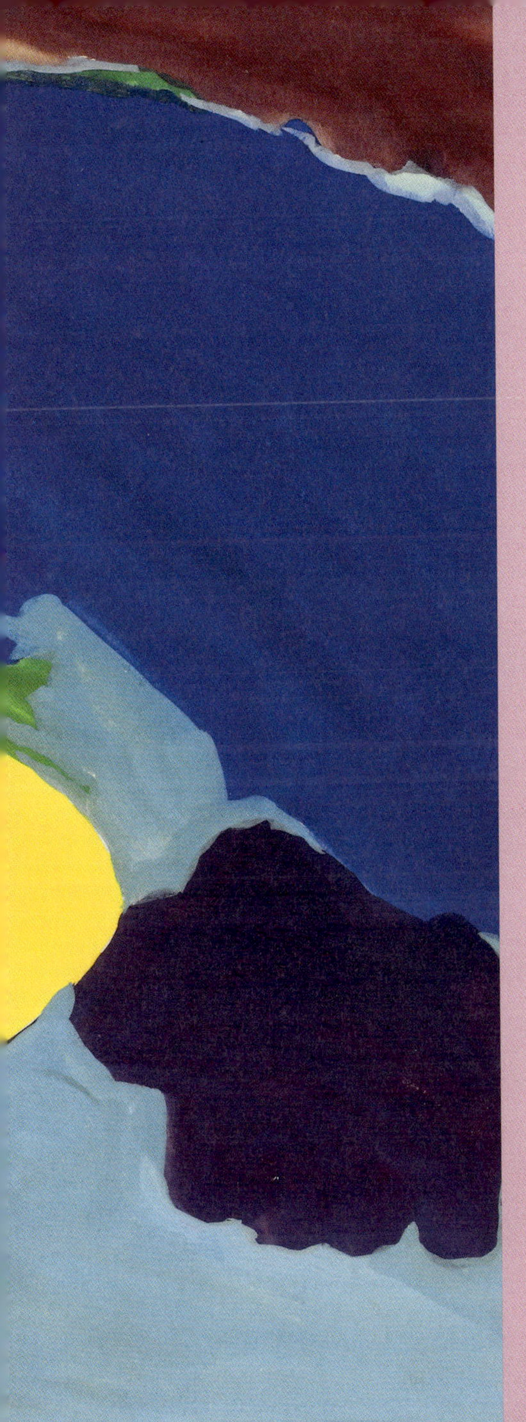

The 'Vache' Period

1948

In early 1948, Magritte was invited to present his first solo exhibition in Paris, at the Galerie du Faubourg. Approaching the age of fifty, the artist was less than ecstatic at such late recognition from the world capital of art. Still, he might have taken advantage of the opportunity to send some of his best works. But his spirit of revenge and desire to make fun of the Parisians prevailed.

He and his friend Louis Scutenaire jumped at the chance to make an impression: 'It was time to make a big splash. Not for a minute was it a question of putting together some paintings in one of the manners that had proved their worth, particularly since Magritte had none on hand. Instead of storing paintings at home, he preferred to let them go at a low price, give them away or even put them in the trash. The point was not to charm the Parisians but to scandalize them.'[29]

In a two-month rush of exhilaration, Magritte painted almost thirty oils and gouaches for his Paris exhibition. He dated some paintings back to 1947 – and one gouache to 1938 – to fool the gallery owner into believing that these works represented his recent production. Turning out a picture nearly every other day, Magritte was not very meticulous with his brushwork. He painted rapidly, approximately. The subjects he chose were related to caricatures, cartoon images and popular literature and were humorous, even vulgar.

In response to this unusual production, referred to as the 'Vache' (literally 'cow' though also meaning 'nasty') Period, Scutenaire wrote a preface to the exhibition catalogue entitled 'Les pieds dans le plat'(a French expression meaning '[to talk] bluntly'). He addressed the Paris public in language full of virulent but barely comprehensible argot, anticipating with irony the outraged reaction these new images would provoke when seen for the first time.

Unsurprisingly, the exhibition was a failure and scandalised both the Paris public and Breton's Surrealist group. The two friends had made their impression.

29   Scutenaire, *Avec Magritte*, op. cit., pp. 109–11.

   The 'Vache' Period

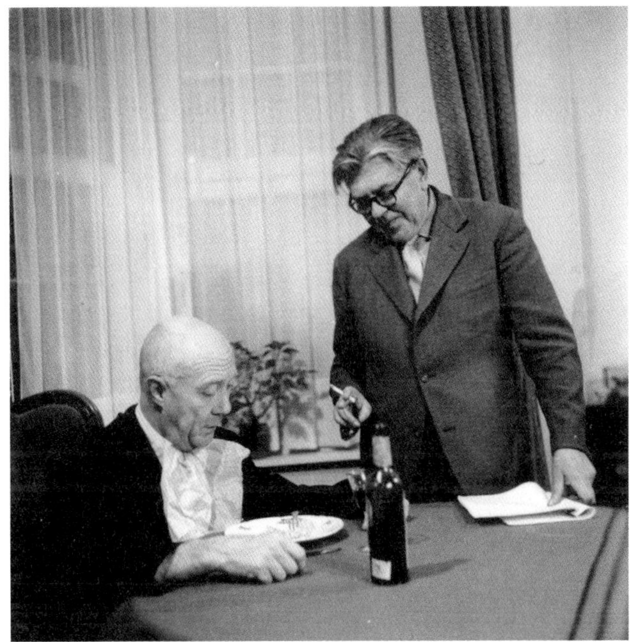

Louis Scutenaire and René Magritte during the filming of
Luc de Heusch's *Magritte ou La leçon de choses*, 1959.

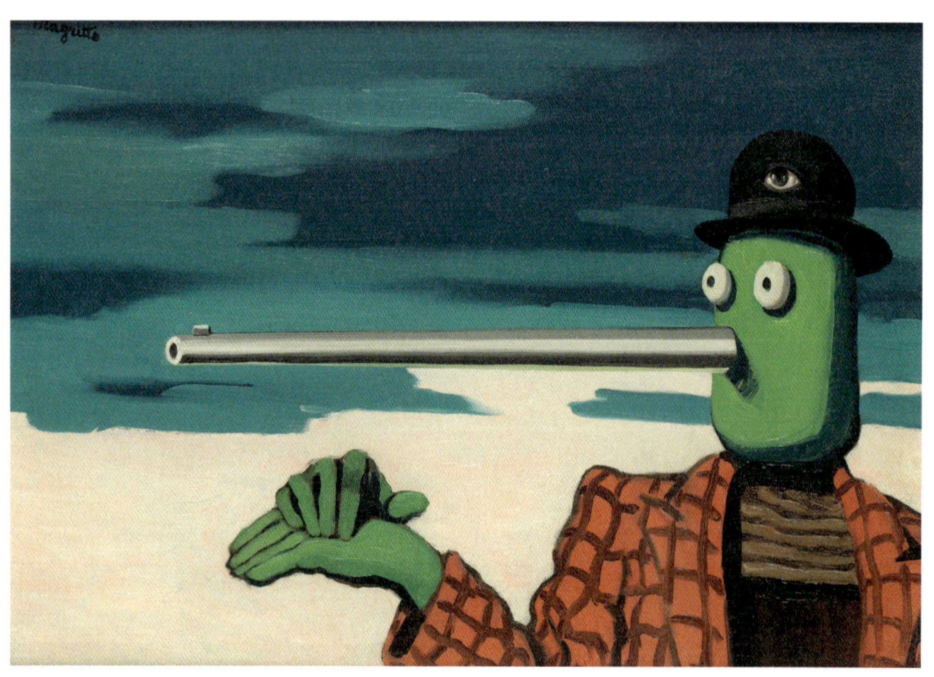

256
The Ellipsis
1948
oil on canvas, 50 × 73 cm

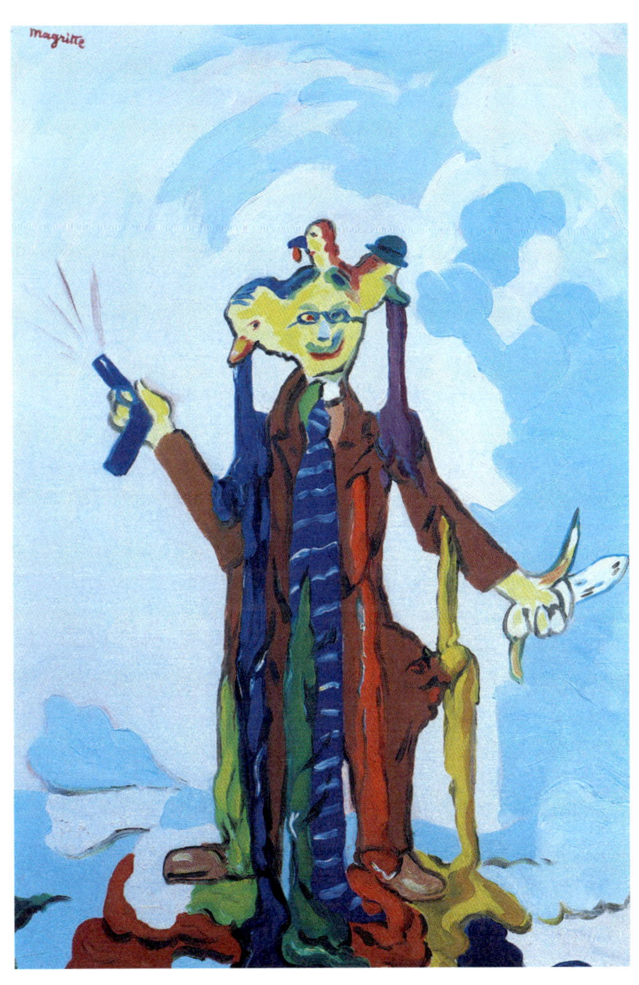

257
Pictorial Content
1948
oil on canvas, 73 × 50 cm

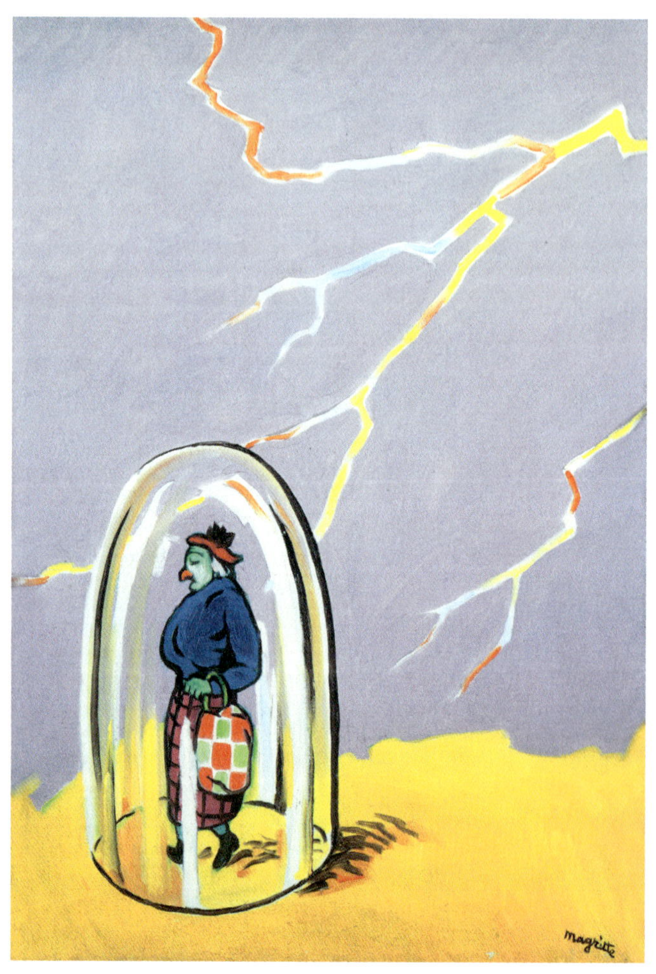

258
The Tow Plug
1948
oil on canvas, 72 × 50 cm

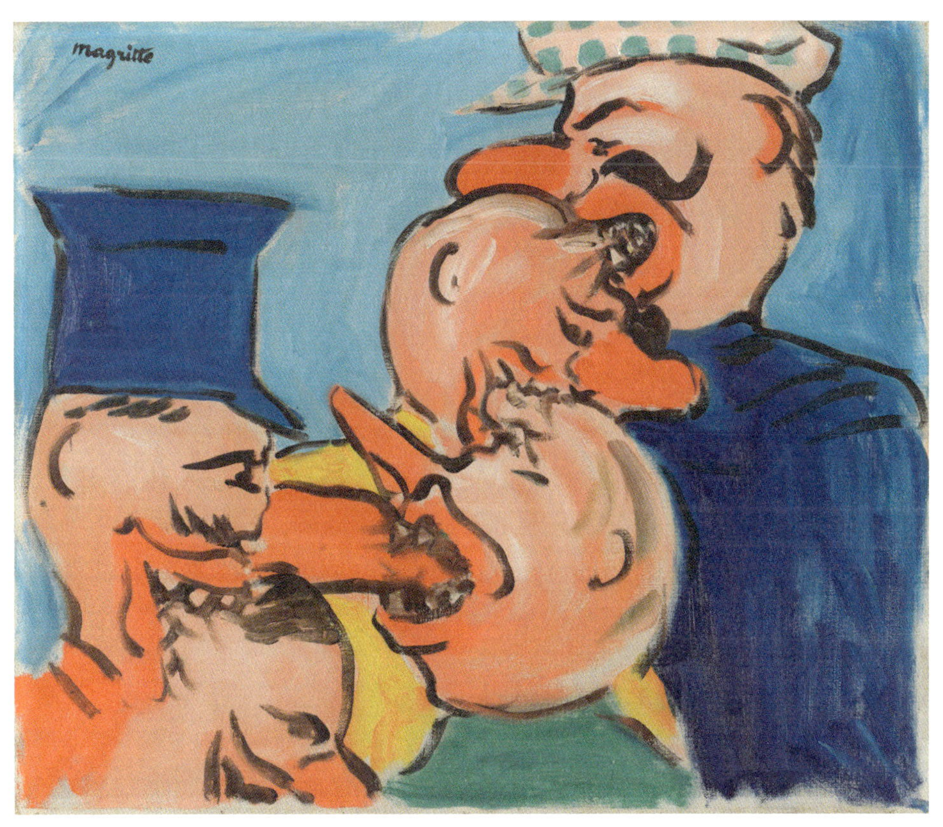

259
Famine
1948
oil on canvas, 46 × 55 cm

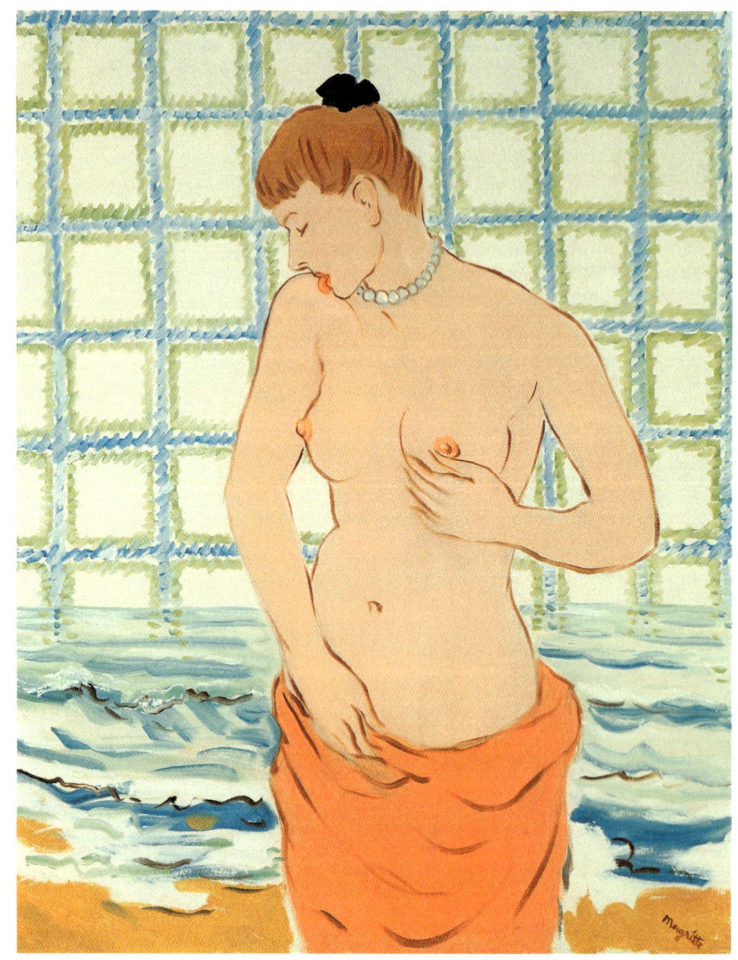

260
The Pebble
1948
oil on canvas, 100 × 81 cm

The 'Vache' Period

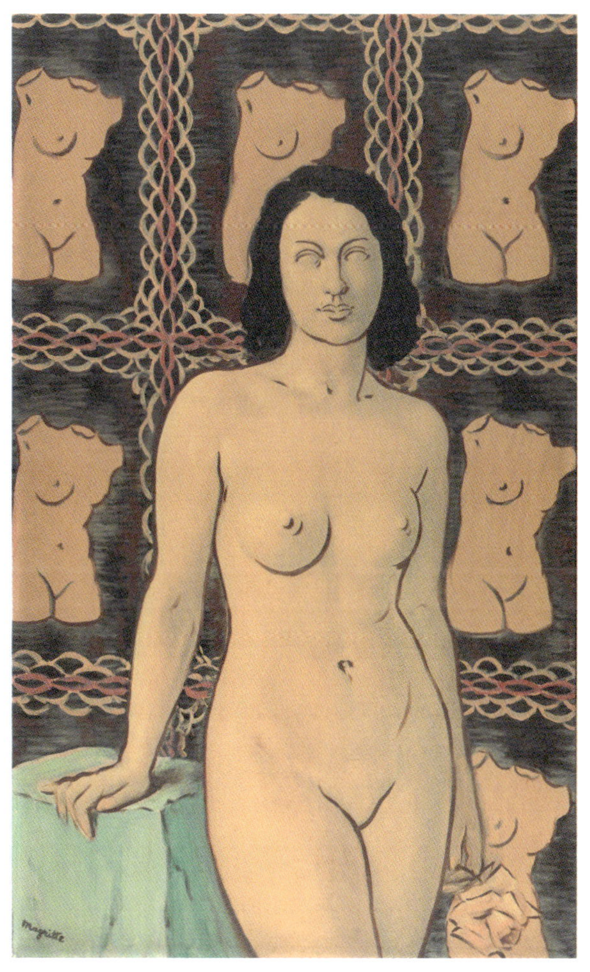

261
Lola de Valence

1948
oil on canvas, 98 × 60 cm

1948

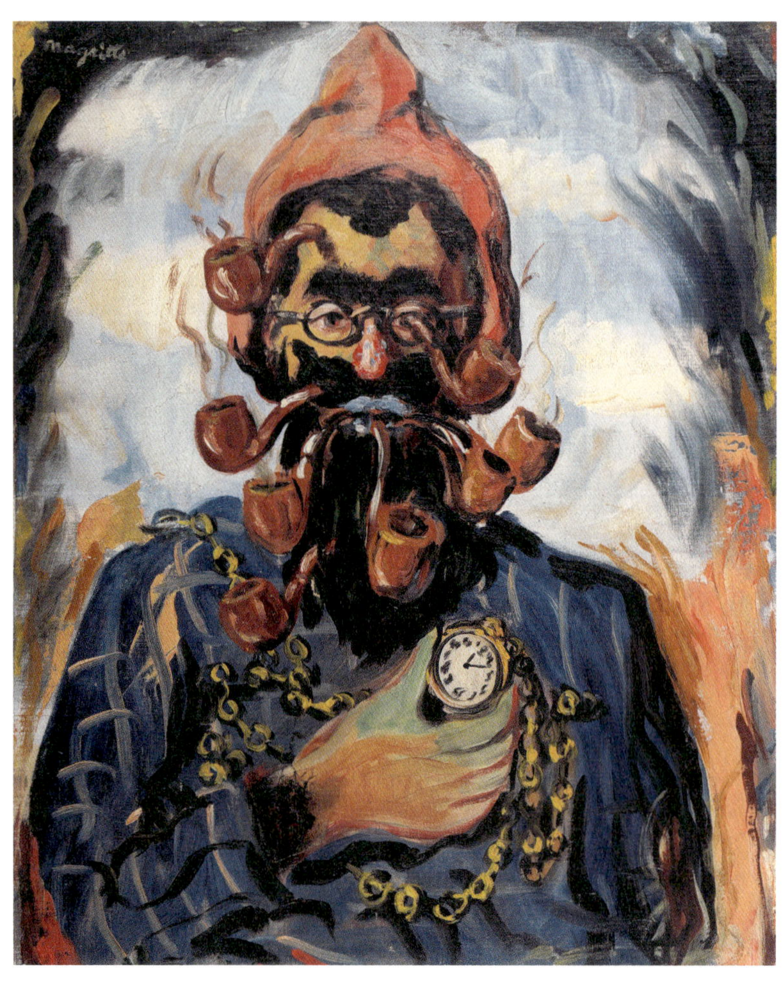

262
The Cripple
1948
oil on canvas mounted on panel, 59.5 × 49.5 cm

The 'Vache' Period

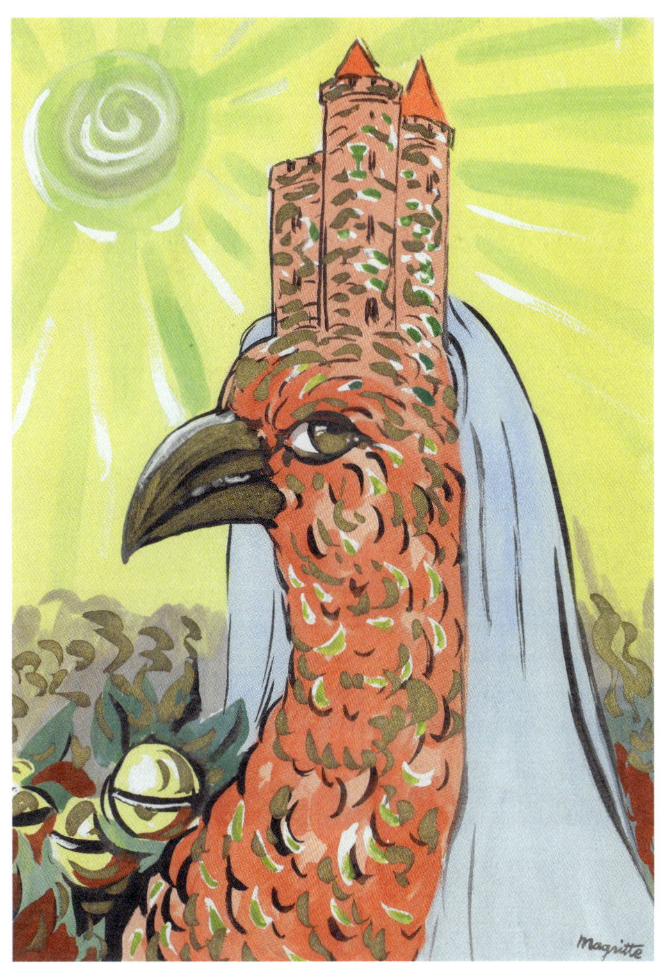

263
Prince Charming
1948
gouache, gold paint, pencil on paper, 45.8 × 32.7 cm

1948

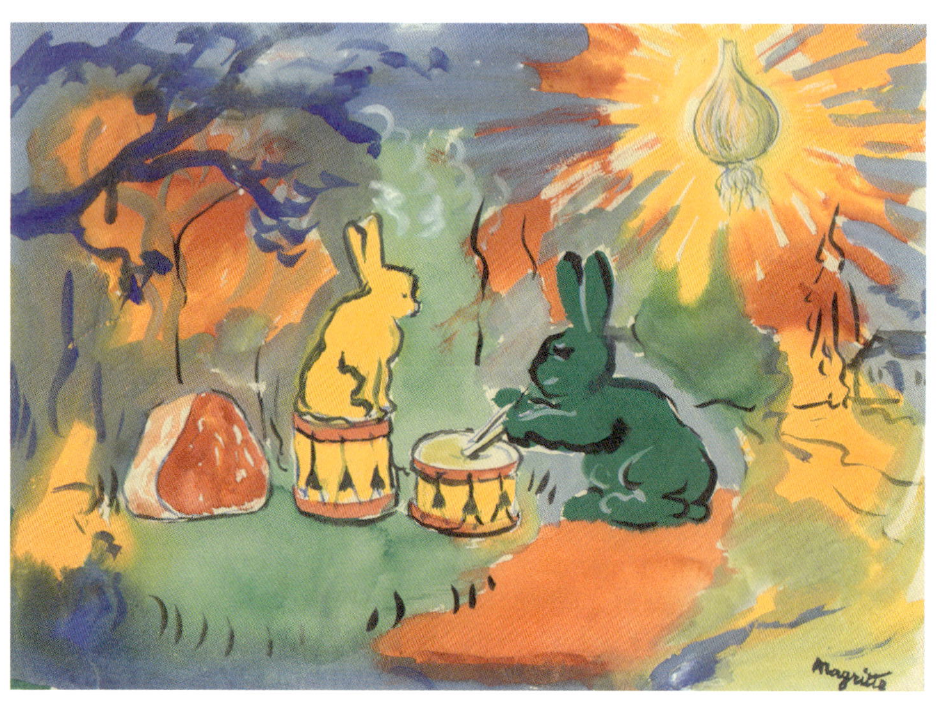

264
Pom' po pom' po pon po pon pon
1948
gouache on paper, 32.8 × 45.9 cm

　The 'Vache' Period

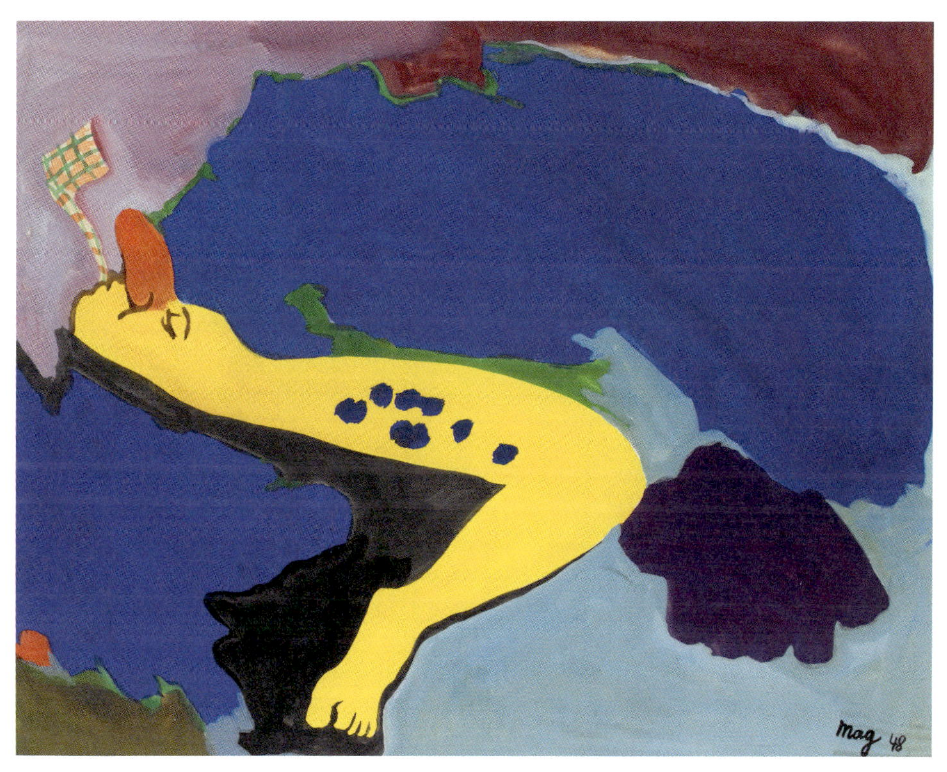

265
The Art of Living
1948
gouache on paper, 57.2 × 74.1 cm

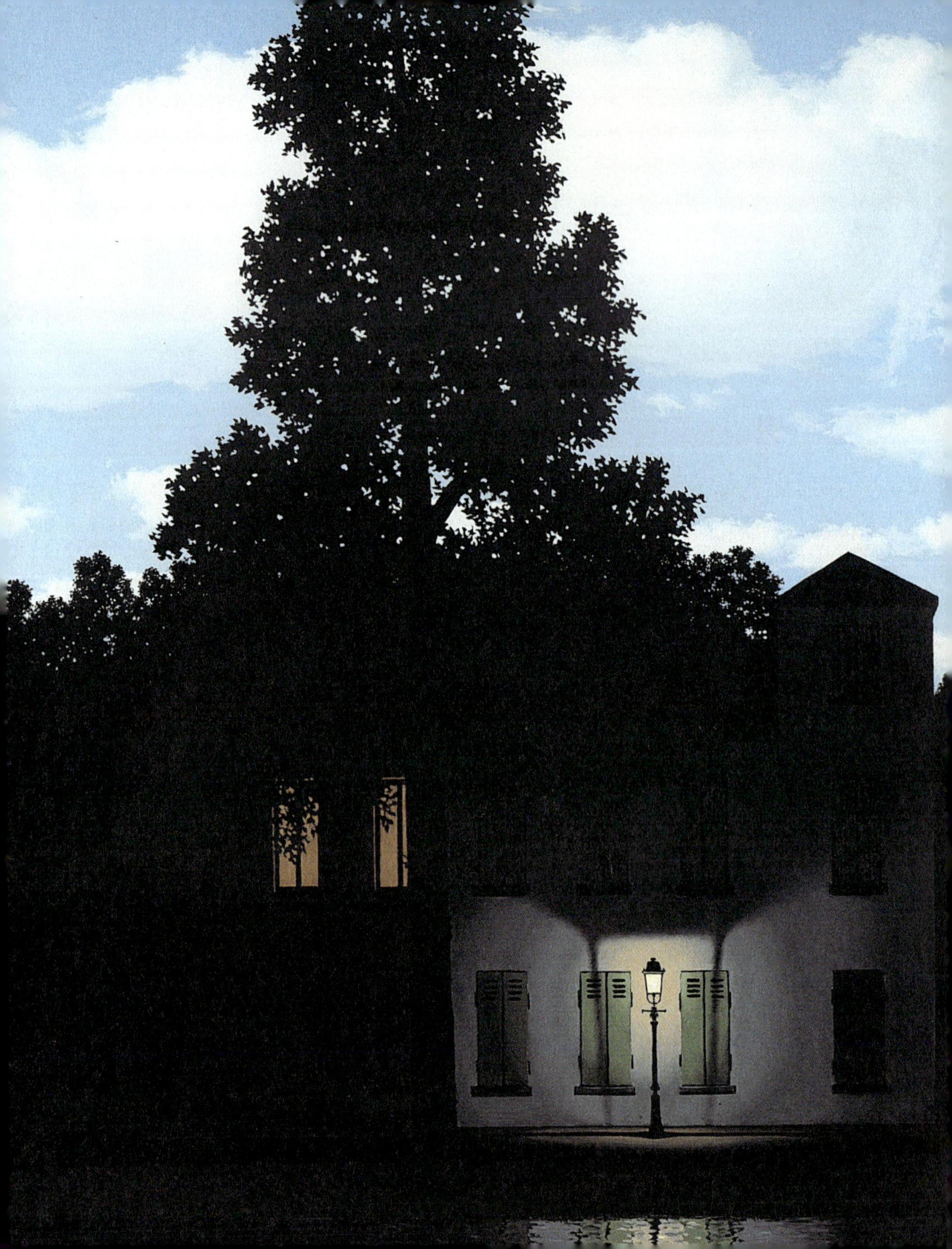

Poetics of the Everyday

1947–1967

After the liberating interlude of the 'Vache' Period, Magritte returned once and for all to the smooth, academic style of his paintings from before 1943. The post-war context encouraged him to do so. In 1946, Magritte came into contact with Alexander Iolas, a Greek-born art dealer who lived in New York. Iolas was enthusiastic about Surrealism and expressed his desire to promote Magritte's work in the United States. Iolas corresponded regularly with Magritte and eventually became his official dealer, greatly contributing to his international fame. During their first exchanges, Iolas insisted on the fact that he wanted to show absolutely no paintings from the Renoir Period in New York, as this style would not be a success in America. This market-dictated imperative, combined with the art milieu's general rejection of Sunlit Surrealism, encouraged Magritte to return to his former style.

Although painting technique was important to Magritte, it was nevertheless far from his primary concern. He often stated that he was bored by the act of painting, as he strove to represent things in precise detail, a necessary condition for his paintings to produce their effect. The main thing for him was to find the image. The rest was mere execution. In 1966, he returned to this original concept: 'In the end, the manner of painting is of little interest. There are after all so many. Instead of looking for a manner of painting that is more or less original, I preferred to get to the bottom of things, make painting a tool for deepening our knowledge of the world, but a knowledge that is inseparable from its mystery. My way of painting is completely ordinary, academic. What is important in my painting is what it shows. I consider it essential to discover how the world can interest us deeply. Now, the world interests us deeply in its mystery. By mystery I mean what cannot be known, what science cannot reduce to knowledge that can be expressed.'[30]

The 'mystery of the world' that Magritte intended to evoke in each of his images was marvellously embodied in 1949 in the first version of *The Dominion of Light* [279], a picture that represents a city scene shrouded in the darkness of night under a daytime sky. The composition is so harmonious that, at first sight, everything seems normal. However, in looking at it more carefully, it becomes obvious: day and night merge in a single image according to a principle of time distortion that defies any attempt at scientific explanation. 'This reference to night and day seems to me endowed with the power to

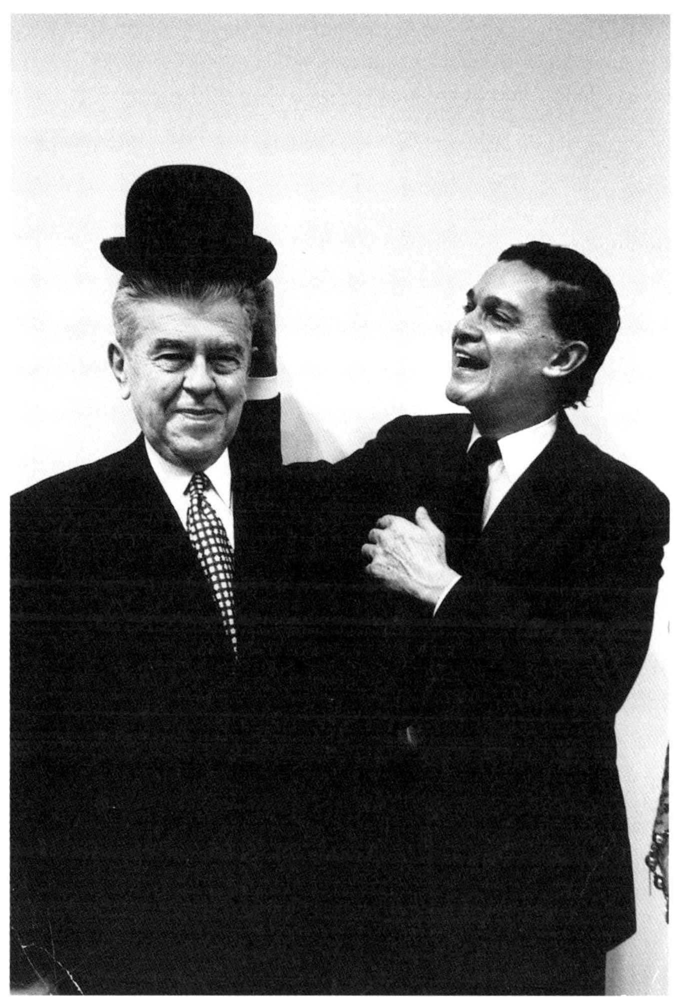

Magritte and Alexandre Iolas, 16 December 1965 (photographed by Steve Shapiro for *Life*).

surprise us and to delight us. I call this power: poetry,' Magritte declared.[31] By reconciling opposites within a single composition, by contradicting all logic, Magritte forces viewers to accept the new reality he proposes to show them. In order to access the image and see this mysterious world that Magritte invites viewers to discover with new eyes, they must let go of their grip and resist the persistent human desire to understand and explain everything.

Magritte's methods for shaking up the world expanded in the last twenty years of his career. From 1950 onwards, he introduced a change of material to his paintings, specifically by depicting the objects in his work in a state of petrification. The transformation of materials was one of the means Magritte had used since the late 1920s to render objects 'disturbing'. Turning them to stone, however, was new. *The Legend of the Centuries* (1950) [282] depicts a stone chair in a rocky landscape. The monumental size of the chair is obvious, as the scale is indicated by a wooden chair placed on its seat. This petrification of materials soon extended not only to other objects (*Memory of a Journey*, 1951 [296]) but also to natural phenomena (*The Haunted Castle*, 1950 [290]) and even human beings. In *Private Diary* (1951) [297], Magritte portrays two men in suits, one apparently trying to remove something from the other's eye. The image is even more arresting than those that depict a petrified object, as in this work the human beings' mobility seems fixed in place for eternity through their bodies' transformation into stone, and through the petrification of the entire landscape that surrounds them.

In addition to petrification, Magritte also exploited a change of scale, particularly in works made during the early 1950s. The process reached a peak in *The Listening Room* (1952) [304], in which a green apple occupies an entire room from floor to ceiling. It seems almost on the point of bursting, so vividly does it convey the impression that it is swelling. This image is no doubt a reference to Lewis Carroll's *Alice's Adventures in Wonderland* (1865), a book that the Surrealists especially liked.

Alongside these new means introduced after the war, Magritte continued to pursue his problematological approach. He found the solution to the problem of water in *The Seducer* [288, 293, 309], an image painted for the first time in 1950. Magritte referred to this

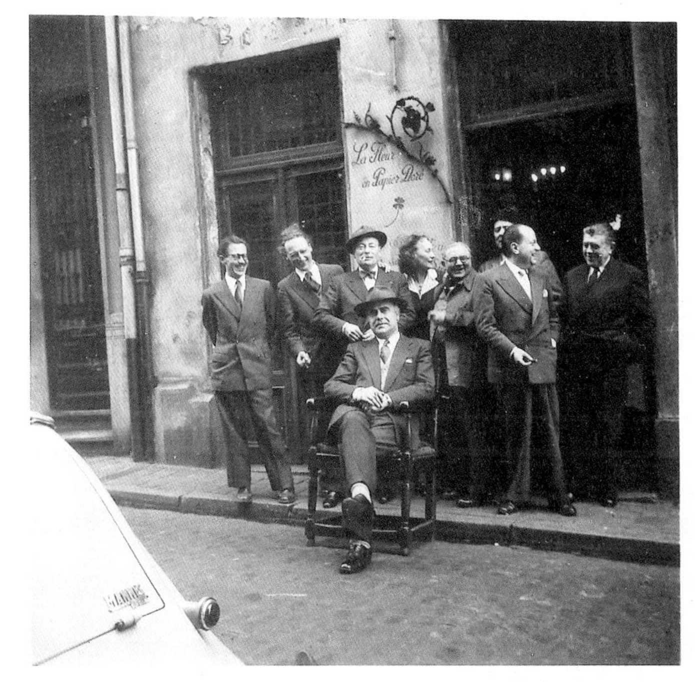

The Surrealists at the café La Fleur en Papier Doré, Brussels, 1953. Left to right:
Marcel Mariën, Albert Van Loock, Camille Goemans, Georgette Magritte, Geert Van Bruaene,
Louis Scutenaire, E. L. T. Mesens and René Magritte. Seated: Paul Colinet.

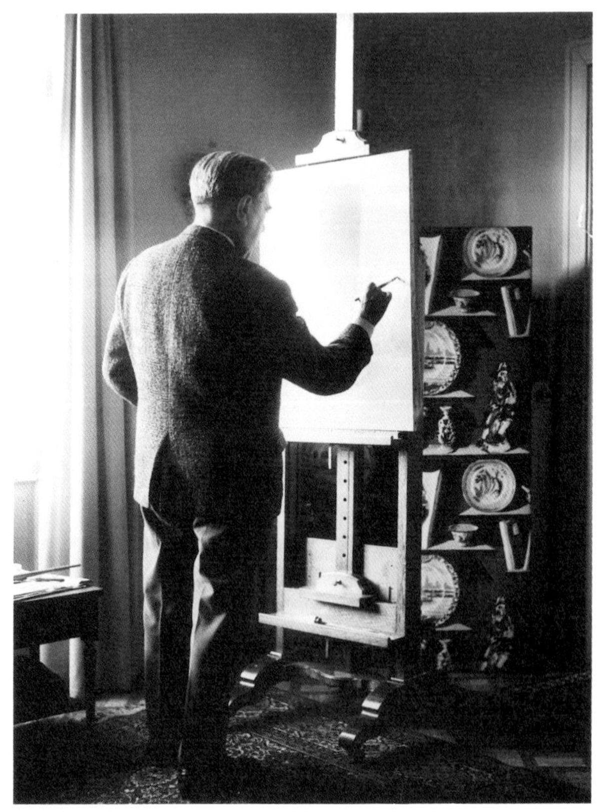

Shunk-Kender (photographers), René Magritte painting *The Well of Truth*,
Brussels, Rue des Mimosas, 1962.

Poetics of the Everyday

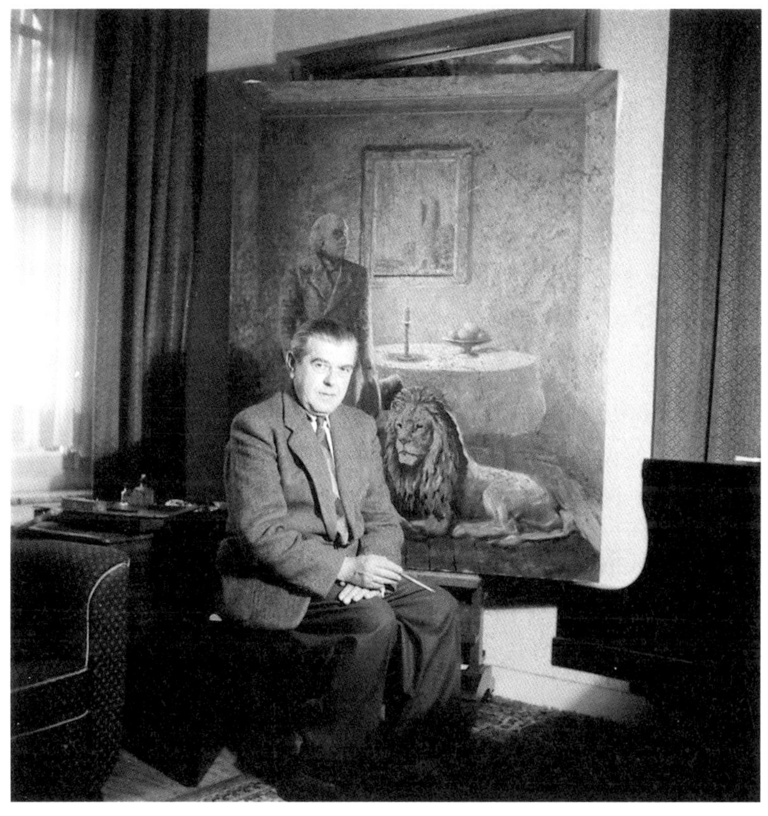

Georges Thiry (photographer), René Magritte
painting *Memory of a Journey*, c. 1955.

picture in a letter to a friend explaining how he arrived at the image: 'The Seducer is the answer I found to the "question of water", the research consisting of a sort of "frenzied contemplation" of the question, as you so aptly put it. In practical terms, it progressed through days of almost always identical drawings representing water, until the day when in one drawing, the idea of the form of water appears. The rest was only a matter of technique.'[32]

In his interviews, Magritte was regularly asked to reveal his pictures' inside story. Speaking of *The Heartstring* (1960) [344], which solves the problem of the cloud, Magritte reconfirmed his method: 'I keep a sketchbook of drawings at hand. Inspiration gives me an image: I feel like painting a cloud. So I draw clouds, perhaps a hundred. And I surround each of them with forms whose meaning I do not know until inspiration visits me again and I know what would be suitable under this cloud: a crystal glass.'[33]

At this time, Magritte broadened his repertoire of objects to include heavenly bodies, the Sun and the Moon being summoned several times to appear in some signal works. In *The Masterpiece or The Mysteries of the Horizon* (1955) [316], Magritte raises the paradoxical question of individual perception of the Moon. Although there is only one Moon, everyone forms their own idea of it, its oneness being divided into as many different perceptions as there are human beings. This is why Magritte says he gave each of the three men represented his own moon.[34]

These heavenly bodies also appear in several works entitled *The Banquet* (1956) [324] and *The Sixteenth of September* (1956) [321, 322]. Each of the variants Magritte painted follows the same principle: the Sun or the Moon in the foreground is superimposed over the leaves of vegetation that should be concealing it. These images are important because they convey a principle that regulates the conditions of the appearance of the objects in our environment: 'These paintings owe their interest to the existence – which we suddenly become aware of – of the apparent visible and the hidden visible, which are never separate in nature. Something visible always hides something else visible. But these paintings immediately show this state of things, and in an unexpected way. Something happens between the visible shown us by the world and what this visible hides, but that is visible.'[35]

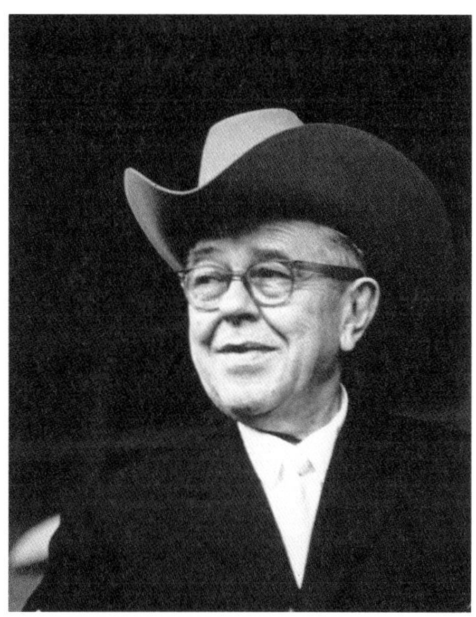

René Magritte, Houston, Texas, 1965.

These thoughts about the hidden visible and the apparent visible are at the centre of several paintings from the 1960s. One of the most famous is *The Son of Man* (1964) [376] and its close variant *The Great War* (1964) [377]. They depict a man seen from the front wearing a suit. His face is masked by an apple. Despite seeming like another failed portrait, it is an altogether different matter. Magritte clarified his intentions in an interview in 1964: 'I hope to rid the things that I show of all symbols. For example, take this painting entitled The Great War, where we see a person in a bowler hat whose face is hidden by a large apple. There is no need to tell you that I was not thinking of war while I painted it. The apple is the apparent visible hiding the hidden visible (the man's face). In the world, everything always happens like that. So it is a sort of tension or war: our mind seeks to see what we cannot see. I would also like for the viewer of my painting to be in a poetical state; as if disturbed by poetry.'[36]

Although reason cannot provide the viewer with any hint to understanding the works, poetry on the other hand is revealing. In a picture like *The Battle of the Argonne* (1959) [335], no explanation presents itself. Above a barely inhabited country landscape, a huge boulder floats in the sky next to a cloud. Magritte attributes this miracle to poetry: 'Now if for example weight can play a role in poetry, it is evoked by a boulder (as in *The Battle of the Argonne*). It is weight that is evoked and not the laws of gravity – it is evoked without physics. The sensation, the feeling or the idea of weight is enough for poetry, the laws would be superfluous and there would be an excess as soon as physics entered into it.'[37]

In art, Magritte recognised no boundaries. There is nothing he would not subject to upheaval. However, his life was just the opposite. After the war, he began to live comfortably with his wife, Georgette, benefiting from the success of his work in the United States. He continued to paint at home, wearing a suit and house slippers. He never had a studio. Nothing protected the floor when he was painting, so carefully did he proceed. His painting activity was regular, almost routine, interspersed with a game of chess or walking the dog. Saturday evenings, he was in the habit of gathering his friends at his home to discuss his new paintings, for which they gleefully came up with poetic titles that resisted all explanation. The life of a middle-class homebody set in his ways seems a thousand leagues away from the artist who systematically endeavoured to undermine all certainties. His friend and Surrealist colleague Marcel Mariën said in this regard, 'I don't think that in Magritte's case the everyday aspect of his life can be considered important or be criticized, as is commonly done, as a bourgeois thing. It was not that at all. In order to paint, he did not necessarily have to dress as if he were poor and loiter in the cafés of Paris until midnight, like some artists. As if it were almost perverse to have a regular, well-ordered life. It's like Kant, who lived a very regular life.'[38]

Magritte died on 15 August 1967 from cancer of the pancreas. His unique oeuvre remains one of the most mysterious in all of art history.

30   Pierre Du Bois, Interview with René Magritte, *Gazette littéraire* [Lausanne], 1966, quoted in Magritte, *Écrits complets*, op. cit., p. 652.

31   René Magritte, 'L'Empire des lumières', unpublished manuscript, AACB, inv. 342.

32   René Magritte, Letter to Gaston Puel, 13 November 1953, quoted in Magritte, *Écrits complets*, op. cit., p. 327.

33   Pierre Descargues, 'René Magritte, le plus célèbre des surréalistes belges parle du mystère', *Feuille d'avis de Lausanne-Magazine*, 1 November 1961, quoted in Magritte, *Écrits complets*, op. cit., p. 544.

34   Anonymous, 'The Enigmatic Visions of René Magritte', *Life*, vol. 60, no. 16 (22 April 1966).

35   Patrick Waldberg, *René Magritte* (Brussels: André De Rache, 1965), pp. 247–8.

36   Pierre Mazars, 'Magritte et l'objet', *Le Figaro littéraire*, 19 November 1964, quoted in René Magritte, *Écrits complets*, op. cit., p. 599.

37   René Magritte, Letter to André Bosmans, 24 July 1961, quoted in René Magritte, *Lettres à André Bosmans, 1958–1967* (Brussels: Éditions Seghers-Brachot, 1990), p. 181.

38   Interview with Marcel Mariën, 9 March 1981, Brussels, in Levy, *Decoding Magritte*, op. cit., p. 216.

     Poetics of the Everyday

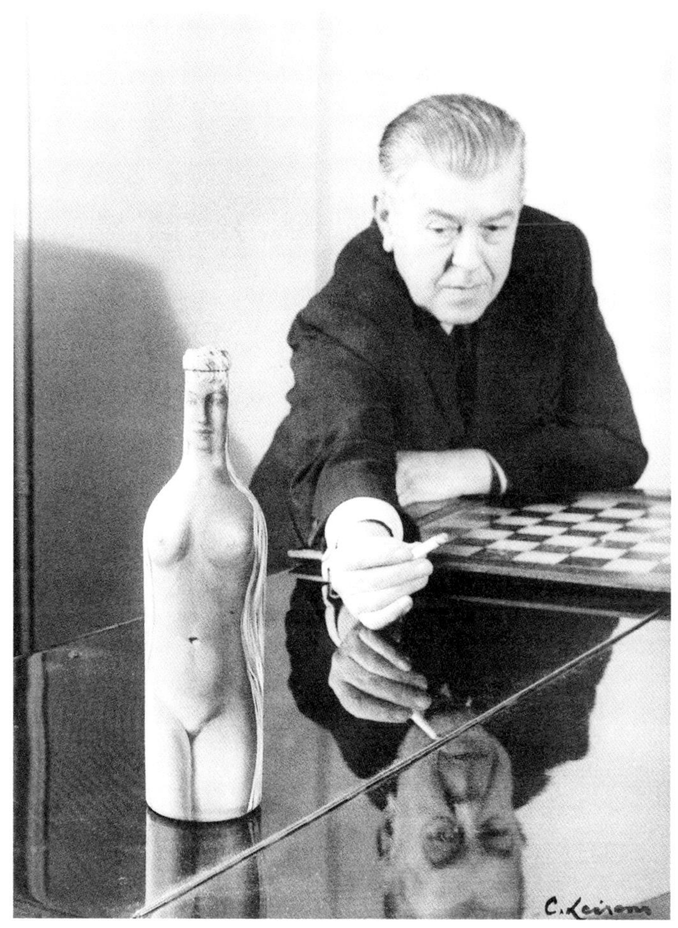

Charles Leirens (photographer), René Magritte, *c.* 1959.

1947–1967

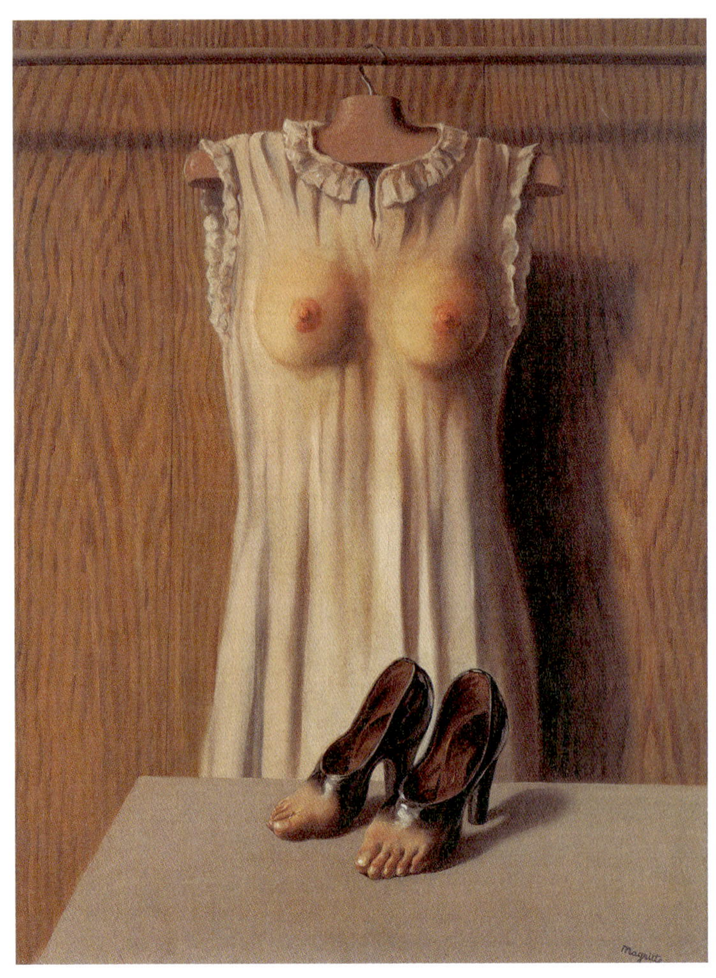

266
Philosophy in the Boudoir
1947
oil on canvas, 80 × 60 cm

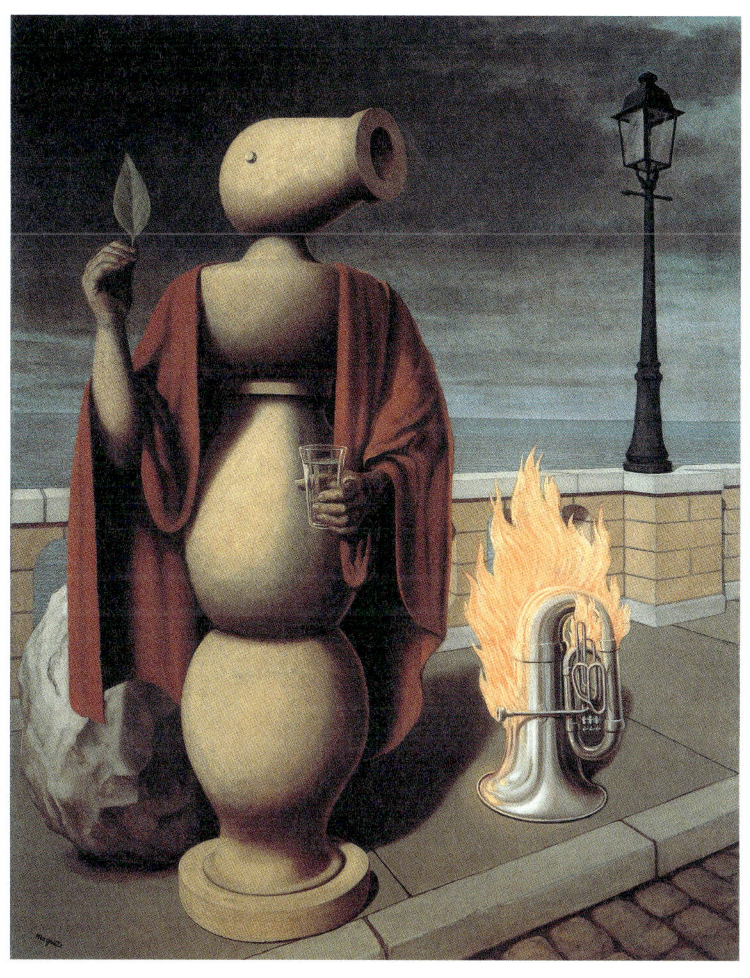

267
The Rights of Man
1948
oil on canvas, 146 × 114 cm

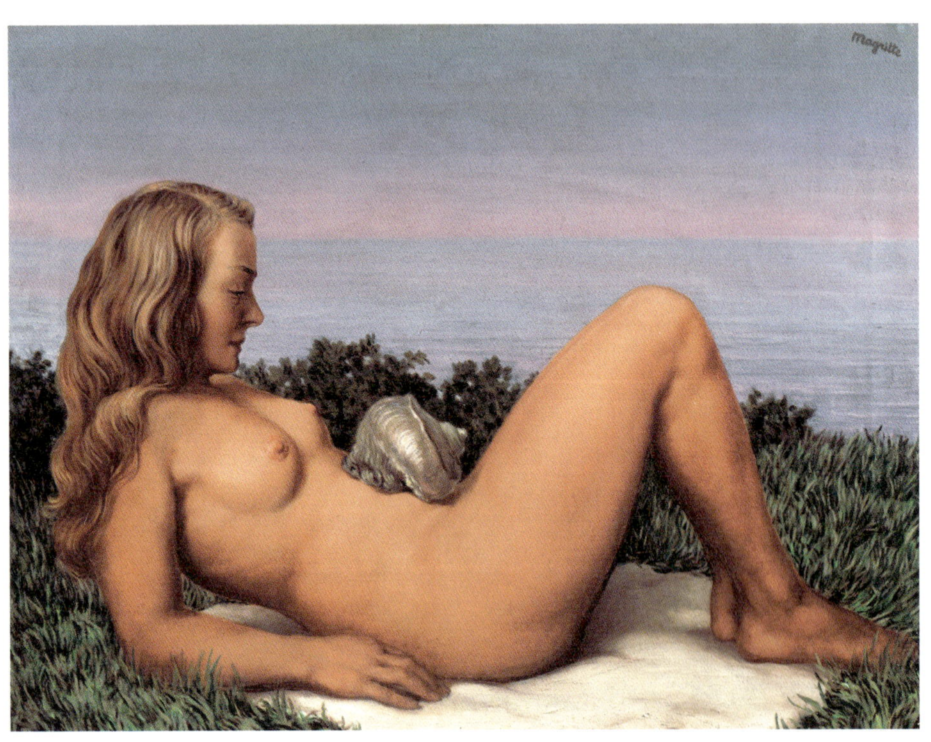

268
Olympia
1948
oil on canvas, 60 × 80 cm

    Poetics of the Everyday

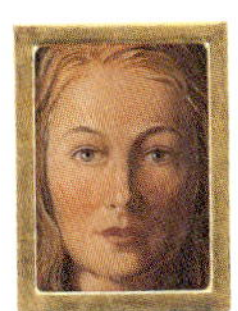

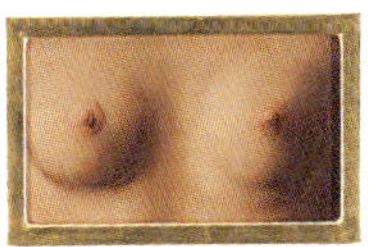

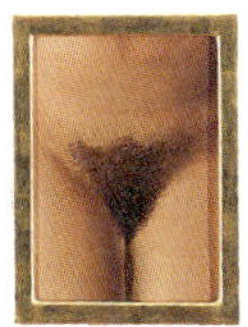

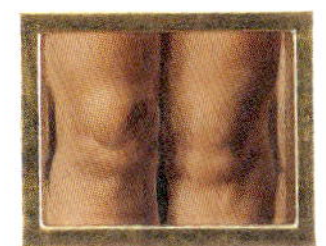

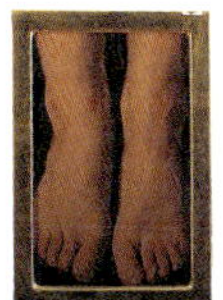

269
The Eternally Obvious
1948
oil on canvas laid on board, five panels framed and mounted on a sheet of
glass: 25.5 × 19.5 cm; 19.3 × 32 cm; 27 × 20.2 cm; 20.5 × 26.6 cm; 26 × 18 cm

1947–1967

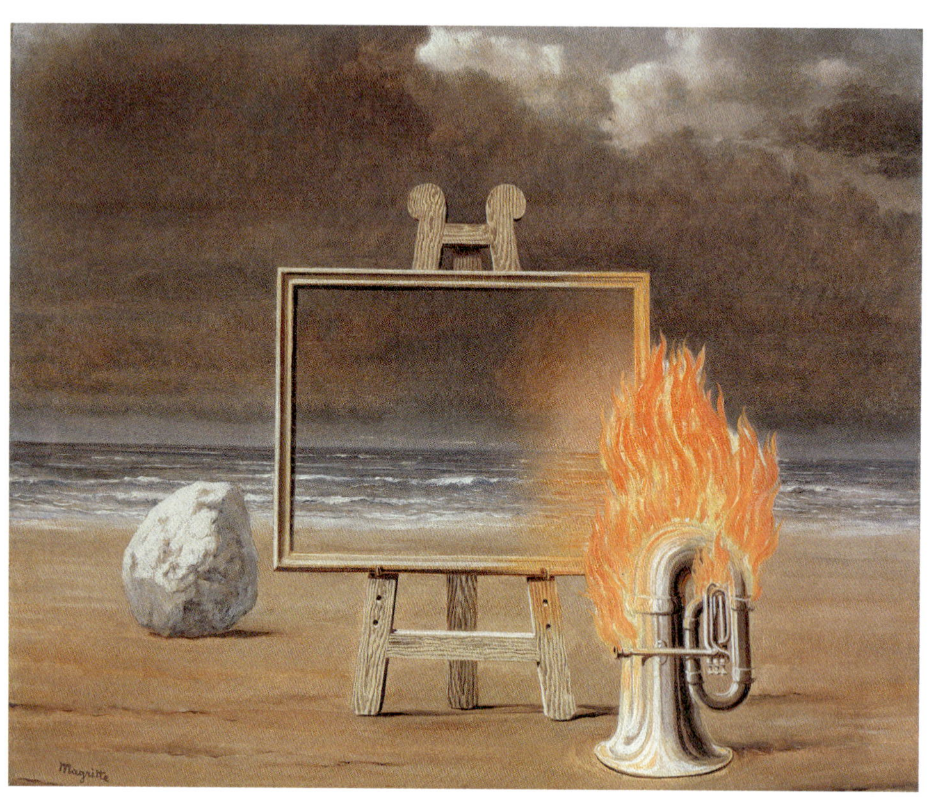

270
The Fair Captive
1948
oil on canvas, 54 × 65 cm

     Poetics of the Everyday

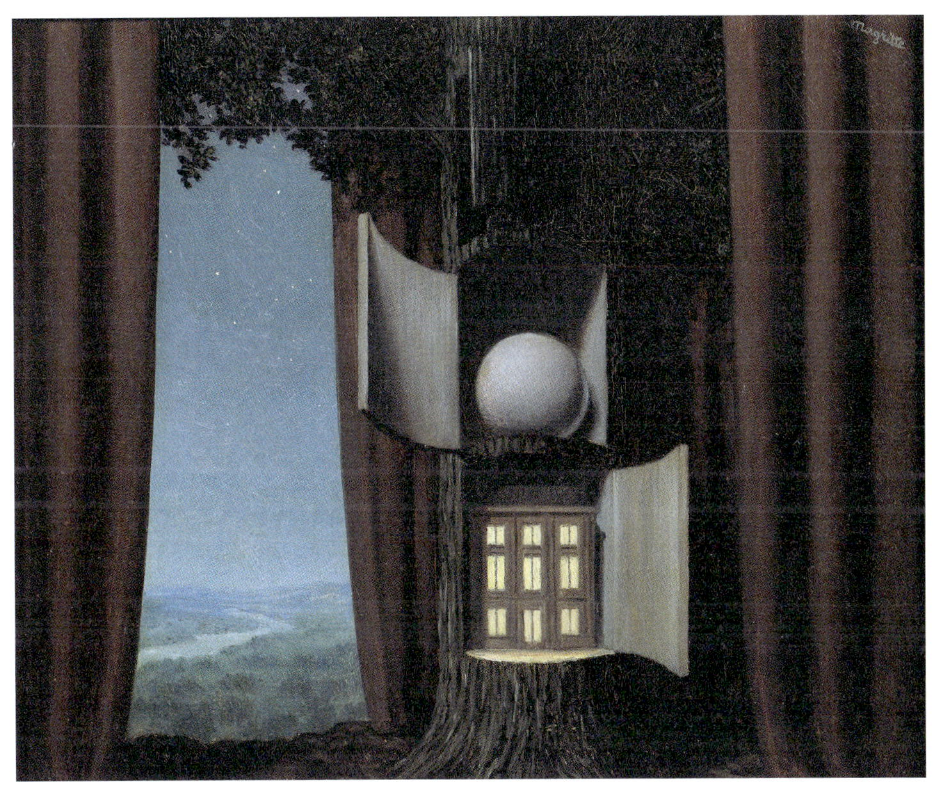

271
Blood Will Tell
1948
oil on canvas, 50 × 60 cm

     1947–1967

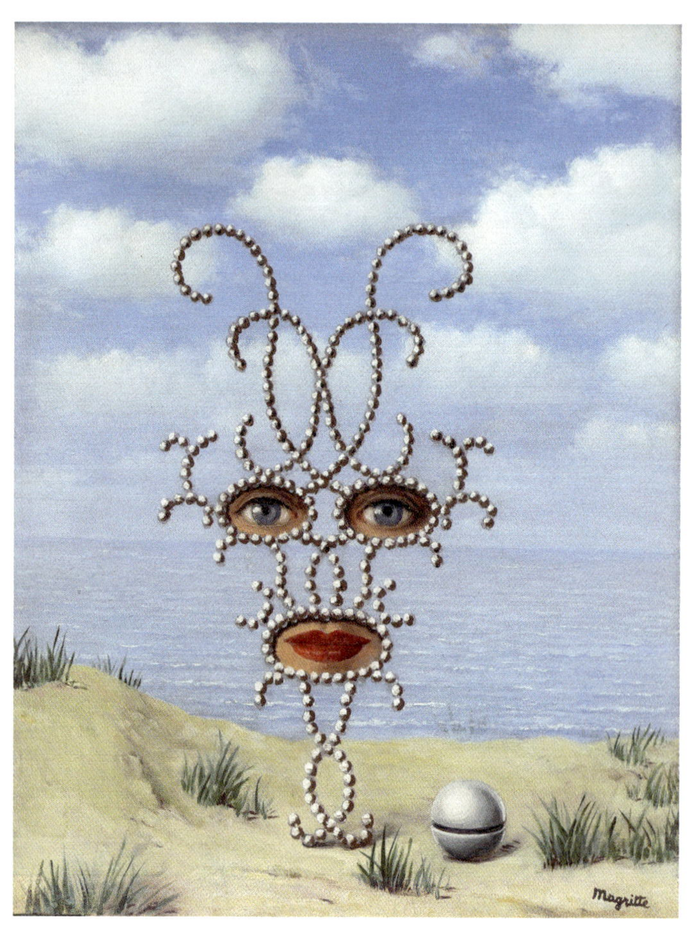

272
Sheherazade
1950
oil on canvas, 40 × 30 cm

     Poetics of the Everyday

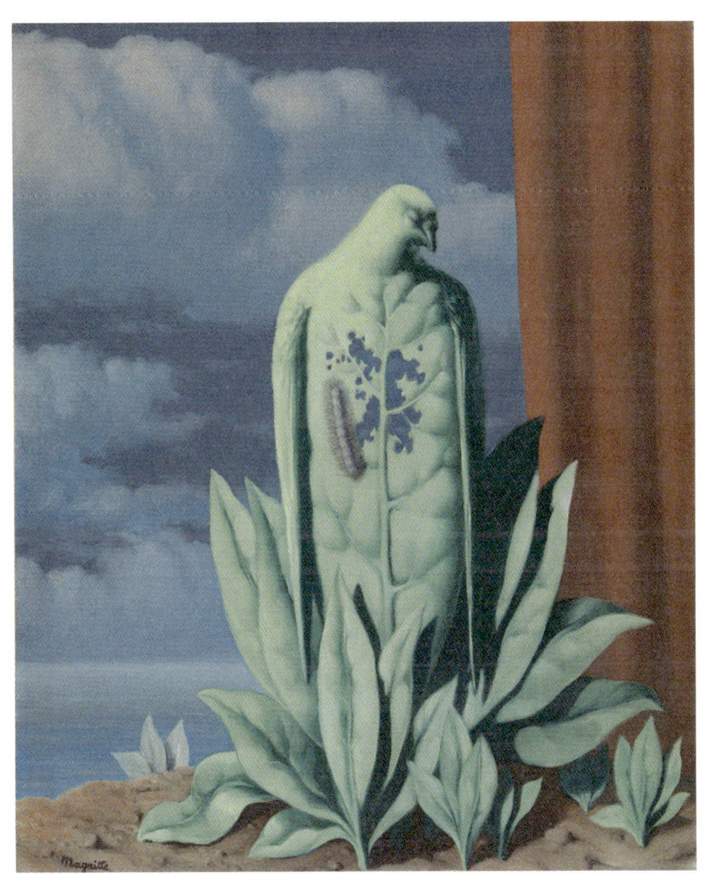

273
The Flavour of Tears
1948
oil on canvas, 60 × 50 cm

     1947–1967

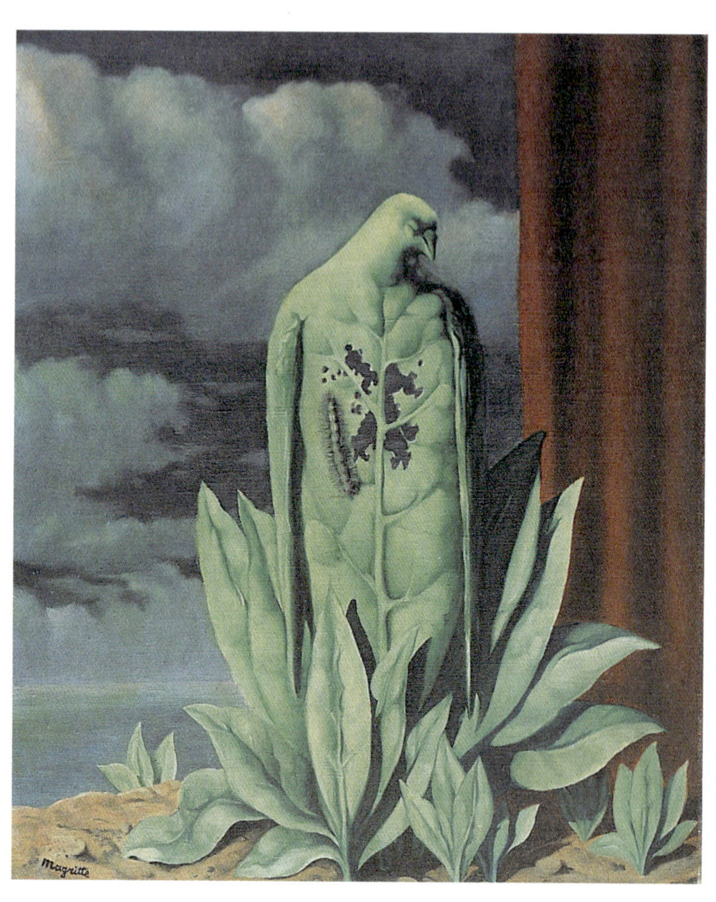

274
The Flavour of Tears
1948
oil on canvas, 60 × 50 cm

   Poetics of the Everyday

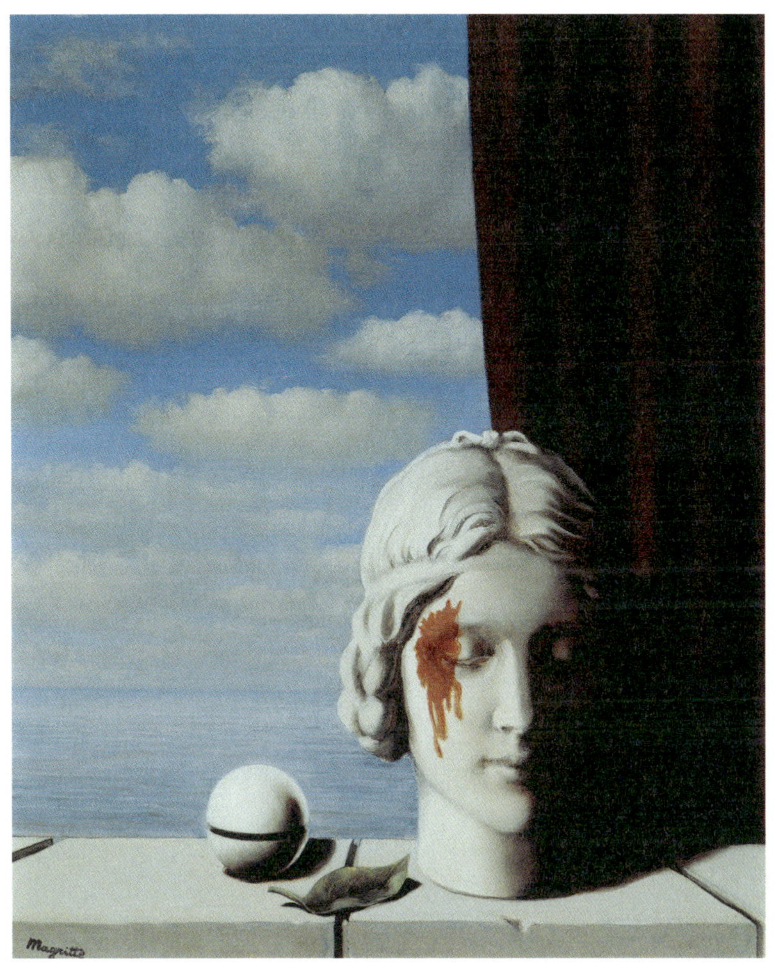

275
Memory
1948
oil on canvas, 60 × 50 cm

     1947–1967

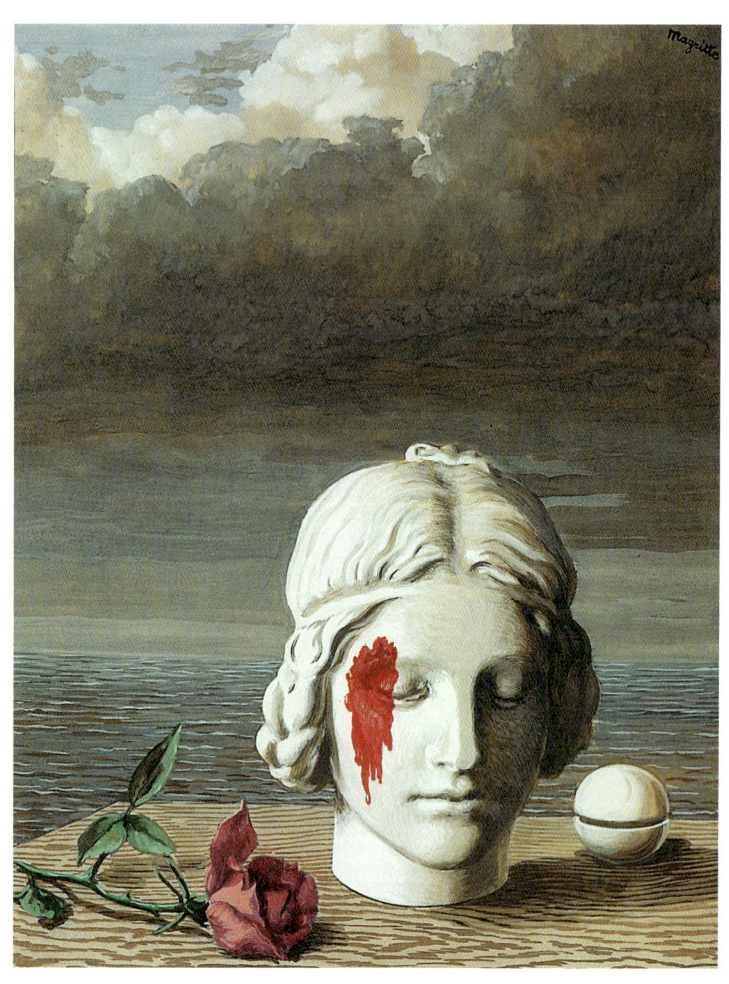

276
Memory
1948
gouache on paper, 46.5 × 37 cm

Poetics of the Everyday

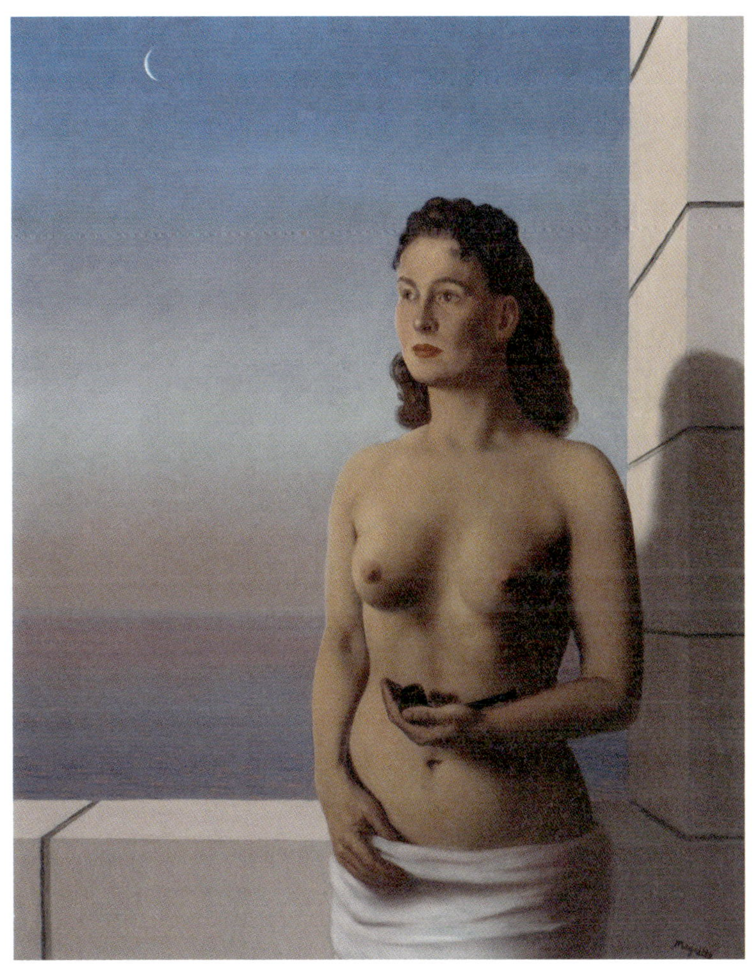

277
Freedom of Mind
1948
oil on canvas, 100 × 80 cm

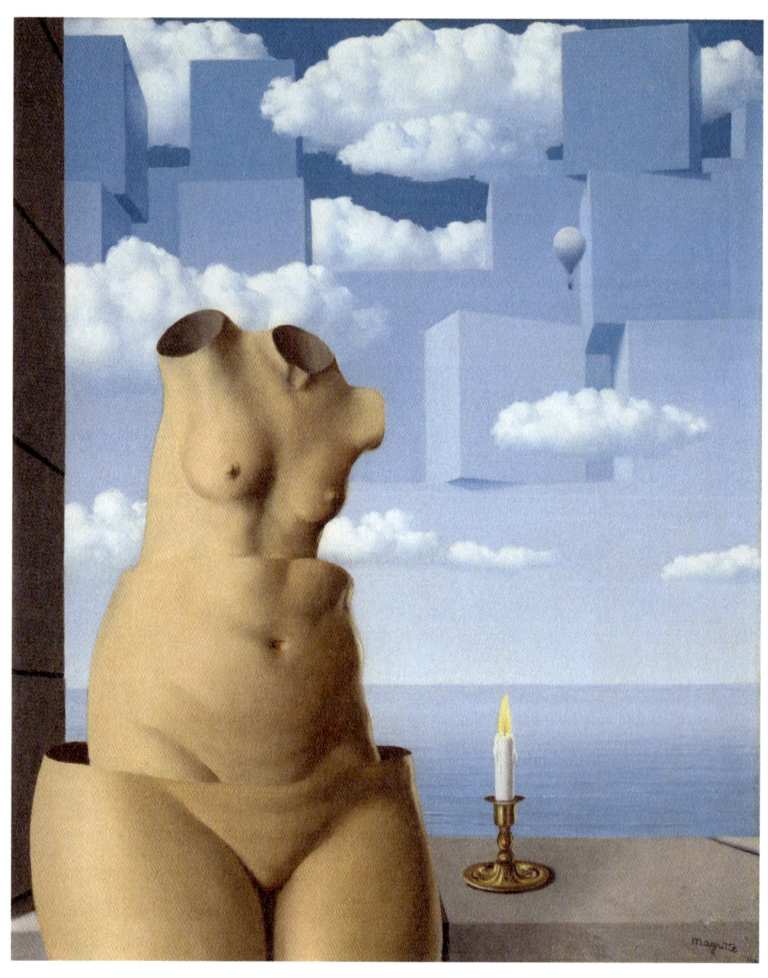

278
Megalomania
1948 or 1949
oil on canvas, 100 × 80 cm

   Poetics of the Everyday

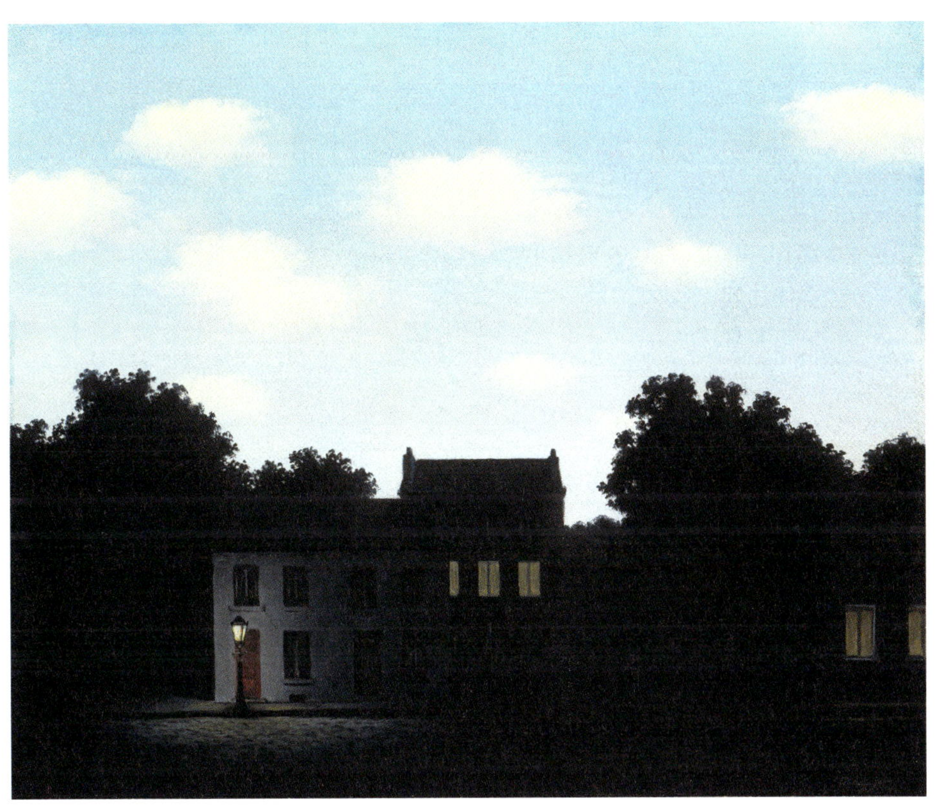

The Dominion of Light
1949
oil on canvas, 50 × 60 cm

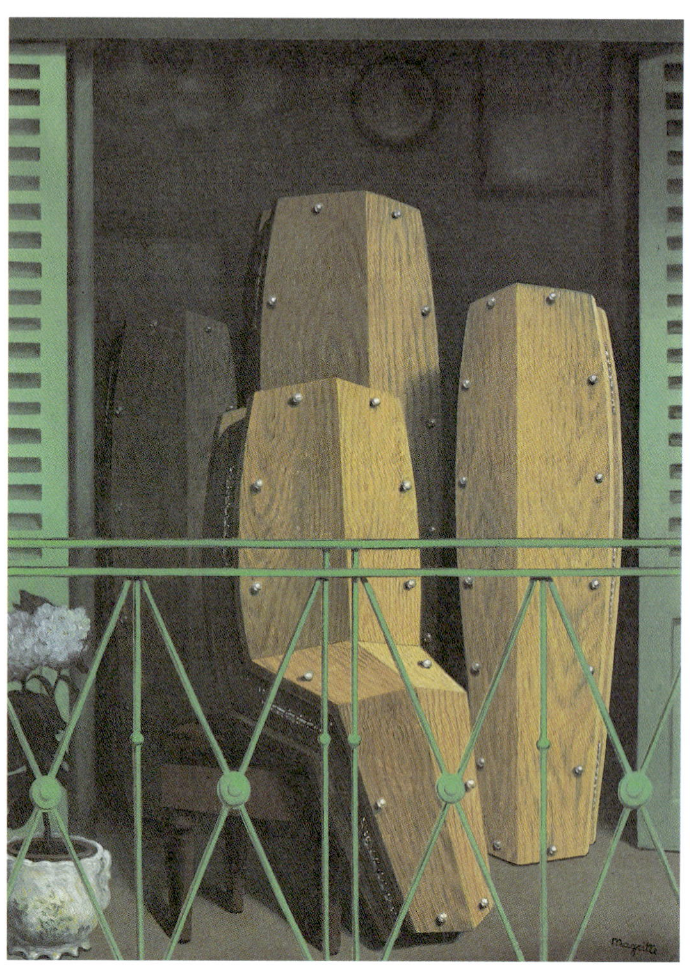

280
Perspective: Manet's Balcony
1950
oil on canvas, 80 × 60 cm

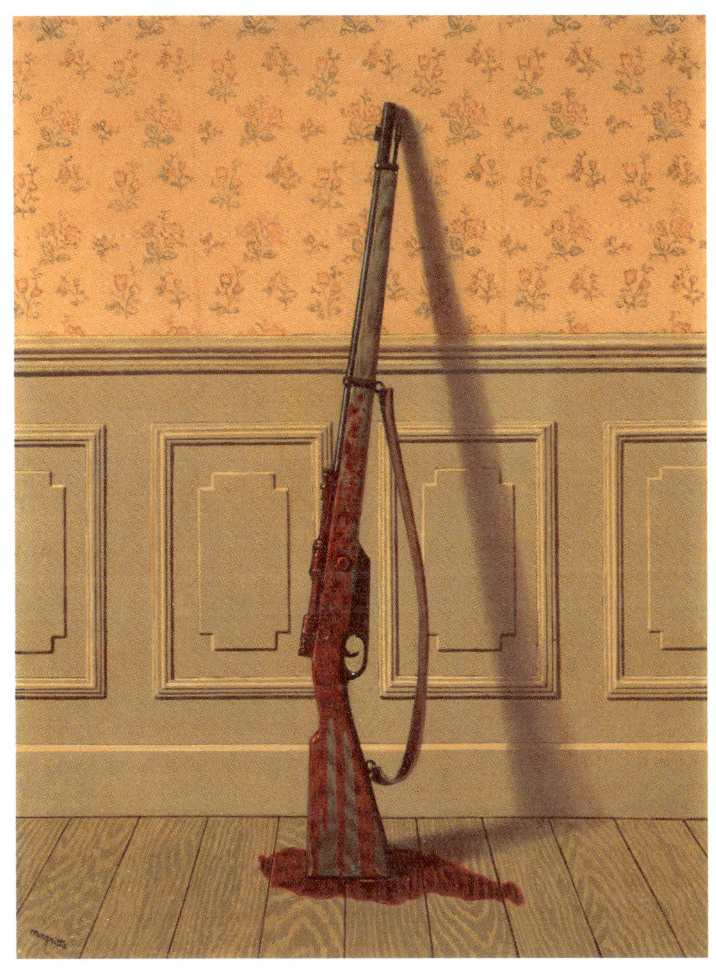

281
The Survivor
1950
oil on canvas, 80 × 60 cm

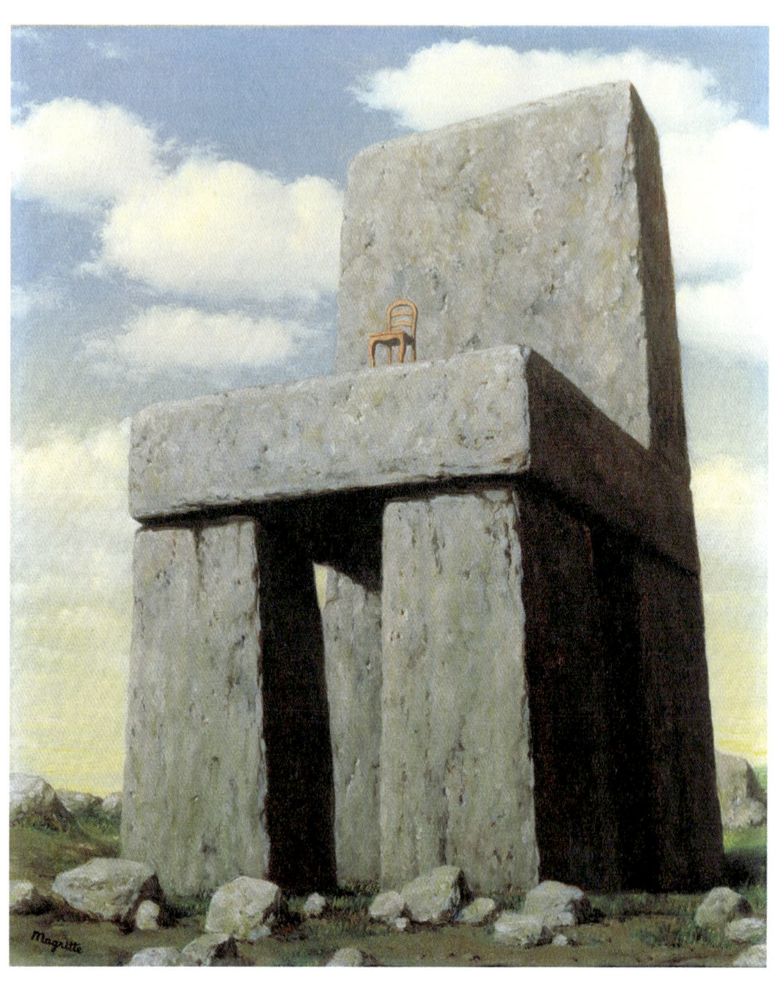

282
The Legend of the Centuries
1950
oil on canvas, 55 × 46 cm

     Poetics of the Everyday

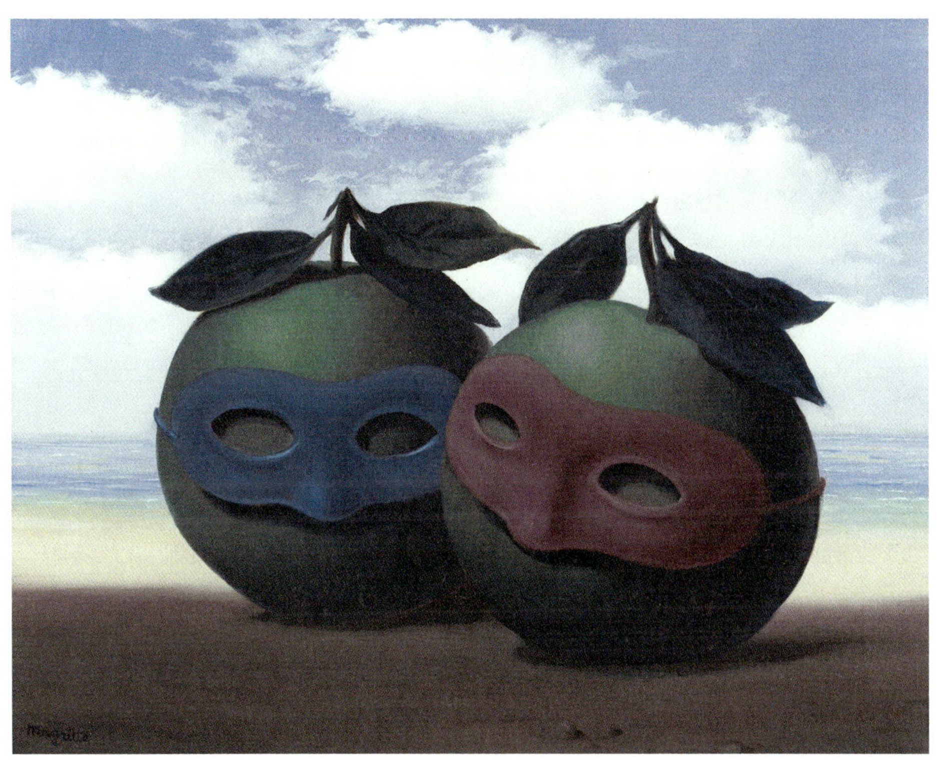

283
The Hesitation Waltz
1950
oil on canvas, 35 × 46 cm

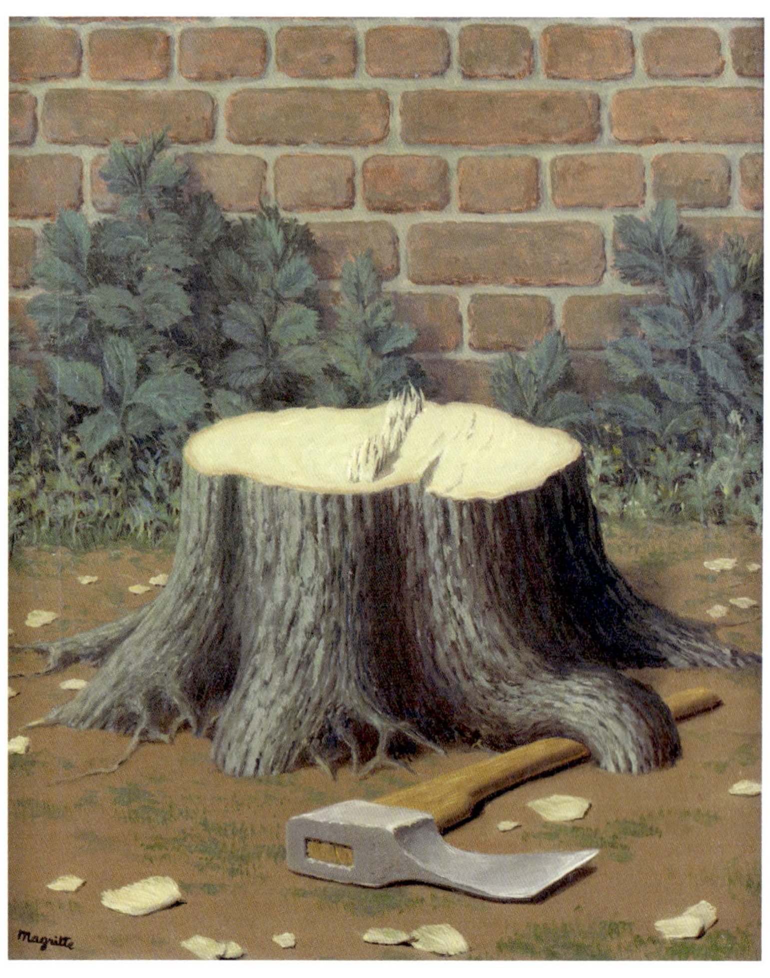

284
The Labours of Alexander
1950
oil on canvas, 58 × 48 cm

     Poetics of the Everyday

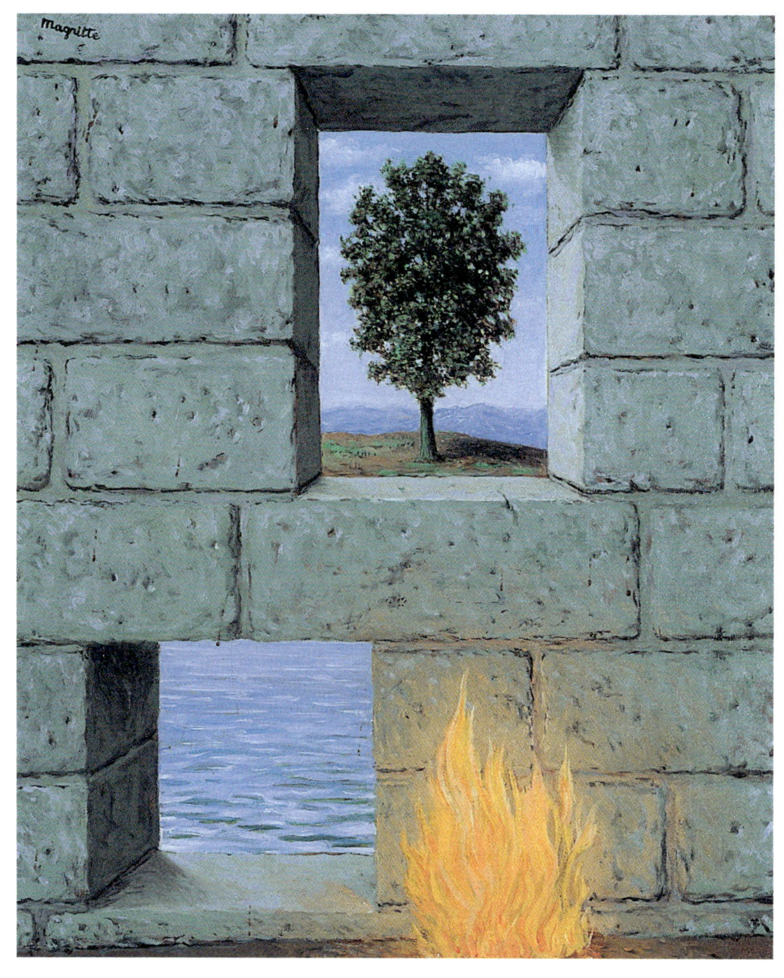

285
Mental Complacency
1950
oil on canvas, 46 × 38 cm

   1947–1967

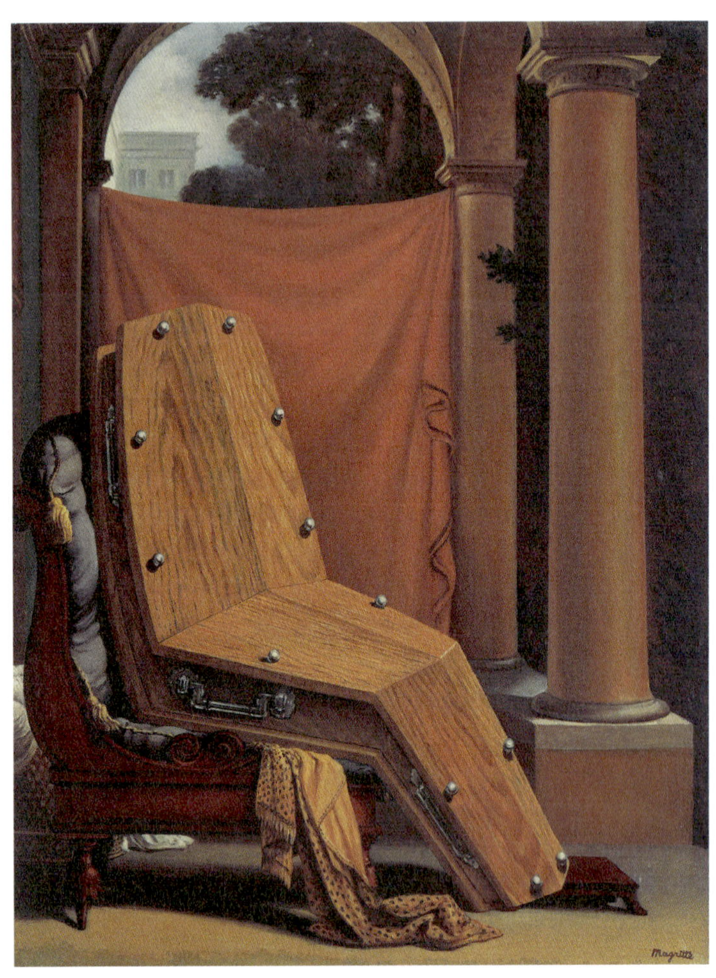

286
Perspective: Gérard's Madame Récamier
1950
oil on canvas, 65 × 50 cm

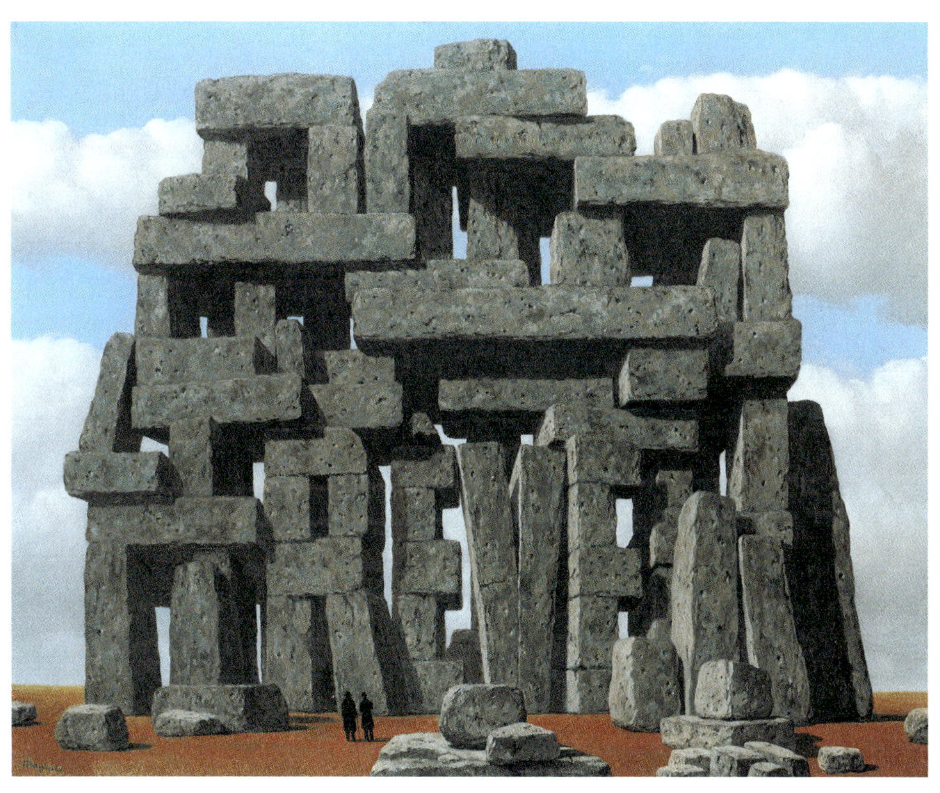

287
The Art of Conversation
1950
oil on canvas, 65 × 81 cm

  1947–1967

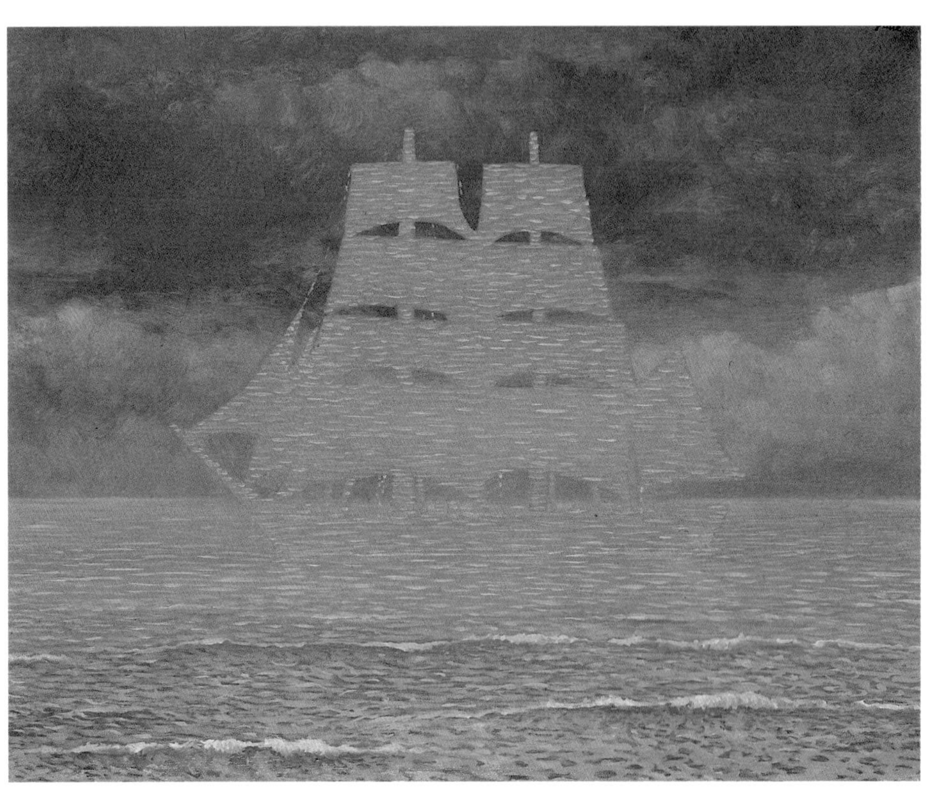

288
The Seducer
1950
oil on canvas, 50 × 60 cm

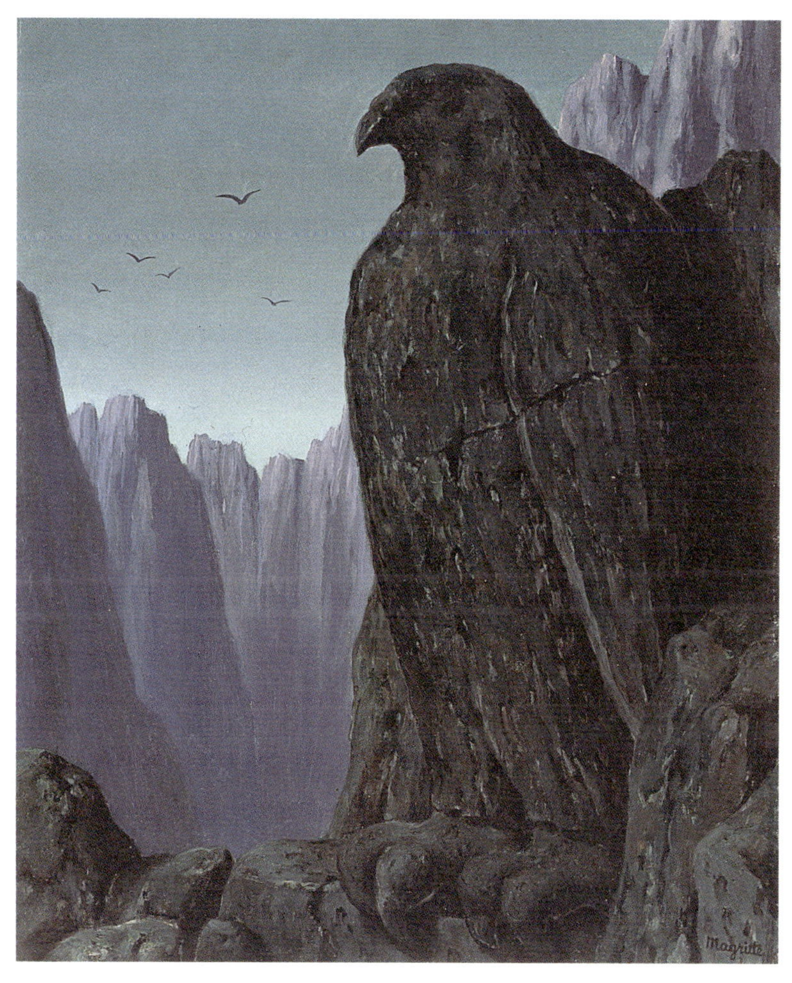

289
The Wasted Footsteps
1950
oil on canvas, 55 × 46 cm

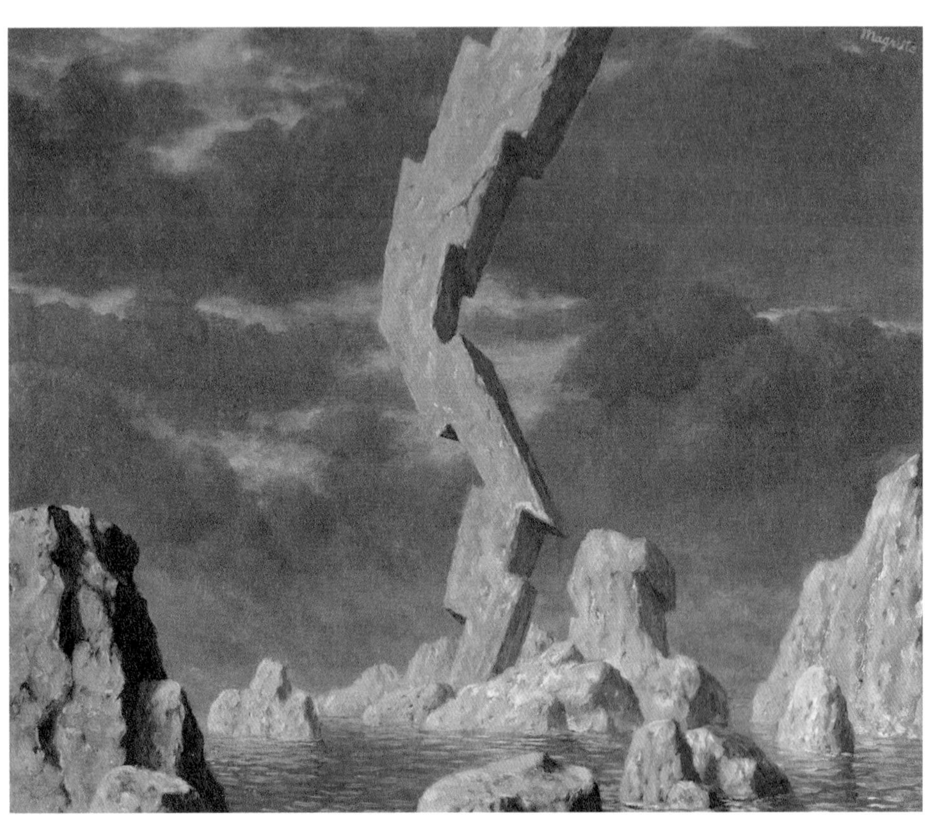

290
The Haunted Castle
1950
oil on canvas, 38 × 46 cm

    Poetics of the Everyday

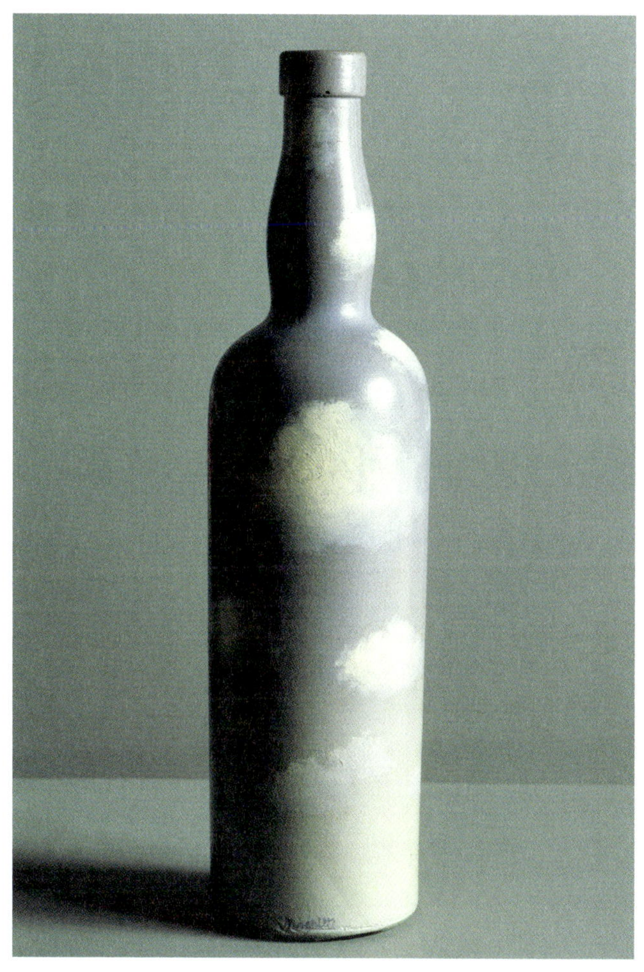

291
The Curvature of the Universe
1950
oil on glass bottle, ht. 29.2 cm

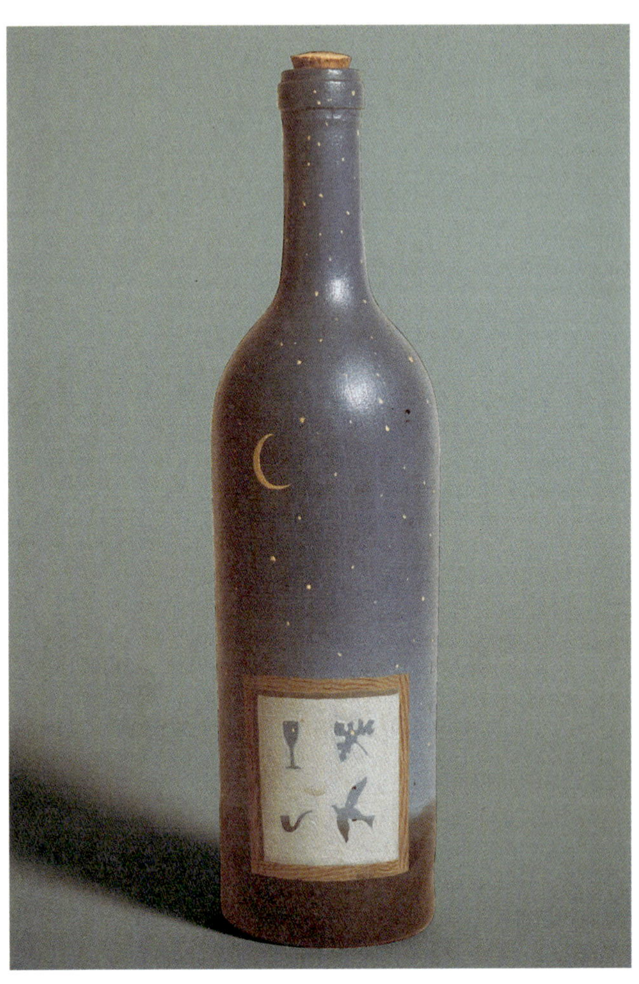

292
(Night Sky with Painting)
1950
oil on glass bottle, ht. 30 cm

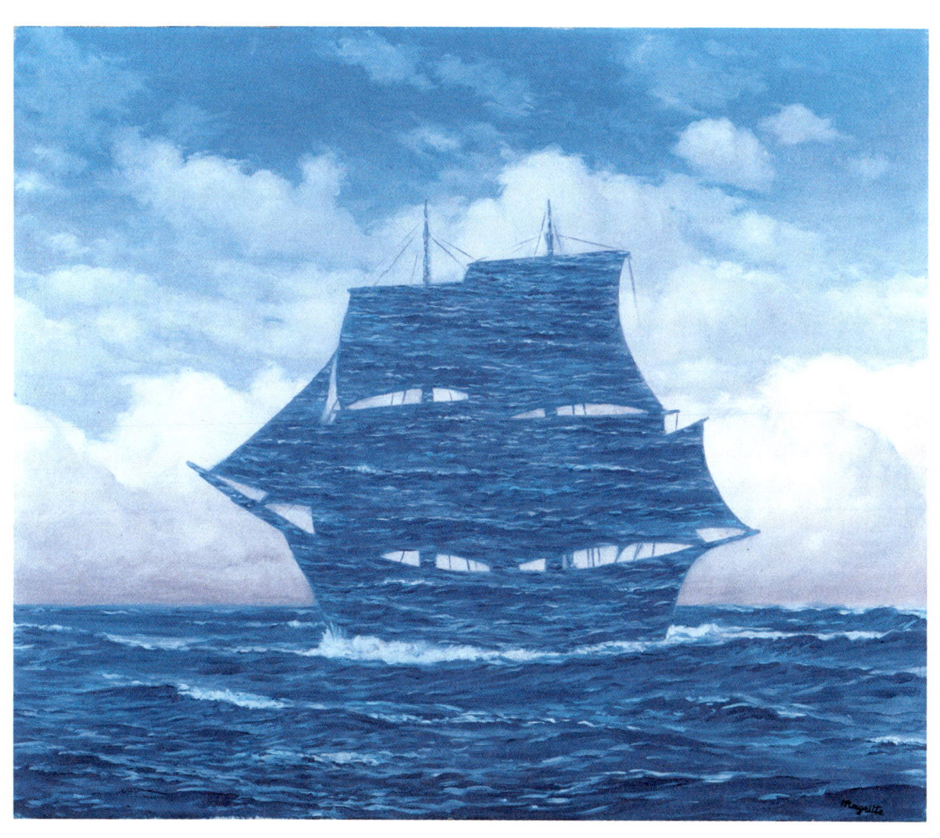

293
The Seducer
1951
oil on canvas, 50 × 60 cm

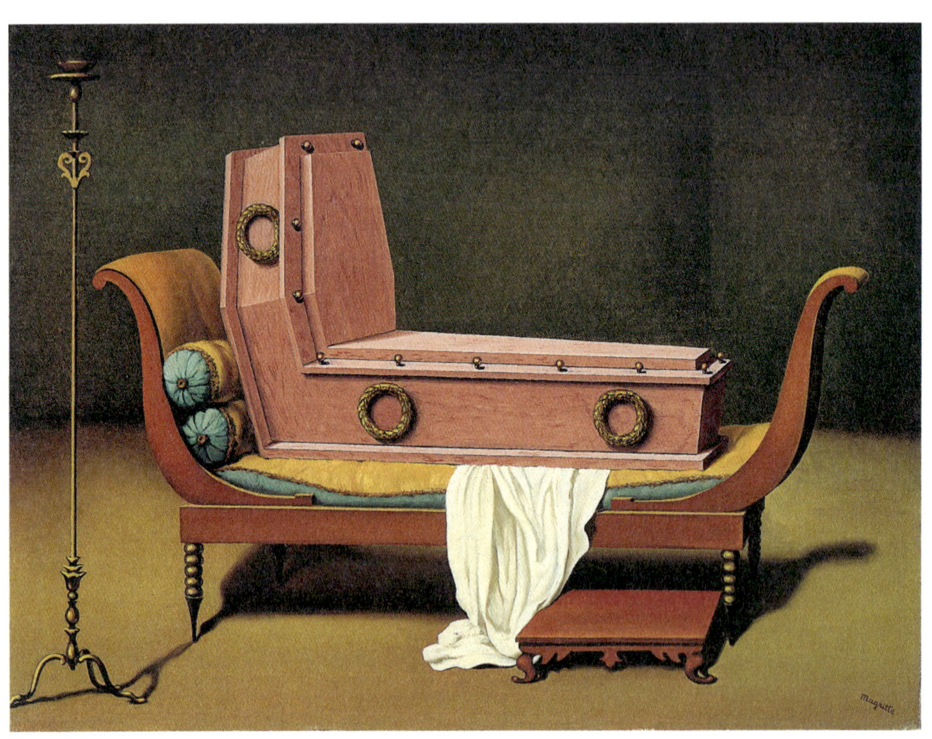

294
Perspective: David's Madame Récamier
1951
oil on canvas, 60 × 80 cm

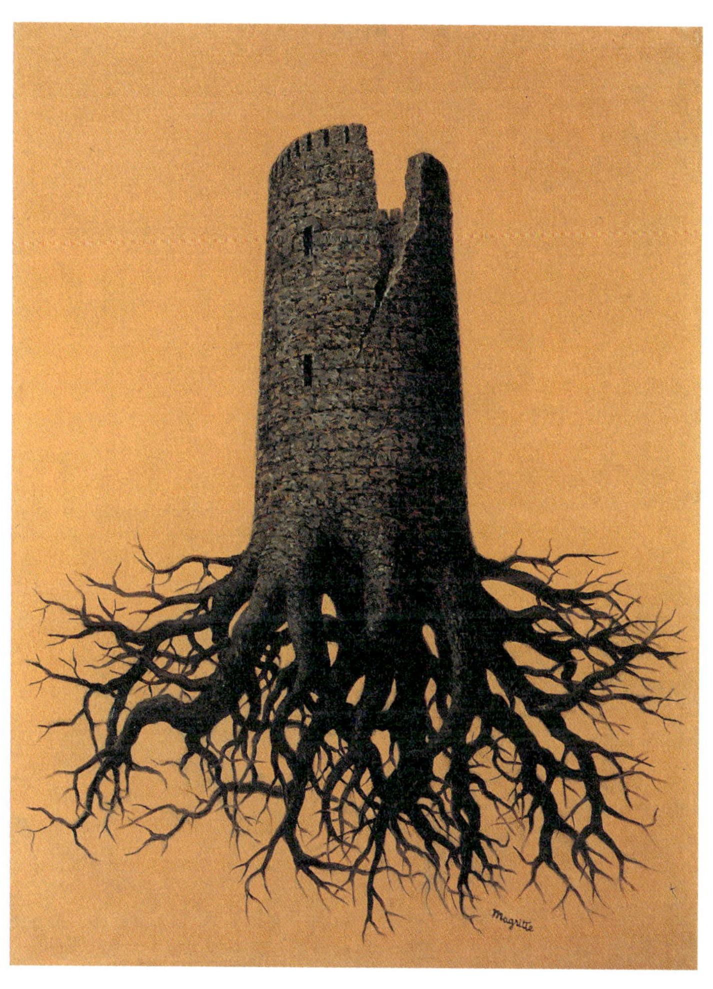

295
Almayer's Folly
1951
oil on canvas, 80 × 60 cm

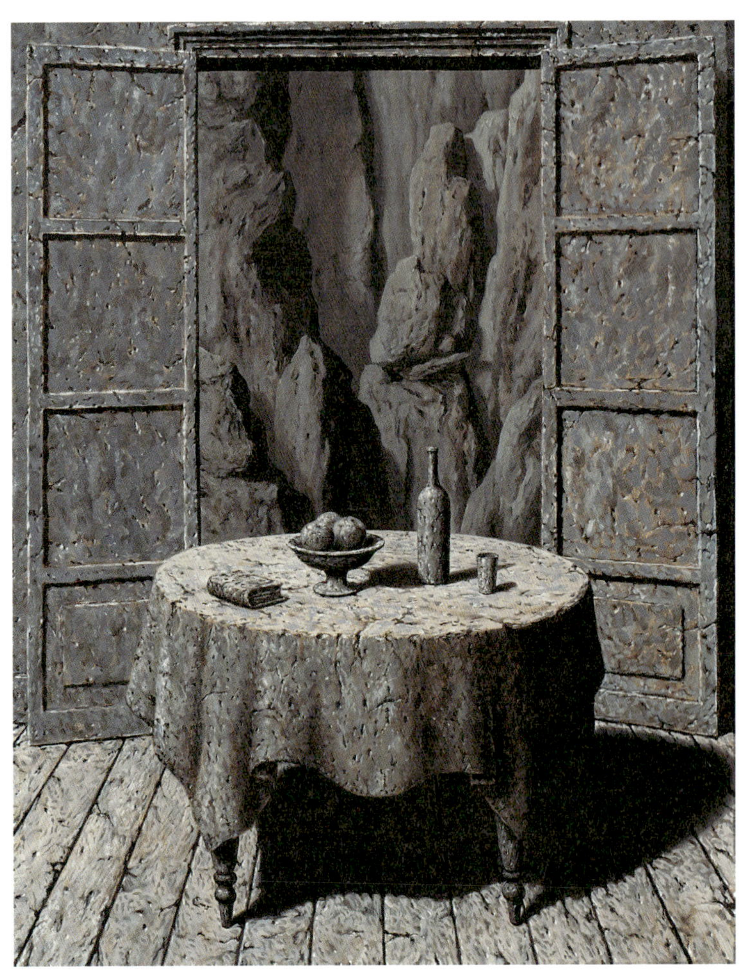

296
Memory of a Journey
1951
oil on canvas, 80 × 65 cm

 Poetics of the Everyday

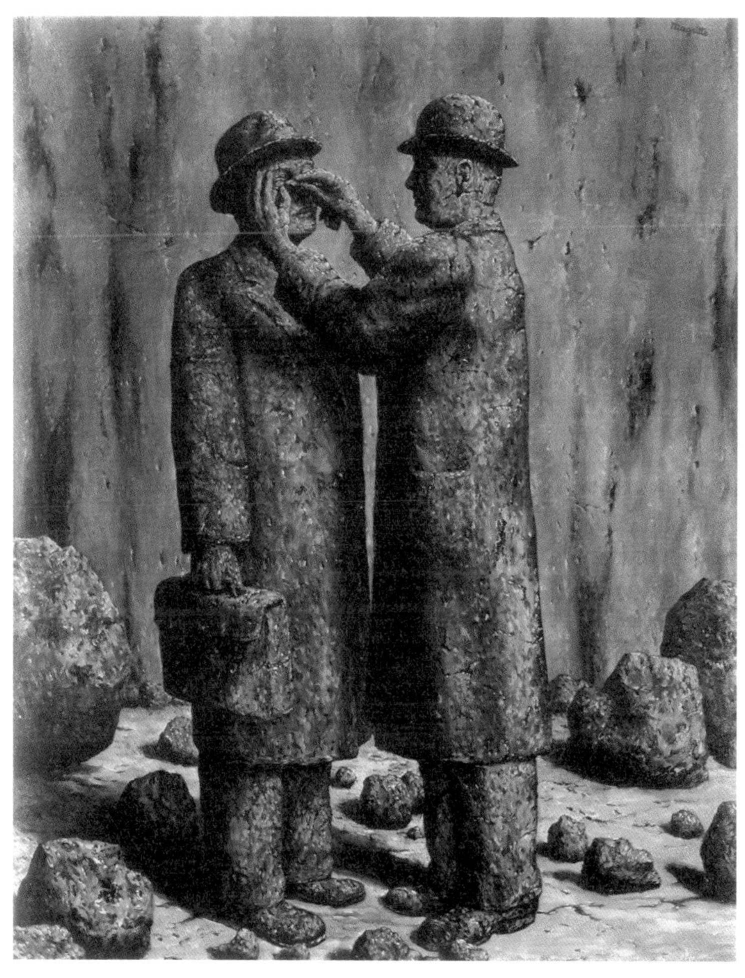

297
Private Diary
1951
oil on canvas, 80 × 65 cm

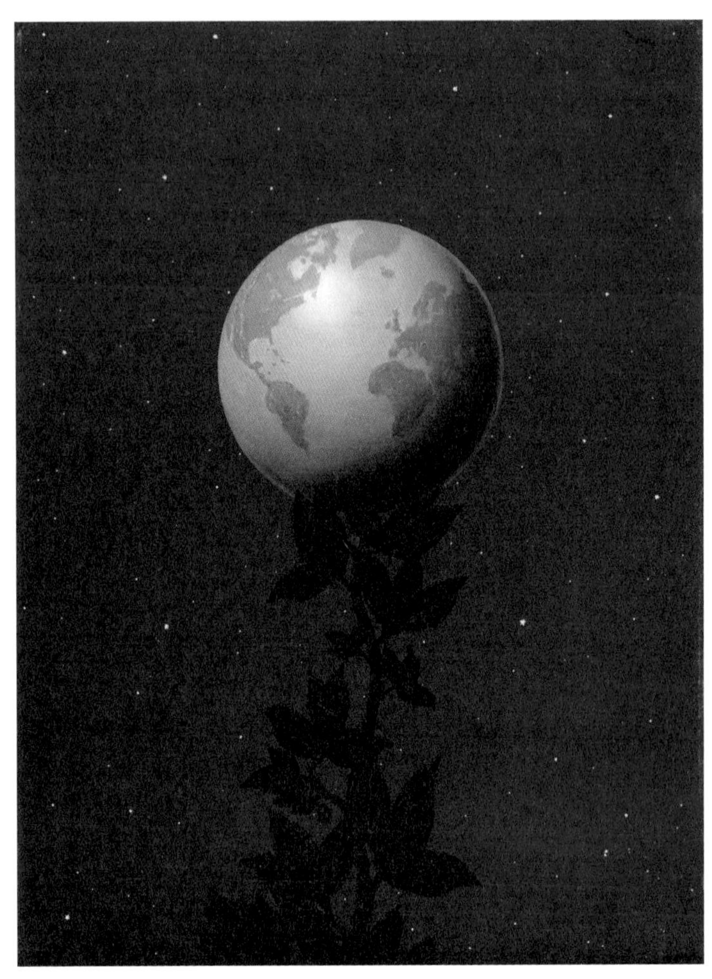

298
The Great Style
1951
oil on canvas, 80 × 60 cm

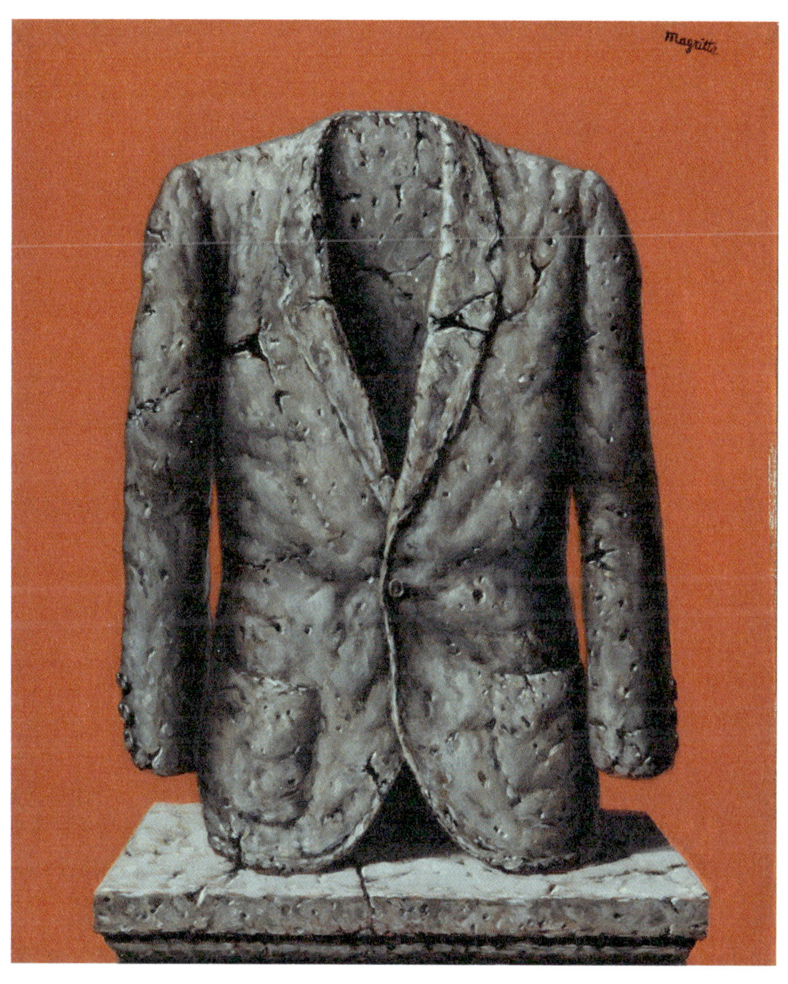

299
The Philtre
1951
oil on canvas, 46 × 38 cm

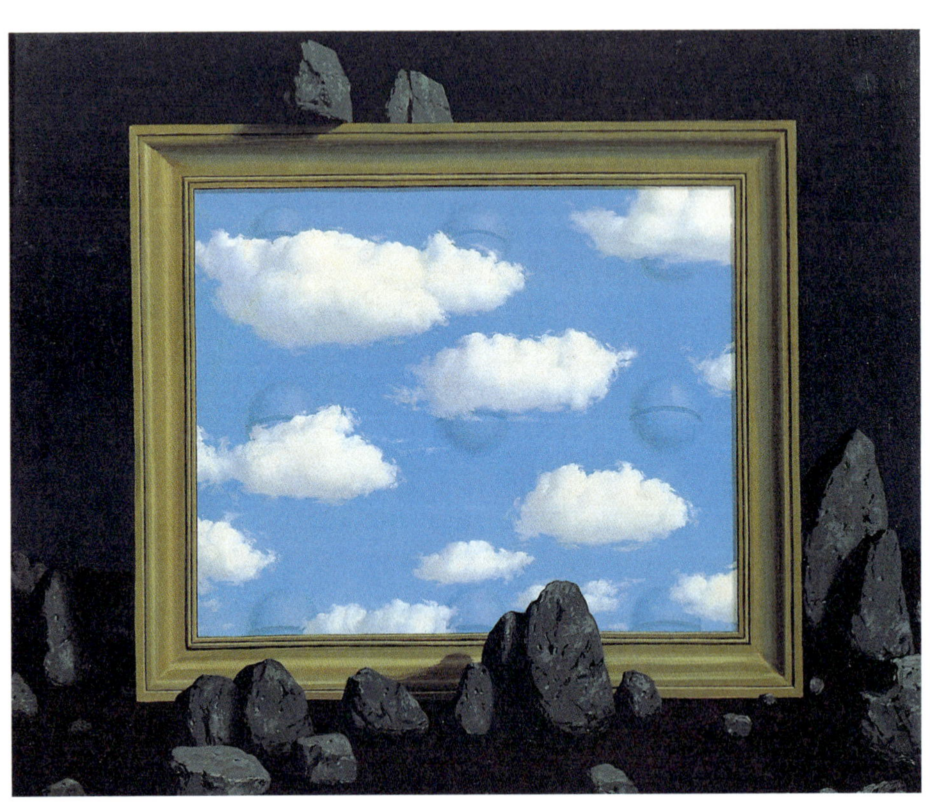

300
The Spring Tide
1951
oil on canvas, 65 × 80 cm

 Poetics of the Everyday

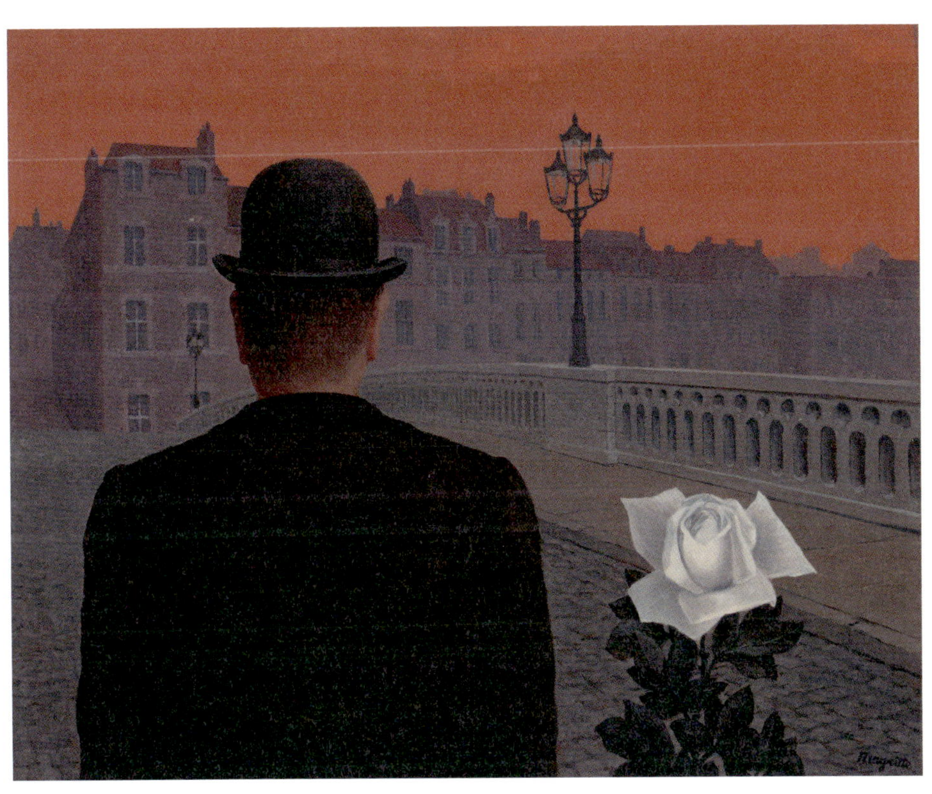

301
Pandora's Box
1951
oil on canvas, 45 × 55 cm

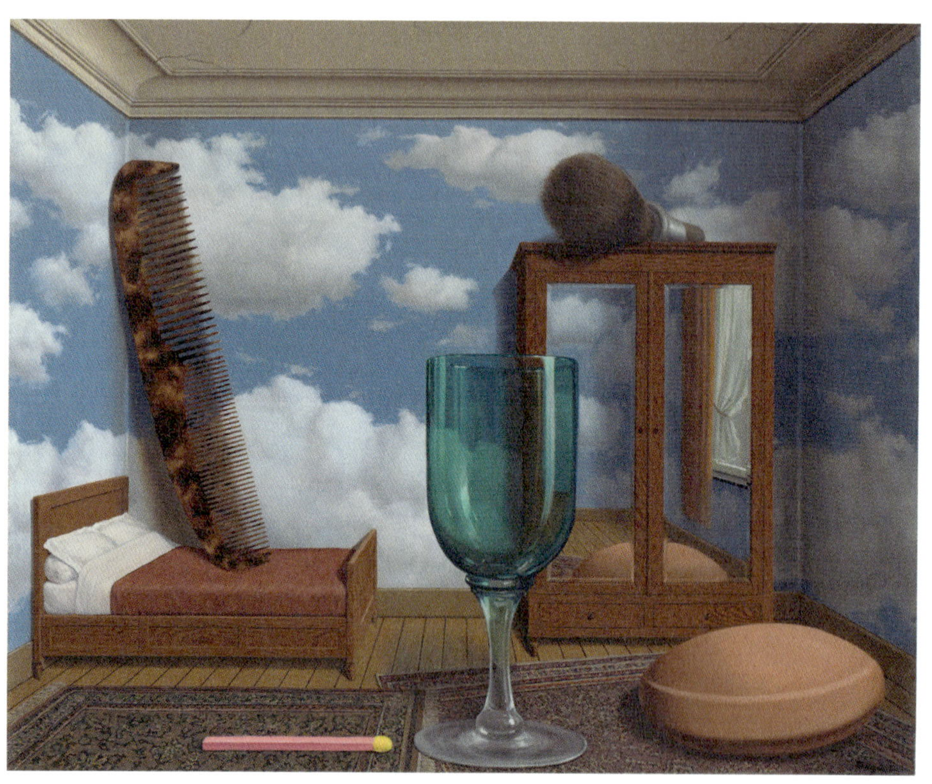

302
Personal Values
1952
oil on canvas, 80 × 100 cm

 Poetics of the Everyday

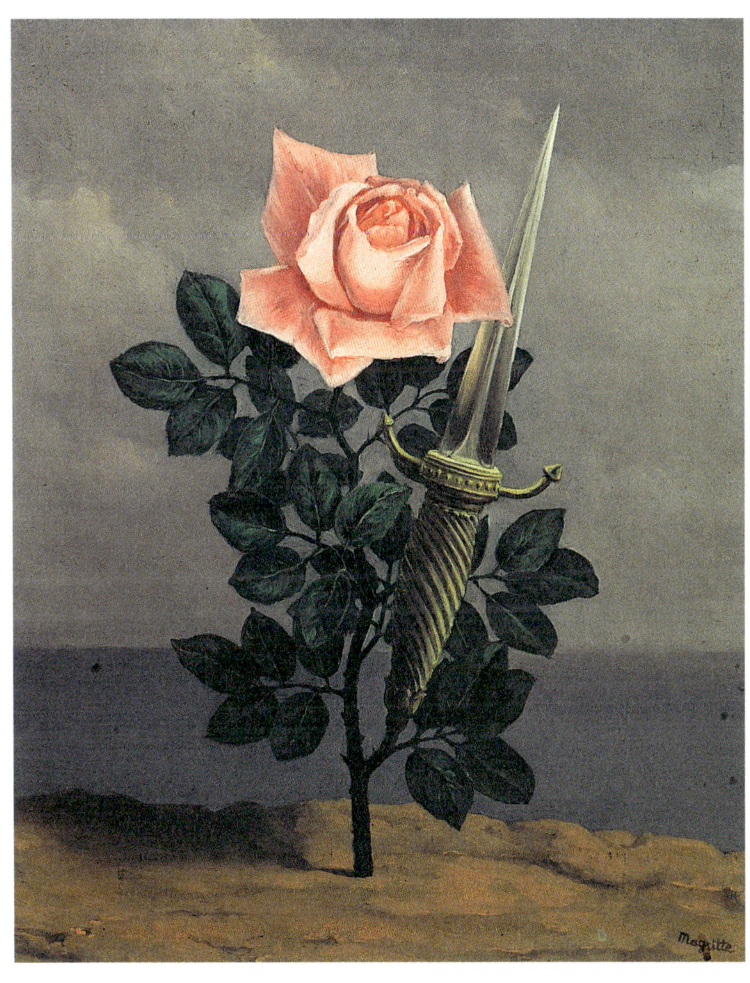

303
The Blow to the Heart
1952
oil on canvas, 46 × 38 cm

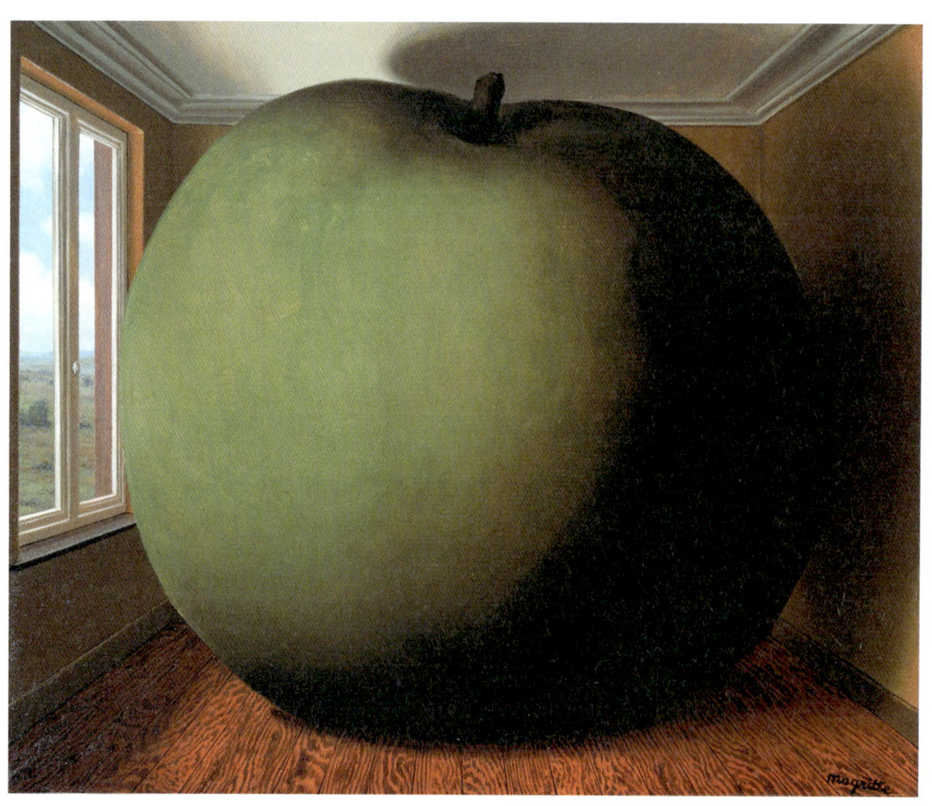

304
The Listening Room
1952
oil on canvas, 45 × 55 cm

     Poetics of the Everyday

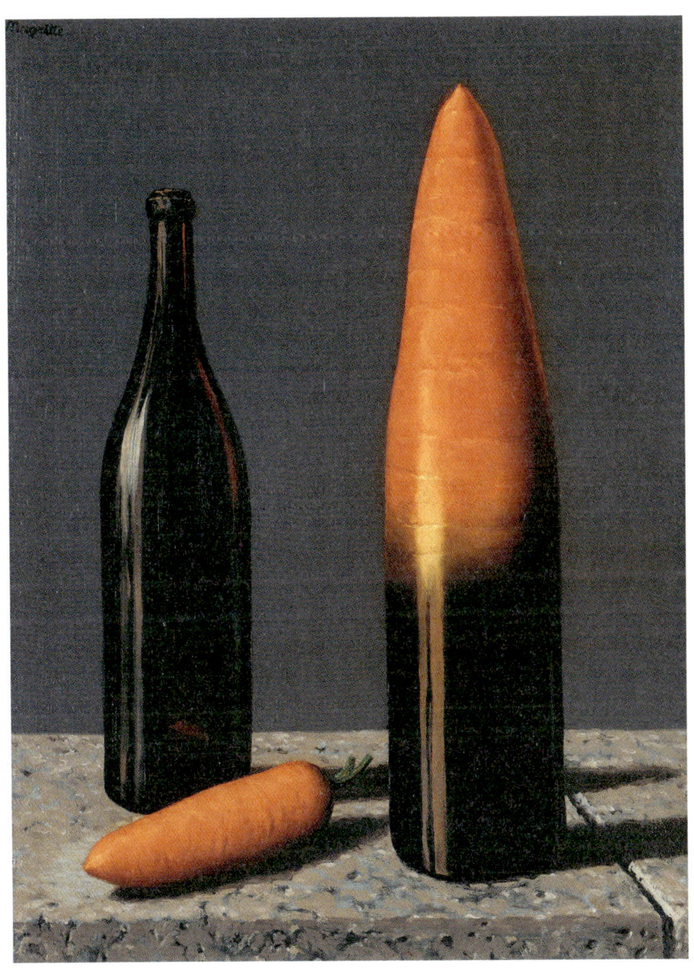

305
The Explanation
1952
oil on canvas, 46 × 35 cm

373

1947–1967

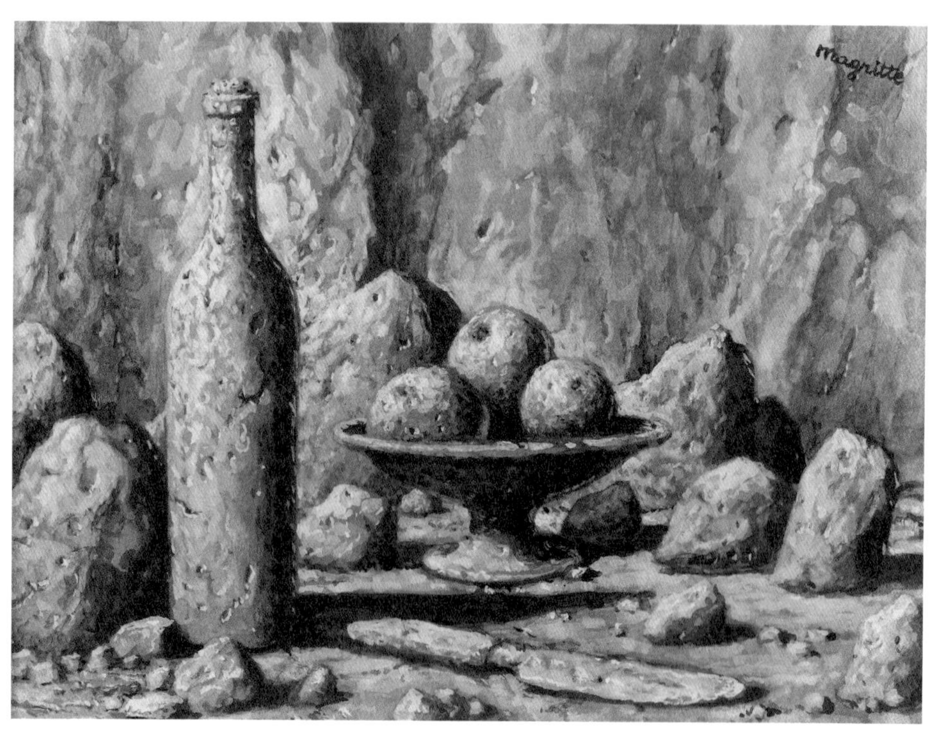

306
Memory of a Journey
1952
gouache on paper or card, 14.3 × 19 cm

     Poetics of the Everyday

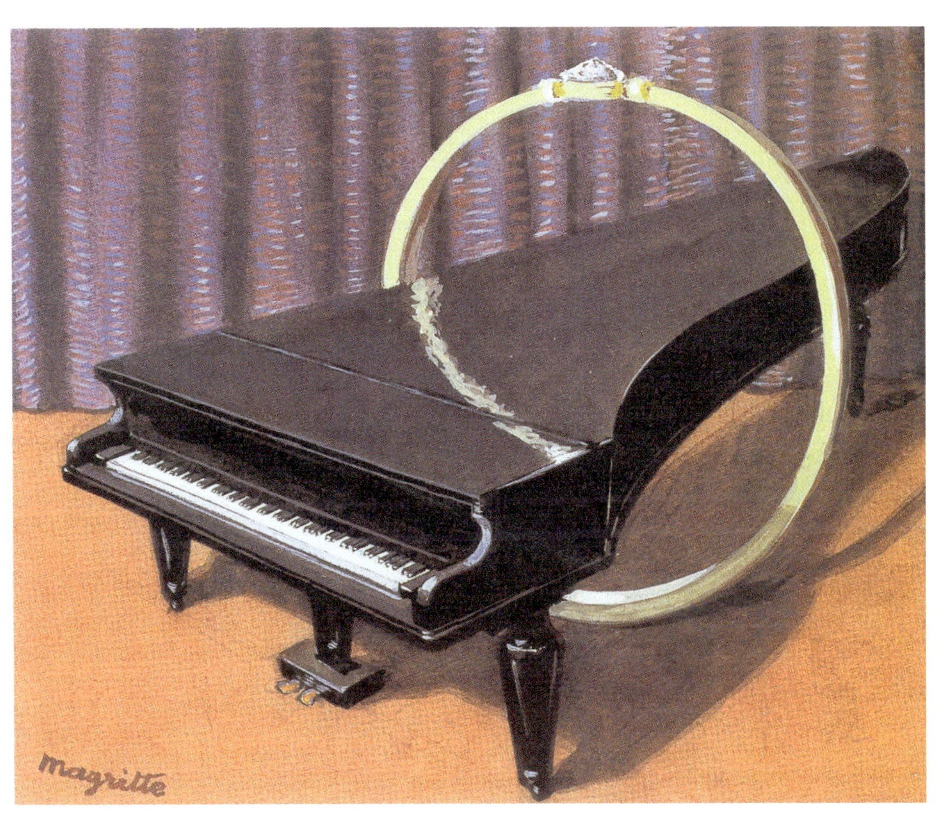

307
The Happy Hand
1952
gouache on paper, 15 × 18 cm

 1947–1967

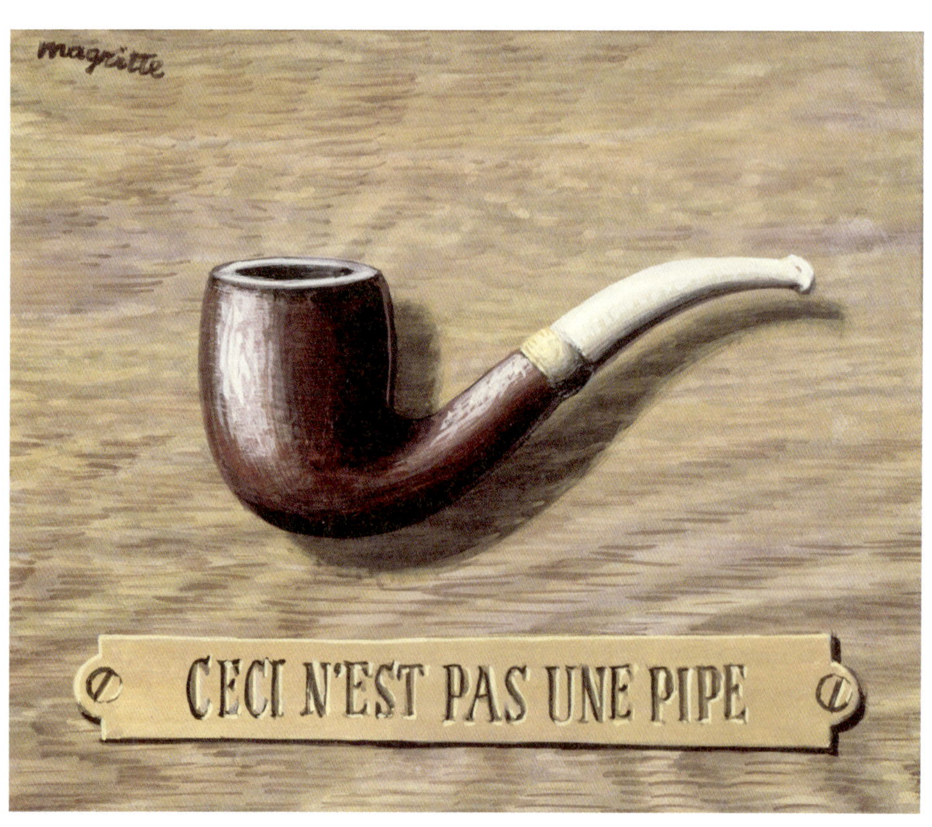

308
(The Treachery of Images)
1952 or 1953
gouache on paper, 14 × 16.5 cm

Poetics of the Everyday

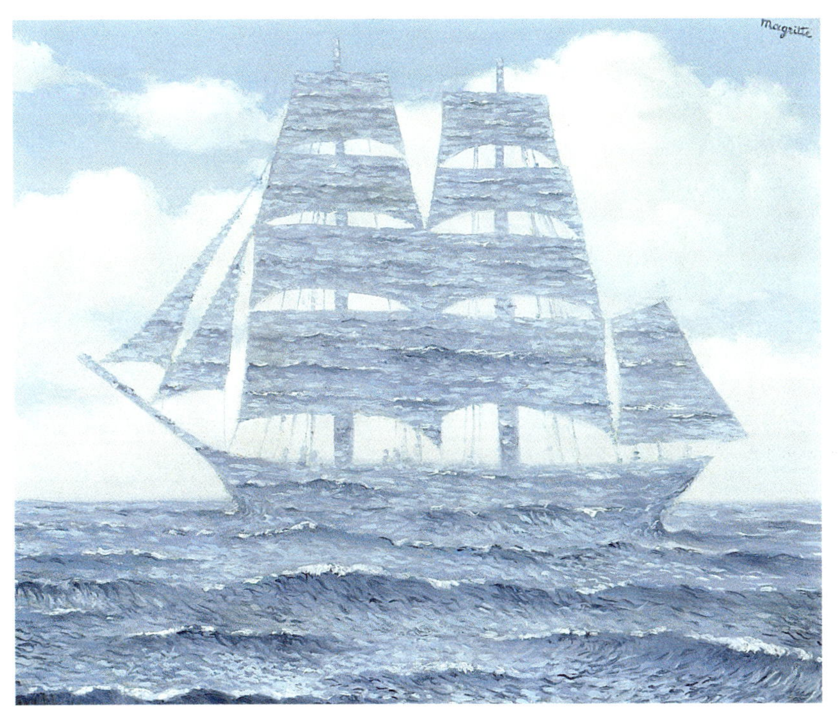

309
The Seducer
1953
oil on canvas, 38 × 46 cm

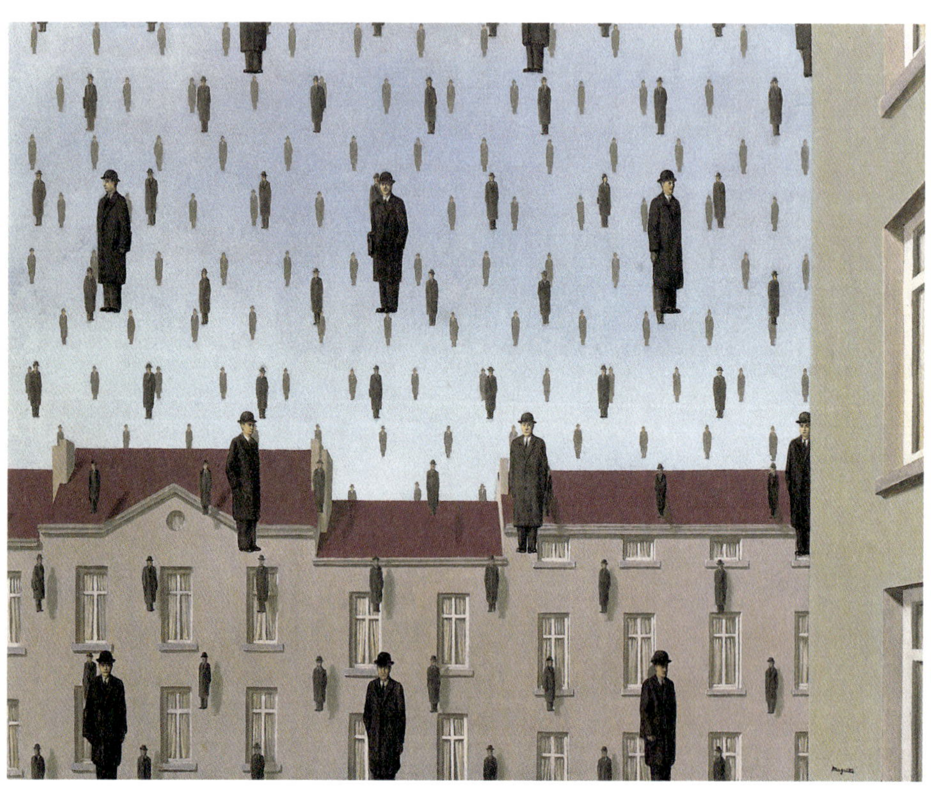

310
Golconda
1953
oil on canvas, 80 × 100 cm

Poetics of the Everyday

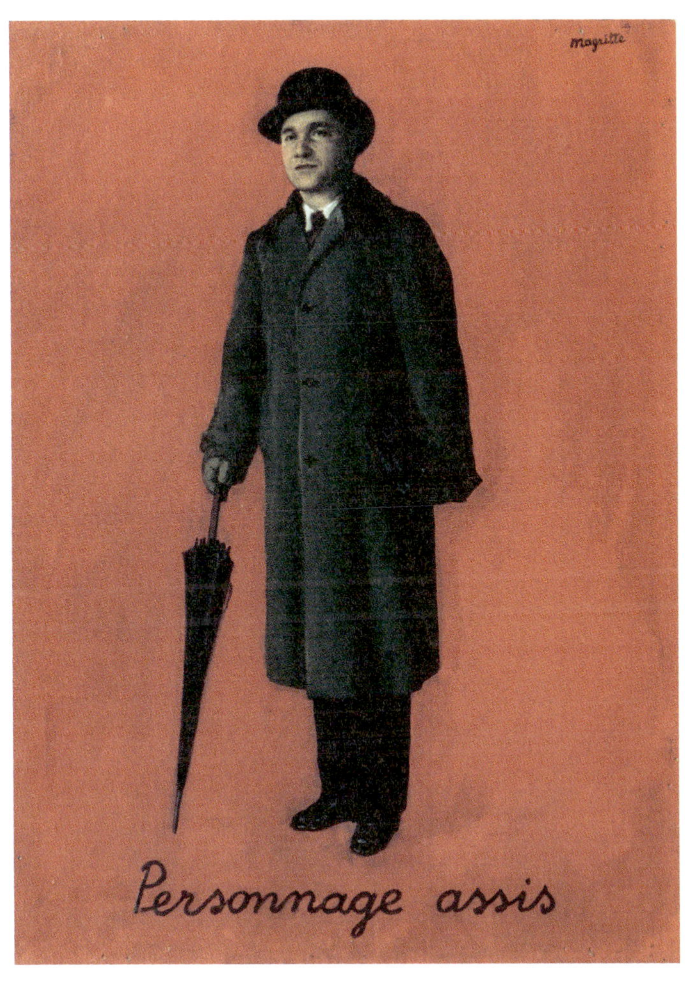

311
The Good Example
1953
oil on canvas, 46 × 33 cm

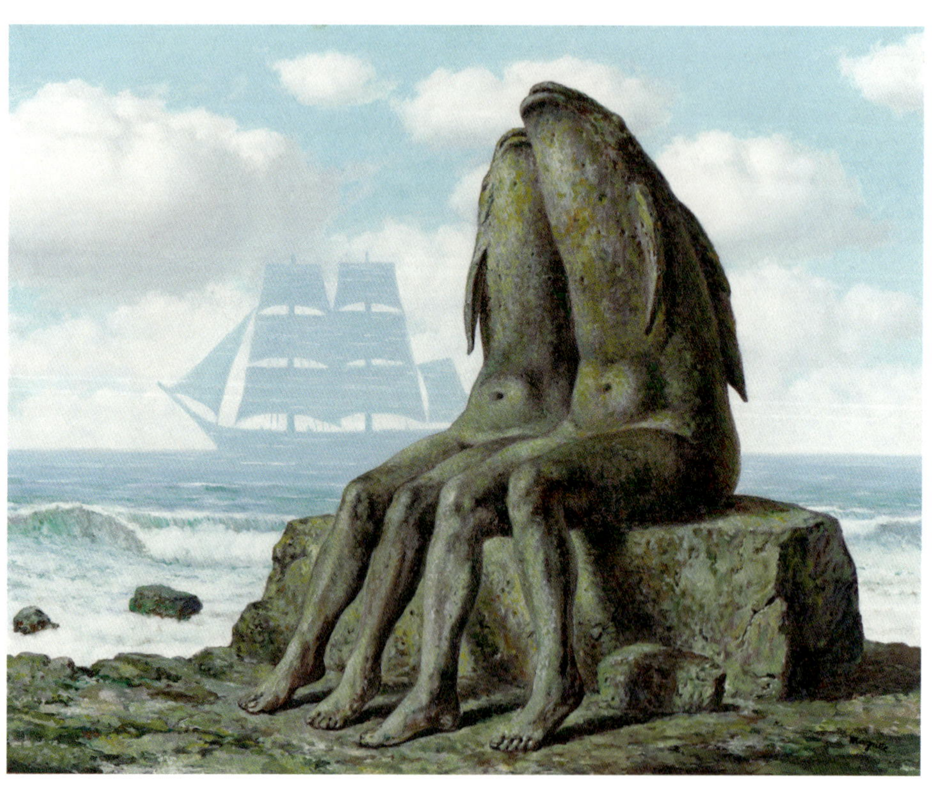

312
The Wonders of Nature
1953
oil on canvas, 80 × 100 cm

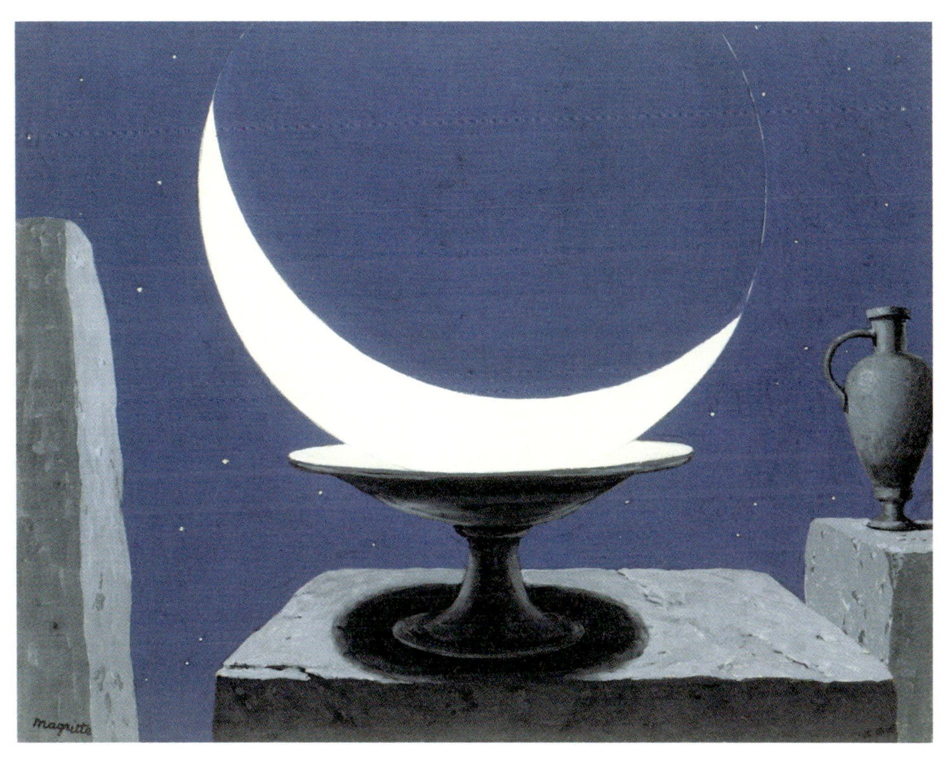

313
Melusine's Window
1953
gouache on paper, 26.4 × 34.7 cm

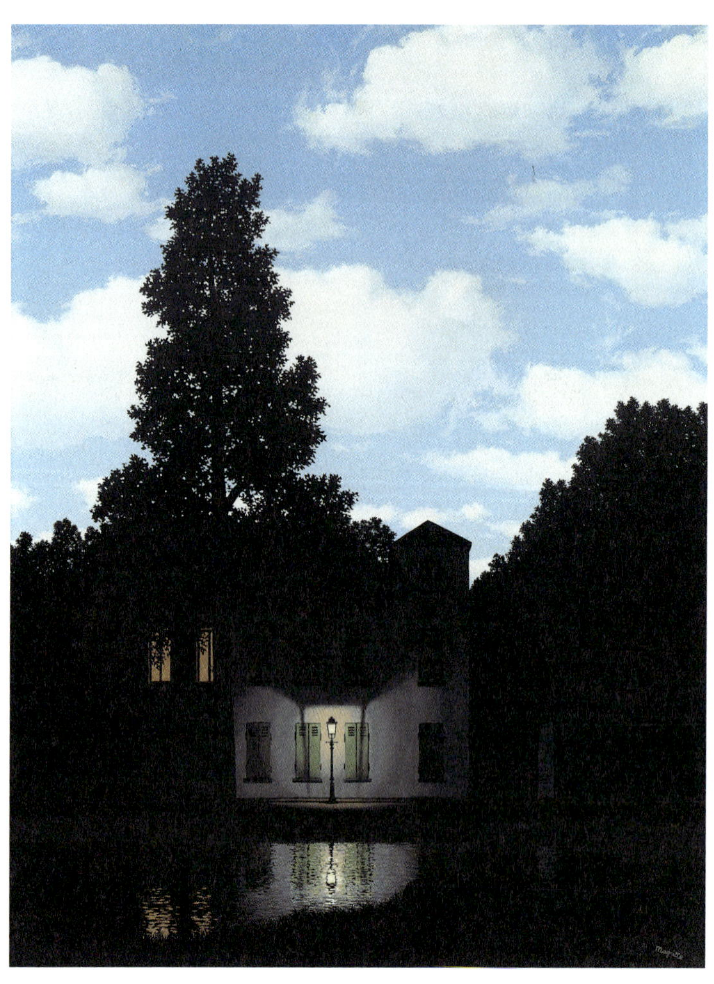

314
The Dominion of Light
1954
oil on canvas, 146 × 114 cm

          Poetics of the Everyday

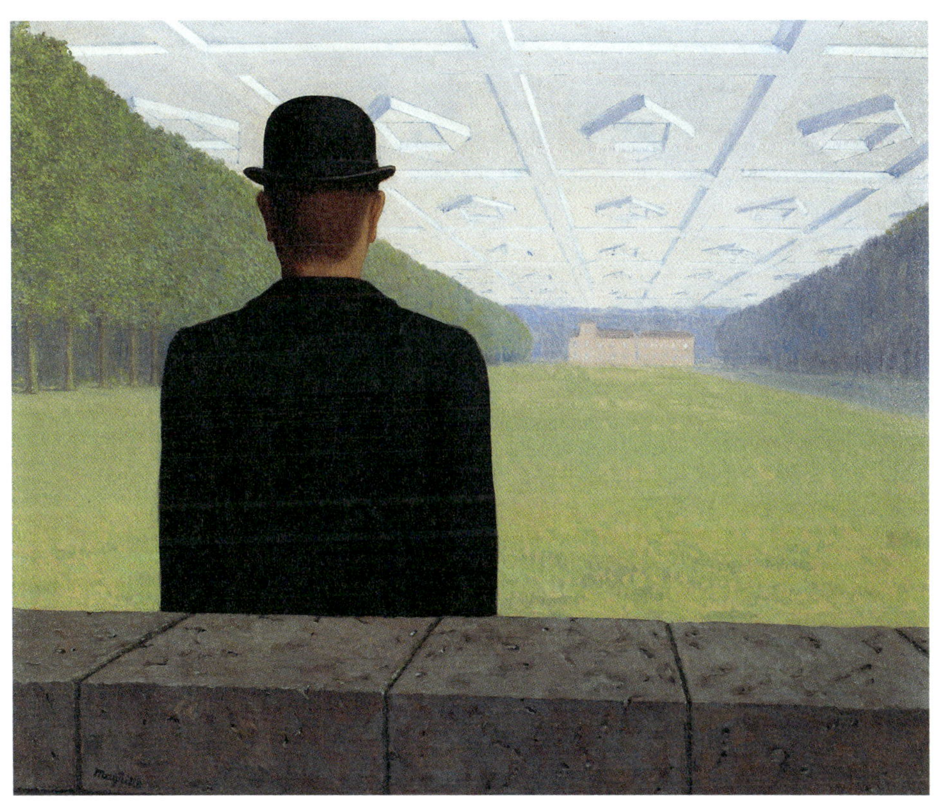

315
The Great Century
1954
oil on canvas, 50 × 60 cm

                1947–1967

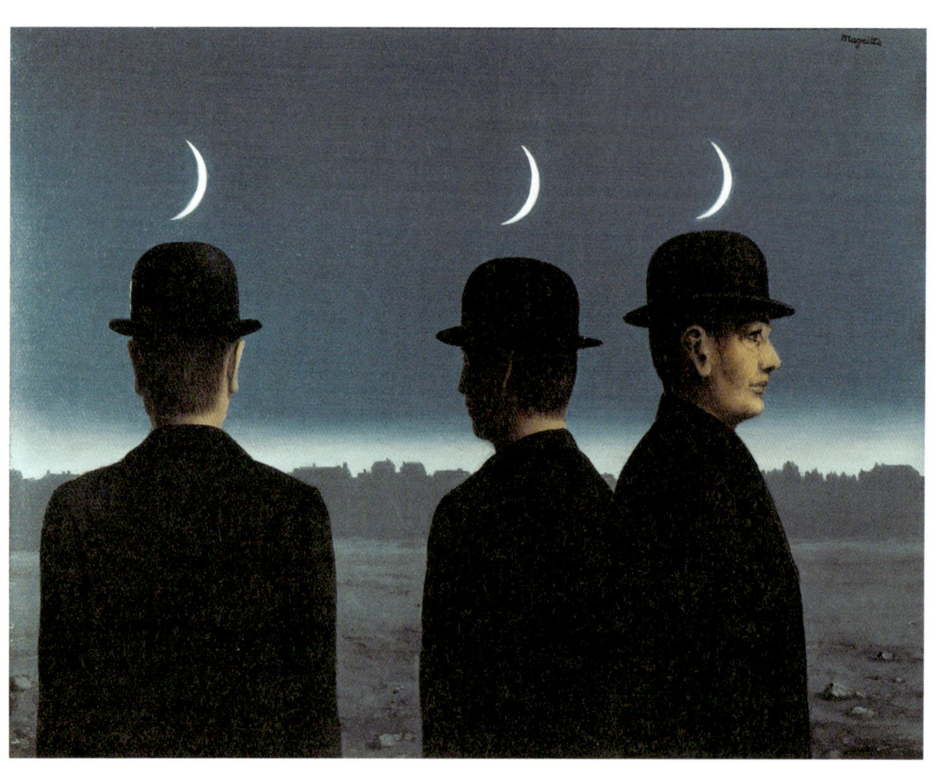

316
The Masterpiece or The Mysteries of the Horizon
1955
oil on canvas, 50 × 65 cm

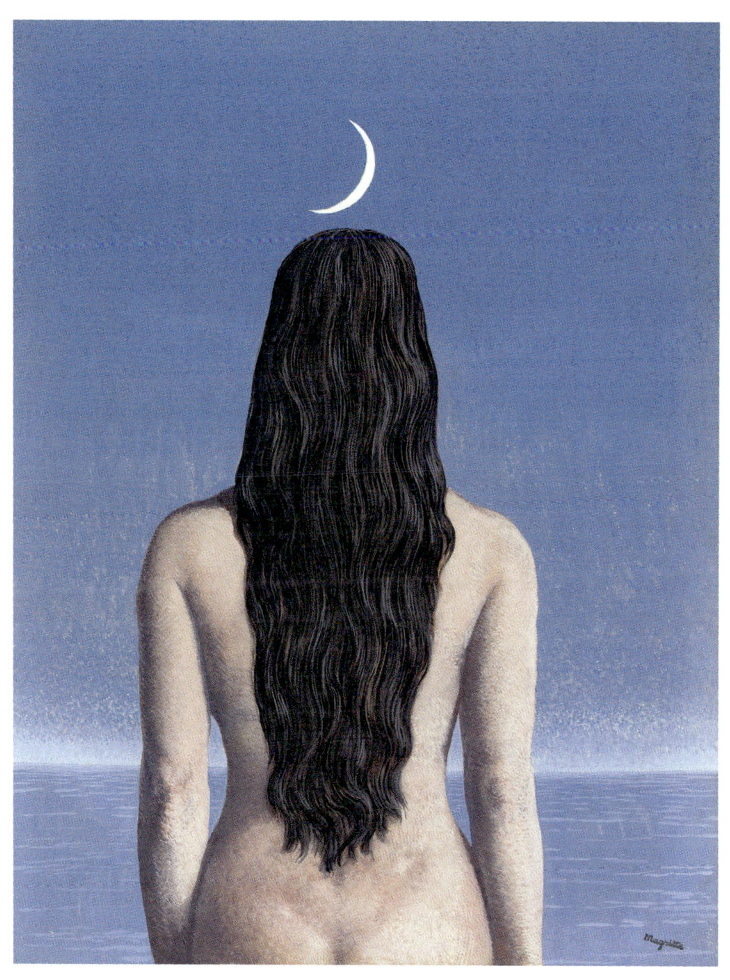

317
The Evening Gown
1955
oil on canvas, 65 × 50 cm

     1947–1967

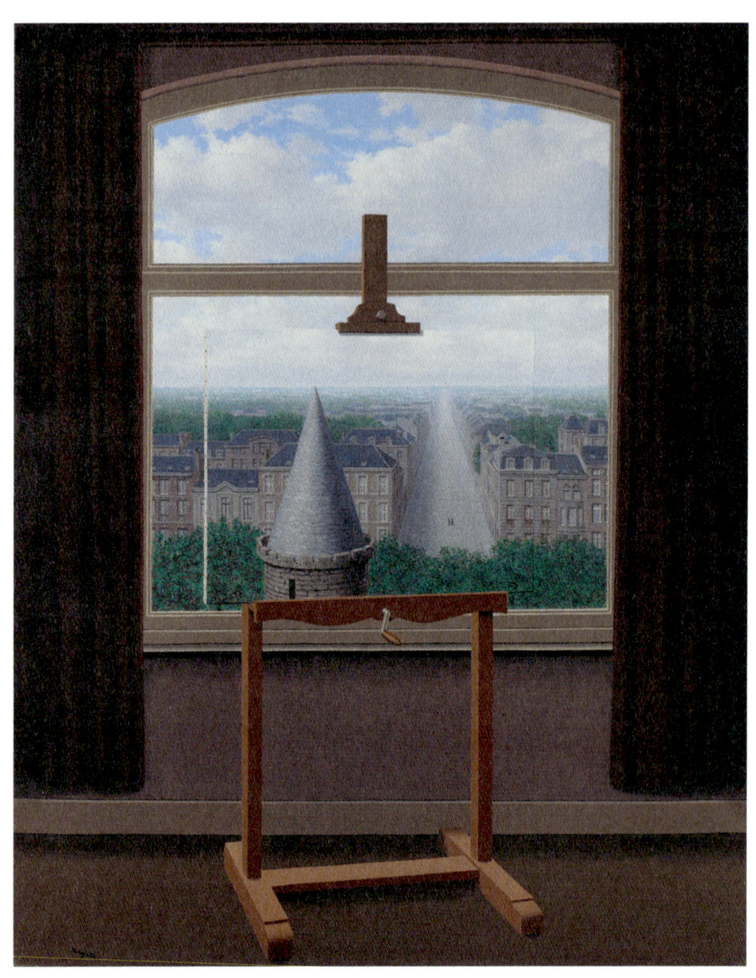

318
Where Euclid Walked
1955
oil on canvas, 162 × 130 cm

     Poetics of the Everyday

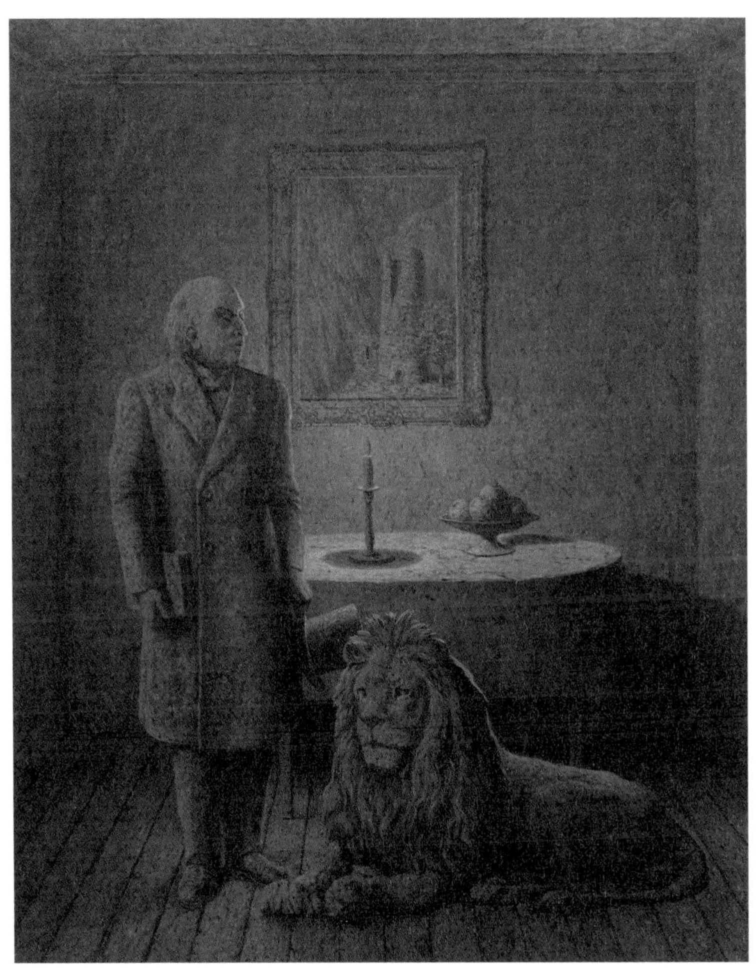

319
Memory of a Journey
1955
oil on canvas, 162 × 130 cm

  1947–1967

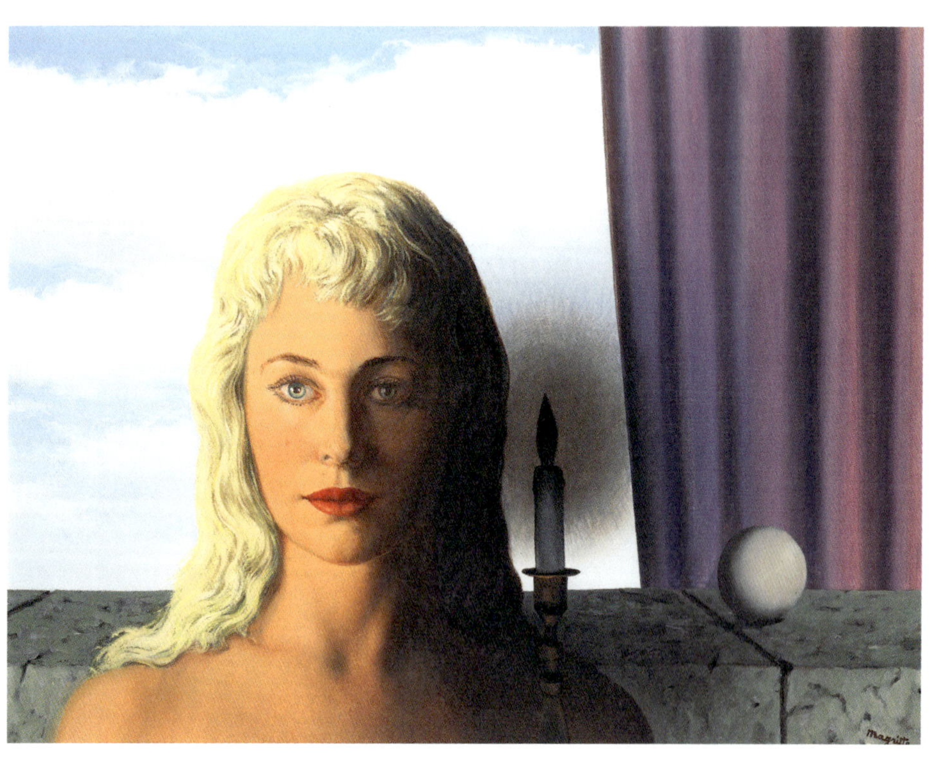

320
The Ignorant Fairy or Portrait of Anne-Marie Crowet
1956
oil on canvas, 50 × 65 cm

Poetics of the Everyday

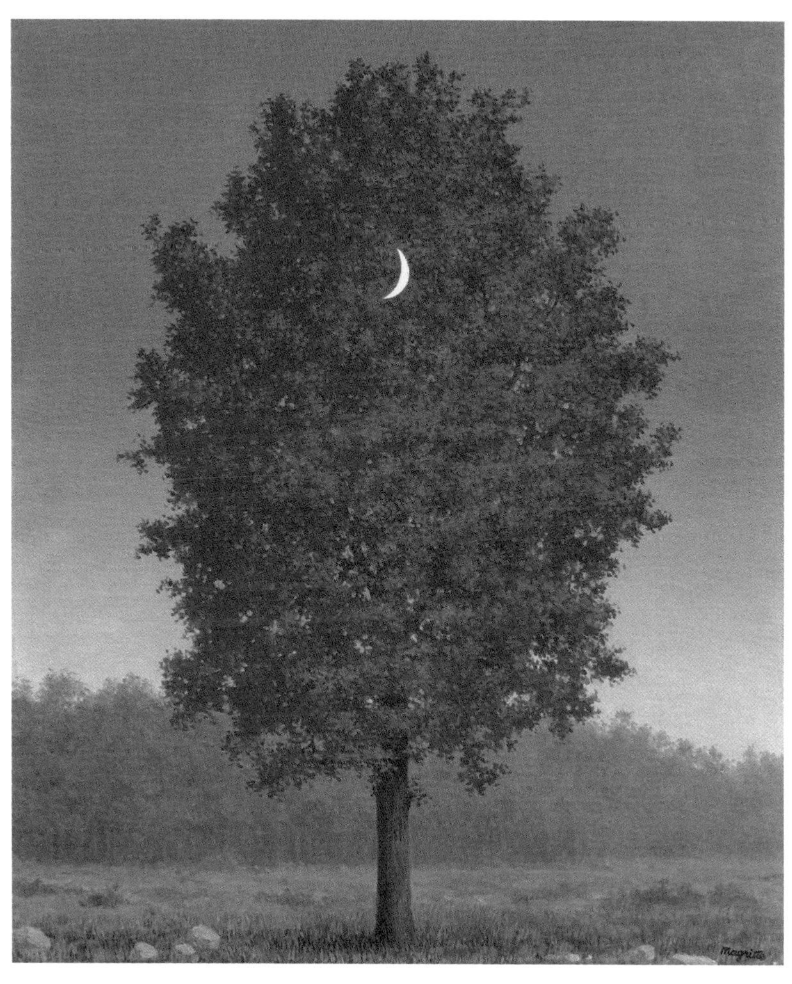

321
The Sixteenth of September
1956
oil on canvas, 60 × 50 cm

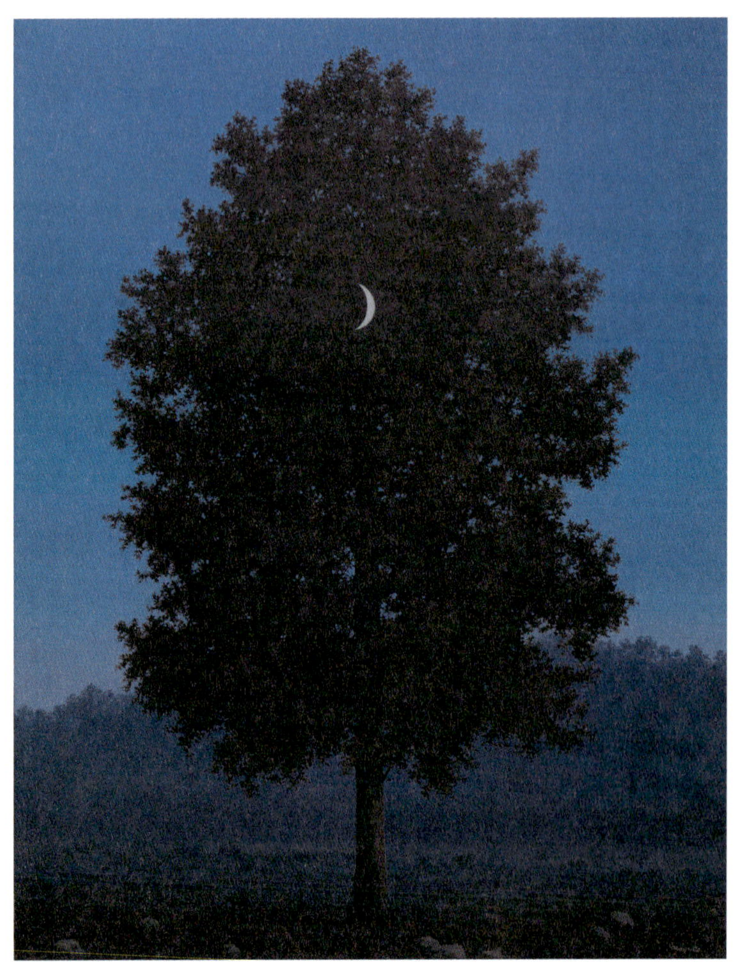

322
The Sixteenth of September
1956
oil on canvas, 116 × 89 cm

Poetics of the Everyday

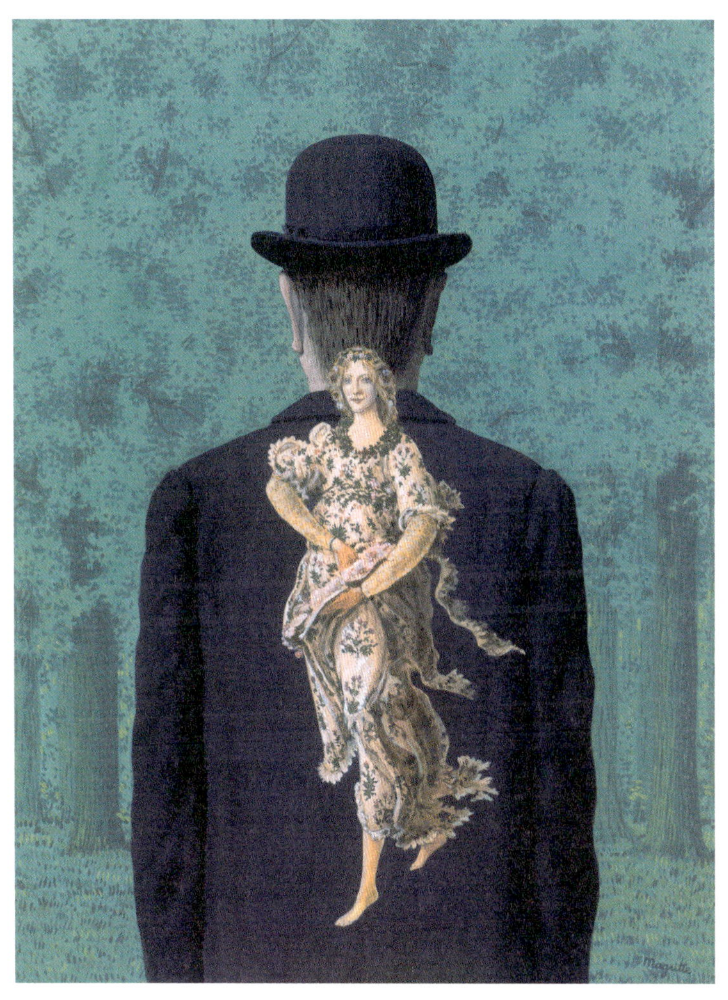

323
The Ready-Made Bouquet
1956
gouache on paper, 46 × 34 cm

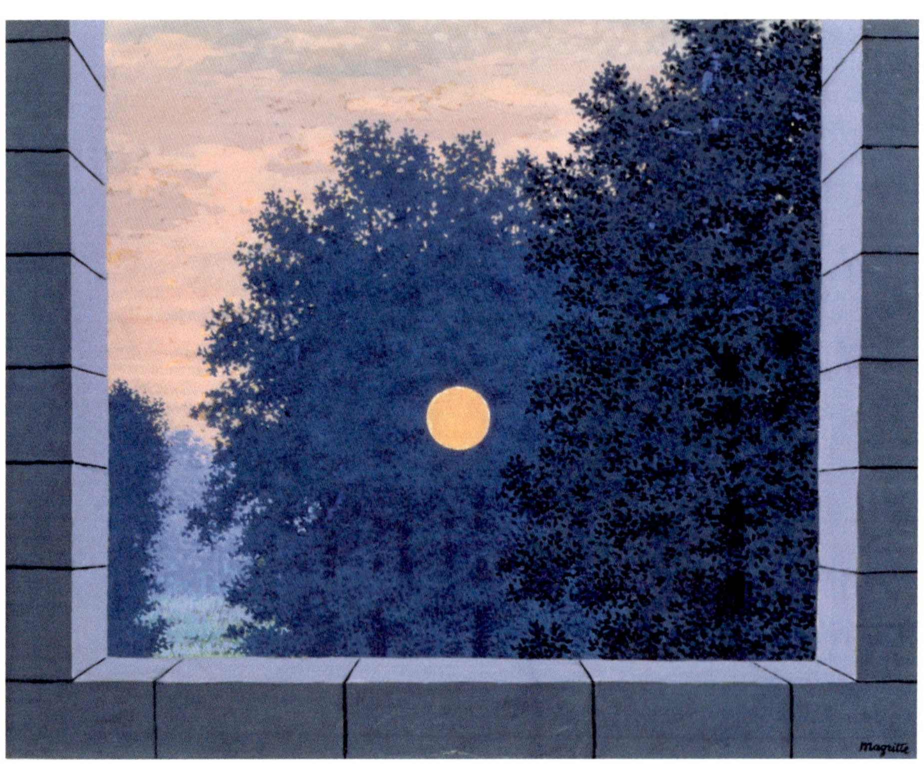

324
The Banquet
1956
gouache on paper, 35.9 × 46.4 cm

          Poetics of the Everyday

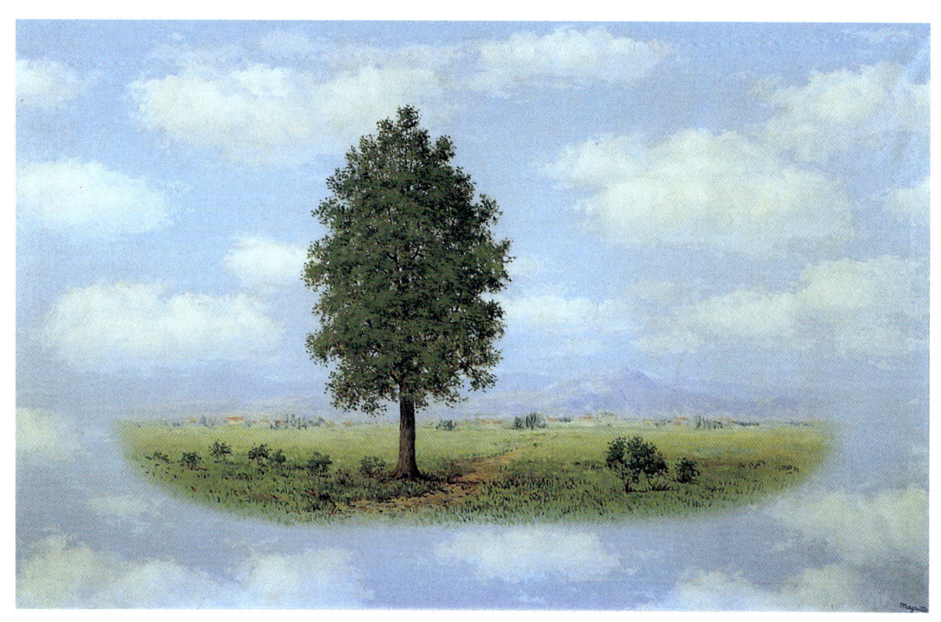

325
The Territory
1957
oil on canvas, 75 × 120 cm

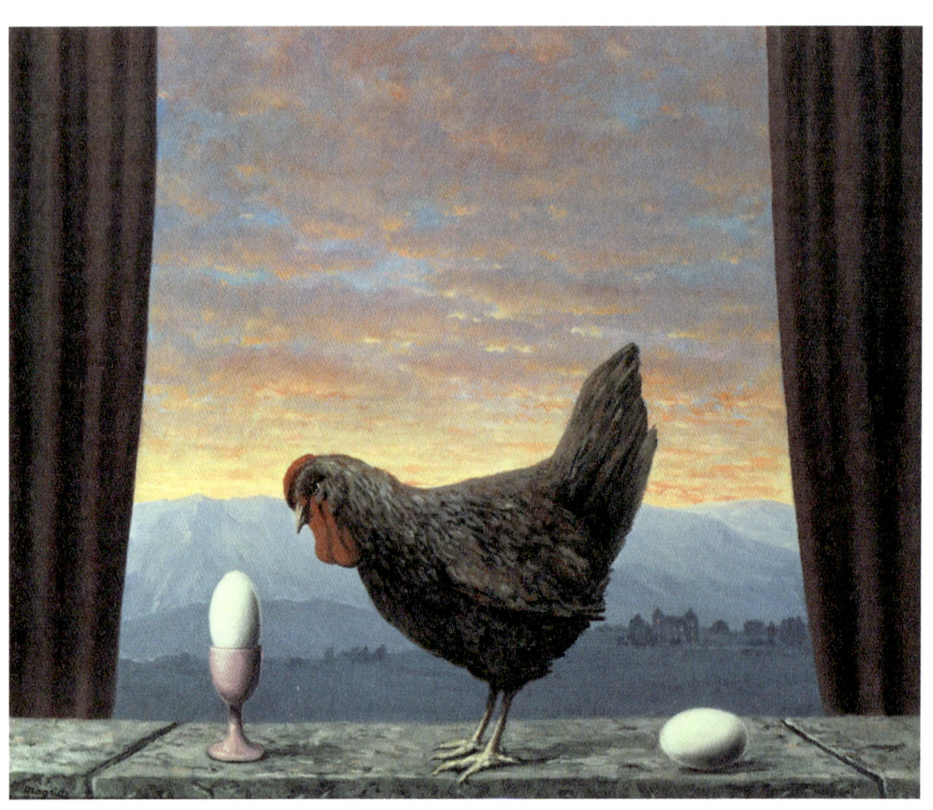

326
A Variation on Sadness
1957
oil on canvas, 50 × 60 cm

    Poetics of the Everyday

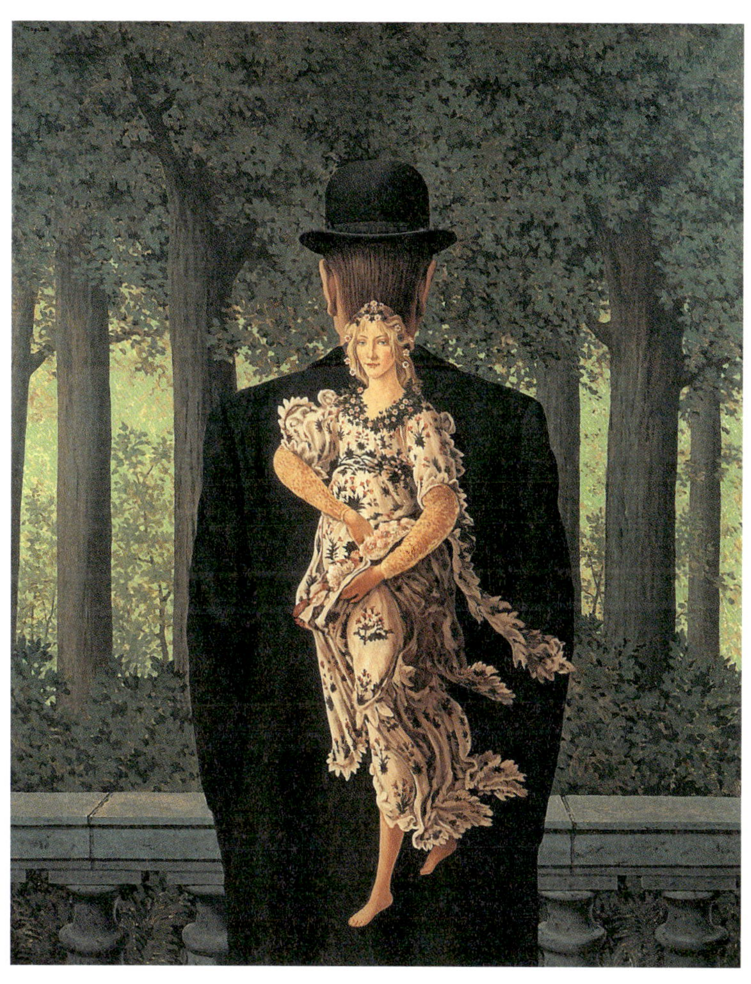

327
The Ready-Made Bouquet
1957
oil on canvas, 162 × 130 cm

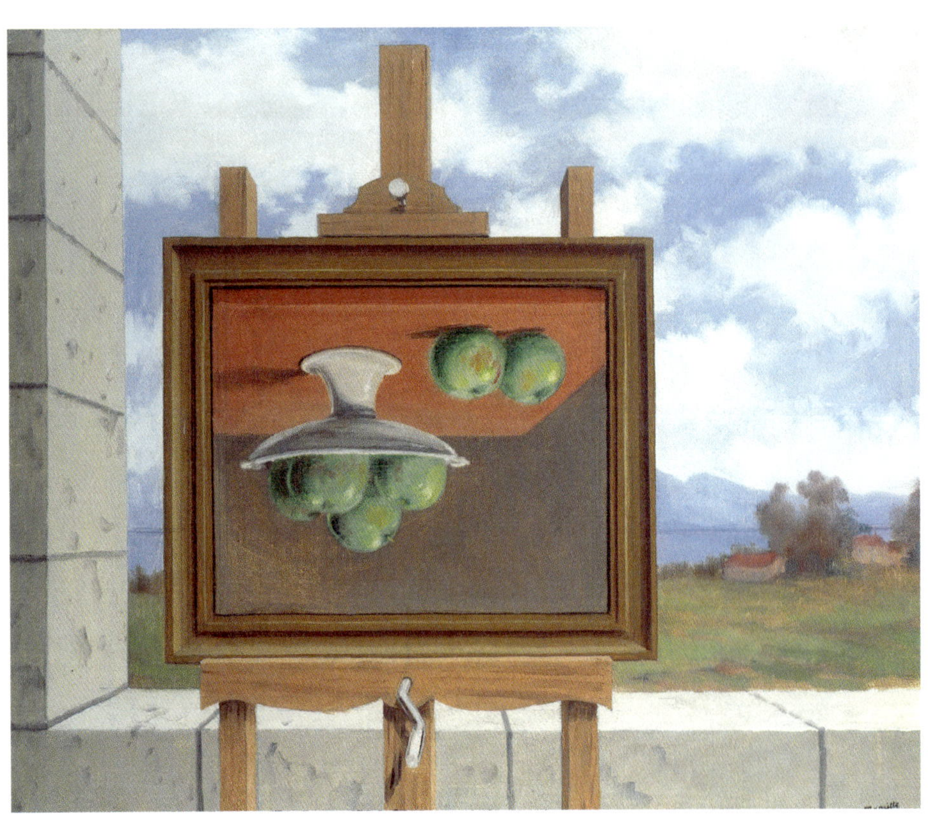

328
The Alarm Clock
1957
oil on canvas, 50 × 60 cm

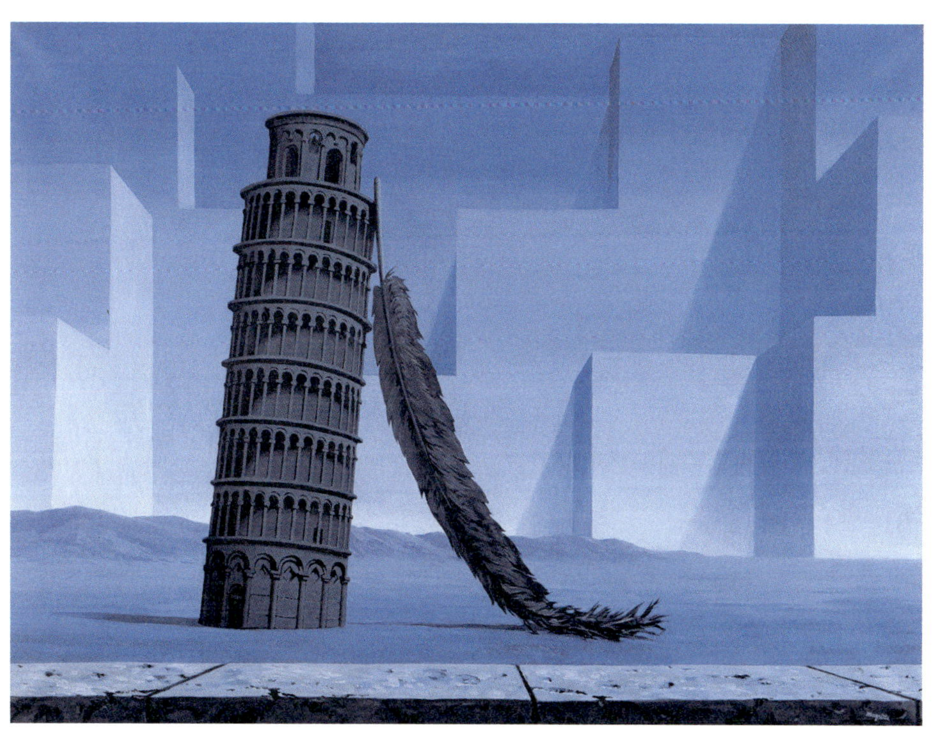

329
Night in Pisa
1958
oil on canvas, 97 × 130 cm

 1947–1967

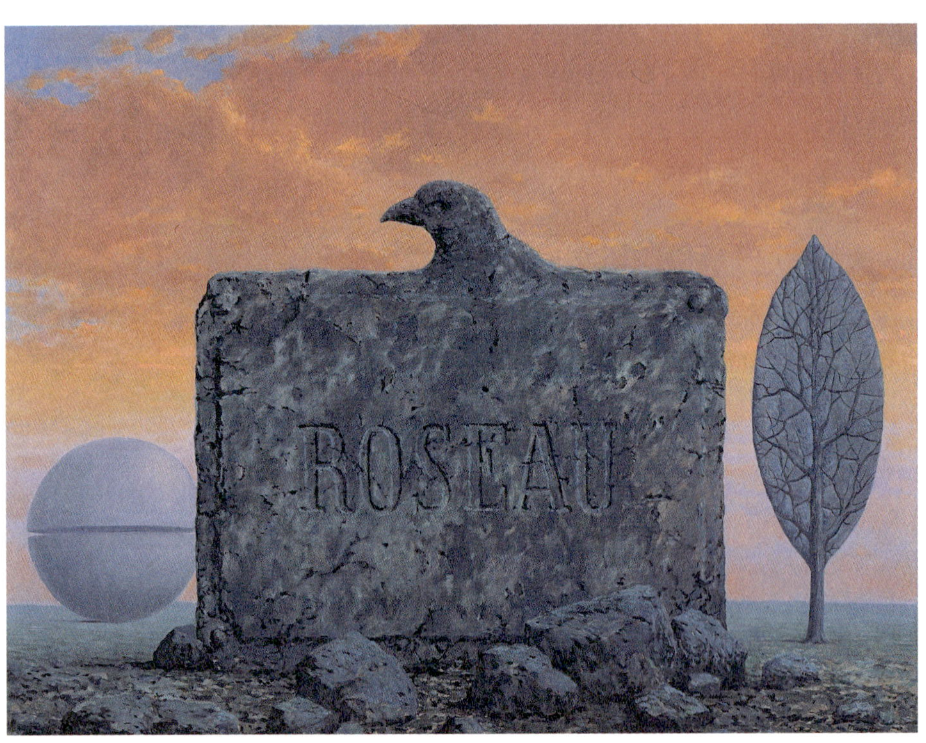

330
The Fount of Youth
1958
oil on canvas, 97 × 130 cm

Poetics of the Everyday

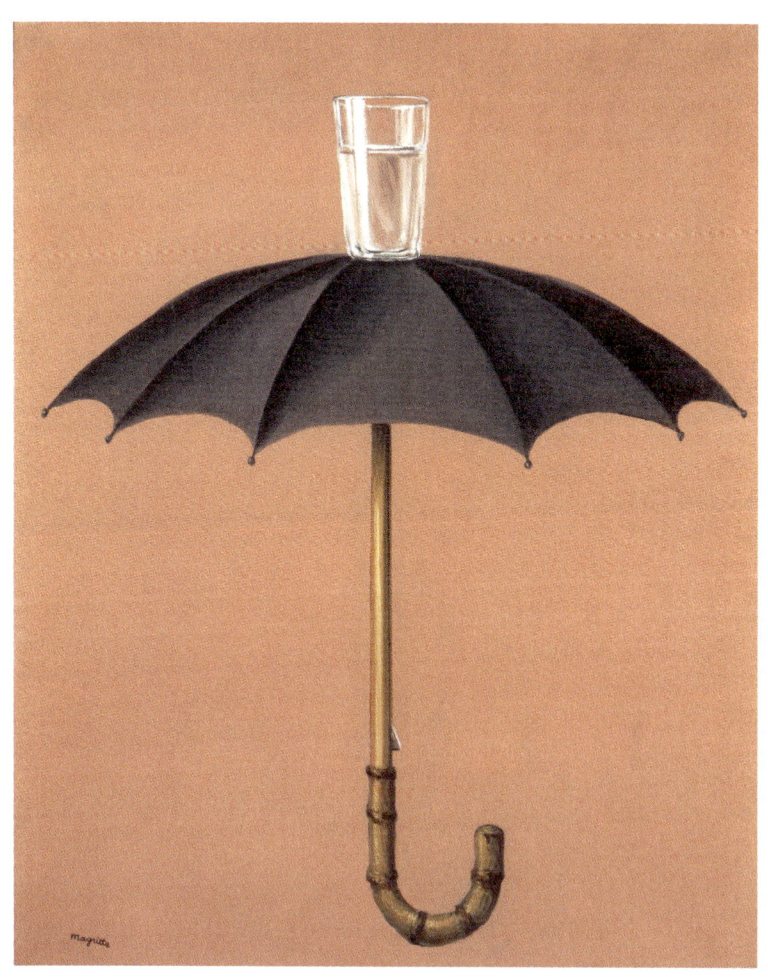

331
Hegel's Holiday
1958
oil on canvas, 60 × 50 cm

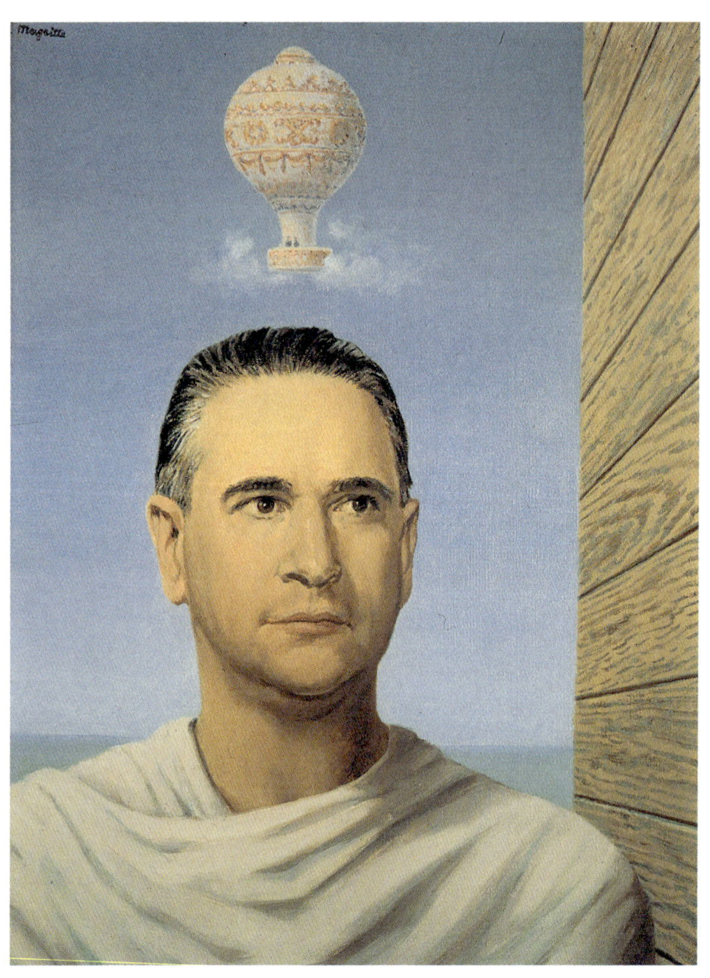

332
Harry Torczyner or Justice has been done
1958
oil on canvas, 40 × 30 cm

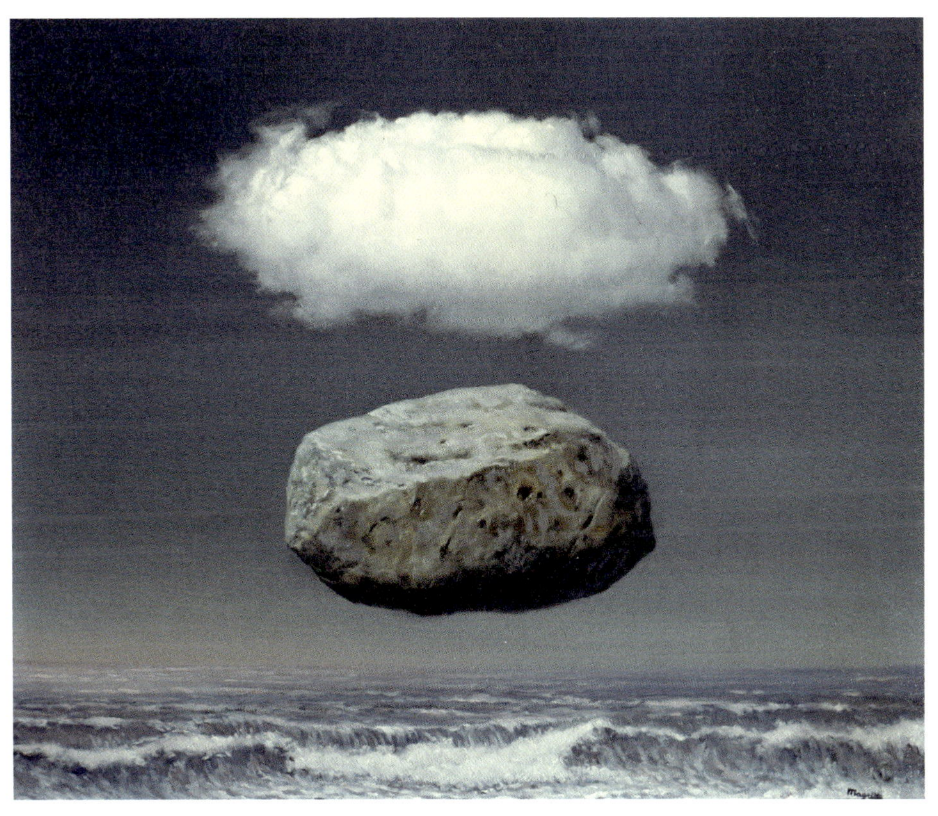

333
Clear Ideas
1958
oil on canvas, 50 × 60 cm

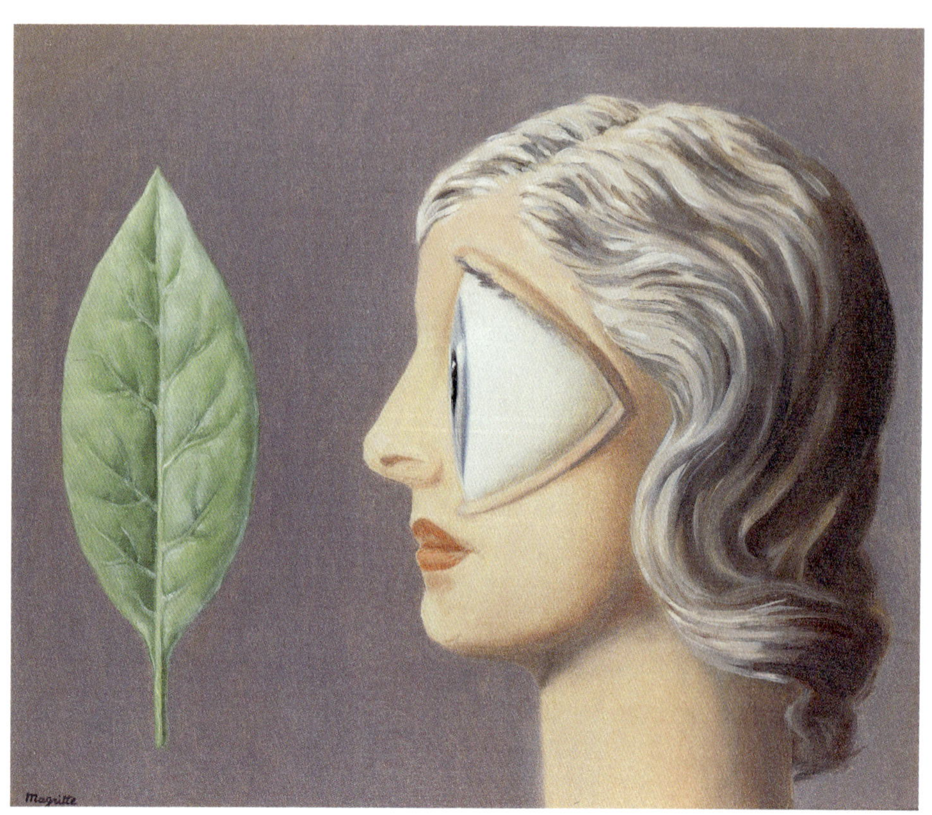

334
The Mason's Wife
1958
oil on canvas, 35 × 41cm

          Poetics of the Everyday

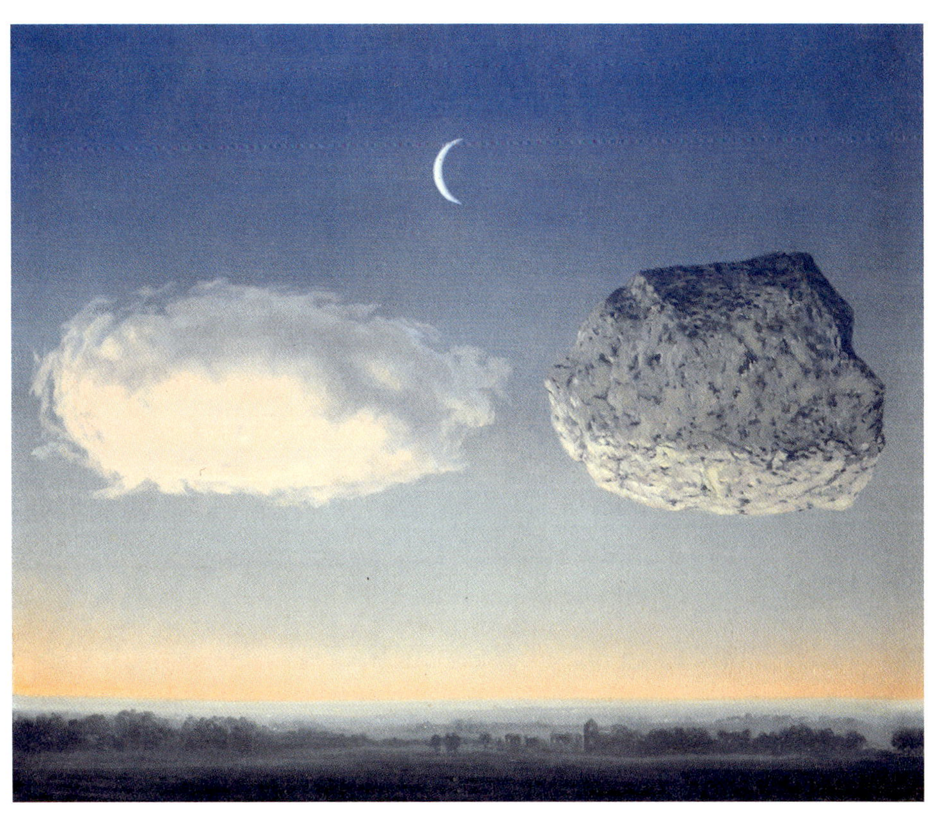

335
The Battle of the Argonne
1959
oil on canvas, 50 × 61 cm

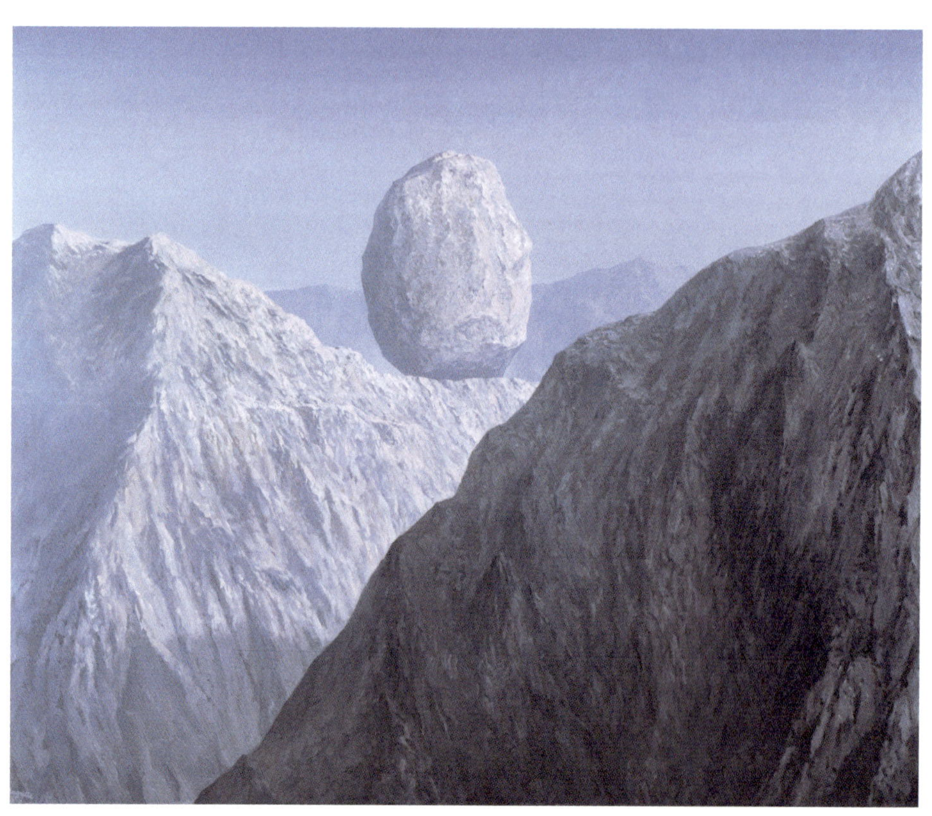

336
The Glass Key
1959
oil on canvas, 130 × 162 cm

Poetics of the Everyday

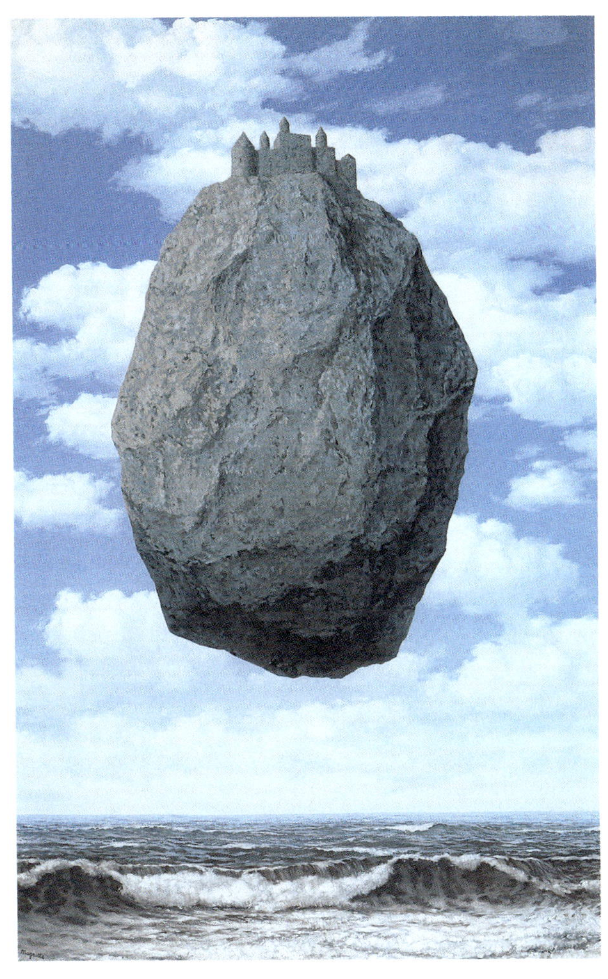

337
The Castle in the Pyrenees
1959
oil on canvas, 200.3 × 130.3 cm

 1947–1967

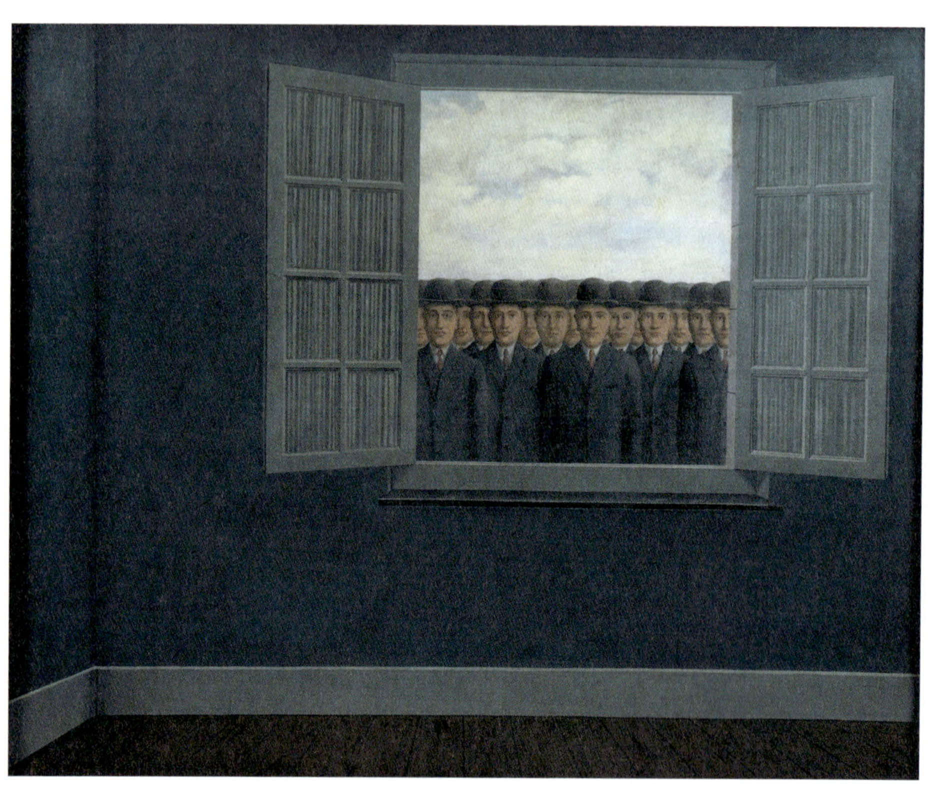

338
The Month of the Grape Harvest
1959
oil on canvas, 130 × 162 cm

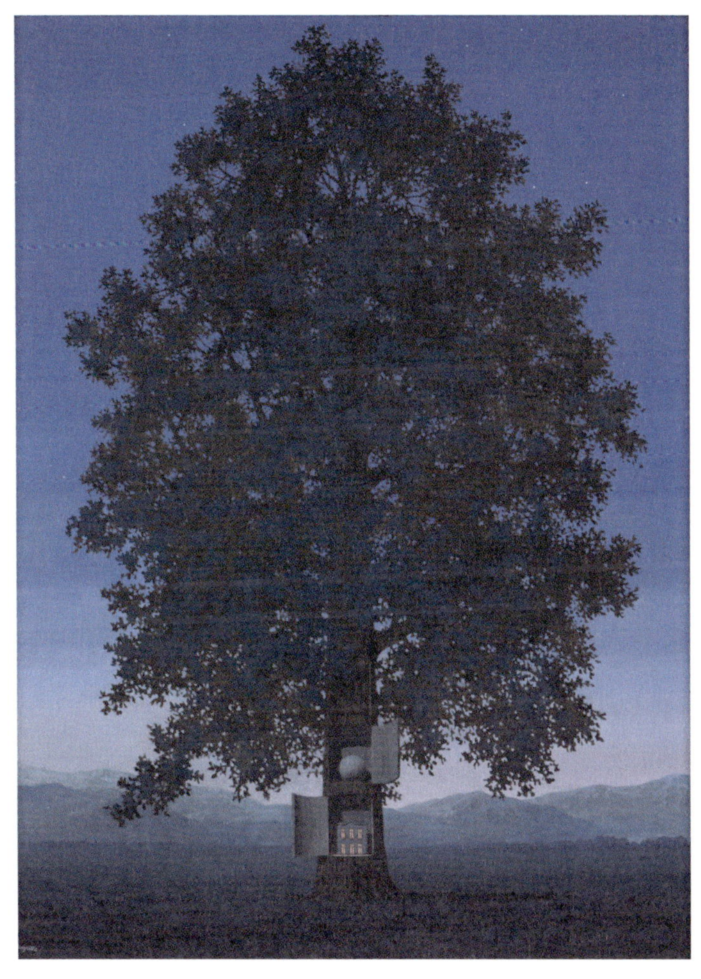

339
Blood Will Tell
1959
oil on canvas, 116 × 89 cm

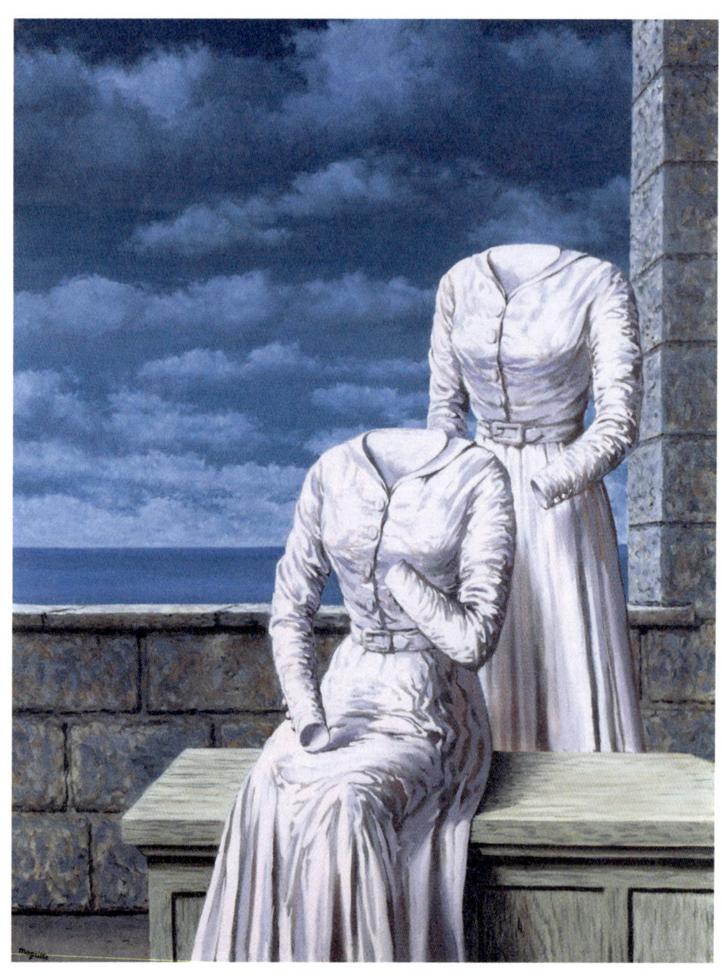

340
The Horns of Desire
1960
oil on canvas, 116 × 89 cm

Poetics of the Everyday

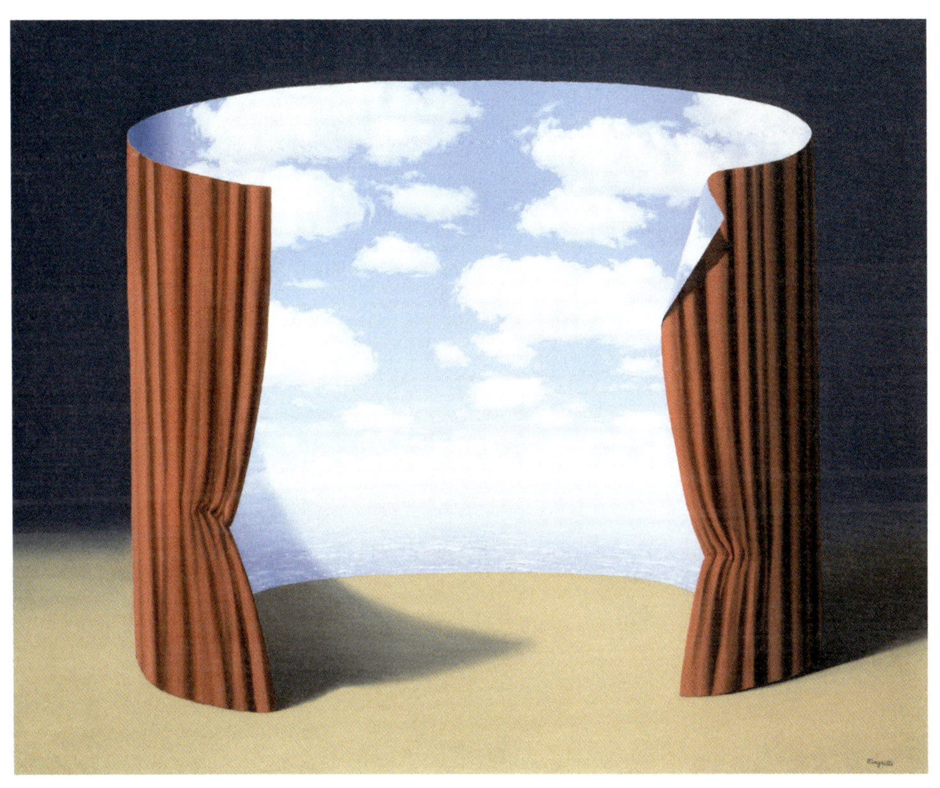

341
The Memoirs of a Saint
1960
oil on canvas, 80 × 100 cm

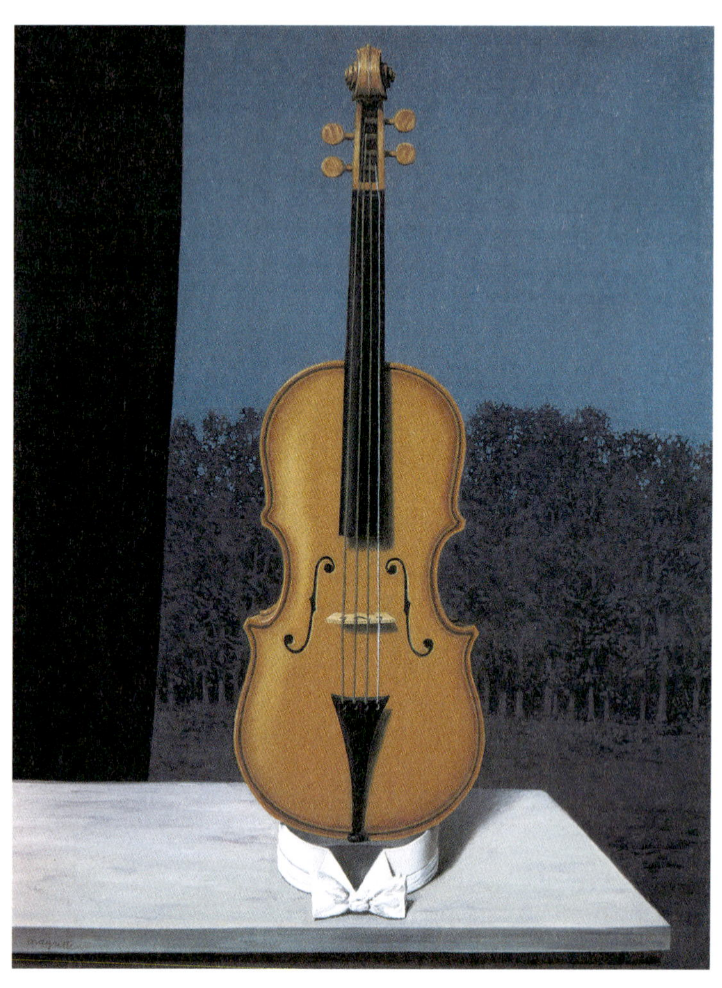

342
A Little of the Outlaws' Souls
1960
oil on canvas, 65 × 50 cm

    Poetics of the Everyday

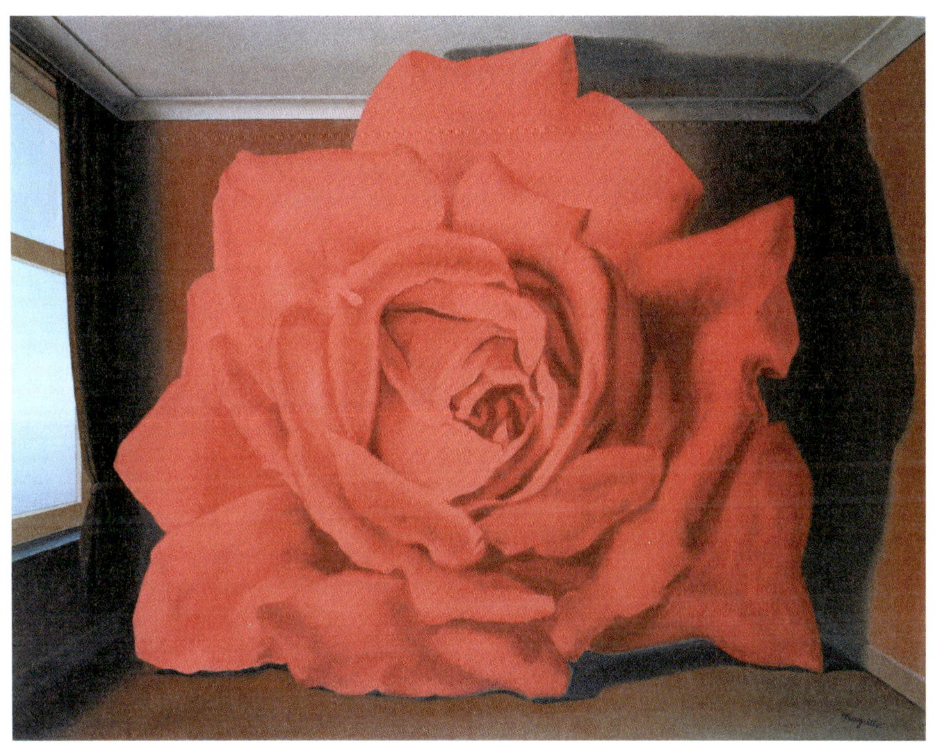

343
The Tomb of the Wrestlers
1960
oil on canvas, 89 × 116 cm

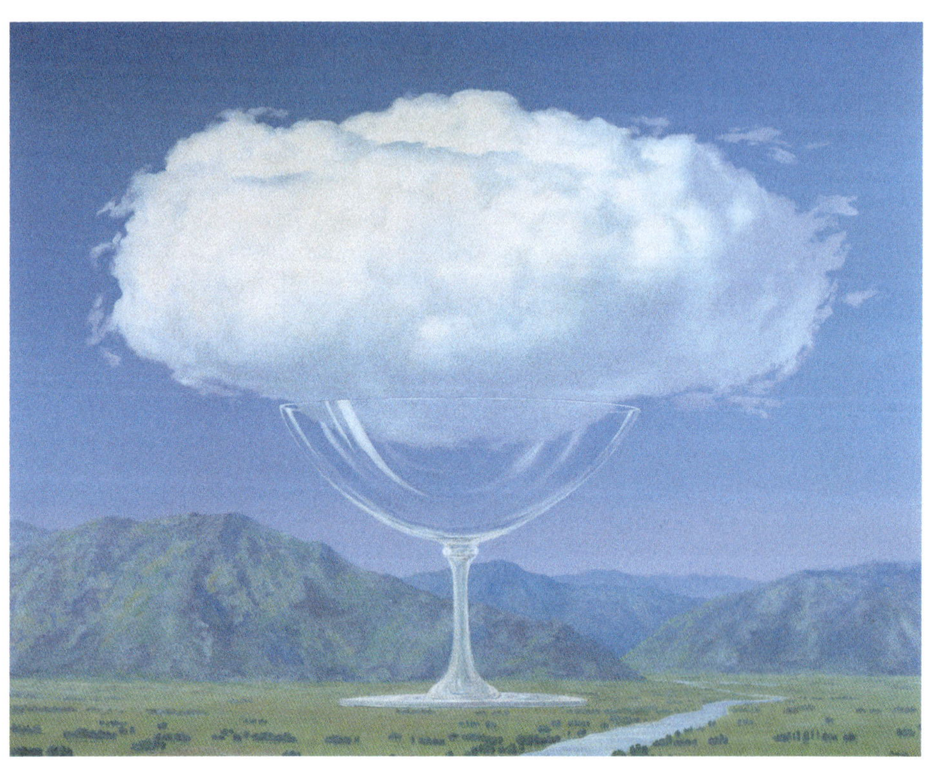

344
The Heartstring
1960
oil on canvas, 114 × 146 cm

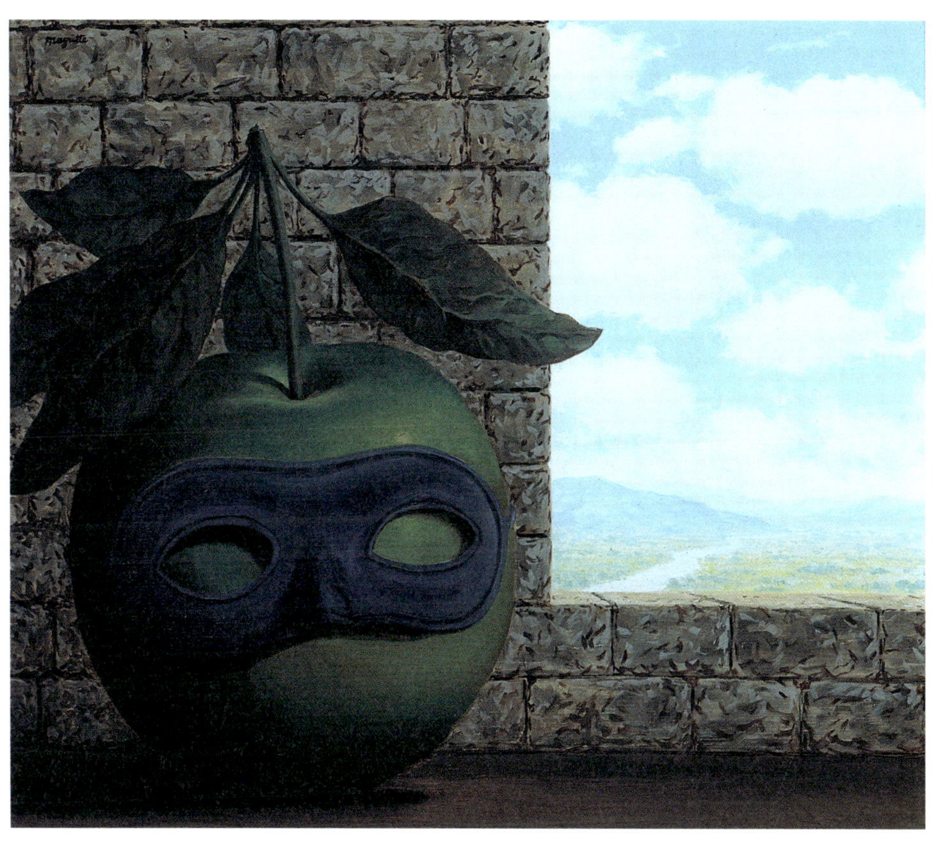

345
The Married Priest
1960
oil on canvas, 46 × 55 cm

346
(The Curse)
1960?
oil on canvas, 33 × 41 cm

  Poetics of the Everyday

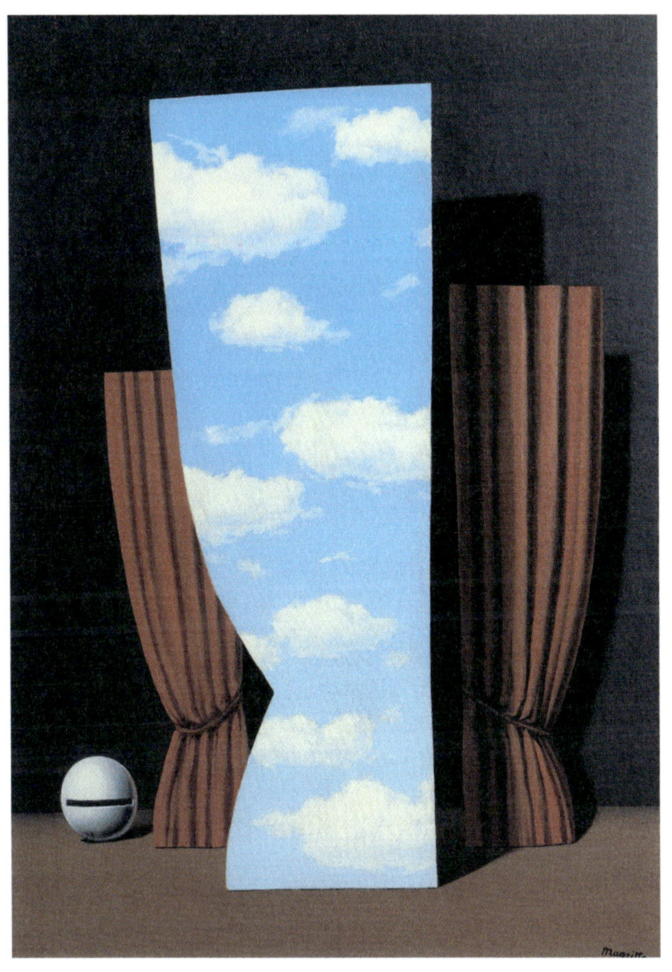

347
Mona Lisa
1960
oil on canvas, 70 × 50 cm

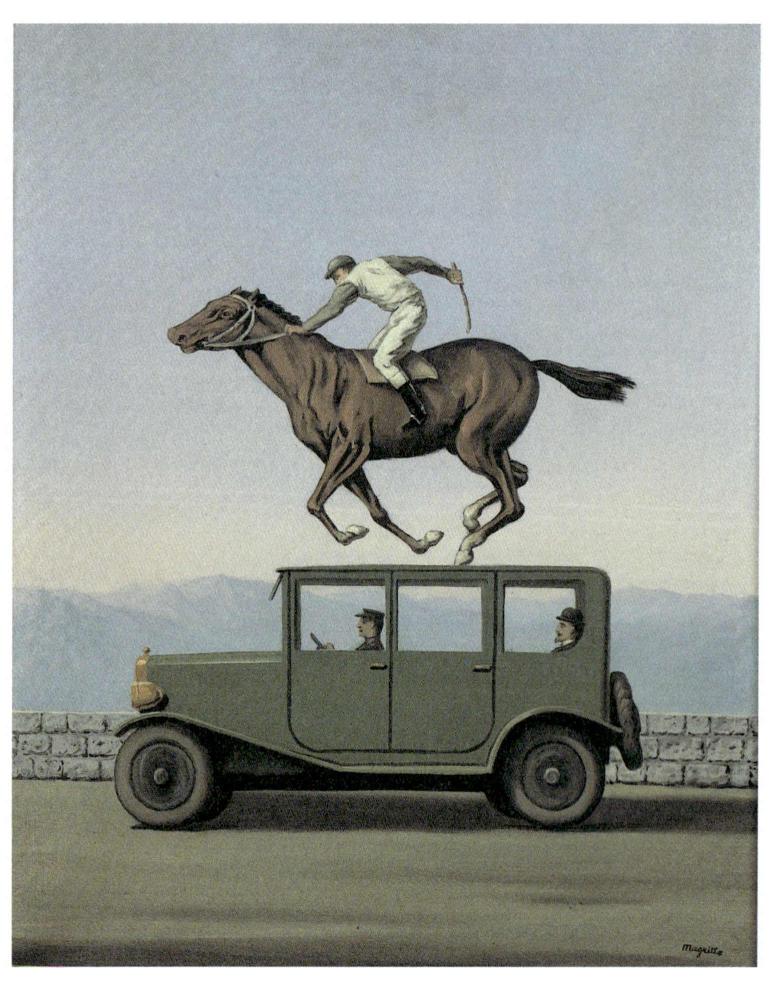

348
The Anger of the Gods
1960
oil on canvas, 61 × 50 cm

 Poetics of the Everyday

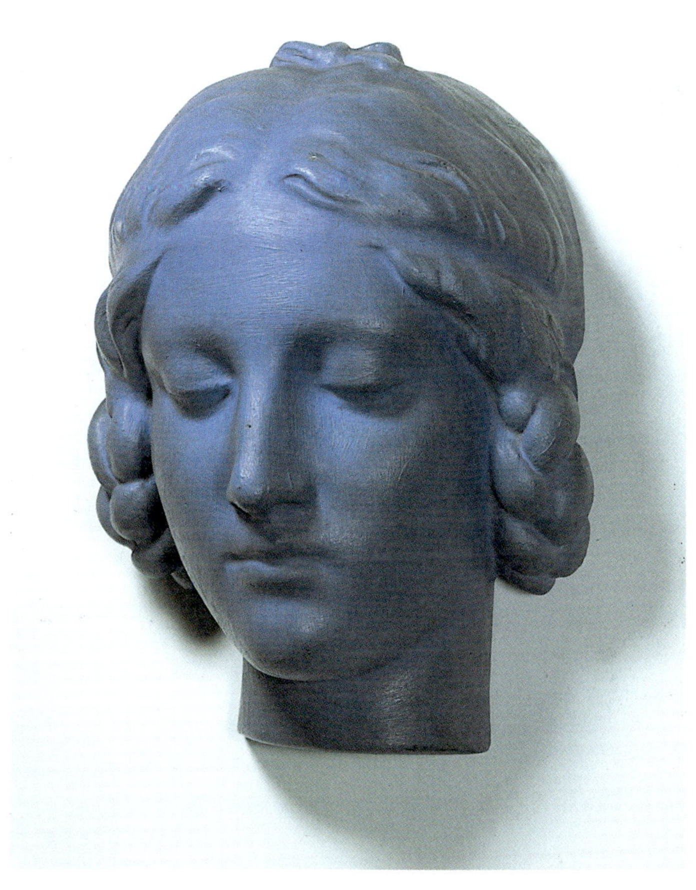

349
(Head)
1960
oil on plaster cast, ht. 25 cm

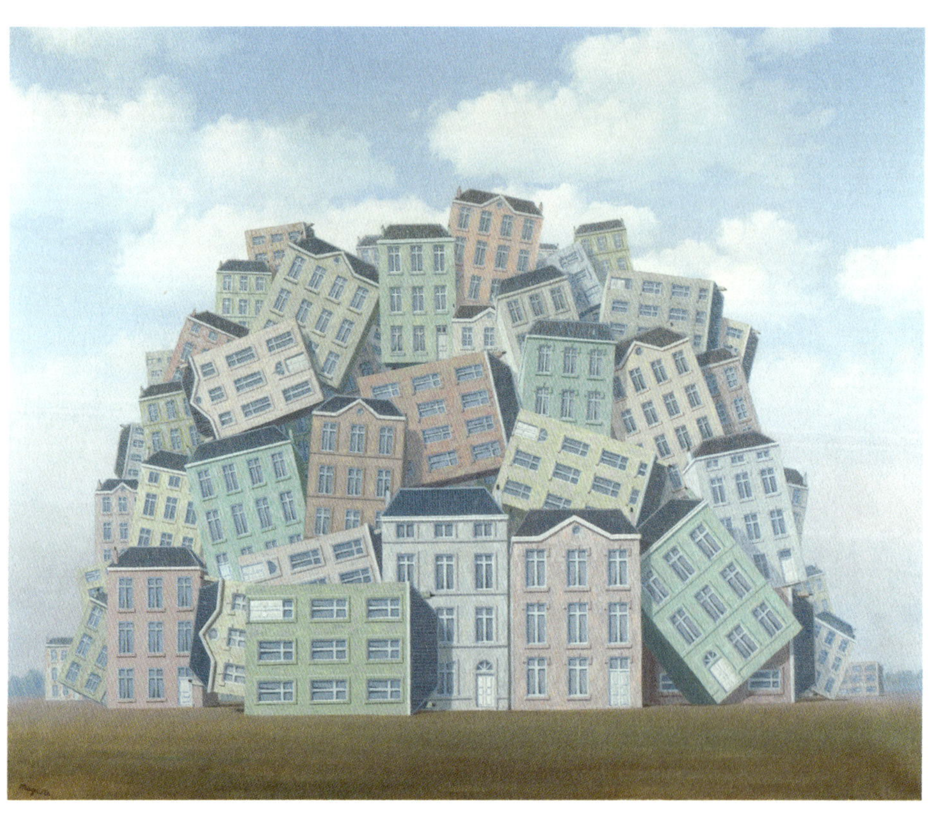

350
The Breast
1961
oil on canvas, 90 × 110 cm

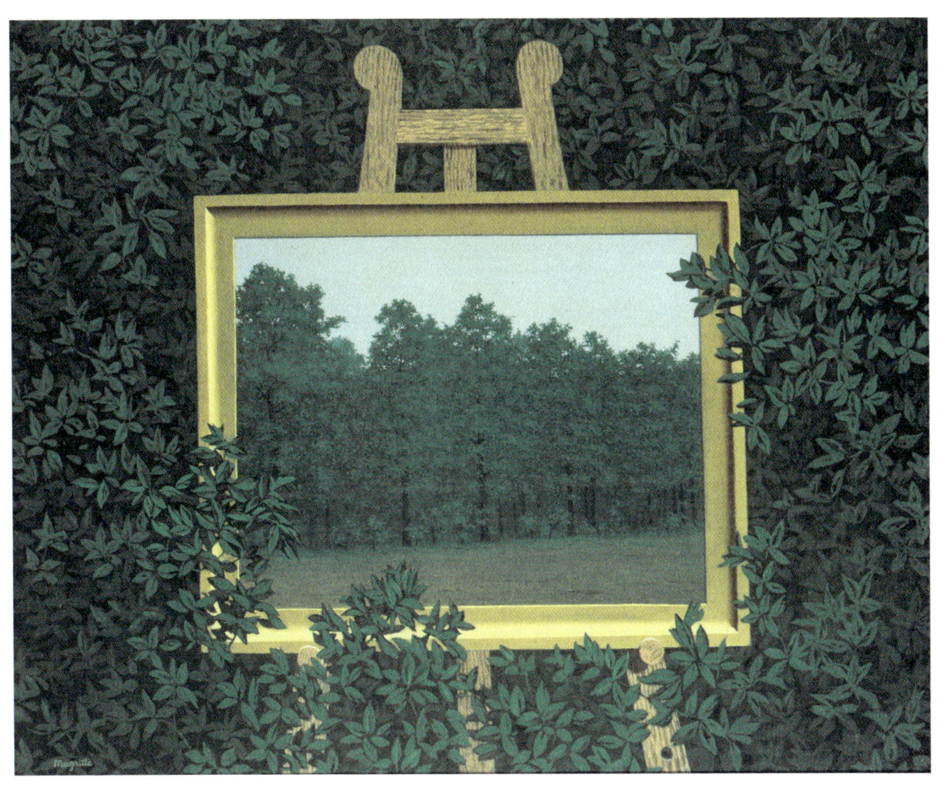

351
The Waterfall
1961
oil on canvas, 81 × 100 cm

1947–1967

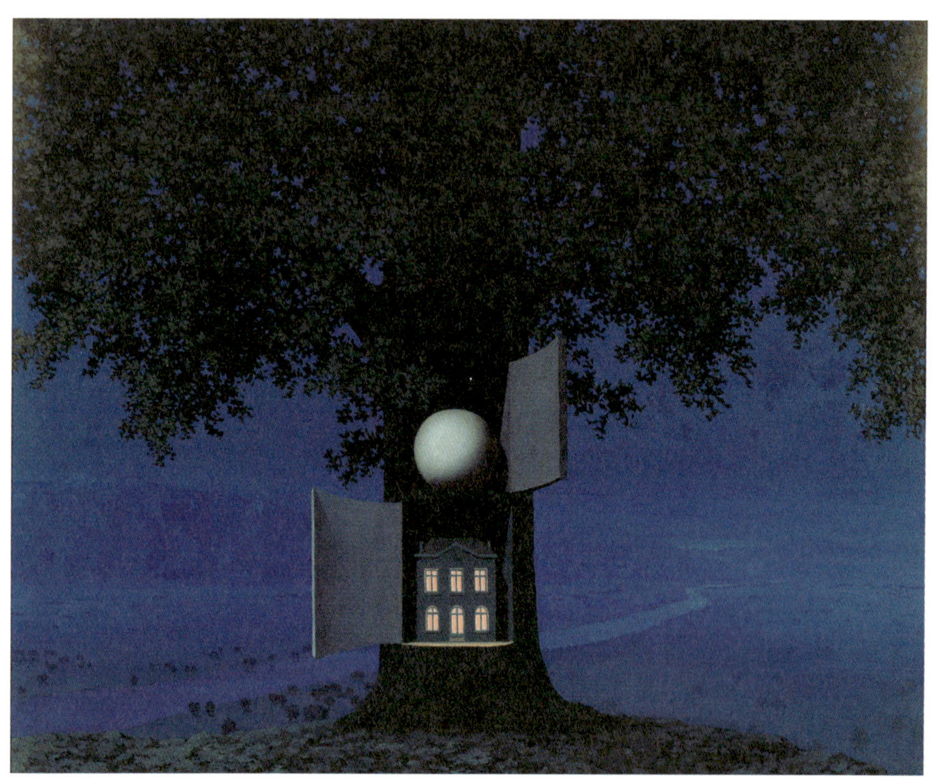

352
Blood Will Tell
1961
oil on canvas, 90 × 110 cm

     Poetics of the Everyday

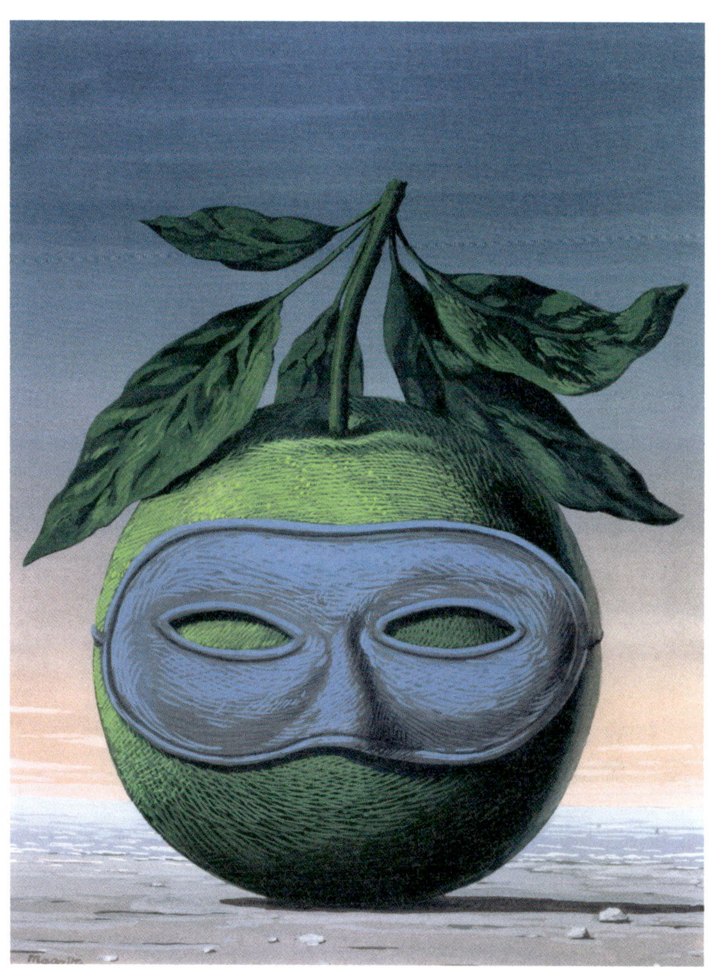

353
Memory of a Journey
c. 1961
gouache on paper, 35.9 × 27 cm

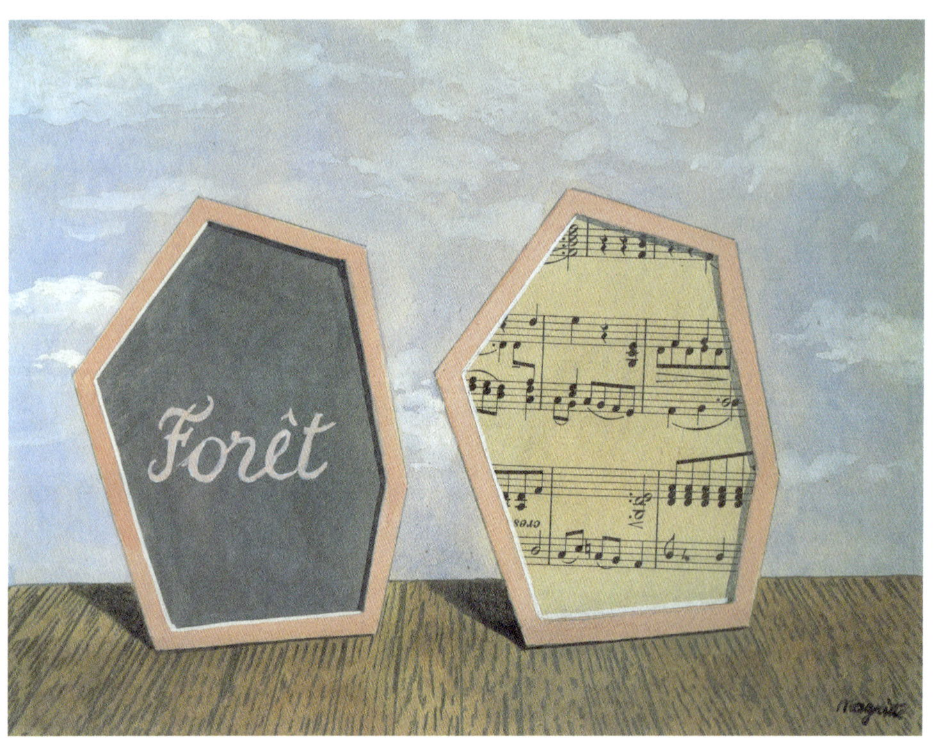

354
The Literal Meaning
1961
pasted paper and gouache on paper, 19 × 25 cm

Poetics of the Everyday

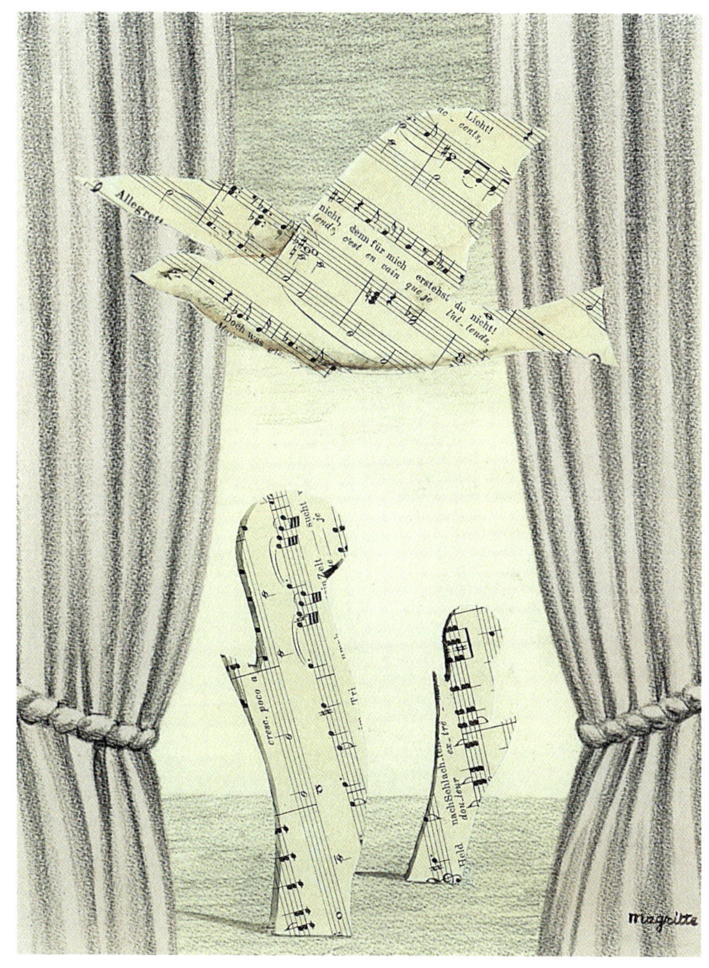

355
Moments musicaux
1961
pasted paper, watercolour, conté crayon on paper, 34.1 × 26 cm

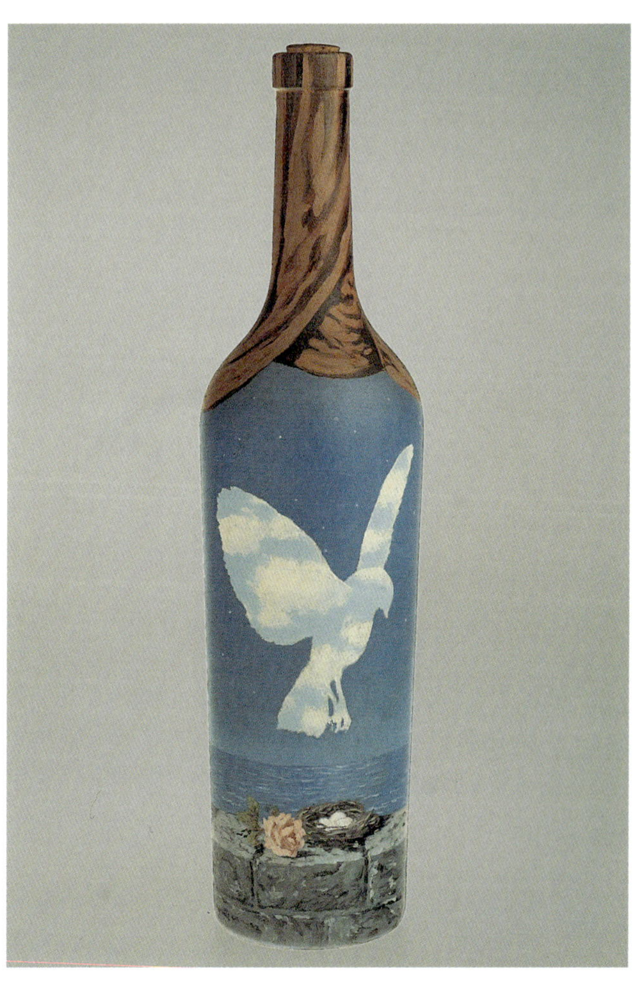

356
(Seascape with Sky-Bird)
1961
oil on glass bottle, ht. 29 cm

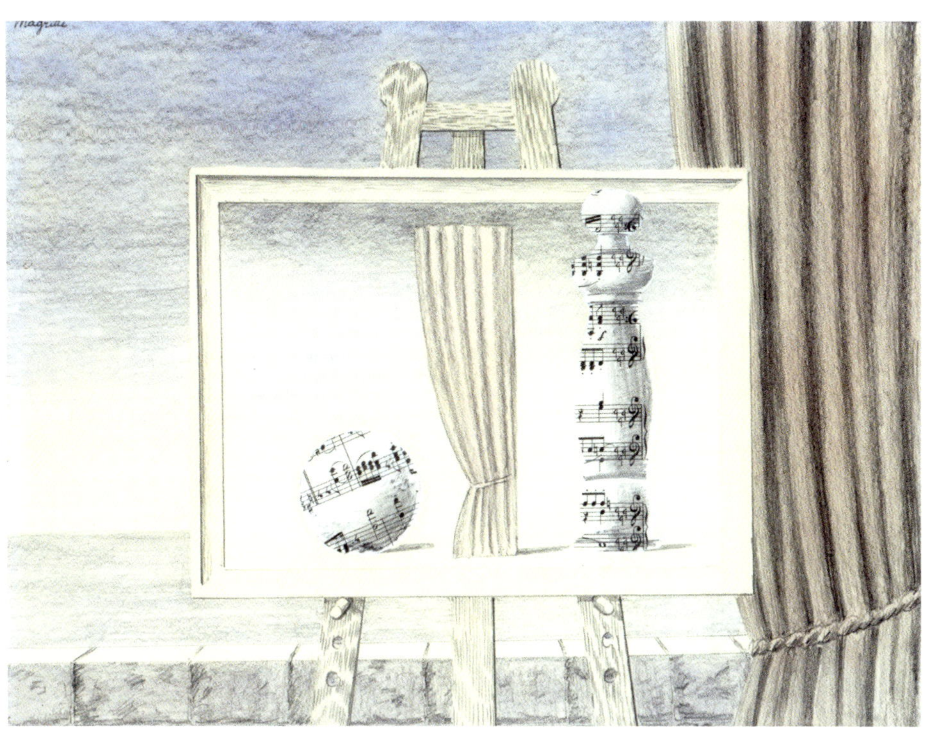

357
(Title unknown)
1961 or 1962
pasted paper, watercolour, pencil, pen, black ink, crayon on paper, 30.5 × 40.6 cm

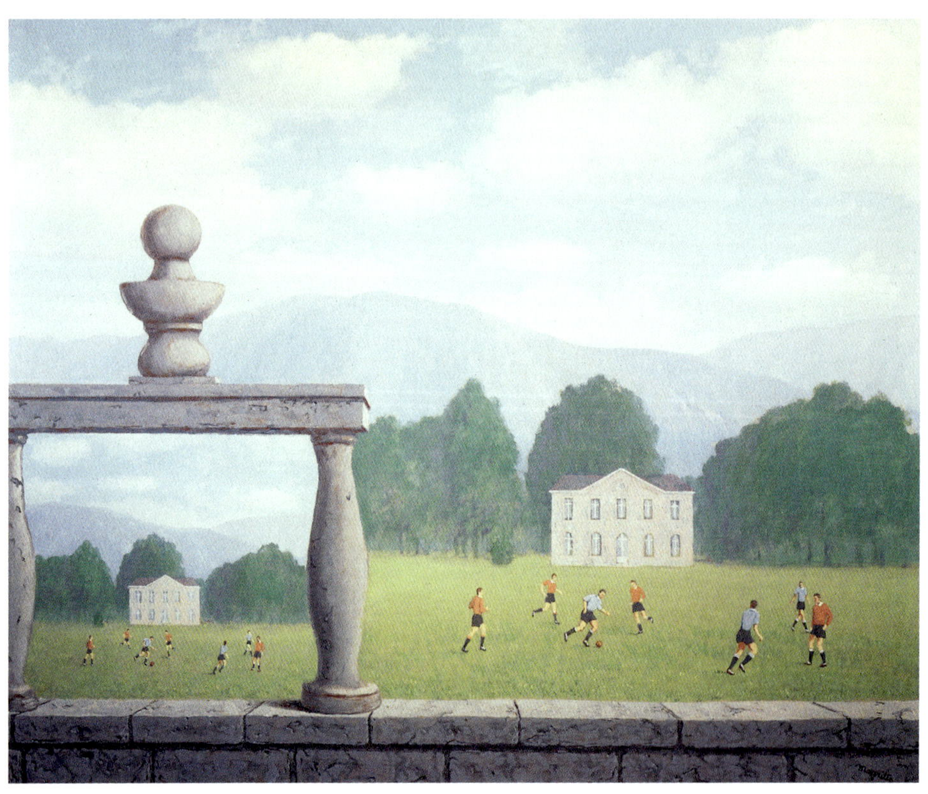

358
Representation
1962
oil on canvas, 81 × 100 cm

     Poétique du quotidien

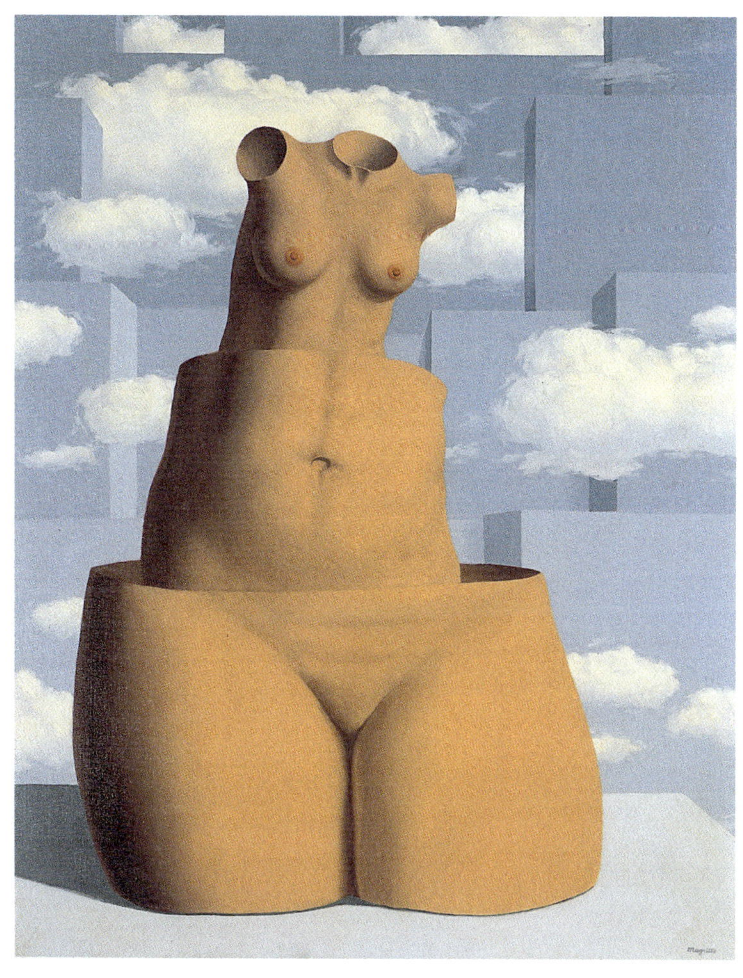

359
Megalomania
1962
oil on canvas, 100 × 81 cm

1947–1967

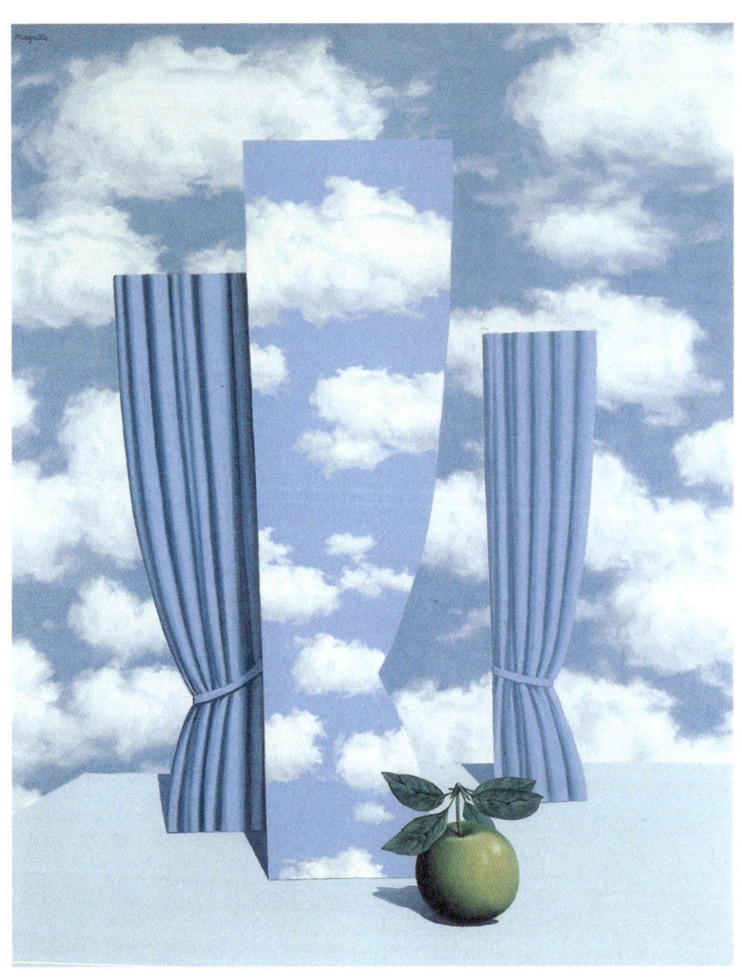

360
High Society
1962
oil on canvas, 100 × 81 cm

361
Towards Pleasure
1962
oil on canvas, 46 × 55 cm

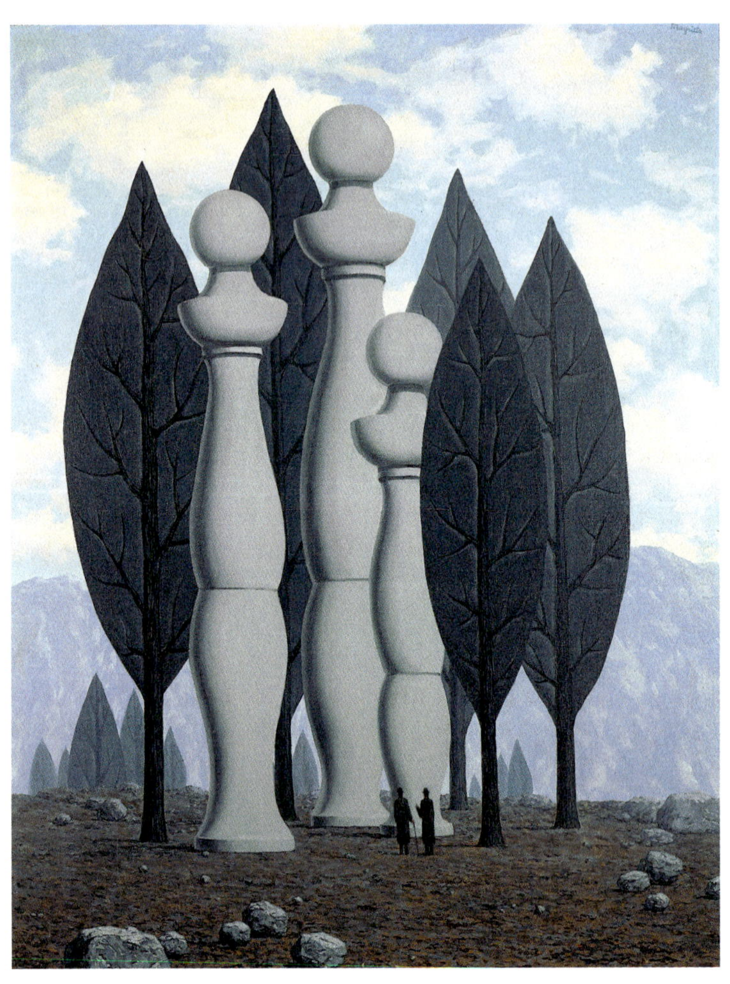

362
The Art of Conversation
1962
oil on canvas, 81 × 65 cm

Poetics of the Everyday

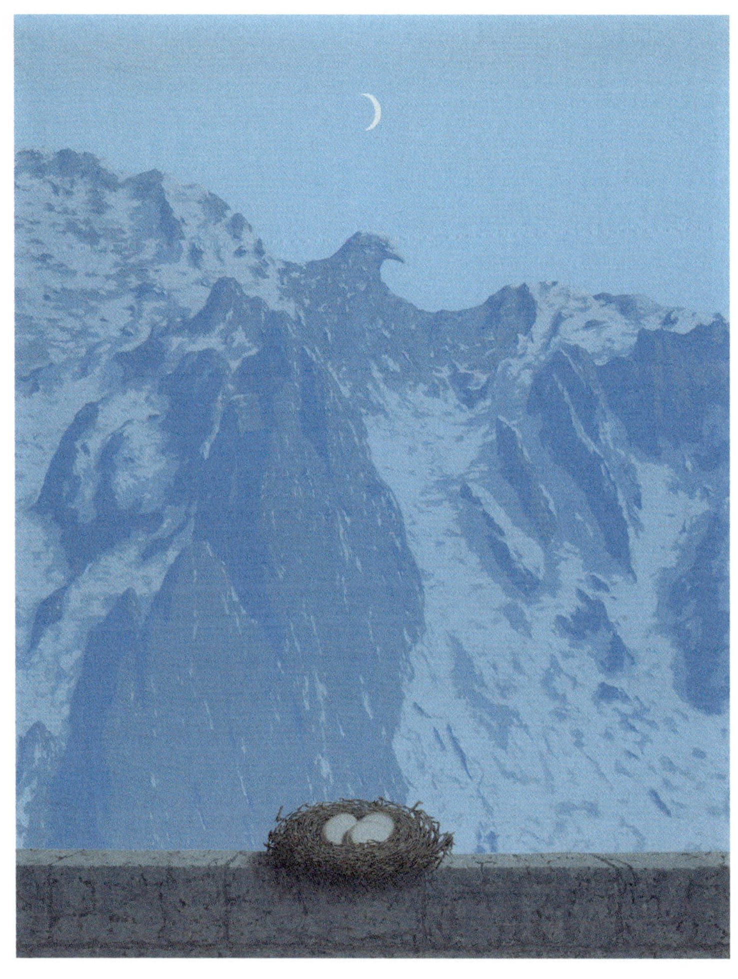

363
The Domain of Arnheim
1962
oil on canvas, 146 × 114 cm

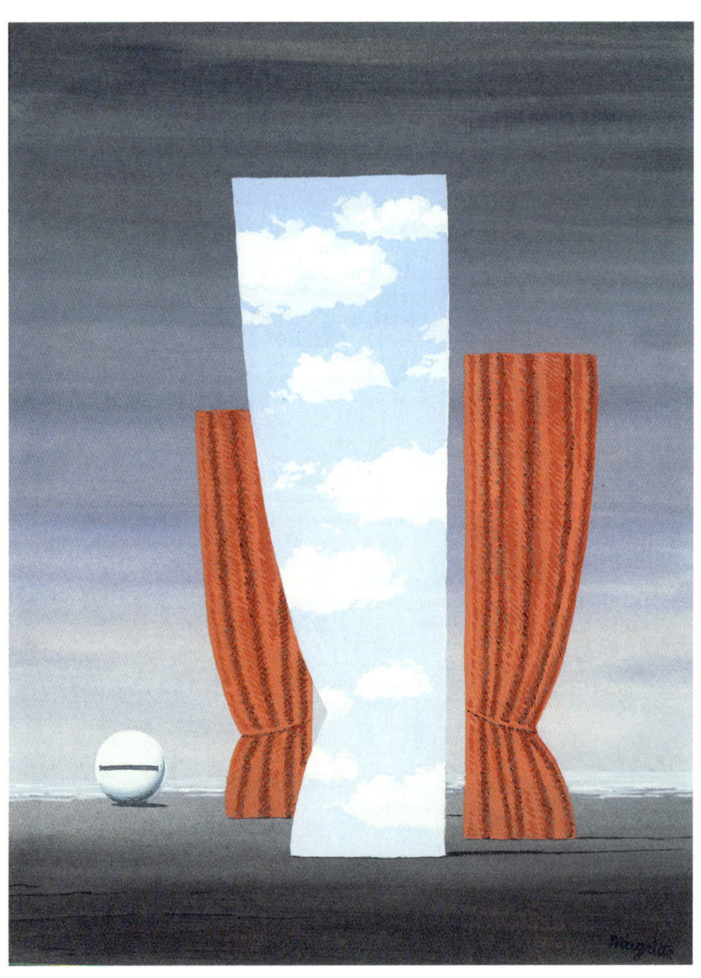

364
Mona Lisa

c. 1962
gouache on paper, 35.2 × 26.5 cm

Poetics of the Everyday

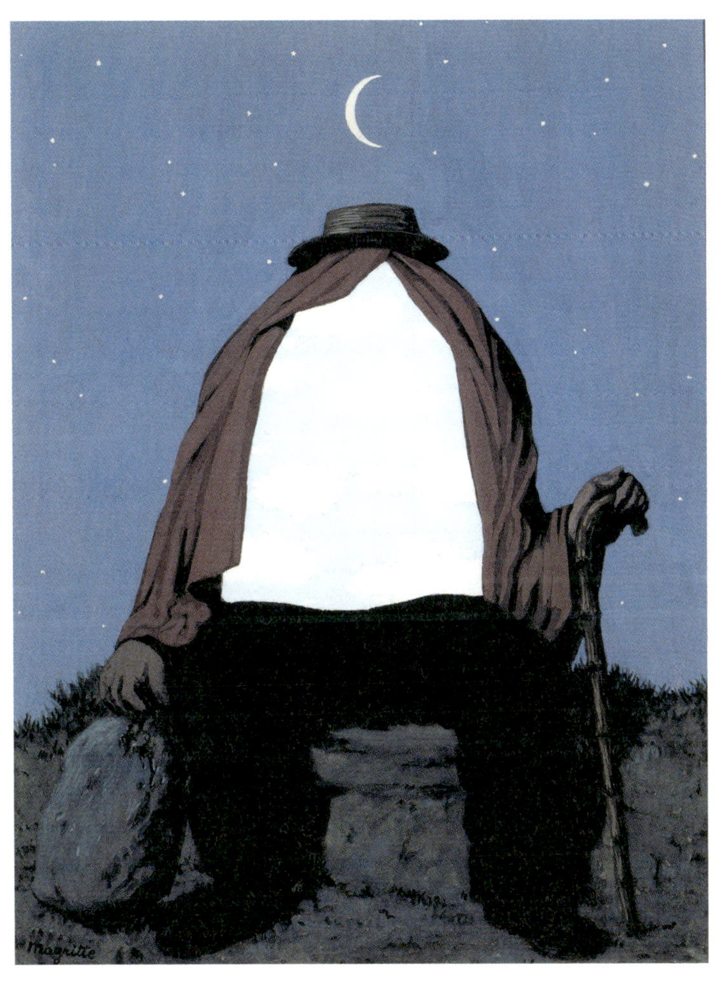

365
The Healer
1962
gouache on paper, 35.5 × 27.5 cm

1947–1967

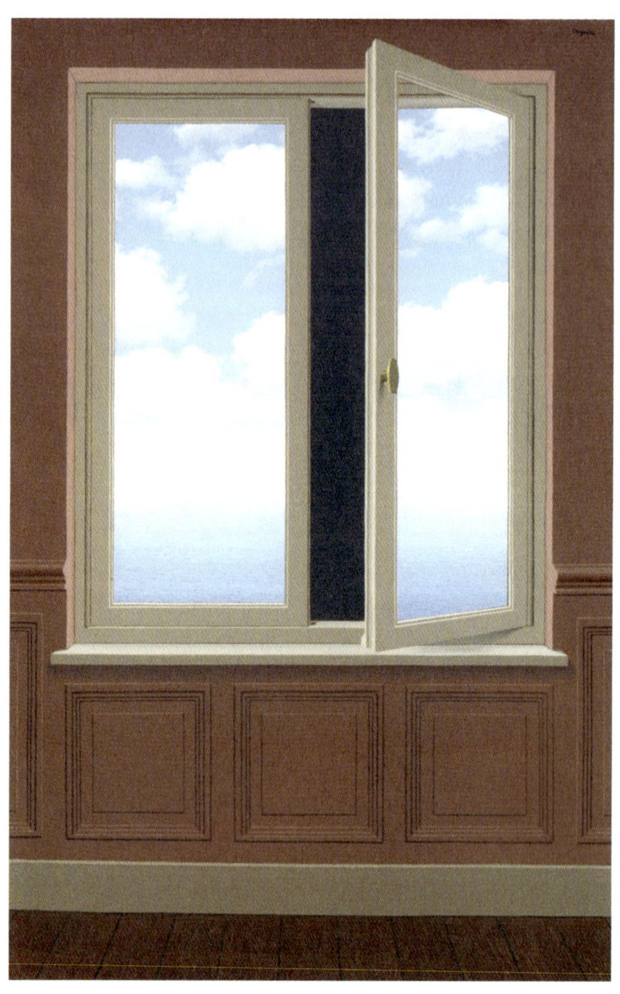

366
The Field-Glass
1963
oil on canvas, 175.5 × 116 cm

     Poetics of the Everyday

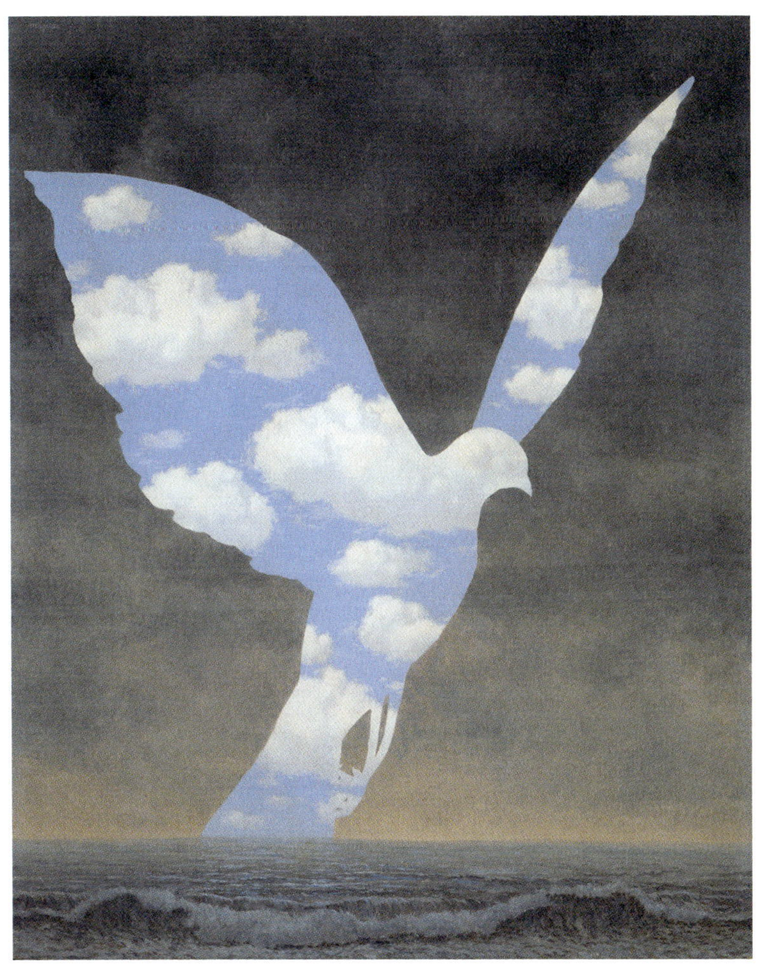

367
The Great Family
1963
oil on canvas, 100 × 81 cm

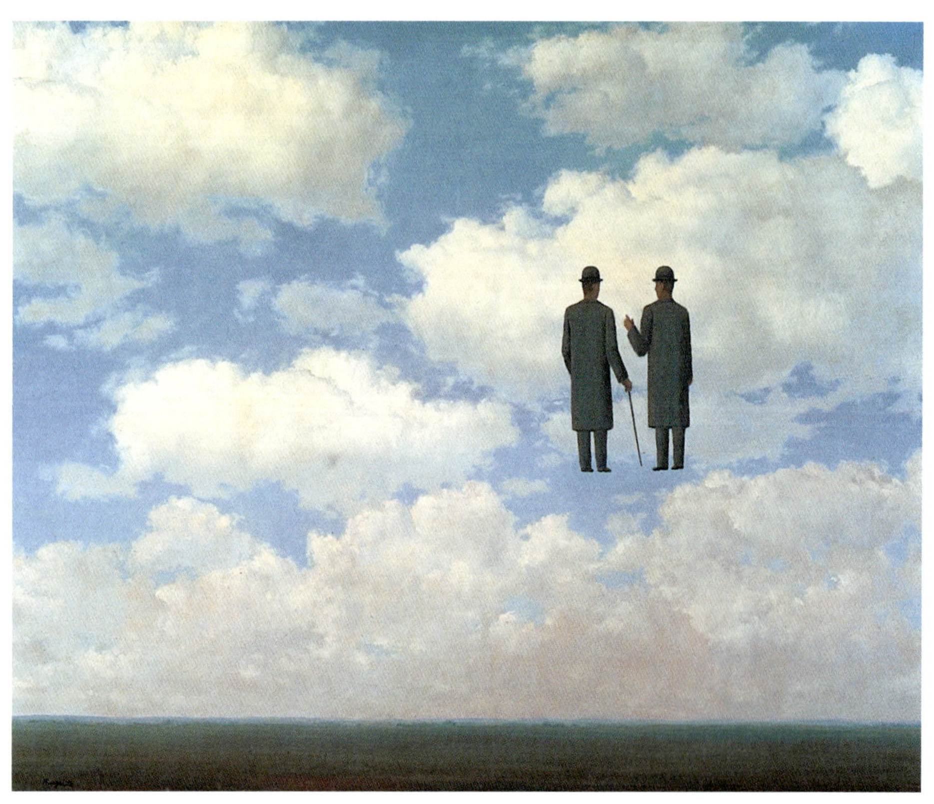

368
Reconnaissance without End
1963
oil on canvas, 81 × 100 cm

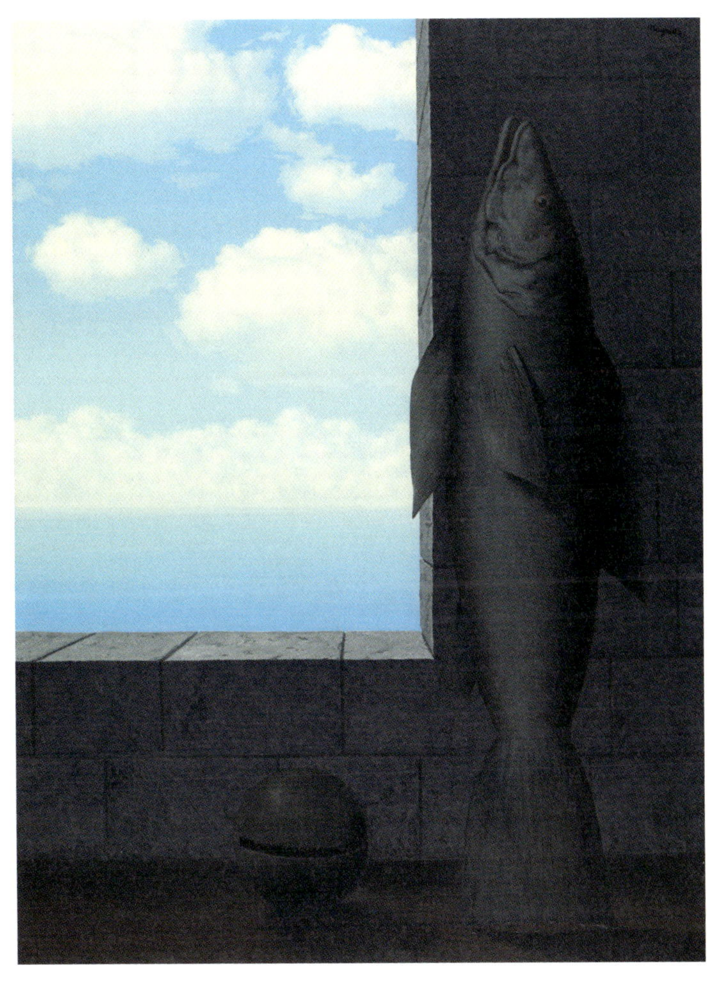

369
The Search for Truth
1963
oil on canvas, 130 × 97 cm

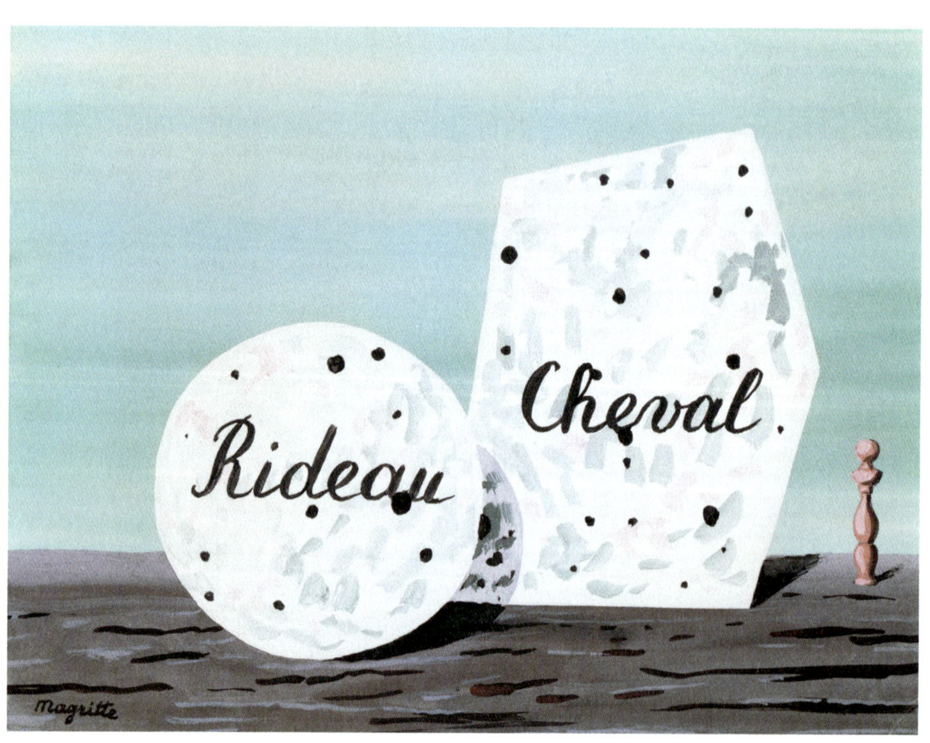

370
The Literal Meaning
1963
gouache on paper, 21.5 × 29.3 cm

    Poetics of the Everyday

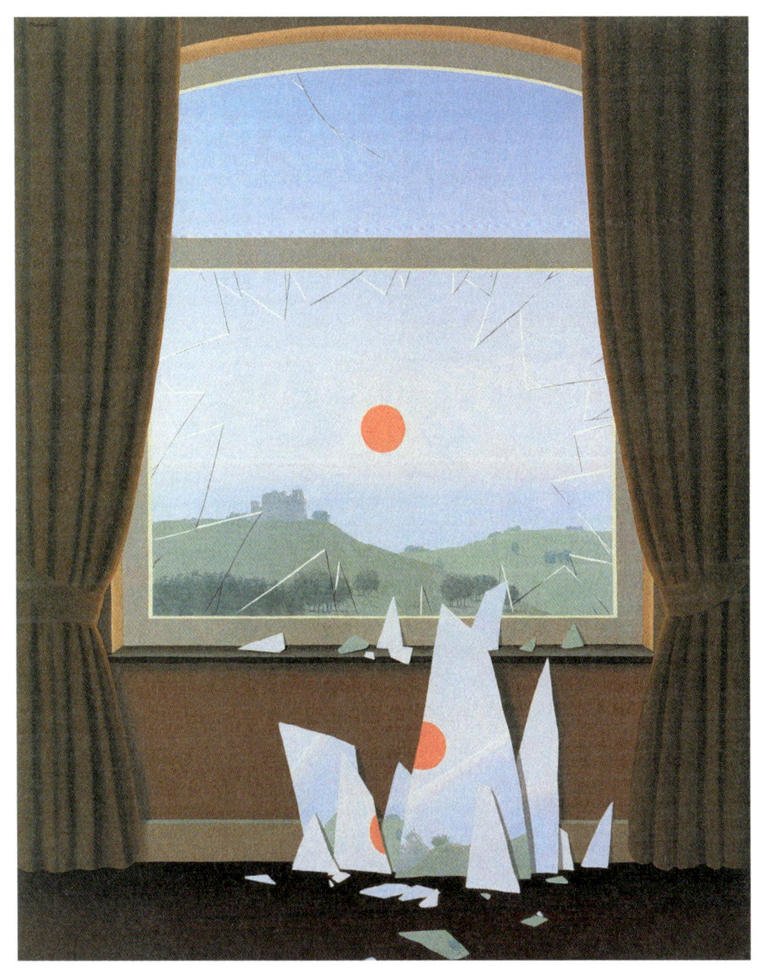

371
Evening Falls
1964
oil on canvas, 162 × 130 cm

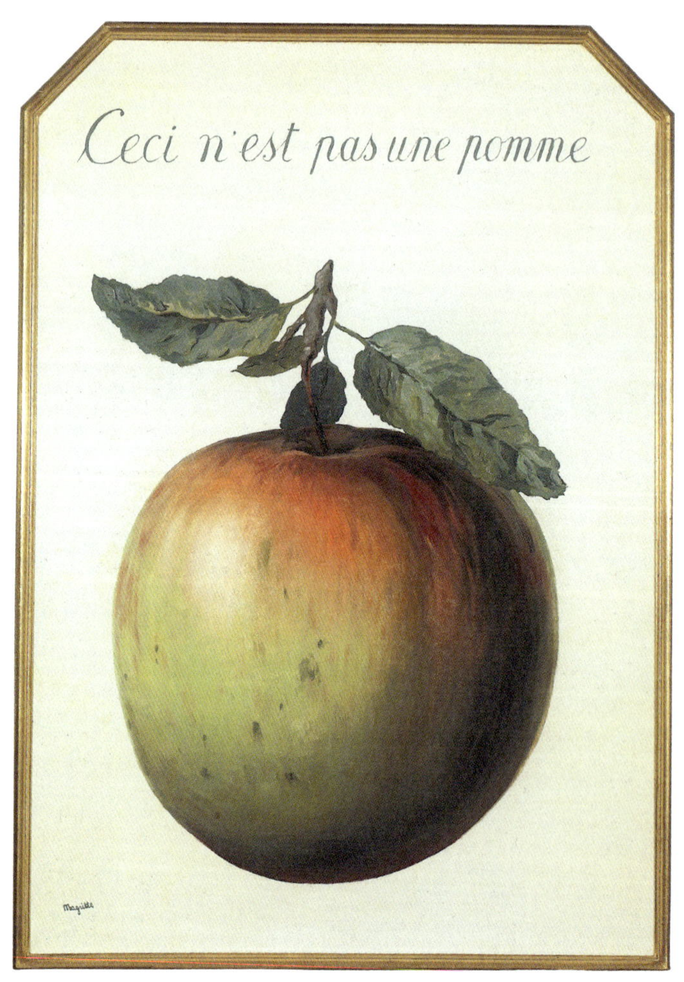

372
(This Is Not An Apple)
1964
oil on Unilite, 142 × 100 cm

     Poetics of the Everyday

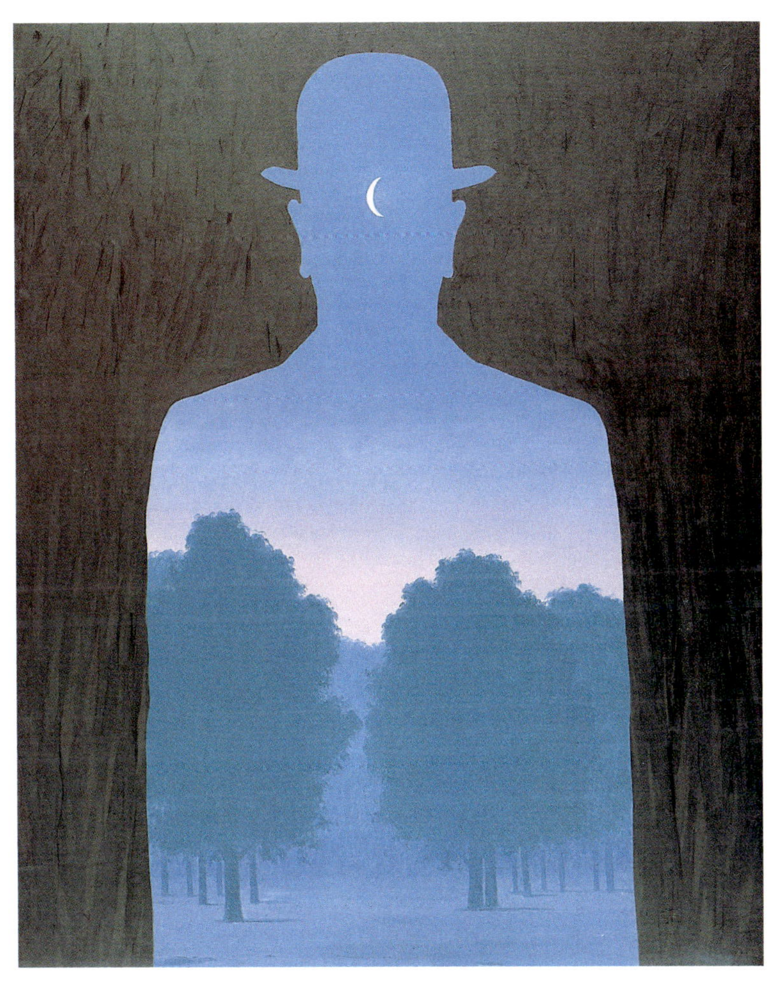

373
The Upholder of the Law
1964
oil on canvas, 100 × 81 cm

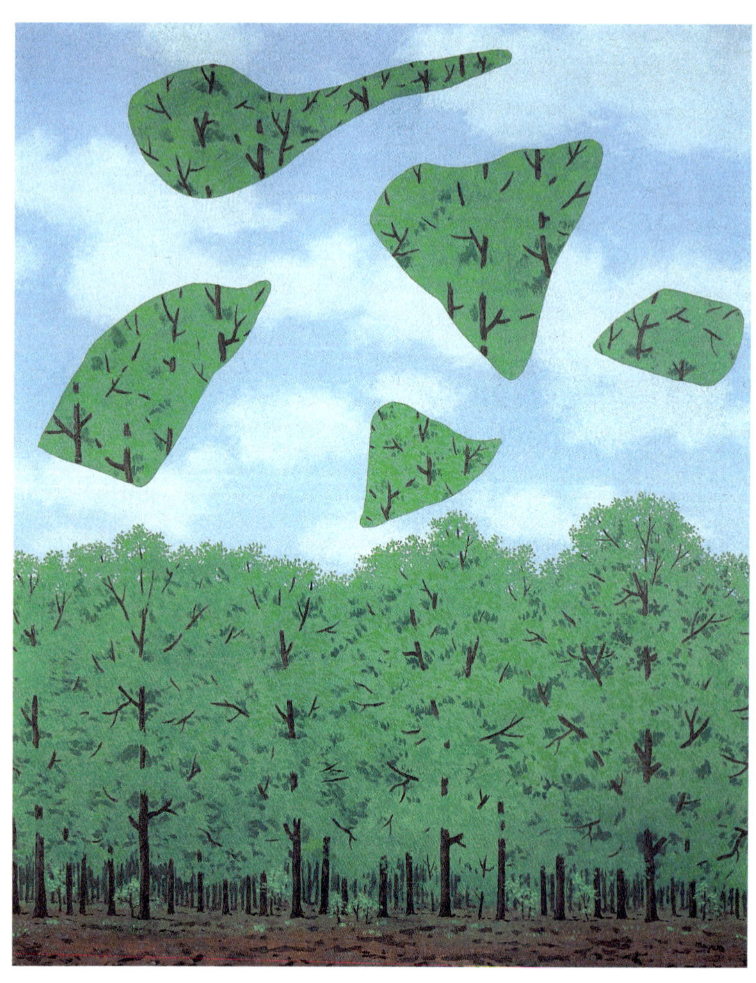

374
The Chorus of the Sphinxes
1964
oil on canvas, 100 × 81 cm

 Poetics of the Everyday

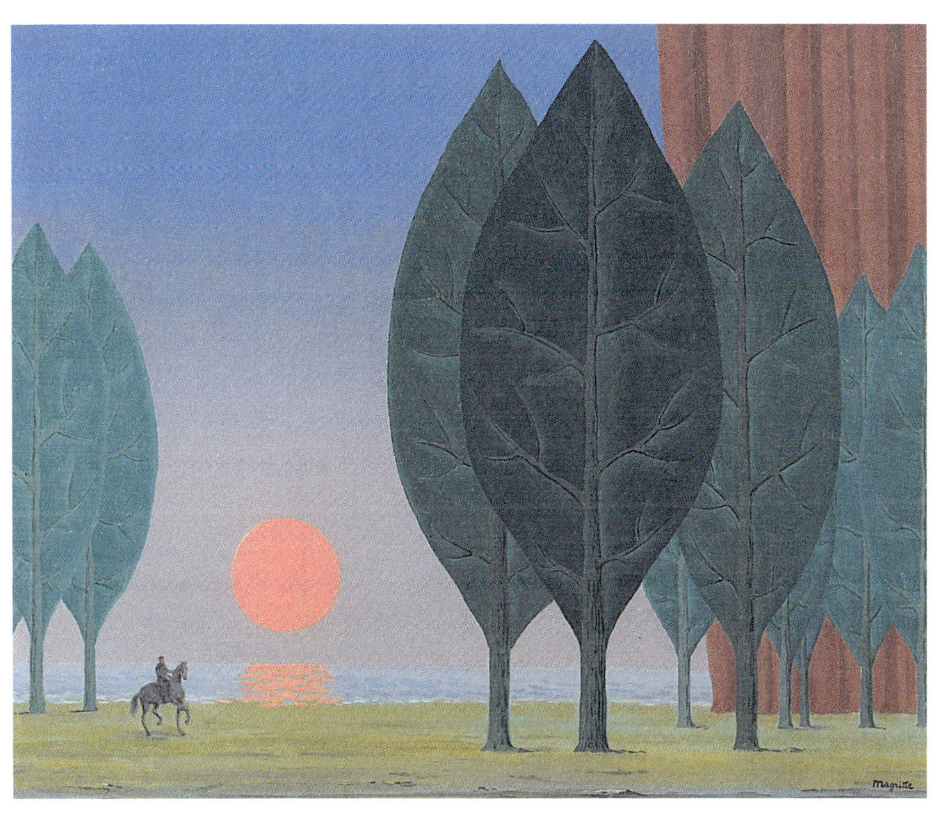

375
The Forest of Paimpont
1964
oil on canvas, 46 × 55 cm

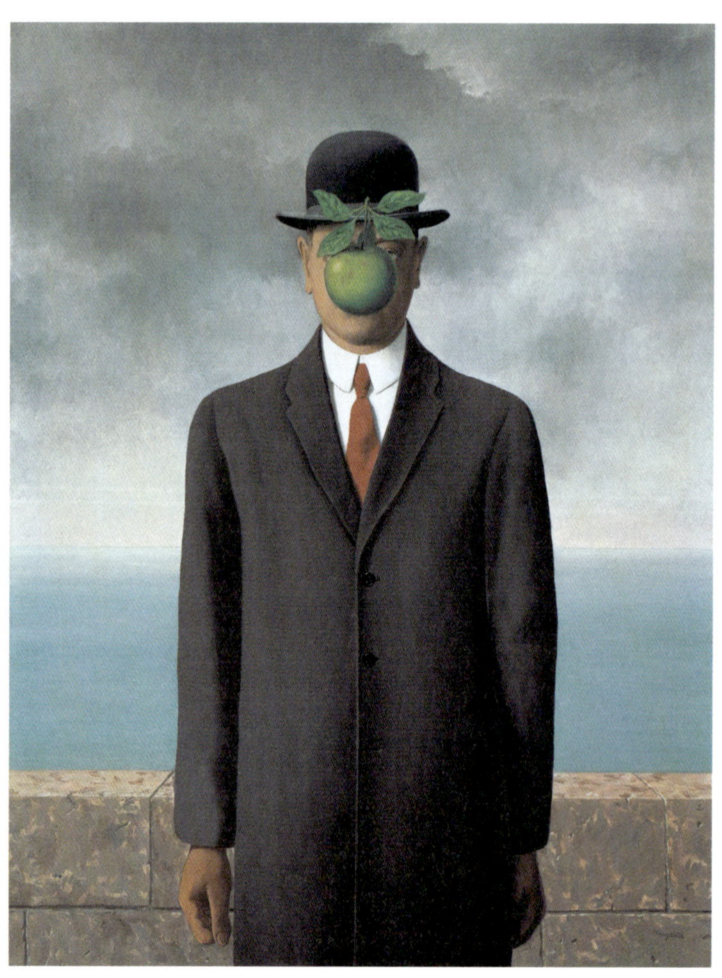

376
The Son of Man
1964
oil on canvas, 116 × 89 cm

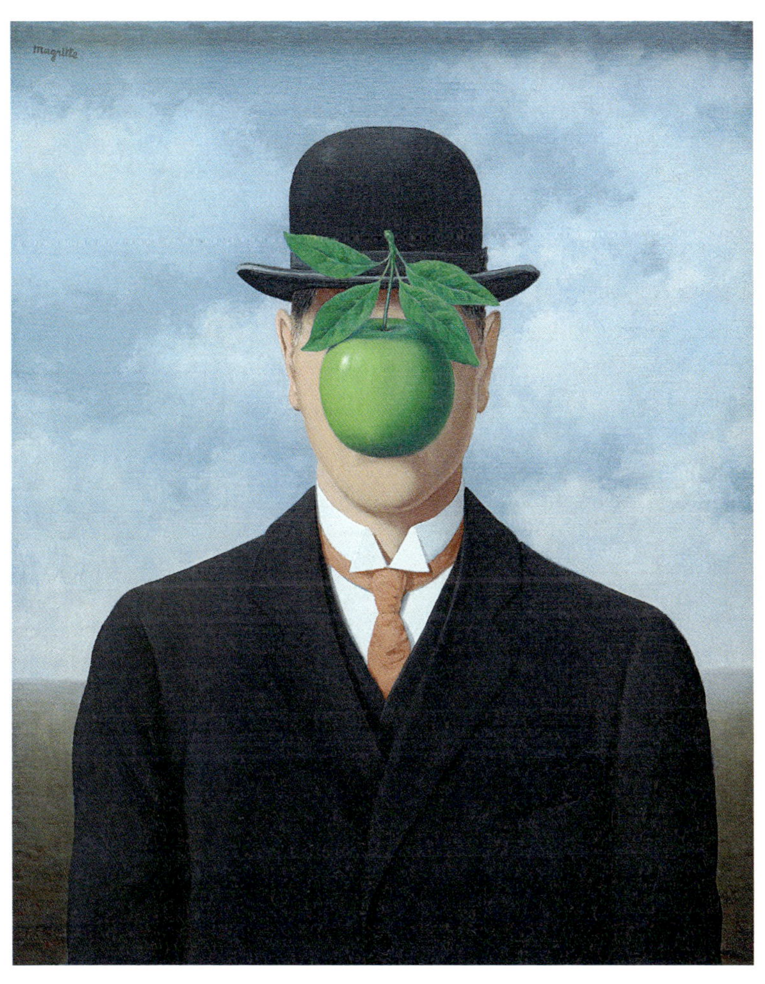

377
The Great War
1964
oil on canvas, 65 × 54 cm

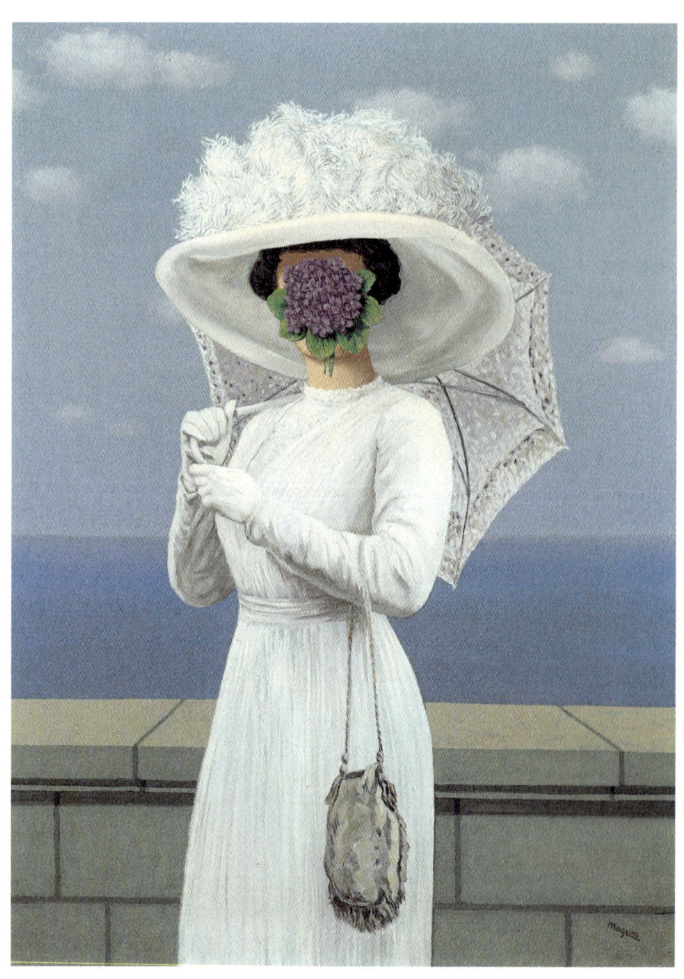

378
The Great War
1964
oil on canvas, 81 × 60 cm

    Poetics of the Everyday

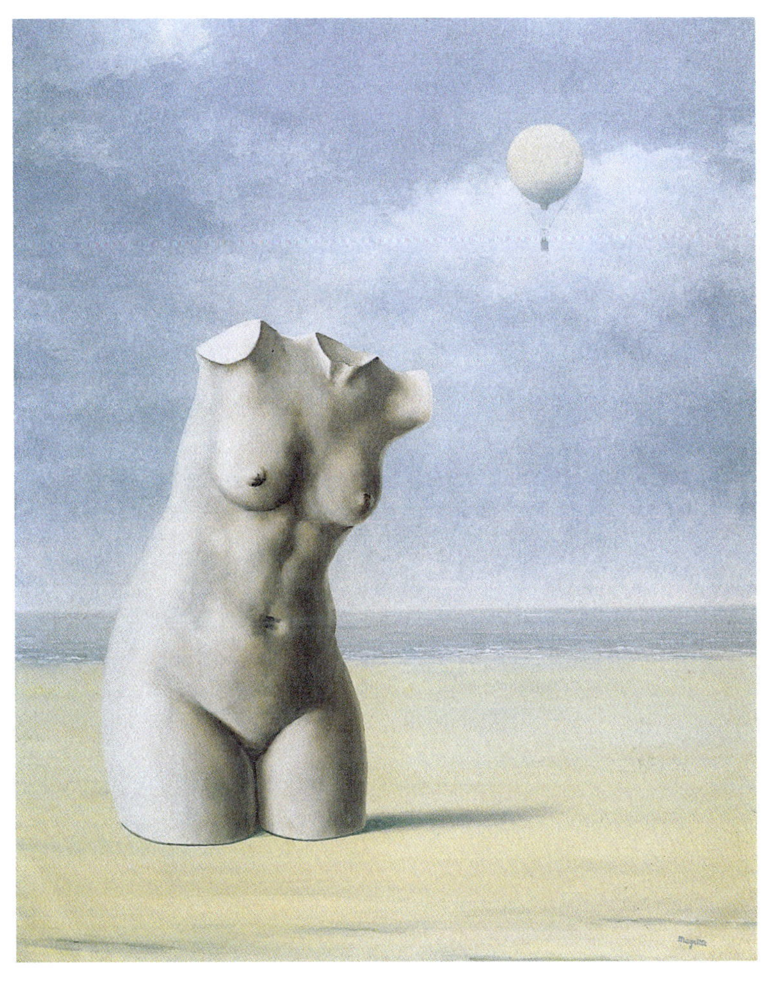

379
When the Hour Strikes
1964 or 1965
oil on canvas, 100 × 81 cm

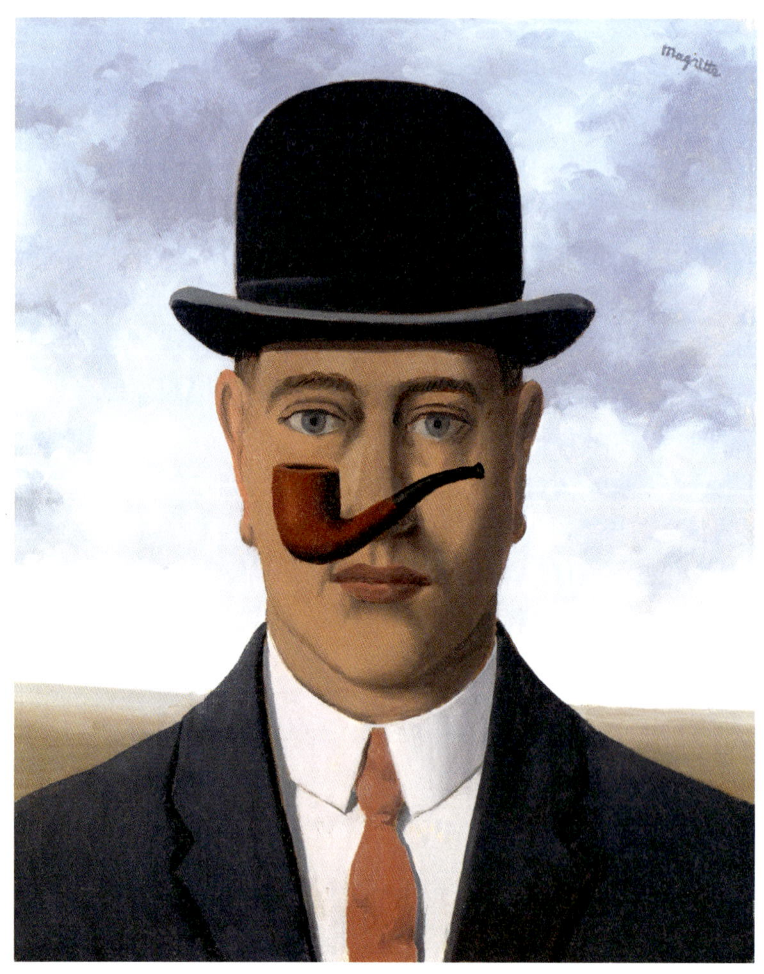

380
Good Faith
1964 or 1965
oil on canvas, 41 × 33 cm

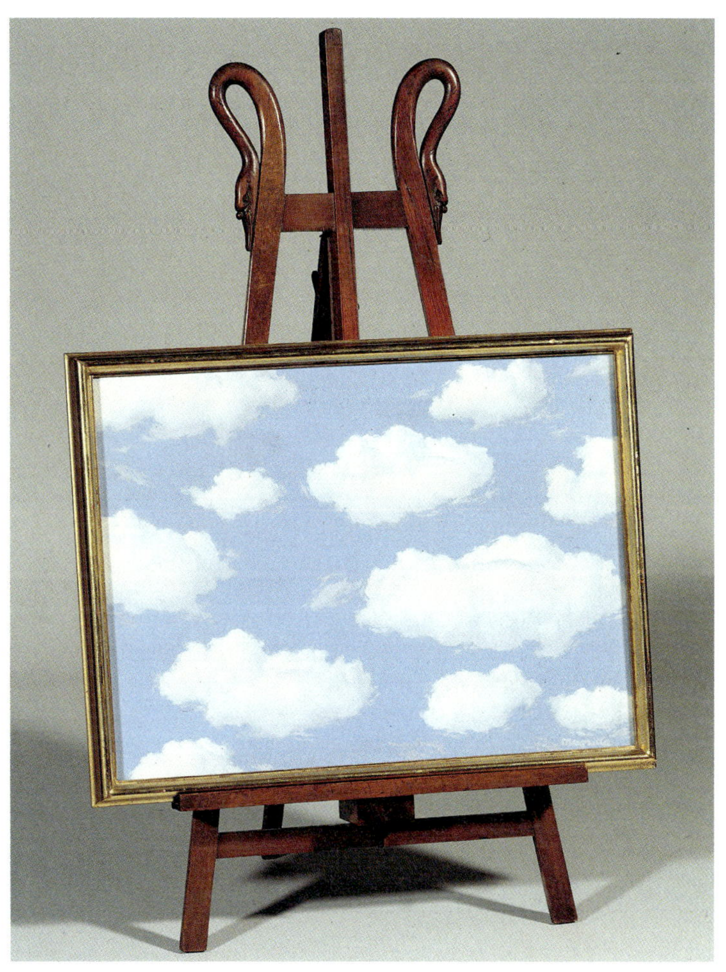

381
The Somersault
1964 or 1965
oil on canvas, 28 × 38 cm

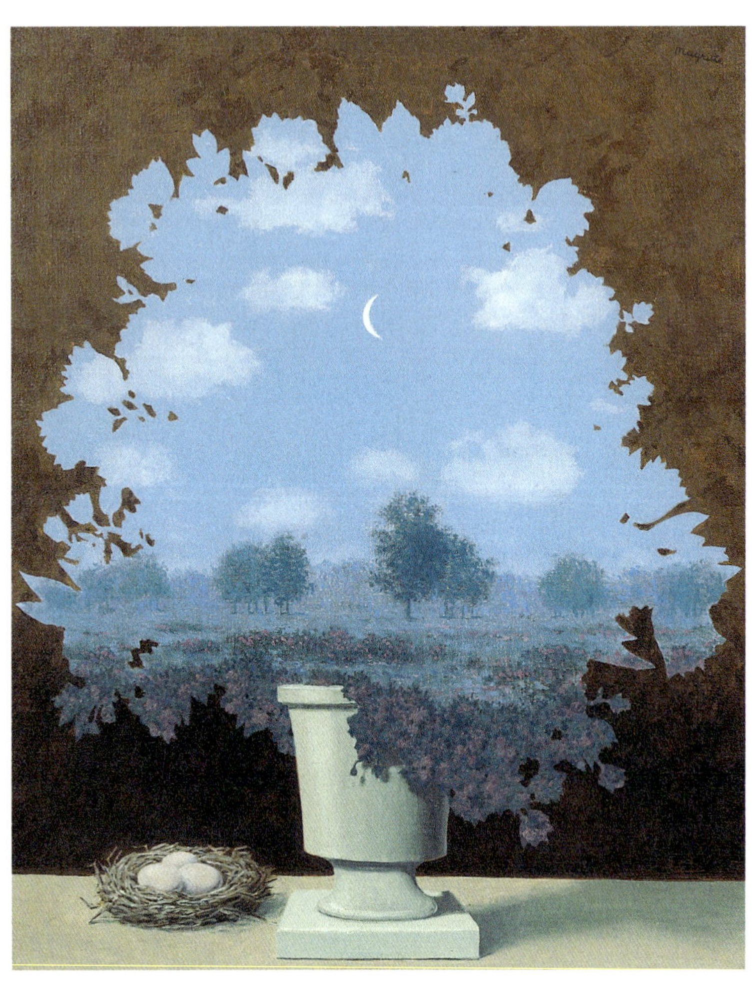

382
The Land of Miracles
1964 or 1965?
oil on canvas, 55 × 46 cm

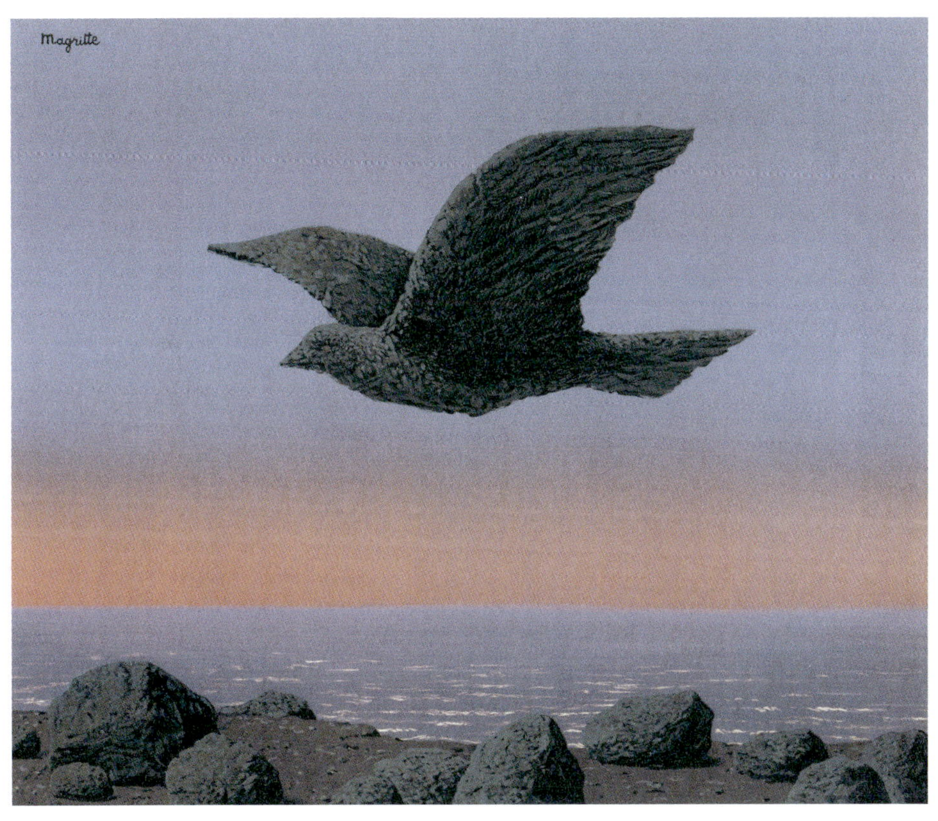

383
The Idol
1965
oil on canvas, 54 × 65 cm

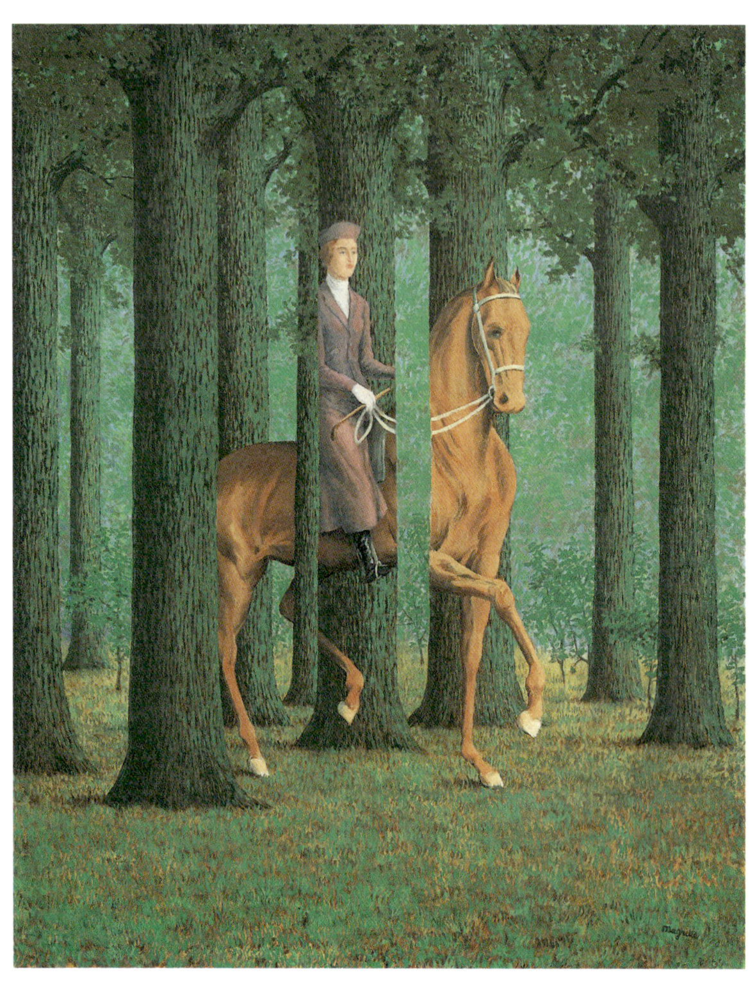

384
Carte blanche
1965
oil on canvas, 81 × 65 cm

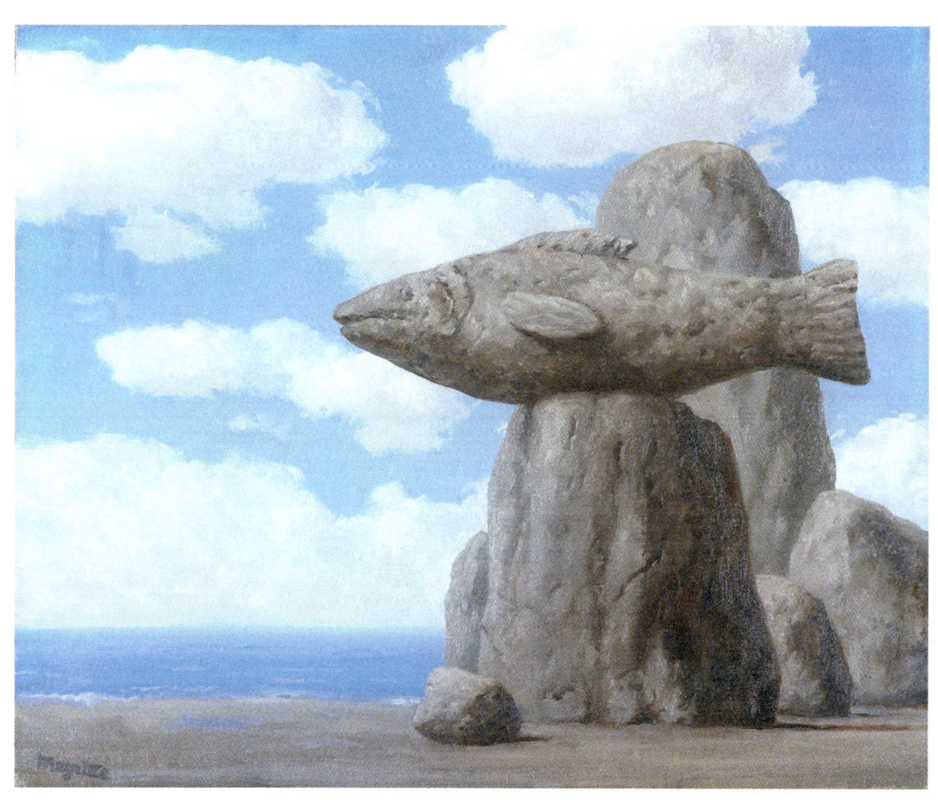

385
Connivance
1965
oil on canvas, 33 × 41 cm

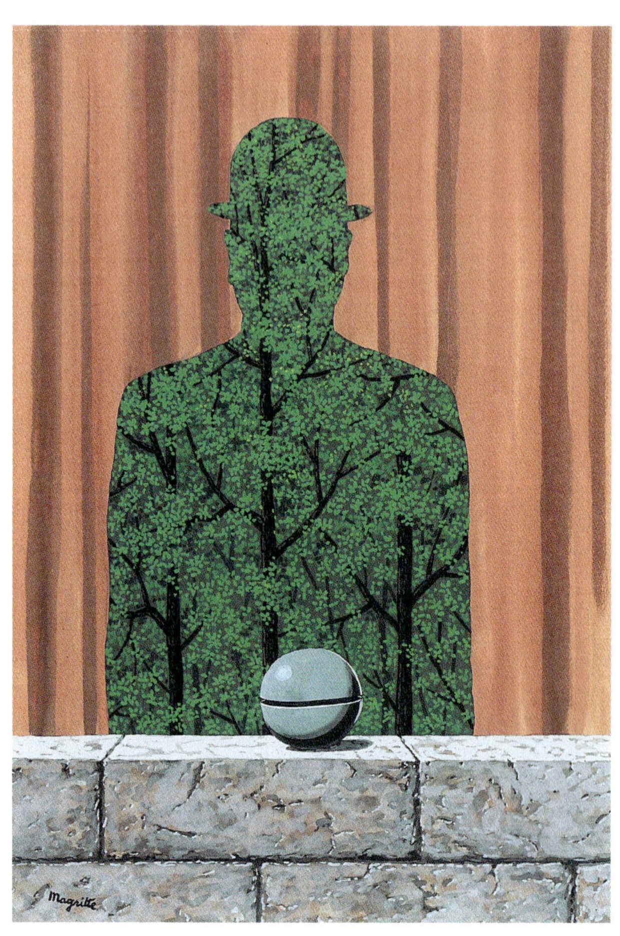

386
Man and the Forest
c. 1965
gouache on paper, 49 × 29 cm

          Poetics of the Everyday

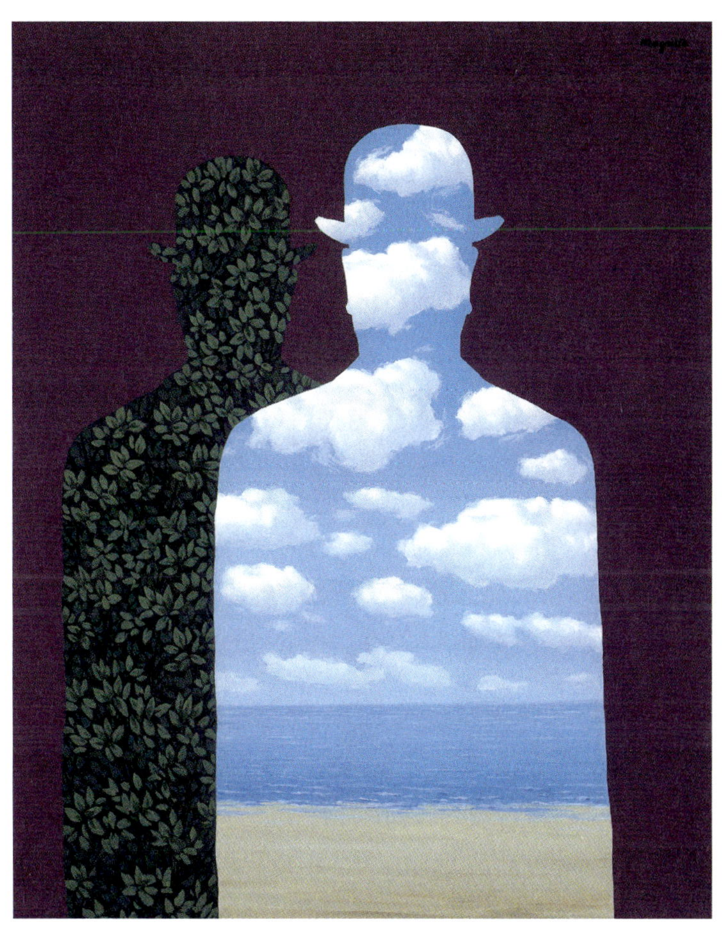

387
High Society
1965 or 1966
oil on canvas, 81 × 65 cm

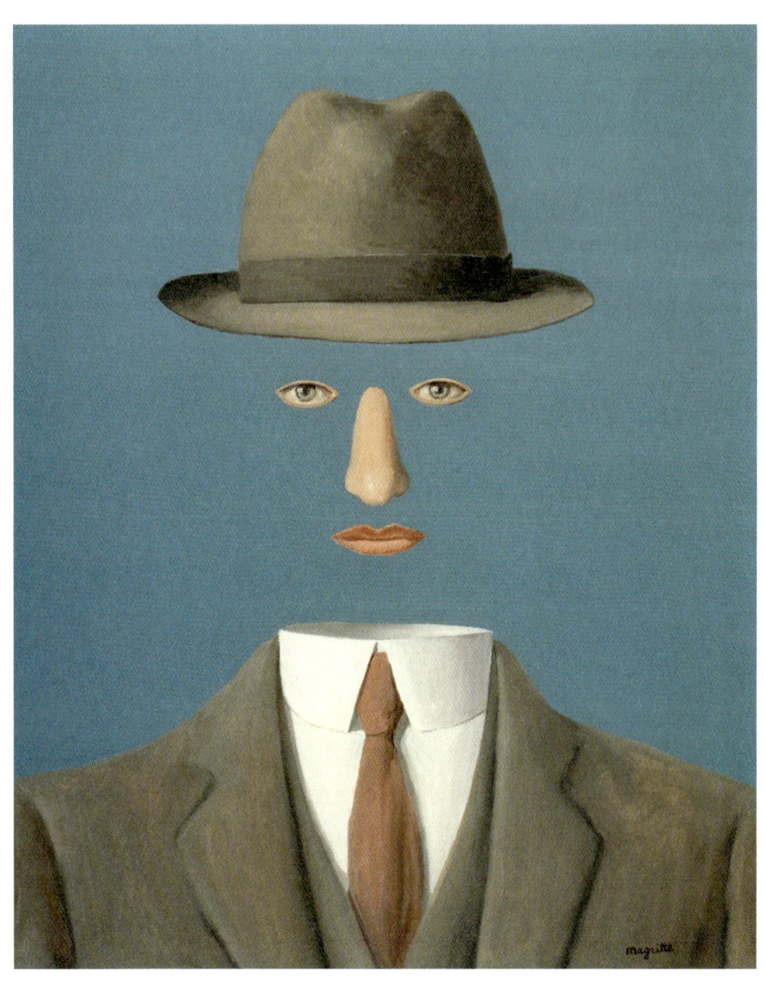

388
Baucis's Landscape
1966
oil on canvas, 55 × 45 cm

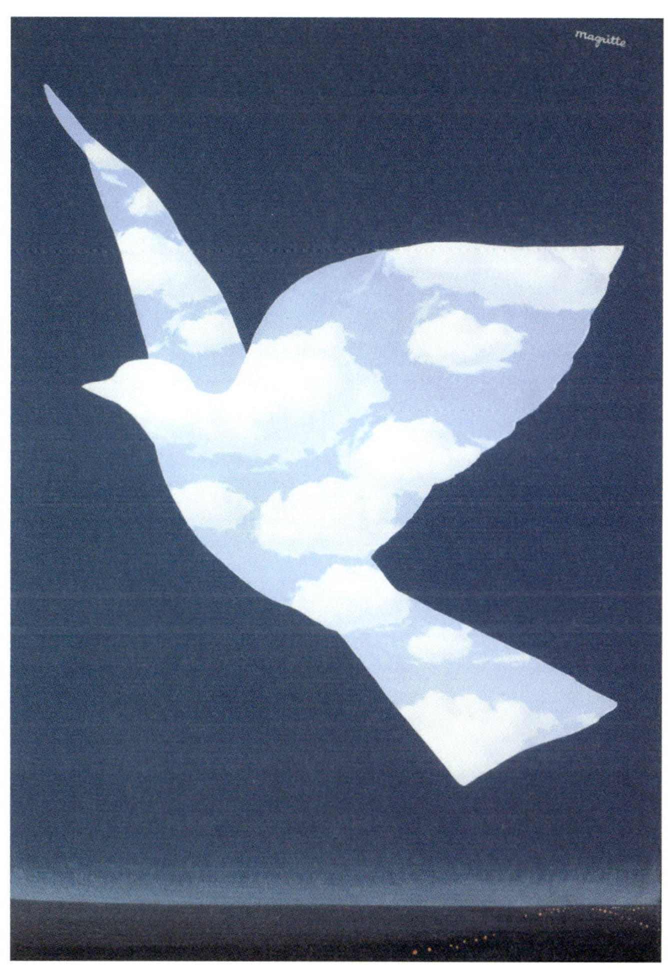

389
Sky Bird
1966
oil on canvas, 68.5 × 48 cm

 1947–1967

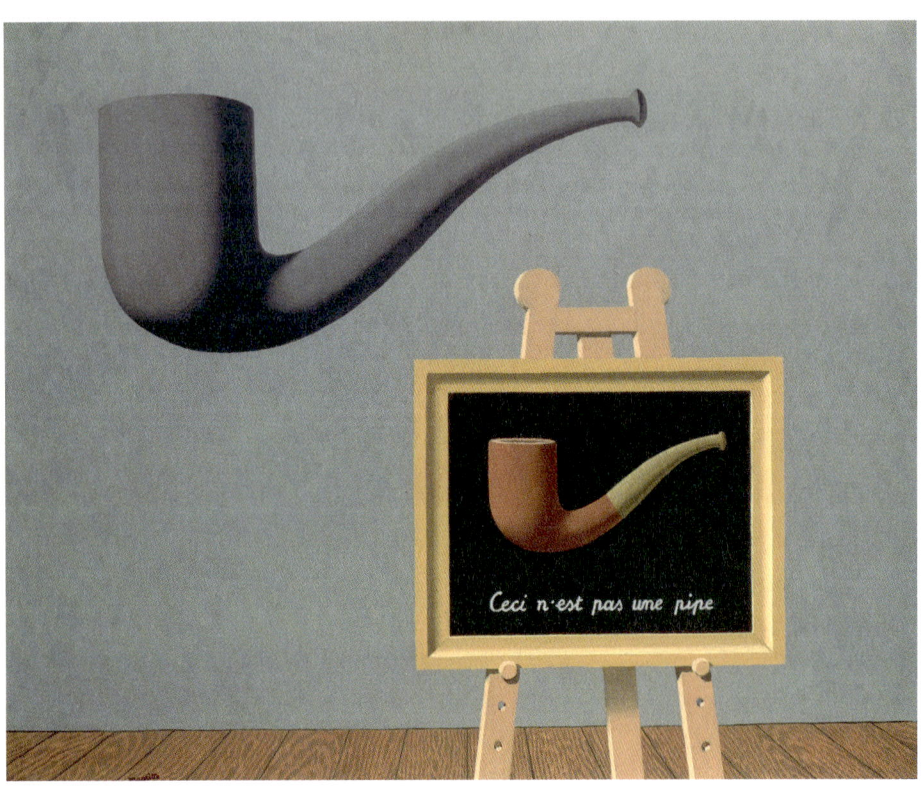

390
The Two Mysteries
1966
oil on canvas, 65 × 80 cm

 Poetics of the Everyday

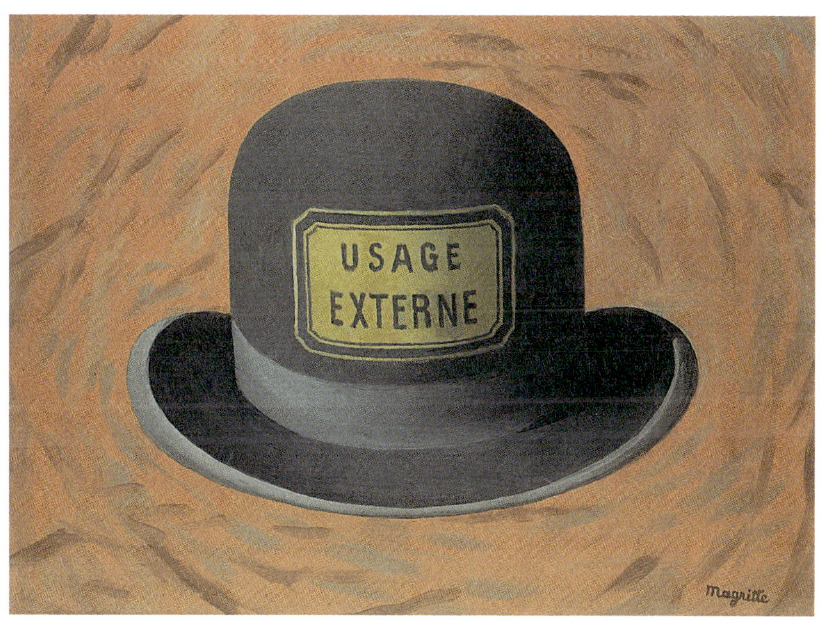

391
The Horrendous Stopper
1966
oil on canvas, 30 × 40 cm

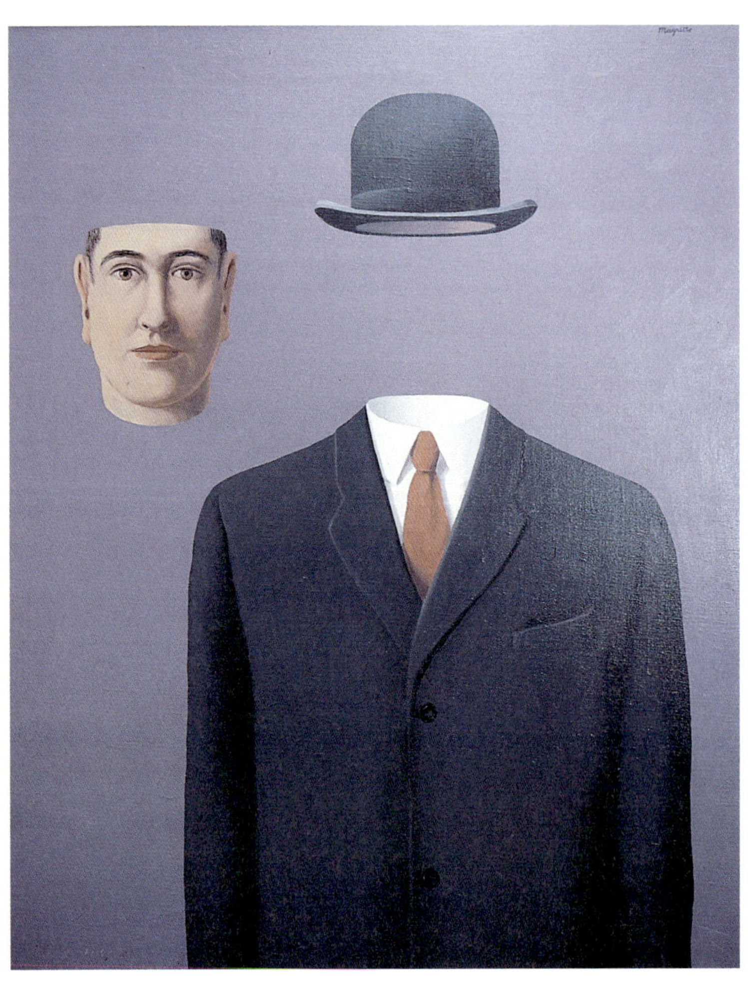

392
The Pilgrim
1966
oil on canvas, 81 × 65 cm

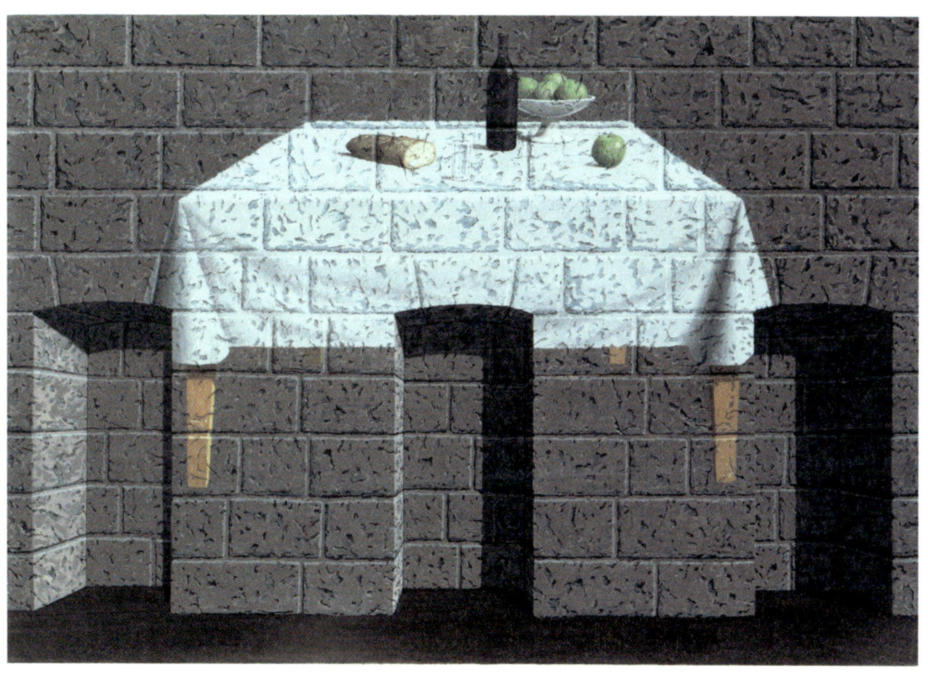

393
The Endearing Truth
1966
oil on canvas, 89 × 130 cm

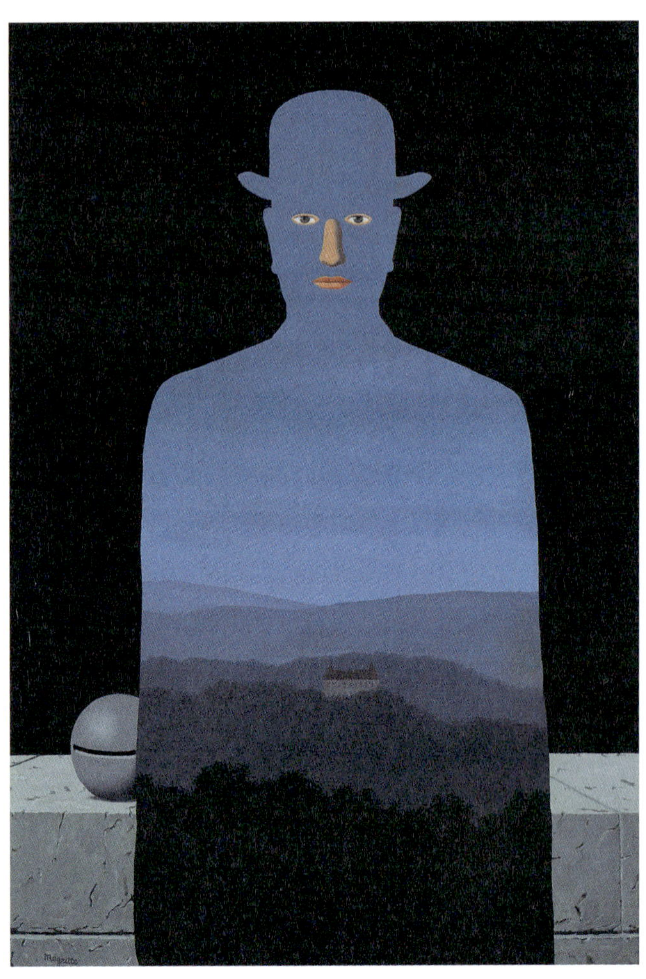

394
The King's Museum
1966
oil on canvas, 130 × 89 cm

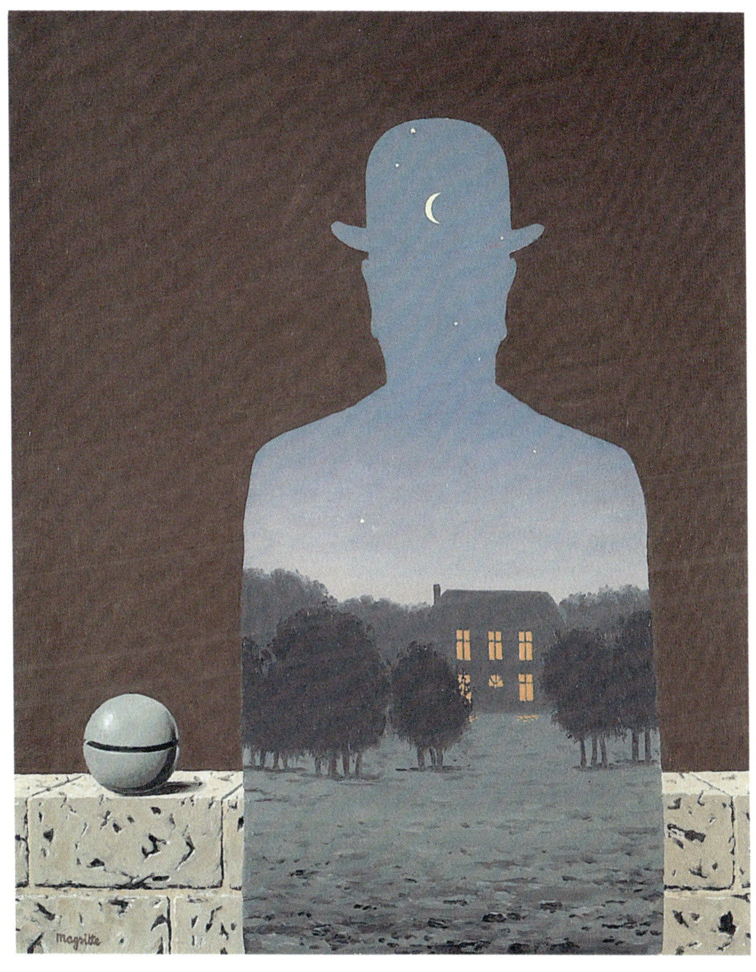

395
The Happy Donor
1966
oil on canvas, 55 × 45 cm

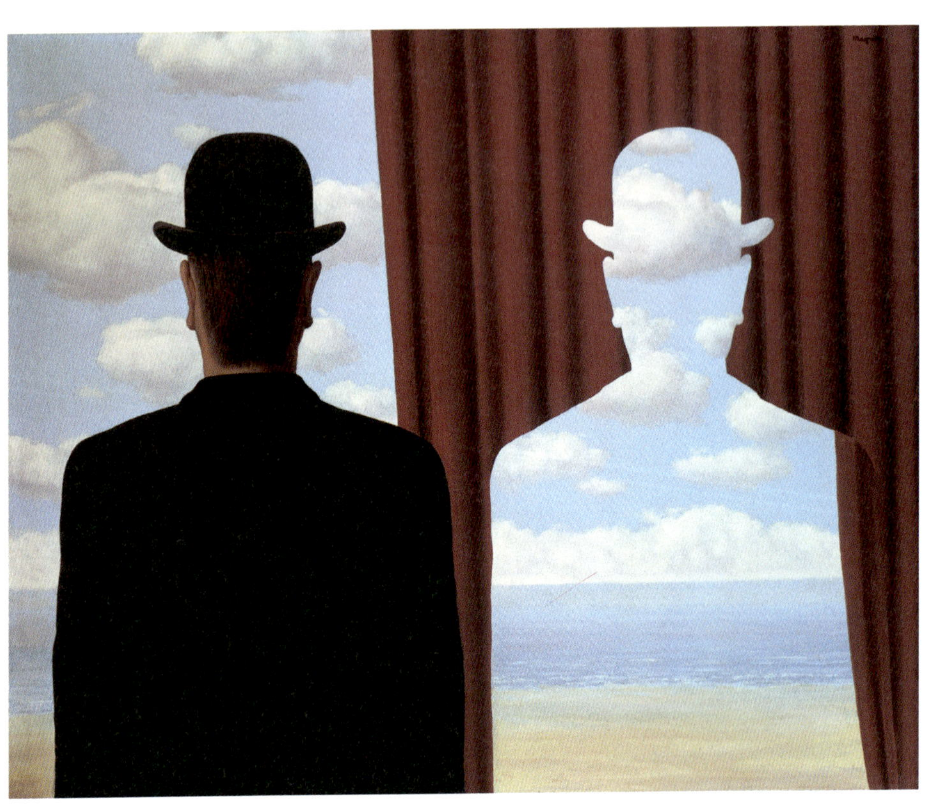

396
Decalcomania
1966
oil on canvas, 81 × 100 cm

  Poetics of the Everyday

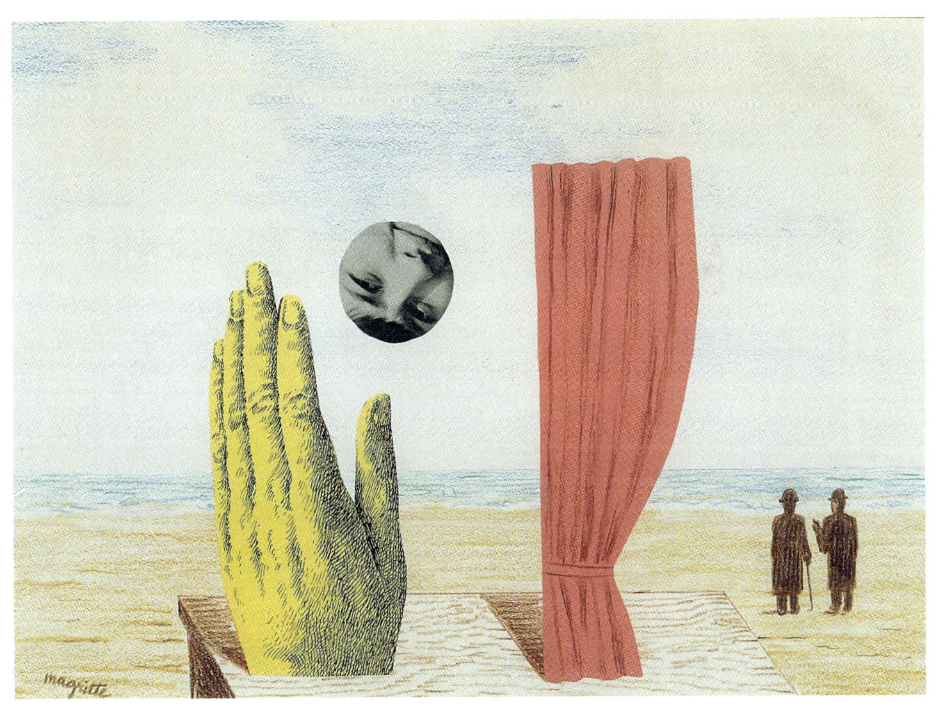

397
(Title unknown)
1966
pasted paper, chalk and crayon on paper, 29 × 41 cm

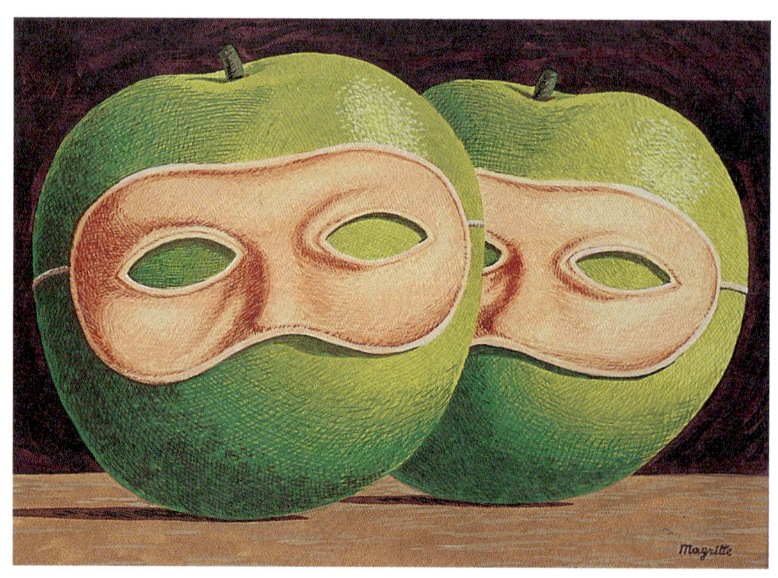

398
The Married Priest
c. 1966
gouache on paper, 28.8 × 41 cm

Poetics of the Everyday

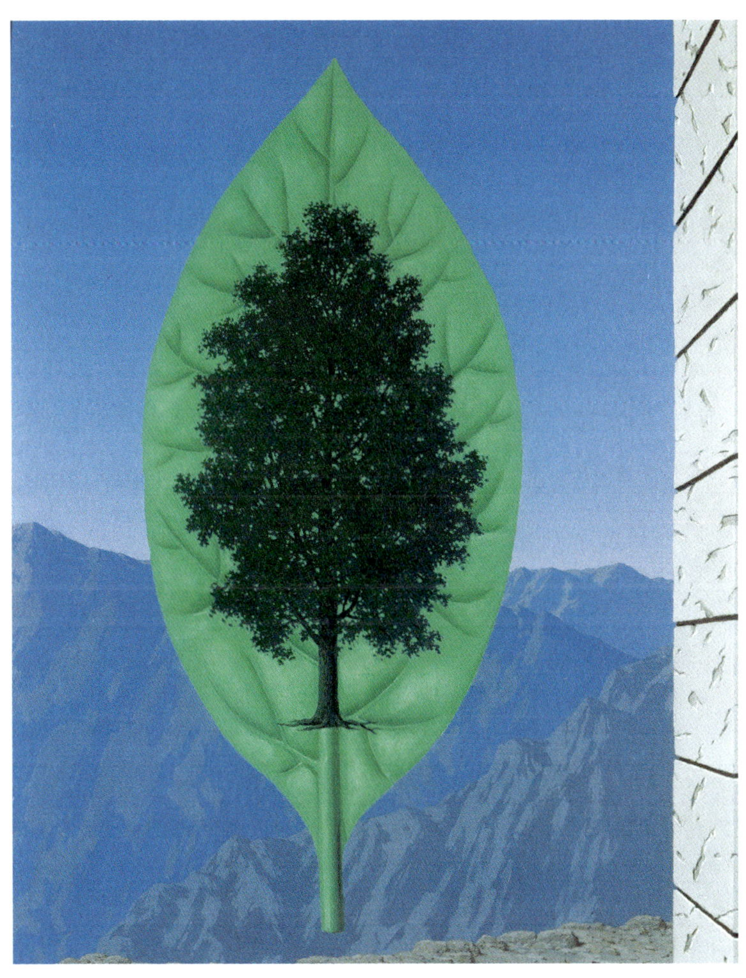

399
The Latest Thing
1967
oil on canvas, 81 × 65 cm

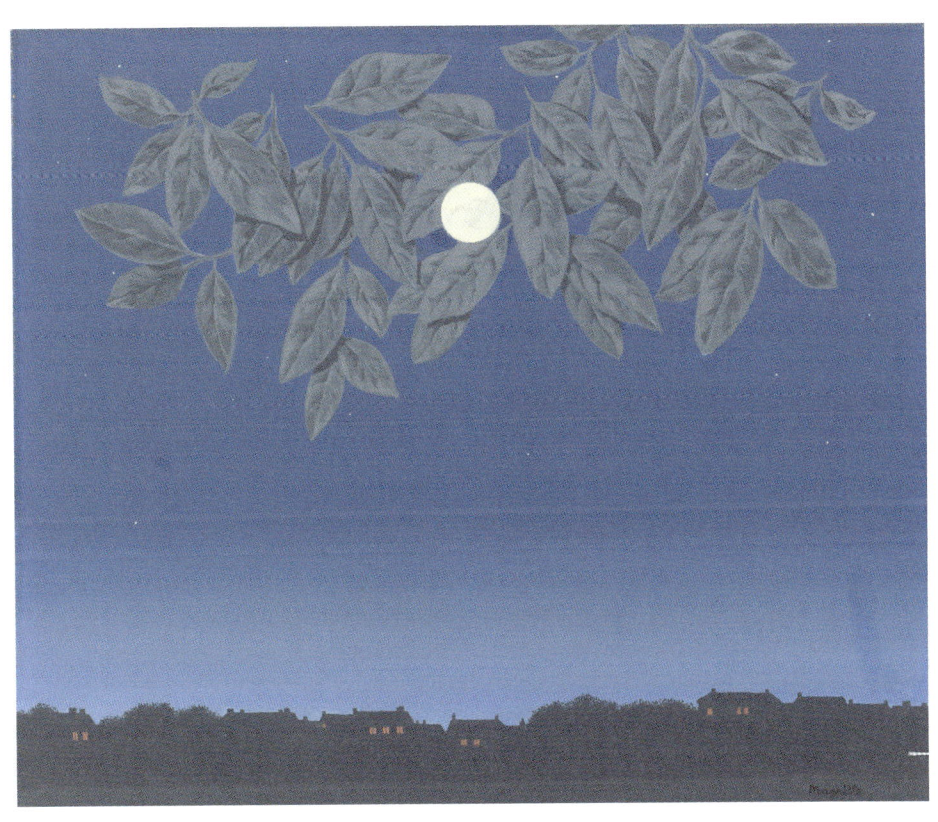

400
The Blank Page
1967
oil on canvas, 54 × 65 cm

Biography

1898
21 November: René Magritte is born in Lessines, Belgium. His brothers Raymond and Paul are born in 1900 and 1902, respectively.

1910
Takes his first painting lessons, in Châtelet, Belgium.

1912
February: Suicide of his mother by drowning in the River Sambre.

1913
Meets Georgette Berger, his future wife, at the annual fair in Charleroi.

1916
Begins to attend drawing and painting classes at the Royal Academy of Fine Arts, Brussels.

1920
Exhibits his first abstract paintings and posters at a Brussels art centre.
Meets E. L. T. Mesens. Makes contact with the Italian Futurists and the Dadaists.

1922
28 June: Marries Georgette Berger in Brussels.

1923–4
Discovers the painting *The Song of Love* (1914) by Giorgio de Chirico through his friend Marcel Lecomte and is profoundly affected by it.

1925
Makes his first Surrealist paintings under the influence of de Chirico and Max Ernst. Makes his first collages.

1926
Signs his first contract, with the dealer Paul-Gustave van Hecke.
Autumn: A Brussels Surrealist group is formed including E. L. T. Mesens, Paul Nougé, André Souris, Camille Goemans and René Magritte.

1927
Presents his first solo exhibition at the Galerie Le Centaure, Brussels.
Meets Louis Scutenaire, who joins the Surrealist group; a long friendship begins.
September: Moves to the Paris suburb Le Perreux-sur-Marne.

1928
Makes contact with André Breton and the Surrealist group in Paris.

1929
Publishes 'Les Mots et les images' in the twelfth issue of *La Révolution surréaliste*.

1930
His contract with the Galerie Goemans, Paris, ends due to the gallery closing. He is forced to return to Brussels for financial reasons.
Founds an advertising agency, Studio Dongo, with his brother Paul, and returns to his activity as a commercial artist.

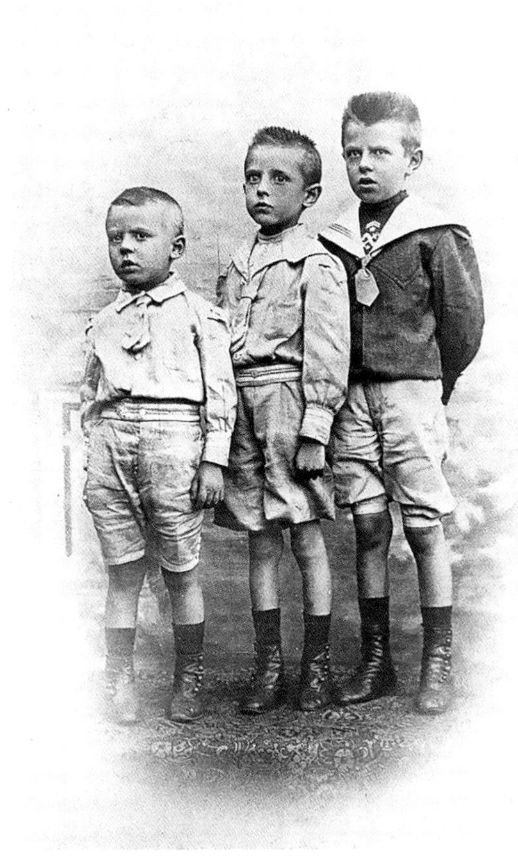

Left to right: Paul, Raymond and René Magritte, c. 1905.

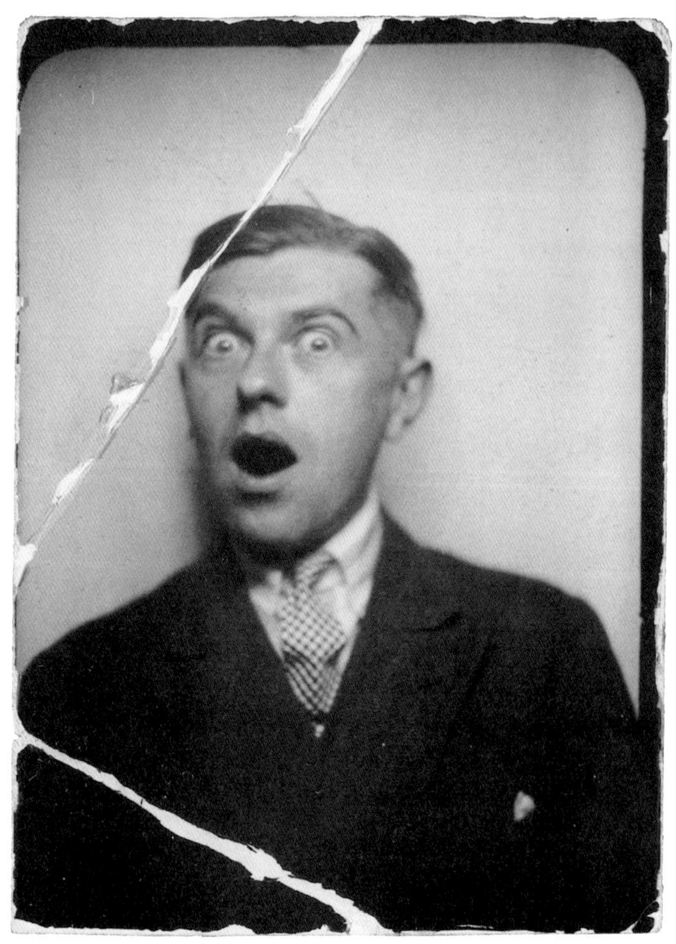

Flirtatiousness, René Magritte at the Jardin des Plantes, photo-booth photo, 1929.

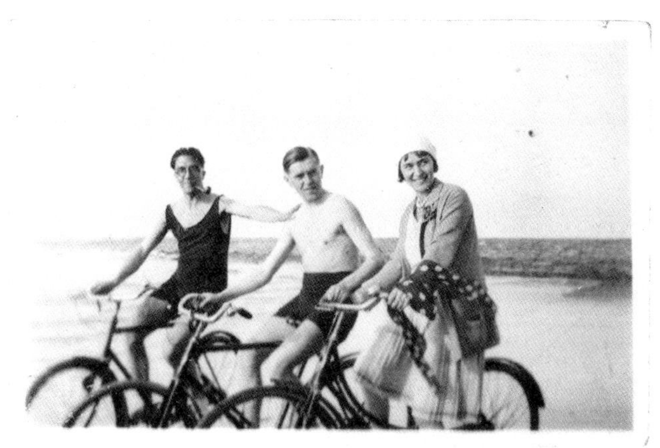

Left to right: Paul Nougé, René and Georgette Magritte on the Belgian coast, 1932.

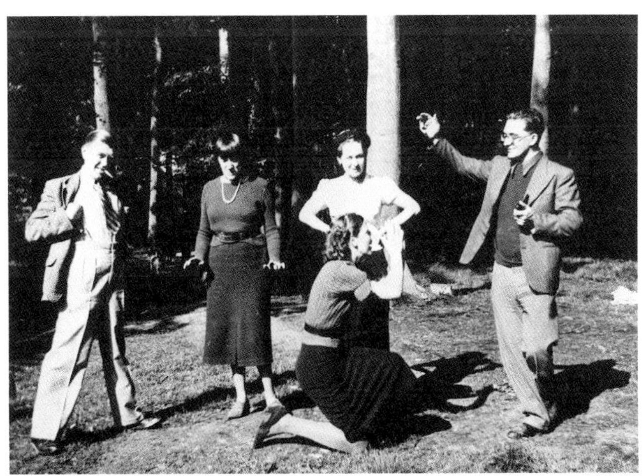

Left to right: René Magritte, Marthe Beauvoisin, Georgette Magritte and Paul Nougé.
Kneeling: Betty Magritte. Brussels, Sonian Forest, 1939.

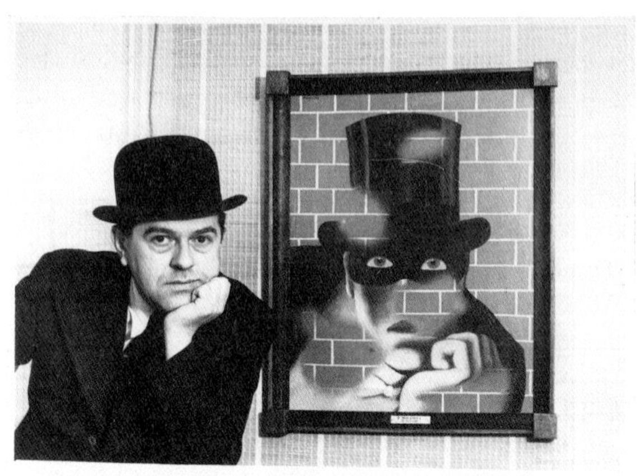

René Magritte and *The Barbarian*, London Gallery, London, 1938.

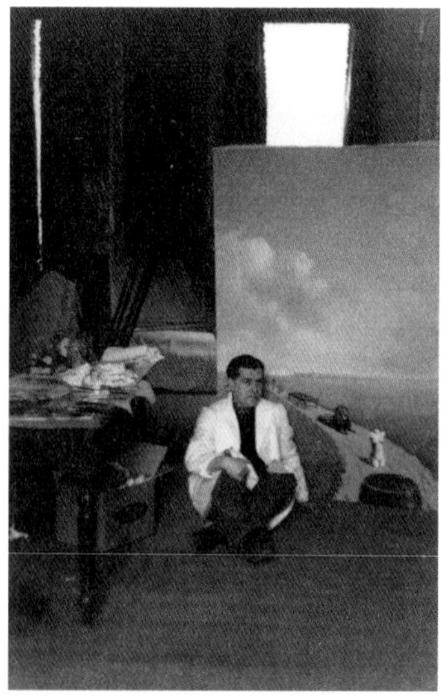

René Magritte painting *Youth Illustrated* at the
home of Edward James, London, 1937.

1931

Presents his first solo exhibition at the Palais des Beaux-Arts, Brussels.

1933

Introduces a new method of exploring reality, 'elective affinities', aimed at finding the solution to the problem raised by an object.

1936

Participates in several international group exhibitions in New York, London, The Hague and Paris.

1937

Meets Marcel Mariën, a new Surrealist kindred spirit.

1938

Participates in the *Exposition internationale du surréalisme* in Paris organised by André Breton, Paul Éluard and Marcel Duchamp.
Has a retrospective at Mesens's London Gallery.
November: Gives the lecture 'La Ligne de vie' at the Royal Museum of Fine Arts, Antwerp.

1940

May: Makes an exodus to Carcassonne with the Scutenaires following the German invasion.
August: Returns to Brussels, where Georgette had remained.
Creates his first painted bottles.

1943

Begins the Sunlit Surrealism' (or 'Renoir Period'), a period characterised by a change of style inspired by the Impressionist palette and technique.

1945

The exhibition *Surréalisme*, including Belgian and French artists, is held at the Galerie des Éditions La Boétie, Brussels. Magritte becomes the main Belgian exponent of Surrealism.

1947

Has a solo exhibition at the Hugo Gallery in New York, directed by Alexander Iolas, his American agent, which initiates a series of exhibitions in the United States that herald international recognition.

1948

Has his first solo exhibition in Paris, at the Galerie du Faubourg, presenting of the 'Vache' Period paintings, which were intended to shock the Paris public.

1952

Founds the magazine *La Carte d'après nature*, which continued publishing until 1956.
Breaks with Paul Nougé.

1954

Has a major retrospective at the Palais des Beaux-Arts, Brussels.

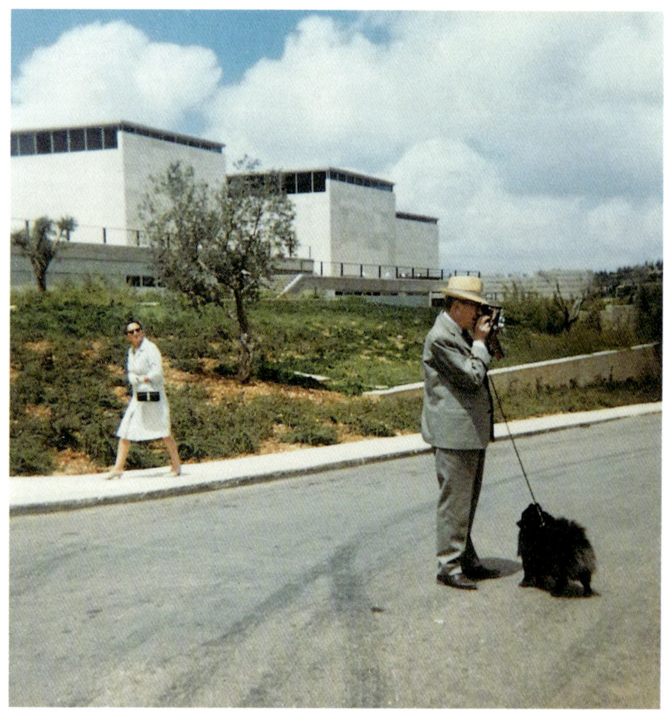

René Magritte, Jerusalem, 1966.

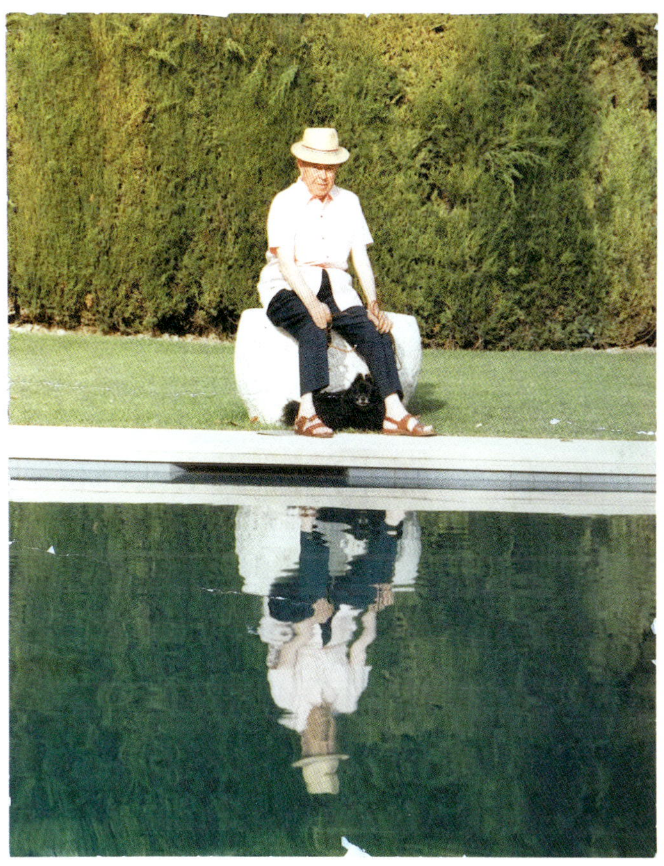

René Magritte, Verona, 1967.

1956

Purchases a camera and makes short films with his wife, Georgette, and close friends, including Louis Scutenaire, Irène Hamoir and Paul Colinet, as actors.
December: Signs an exclusive contract with Iolas.

1957

Meets the Antwerp-born New York lawyer Harry Torczyner, who becomes his legal advisor, his intermediary with Iolas and one of his main collectors.
Moves to a comfortable home on Rue des Mimosas in Schaerbeek.

1959

Filming of *Magritte ou La leçon des choses* by Luc de Heusch.

1960

Beginning of a travelling retrospective in Dallas and Houston, Texas, at the initiative of Iolas.

1961

Publication of the first issue of *Rhétorique* (1961–6), founded by André Bosmans.
Takes part in London exhibitions at the Grosvenor Gallery, organised by Mesens, and the Obelisk Gallery, for which André Breton writes a substantial text.

1962

Retrospective at the casino in Knokke, Belgium. Marcel Mariën issues the leaflet 'Grande Baisse', falsely signed by René Magritte, to denounce his friend's commercial success and his practice of the variant.
Retrospective co-organised by Harry Torczyner at the Walker Art Center, Minneapolis, Minnesota.

1964

Retrospective at the Arkansas Art Center, Little Rock, Arkansas. Catalogue preface by André Breton.

1965–6

Major retrospective at the Museum of Modern Art, New York, subsequently shown in Waltham, Massachussets; Chicago; and Pasadena and Berkeley, both California.
The Magrittes' first trip to the United States, to New York and Houston, Texas.

1967

Designs sculptures based on a selection of eight subjects from his paintings.
June: Visits the Gibiesse foundry in Verona, Italy, to supervise the wax models.
July: Hospitalised at the Edith Cavell clinic in Uccle, Belgium, suffering from cancer of the pancreas.
15 August: Magritte dies at home and is buried three days later in the Schaerbeek cemetery, Belgium.

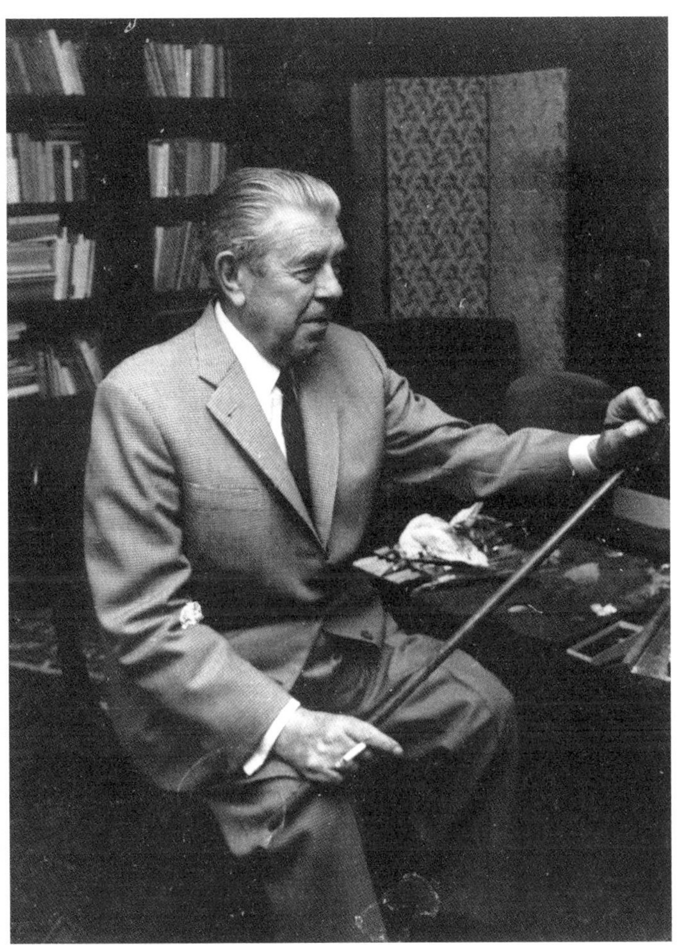

René Magritte, Brussels, Rue des Mimosas, 1966.

Colophon

Text
Julie Waseige

Translation
Donald Pistolesi

Editing
Sarah Auld

Proofreading
Robert Anderson

Coordination
Ruth Ruyffelaere

Cover design
Tim Bisschop

Graphic design
Dylan Van Elewyck

Typesetting
Lieve Lenaerts

Printing
Graphius

D/2021/6328/3
ISBN 978-94-9303-916-2

Cover: *The Son of Man*, 1964 (detail)

Photographs
© Photothèque R. Magritte / Adagp Images, Paris, 2021
© Ludion Image Bank, Brussels, 2021

First published 2021
Fourth printing 2025

Also available in the same series:

Dalí in 400 Images
Text by William Jeffett
ISBN 978-94-6478-114-4

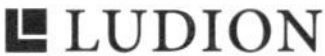